Professional Windows Forms

Jason Bell
Benny B. Johansen
Jan D. Narkiewicz
Gerry O'Brien
Ranga Raghunathan
Simon Robinson
John Timney
Eric White

Wrox Press Ltd. ®

Professional Windows Forms

Published by Wrox Press Ltd,
Arden House, 1102 Warwick Road, Acocks Green,
Birmingham, B27 6BH, UK
Printed in the United States
ISBN 1861005547

Trademark Acknowledgements

Credits

Authors
Jason Bell
Benny B. Johansen
Jan D Narkiewicz
Gerry O'Brien
Ranga Raghunathan
Simon Robinson
John Timney
Eric White

Additional Material
Mark Mamone
Sariya Binsaleh
Christian Nagel

Technical Architect
David Mercer

Technical Editors
Claire Brittle
Allan Jones
Gerard Maguire
Jake Manning
Caroline Robeson

Category Manager
Steve Farncombe

Index
Martin Brooks

Production Coordinator
Pip Wonson

Figures
Paul Grove

Cover
Dawn Chellingworth

Proof Reader
Fiona Berryman

Author Agents
Avril Corbin
Laura Jones

Project Administrator
Cathy Succamore

Technical Reviewers
Fred Barwell
Jason Bell
Robert Chang
Paul Churchill
Chris Crane
Jeff Gabriel
John Godfrey
Mark Harrison
Mark Horner
Benny B. Johansen
Mark Mamone
Frank Miller
Gerry O'Brien
Phil Powers De-George
Jawahar Puvvala
Ranga Raghunathan
Scott E. Robertson
Simon Robinson
Juan Ramon Rovirosa
Larry Schoeneman
David Schultz
Trevor D. Scott
Keyur Shah
Adrian Sloan
Ben Taylor
Kent Tegels
Eric White

Production Manager
Liz Toy

About the Authors

Jason Bell

Jason Bell started learning computer programming back in 1981 on his father's TI-99/4A with an incredible 16KB of RAM and a panoramic 10" display supporting resolutions of up to 256x192. After eight years of developing software for the U.S. Air Force, Jason is now an MCSD working as a consultant for Stroudwater NHG, a Microsoft Certified Partner located in Portland, ME. When he's not busy donating out-of-date computer books to the library or reformatting his computer's hard drive to install more beta software; Jason enjoys piloting small aircraft, driving his vintage Porsche, and dreaming about going back to school someday to work toward a PhD in Physics.

Benny B. Johansen

Benny B. Johansen is V. P. of Software Development at Sound ID, a Palo Alto based startup using innovative technology to 'enhance the appreciation of sound'. He has a B.Sc. in Computer Science, an MBA in Corporate Strategy, and finally got his MCSD just in time, before it will be replaced with a new .NET based curriculum. When not developing, delegating or cracking the whip at Sound ID, he enjoys running, cooking and trying to improve his piano playing. He can be reached at bjohansen@soundid.com or benny@etvoila.com.

Jan D. Narkiewicz

Jan D. Narkiewicz is Chief Technical Officer at Software Pronto, Inc. (jann@softwarepronto.com). Over the years Jan managed to work on an email system that resided on 17 million desktops, helped automate factories that make blue jeans you have in your closet (trust me, you own this brand), and kept the skies over the Emirate of Abu Dhabi safe from enemy aircraft.

Presently he works in MPEG streaming. If you're watching a national channel on cable TV and see a commercial for a local business miraculously inserted, Jan was likely involved (90% probability for the U.S. cable market). His technologies of choice include COM/DCOM, COM+, C++, VB, C#, ADO, SQL Server, Oracle, DB2, ASP.Net, ADO.Net, Java, Linux and XML. In his spare time Jan is Academic Coordinator for the Windows curriculum at U.C. Berkeley Extension, teaches at U.C. Santa Cruz Extension, writes for ASP Today.

Gerry O'Brien

Gerry O'Brien has been working with computers for over 14 year, and has over 5 years of experience in Network Administration using Windows NT 4.0 and Windows 2000. His programming experience started when he got hooked on programming with GW Basic and Quick Basic from the DOS days. He started Windows programming with Visual Basic 3 and has used VB for most of his programming tasks since then. Of course, the natural extension to VB was Visual Basic for Applications and VBScript, which he used in customizing office applications, and creating Active Server Pages for various companies.

He presently works full-time as a Facilitator with ITI Information Technology Institute, where he teaches HTML, Project Management, FrontPage, RDBMS theory, Microsoft Access, VBA, VBScript and Distributed Application Design with Visual Basic. He holds an MCP in Windows NT 4.0 and Visual Basic.

Gerry also has a part-time consulting company, as well as being a beta tester for Microsoft Operating Systems and Visual Studio.NET.

Ranga Raghunathan

Ranga Raghunathan is currently developing an ERP application for Trinity Industries, Dallas using Microsoft Technologies. He has a Bachelor's degree from Birla Institute of Technology and Science, Pilani, India and a Masters degree from Virginia Tech, USA. He lives in Richardson, Texas with his little son Vivek and wife Radha. He dedicates his contributions to this book to his late father. You can reach Ranga at ranga1@msn.com

Simon Robinson

Simon Robinson lives in Lancaster in the UK, where he shares a house with some students. He first encountered serious programming when he was doing his PhD in physics, modeling all sorts of weird things to do with superconductors and quantum mechanics. The experience of programming was nearly enough to put him off computers for life (though, oddly, he seems to have survived all the quantum mechanics), and he tried for a while being a sports massage therapist instead. But he then realized how much money was in computers compared to sports massage, and rapidly got a job as a C++ programmer/researcher instead. Simon is clearly the charitable, deep, spiritual type, who understands the true meaning of life.

His programming work eventually lead him into writing, and he now makes a living mostly from writing great books for programmers. He is a great enthusiast for C#, which he firmly believes is set to revolutionize programming. His spare time is spent either at dance classes (he loves performing arts) or on his pet project writing a computer strategy game. And with what little time is left, he is an honorary research associate at Lancaster University, where he does research in computational fluid dynamics with the environmental science department. You can visit Simon's web site at http://www.SimonRobinson.com.

John Timney

John lives in the UK with his lovely wife Philippa in a small town called Chester-Le-Street in the North of England. He is a Postgraduate of Nottingham University, having gained an MA in Information Technology following a BA Honors Degree and a Postgraduate Diploma from Humberside University. John specializes in Internet Solutions and his computing expertise has gained him a Microsoft MVP (Most Valuable Professional) award. His hobbies include Martial Arts, and he has black belts in two different styles of Karate.

> *"Thanks to my parents Ann and John for being the best in the world, and to my wife Pippa for always being my best friend and favorite person".*

Eric White

Eric White is an independent consultant, specializing in managing offshore development with some hotshot developers in India. Having written well over a million lines of code, Eric has over 20 years experience in building Management Information Systems, accounting systems, and other types of fat client and n-tier database applications. Eric has particular interest in Object-Oriented design methodologies, including use case analysis, UML, and design patterns. After years of working with too many varieties of technologies to list, he is currently specializing in C#, VB.NET, ASP.NET, ADO.NET, XML, COM+, GDI+, SQL Server and other Microsoft technologies.

He loves meeting new people and traveling to far-flung places, and is equally at ease wandering around the streets of Bangalore, London, and San Francisco. When he is not in front of a computer, he loves hiking in the mountains of the US and India. He can be reached at eric@ericwhite.com.

Table of Contents

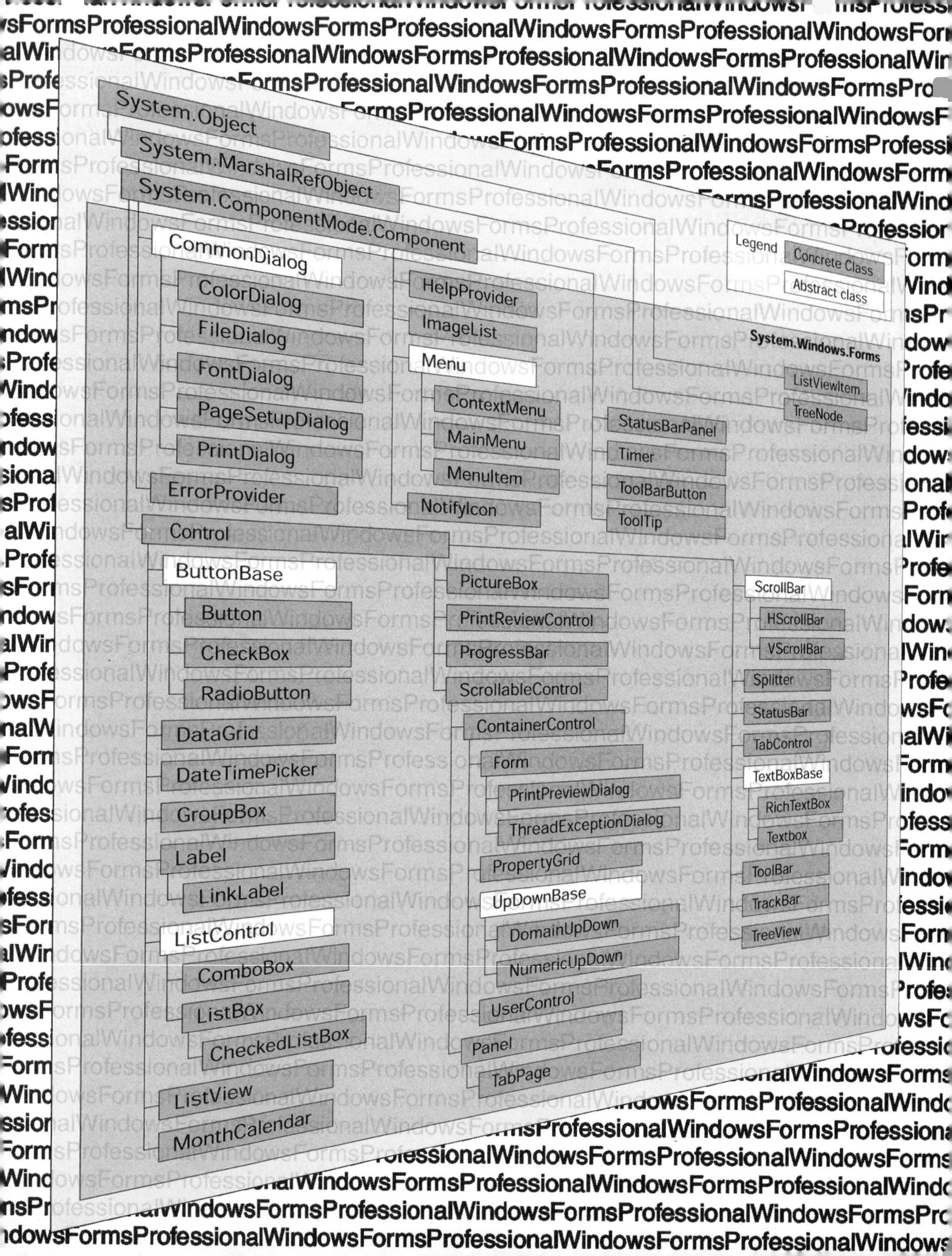

System.Object
System.MarshalRefObject
System.ComponentMode.Component

Legend
Concrete Class
Abstract class

System.Windows.Forms

CommonDialog
ColorDialog
FileDialog
FontDialog
PageSetupDialog
PrintDialog
ErrorProvider

HelpProvider
ImageList
Menu
ContextMenu
MainMenu
MenuItem
NotifyIcon

StatusBarPanel
Timer
ToolBarButton
ToolTip

ListViewItem
TreeNode

Control
ButtonBase
Button
CheckBox
RadioButton
DataGrid
DateTimePicker
GroupBox
Label
LinkLabel
ListControl
ComboBox
ListBox
CheckedListBox
ListView
MonthCalendar

PictureBox
PrintReviewControl
ProgressBar
ScrollableControl
ContainerControl
Form
PrintPreviewDialog
ThreadExceptionDialog
PropertyGrid
UpDownBase
DomainUpDown
NumericUpDown
UserControl
Panel
TabPage

ScrollBar
HScrollBar
VScrollBar
Splitter
StatusBar
TabControl
TextBoxBase
RichTextBox
Textbox
ToolBar
TrackBar
TreeView

Introduction

With all the talk about the way in which the .NET technologies are going to revolutionize Web based applications, it's easy to lose sight of the fact that Microsoft has invested a large amount of time in improving the ways in which we develop traditional windows style applications.

Windows Forms is the new Microsoft endeavor that allows us to create sophisticated, rich, and data-aware user interface applications. While impressive, many people may feel that having 'expensive' client applications is still not feasible. Under .NET, this is not really the case, since a simple XCOPY deployment means that deployment and support of Windows Forms applications is cheaper. The upshot of this is that Windows Forms applications may well begin to replace browser based applications that were previously used, even though they suffered from weaker user interfaces.

At any rate, there is no denying that with a host of new features, all the benefits afforded by the .NET Framework, and plenty of improvements and upgrades, means that Windows Forms is going to be the tool of choice for building our Windows based interface applications. Have fun!

What Does This Book Cover?

Chapter 1 sets the stage for the rest of the book by giving an overview of the .NET Framework. It discusses the various components of the Framework, and pays particular attention to the place that Windows Forms holds within it.

Chapter 2 is all about Visual Studio.NET, and how we can use it to make our programming lives so much easier. This chapter shows us everything we will need to know in order to effectively program Windows Forms applications. Starting with creating solutions, projects and files, running through features such as 'intellisense', and finishing up with building and debugging. Finally, it takes a look at command line compiling in .NET.

Chapter 3 looks at the important language features inherent in the new .NET languages. The main topic discussed is Object Oriented programming, but even seasoned C and C++ programmers may find some interesting topics, like Visual Inheritance in Windows Forms, or how the support for established principles has been upgraded.

Chapter 4 is the first chapter dedicated to Windows Forms. It looks more closely at how we create them, including some basic examples of coding forms by hand. In this chapter, we dissect the code that is generated by Visual Studio.NET for a basic form in order to get a better idea of what is going on 'under the hood'. We also begin developing our first application, and specifically take a look at how we place and arrange controls on a form.

Chapter 5 talks about human-computer interaction and shows how Windows Forms implicitly support the principles of good design. As well as discussing the theory and practicalities of interface design, we also look at the range of forms available to us, and how we can use them to control the flow of our applications.

Chapter 6 deals with events. Since, with all event driven applications, it is important to understand how we implement the use of events, this chapter takes a look ' under the hood' and explores the underlying mechanisms involved. For example, we see how to program with delegates, and how to write event handlers in VB.NET and C#

Chapter 7 delves into the world of data. We cover the controls provided by Visual Studio.NET for connecting to data sources, as well as looking at the ADO.NET architecture. As well as this, we look at simple and complex data binding, and how to bind to collections and arrays through a series of examples.

Chapters 8, **9**, and **10,** deal with the various different controls available to Windows Forms. These chapters present all the controls available in several different applications, and then discuss their more important methods and properties. We also show how to use ActiveX controls in our Windows Forms programs. It should be noted however, that due to the sheer number of properties and methods contained in these controls, we only cover the more important or useful ones.

Chapter 11 introduces us to Windows Forms components. We show the various different uses of all the available components, and how we can incorporate them into our applications to enhance their functionality. Topics covered range from monitoring file systems and event logs to incorporating crystal reports into our forms.

Chapter 12 on GDI+ begins with an overview of graphical drawing. After which, we talk about important issues concerning drawing, including coloring, sizing, and how to draw paths like Bezier curves. From here we show, in a series of examples, drawings created using varying methods, like drawing with pens and texture brushes.

Chapter 13 covers the topic of internationalization. It is now increasingly important to develop applications that can support an international array of users and because of this, Microsoft now provides excellent support . Specifically, this chapter introduces two important aspects of internationalization, namely globalization and localization, and shows how we can use them effectively in our applications.

Chapter 14 shows us how to debug our applications. We talk about the new debugging features in .NET, and look at how to use the debugger effectively. We then, by way of an example, show the different debugging windows and round off the chapter with a look at how we can optimize our applications.

Chapter 15 deals with how we package and deploy our applications. The chapter focuses on how we can use Visual Studio.NET to package our Windows Forms applications. Amongst other things, we also cover the Windows Installer, uninstalling Windows Forms applications, and deployment using XCOPY.

Chapter 16 shows us that Web Services aren't the sole property of ASP.NET. In this chapter, we create a Web Service, and then consume it with an ASP.NET Web Form and a Windows Form. This chapter also uses the command line to compile and run code to demonstrate how we can implement a non Visual Studio application.

Chapter 17 looks at how easy it is to expose our forms and controls in a browser. In particular, we have an overview of mobile code, set up IIS, and show several examples demonstrating the different abilities of mobile code.

Chapter 18 is a case study in which we create a sophisticated Windows Form application. The application is a (WDE), or Website Development Environment that incorporates many of the topics covered in the rest of the book. Specifically, it uses a Multiple Document Interface to present the source, HTML, and browser views of the individual pages. It also uses an explorer style form, which allows us to keep track of the Web pages in our site, and thereby support efficient site maintenance.

Who Is This Book For?

This book is aimed at developers who have some experience of C# or Visual Basic.NET. It is not aimed at beginners and consequently does not cover C# or VB.NET programming techniques, or the basics of these programming languages. Having said this, every effort has been made to ensure that all the information required to use the Window Forms technology is present.

To this end, we begin the book by taking a high level view of the role Windows Forms play in the grand scheme of things. This is followed by a thorough investigation of the features that they provide, and how we can use Visual Studio.NET (and the command line) to manipulate them. The book is then rounded up with some excellent practical Windows Forms applications.

In general, so long as you are familiar with the basics of a .NET language, you will be able to use this book, in conjunction with Visual Studio.NET, and require no further reference material. Since the remit of Windows Forms overlaps that of others, you will need to have a generic familiarity with Microsoft software in order to use a couple of the applications demonstrated. The sample code in this book is presented in both VB.NET and C#, in places where it is necessary to point out differences between the two languages.

What you Need to Use this Book

To run the samples in this book you need to have the following:

- Windows 2000 or Windows XP
- Visual Studio.NET

> **Due to the nature of the technology presented in this book, it is strongly suggested that you have the source code download to work with.**

Conventions

We've used a number of different styles of text and layout in this book to help differentiate between the different kinds of information. Here are examples of the styles we used and an explanation of what they mean.

Code has several fonts. If it's a word that we're talking about in the text – for example, when discussing a `For...Next` loop, it's in this font. If it's a block of code that can be typed as a program and run, then it's also in a gray box:

```
<?xml version 1.0?>
```

Sometimes we'll see code in a mixture of styles, like this:

```
<?xml version 1.0?>
<Invoice>
   <part>
      <name>Widget</name>
      <price>$10.00</price>
   </part>
</invoice>
```

In cases like this, the code with a white background is code we are already familiar with; the line highlighted in gray is a new addition to the code since we last looked at it.

Advice, hints, and background information comes in this type of font.

Important pieces of information come in boxes like this.

Bullets appear indented, with each new bullet marked as follows:

- **Important Words** are in a bold type font.
- Words that appear on the screen, or in menus like the Open or Close, are in a similar font to the one you would see on a Windows desktop.
- Keys that you press on the keyboard like *Ctrl* and *Enter*, are in italics.

Customer Support

We always value hearing from our readers, and we want to know what you think about this book: what you liked, what you didn't like, and what you think we can do better next time. You can send us your comments, either by returning the reply card in the back of the book, or by e-mail to feedback@wrox.com. Please be sure to mention the book title in your message.

How to Download the Sample Code for the Book

When you visit the Wrox site, http://www.wrox.com/, simply locate the title through our Search facility or by using one of the title lists. Click on Download in the Code column, or on Download Code on the book's detail page.

The files that are available for download from our site have been archived using WinZip. When you have saved the attachments to a folder on your hard-drive, you need to extract the files using a de-compression program such as WinZip or PKUnzip. When you extract the files, the code is usually extracted into chapter folders. When you start the extraction process, ensure your software (WinZip, PKUnzip, etc.) is set to use folder names.

Errata

We've made every effort to make sure that there are no errors in the text or in the code. However, no one is perfect and mistakes do occur. If you find an error in one of our books, like a spelling mistake or a faulty piece of code, we would be very grateful for feedback. By sending in errata you may save another reader hours of frustration, and of course, you will be helping us provide even higher quality information. Simply e-mail the information to support@wrox.com, your information will be checked and if correct, posted to the errata page for that title, or used in subsequent editions of the book.

To find errata on the web site, go to http://www.wrox.com/, and simply locate the title through our Advanced Search or title list. Click on the Book Errata link, which is below the cover graphic on the book's detail page.

E-mail Support

If you wish to directly query a problem in the book with an expert who knows the book in detail then e-mail support@wrox.com, with the title of the book and the last four numbers of the ISBN in the subject field of the e-mail. A typical e-mail should include the following things:

- The **title of the book, last four digits of the ISBN**, and **page number** of the problem in the Subject field.
- Your **name, contact information**, and the **problem** in the body of the message.

We *won't* send you junk mail. We need the details to save your time and ours. When you send an e-mail message, it will go through the following chain of support:

- Customer Support – Your message is delivered to our customer support staff, who are the first people to read it. They have files on most frequently asked questions and will answer anything general about the book or the web site immediately.
- Editorial – Deeper queries are forwarded to the technical editor responsible for that book. They have experience with the programming language or particular product, and are able to answer detailed technical questions on the subject.
- The Authors – Finally, in the unlikely event that the editor cannot answer your problem, he or she will forward the request to the author. We do try to protect the author from any distractions to their writing; however, we are quite happy to forward specific requests to them. All Wrox authors help with the support on their books. They will e-mail the customer and the editor with their response, and again all readers should benefit.

The Wrox Support process can only offer support to issues that are directly pertinent to the content of our published title. Support for questions that fall outside the scope of normal book support, is provided via the community lists of our http://p2p.wrox.com/ forum.

p2p.wrox.com

For author and peer discussion join the P2P mailing lists. Our unique system provides **programmer to programmer™** contact on mailing lists, forums, and newsgroups, all in addition to our one-to-one e-mail support system. If you post a query to P2P, you can be confident that it is being examined by the many Wrox authors and other industry experts who are present on our mailing lists. At p2p.wrox.com you will find a number of different lists that will help you, not only while you read this book, but also as you develop your own applications. Particularly appropriate to this book are the pro_windows_forms and the vs_dotnet lists.

To subscribe to a mailing list just follow these steps:

1. Go to http://p2p.wrox.com/.
2. Choose the appropriate category from the left menu bar.
3. Click on the mailing list you wish to join.
4. Follow the instructions to subscribe and fill in your e-mail address and password.
5. Reply to the confirmation e-mail you receive.

- Use the subscription manager to join more lists and set your e-mail preferences.

Why this System Offers the Best Support

You can choose to join the mailing lists or you can receive them as a weekly digest. If you don't have the time, or facility, to receive the mailing list, then you can search our online archives. Junk and spam mails are deleted, and your own e-mail address is protected by the unique Lyris system. Queries about joining or leaving lists, and any other general queries about lists, should be sent to `listsupport@p2p.wrox.com`.

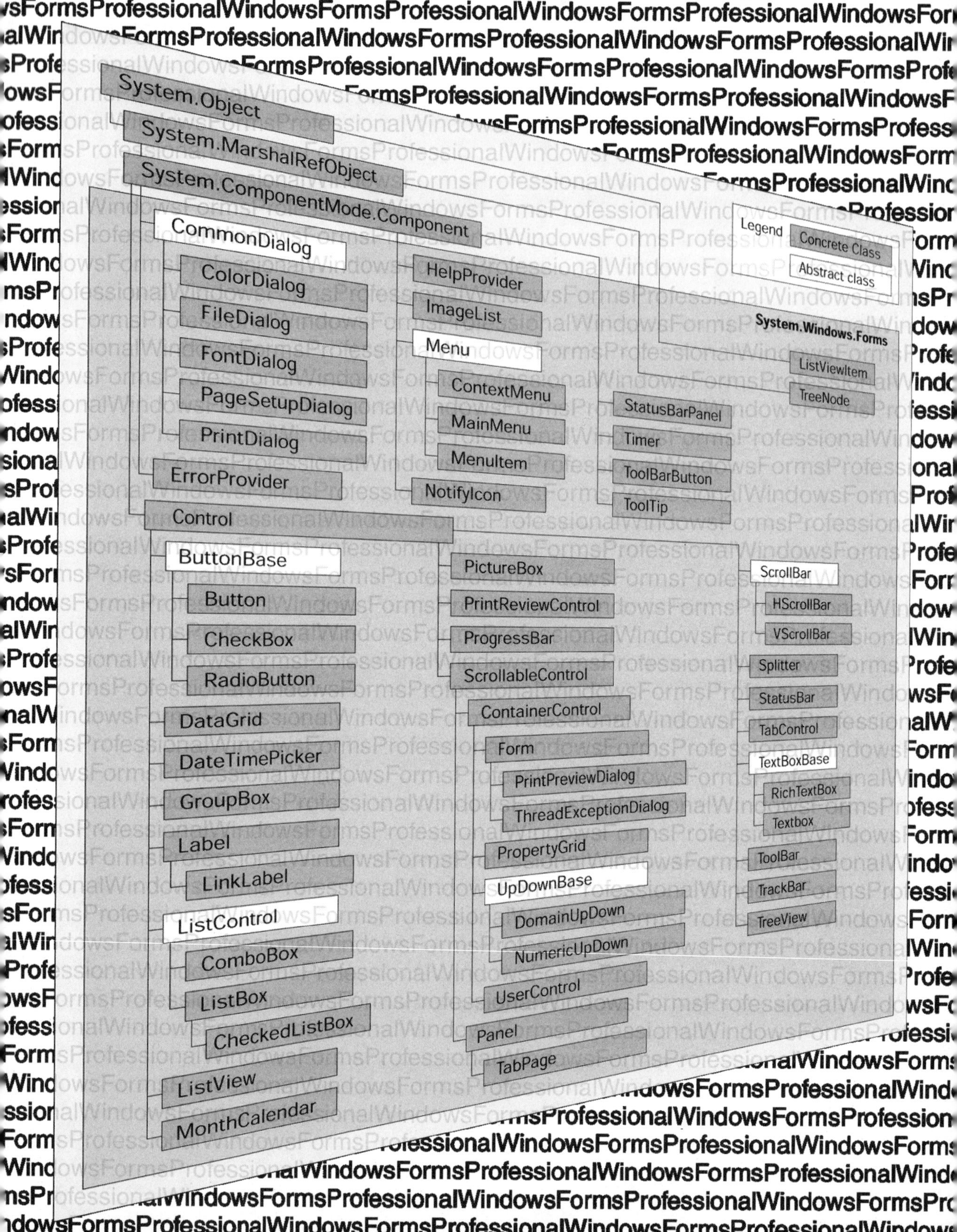
System.Object
System.MarshalRefObject
System.ComponentMode.Component
CommonDialog
ColorDialog
FileDialog
FontDialog
PageSetupDialog
PrintDialog
ErrorProvider
HelpProvider
ImageList
Menu
ContextMenu
MainMenu
MenuItem
NotifyIcon
StatusBarPanel
Timer
ToolBarButton
ToolTip
Legend
Concrete Class
Abstract class
System.Windows.Forms
ListViewItem
TreeNode
Control
ButtonBase
Button
CheckBox
RadioButton
DataGrid
DateTimePicker
GroupBox
Label
LinkLabel
ListControl
ComboBox
ListBox
CheckedListBox
ListView
MonthCalendar
PictureBox
PrintReviewControl
ProgressBar
ScrollableControl
ContainerControl
Form
PrintPreviewDialog
ThreadExceptionDialog
PropertyGrid
UpDownBase
DomainUpDown
NumericUpDown
UserControl
Panel
TabPage
ScrollBar
HScrollBar
VScrollBar
Splitter
StatusBar
TabControl
TextBoxBase
RichTextBox
Textbox
ToolBar
TrackBar
TreeView

1

Introduction to the .NET Framework

According to a leading industry CIO, 99% of all Internet applications have yet to be written. Considering the rate of technology advancement, changes in the market, and changes in the expectation of Internet users, as we look forward 5, 10, and 20 years, this very well may be a conservative estimate.

As the hype and excitement around the irrationally exuberant .com boom (and bust) settles, we are moving into another era where the Internet will be seen for what it is – another tool (albeit a very important one) in the Information Technologist's toolbox. This technology will be the platform for many generations of applications in the years to come, and it's not just a platform for building browser-based applications. The expectations of users have changed, and modern applications are ever more frequently required to interact with the world at large, rather than relying on local machine resources. This involves communicating with other machines via a network, which often means enabling those applications to talk to the Internet.

In fact, the era of monolithic applications that cannot access resources on the Internet is just about over, and one prominent thread that is woven throughout the whole fabric of Microsoft's .NET vision is the facilitation of distributed computing. Portions of a distributed application are executed on different computers, and data presented in the application may come from many different sources on the network.

The .NET Framework is a development platform designed to make it relatively straightforward to build an enormous variety of applications. All the same, if it were merely a few evolutionary steps ahead of MFC, Visual Basic, PowerBuilder, Visual FoxPro, or any of the other software development frameworks of the past, it would probably not be that big a deal. There are several reasons why it's causing such a stir amongst Windows developers: one is the aforementioned emphasis on distributed computing; another is the high quality of its hierarchical class library and the associated .NET tools, foremost of which is Visual Studio .NET.

Whether we are building Windows applications or Web applications in .NET, there are certain features of the Framework that will almost certainly come into play at some point, so deeply entrenched are they in the .NET vision. Together, they bring an unparalleled level of Internet awareness to our .NET-based applications, and as such are vital to the overall .NET vision. Therefore, although it's not strictly necessary to know about these technologies before we start to build Windows Forms applications, we shall take a brief, high-level look at them. Specifically, in this chapter we will cover:

- The Common Language Runtime (CLR)
- Building User Interfaces in .NET
- XML
- Web Services
- Component services through COM+

Finally, with Visual Studio .NET, Microsoft has raised the bar with regards to the quality and capabilities of an Integrated Development Environment (IDE). In this chapter, we'll take a quick look at some of the highlights of the new features of this tool. Other chapters in this book will give a detailed examination of the capabilities and usage of Visual Studio .NET.

What's So Great About .NET?

The requirements of a distributed application dictate that our code run in the context of a runtime that can manage security, object creation and destruction, and cross-platform interoperability. The only other development environment that has such a runtime is Java, which is .NET's closest competitor. However, Microsoft believes that .NET has significant advantages over Java and J2EE. Here's a partial list:

- We will have to wait until the final release of .NET to develop and compare performance benchmarks, but ad hoc tests show that, even with the beta versions, .NET is considerably more efficient than Java. In addition, the runtime allows interoperability between languages at a level not seen before. We can write classes in one language and use them or derive from them in another.
- Visual Studio .NET is a very advanced Integrated Development Environment (IDE). It hosts all of the .NET languages in a single IDE. Automatic code completion and a code editor that allows collapsing and expansion of sections of code make it much more convenient to edit code. With Visual Basic .NET, background compilation can give the appearance of instantaneous compilation.The framework for building web applications (ASP.NET) compares very favorably with the JSP and Servlet technologies. As this book is about Windows Forms, we will not see much about ASP.NET in this book, however. For an in-depth look at this subject, try *Professional ASP.NET* (ISBN *1861004885)*, also from Wrox Press.
- The Windows Forms class hierarchy is rich, and offers improvements over the Java AWT and Swing class hierarchy – we'll take a look at these shortly.

Having said all that, we should point out that at the time of writing, .NET is only available for installation on the Windows platform; consequently Java has the advantage of greater cross-platform compatibility (running on UNIX-based systems for example). Although there is plenty of talk of the .NET Framework being ported to other operating systems at some time in the future, Java will continue to hold that point over .NET until such time as it actually happens.

The Windows Forms Class Hierarchy

The Windows Forms class library is one of the main components of the .NET Framework. It defines numerous object classes that can be used to build rich client applications that look like traditional Windows applications (as built using MFC, Visual Basic, or one of the many other Windows application development toolkits). It provides us with the most modern way to build Windows applications, having built on lessons learned from the Microsoft Foundation Classes (MFC), previous versions of Visual Basic, the Win32 API, and the many other technologies and libraries used to build Windows style applications.

The Windows Forms class hierarchy is specifically designed to fit in with the other .NET classes to build both distributed and non-distributed computing applications. As we examine the .NET Framework, we'll place Windows Forms within the context of the entire .NET vision.

.NET Distributed Application Technologies

In this section, we'll take an overview of some of the technologies underlying .NET. They all have one thing in common: they help us to build high quality distributed applications with good user interfaces. Below is a diagram showing the components that make up the .NET Framework:

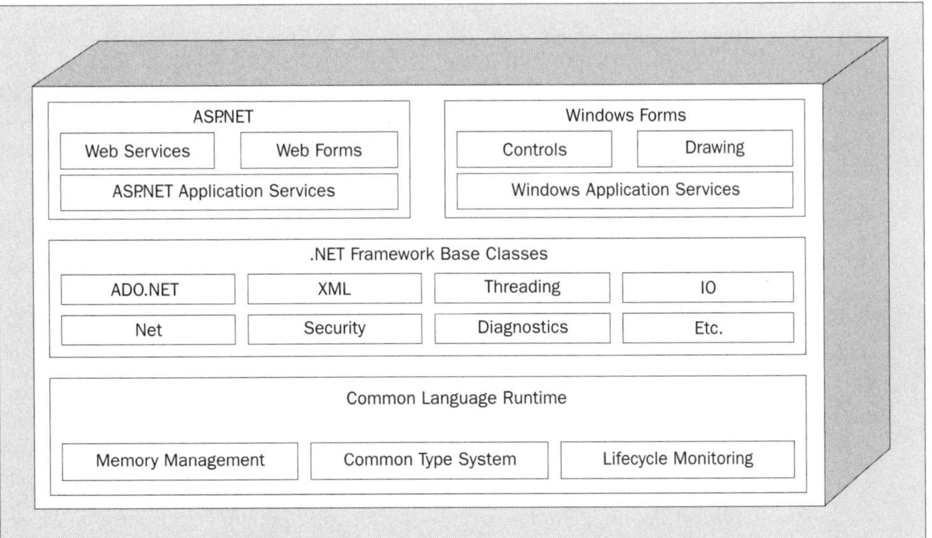

In order to build robust distributed n-tier applications, it is important that we make them **loosely coupled**. That is, we design them so that it's possible to modify one tier, without having any impact whatsoever on the other tiers. For example, in a loosely coupled system, we could replace the database engine in one tier without impacting the user interface tier at all. To build more robust systems, we want to reduce the interconnectedness of the system. Many of the technologies in .NET are specifically designed to aid us in building loosely coupled systems.

- **Common Language Runtime (CLR):** Sometimes referred to as the .NET runtime, the CLR is the foundation for all other .NET technologies. With regards to distributed applications, it provides facilities for mobile code (code that can execute across the network). It also integrates security at the deepest level, which is a vital component of distributed apps. In addition to its distributed application features, the CLR is state-of-the-art with regards to building modern object-oriented (OO) applications. We'll examine the CLR in detail in this chapter.

- **ASP.NET Web Applications:** Formerly known as ASP+, ASP.NET is Microsoft's latest offering for building interactive web applications. Using a non-procedural, declarative approach to web page construction, it provides a powerful infrastructure for building scalable, maintainable, and secure web sites with a rich user interface. ASP.NET code also runs as compiled rather than interpreted code, allowing high performance in web applications.

- **Rich Client Distributed Applications:** Using Windows Forms in combination with technologies such as Web Services, Remoting, Messaging, and COM+, these applications look like a traditional application, but provide a distributed computing experience that accesses data and functionality from many sources on the network.

- **.NET applets:** Windows Forms can be integrated with a web application using Browser Controls. This technology, similar to Java Applets (although at present only available on the Windows platform), facilitates opening Windows Forms from within the context of a web page, either embedded directly in the web page, or opened as a new window on top of the browser.

- **Web Services:** By providing a means by which applications of all kinds can instantiate remote objects and execute methods on those objects, Web Services enable building loosely coupled distributed applications on heterogeneous networks. Because Web Services use HTTP as the protocol to communicate to and from remote objects, they can be implemented so that they easily can be accessed across firewalls.

- **.NET Remoting:** Similar to Web Services, but more tightly coupled, .NET Remoting gives a greater degree of control when instantiating remote objects and executing methods on them. It supports passing objects by value or by reference. It can use a variety of protocols (HTTP, TCP, etc.), and formats (SOAP or Binary). In some cases, it may be more efficient, providing better performance. .NET remoting provides a replacement for the older DCOM technology on Windows.

- **Security:** .NET provides an 'evidence based' security system, comprised of two parts:

  - Code Access Security identifies who wrote the code (what digital signatures it has), what it will try to do, and where it came from.

  - Role-Based Security controls permissions based on the identity of the user.

  This gives system administrators a much finer degree of control when configuring security on their system. This also relieves the user from making trust decisions as to whether or not they should install a component.

- **Enterprise Services using COM+:** Enterprise applications require facilities such as Transactions, Object Pooling, and Security. When distributed applications are on a network where availability of remote systems is not guaranteed, transactions provide database integrity. When the number of users connecting to a system may be in the hundreds or thousands, Object Pooling provides tools for implementing scalability. When code is available for remote execution on a public network, the security services of COM+ authenticates users and disallows unauthorized access.

- **Data Access:** ADO.NET provides a programming model that is suited to building distributed applications in a disconnected environment. It provides mechanisms whereby connections to the database don't need to be kept open, and data can be retrieved, updated, and reconciled in a loosely coupled, distributed system with less than high network availability. We can use ADO.NET to access any number of SQL database engines, of course including MS SQL Server. We can also access any database that has ODBC access.

- **Messaging with MSMQ:** This is an asynchronous messaging service that facilitates building robust distributed applications. The asynchronous nature of MSMQ means that applications can send a message, and if the network is not currently available, the message will get delivered when the network becomes available. In contrast, synchronous messaging means that a message and its response must happen in a timely fashion, otherwise there is a malfunction of the system. In a system where network availability is low, asynchronous messaging provides increased robustness.
- **Network Communication:** These are more low-level facilities that the Framework provides as programming interfaces to many protocols, such as DNS, HTTP, TCP, UDP. These APIs are the basis for all of the distributed application capabilities in .NET, and are the foundation for building advanced Peer-to-Peer applications.

This is an extremely impressive set of resources for building distributed applications, but this is not all that .NET offers. Another area of extreme interest to the Information Technologist is programmer productivity.

Programmer Productivity

In days past, I had a manager with this sign on his wall:

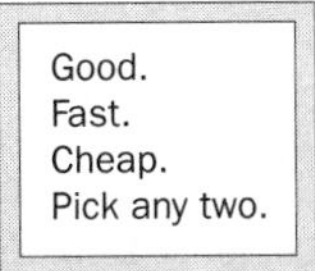

This was an amusing way to articulate the problem that we all face: how to get more done, with higher quality, in less time. The .NET platform makes some important inroads into this problem.

There are a number of studies that show that developers can write Java code, on average, twice as fast as they can write C++ code. My own subjective experience agrees with this conclusion.

While Java was a step forward from C++, Java has some problems, performance being the largest of them. Java byte code was not specifically designed for ease of compilation to native machine code. Another problem is application appearance. Rich client applications written in Java look 'clunky' when run on a Windows machine. They don't have the same look and feel, and they don't have the same level of polish. Windows users expect a certain level of behavior – for example: popup menus should behave in a certain way when activated at the bottom or right edge of the screen; the clipboard should always be available when the user right-clicks on text boxes, and so on. The end result is that very few of the commercial applications available for the Windows platform are actually written in Java – the vast majority are written using tools such as VC++ and VB, which are targeted specifically at Windows-based development.

.NET applications can be written in any number of compliant languages, including C#, Visual Basic.NET, JScript.NET, and managed C++. As we'll discuss shortly, all source code is compiled to a common MS Intermediate Language (IL) prior to execution, so it's even possible to mix and match languages within a single application. Programmers can therefore pick and choose their language with complete freedom.

As part of the .NET Framework, Microsoft provides compilers for each of the languages listed above, while compilers for other languages are currently being developed by third parties.

In this book we shall be focusing on C# and VB.NET. C# and VB both have similar characteristics to those that make Java so productive: a good inheritance model, garbage collection, no pointers (mostly), a cleaner syntax, and a single set of standard libraries. It is interesting to note these similarities between C# and VB.NET. The languages are so similar that there are even rough tools that can translate some VB.NET code to C#.

The better inheritance model is the one that the foremost object-oriented language design experts have advanced: single implementation inheritance and multiple interface inheritance. Multiple implementation inheritance is available in C++ but brings in a whole host of problems, particularly in the area where one class inherits twice from another class, but through two different inheritance paths.

Another area of innovation of both C# and VB.NET is the inclusion of properties and events as first-class citizens in the type system. Component-based software requires both properties and events, and their integration at the foundation of .NET removes the necessity of magic naming conventions, that is, in Java a property *must* be implemented by a function named `get_____()`, for example `getHeight()`. Rather, in .NET we would simply have a property named `Height`. Events implemented via delegates (which are similar to pointers to functions) provide a similar benefit. See Chapter 6 on Events for more information on delegates. Another benefit is that this feature enhances automatic documentation generation.

C# includes a few features in the language that make programming somewhat easier, such as an implementation of enums, limited operator overloading, and delegates. These features are not **must have** features, and we can certainly write applications without them. However, their absence removes an element of expressiveness that makes programs easier to read and maintain.

C# and VB.NET also have the advantage of being implemented on top of the **Common Language Runtime**, which provides performance gains over Java.

Common Language Runtime (CLR)

One way to think of the **.NET Common Language Runtime** (often referred to as the **CLR** or **.NET Runtime**) is as an elaborate virtual machine on which compiled code is executed. By handling many crucial low-level processes such as resource allocation, thread management, and garbage collection, it hides away many of the necessary but time-consuming coding tasks that you (as a developer) might otherwise have spent sleepless nights over. What's more, the fact that the CLR effectively **supervises** the executing code means that we have security facilities far beyond unmanaged languages such as C++. Here's a brief list of some of the features it offers:

- Code access security
- Object lifetime management (object creation and garbage collection)
- Process and thread management
- Cross-language integration
- Debugging support
- Profiling support

It is very useful to have a basic appreciation of the architecture of the CLR, and to understand the most important terms and acronyms used in reference to its various elements. However, an in-depth exploration could fill an entire book, and is not necessary here. We'll now explore just enough to give you a rough idea of what is going on under the hood when we come to build and run our Windows Forms applications.

Runtimes

The concept of **runtimes** is nothing new – many programming languages have them, including Visual Basic (`VBRUN.dll`), Visual C++ (`MSVCRT.dll`), as well as Java, JScript, Visual FoxPro, SmallTalk, and Perl. A runtime is code or libraries that run in addition to, or in conjunction with, our program, and provide many of the core services, such as libraries for basic IO, memory protection, etc. Sometimes, the runtime actually interprets the targeted language, as is the case with Visual Basic when not compiled to machine code. One thing that makes the .NET Runtime different from all of these is that it is a unified runtime for many programming languages. Another thing that sets this runtime apart, is the high quality of the technology it contains, such as the very fast garbage collector.

One of the problems with runtimes in the past has been installation and versioning issues. Once the .NET runtime is integrated into the operating system, and ships with it by default, the distinction between the runtime and the rest of the machine and operating system will start to blur. We will be able to always rely on it being installed and available. Microsoft has said that the CLR will ship with operating systems sometime in 2002. In the meantime, it can be easily downloaded from Microsoft's web site and installed.

Managed Code

Any code that runs within the CLR is called **managed code**. Examples of managed code include C# and Visual Basic .NET code. Examples of unmanaged code are legacy DLLs and COM components. We can use them, but they do not receive the benefits of managed code, including garbage collection, security, debugging support, and profiling support, as we mentioned previously.

Intermediate Language

C#, Visual Basic .NET, and many other languages are compiled to Microsoft Intermediate Language (MSIL), often called just **Intermediate Language**, or simply **IL**. IL is the language for an abstract stack-based virtual machine, and is the input to a JIT (Just-In-Time) compiler.

Some of the main characteristics of IL are:

- It is intrinsically object-oriented with single implementation inheritance and multiple interface inheritance. It has support for object management (object creation and garbage collection).
- It has support for both value types (integers, floats, strings, etc.), and reference types (classes).
- It is strongly typed.
- It is specifically designed for fast and effective translation to native machine code.
- It supports verifiability. An application cannot attempt to access private variables.

One of the responsibilities of the CLR is to load and run code. When it loads code, IL is what the CLR expects to find. The CLR invokes one of the JIT compilers to convert IL to native machine code. The JIT compiler leads to high performance, since it compiles each portion of code the first time it is actually called, and then retains the compiled native machine code in memory while the application runs. This means that only the parts of the application that are actually used are compiled, and each line of code is only compiled once, no matter how many times it is executed. IL is designed to be very easily compiled to machine code, meaning that performance is almost as good as if native executable instead of IL had been supplied.

The IL approach to delivering executable code is by far the best approach for distributed applications. When looking at the domain of solutions that can deliver executable code, there are primarily five possible alternatives:

- We could deliver executables and DLLs compiled for a particular platform. This solution (the traditional one for Windows since its inception) of course makes efficient cross platform delivery impossible. In addition, because the code is not managed, security issues can't be dealt with. This is the reason that we see messages when installing ActiveX controls such as 'Do you trust this software from the XYZ Corporation?'
- We could deliver source code that is interpreted on the client machine. This has serious performance problems. In addition, there are source code confidentiality issues. JavaScript embedded in a web page is an example of this type of source code delivery.
- We could deliver source code that is compiled on the client machine. This brings source code confidentiality issues, compilation time issues, and client machine configuration issues. Full-blown development compilers would need to be on the client machine. This solution is basically out of the question.
- We could deliver intermediate language that is interpreted on the client machine. This is the Java Byte Code solution. This has performance issues. The IL should be designed from the ground up with JIT compilation in mind.
- Finally, we could deliver intermediate language that is designed for very fast compilation to native code on the client machine. This is the only reasonable alternative. Source code is compiled to an intermediate language on the developer's machine. This protects the confidentiality of the source code. It also places the burden of the bulk of the compilation on the developer's machine. Because this intermediate language is designed for fast compilation or translation to efficient machine code, we get high performance from our applications, and because this intermediate language could potentially be compiled for different processors, we could get platform independence. Microsoft has not stated that platform independence is a main goal of .NET, other than compilation for small devices such as PDAs and cell phones, but the potential is there.

The most convenient way to implement this last method is to integrate it into the operating system, so that the mechanism of JIT compilation and caching the compiled machine code is hidden from the view of the user. It is not the only way, but it eliminates one element of complexity from the view of the user. This is .NET's approach.

IL actually has the potential to deliver better performance than code that is compiled to native machine code. This is because there could be JIT compilers that understand the class of machine that it is compiling for. So for example if JIT-compiling on a Pentium 4 class machine we could compile IL so that it takes advantage of advanced Pentium 4 instructions. In addition, the various Pentium architectures may perform better when machine code is organized with the architecture in mind, and the JIT compiler potentially could do this. This is not possible if compiling to native executable on the developer's machine, since the compiler in that case does not know what machine the code will run on, and so cannot optimize for any particular hardware.

Assemblies and Manifests

Compilers place IL into **assemblies**. An assembly is a collection of classes (stored in one or more files) that form a unit of functionality. In the process of resolving external references (a process similar to linking), the runtime loads and binds together one or more assemblies to run an application. Assemblies are somewhat analogous to executables (EXEs) or Dynamic Link Libraries (DLLs), but with some important differences.

Assemblies are self-describing via something called a **manifest**. The manifest is a part of the assembly that stores information about its containing assembly. The result is that:

- It establishes the assembly identity. The identity comprises a text name, version, culture, and optionally a digital signature if the assembly will be used by other applications.
- An assembly can be spread across multiple files, and the manifest defines the files that make up the assembly.
- The assembly may have dependencies on other assemblies. The manifest specifies this dependency.
- The manifest works with the security features of the CLR by specifying what security permissions are required for the assembly. The security system of the CLR applies Code Access Security permissions at the granularity of an assembly. When running a program, the CLR can determine the assembly for any instantiated object, as all classes are loaded in the context of an assembly, and it uses this information to grant permissions.

An assembly can be stored in a DLL file or it can be stored in an EXE file if we intend for a user to execute it, instead of another program. EXE files created in this fashion are called **Portable Executable** (**PE**) files.

The classes and types within an assembly are marked indicating whether they are accessible outside of the assembly. The public interface to the assembly can be discovered through an API or through external utilities.

The self-describing nature of assemblies (the type information plus the manifest information) enables assembly installation that doesn't need to modify the registry or any directory outside of the application. This is sometimes called **zero-impact install** or **xcopy deployment**. Assembly deployment can be as easy as copying files to the client system.

There are also facilities for validating the integrity of assemblies. This should prevent malicious code from tampering with an assembly.

Because part of the assembly identity is a version number, the CLR can load and run two different versions of an assembly simultaneously. This is part of the solution to 'DLL hell', where a component is updated on a system where other software is relying on a bug that exists in a previous version of the same component. Allowing simultaneous access to multiple versions improves system stability.

Common Type System

An integral part of IL is the **Common Type System** (**CTS**). In the past, we have seen situations where types are not compatible between various languages and compilers. A long integer would be defined as 32 bits using one C compiler, and 64 bits using another. The differences between types even more pronounced when moving from language to language.

The CTS defines a standard set of types that are supported by IL, that is, the CLR knows how to create and manipulate these types. This list is exhaustive, and is quite sufficient for all general purpose programming needs. The CTS also defines rules for creating new types, such as classes, and the CLR knows how to instantiate and execute these types. The compilers for the .NET Framework make use of standard facilities in the CLR to define classes, manage instances of those classes, and make method calls into those classes, instead of inventing their own class and instance infrastructure.

Common Language Specification

A standard that is applied to the CLR is the **Common Language Specification** (**CLS**). The CLS defines a particular subset of the CLR that compilers must support so that languages can interoperate. The standard sometimes can be said to apply to a compiler, that is, the compiler generates CLS compliant code. The standard also sometimes can be said to apply to a class library: the library is or is not CLS compliant. Examples of the CLS:

- No global methods or variables are permitted.
- Certain data types can only be defined if they are private, and therefore are not visible to any client code (signed byte integer, unsigned short integer, unsigned integer, or unsigned long integer). This is to allow interoperability with languages (such as VB.NET) that do not recognize those data types.
- Public names must differ in more than case.

The CTS combined with the CLS gives us language interoperability. Classes written in one language can inherit from classes written in another. A method written in one language can throw an exception that is caught in a method written in another. Debugging and profiling work seamlessly across languages. This gives a great degree of leverage. Having once learned the .NET Framework, we can use it from a variety of languages, eliminating the need to learn new class hierarchies when we move from language to language. If developers writing commercial components restrict their classes such that they only expose CLS-compliant features, they can market their component to users of any CLS compliant language.

There is nothing to prevent MC++ and C# coders from declaring types that are not compliant with the CLS. However, the classes most probably will not be accessible from other languages.
Other languages that have now been implemented on the CLR, or are in the process of being implemented on the CLR, include:

- APL
- Cobol
- Eiffel
- Fortran
- Pascal
- Perl
- Python
- Smalltalk

There are many other languages also being ported to the CLR. For more information on porting efforts, see www.gotdotnet.com.

Class Libraries

There are many class libraries that are part of the .NET Framework, and it is useful to understand some subdivisions, and what the functionality of each of the subdivisions is. There are a lot of acronyms in this section, and getting a clear understanding of them will help a lot.

The **Framework Class Library** (**FCL**) is the class library that CLS compliant languages can use. The FCL is broken down into five parts:

- Base Class Library (BCL)
- ASP.NET
- Windows Forms
- ADO.NET
- XML

The **Base Class Library** (**BCL**) is a subset of the FCL. Functionality present in the BCL is:

- `Collections`
- `Configuration`
- `Diagnostics`
- `Globalization`
- `IO`
- `Net`
- `Reflection`
- `Resources`
- `Security`
- `ServiceProcess`
- `Text`
- `Threading`
- `Runtime` (InteropServices, Remoting, Serialization)

Microsoft has submitted C#, the CLR, and a subset of the FCL to ECMA, an international standards organization. This is referred to as the **Common Language Infrastructure** (**CLI**). The class libraries that they have submitted include:

- Runtime Infrastructure Library
- Base Class Library (BCL)
- Network Library
- Reflection Library
- XML Library
- Floating-Point Library
- Extended Array Library

Application Domains

There is an old saying, 'Good fences make good neighbors'. In the past, isolation between applications was typically accomplished through the use of multiple processes. This certainly creates a good fence, but when it is necessary to climb over the fence it involves a process context switch at the operating system level, which is time consuming. Another interesting and innovative feature of the CLR is **application domains**. This facility of the CLR enables us to put two applications into the same process, but because the code is managed and type safe, the fence is intact. In effect, the fence is provided by the CLR instead of the operating system. This allows extremely fast inter-application communication.

Evidence Based Security

The .NET Framework security infrastructure provides a great degree of control over what code can or cannot do based on the identity of the user, who wrote the code, what the code is trying to do, and where it came from.

Security based on the identity of the user is called **role based security**. We use this type of security to allow or deny access to a protected resource, such as confidential pages on a web site.

Security based on who wrote the code, what the code is trying to do, and where it came from is called **code access security**. We use this type of security to allow or deny code the permission to run. This is the technology that protects us from malicious code. A **Trust Policy** defines security permissions based on code access security.

Role Based Security

There are two fundamental concepts in role based security: **authentication** and **authorization**.

When we authenticate a user, we validate a set of user credentials against an authority. If the credentials are valid, then the user has an **Identity**. There are several ways to authenticate a user:

- Basic
- Digest
- Microsoft Passport
- Integrated Windows authentication (also known as Windows NT LAN Manager, or NTLM)
- Custom authentication

Basic authentication is the least secure method of performing authentication. User information is sent over the Internet using clear text. The user name and password use a base64-encoded string. Microsoft does not recommend this method.

Digest Authentication uses a more sophisticated scheme than basic authentication. The server challenges using something called a nonce, which is a string specified by the server. The client must formulate and send a valid response, which is a checksum of the user name, the password, the nonce, the HTTP method, and the requested **Uniform Resource Identifier** (**URI**). A URI is an address on the Internet. It would be rather difficult for a malicious interlocutor to decode the user name and password from an intercepted checksum, even if the nonce has been previously intercepted. This method works across proxy servers and firewalls.

Microsoft Passport Authentication is a service provided by Microsoft. When the user makes a request for a protected resource, the server looks for a valid Passport ticket. If there is no ticket, the user is re-directed to the Passport Logon Service. Information about the original request is passed in an encrypted form to the Passport Logon Service. The user logs on to the logon service using Secure Sockets Layer (SSL). After a successful logon, the logon service redirects the user back to the original URI with the ticket encrypted in the query string, and the protected resource is made available to the user. All communications made in the process of Microsoft Passport authentication are encrypted. This method is very secure.

Integrated Windows Authentication uses the current user's credentials from a domain logon. If the user is not a valid one on the server, the user will be prompted for a user name and password via a dialog box. The user's password is never passed from the client to the server. This is an appropriate method when we have a web site with a known, finite list of authorized users.

With **custom authentication**, programmers can design their own authentication mechanisms. This enables us to use a custom database or other source for user authentication.

After a user is authenticated (has an identity), **authorization** is the process of using that identity to grant or deny access to a protected resource.

We write the application program in the same way, regardless of the type of authentication that we are using.

Code Access Security

Code access security refers to the process of granting permissions to a particular assembly to do some operation – write to a file, draw to the screen, etc.

The evidence for code access security is:

- Who wrote the code. The code may have a digital signature.
- What the code is trying to do. Does it attempt to write to the file system? Does it attempt to do network access?
- Where it came from. Did it come from a trusted site on the Internet, an unknown site on the Internet, from a site on the LAN, or from our own hard disk?

This evidence is passed, along with a Trust Policy, to the Security Policy System, which makes a trust decision based on the policies previously established. This removes the responsibility to make a decision of whether or not to trust the code from the user.

Cryptography

The .NET Framework provides a library of cryptographic functionality, including symmetric and asymmetric encryption algorithms. This library contains the building blocks for the .NET security system.

Garbage Collection

The CLR supports garbage collection. The Garbage Collector (GC) traces through all references to actively used objects, and by a process of elimination, it locates all objects that can't be reached. It rearranges memory to defragment the heap. Most professional programmers are familiar with the benefits of garbage collection, but to reiterate, garbage collection solves the problem where code never frees memory, causing a memory leak. It also solves the problem where code prematurely frees memory, and there still exists a reference to the memory. This problem leads to memory corruption. Both problems are time-intensive to solve.

The garbage collector also rearranges memory for the purposes of efficiency, organizing objects by the length of time that they have been in existence. By far, most objects are very short lived. They are created and destroyed very quickly. If an object lasts for a longer period of time then it is moved to a different part of the heap where garbage collection is done much less frequently. The garbage collector runs most often in the portion of the heap that contains short-lived objects, and less frequently in the portion of the heap that contains long-lived objects.

There are some situations where we might desire to keep some very large objects in memory for efficiency. We may be done with the objects, but it is possible that we will need them again. We have the ability to register 'weak references', where we essentially tell the CLR that we may still want this object, but if it requires, it can destroy it and recover its memory. Later, if and when we want the object again, we ask for the object. If it still exists, we get a reference to it, and it no longer is a weak reference, but is a normal reference. Alternatively, we may be told that the object no longer exists, and then we need to recreate it again from the original source. Caching for a web browser is a good example where this technique would be valuable.

Summary of Acronyms and Terms in the CLR

Acronym/Term	Meaning
Application Domain	A partition in a process, such that two applications can share the same process
Assembly	A collection of managed classes
Authentication	The process of identifying a user
Authorization	The process of granting permission to a user for a resource
BCL	Base Class Library
Byte Code	The Java equivalent to IL
CLI	Common Language Infrastructure (what is being standardized by ECMA)
CLR	Common Language Runtime
CLS	Common Language Specification
Code-Based Security	Security that allows or denies permission for code to run
CTS	Common Type System
FCL	Framework Class Library
GC	Garbage Collector
Identity	The identity of a user after authentication
IL	Intermediate Language
JIT	Just-In-Time, as in JIT Compiler
Language Interoperability	The capability for a language to derive a class from one written in another language, and to use a type defined in another language
Managed Code	Code that runs in the context of the CLR
Manifest	A part of an assembly that describes the assembly
MSIL	Microsoft Intermediate Language, more often referred to as IL
PE	Portable Executable
Role-Based Security	Security that allows or denies access to a protected resource based on the identity of the user
URI	Uniform Resource Identifier (an address on the Internet)

Building User Interfaces in .NET

Java and C++ have proved that the effective use of object-oriented technology *must* include the development of comprehensive class libraries that facilitate many aspects of application development, including user interfaces, data storage, and IO. Good hindsight has given the .NET Framework designers the chance to clean up and rework past approaches, providing the best class libraries seen yet.

We have two choices when developing user interfaces using .NET. Windows Forms (the topic of this book) allows us to develop rich user interfaces that have a traditional Windows look and feel. Web Forms is Microsoft's new system for developing browser-based applications.

We'll present a small overview of each of the technologies, and then talk about the considerations that play in the choice between the two.

Windows Forms

Windows Forms is the next step in the evolution of class hierarchies for building traditional Windows applications or for building rich client tiers in n-tier applications. It builds on the experience of MFC, the Win32 API, and other frameworks to provide a very clean and powerful class hierarchy. It has a number of very good features:

- **Rich set of controls with a new look**: Windows Forms provides a rich set of controls that give a new, pleasing, modern look to applications. In addition to all of the standard controls that we expect as part of a Graphical User Interface API, these controls include a comprehensive grid control and a tree control.
- **Layered approach**: A layered approach offers the advantages of better performance, a true native look and feel, and a clean class hierarchy.

  A layered approach means that native controls from the Win32 API, such as text boxes, buttons, combo boxes, etc. are wrapped in the new API. This approach actually uses the real native controls.

  In contrast, an emulated approach makes use of some of the facilities in the native windowing system, such as windows, child windows, graphical functions, mouse events, and character events. However, for the controls in the window, this approach uses drawing functions to create the appearance of the controls, and handles mouse and character events to implement their behavior.
- **Clean, homogenized programming model** Windows Forms eliminates many of the inconsistencies of the Windows API. For example, sometimes a certain window style can only be applied to a window when it is created. In Windows Forms. If we apply such a style, Windows Forms will quietly destroy and re-create the window behind the scenes with the new style.

  Delegates provide the cleanest programming model for handling events yet seen. We can easily have multiple event handlers for an event without the need to declare or derive new classes.
- **Same API from Multiple Programming Languages** Because it uses the CLR, regardless of whether we use C#, Visual Basic .NET, managed C++, or other languages, we use the same API to write our application.

- **Forms Inheritance** Because of the technical approach taken by Windows Forms, it is possible to derive from another form and add a few controls to the form. For example, in a database application, we could have a base class that puts up the controls for data navigation, such as first record, next record, previous record, and last record. The classes that do the actual data maintenance would then derive from this base class and we wouldnot need to re-declare these controls.

Windows Forms applications can *look* like traditional Windows applications, but they can differ in almost every other respect. By taking advantage of all of the distributed computing capabilities in .NET, Windows Forms can be part of an n-tier, loosely coupled distributed application, with all of the deployment characteristics of browser-based applications.

A particularly interesting capability of Windows Forms is the ability to put up Windows Forms from within a web page in IE6 using mobile code. These forms are similar to Java applets, but with some important differences: They perform better, due to the compiled nature of .NET applications vs. the interpreted nature of Java byte code. In addition, they are cached easily on the local machine. This can be done with Java applets, but is more difficult. Unfortunately though, they can only be used on Windows clients.

To see examples of some of these advanced capabilities, see Chapter 17, *Windows Forms in Web Pages.*

Web Forms

One of the most revolutionary and visionary parts of .NET is the new approach that Microsoft has taken for building web pages and web applications. ASP.NET is a non-procedural, declarative model for building web pages. Further, it is a model that we can easily extend, building components that implement abstractions that give us unparalleled expressiveness when solving our own particular problems. We can build our own specialized application development infrastructure. It embraces the idea of 'Don't build applications. Build tools, and then use the tools to assemble your applications.'

As an example, an Internet-based newspaper could implement a 'news story' abstraction that provides the standard formatting that they want for a news story. This abstraction could include references to pictures, references to embedded advertisements, keywords for links to a search engine for automatic inclusion of a list of other stories to also see, etc.

Another example is a company that publishes databases. They could build up a 'database maintenance' abstraction, such that they only need to provide the name of the table, and their custom .NET control would automatically generate all of the input fields, buttons, etc., that allow the user to add, delete, and update records in their database. Adding new tables to the database then becomes very easy.

These abstractions are processed on the server, and can make presentation decisions based on the capabilities of the client's browser. If the browser is a down-level browser, it can generate HTML 3.2. If the browser is IE 4.0 or later, it can generate DHTML.

These abstractions can also provide device independence. For instance, if the abstraction determines that the browser is a mobile device, such as a PDA, connected over a digital cellular network, it can make formatting decisions more appropriate to the small screen of the PDA, and delay transmission of pictures that accompany the story until the user requests them.

Business logic code can be cleanly separated from the presentation code, which makes for a much more maintainable web application. It also separates the code so that programmers and presentation or business experts do not need to maintain the same files. This is a more effective and clean separation of the business logic from the presentation.

Another advantage of Web Forms is its inclusion in a framework that provides a real object-oriented architecture. When building a small web application, there is not a lot of difference between using an OO approach or not, but when building large applications using a non-OO approach, maintainability suffers. The applications get 'brittle'; small changes in one part of the application have the potential to impact many other parts of the application.

When we use Visual Studio .NET to build web applications using Web Forms, we get a Rapid Application Development (RAD) environment that gives us drag and drop design capabilities. It also gives us an event-based programming model similar to building Visual Basic applications that makes it very easy to build and debug web applications.

Which Should We Use: Windows Forms or Web Forms?

Since this is a book on Windows Forms, it is helpful to understand the considerations about whether to use Windows Forms or Web Forms.

Sometimes the decision is clear. If we are building an application for the Internet that users will access from browsers, such as an e-commerce application, then we must use Web Forms. If we are building a processing-intensive application that needs to take advantage of fast processors on the client machine, then a Windows Form application will be more appropriate. If the decision is not clear, some of the following considerations may apply:

- **User Preference**: The nature of the two styles of user interface is quite different. Sometimes the users of the application know that they want a traditional rich client user interface, or a browser interface.
- **CPU Processing Requirements**: A Windows Forms application would be used when most of the processing will be done on the client. Some examples are CAD/CAM applications, games, high volume heads-down data entry applications, word processors, spreadsheets, and point-of-sale systems.
- **Deployment Cost Requirements**: Web Form applications are easy to write such that they have minimal deployment cost. They only require a compatible browser on the client. It is possible to write a Windows Form application with no deployment costs, but it takes somewhat more effort, and the client is restricted to one of the Windows operating systems, and must have the .NET runtime installed.

  Regardless of whether a Windows Forms application is distributed on demand from a server, or distributed via download or physical media, it requires the installation of the .NET runtime on the target machine. It will be several years before we can assume the existence of the .NET runtime on all client machines. As it is right now, it is not possible to build a small Windows Forms application, put it on a floppy disk, and send for installation if the client machine doesn't have the runtime installed.
- **Non-connected Applications**: If an application may need to run when the computer is not connected to the network, we need to build a Windows Forms application.
- **Applications that require access to local resources**: If an application needs access to the local file system, the registry, IO ports, etc., it must be written using Windows Forms.

- **Interactive Graphical Applications**: If we are building a graphical application where there should be a high degree of responsiveness to the user, such as a drawing application, a Windows Forms application is appropriate. A Web Form application can use draw graphics and serve them to the browser on the client, but interactive operations require a message to be sent to the server and a response sent back to the client (this is often called a 'Round Trip'). Latency and bandwidth considerations may require that this portion of an application be written using Windows Forms.
- **Formatted Text Applications**: Some applications may be oriented around formatted text. A document presentation application might be an example of this type of application. These applications sometimes are naturally suited for a Web Forms implementation, where they can take advantage of all of the formatting capabilities of HTML.
- **High Concurrency Control Applications**: Database applications that require a high degree of concurrency control, such as pessimistic record locking, may be better implemented using Windows Forms.

There are even certain situations where we may want to build a hybrid application, where a portion of the application is a browser-based application, but certain functionality is put up in Windows Forms.

XML

XML is a markup language where application developers can define their own tags. It is a subset of SGML that is a generalized format for describing data. This format is useful in a variety of contexts, such as transmitting data, describing remote objects, serializing objects, and separating data in a web page from its presentation.

Microsoft has stated that XML is a central part of their strategy for building distributed applications. There are many parts of the .NET Framework that provide facilities using XML. We will place their usefulness in the context of the entire Framework, and examine the potential for using them in combination to gain additional power.

Following is a list of the uses of XML in the .NET Framework and tools:

- **Presentation of data in a web page**: With XML, we can use the XML Web Server Control to present data in a browser. If we supply an XSLT document, the XML will be transformed before its contents are written to the output stream. XML separates the data from the presentation, which allows us to take the same data and present it in a variety of ways.
- **Web Services**: Early on in this chapter, we saw how web services allow us to create and access remote objects. XML is the technology underneath web services. Simple Object Access Protocol (SOAP) is an XML based protocol for calling methods and transferring data over the web.
- **Datasets**: In ADO.NET, datasets can be converted to and from XML. This gives us the capability to do a query on a database, which gets us a dataset. We can then use the XML representation of that `DataSet` in a variety of ways, including transmitting it over the web, formatting it for inclusion on a web page, caching it for performance reasons, or re-creating another ADO.NET `DataSet`, perhaps on a remote machine.
- **Serialization**: Sometimes we need to save the state of some objects in our software system. This technique could be used to save a complex document onto disk, to be reloaded later. Serialization can use either a binary format or SOAP, in which case it uses XML.

- **Documentation**: When using C#, we can document our code using XML. C# is the only programming language in the .NET Framework that natively supports this feature.
- **Configuration Files**: There are various files that let us specify configuration options for the entire machine, or for a single application. There is also a separate configuration file for specifying security options. All of these configuration files are in XML.
- **Programming Interfaces to XML**: When writing our application, we can make use of classes that facilitate reading XML files into memory, modifying the data, and writing the XML file to some destination on the local machine, to a string in memory, or to a stream across the network. **Document Object Model** (**DOM**), **Simple API to XML** (**SAX**), and **SAX2**, the latest incarnation of SAX, are the APIs for programming with XML.
- **XML Designer**: This tool allows us to directly edit XML and **XML Schemas Definition** (**XSD**) files from within Visual Studio .NET. There are two views for maintaining XML and XSD files. One is an intelligent text editor that provides color-coding and IntelliSense, which provides automatic property completion and drop-down lists when inserting new properties. Another view for editing XML and XSD is the Data view, which allows us to edit them in a structured data grid.
- These are not all of the ways that XML is used in this system, but this is a rather impressive list. There will certainly be developers out there who will combine the use of several of these facilities in ways that the designers never imagined, and in doing so, create a level of leverage and functionality that will surprise everyone.

Web Services

Web Services, which we have seen mentioned in a couple of different contexts previously in this chapter, goes beyond just another remoting technology. Its platform-agnostic approach, embodied in its use of SOAP and XML transmitted over HTTP, give it a generic flavor and accessibility that invite its use across platforms and technologies. We can choose one of many technologies to implement our Web Service, and then consume it from an entirely different technology.

Web Services will change the landscape of the Internet. New business models for Internet companies are made possible by this technology.

Consider the case of a vendor of mapping technology. They now can inexpensively provide mapping facilities to many other web sites by implementing a Web Service. They don't need to expose their mapping technology to others. They don't need to deliver large map description files to their customers. They simply need to write a Web Service so that when an end user requests a map from one of their customer's web sites, their customer's web site accesses their Web Service, passing addresses, level of detail, and other pertinent information, and the mapping company can deliver the map, to be included seamlessly into their customer's web site.

Or consider the case of a shipping company. Let's say that we have just ordered our new dream computer. It has now been built and shipped by the computer vendor. We could find out the shipping status of our computer in a seamless way. When we visit the computer vendor's web site, it uses a Web Service published by the shipping company, and reports on the last checkpoint of our computer, and a continuously updated projected arrival date and time.

Or a private hospital that uses a Web Service published by a flower merchant. When checking the status of loved ones in the hospital, we could order flowers to be sent to them, along with a customized note, without leaving the hospital's web site.

Sometimes this is referred to as the arms merchant business model. They don't really care who wins the war, because they sell weapons to both sides of the conflict.

Web Services also promote loosely coupled systems. We can change an already implemented Web Service, perhaps changing underlying algorithms, or even changing the entire underlying technology, so long as we don't change the published public interface to our Web Service.

There are times that Web Services are not the best choice due to performance considerations. If high performance is required, Remoting Services, using a binary protocol, is more efficient.

Component Services through COM+

COM+ provides a number of facilities that are necessary for building enterprise scale applications. There are three primary services that we want to discuss here.

Transaction Processing

We may have a set of operations or tasks where we want them all to succeed or fail as a unit. If we take an e-commerce site as an example, a purchasing transaction consists of taking the customer's money, sending notice of the sale to the shipping department, and adjusting inventories to reflect the current stock. We want all of these operations to succeed or fail together.

When we speak about transaction processing, we say that a transaction either commits or aborts. For a transaction to commit, all of the operations that make up the transaction must guarantee that their changes to data will be permanent. These changes must take effect regardless of any extraneous circumstances, including whether the system crashes.

COM+, the successor to **Microsoft Transaction Server** (**MTS**) provides this functionality to the .NET Framework.

Object Pooling

Object pooling is an important technique when creating web sites that scale so that they handle thousands of users. It is a service provided by COM+ that enables us to configure a component so that instances of it are kept in a pool. Any client that requests this component is given one from the pool.

There are administration options to configure and monitor the pool, so that we can specify such things as the pool size. When our application is running, COM+ manages the pool, serves up objects, and manages reuse.

Some key advantages of object pooling are:

- Speed up object use time. This technique separates the time and processing for initialization and resource acquisition from the actual work that the component does for clients of the component.
- Share the processing cost for creating expensive resources, such as database connections, socket connects, etc., across many clients.
- Move some of the object creation time to application startup.

We can use C#, Visual Basic .NET, or any other .NET language to create classes that are managed by COM+ and object pooling.

Queued Components

Queued components, based on **Microsoft Message Queuing Services** (**MSMQ**), provide a way to execute methods on components asynchronously. Messages can be sent or received regardless of the availability of either the sender or receiver. The increase in use of laptops and palmtops in enterprise systems, where the laptops and palmtops are not always connected, prescribes the use of queued components.

The messages can be sent synchronously in real-time, or asynchronously using queues. The components don't need to be aware of which method is currently working.

An example of an application that would benefit from this technology is a sales application. Sales people could take their laptop and portable printer with them on sales calls. When the customer confirms the sale, the sales person enters the sales details into their Windows Forms application. They can print out the sales receipt for the customer. The notification that the sale took place is sent through MSMQ, and the next time that they connect to the network, the message is sent to the server, which enters the sale into the database.

Visual Studio.NET

Our discussion of the technologies of the .NET development environment would not be complete without a quick summary of the new features and benefits of Visual Studio .NET:

- Support for Multiple Languages: In this one environment, we can edit and build modules written in any of the .NET languages. Debugging across language boundaries is seamless.
- The code editor in .NET is very advanced. IntelliSense provides automatic statement completion, and drop-down lists of available options when editing. In addition, the code editor provides the ability to collapse and expand sections of code, so that we can focus exclusively on the code that requires our attention.
- We use this one environment regardless of whether we are building Windows Forms applications or Web Forms applications. This leverages our learning time – we don't need to learn a new environment for each type of application.
- Direct editing of XML and XSD files in Visual Studio makes it more convenient to build applications that use XML and its associated tools.
- Visual Studio is customizable and extendible at multiple levels. Users can easily customize it using the built-in macros. Vendors can create 'Add-Ins' or Wizards that extend functionality. Some vendors who want to add features such as support for a new project type, customized editors, or advanced debugging features can join the Visual Studio Integration Program (VSIP).

We will look at Visual Studio.NET in detail in the next chapter.

Summary

In this chapter, we have taken a look at the distributed computing capabilities of the .NET Framework. We have seen a very wide range of tools that we can use to build connected applications that meet the demands of today's market.

We have reviewed Windows Forms and Web Forms, and understood some of the considerations that drive the decision about which one to use.

We have reviewed the use of XML in the Framework, and seen how extensive its use is.

Web Services is an integral part of Microsoft's vision, and it is easy to see why. Web services provide a way for companies to integrate functionality in ways not imagined before.

We have seen how COM+ provides three areas of functionality that are vital for building enterprise level applications: Transaction Processing, Object Pooling, and Asynchronous Messaging.

Most programmers in the world will be impacted by .NET in the next few years, either by working directly with it, interfacing with web services written in .NET, or using applications and tools written in .NET. This book aims to give clear insights into the use of the Windows Forms class hierarchy, as well as perspective on how Windows Forms fits into the entire .NET vision.

Sometimes the rules change enough that the old ways of doing things must be discarded. With this framework, Microsoft has taken a fresh look at the problem of application development. Some parts are evolutionary, such as C# and the CLR. Some parts are really quite revolutionary, such as the non-procedural, declarative nature of ASP.NET. They have made a valid and impressive effort to revamp software development.

Legend: Concrete Class / Abstract class

System.Windows.Forms

- System.Object
  - System.MarshalRefObject
    - System.ComponentMode.Component
      - CommonDialog
        - ColorDialog
        - FileDialog
        - FontDialog
        - PageSetupDialog
        - PrintDialog
      - ErrorProvider
      - HelpProvider
      - ImageList
      - Menu
        - ContextMenu
        - MainMenu
        - MenuItem
      - NotifyIcon
      - StatusBarPanel
      - Timer
      - ToolBarButton
      - ToolTip
      - Control
        - ButtonBase
          - Button
          - CheckBox
          - RadioButton
        - DataGrid
        - DateTimePicker
        - GroupBox
        - Label
          - LinkLabel
        - ListControl
          - ComboBox
          - ListBox
            - CheckedListBox
        - ListView
        - MonthCalendar
        - PictureBox
        - PrintReviewControl
        - ProgressBar
        - ScrollableControl
          - ContainerControl
            - Form
              - PrintPreviewDialog
              - ThreadExceptionDialog
            - PropertyGrid
            - UpDownBase
              - DomainUpDown
              - NumericUpDown
            - UserControl
          - Panel
            - TabPage
        - ScrollBar
          - HScrollBar
          - VScrollBar
        - Splitter
        - StatusBar
        - TabControl
        - TextBoxBase
          - RichTextBox
          - Textbox
        - ToolBar
        - TrackBar
        - TreeView
  - ListViewItem
  - TreeNode

2

Visual Studio.NET Overview

Developing software for Microsoft platforms is no longer bound by the fiefdoms of Visual C++, Visual Basic and Visual Interdev. There is just one development environment and it encompasses all languages (C#, VB, C++, etc.), and all types of applications (database, traditional client applications, web development, etc). Its name is Visual Studio.NET. For the purposes of this chapter, our languages are C# and VB.NET, and our target software is client applications using Windows Forms.

Before assaulting the broad topic of Windows Forms, an introduction to the great unifier, Visual Studio.NET, is in order. This development tool handles the configuration and building of applications (solutions) composed of multiple projects. Specific files are created and managed by Visual Studio.NET. Various wizards and tools are exposed by Visual Studio.NET to expedite the development process. These tools include a designer for user interfaces and wizards that support the development of dialogs and visual controls to reside on these dialogs. Building and debugging applications is also facilitated with a large number of new debugging features not present in previous version of Visual Studio.

We also take a brief look at how to use Visual Studio .NET's help. Before scoffing at something so trivial, help has added some useful new features that make help more helpful.

The main topics we will cover in this chapter are:

- Solutions, projects, and files
- The View menu
- How to write code (specifically IntelliSense and code wizards)
- Project management and the project menu
- An overview of debugging
- Help
- Command line development

A First Project

Since the dawn of time, Visual Studio projects have been created using the File, New menu item. Visual Studio.NET continues this rich tradition, as is shown below in the New Project dialog (displayed using, File | New | Project):

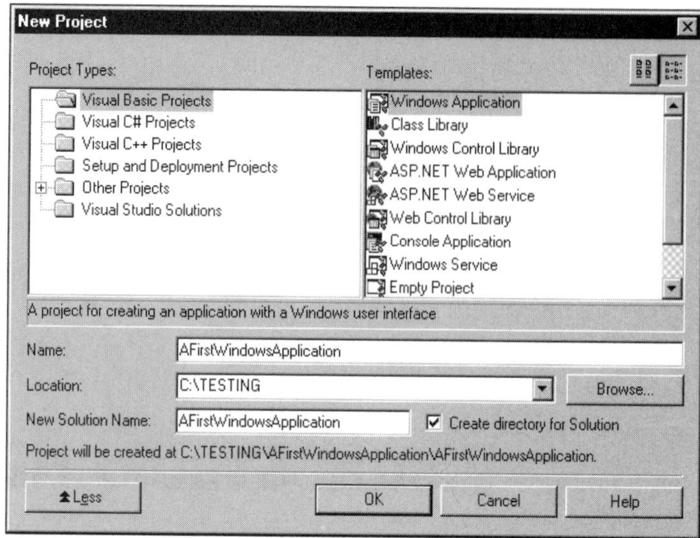

Under Project Types, Visual Basic Projects is highlighted. Actually, Visual C# Projects could also have been highlighted. Both these languages support exactly the same project types. For the sake of this example we select Windows Application in conjunction with Visual Basic Projects and then click on OK.

Once OK is selected, the newly created project will appear in Visual Studio and look something like the following:

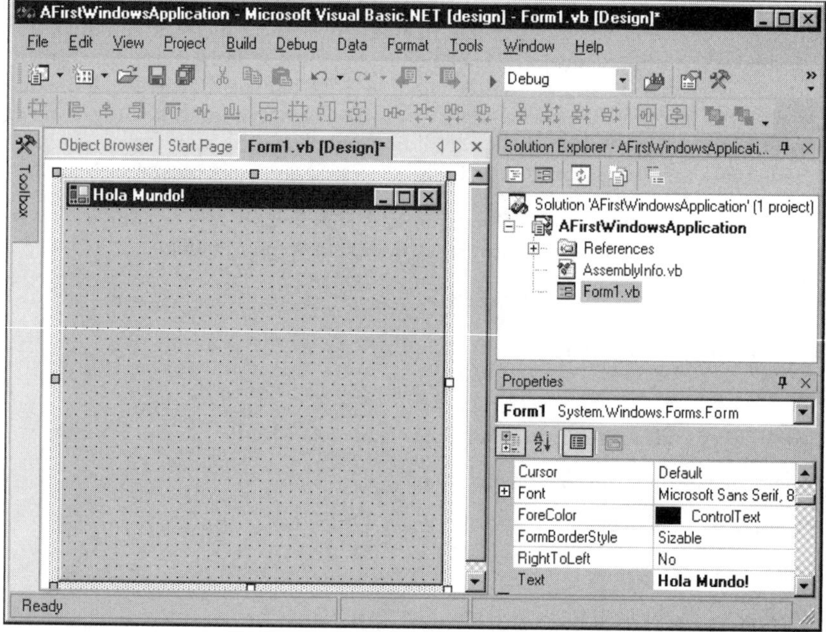

The title of Visual Studio is significant:

AFirstWindowsApplication – Microsoft Visual Basic.NET[design] – Form1.vb[Design]*

This title shows us the following:

- AFirstWindowsApplication: The current project is `AFirstWindowsApplication`.
- Microsoft Visual Basic.NET[design]: This project is a VB.NET project and not a C# project. We are designing the project, [design], not running it, [run], and not stopped at a breakpoint, [break].
- Form1.vb[Design]: The current file being accessed is `Form1.vb`. The current mode associated with this file is [Design] which means we are designing the form and, behind the scenes, Visual Studio is writing the code. If we did not see [Design] we would actually be editing the source code associated with `Form1.vb`.
- *: The asterisk at the end of the title indicates that the work is unsaved.

The current project, current file, and their respective states (for example, [Design]) determine the features exposed by Visual Studio, including which menus are visible, which menu items are visible or grayed-out, and which toolbars are visible.

Within our Visual Studio screenshot, the windows visible are Solution Explorer (top right), Designer (left), and Properties (bottom right). We can use the View menu to ensure these windows are displayed. The intricacies of these windows will be discussed later in this chapter. Within our first application, we need to make one slight modification to the default. Under the Properties window, the `Text` property is changed to `Hola Mundo!` (Hello World!). The properties displayed are for the form shown in the Designer window.

The Solution Explorer window contains a list of the projects contained in the solution. Underneath each project is a list of the files and directories contained in said project. Information such as what assemblies a project references (the References folder) are also included. The Solution Explorer window serves another more subtle purpose. This window shows what element within Visual Studio we are currently working with. In our screenshot of Visual Studio, the file `Form1.vb` is in bold as it is the current element being operated on.

At this stage it might be pertinent to talk about the source code. There is source code but for our example we let Visual Studio write it for us. Within the source file `Form1.vb`, Visual Studio wrote a slew of code including a line of code corresponding to changing the `Text` property associated with the form, like this:

```
Me.Text = "Hola Mundo!"
```

To compile and run our 'Hello World' variant, we:

- Select the Build option from the Build menu item. This creates the executable `AFirstWindowsApplication.exe`.
- Select the Debug | Start menu item. This step starts the program's execution under the debugger. Had we not initially built the solution (the previous step), the solution would have been built so that there would be something to debug. Starting the debugger using the Debug menu runs the executable `AFirstWindowsApplication.exe` and displays our form.

Clearly, the window displayed by our application is on the dull side. Chapter 4 will look at the structure of a basic form in more depth, and show how to place Windows Forms controls (buttons, labels, textboxes, etc.) on a form to develop real applications. For now though, let's continue with Visual Studio.NET.

Solutions, Projects, and Files

When we first created our sample application, `AFirstWindowsApplication`, we saw the New Project dialog (File, New, Project). The New Project dialog lists a variety of project types that can be created. The project types particular to the development of Windows Forms applications are:

- Windows application: This style of project generates an executable primed and ready to display a graphical user interface (GUI).
- Class library: This style of project generates a .NET assembly (a dll in classic Windows terminology) that contains classes. These classes can themselves contain forms or controls that can be displayed by an executable. The Windows Forms classes can be used as base classes to other Windows Forms classes. This Windows Forms development technique is called inheritance and is discussed in Chapter 3.
- Console application: This style of project generates an executable that displays a console window. There is a common misconception with console applications, that since they are console applications they cannot display windows. This is wholly untrue. Console applications are Windows applications and are subject to all the laws of nature that govern Windows applications. This includes such abilities as the creating and displaying of Windows Forms.

Selecting OK from the New Project dialog with Windows Application selected (ether C# or VB.NET) creates the files necessary to create a simple Windows Forms application. What Visual Studio has generated for us includes:

- Solution file: `AFirstWindowsApplication.sln`, refers to the solution that contains our project. A solution contains one or more projects, and maintains the dependencies between projects. Projects are specific .NET assemblies (a console executable, a Windows Forms executable, a class library *.dll).
- Project file: `AFirstWindowsApplication.vbproj`, specifies the (VB) project. The project file contains configuration settings and information such as a list of the source files and references to components used to build our application. The configuration settings of the project specify that an executable that displays a GUI will be generated.
- Other files: Windows Forms applications work with files containing source code. Visual Basic source files have extension `.vb` and C# source file have extension `.cs`. Visual Studio and Windows Forms use a variety of other file types: icon (`*.ico`), bitmap (`*.bmp`), resource file (`*.rct`), etc.

File Menu

Creating, saving, and opening solutions, projects and files, is the domain of Visual Studio's File menu. Most of File's menu items are self-explanatory (Close, Open Solution, Close Solution, Print, Exit, etc.) The File menu's New menu item does expose a large amount of functionality. This menu item can create a new Project such as a Windows application, class library, Web project, etc. When this project is created it can be added to an existing solution or a solution can be created in conjunction with the project.

The **File** menu's **New** menu item can also create a **Blank Solution**. Such a solution contains no projects initially but projects can be added to it (again using the **File** menu's **New** menu item). As well as this, the **New** menu can create files such as icon, bitmap, cursor, resource files, etc. When a new file is created, the file is not actually added to the project. Adding these files to the project is the purview of the **Project** menu's **Add Existing Item** menu item.

Notice that when discussing creating new files, no mention was made of creating a new VB.NET or C# source file. New source files are added using other mechanisms such as the **Project** menu's, **Add Class...** menu item.

The **File** menu of Visual Studio and its submenus change based on context. For example, if the code of a source file is being edited, the file menu contains the following menu items: **Advanced Save Options**, **Print**, and **Page Setup...** The dialogs displayed by menus and submenus are also dynamic with respect to their content. For example, the **New Project** dialog exhibits slightly different behavior when a new project is created whilst an existing project is open. Under these circumstances this dialog contains two radio buttons:

- **Add to Solution**: Selecting this option creates a new project within the existing solution.
- **Close Solution**: The present solution open is closed. The new project created is contained in a new solution.

In order to demonstrate the concept of adding to a solution, we will use the **File | New** menu item to create a new project. The dialog displayed by this is shown below. This time we have selected **Visual C# Projects** with respect to **Project Types**, and **Class Library** with respect to **Templates**:

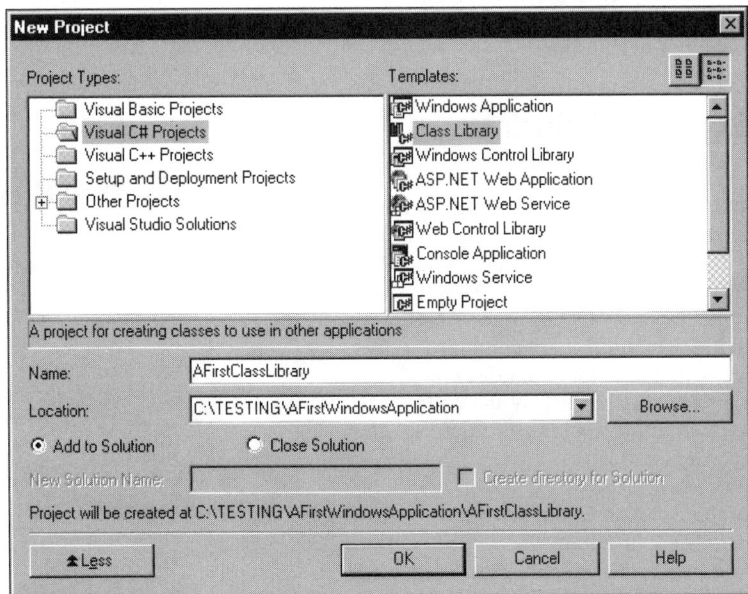

As shown in the above screenshot, we selected the radio button, **Add to Solution**. This means that the new project created, `AFirstClassLibrary`, is contained in our original solution, `AFirstWindowsApplication`. This new project will be used later in the chapter to demonstrate how multiple projects within a solution interact. It also serves to demonstrate how one solution can support multiple languages (VB.NET and C#).

The types of projects created so far are pertinent to Windows Forms development (Windows Applications and Class Libraries). The other project type that will commonly be used by Windows Forms developers is Windows Control Library. This project style corresponds to a user created control. Windows controls subsume the functionality previously the domain of ActiveX controls. Legacy controls (ActiveX controls) can still be used in development but controls developed as Windows Control Libraries have all the bells and whistles of .NET (improved memory handling, cross language development, simplified installation, etc.).

View Menu

Visual Studio offers a variety of different windows that perform a plethora of useful and critical tasks. The View menu is used to display each of these windows. New users of Visual Studio may feel inundated with windows, all of which perform a task crucial to the development of a Windows Forms application. There is nothing more frustrating to a Visual Studio user than to lose a window crucial to development. Such windows are not really lost. They have just been closed and require re-opening. The View menu is invaluable when navigating through the windows associated with Visual Studio's rich suite of features.

Remember that the contents of the View menu, and every Visual Studio menu, are dynamic. For example, if a solution is selected in the Solution Explorer window, the View menu contains a Property Pages menu item. If a project or a source file is selected, Property Pages is not a menu item of the View menu.

A variety of the menu items found in the View menu are helpful in the development of Windows Forms applications. An oft-used subset of these menu items is reviewed in this section. The View menu items not reviewed can be categorized as more self-explanatory in nature or not as directly applicable to Windows Forms development. Menu items that are exposed by the View menu but not discussed in this section include: Open, Open With..., Server Explorer, Pending Checkins, Navigate Backwards, Navigate Forwards, and Refresh.

Solution Explorer Window

The Solution Explorer window is exposed by the View | Solution Explorer menu item. This window's function is roughly analogous to the windows utility, Windows Explorer. The Solution Explorer displays a hierarchy, the root of which is a solution. The projects of a solution are contained as branches of the solution tree, and the source files of a project are contained under each project. A virtual directory contains the references for a particular project. When a file-centric view of a solution and its projects is desired, Solution Explorer is the window to use.

An example of the Solution Explorer window is shown as follows, where the solution is `AFirstWindowsApplication` (solution associated with our first Visual Basic application), and the projects are `AFirstWindowsApplication` (first VB.NET windows application) and `AFirstClassLibrary` (the C# class library):

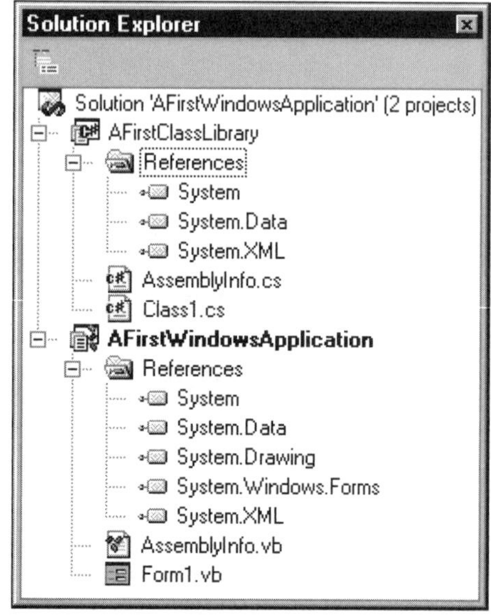

Yes, the solution (`AFirstWindowsApplication`) and the project associated with the Visual Basic windows application (`AFirstWindowsApplication`) have the same name. Remember that they are different entities and represented by different file names: `AFirstWindowsApplication.sln` and `AFirstWindowsApplication.vbproj` respectively.

An icon that specifies whether the item is a source file, form, reference assembly, etc, prefixes each item in the **Solution Explorer** window. For example, you'll notice that the C# source file looks like a piece of paper with 'C#', superimposed on it.

We have seen that highlighting a solution, a project or a source file changes everything from menu items to what is displayed in the Properties window. Right-mouse-clicking on each of these entities within Solution Explorer is a shortcut to a plethora of pertinent features. Right-mouse-clicking on source file, `Form1.vb`, displays the following context menu:

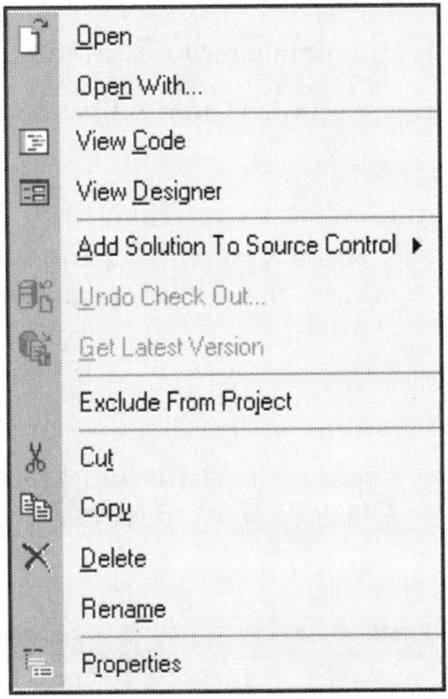

Double-clicking on `Form1.vb` would have resulted in the file being opened in the Design view. The alternative would be to select the **Open** menu item from the context menu. Let's quickly run through these properties:

- **Open With** allows an application besides Visual Studio to open the file.
- The **View Code** menu item is equivalent to the **View** menu's, **Code** menu item.
- The context menu's **View Designer** menu item is equivalent to the **View** menu's **Designer** menu item in that it displays the form in the Windows Forms Designer.
- **Properties**, displays the Properties window and the properties associated with `Form1.vb`.
- **Add Solution to Source Control** places the solution under source code control.

There are some subtleties with respect to the items remaining in this context menu. For example, **Exclude From Project** will delete the file from the project but the file will remain on disk. The **Delete** menu item will both delete the file from the project and delete the file from disk. At the same time the resource file (`Form1.resx`) corresponding to the source file will also be deleted. **Cut**, **Copy** and **Rename** behave for our solution just like Cut, Copy and Rename behave in Windows Explorer. These menu items allow files within our solution to be managed. Once a **Cut** or **Copy** menu item is selected, a **Paste** menu item will be displayed on our context menu.

The context menu previously shown was displayed by right-clicking on a class within Solution Explorer. Right-clicking on a project (for example, `AFirstClassLibrary`) reveals a menu containing items such as:

- Build: Builds the selected project and all its dependencies. The build only occurs if said project and/or its dependencies are out of date and require building. This menu item is identical to the Build Project menu item exposed by the Build menu.
- Rebuild: Rebuilds current project and all its dependencies. A rebuild builds even if a project has not been changed in a manner requiring that it be rebuilt. This menu item is identical to the Rebuild Project menu item exposed by the Build menu.
- Set as Startup Project: Specifies that the currently selected project will be run when a project is executed. This includes stand-alone execution and running the program within the debugger. For example, if a solution contained a server executable and a client executable, this would allow us to select which one to debug.
- Debug: This submenu allows the debugger to Start new instance or Step Into new instance.
- Add: This submenu allows a new class, virtual folder, Windows Form, Component, etc. to be added to the project.
- Add References: This menu item adds a reference to a .NET assembly, legacy COM component, or to the assembly associated with a particular Visual Studio project. It allows the project to resolve external dependencies – classes, methods, properties, enumerations, etc.

Class View Window

A typical project is composed of one or more classes. When a class-centric view of a project is desired, Class View is the window to use. The Class View window for solution, `AFirstWindowsApplication`, is as follows:

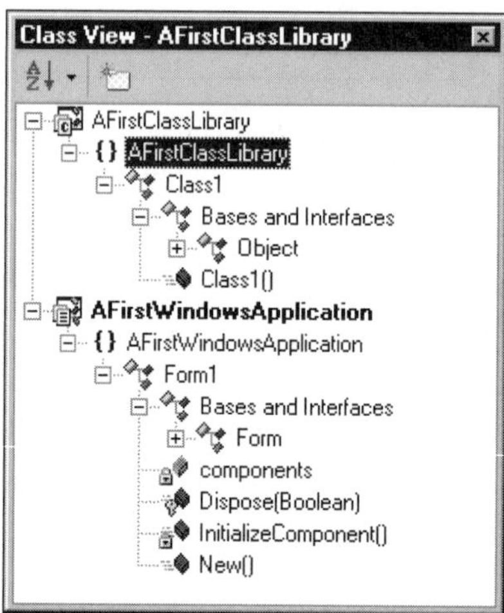

Each icon in the previous screenshot is significant. These icons represent entities such as a VB.NET windows application project, C# windows application project, namespace, class, method and property. For example the icon that looks like starting and ending curly braces, that is, {}, refers to the namespace for the project. This namespace is used to limit the scope of the classes, interfaces, and enumerations declared by the project.

By right-mouse-clicking on a class name, a context menu is displayed that exposes a variety of features, shortcuts, and actions pertaining to the current class:

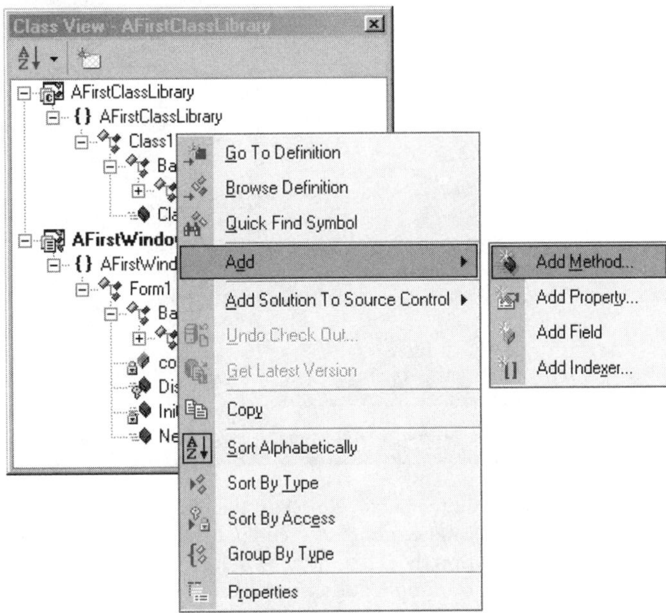

The individual features of the per-class context menu are for the most part self-documenting. The Add submenu was exposed to demonstrate a shortcut that allows methods, properties, fields and indexers to be added to a class. The Go To Definition menu item of our context menu goes to the corresponding line of source code where the class is declared (for example, `public class Lower`).

Code Menu Item

This menu item is displayed when a source file is highlighted in Solution Explorer. Selecting the Code menu item causes the source code associated with a source file to be displayed for editing. For our example, `AFirstWindowsApplication`, the source code for `Form1.vb` is as follows:

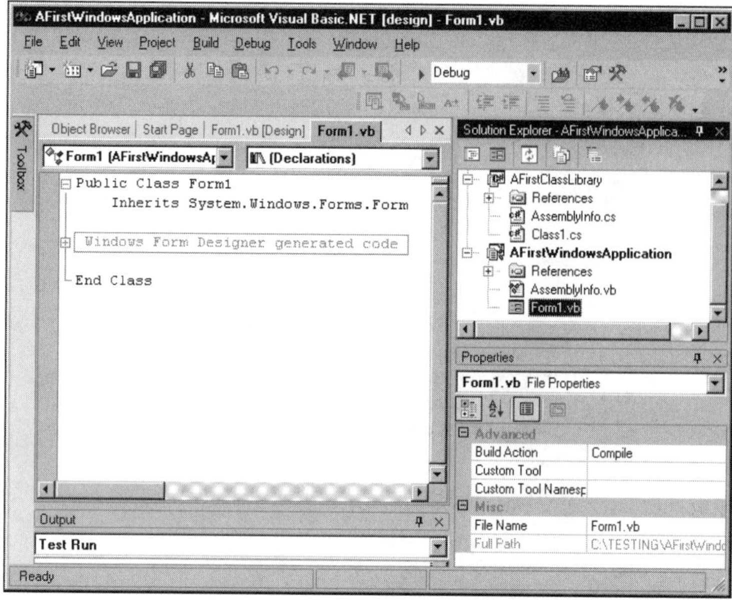

The source code for our example is quite sparse. Notice in the above source code that a portion of the code is labeled as 'Windows Form Designer generated code'. Microsoft strongly recommends that developers do not modify this code directly. There is a '+' before this section. Clicking the mouse on this '+' expands the code written for our application by the Windows Form Designer. When expanded the code takes the following form where the actual implementation of the subroutines has been replaced by comments:

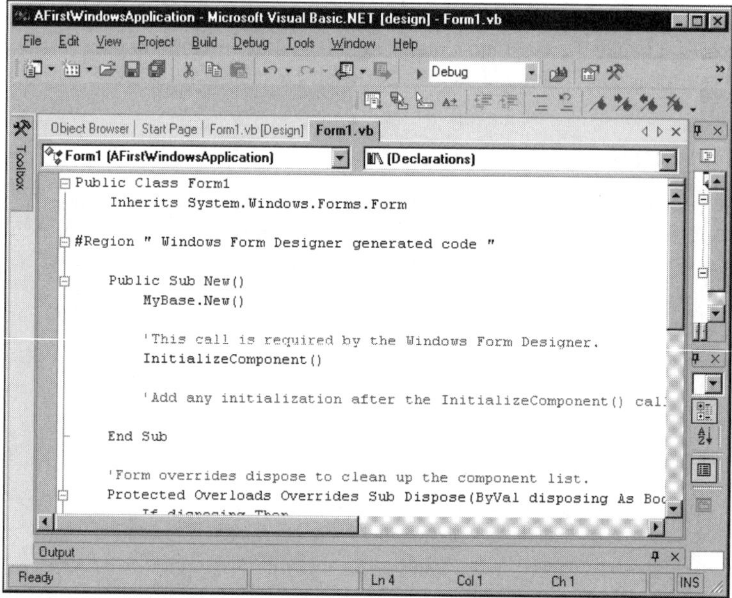

If the sample application had been developed in C#, the same style of view/hide regions are supported. A bit more code would be initially visible but the grayed out 'Windows Form Designer generated code' prefixed but a '+' would still be there. The '+' means that C# methods can also be collapsed and expanded as need be. Regardless of the language (C++, JScript.NET, VB.NET, C#, etc.), the region directives are an extremely useful new feature.

Designer Menu Item

The Designer menu item is displayed when a source file is double-clicked in Solution Explorer, or when we open up a new project (as we saw earlier in the chapter). Selecting the Designer menu item causes the form associated with a source file to be displayed for editing. The Designer menu item is only visible for source files that are ultimately derived from the `System.Windows.Forms` namespace's `Form` class (windows application) or `Component` class (user defined components).

Toolbox Menu Item

Developing a Windows Forms application without the **Toolbox** window is akin to attending an opera performed by mimes. The **Toolbox** menu item ensures that the **Toolbox** window is displayed. The screenshot below shows a small portion of the dozens and dozens of Windows Forms controls exposed by the **Toolbox** window:

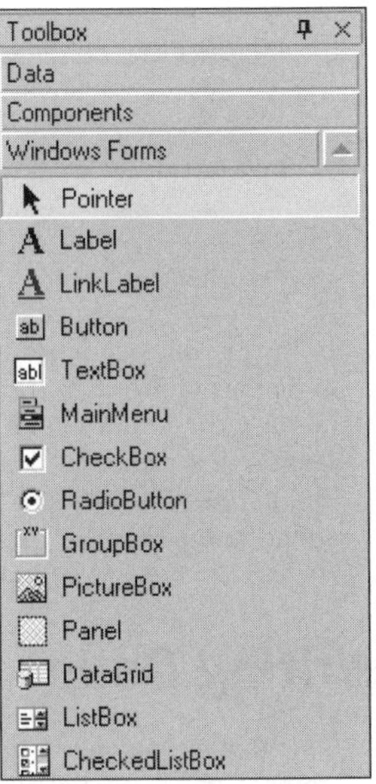

It is possible to place a `Button`, `Textbox` or `CheckBox` control on a form without using the Toolbox. An object of the Windows Forms control type (for example, `Button`) would have to be created; the position and size of the object would have to be specified along with properties such as Text. To demonstrate the raw power of the Toolbox window, all we need to do is drag a button from the Toolbox and drop it on the form associated with application, `AFirstWindowsApplication`:

The simple act of dragging a button from Toolbox to form results in several lines of code written by Visual Studio and more importantly, not written by you (code in boldface was added):

```
Friend WithEvents Button1 As System.Windows.Forms.Button

'Required by the Windows Form Designer
Private components As System.ComponentModel.Container

<System.Diagnostics.DebuggerStepThrough()> Private Sub InitializeComponent()
    Me.Button1 = New System.Windows.Forms.Button()
    Me.SuspendLayout()
    '
    'Button1
    '
    Me.Button1.Location = New System.Drawing.Point(88, 48)
    Me.Button1.Name = "Button1"
    Me.Button1.TabIndex = 0
    Me.Button1.Text = "Button1"
    '
    'Form1
    '
    Me.AutoScaleBaseSize = New System.Drawing.Size(5, 13)
    Me.ClientSize = New System.Drawing.Size(292, 273)
    Me.Controls.AddRange(New System.Windows.Forms.Control() {Me.Button1})
    Me.Name = "Form1"
    Me.Text = "Hola Mundo!"
    Me.ResumeLayout(False)

End Sub
```

In the previous code snippet, the first highlighted line creates a button data member, which is declared to be part of the class `System.Windows.Forms.Button`. Then, an instance of this button is created in the second highlighted line. Some properties of this button are also set in the third highlighted section. For example, the final line `Me.Button1.Text = "Button1"` sets the text to be displayed on the button. The button is then associated with the `Form` (in the final highlighted line) because it was added to the Form's `Components` collection. This is an impressive bit of work for a drag-and-drop.

Writing Code

Now that we can get to the stage of sitting down and writing some code, let's take a look at some of the features, which Visual Studio provides to make our lives easier. Start up a new Visual Basic project, and get to the code view of `Form1.vb`. Now, add the following line below the Windows forms Designer generated code:

```
Public Sub ProvideSomeInformation()
```

We are now ready to look at some helpful features of Visual Studio.NET.

IntelliSense

When writing code, the IntelliSense feature of Visual Studio is quickly noticeable. For example, when typing in our source file `Form1.vb`, the following IntelliSense window pops up when `MessageBox` is typed followed by a period:

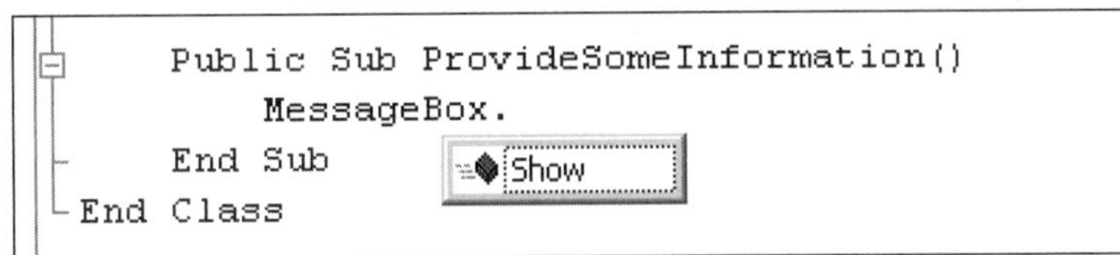

Just like that, we see whatever methods, properties, enumeration, fields and indexes can found in the `MessageBox` class. Here `MessageBox` only contains one public shared method (static methods in C#), which is `Show`. For classes that have more than one option, we can move up and down the displayed list using the up and down arrow keys. Another way to move through the list is by typing letters corresponding to an element in the list.

Once the left parentheses character is typed after `Show`, IntelliSense kicks in again. This time it displays the parameters associated with the `Show` method and highlights using boldface the first parameter in the list:

```
    Public Sub ProvideSomeInformation()
        MessageBox.Show(
    End  ▲6 of 12▼  Show (text As String) As System.Windows.Forms.DialogResult
End Class
```

In the above screenshot, IntelliSense shows the sixth of twelve overloaded versions of the `Show` method. Of course, we can move through the list of `Show` overloads using the up and down arrow keys.

If we had chosen another option, and decided to use more than one parameter, then after the first parameter of `Show` is typed, IntelliSense remains active. The next parameter is marked in boldface after the comma is typed following the first parameter. Each subsequent parameter is highlighted in boldface so a developer can keep track of where they are in a lengthy parameter list:

```
    Public Sub ProvideSomeInformation()
        MessageBox.Show("Hi",
    End  ▲5 of 12▼  Show (text As String, caption As String) As System.Windows.Forms.DialogResult
End Class
```

IntelliSense also kicks in when declaring parameters for a subroutine or function. In the following code snippet the `ShowMore` subroutine is to be written with a parameter, `parm1`. When the type for `parm1` is being typed, IntelliSense simplifies the parameter declaration process as follows:

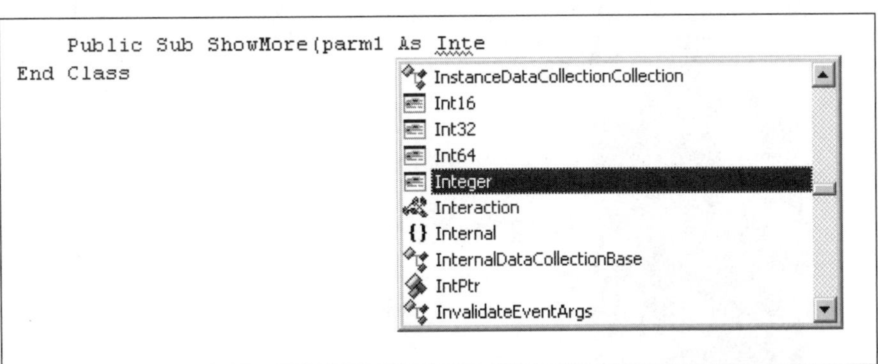

When declaring parameters in C#, Intellisense will also provide type information. Regardless of the language IntelliSense lists class members, structure members, method parameters and enumeration values. IntelliSense is by of the most useful and time saving features of Visual Studio.

Using Code Wizards

As mentioned previously, Visual Studio provides a set of wizards designed to help add code (projects, classes, methods, properties, fields, indexers, etc.). Using the Class View window we can highlight our C# class library project, `AFirstClassLibrary`. With a right click and a bit of menu navigation we can select Add Class, as shown in the adjacent screenshot:

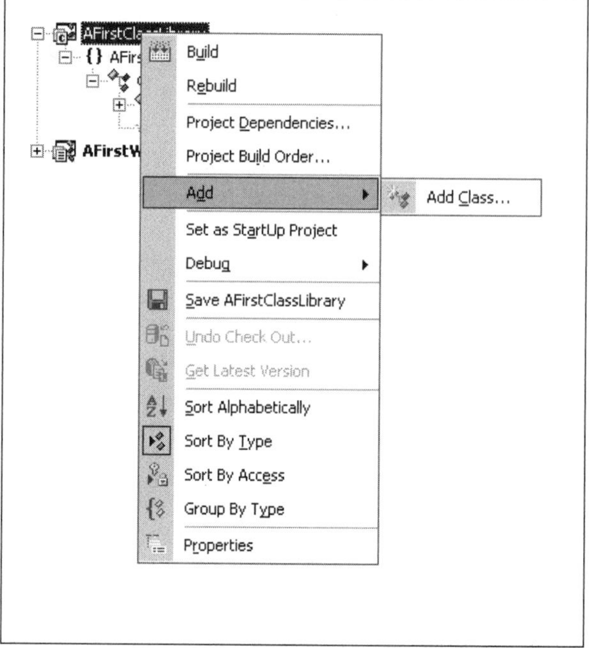

The Add Class menu item ultimately displays the Add Class Wizard as follows:

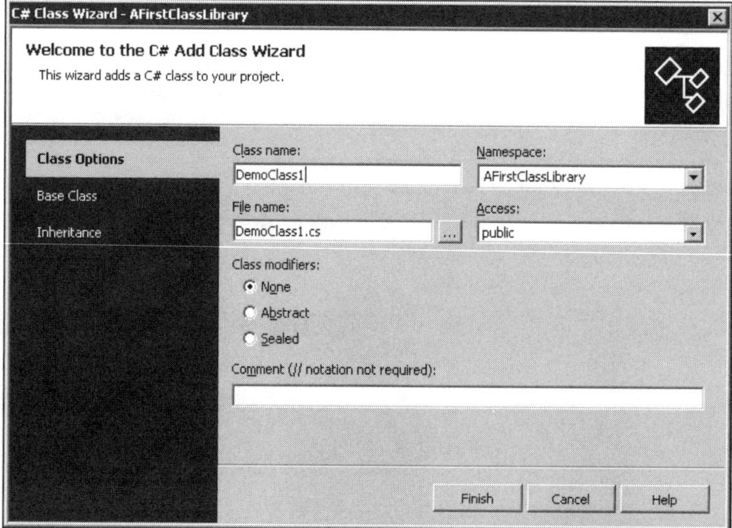

Along the left side of the Add Class Wizard a set of configuration settings is provided:

- Class Options: The first configuration selected allows our class name to be specified, `DemoClass1`, which will be placed in a source file of the same name plus the `*.cs` file extension. We have decided to make access to this class `public`. Class modifiers such as `abstract` and `sealed` could also be selected.
- Base Class: This view of the Add Class Wizard allows a namespace to be selected and from this namespace allows base classes to be selected.
- Inheritance: This view of the Add Class Wizard allows a namespace to be selected and allows one or more interfaces to be inherited from it. It is possible to inherit multiple interfaces from multiple namespaces.

We can display `DemoClass1` in the Class View window now. Right-clicking on it will display the context menu, which contains an Add menu item that contains Add Method, Add Property, Add Field, and Add Indexer. Actually this context menu is only displayed for C# projects and not VB.NET (the feature is not yet in VB.NET). Each of these add menu items displays a wizard designed that adds a method, property, field or index. So developers use these menu items to write a good portion of their code. Other developers find them cumbersome and feel that they slow down development, so you will have to make up your own mind on this.

Edit Menu

Most tasks presented in the Edit menu are so common place that developers do not access them via the Edit menu but instead use shortcuts. Most Visual Studio commands can be accessed using shortcuts but since the Edit menu's shortcuts apply to many different windows application this category of shortcuts are frequently used.

The Edit menu does expose the highly useful Find and Replace submenu. This submenu contains the following items:

- Find: Finds a particular string in the current file.
- Replace: Finds a matching string and replaces it.
- Find in Files: Finds a string in a set of files. The files can be filtered by type (by extension) and sub-directories may or may not be included in the search. The Find in Files dialog contains a Use: label that allows either Regular expressions or Wildcards to be used in matching the specified search string. The Find in Files dialog is as follows:

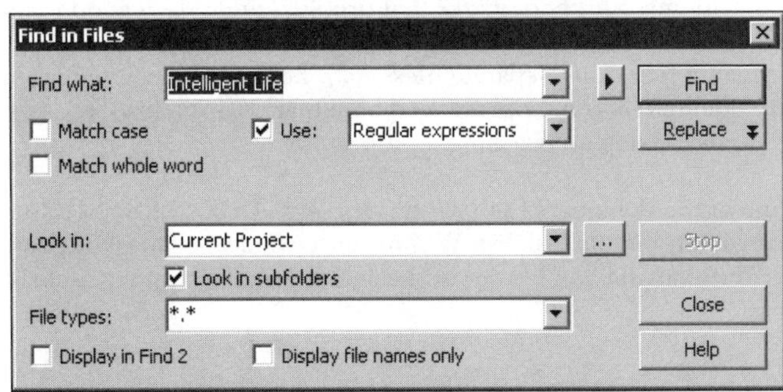

- Replace in Files: Searches sets of files for a matching string and replaces it. This is a great way to rename a project and its contents after a name is changed or due to a misspelling. Imagine we are developing an application named `RecieveServer`, and this name is used dozens of places throughout our source code hierarchy. Then some smarty in marketing points out that the correct spelling is `ReceiveServer`. Using the Replace in Files feature of Visual Studio is vastly more plausible than attempting to convince marketing that `RecieveServer` uses the Canadian spelling of the word receive.
- Find Symbol: The Find Symbol feature is also exposed by the Class View's context menu. Find Symbol finds all instances of that symbol within the current project and every assembly the project references.

The remaining submenus of the Edit menu do expose some interesting features. For example, the Advanced submenu contains menu items Comment Selection and Uncomment Selection. Imagine some software is just about to ship when some issues are noticed with some non-critical source code such as:

```
Public Sub PhilWentOnVacationAndLeftABug()
End Sub

Public Sub NoOneUnderstandsRaysCode()
End Sub

Public Sub FeatureNotSupportedInThisVersion()
End Sub
```

Simply select the offending region of code and then bring up the Edit menu's Advanced submenu and its Comment Selection option:

```
' Public Sub PhilWentOnVacationAndLeftABug()
' End Sub

' Public Sub NoOneUnderstandsRaysCode()
' End Sub

' Public Sub FeatureNotSupportedInThisVersion()
' End Sub
```

Bingo! Just like that, instant comments and a reduced chance of developing metacarpal tunnel syndrome.

The Bookmarks submenu manages bookmarks that provide quick navigation to marked locations in the source code. Imagine we are working five or six sections of the code at once (the top of one file, the bottom of the same file, in four other separate files, etc.). Bookmarks can be placed at key locations within files. You can then move from bookmark to bookmark. This allows you to jump to precisely the region of code that needs looking at, tweaking, or a rewrite.

Nestled at the bottom of the Bookmarks submenu is the Add Task List Shortcut menu item. Selecting this menu item adds an entry to the task list. Within source code, such task list entries are indicated by a 'right turn ahead' arrow along the left border of the source window. An example of such a task list entry is as follows:

```
public class DemoClass1
{
    public DemoClass1()
    {
```

The Edit menu's Outline submenu controls how portions of the code marked by the region directive are displayed. This submenu can toggle selective outlining or all outlining, and can even disable and re-enable outlining.

The Edit menu's IntelliSense submenu facilitates direct control over Visual Studio's IntelliSense feature. For example, selecting the List Member menu item when the `Text` method of class `Button1` (from our `AfirstWindowsApplication`) is highlighted shows all the shared methods (static in C# terms) of the `Button1` class. The following screenshot demonstrates this:

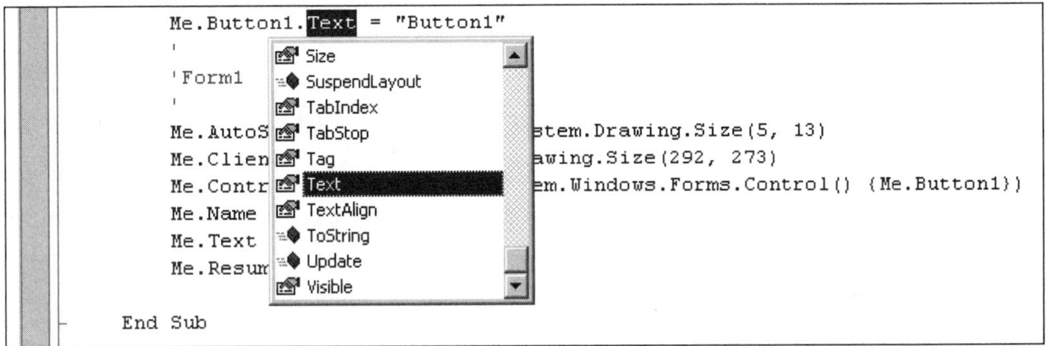

Project Management and the Project Menu

How a project is built, runs, and interacts with other projects is a critical aspect of the development process. Specifying these categories of project behavior is known as Project Management and is the domain of the Project menu. To better understand project management, let's create yet another project with Visual Studio.NET. The project type created will be a Visual Basic Project using the Console Application template. This new project will be named `AFirstConsoleApplication`. Project `AFirstConsoleApplication` will be added to our existing solution, `AFirstWindowsApplication`. To this new project we will add a message box to the main subroutine of source file, `Module1.vb`:

```
Module Module1
    Sub Main()
        MessageBox.Show("A demonstration")
    End Sub

End Module
```

An observant developer may have noticed that after typing `MessageBox.` in the previous code snippet, no Intellisense was displayed. Something was clearly amiss in the previous code snippet. This is what it is:

```
Sub Main()
    MessageBox.Show("A Demonstration")
End Sub        The name 'MessageBox' is not declared.
```

To resolve this issue our newly created project must be given knowledge of where to find the assembly that contains class `MessageBox`. To be specific the Windows Forms assembly, `System.Windows.Forms`, contains this definition. Our project not having knowledge of the assembly is why Intellisense failed to work when `MessageBox.` was typed. Let's look at the solution to this.

Inter-Project Management

Remember that `AFirstConsoleApplication` is a console application and not a Windows Forms application. Visual Studio did not bother to set up a reference to the Windows Forms assembly, `System.Windows.Forms`, which contains the class `MessageBox`. To resolve this issue we select the Project menu's **Add Reference** menu item. This menu item displays the following **Add Reference** dialog:

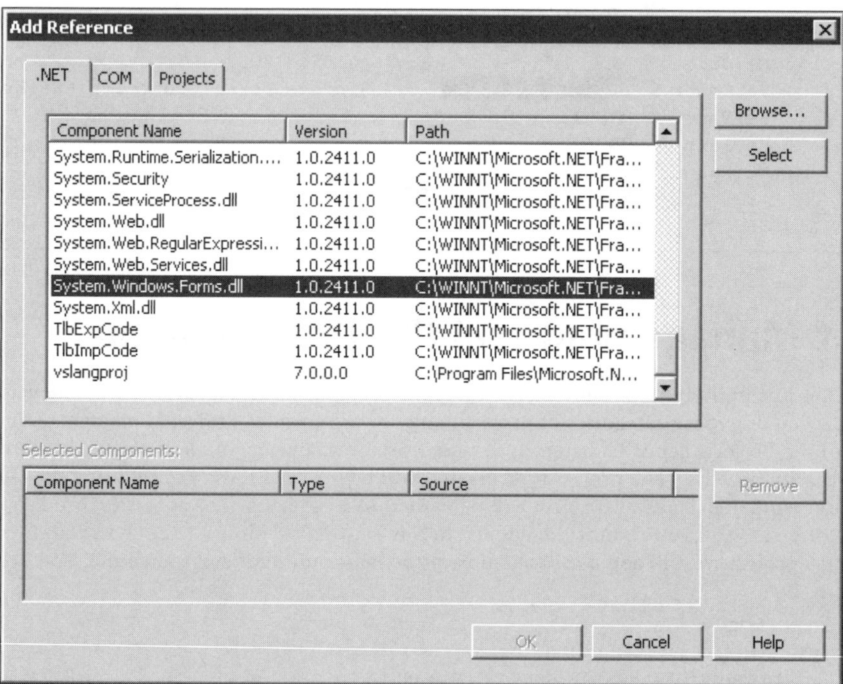

Clicking **Select** followed by **OK** adds the reference to our project. This reference means that all classes exposed by the namespace `System.Windows.Forms` can be used by our project.

We do have one final modification to make to our source file `Module1.vb`, namely adding an `Imports` statement that makes the contents of `System.Windows.Forms` available in the global namespace. More simply, the `Imports` directive means that each class from the Windows Forms namespace does not need to be fully qualified, such as: `System.Windows.Forms.MessageBox`.

Adding this `Imports` statement in VB.NET is equivalent to the `using` statement in C#. The source file `Module1.vb` is shown here containing the `Imports` directive:

```
Imports System.Windows.Forms
Module Module1

    Sub Main()
        MessageBox.Show("When Max put on his wolf suit")
    End Sub

End Module
```

For VB.NET projects, the project's properties menu includes a setting for `Imports`. Most VB.NET projects will likely use the project property rather than manually setting the `Imports` directive. This is because specifying the project property makes the `Imports` directive apply to every source file in the project.

The Project menu also exposes the menu item **Add Web References** This menu item allows references to web services to be setup and maintained.

Now that the references for our new project are resolved we can start configuring how the solution will build each project. For our solution the following is true:

- Project `AFirstWindowsApplication` depends on class library `AFirstClassLibrary`.
- Project `AFirstConsoleApplication` will depend on class library `AFirstClassLibrary`.

The **Project Dependencies** menu item of the Project menu can resolve our inter-project relationship troubles. When this menu item is selected, the following dialog is displayed:

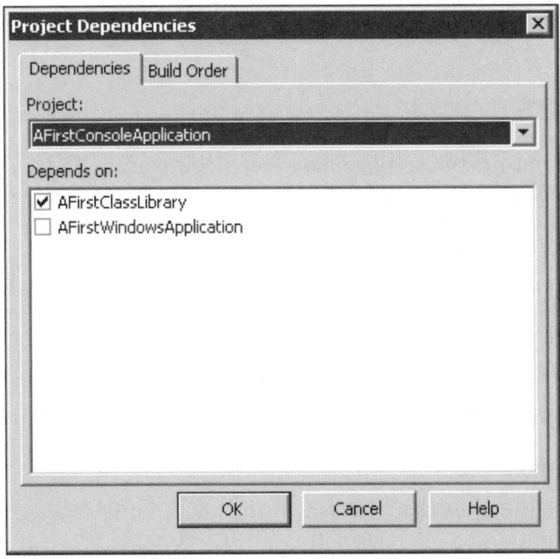

Since the project displayed in the Project combo box is `AFirstConsoleApplication`, we have gone to the Depends on panel and checked the box next to `AFirstClassLibrary`. Using the Project dropdown, we can select project `AFirstWindowsApplication` and make this project also depend on `AFirstClassLibrary`. At this stage our solution is cognizant of the inter-project dependencies. What this means is that the solution will build the dependencies (for example, `AFirstClassLibrary`) before dependant projects are built (`AFirstConsoleApplication` and `AFirstWindowsApplication`).

Selecting the Build Order tab in the Project Dependencies dialog displays the build order of the projects. This build order is dictated by the dependency relationships specified. The Project Build Order... menu item of the Project menu could also have been used to display the Project Dependencies dialog with the Build Order tab selected. The build order information is displayed as follows:

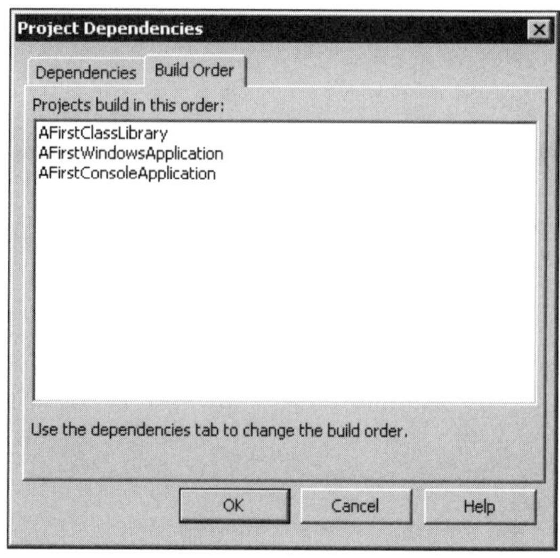

The Project menu contains other menu items that 'fine tune' how projects are built. Remember that the menu items displayed in the Project menu change depending on whether the solution, a project, or a source file is currently highlighted in Solution Explorer or Class View.

The Project menu also includes a menu item, Set as Startup Project. To understand this menu item, remember that a Visual Studio.NET solution can contain multiple projects. Precisely which project is launched when the Debug menu's Start menu item (function key, *F5*) is selected, is specified by this menu item.

Project Properties

Using references, certain per-project settings have been configured. There are a great many more per-project options that can be specified using the Project menu's Properties menu item. This menu item displays the Project Properties dialog. Before reviewing the various options that can be set with this dialog, there is an extremely important distinction to be made. The options set using the Tools menu's Options menu item are completely separate from the options set using the Project menu's Properties menu item. Tools | Options specifies how the tool is configured while Project | Properties specifies how a project is configured. This may sound obvious but consider the following scenario:

1. A developer named Naïve uses their Tools Options to specify that C++ projects should search directory `SomeDirectory` for include files.

2. Developer Naïve then checks a project into source code control (project `UsedByEveryDeveloper`) that uses this directory.

3. A developer named Crafty Veteran then retrieves project `UsedByEveryDeveloper` from source code control and attempts to build the project. The project won't build because Crafty Veteran does not have the same Tools Options settings as developer Naïve. The way to avoid this issue would have been to use the Project Properties in order to specify the include directories used by the C++ project.

The lesson here is that the Tools menu's Options menu item configures only the local developers Visual Studio.NET environment and not the project being developed. The Project menu's Properties menu item configures its namesake, the project.

The Project Properties dialog is displayed using the Project menu's Properties menu item. The Properties menu item is only available when a project, or the solution, is highlighted in the Solution Explorer. The properties associated with a solution include setting the startup project, specifying inter-project dependencies, and setting the path to debug source files and symbols. It should be noted that the project properties change based on project type and project language.

In previous versions of Visual Studio a vast number of properties could be set for a project. There were so many that could be set that most developers ignored most of them. When some over zealous developer tweaked a little known option, there were usually unforeseen side effects. Visual Studio.NET took great pains to remedy this situation. The solution was simple – have significantly fewer project properties that can be changed.

The properties associated with a project are configured using the following Property Pages dialog:

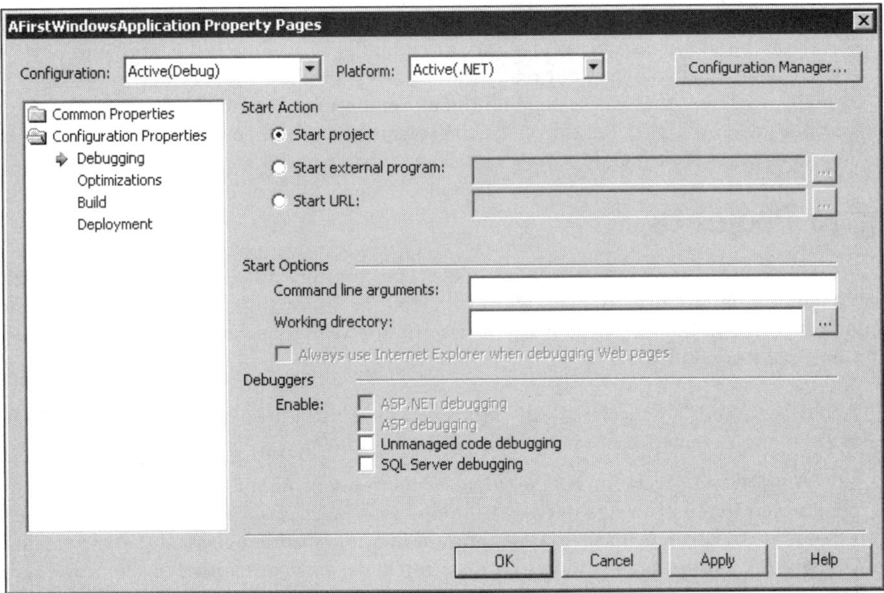

The previous screenshot shows that the properties for a project are broken down into two categories: Common Properties and Configuration Properties. From the Configuration Properties category, the Debug subcategory was deliberately selected because it contains several important properties:

- Start Project: Specifies that the executable for the project should be started at time of debug.
- Start External Program: When the project is debugged, Visual Studio launches an external program. For example if the project is an e-mail server, we could launch a client application that attempts to read and send mail using the e-mail server we are debugging.
- Command line arguments: The command-line arguments to the application can be specified here.
- Working Directory: Allows the directory, where an application will look for its files by default, to be specified (the project's working directory).

Between the categories, Common Properties and Configuration Properties, there are a fair number of additional properties that can be configured. Some examples of such properties include:

- Common Properties | General | Startup object: For an executable containing more than one entry-point function `main`, specifies which object containing `main` is launched at startup.
- Common Properties | Build | Application icon: Specifies the icon displayed for an executable application.
- Common Properties | Imports: For Visual Basic projects, adds an `Imports` directive. For our project `AFirstConsoleApplication` we specified `Imports System.Windows.Forms` in the source file, `Module1.vb`. Using this project property we could have specified that `System.Windows.Forms` be imported without specifying `Imports` in the source code.
- Configuration Properties | Optimizations | DLL base address: For class libraries, specifies the default base address where the DLL is loaded in memory. The basic idea of this setting is that applications load faster if their DLLs use the same default addresses. This is because collisions in address spaces result in address recalculation before the DLL can be loaded.
- Configuration Properties | Build | Treat compiler warnings as errors: Causes warnings to 'break the build'. A warning is given if, for example, a variable is declared and never used. This is syntactically correct but really should be cleaned by a developer so the code only contains variables that are used. With the aforementioned setting, projects containing warnings will no longer build because the warnings are treated as errors. This is an excellent way to encourage (force) developers to clean up their pesky warning messages.

Adding to Projects

A larger number of the Project menu's items add programming entities to a project. The Add Reference menu item has already been addressed, but the following other add-related menu items are found in the Project menu. These menu items are not available if the solution is selected within the Solution Explorer windows:

- Add Class: Adds a new class to the project. If the class added is ABC then a source file of the same name is created (`ABC.vb` for Visual Basic and `ABC.cs` for C#).
- Add Windows Form: Performs the same functionality as menu item Add Class, except that the class added to the project is derived from `System.Windows.Forms.Form` and the code generation wizard sets up several methods of the newly added class. If the project does not contain the appropriate Windows Forms references, these are added to the project (assemblies `System.Windows.Forms`, `System.Data`, `System.XML` and `System.Drawing`). Access is made available to the appropriate namespaces within these assemblies. In a C# project this means that Visual Studio.NET adds the appropriate `using` statements to the source file, and in Visual Basic the appropriate `imports` statements are added.
- Add Inherited Form: Performs the same functionality as menu item Add Windows Form, except that an Inheritance Picker dialog is displayed. This dialog allows the base-class for the form to be specified.
- Add Control: Performs the same functionality as menu item Add Class, except that the class added to the project is derived from `System.Windows.Forms.UserControl` and the code generation wizard sets up several methods of the newly added class. A control is a user-interface element such as Button or TextBox. Just like menu item Add Windows Form, Add Control ensures that the appropriate references are set up and that the namespaces are made visible (using `imports` in Visual Basic and `using` in C#).

- Add Inherited Control: Performs the same functionality as menu item Add Control, except that an Inheritance Picker dialog is displayed. This dialog allows the base-class for the control to be specified.
- Add New Item: This menu item is a generic Add New, capable of adding entities that are supported by specific menu items such as a new Windows form, class, module, component class, and user control. The Add New Item menu can add a variety of other entities including a new text file, code file, transaction component, assembly resource file, bitmap file, cursor file, icon file, XML file, JScript file, VB script file, or Windows scripting host file. The new items that can be added are dependent on what is currently highlighted in Solution Explorer (solution, project, or file of project). Entities such as a new text file or JScript file could be added to a solution. A class, Windows Form, or component class cannot be added to a solution.
- Add Existing Item: This menu item is a generic Add for entities, of types as listed in Add New Item, that already exist. The new items that can be added are dependent on what is currently highlighted in Solution Explorer (solution, project or file of project). The overview of the menu item Add New Item presents a subset showing which existing items pertain to a solution and which ones do not.

This menu also contains a variety of other menu items not as directly germane to Windows Forms development.

Build Menu

The Build menu offers the following menu items:

- Build Solution: Builds every project in the entire solution based on the current configuration. The default configurations provided with a solution are Debug and Release. The current configuration is set using the dialog displayed by the Build menu's Configuration Manager menu item. The Build menu does not necessarily build every project in the solution. A project that is up-to-date (which has experienced no changes to itself or its dependencies since the last build) is not built. The Standard toolbar contains the Solution Configurations dropdown, which corresponds to the current configuration.
- Rebuild Solution: Rebuilds the current configuration of the entire solution. See the discussion of menu item Build Solution, for a review of how to specify current configuration. Even if a project is up-to-date, Rebuild Solution causes the project to be cleaned and built.
- Deploy Solution: This menu item is reviewed in a dedicated subsection of the current section of this chapter (see below).
- Build *project*: Builds the currently active project and all its dependencies. The project and/or its dependencies will only be built if they are not up-to-date. If `AFirstWindowsApplication` were the currently active project, this menu item would be displayed as Build AFirstWindowsApplication.
- Rebuild *project*: Rebuilds the currently active project and all its dependencies. If `AFirstWindowsApplication` were the currently active project, this menu item would be displayed as Rebuild AFirstWindowsApplication.
- Batch Build...: The Batch Build menu item should actually be named, 'Batch Build, Rebuild, Clean'. This menu item allows multiple projects and solutions (Debug or Release) to be built, rebuilt, or cleaned with the press of a single button. The Batch Build dialog is as follows:

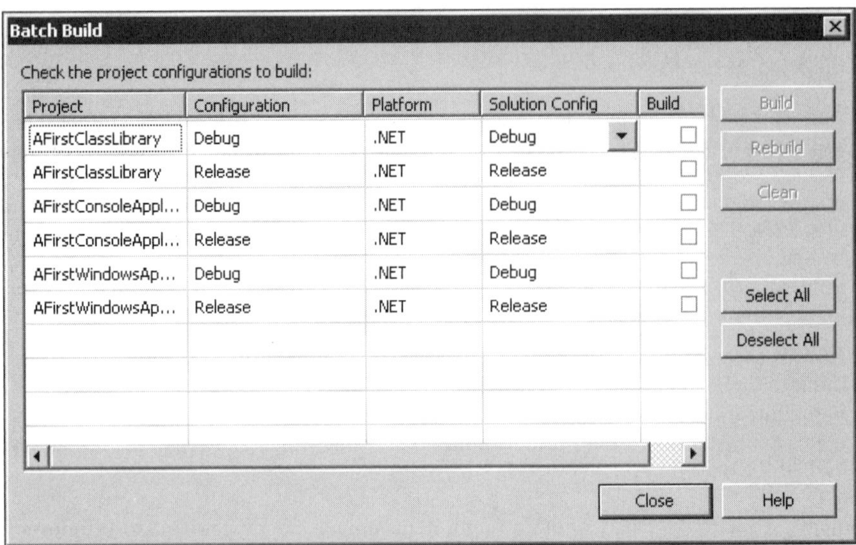

- Configuration Manager...: This specifies the active solution configuration using the combo box labeled Active Solution Configuration. The active solution configuration is either Debug or Release. When the Build menu's Build or Rebuild menu item is selected it is this active solution configuration that is built. For example if Debug were the active solution configuration, then only the Debug versions of the projects would be candidates to be built. The combo box, Active Solution Configuration, contains an entry that allows new configuration to be created, <New...>, and for existing configurations to be edited, <Edit...>. The Configuration Manager dialog is as follows:

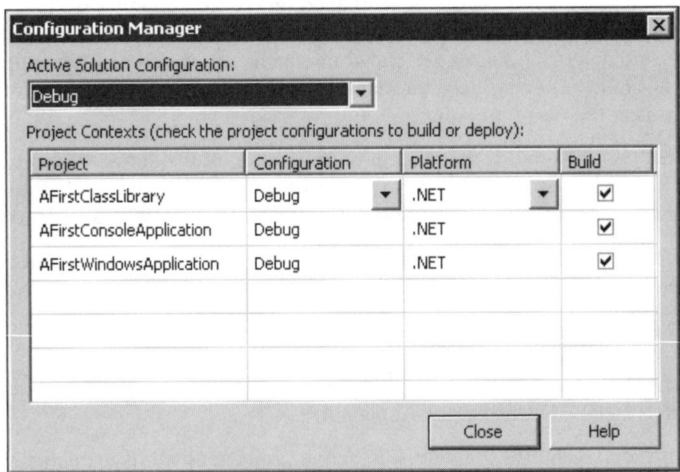

A great many developers rely on the Build toolbar:

From left to right the icons on the Build toolbar are Build Project, Build Solution, and Cancel build. Unless the build is in progress, the Cancel icon is grayed out. While the build is in progress the Build Project and Build Solution are grayed out.

The Debug Menu

It should come as no surprise that the Debug menu is used to control the debugging of a solution and its projects. The menu items exposed by the Debug menu are:

- Windows: Contains a submenu that allows a variety of debug-related windows to be displayed.
- Start: Starts debugging the project specified as the start project. If this project and its dependencies are out of date or have not been built, then the project and its dependencies are built.
- Start Without Debugging: Starts an application but does not run the application inside Visual Studio.NET's debugger. This means that breakpoints and other debugger features are not available to the running application.
- Processes: Displays a dialog that allows Visual Studio to debug multiple processes, processes that are already running, and processes that may reside on another machine. An entire section of this chapter is dedicated to this menu item.
- Step Into: Single steps execution and steps into functions.
- Step Over: Single steps execution and steps over functions.
- New Breakpoint...: Adds a new breakpoint that stops debug execution when a particular function is called, a line number in a source file is reached, a specific instruction address is reached, or a given variable changes value.
- Clear All Breakpoints: Clears all breakpoints. This menu item is only available once a breakpoint exists.
- Exceptions: Specifies how Visual Studio handles exceptions.

We will go no further with debugging here, but for more information on this see Chapter 14, which covers debugging and optimization in detail.

Tools

The Tools menu provides developers with access to a set of external tools and a mechanism with which to configure their Visual Studio experience. Visual Studio is composed of more than just the IDE. The menu items of the Tools menu correspond to the external tools available to the developer that include:

- Error Lookup: Displays the Error Lookup dialog that can be used to enter an error number. This can be looked up behind the scenes using the Win32 function, FormatMessage. This dialog is extremely useful when calling legacy functions or COM objects. It looks like this:

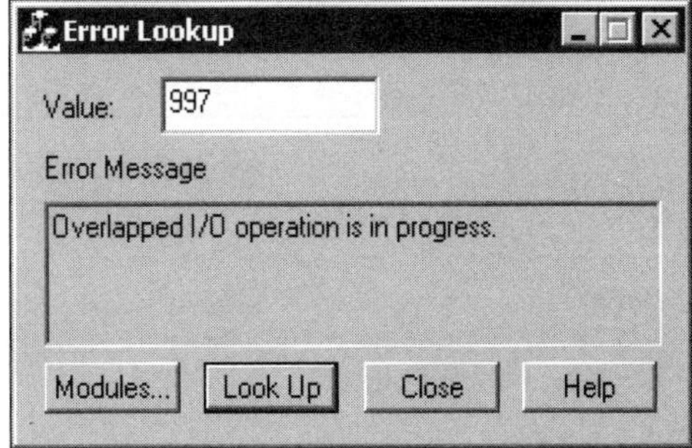

- Spy++: Launches the Spy++ tool that can be used to monitor a process's windows, threads and processes.
- OLE/COM Object Viewer: Launches the OLE/COM Object Viewer application that is useful in retrieving information on COM classes, program IDs, interfaces, and type libraries.
- ActiveX Control Test Container: Launches a tool that serves as a test container for ActiveX controls.
- MFC/ATL Trace Tool: Launches a tool that configures what MFC and ATL trace output will be displayed.

Configuring Visual Studio is a great way to increase productivity. Using the Tools menu and its Customize Toolbox menu item, we can do things like add new controls or remove unused controls. External applications can be added as menu items of the Tools menu. Using the External Tools menu item of the Tools menu supports this customization. The Customize menu item from the Tools menu provides a mechanism for customizing toolbars, Visual Studio commands and basic Visual Studio options.

The Options menu item from the Tools menu allows Visual Studio to be customized for a particular user on a particular computer. It is important to recognize that such customizations apply to Visual Studio and are not affiliated with any solution or project shared with co-workers. This section will not attempt to go into every minute detail of options configuration but will touch on certain highly desirable options. Specifying options applies only to the behavior of your tool on your machine. The dialog displayed by selecting Options from the Tools menu is as follows:

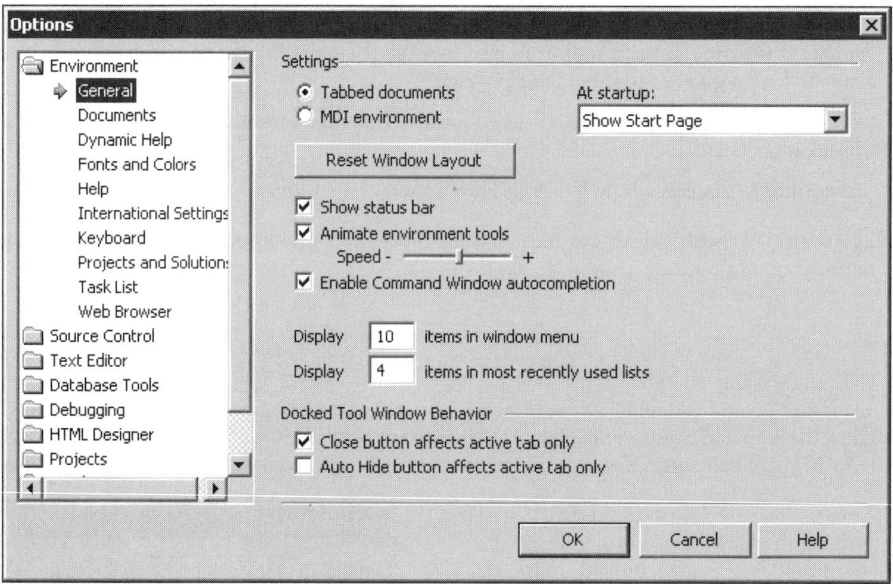

The specific categories of options that can be configured are in the left panel. Notice that under Environment the General selection is highlighted. The panel on the right side of the dialog corresponds to configuring Environment, General options. Of interest on this screen is At startup: which allows the behavior of Visual Studio at startup to be specified. The choices include Show empty project, Load last loaded solution, Show Start Page, etc.

Help

Using the My Profile setup in Visual Studio's Start Page, we can specify whether help is displayed within Visual Studio (internally) or not. Legacy versions of Visual Studio dictated whether help was part of the IDE or run in a separate application. It was not configurable by the developer.

Visual Studio's Help menu contains menu items such as: Contents, Search, Index, Index Results and Search Results. Each of these menu items corresponds to a specific section of the help provided within Microsoft document explorer. For example, if the Help menu's Contents menu item is selected, the following is displayed:

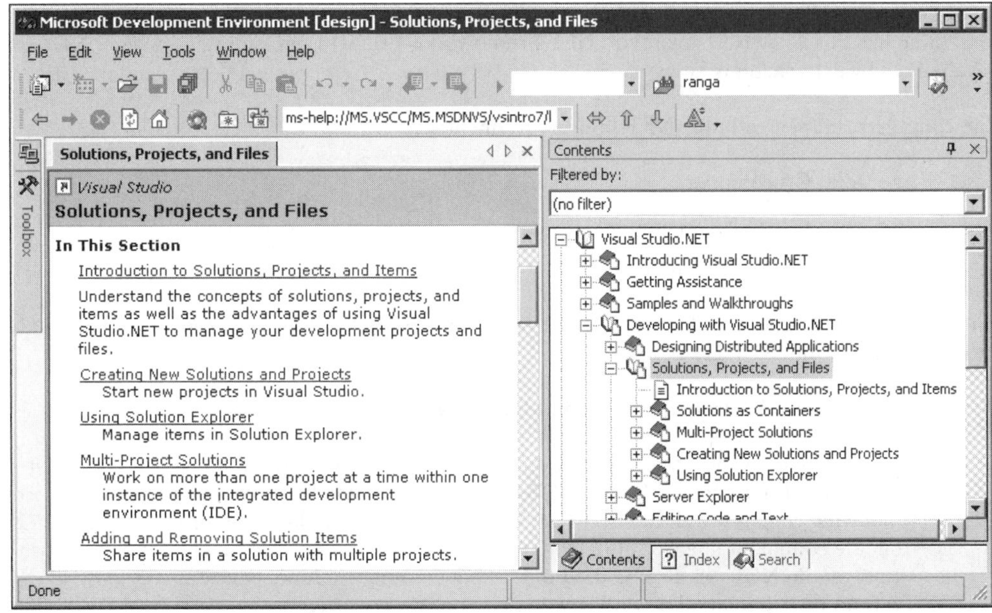

The navigation window (right pane of dialog) displayed within the help application is the Contents window. Contents are selected using the Contents tab at the base of the navigation window.

When looking at the Contents pane within help pay particular attention to the Filter by: drop-down menu. Notice that (no filter) is specified and the help available in the Contents window is extensive. By setting Filter by: to Visual Basic, our view of help is much more limited, since we see only VB-specific help topics.

It will be easy enough to play around with help and so we will cover it no further here.

Command-Line Development

It has been shown that Visual Studio.NET as an integrated development environment provides extremely powerful build features. Still, there are times when building from the command-line makes sense. Consider an application that uses make to build for a variety of languages, such as Java, C#, and VB.NET on Windows. It just so happens that the Java compiler used is not part of Visual Studio.NET. In order to provide a common build across all languages, make was used to develop the build process. Such applications do exist. Ninety percent of you with cable television receive programs processed by software built in just this manner (a Windows machine running Java compiled with one tool and components developed with Visual Studio).

As of Beta 2 the .NET Framework initially installs three compilers under a directory that will look something like this C:\WINNT\Microsoft.NET\Framework\v1.0.2914 depending on where .NET was installed, and what version is being used:

The compilers shipped with the .NET Framework include:

- `csc.exe`: C# compiler
- `jsc.exe`: JScript.NET compiler
- `vbc.exe`: VB.NET compiler

Noticeably absent is the compiler for C++, `cl.exe`. This compiler ships as part of Visual Studio.NET and not as part of the .NET Framework.

The steps to build with C# from the command-line are as follows:

- Execute the following Start Menu | Programs | Microsoft Visual Studio.NET 7.0 | Visual Studio.NET Tools | Visual Studio.NET Command Prompt. This command launches console windowing containing all the necessary environmental variables set in order to compile C# from the command line (running the C# compiler, `csc.exe`). Two batch files shipped with Visual Studio.NET can also be used to set up a console window's environment to build .NET C# from the command line (`VSVars32.bat` or `VCVars32.bat`).
- From the same console windows ready to compile C#, run the compiler, `csc`.

To demonstrate compilation, consider source file `HiWorld.cs`, which is defined as:

```
namespace ANamespace
{
    class AClass
    {
        static void Main()
        {
            System.Console.Out.WriteLine("Hello world!");
        }
    }
}
```

It is possible to build this program from the command-line:

```
C:\test>csc HiWorld.cs
```

This would build HiWorld.exe, which would display the expected output when run. The executable generated is named HiWorld.exe, because the first source file in the list of files to compile is named HiWorld.cs. Yes, there was only source file specified, but it was still the first file in the list.

The Visual Basic command-line works in the same way as will be demonstrated on the following, HiWorld.vb:

```
Module Module1

    Sub Main()
        System.Console.Out.WriteLine("Hello world!")
    End Sub

End Module
```

This file would be compiled using the Visual Basic compiler, vbc.exe, as follows:

```
C:\test>vbc HiWorld.vb
```

The C# compiler, and the Visual Basic compiler share a variety of command-line options which include:

- /?: Lists the compiler's command-line options.
- /out:*filename*: Specifies the output file generated by the compilation. When creating an executable make sure to include extension, .exe, in the filename and when building a DLL make sure to include extension, .dll. The compilers (csc and vbc) do not automatically add the appropriate extension when the output file name is specified.
- /target:exe: Specifies that the target is a console application (an executable that displays a console window).
- /target:winexe: Specifies that the target is a windows application.
- /target:library: Specifies that the target build is a library (a DLL).
- /unsafe(+| –): If '+' is specified then unsafe code is permitted, and if '–' is specified then unsafe code is not permitted.
- /checked(+| –): If '+' is specified then numeric operations are checked for overflow, and if '-' is specified such operations are not checked for overflow.
- /baseaddress:*xxxxxxxx*: Specifies the base address of the library built. This is used in order to improve application load time by causing libraries not to collide with respect to address range.
- /recurse:[*dir*]*wildcard*: All files in the current directory or the directory specified by *dir* are built. The sub-directories of this root directory are included in the build. A filename can be specified to limit the files included in the build during the recursive search. This file name, *wildcard*, can contain a wildcard or a filename to further control what is built.
- /reference:*filelist*: Specifies a list of assembly files from which metadata will be retrieved. The primary .NET assembly, mscorlib.dll, does not need to be specified. It is assumed be part of the project.
- /debug(+|–): If '+' is specified then a debug version is built, and if '–' is specified then a release version is built (non-debug version). When debugging is enabled a file with extension .pdb is created. The *.pdb file maintains the relationship between the source files and the module for which debug information is generated (the *.exe or *.dll).

- /optimize(+|–): If '+' is specified then optimization is turned on, and if '–' is specified then optimization is turned off.
- /main:*type*: Specifies which type's `Main` method will be used as the executable's entry-point.

Let's run through a couple of examples to show a variety of these options in action.

An example in which all C# files in the current directory and each sub-directory are built using `/recurse` is as follows:

```
C:\test>csc /target:exe /out:BuildItAll.exe /recurse:*.cs
```

In this example, /target was placed before /recurse because the target must be specified before the source files are specified. The /recurse option is the equivalent of specifying source files. If the previous command-line had been run on the directory containing `HiWorld.cs`, this file would have been built but the executable created would have been called BuildItAll.exe (based on the /out parameter).

Before demonstrating further command-line options, we'll create a new source file called `ByeWorld.cs`:

```
namespace ANamespace
{
    class BClass
    {
        static void Main()
        {
            System.Console.Out.WriteLine("Bye world!");
        }
    }
}
```

The `ByeWorld.cs` file contains the `BClass` class that exposes the `Main` method while `HiWorld.cs` exposes the `Main` method via the class, `AClass`. Attempting to compile these two source files together leads to problems:

```
C:\test>csc hiworld.cs byeworld.cs
Microsoft (R) Visual C# Compiler Version 7.00.9254 [CLR version v1.0.2914]
Copyright (C) Microsoft Corp 2000-2001. All rights reserved.

hiworld.cs(5,21): error CS0017: Program 'hiworld.exe' has more than one entry
    point defined: 'ANamespace.AClass.Main()'
byeworld.cs(5,21): error CS0017: Program 'hiworld.exe' has more than one entry
    point defined: 'ANamespace.BClass.Main()'
```

This afore-demonstrated conflict of interest could be remedied using /main command-line switch in order to specify which main is to be used as the executables entry point. In the following example the `Main` method from the `AClass` class of the `ANamespace` namespace is specified as the executable's entry-point (option, /main) is as follows:

```
C:\test>csc /main:ANamespace.AClass HiWorld.cs ByeWorld.cs
```

When specifying which class contains method Main, the class name must be fully qualified, including the namespace in which the class resides (for example, ANamespace.AClass). The executable created by the previous compilation would be HiWorld.exe because HiWorld.cs is the name of the first source file in the compilation list.

The csc, jsc, and vbc compilers can be used to develop class libraries. To demonstrated this consider the following VB.NET file, greet.vb:

```
Imports System.Windows.Forms

Public Class GreetSaidIndividual
    Public Shared Sub Greetings(ByVal greeting As String)
        MessageBox.Show(greeting)
    End Sub
End Class
```

Using the greet.vb source file, a library called greet.dll can be built with debugging enabled:

```
C:\test>vbc /debug+ /reference:system.windows.forms.dll /target:library greet.vb
```

greet.dll uses the MessageBox class, which is found in the system.windows.forms.dll assembly, hence the /reference command-line argument to the vbc compiler. Let's say that HiWorld2.cs is a C# application that makes use of the GreetSaidIndividual class contained in greet.dll is as follows:

```
namespace BNamespace
{
    class CClass
    {
        static void Main()
        {
            GreetSaidIndividual.Greetings("Hello world!");
        }
    }
}
```

A C# executable, HiWorld2.exe, can reference our VB.NET DLL as follows:

```
C:\test>csc /debug+ /reference:greet.dll HiWorld2.cs
```

HiWorld2.exe, was also built with debug information. If we wanted to take our fascination with command-line one step further, we could run the .NET command-line debugger, cordbg.exe. Why a command-line debugger? Such a debugger is extremely useful when the environment being debugged does not support high-resolution graphics like those required by an IDE such as Visual Studio.NET. The following demonstrates launching the command-line debugger with our HiWorld2 executable and running said executable within the core debugger:

```
C:\test>cordbg HiWorld2
Process 1808/0x710 created.
Warning: couldn't load symbols for c:\winnt\microsoft.net\framework\v1.0.2914\mscorlib.dll
[thread 0x4c8] Thread created.
```

```
007:         GreetSaidIndividual.Greetings("Hello world!");
(cordbg) g
Warning: couldn't load symbols for c:\winnt\assembly\gac\system.windows.forms\1.
0.2411.0__b77a5c561934e089\system.windows.forms.dll
Warning: couldn't load symbols for
   c:\winnt\assembly\gac\system\1.0.2411.0__b77a5c561934e089\system.dll
Warning: couldn't load symbols for
   c:\winnt\assembly\gac\system.drawing\1.0.2411.0__b03f5f7f11d50a3a\system.drawing.dll
[thread 0x634] Thread created.
[thread 0x6b8] Thread exited.
Process exited.
(cordbg)
```

A bit of user interaction was required before the line, [thread 0x634] Thread created, could be displayed. Remember that the `Greetings` method contains a message box. The program being debugged blocks in the debugger until this message box is closed. At this stage the line, [thread 0x634] Thread created, is displayed.

Don't be intimidated by the warnings in the previous screen text. This is simply informing the developer that the primary DLL of the .NET Framework (`mscorlib.dll`) does not contain debugging symbols. Similarly the assemblies, `system.dll` and `system.drawing.dll`, also do not contain debug symbols. This simply means that the code exposed by `mscorlib.dll`, `system.dll`, and `system.drawing.dll` cannot be debugged.

The final line of the previous screen text is `cordbg`'s prompt. The (cordbg) g before this ran the program (where g stands for go). An '`s`' would step into the program, including the VB.NET DLL if '`s`' was entered enough times. Yes, it is permissible to debug multiple languages from the command-line! A '`b`' displays or sets breakpoints, while a '`t`' sets or displays the current thread. Naturally, try the '`?`' which stands for help and subsequently lists all the commands permissible for the command-line debugger, `cordbg.exe`.

Visual Studio.NET supports command-line compilation, but developers should not go out of their way to adopt this style of project compilation. If, however, you wish to see a further example of developing using the command line and coding by hand, then see Chapter 16 on Windows Forms and Web Services, which uses the command line to compile its example applications.

Summary

In closing we turn to Dickens: 'It was the best of times.' Those who were expecting the remainder of the Tale of Two Cities quote, 'It was the worst of times', clearly did not read this chapter. The reasons to fall in love with Visual Studio.NET are plentiful:

- One development environment supporting many languages
- Improved code generation wizards
- Simpler installation and deployment
- A more logical menu organization than past Visual development tools
- Easier GUI development
- Provides a means to exploit the plethora of features provided with the .NET Framework

Just remember that Visual Studio.NET is very powerful and may appear to be intimidating at first. Don't get overwhelmed by this robust feature set. When all else fails reread this chapter, or if you cannot see the window you need, return to the View menu.

Legend: Concrete Class / Abstract class

System.Windows.Forms

- System.Object
  - System.MarshalRefObject
    - System.ComponentMode.Component
      - CommonDialog
        - ColorDialog
        - FileDialog
        - FontDialog
        - PageSetupDialog
        - PrintDialog
      - ErrorProvider
      - HelpProvider
      - ImageList
      - Menu
        - ContextMenu
        - MainMenu
        - MenuItem
      - NotifyIcon
      - StatusBarPanel
      - Timer
      - ToolBarButton
      - ToolTip
      - Control
        - ButtonBase
          - Button
          - CheckBox
          - RadioButton
        - DataGrid
        - DateTimePicker
        - GroupBox
        - Label
          - LinkLabel
        - ListControl
          - ComboBox
          - ListBox
            - CheckedListBox
        - ListView
        - MonthCalendar
        - PictureBox
        - PrintReviewControl
        - ProgressBar
        - ScrollableControl
          - ContainerControl
            - Form
              - PrintPreviewDialog
              - ThreadExceptionDialog
            - PropertyGrid
            - UpDownBase
              - DomainUpDown
              - NumericUpDown
            - UserControl
          - Panel
            - TabPage
        - ScrollBar
          - HScrollBar
          - VScrollBar
        - Splitter
        - StatusBar
        - TabControl
        - TextBoxBase
          - RichTextBox
          - Textbox
        - ToolBar
        - TrackBar
        - TreeView
  - ListViewItem
  - TreeNode

3

Inheritance and Other Important New Language Features

One of the many advantages of Microsoft's new .NET initiative is that it is language agnostic. As we have already seen, Visual Studio ships with full support for both VB.NET, C# and C++. In addition Microsoft is working with over 30 different companies to port other languages, both commercial and academic, onto the .NET platform, giving the developer the option to pick the language he or she is most familiar with.

While Microsoft promotes comprehensive language support, it's clear that the company's main thrust is concentrated on VB.NET and C#. In reality, there is very little difference between the two languages, apart from a few naming conventions. VB.NET has been extended to support almost all of the language constructs that are available in C# (and previously in C++).

Probably the most important extension is the introduction of full support for the Object-Oriented (OO) programming paradigm. While classes have been supported since VB4, and COM classes have been around even longer, support for other features like inheritance and polymorphism were sorely lacking from within VB. We will spend most of this chapter discussing various aspects of object-oriented programming in VB.NET. To fully benefit from this, it is not only important to learn the relevant language constructs. Those who are new to the concept of OO must also take a 'leap of faith', and maybe change their program design methods. Throughout, we will therefore try to cover both the **how** and **why** of OO, using three examples:

- `WroxGraph`: A fairly comprehensive graph control in only 200 lines of code. It demonstrates the power of OO, while also showcasing many of the language constructs.
- `WroxTest`: This sample demonstrates Visual Forms inheritance, the ability to reuse the visual design, and basic functionality in a complete Form.
- `WroxInterface`: This sample demonstrates how to define, implement and use so-called interfaces.

The final part of the chapter is devoted to Structured Error Handling. This is a much better way to write robust code. We have also included a sample application to demonstrate this:

- `WroxExcept`: A very simple application, which throws and catches a couple of exceptions.

Experienced C++ programmers moving to C# may want to just skim this chapter, since a lot of it will be slightly 'old hat'. Alternatively, developers may want to download the sample VB.NET code, just to see how much similarity there is between the two languages.

Introduction to Object-Oriented Programming

When we think about it, it's really quite amazing that it's possible to make computers do anything remotely useful. At the hardware level, today's CPUs are still only able to work with binary data, and perform a small set of simple generic operations. The operations are CPU-specific, and only understood by the very few people who specialize in machine level programming. Fortunately, the computer can perform these operations *very* quickly, and it is possible to organize the generic operations into blocks, which can perform more complex operations. The third saving grace for modern software development is the fact that we can reuse complex operations built by ourselves, or most often by others. These include the BIOS, the whole Windows API, and the .NET Framework, as well as compilers, word processors, etc. Without the ability to reuse, we would have to directly specify each of the 1 billion instructions that a modern CPU executes every second!

At the same time, today's business problems can be very complicated. They very often require knowledge not directly available to the person or team developing the application. Say you are called in to write software for an air traffic control system. You may be the world's best programmer, but there is no way you can write this program in a vacuum. You need to interview many different users and people with expert knowledge about air traffic control to understand what the requirements are for the system. Through this you will then learn about airplane trajectories, flight paths, approach procedures, wind directions, security procedures, schedules, etc.

So, it's all about abstractions. Starting from the top, the different users and experts in the problem domain (that is, those who know what the system should do) must describe the problem to the software developer. The developer organizes the program into smaller modules. These may again be sub-divided until they can finally be implemented through reuse of code available in the framework. It should now be evident that a good programming language must have at least two types of qualities. A language should:

- Facilitate efficient reuse: A good programming language makes it easy to write a block of code once, but then reuse it when a similar problem needs to be solved in another application. The developer will often want to 'tweak' the module a little to fit the new application, and we should be able to do this without breaking other applications that depend on the same code.
- Facilitate efficient modeling and discussion: Since programming is definitely a team sport nowadays, it would be beneficial if the program could be structured to correspond to the concepts embodied in the business problem to be solved. If an air traffic control system is explained using terms like airplane, flight path, etc. we should also be able to find these terms in the program design, and possibly in the code. This would make it easier to understand, easier to maintain and, as it turns out, more resilient to change.

Ease of understanding and ease of maintenance is achieved because a design based on real-world concepts immediately gives everyone some idea of what different parts of the code mean, and what they are supposed to do. When we write a design and a program that includes a function like `AirPlane.AssignFlightPath(pathno)`, most people can get some understanding of what is going on. The function is probably going to assign a flight path to an airplane, and the airplane will then probably start following that path after proper course correction has taken place. Most people will also quickly spot a potential problem, if we design a function like `AirPlane.SwitchOffRunwayLight(RunwayNo)`. Clearly, the switching off the runway lights has nothing to do with the airplane, but with another part of the system.

The system's increased resilience to change stems from the fact that these real-world concepts have been around for a long time. They are usually the result of many years of experience, and therefore are known to be stable. If we can build an air traffic control around airplanes, flight paths, schedules, etc., chances are that these concepts and their interrelation will still be valid 10 years from now. There may be more airplanes, they may fly faster, and the flight paths may be more complicated, but, an airplane will still follow a flight path, and it will still fly according to a schedule. Consequently, the overall architecture can survive for a long time.

In the following section, we will put forward the case that the object-oriented features now available in VB.NET (and C#) have these qualities in great abundance.

Objects and Classes

A fundamental concept of OO modeling and programming is the **object**. In good designs, an object in the program corresponds to a similar object or abstraction in the real world. For example, our air traffic control system will have objects like airplanes, runways, etc. An inventory system will have objects like accounts, invoices, debtors, and creditors. And, as we shall see later, a graph control may have shapes, lines, squares, and triangles.

All objects are an instance of some **class**. The class defines what type of object it is. Once we know an object's class, we know its **interfaces** and its **behavior**. The interfaces define how we (or other parts of the program) can interact with any object of this class. The behavior defines what the object will do in response to such interaction.

A Sample 'Line' Class

A sample `Line` class is shown below using UML (Unified Modeling Language) notation. The UML symbol for a class is a rectangle with three compartments (for further information on UML, see *Instant UML* by Wrox Press, *ISBN 1861000871*):

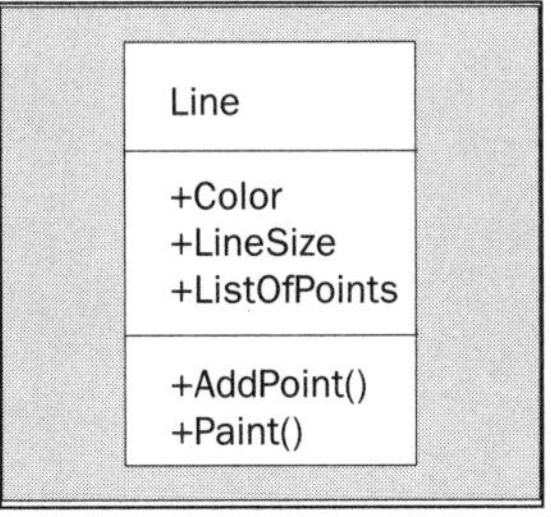

A class is generally described by its **name**, **properties**, and **methods**:

- The name identifies the class. The class name is shown in the top of the three compartments.
- A property is normally a simple value, which can be assigned and/or read by other classes. In our example the `Line` class has properties like `Color`, `LineSize` and `ListOfPoints`. Properties are listed in the second compartment of the class symbol. The + in front of `Color` and `LineSize` is a 'public' access specifier. It indicates that objects of other classes can access these properties. The '–' in front of `ListOfPoints` indicates that objects of other classes cannot access this property. The property is said to be 'private'.
- A method is a more complex operation, which may or may not affect the state of the class itself. In our example, methods include `AddPoint`, which adds another point to the line, and `Paint`, which paints the line onto the selected output device. Methods are listed in the bottom compartment of the class symbol. Just like properties, methods are also prefixed with an access specifier (+ in this case).

Objects of the same class have the **same interfaces and behavior**. With respect to interface, all instances of the `Line` class will allow us to get and set the values of its `Color`, and `LineSize` properties. We may also call `AddPoint` to add another point or `Paint` to get the line painted. With respect to behavior, we are assured that the act accessing any of the properties or calling any of the methods will have the same effect for all instances of the `Line` class.

However, they do **have different identities and maintain their own state**. Even if two lines have identical `Color, LineSize`, etc., they still have different identities. At the very least, they may have different locations in the computers memory. It will be possible to find one line, and modify its color without also modifying the other. By the same token, all objects maintain their own state. Note that we refer to state as the combined value of all the object's properties. A red line comprising three points does not have the same state as a red line comprising four points. Neither does a yellow line comprising nine points have the same state as a blue line also comprising nine points.

In summary, a red and a blue line will both have an `AddPoint` and a `Paint` method. But, they are obviously two different lines, which can be treated individually.

Associations

Once we have defined the individual classes, it's time to think about how they are associated in our model. For example, a debtor in our accounting system will have a list of outstanding invoices. Each of the invoices may comprise a list of billable item's etc. Similarly, our graph control has a collection of lines, and each of the lines has a collection of points.

This is illustrated below:

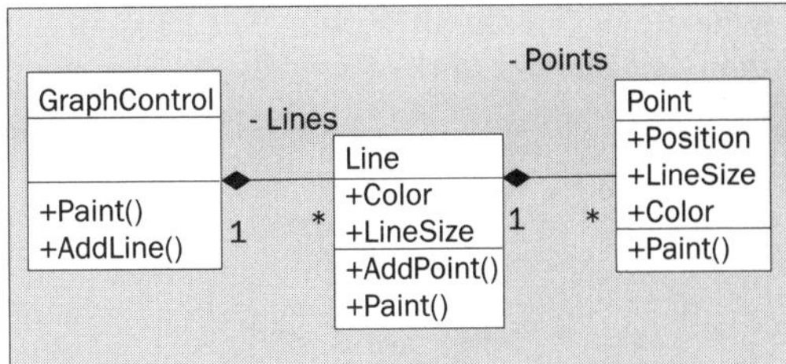

Associations between classes are show by connecting the classes with lines. The lines are then annotated to indicate a couple of important characteristics of the association:

- **Multiplicity**. Both of the relations in our graph example are **one-to-many relations**. Each graph control can include many lines, and a line can include many points. But any line can only be associated with one graph, and any point can only be associated with one line. In UML this is shown by placing a 1 and a * respectively at each end of the relation. Other relations include **one-to-one relations** and **many-to-many relations**. One-to-one relationships are indicated by placing a '1' at both ends, and many-to-many relationships are indicated by placing an '*' at both ends.
- **Strength of relationship**. An 'equal' association between two classes, where both classes were at the same level, would have been modeled with a straight line. This is sometimes called a **uses-relationship**. A possible uses-relationship would be the association between an airplane and the runway. At some point in time the airplane will use the runway, but they are really two separate entities, and one is not 'more' than the other.

By contrast, we may sometimes want to model a 'whole/part' relationship where a top-level class (the whole) is made up of several smaller things (the parts). Consider our graph control. Here our graph is made up of lines, and the lines are made up of points. These kinds of relationships are called **aggregations**. They are also sometimes called '**has-a**' relationships to indicate that the whole object has some objects of the part. Aggregations are indicated by placing a **white diamond** at the end of the line next to the whole object.

The **black diamond** at the left of the association lines in this diagram indicates a so-called **composition**. Composition is the strongest possible association between two classes. We may read the diagram to mean that our graph control **is composed of** a number of lines, and each line **is composed of** a number of points. Compared to aggregations, compositions infer that the lifetime of the part will be dependent on the lifetime of the whole. In other words, if we delete an instance of the graph control object, it will in return delete all its lines, and they will in return delete all their points.

Divide and Conquer!

We can probably already appreciate that OO programs are structured so that they solve the problem through collaboration. Each class is designed to be essentially self-sufficient. At the lower level a class will offer rich functionality within limited scope of responsibility, while at a higher level, another class will offer broader functionality by calling upon classes at the lower level and coordinating their behavior.

When the `Paint` method is called on our `GraphControl`, it will simply iterate its collection of lines and call the `Paint` method on each `Line` object. In the same vein, when the `Paint` method is called on a `Line` object, it will simply iterate its `Points` collection. The `Line` object will first draw the line between points, but it will then delegate the work of actually drawing the point marker by calling `Paint` on each of the `Point` objects.

Very simple to implement; yet very effective!

Inheritance

While life is good now, there is still room for improvement. One of the problems is that we cannot insert a single point directly on the `GraphControl`. Instead, we have to first insert it into a line, and then insert the line into the control.

We could remedy this by adding an `AddPoint` method and a `Points` collection to the `GraphControl`. But this is a short-lived solution, because we have just doubled the work in the graph controls `Paint` method. It must now iterate both the `Lines` collection and the `Points` collection.

Additionally, what happens when we decide that we also want the ability to insert squares, circles, or textual tags? If we follow this model, we will have to add a new collection to both the `GraphControl` and the `Line` class, each time we get a new creative idea.

Another problem is that we are not reusing any code between the points, squares, circles, etc, even if they are very similar.

This is where **inheritance** comes in. Inheritance allows us to express that class B **is a kind of** class A. We will say that class B inherits from class A. We may also say that class A is a **generalization** and class B is a **specialization** (of the concept), or that class A is a **base class** and class B is the **sub class**. Or we may say that B is **derived** from A, or that A is a **superclass** of B:

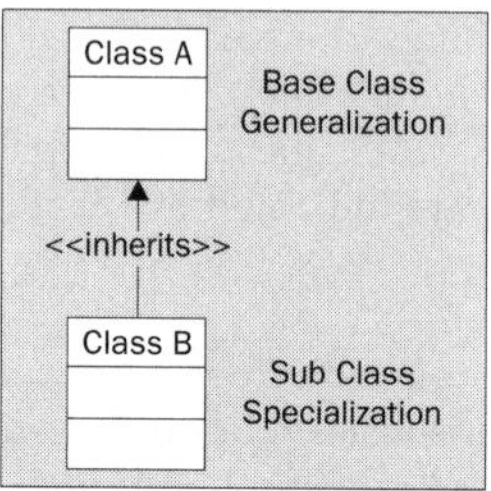

When class B inherits from class A, it inherits all properties and methods from the base class. It is then able to extend and/or modify these. To illustrate the importance of inheritance with a real life example, let's think again about our airplane. When Boeing's engineers decided to develop the 747-200, they probably did not start totally from scratch. Instead, they very likely said: 'The 747-200 is a kind of 747-100 with the following additions and modifications'. This realization, that they could reuse almost all of the design from the base model 747-100, obviously translated into huge savings. As we will discuss in the next section (under polymorphism), these savings are not just limited to the engineering effort required to create the 'specialization'. The benefit is equally applicable to the users of this new class.

While the illustration above uses UML notation, the documentation available in the .NET help system uses simple text indentation:

```
Class A
     Class B
```

Introducing 'Shape' as a Generalization

Inheritance allows us to introduce the generalized concept of a `Shape`. We can say that the text, several variations of points, and a line are special types of shapes. This simplifies the problem tremendously:

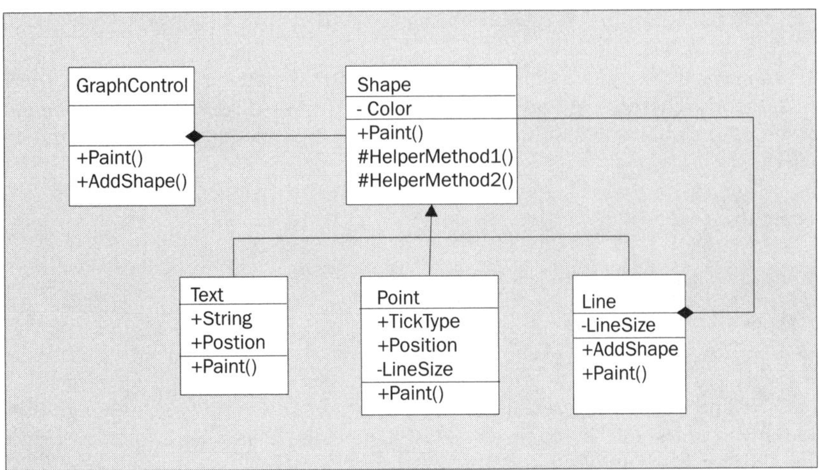

The `GraphControl` can now maintain only one collection, a `Shapes` collection, no matter how many new types of shapes we may want to come up with in the future. The `GraphControl` does not even know that different types of shapes exist. Further, it does not have to differentiate between a simple `Point`, and say, a complex object like `Line`, which again is a collection of `Shapes`. The same holds true for the `Line` object. Since this now also maintains a collection of `Shapes`, instead of `Points`, it will also be unaffected by any future creativity with respect to new draw-able objects. As long as new draw-able objects inherits from `Shape`, those objects can also be inserted in the `Shapes` collection owned by the `GraphControl` as well as the `Shapes` collection owned by the `Line`.

Inheritance also allowed us to push the `Color` property from the `Point` and `Line` classes up to the `Shape` class. All classes derived from `Shape` will now share this.

Finally, it can be seen that we have introduced two helper methods. If any code is shared between some of the derived classes, we can quite conveniently create methods in the base class and move the shared code up.

Experienced C++ programmers may be wondering what happened to multiple inheritance. Multiple inheritance is not directly supported in .NET. We can, however, define a class to implement several so-called interfaces. Interfaces will be discussed later in this chapter.

Polymorphism

The real benefit of inheritance is not reaped until we combine it with the concept of **polymorphism**. Polymorphism is the ability of an object to take on different behavior, depending on which class was used to instantiate the object.

Consider the code below:

```
Dim aText As Text = New Text(…)
Dim aPoint As Point = New Point(…)
aText.Paint()
aPoint.Paint()
```

This code instantiates aText and aPoint objects, as instances of the Text and Point classes, and calls their Paint methods. There should be no surprises here. In line three we call the code in the Paint method for the aText object, and in line four we will call the code for the Paint method in the aPoint object.

But what about this code:

```
Dim aText As Shape = New Text(...)
Dim aPoint As Shape = New Point(...)
aText.Paint()
aPoint.Paint()
```

This time, aText and aPoint are declared to be of the generic Shape type, although they are assigned instances of the Text class or the Point class, just like before. This is legal, since aText 'is a kind of' Shape, and aPoint 'is a kind of' Shape.

Because of polymorphism, the call to the Paint method will still be routed to the code in the derived class, even if the object is declared to be of the base class. The beauty of this concept is that we can now write the code in the GraphControl to only deal with generic Shapes. The runtime system will automatically determine which sub class of Shape it is, and automatically call the relevant Paint method.

The act of redefining the function of a method in a sub class is called **overriding** the method. The main purpose for including Paint in the Shape base class was to make it available for GraphControl to call. Once the 'place holder' method is declared in the base class, we can then go ahead and implement the real behavior for the method in a sub class.

This allows us to write something like this:

```
For I = 0 To Shapes.Count - 1
   Dim aShape As Shape = Shapes.Item(I)
   aShape.WroxPaint(…)
Next
```

This will request every shape attached to the graph control to paint itself using the implementation of Paint pertaining to the actual shape in question. This code will not have to change when we introduce new sub classes derived from the Shape class.

Methods that are defined in a base class and overridden in a derived class are called **virtual methods**. Returning to our real world example, consider a pilot who is certified to fly a 747-100. As long as the 747-200 has exactly the same navigational interface and flight behavior as the 747-100, the pilot will also be able to fly the 747-200. An even better example may be that of a car. Although most models have different engines, different bodies, different looks, etc., they still share the basic interface of a steering wheel, a brake, a speeder, indicator lights, etc. A driver may therefore be able to drive any car (within limits). If a new manufacturer produces a completely new car model, our driver will also be able to drive that car as long as its interface is derived from the base car model.

Similarly, if we create a new draw-able object, say a bitmap, this object can still be inserted into the `Shapes` collection and be used by the `GraphControl`, as long as our new object is an instance of a class derived from `Shape`.

Abstraction, Encapsulation and Code Reuse

Before we jump into the code, it's time to reflect on some of the benefits offered by truly object-oriented languages like VB.NET.

First of all, we have seen that it supports **abstraction** at different levels. We can build systems where code is structured around real-world entities, like 'airplane', or 'account'. We can also introduce additional abstractions within our program to share common behavior, like we did with the `Shape` class.

Another important attribute is that of **encapsulation** and **information hiding**. As we have just seen, we can write the graph control to only deal with the `Shape` class. It does not have to know anything about any sub classes of the `Shape` class to do its job. In fact, it does not even have to know how the `Shape` class or any of its sub classes are implemented. We can completely change the implementation, without affecting the `GraphControl`.

Finally, object-oriented languages offer excellent opportunities for **code reuse**. We can reuse individual classes, or whole frameworks of classes. A well-designed OO program will distribute 'intelligence' over all classes and try to make them self-sufficient. Classes can be reused through simple association, like the `GraphControl` uses a collection of `Shapes`. In addition, we can inherit from a class and extend its behavior with additional methods. Alternatively, we can modify it by overriding an existing method, as we did with the `Paint` method.

WroxGraph: Extending a Control

It is time to see how this works in practice. In this example, we will demonstrate how to implement a simple graph control using the principles discussed above. Along the way, we will discuss the various OO-related language constructs that are used.

Please note that this is not a real 'professional' control. We have had to make a couple of compromises to keep the example small. We also wanted to postpone an in-depth discussion of GDI+, the new Graphics Device Interface that is part of the .NET Framework, to Chapter 12.

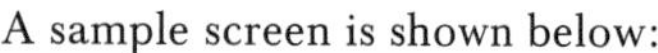

A sample screen is shown below:

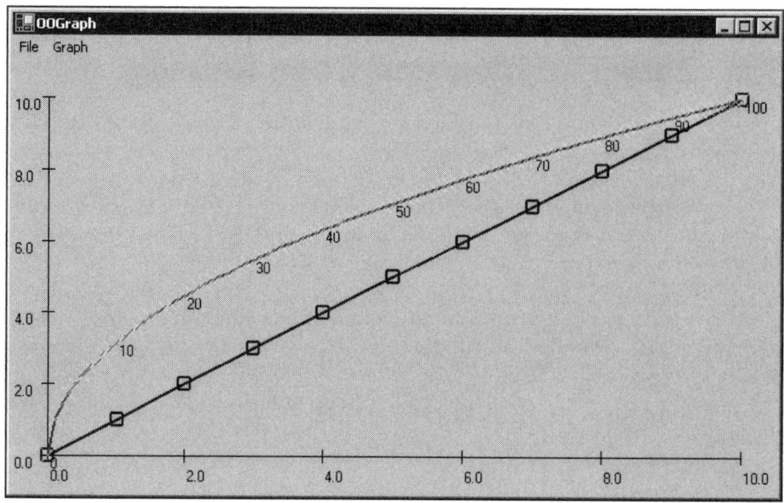

Our control is created on the basis of a `Panel` control. This was first inserted into the form using the IDE, and its `Dock` attribute was set to `DockStyle.Fill`, so it would take up all available space. We then manually modified the code to instantiate a `MyGraph` object instead of a `Panel` object.

The following code was auto-generated within the IDE:

```
...
Friend WithEvents Panel1 As Panel
...
...
Me.Panel1 = New Panel()
...
```

This was changed to:

```
...
Friend WithEvents Panel1 As MyGraph
...
...
Me.Panel1 = New MyGraph()
...
```

The graph is composed of the following objects:

- Two axes. Both of these are created as simple lines (of class `WroxLine`). Each line has a `WroxPoint` and a `WroxText` object inserted at appropriate values. A `WroxPoint` can have different `TickStyles`. For the `X-axis` we have set the `TickStyle` to Vertical, and for the Y-axis the `TickStyle` is Horizontal.
- Two lines. One line has a number of `WroxPoint` objects with their `TickStyle` set to `Square`. The other has both a number of `WroxPoint` objects with `TickStyle` set to `Cross` and for each tenth point we have also inserted a `WroxText` object.

A Two-Minute Primer on Controls and GDI+

While this chapter is not about Controls or GDI+, we need to spend a few lines on how Windows Forms renders forms, and how GDI+ supports graphical information. See Chapter 12 for further information on GDI+.

The 'OnPaint' Method

This is really quite simple. A Windows Form contains a collection of `Controls`. In order to render itself, the form will iterate its `Control` collection and ask each control to render itself. Sounds familiar, doesn't it?

To ask a control to render itself, the `Form` will send out a `Paint` event. This will eventually be translated into a call to an `OnPaint` method implemented by the control. In order for us to implement our graph control all we need to do is:

- Derive our graph control from the `Control` class (or a descendant thereof).
- Override the `OnPaint` method to draw what we want. This, of course, works because of polymorphism.

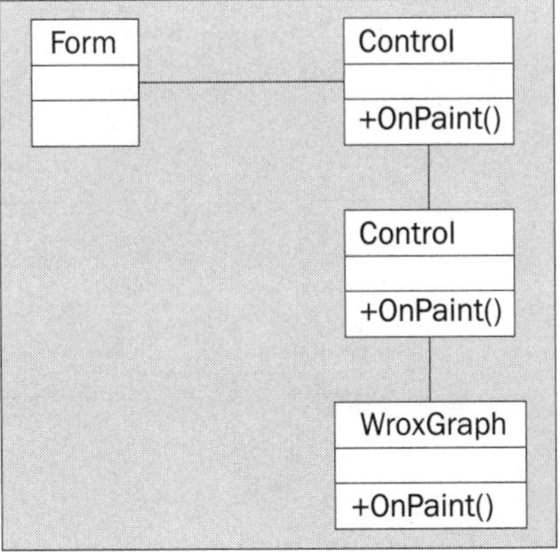

About GDI+

In order to avoid too much exposure to GDI+, we have implemented a couple of methods in the `WroxGraph` class to handle the drawing of texts and lines. The rest of the application will use these, so there are only a few things we need to know.

First, when a `Control` needs to render itself, it is handed an object of the `Graphics` class. The `Control` can now use methods on this object to draw lines, text, etc. If `aGraphics` is a `Graphics` object, the following code will draw a line from the position `CurrentPoint` to `aPoint`, using style `aPen`:

```
        aGraphics.DrawLine(aPen, aCurrentPoint, aPoint)
```

Lines and text are rendered using Pen's and Brushes. For example, a Pen is specified by its color, thickness, and whether or not it is solid or hatched. The position of the control is specified by a Point object, which has X and Y members, and finally, the size of a control is specified in pixels. This means that if a Control is 200 pixels wide and 400 pixels high, the point at the upper left corner will be (0,0) and the point at the lower right corner will be (199,399). If we go through the code we will see that a function has been included in WroxGraph to, firstly, invert the coordinate system so the value for Y increases as we move up the graph control, instead of down. Secondly, it will scale between the values that we will be using internally to represent data points, and the number of pixels available on the Control.

The Complete Application

The class diagram for the complete application is shown below:

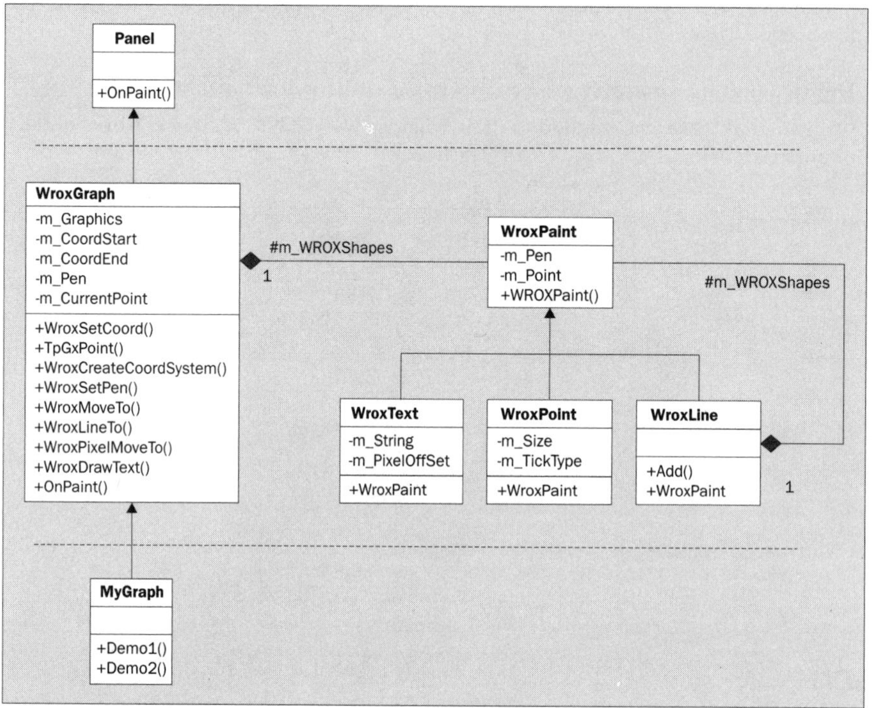

- WroxGraph is derived from Panel, and is responsible for painting the control. In order to shield us from GDI+, it also implements WroxSetPen, WroxMoveTo, WroxLineTo, WroxPixelMoveTo, WroxPixelLineTo, and WroxDrawText. The other classes use these instead of the real GDI functions.
- WroxGraph has a collection of WroxShape objects. It calls the WroxPaint method on the shapes to ask them to render themselves.

- WroxText, WroxPoint, and WroxLine are all descendants of WroxShape. Each inherit the m_Pen and m_Point member variable from WroxShape. They also override the WroxPaint method to implement their own rendering.

Together, all the Wrox... classes comprise a small generic framework that can render a graph, once the graph is defined. We must define the graph by creating WroxShape objects and adding them to the m_WroxShapes collection. We have deliberately introduced a prefix, namely Wrox, in order to distinguish methods created by us as opposed to methods that are already available in the .NET Framework.

In this application, we have chosen to reuse the framework by creating MyGraph as a sub class of WroxGraph. While WroxGraph stays generic, MyGraph has two added methods – Demo1 and Demo2, which are used to populate the m_WroxShapes collection in various ways.

The code for most of MyGraph is shown below:

```
Public Class MyGraph
    Inherits WroxGraph

    Sub Demo1()

        'clear shapes collection
        m_WroxShapes.Clear()

        'setup coordinate system
        WroxSetCoord(New PointF(0, 0), New PointF(10, 10))
        WroxCreateCoordSystem(2, 2, True)

        'add a line
        Dim aWroxLine As WroxLine = New WroxLine(New Pen(Color.Blue, 2))
        Dim I As Integer
        For I = 0 To 10 Step 1
            aWroxLine.Add(New WroxPoint(New PointF(I, I), New Pen(Color.Blue, 2),_
            WroxPoint.WroxTickType.Square))
        Next
        m_WroxShapes.Add(aWroxLine)

        'add another line
        Dim bWroxLine As WroxLine = New WroxLine(New Pen(Color.Red, 2))
        For I = 0 To 100 Step 1

            'add point
            bWroxLine.Add(New WroxPoint(New PointF(I / 10, Math.Sqrt(I)), _
            New Pen(Color.Yellow, 1), WroxPoint.WroxTickType.Cross))

            'Add text
            If I Mod 10 = 0 Then
                bWroxLine.Add(New WroxText(New PointF(I / 10, Math.Sqrt(I)),_
                I.ToString()))
            End If
        Next
        m_WroxShapes.Add(bWroxLine)
        Invalidate()
    End Sub
    ...
End Class
```

Specifying Inheritance

Inheritance is specified using the Inherits keyword:

```
Public Class MyGraph
    Inherits WroxGraph
     ...
End Class
```

MyGraph inherits all public and protected properties (more about access later), and methods from the WroxGraph Class. For example, it can access the Clear method on the m_WroxShapes collection, and it can call SetCoord, which is implemented in WroxGraph:

```
Sub Demo1()

    'clear shapes collection
    m_WroxShapes.Clear()

    'setup coordinate system
    SetCoord(New PointF(0, 0), New PointF(10, 10))
...
```

'MustInherit'

Consider the implementation of the WroxShapes control, shown below:

```
Public MustInherit Class WroxShapes
    Protected m_Pen As Pen
    Protected m_Point As PointF
    Public ReadOnly Property Point() As PointF
        Get
            Return m_Point
        End Get
    End Property

    Protected Sub New(ByVal aPoint As PointF, ByVal aPen As Pen)
        m_Point = aPoint
        m_Pen = aPen
    End Sub
    Public MustOverride Sub WroxPaint(ByRef aWroxGraph As WroxGraph)
End Class
```

WroxShape is not a concrete class by itself. It was introduced to serve as a base class for the 'real' classes WroxPoint, WroxText and WroxLine. We should not be able to instantiate WroxShape, and applying the MustInherit keyword at the start of the class specification can specify this.

Specifying Override Ability

When we implement a method in a sub class with the same name and signature (that is, same number and types of parameters) we are said to override the method. In order to implement this:

- The method in the base class must be marked `Overridable` or `MustOverride`. `Overridable` means that the method can be overridden. `MustOverride` means that a sub class must override the method, if that class is to be instantiated.
- The method in the sub class must be marked `Overrides`.

If a class has any methods marked `MustOverride`, we must also place a `MustInherit` keyword at the top of the class declaration. If a method is marked `MustOverride`, we should not supply an implementation for it in the class, as can be seen from the `WroxShapes` class. Such a method is also sometimes referred to as a **pure virtual method**.

Abstract Base Classes and Interfaces

If a class is marked `MustInherit`, and has at least one pure virtual method, it is called an **abstract base class**. We may choose to define an abstract base class for two reasons:

- **Implementation inheritance**. We employ implementation inheritance when we collect methods and properties in a base class, so they can be reused in the derived classes. This allows us to reuse the implementation of the code already written in the base class. The only reason we are making the base class abstract is because a couple of the methods that are truly shared by the derived classes cannot be implemented in the base class. This is the case with our `WroxShape` class. It doesn't make sense to even attempt an implementation of the `Paint` method. That should obviously be implemented in the derived classes only.
- **Interface inheritance**. A special form of abstract base classes is one that does not include any properties, and where all the methods in the class are pure virtual. Such base classes obviously do not allow us to reuse any implementation. But, they do allow us to share the **interface**. Over the years, the use of such pure abstract base classes has been touted as perhaps the most important OO technique to enforce encapsulation. A good design rule is to implement any high level conceptual class as an abstract base class, and always put any implementation in a sub class.

The .NET framework relies heavily on interface inheritance and both VB.NET and C# have elevated the concept of interfaces and interfaced programming by introducing a couple of special language constructs. We will discuss this further, under the Interfaces section later in this chapter.

Specifying Access and Properties

As we discussed the section on abstraction and code reuse, we could write the `GraphControl` class without any knowledge of how `Shape` or any of `Shape's` sub classes are implemented. This is a very important quality. It allows us to reuse the whole `GraphControl` class in other applications, if that other application also incorporates a `Shape` class, even if it is implemented differently.

To preserve this quality – loose coupling between a user of a class (`GraphControl`) and the used class (`Shape`) – we must try to ensure that `GraphControl` really is implemented without knowledge about the internals of the `Shape` control. We must encapsulate and hide the implementation details in the `Shape` class from the `GraphControl` class.

Consider the following excerpt from the implementation of the `WroxGraph` class:

```
Public Class WroxGraph
    Inherits Panel
```

```
    Private Const XOffset = 30
    Private Const YOffset = 30

    Private m_Graphics As Graphics
    Private m_CoordStart As New PointF(0, 0)
    Private m_CoordEnd As New PointF(100, 100)
    Private m_Pen As New Pen(Color.Black, 1)
    Protected m_WroxShapes As New ArrayList()
    Friend m_CurrentPoint As New Point(0, 0)

    Public Sub WroxSetCoord(ByVal CoordStart As PointF, ByVal CoordEnd As PointF)
        m_CoordStart = CoordStart
        m_CoordEnd = CoordEnd
    End Sub
...
```

This shows a very important aspect of encapsulation and information hiding – the ability to control access to properties and methods of a class. Access is determined by use of the keywords shown in the excerpt, which are discussed in the following sections.

'Private'

A `Private` variable, property or method is only accessible to methods that are part of the class itself. Other classes, such as derived classes, and classes that may use the `WroxGraph` class, do not have access to the internal `m_Graphics`, `m_Coordxxx` or `m_Pen` variables. This makes sense. These are just 'helper variables', used by `WroxGraph` to implement its designed functionality. They are not intended for external modification or inspection.

'Protected'

The `Protected` keyword opens up access for derived classes, but not for external classes that just use the class. For example, the `m_WroxShapes` collection is marked `Protected`. This allows us to implement the derived `MyGraph` class, and have `MyGraph` insert new objects directly into `m_WroxShapes`.

Note that this may not always be a suitable design choice. The derived class will now have detailed information about the base class implementation and it will probably break if the base class implementation changes.

'Public'

The `Public` keyword opens up access to 'everyone'. We should really only use this for methods and properties that are intended for use by 'clients' of our classes. If a method or property is only to be used by our own framework, we should consider restricting access using one of the other keywords.

'Friend'

`Friend` is somewhere between `Public` and `Protected`. If a variable, property or method is marked with the `Friend` keyword, it can be accessed from another class if:

- The other class is derived from this class (just like `Protected`).
- The other class is in the same code module as this class. Since `WroxText` is implemented in the same code module (`WroxGraph.vb`) it has access to the `m_CurrentPoint` member variable, even if `WroxShape` is not derived from `WroxGraph`.

```
Public Class WroxText
    Inherits WroxShape
   . . .

    Public Overrides Sub WroxPaint(ByRef aWroxGraph As WroxGraph)
        aWroxGraph.WroxMoveTo(m_Point)
        Dim TextPoint = aWroxGraph.m_CurrentPoint
        TextPoint.X += m_PixelOffset.X
        TextPoint.Y += m_PixelOffset.Y
        aWroxGraph.WroxPixelMoveTo(TextPoint)
        aWroxGraph.WroxDrawText(m_String)
    End Sub

End Class
```

The design assumption here is that, since WroxShape and WroxGraph are in the same code module, whoever coded WroxShape probably has some knowledge about (and responsibility for) WroxGraph. It is therefore acceptable to expose the 'internals' of a class to a 'friend'. Just like Protected, the use of Friend opens up our class internals, and increases the potential for tighter coupling within our programming framework. So we should use it judiciously.

About Properties

It is good practice never to declare member variables Public. Rather, we should make them Private or Protected and 'hide' them behind a Property declaration. When we declare a property, we must also specify a Get and/or a Set method. We then use these to access or modify the 'internal' variable, which is kept Private. Specifying two methods in addition to the variable may seem to be a lot more work than just declaring the variable Public, but the IDE provides a lot of help, and the added protection of our class' integrity is well worth the effort in the long run.

We can, for example, ensure that an outsider can read, but not write to the variable, as we did for WroxShape:

```
...
Public ReadOnly Property Point() As PointF
    Get
        Return m_Point
    End Get
End Property
...
```

Alternatively, we can ensure that a variable is only assigned appropriate values, as in this fictitious Person class:

```
Public Class Person
    Private m_Age As Integer

    Public Property Age() As Integer
        Get
            Return m_Age
        End Get
```

```
        Set(ByVal Value As Integer)
            If Value > 0 And Value < 120 Then
                m_Age = Value
            End If
        End Set
    End Property

End Class
```

Finally, we can actually change the internal representation of the property without affecting any of the other classes using the property. The following is an excellent example of the value of encapsulation and information hiding.

Saved by a Property

Say our fictitious `Person` class is introduced in the computer system used to administer a Social Security system. After an expensive redesign, the new system keeps a list of person objects. Every month it iterates the list and sends checks to people aged 60 and above. A couple of years later an investigation is started to find out why the social security system is now running at such a surplus. With the help of an expensive consulting company, it is discovered that people never age! If someone is originally entered into the system at the age of 18, that age will remain the same forever.

Luckily, the programmers implemented the `Person` class using properties. We can therefore now change the implementation to store the person's date of birth, without affecting any of the external classes that may iterate the person collection and access the `Age` property.

The improved implementation is shown below:

```
Public Class Person
    Private m_BirthDate As DateTime = New DateTime()

    Public Property Age() As Integer
        Get
            Return DateTime.Now.Year - m_BirthDate.Now.Year
        End Get

...
        End Set
    End Property

End Class
```

'Me', 'MyBase' and 'MyClass'

The `Me` keyword (`this` in C#), is used with a class to specify a reference to the object itself. The most common use for this is when we want to supply the object as a parameter for use by another method. We do this in the `OnPaint` method of the `WroxGraph` class. When we call the `WroxPaint` method on shapes in the `WroxShapes` collection, we want the shape to call, in return, functions made available by the calling `WroxGraph` class, when it needs to undertake the actual painting.

The code for `OnPaint` in `WroxGraph` is shown below:

```
...
Protected Overrides Sub OnPaint(ByVal e As PaintEventArgs)
    MyBase.OnPaint(e)

    'called every time control is invalidated
    'setup graphics context
    m_Graphics = e.Graphics

    'Then draw all shapes
    Dim I As Integer
    For I = 0 To m_WroxShapes.Count - 1
        Dim aWroxShape As WroxShape = CType(m_WroxShapes.Item(I), WroxShape)
        aWroxShape.WroxPaint(Me)
    Next

End Sub
...
```

And the code that gets called in, for example, the `WroxText` object, looks like this:

```
Public Class WroxTest
...
Public Overrides Sub WroxPaint(ByRef aWroxGraph As WroxGraph)
    aWroxGraph.WroxMoveTo(m_Point)
    Dim TextPoint = aWroxGraph.m_CurrentPoint
    TextPoint.X += m_PixelOffset.X
    TextPoint.Y += m_PixelOffset.Y
    aWroxGraph.WroxPixelMoveTo(TextPoint)
    aWroxGraph.WroxDrawText(m_String)
End Sub
...
```

As you can see, we use `Me` as the parameter in the call from the `WroxGraph` class to hand the instance of this object over to the `WroxPaint` method in the other class.

'MyBase'

Because of polymorphism, a call to a virtual method will always be routed to the implementation in the most derived class. We have taken advantage of this many times, including in the `OnPaint` method of `WroxGraph`. Even if the rest of the application 'thinks' it's dealing with a collection of `Controls`, the call to `OnPaint` will still get routed to `WroxGraph.OnPaint`.

When we override a method, it is often in order to extend the functionality already implemented by that method. In this case, we will want to first call the method in the base class, and then tag our implementation on at the end:

```
Protected Overrides Sub OnPaint(ByVal e As PaintEventArgs)
    MyBase.OnPaint(e)
    ...
```

This is exactly what happens in `WroxGraph.OnPaint`. We use the keyword `MyBase` to indicate that we first want to call the `OnPaint` method in the base class, instead of our own implementation (which would result in recursion). Then we will follow up with the rest of our implementation.

'MyClass'

MyClass has almost the opposite function of MyBase. We just saw that if a method in any class in the inheritance tree calls a virtual method, it will result in a call to the most derived method in the inheritance tree. If we did not want that to happen, we could use MyBase to point the method call one level up the tree.

Alternatively, we could have used MyClass. MyClass specifies that if we make a function call to a virtual method, the call should **not** be routed to the most derived class. Instead, we want to call the method available **in the same class** as the one in which the call is made. So if WroxGraph had contained a method, CallMe, which included a call to MyClass.OnPaint, this call would be routed to WroxGraph.OnPaint instead of the derived MyGraph.OnPaint.

To better illustrate the function of MyClass consider this code below:

```
Public MustInherit Class MyBaseClass
    Public Overridable Sub VirtualFunction(ByVal S As String)
        MessageBox.Show("Hello from MyBaseClass", S)
    End Sub

    Public Sub CallMe()
        MyClass.VirtualFunction("Using MyClass")
        VirtualFunction("Not using MyClass")
    End Sub

End Class

Public Class MyDerivedClass
    Inherits MyBaseClass
    Public Overrides Sub VirtualFunction(ByVal S As String)
        MessageBox.Show("Hello from MyDerivedClass", S)
    End Sub
End Class
```

If we create an object of the MyDerived class and call the CallMe method, we will get two message boxes:

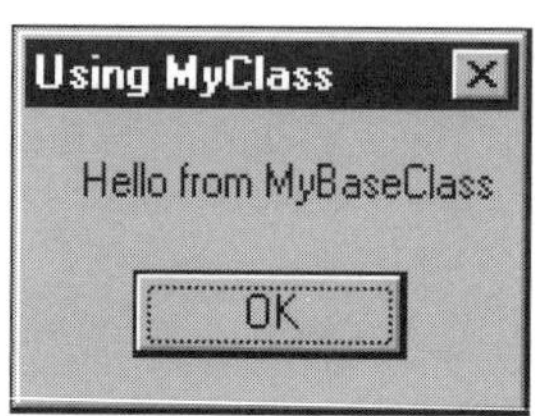

and

Function Overloading

Another aspect of polymorphism is called function overloading. Function overloading is the ability to specify several implementations of the same method with the same name, but with different sets of parameters. It is a very important language feature.

'Overloads'

Overloaded functions or procedures must be marked with the `Overloads` keyword.

Consider this excerpt below:

```
...
Public Overloads Sub SetCoord(ByVal CoordStart As PointF, _
ByVal CoordEnd As PointF)
    m_CoordStart = CoordStart
    m_CoordEnd = CoordEnd
End Sub

Public Overloads Sub SetCoord(ByVal X1 As Double, ByVal Y1 As Double, _
ByVal X2 As Double, ByVal Y2 As Double)
    m_CoordStart = New PointF(X1, Y2)
    m_CoordEnd = New PointF(X2, Y2)
End Sub
...
```

Since we have implemented two different versions of the `SetCoord` method, we can now call it in different ways, depending on what is most convenient:

```
Dim LowerLeft=new Point(0,0)
Dim UpperRight=new Point(100,100)
aWroxGraph.SetCoord(LowerLeft,UpperRight)

'or
aWroxGraph.SetCoord(0,0,100,100)
```

Benefits of Function Overloading

To appreciate the benefit of overloading, consider the alternative. Without overloading, we would have had to name the methods differently, for example:

```
Public Overloads Sub SetCoordPoints(ByVal CoordStart As PointF, _
ByVal CoordEnd As PointF)
```

and:

```
Public Overloads Sub SetCoordXY(ByVal X1 As Double, ByVal Y1 As Double, _
ByVal X2 As Double, ByVal Y2 As Double)
```

This may not seem to be a big deal with only two implementations. However, we can easily imagine further variations, including passing in the complete coordinate system in one `Rectangle` parameter or maybe supplying additional parameters to indicate if an axis is linear or logarithmic. As the number of different parameter lists increase, we are going to be stretched to come up with useful names, and the programmer using our class is going to be equally stretched to remember all of them.

Methods in Windows Forms are heavily overloaded. Luckily, the IntelliSense feature pops up a little window, with arrows allowing us to scroll through the different variations. As we can see from the screenshot below, there are four different function signatures for the `DrawLine` method:

```
Public Sub WroxPixelLineTo(ByVal aPoint As Point)
    m_Graphics.DrawLine(m_Pen, m_CurrentPoint, aPoint)
    2 of 4 DrawLine (pen As System.Drawing.Pen, pt1 As System.Drawing.PointF, pt2 As System.Drawing.PointF)
End pen: The n object that determines the color, width, and style of the line.
```

Object Constructors

An object must be constructed before it can be used. These lines below:

```
Dim aWroxLine As WroxLine
WroxLine.Add(somePoint)
```

will fail. In the first line `aWroxLine` has only been declared as a reference to an instance of a `WroxLine` object. But that instance has not yet been created, and `aWroxLine` is uninitialized.

The correct code is shown below:

```
Dim aWroxLine As WroxLine = New WroxLine(somePen)
WroxLine.Add(someLine)
```

The call to `New` creates the object, and initializes the object with the value or values supplied as parameters.

Simple Object Initialization

We will, of course, want our new object to be initialized to a known state. If this state is the same for all objects, we can declare the initialization as part of the class definition. For example:

```
Public Class WroxGraph
    Inherits Panel

    ...
    Private m_CoordStart As New PointF(0, 0)
    Private m_CoordEnd As New PointF(100, 100)
```

We can also omit this initialization, in which case the .NET runtime system will assign default values. Default values for numeric types and enumerators are '0' (zero), and default values for string types are "" (empty string).

Defining a Constructor 'New'

We can define additional steps to be taken, after the simple initialization, by defining a constructor. A constructor is a `Sub` with the name `New` and 0 or more parameters. Below is the implementation for the constructor in our `WroxLine` class:

```
Public Class WroxLine
    Inherits WroxShape
    Private m_WroxShapes As ArrayList = New ArrayList()

    Public Sub New(ByVal aPen As Pen)
        MyBase.New(New PointF(0, 0), aPen)
    End Sub
...
```

Notice how we can use simple object initialization to create the m_WroxShapes collection. But then we want different lines to be drawn with different Pens. We therefore implement a constructor. As we have seen, this allows the user to specify initialization parameters to be used when the object is created. Notice also how the constructor in WroxLine includes a call up to the constructor in its base class to ensure that any variables in that class also gets initialized.

Overloading the Constructor

It is very common to see overloaded constructors or constructors with optional parameter lists. Consider this code from the initialization of the WroxPoint class:

```
Public Class WroxPoint
    ...
    Private m_Size As Integer
    Private m_TickType As WroxTickType
    Public Sub New(ByVal aPoint As PointF, ByVal aPen As Pen, _
    ByVal aTickType As WroxTickType, _
    Optional ByVal aSize As Integer = 10)
        MyBase.New(aPoint, aPen)
        m_Size = aSize
        m_TickType = aTickType
    End Sub

    Public Sub New(ByVal aPoint As PointF, ByVal PenColor As Color, _
    ByVal PenSize As Integer, ByVal aTickType As WroxTickType, _
    Optional ByVal aSize As Integer = 10)
        MyBase.New(aPoint, New Pen(PenColor, PenSize))
        m_Size = aSize
        m_TickType = aTickType
    End Sub
```

In this somewhat contrived example we have implemented two constructors. In the first constructor, the caller must supply a Pen. In the second constructor the caller must just supply a pen color and size. In addition the last parameter is marked Optional, and a default value of 10 is defined. This means that the caller does not need to include a value for this parameter, in which case it will be assigned the value 10.

Garbage Collection

In .NET we are no longer responsible for destroying objects when we are done with them. This can be a great blessing, since memory leaks are one of the most common problems in programming (especially with C and C++). In VB.NET and C# (and managed C++), we just create an object instance and use it, without having to worry about destroying it.

This is possible because the .NET runtime system incorporates garbage collection. While a program is running, the .NET runtime constantly keeps internal reference count for all instantiated objects. Once an object is no longer referenced, it is considered garbage and will be removed automatically.

In addition to removing a headache for us programmers, it is potentially also faster, since the system can defer the garbage collection until a time when the system is idle. Most applications switch between working very hard retrieving and producing data for the user, and then sitting idle awaiting the user's response. If the destruction of objects and ensuing cleanup of memory is postponed until the idle period, the perceived performance of the system has actually been improved.

Notice however, that garbage collection is not a holy grail. Since objects will be destroyed when the program is deemed 'idle', the developer does not know when that happens. In fact, we don't even know in which order the objects are destructed. This 'feature' is called **non-deterministic finalization**. While the benefits of automatic garbage collection far outweigh this side effect, we should still take that into account when we design programs. We will discuss it further under *Dispose.*

The 'Finalize' Method

When an object is destroyed, the garbage collector will call its `Finalize` method. The `Finalize` method is declared as follows:

```
Protected Overrides Sub Finalize()
        MyBase.Finalize() 'include call to base class Finalize
        'Place additional clean up code here.
End Sub
```

Notice that `Finalize` is protected so it cannot be called directly.

We should only define a `Finalize` method if our class has allocated external resources not managed by the runtime system, like file handles, critical sections and database connections. When we define `Finalize` in a sub class, we must remember to include a call to the `Finalize` method in the base class.

The 'Dispose' Method

One potential disadvantage of garbage collection is that we have no control over when an object gets destroyed. We can certainly not be sure that it will happen 'as quickly as possible' or immediately when the object goes out of scope. This can be a problem if our object allocates expensive external resources, like the above mentioned database connections or communications ports. An orphaned database connection to an external server may not be very expensive for our application, and the garbage collector may not aggressively try to collect it, since it does not affect the application significantly. But if the server we are connecting to only has two available connections, it is quite unfortunate that one of the connections is held up long after it has been used.

In most of the .NET framework classes, Microsoft has introduced the convention to add a method called `Dispose`:

```
    Public Sub Dispose()
        'Place cleanup code here
    End Sub
```

It is now **up to the caller** to call `Dispose` when the object is no longer needed, to force any necessary cleanup. That way, the object may not be destroyed, but at least all the critical resources it has allocated will be released. As the user of an object we will want to call `Dispose` on the object if we know it has allocated expensive resources.

As the programmer of a class, we should remember that there is no guarantee `Dispose` will be called. We should also implement the `Finalize` method to ensure that things will at least get cleaned up eventually.

The Base Object

In .NET everything is an object, and all objects inherit from a class called `Object`. `Object` is the ultimate base class, the mother of all classes. The .NET framework includes a number of general utility classes that all work with the `Object` base class. These include powerful collection classes like `ArrayList`, `SortedList`, and `Queue`, all of which are available in the `System.Collections` namespace. Since these all work with the `Object` base class, they can be used on any class we may create ourselves, in addition to all existing classes. Very convenient!

`Object` implements a couple of member functions. In the interest of saving space, we will only discuss one of these below. Please refer to the online documentation or Wrox's *Professional VB.NET* (*ISBN 1861004974*), for a more complete description.

'Object.ToString'

Probably the most useful member function of `Object` is `ToString`. `ToString` returns a textual representation of any .NET object. There is no specification for what exactly `ToString` must return. This is left up to the implementer of the class. Sometimes it will only return detailed type information. Most of the time, however, it will return a string containing the most important properties of the object. In some instances, we are even able to specify a formatting string to this function.

To demonstrate how this works, and to prove that in .NET everything is indeed an object, take a look at the code that builds the X-axis of the coordinate system of the graph:

```
Public Sub CreateCoordSystem(ByVal XStep As Double, ByVal YStep As Double,_
Optional ByVal ShowValue As Boolean = True)

'compose coordinate system as two lines with ticks and numbers,
     Dim aWroxLine As New WroxLine(New Pen(Color.Black, 1))
     Dim X As Double
     For X = m_CoordStart.X To m_CoordEnd.X Step XStep
         aWroxLine.Add(New WroxPoint(New PointF(X, 0), New Pen(Color.Black),_
                     WroxPoint.WroxTickType.Vertical))
         If (ShowValue) Then
            aWroxLine.Add(New WroxText(New PointF(X, 0), X.ToString("f1"), _
            New Point(0, 10)))
         End If
     Next
     ...
```

The highlighted line creates a text with the value of the coordinate. As we can see, X appears to be a regular double. But we can still call its `ToString` method, and we can in fact supply a formatting parameter to ensure that the number is only written out with accuracy to one decimal place. The reason is of course that `Double` is implicitly derived from the base object. You can verify this by checking the online documentation.

```
Object
   ValueType
      Double
```

This clearly shows that `Double` is derived from `ValueType`, which again is derived from `Object`.

'Object.Equals'

Another important function is Equals. The purpose of Equals is to compare the value of two objects, to determine if they are equal.

Consider this Customer class:

```
Class Customer
    Private m_CustomerID As Integer
    Public Sub New(ByVal CustomerID As Integer)
        m_CustomerID = CustomerID
    End Sub
    ...
End Class
```

And this set of instantiations:

```
Dim Cust1 As Customer = New Customer(35)
Dim Cust2 As Customer = New Customer(35)
```

Without any further work on our part, we can try to compare the two customers using either of the following constructs:

```
Dim b1 As Boolean = Cust1 Is Cust2        'returns false
Dim b2 As Boolean = Cust1.Equals(Cust2) 'returns false
```

Unfortunately, both statements compare the address of Cust1 to Cust2 instead of the customer numbers. To overcome this problem, the developer of the Customer class should overload the Equals method to implement the proper value comparison:

```
Public Overloads Function Equals(ByVal C1 As Customer)
    Return C1.m_CustomerID = m_CustomerID
 End Function
```

The second comparison will now return true.

Casting

As we have now seen many times, OO languages not only allow us to declare references to a base class, but also populate them with instances of a derived class. So far we have postulated this to be a benefit, because our calling program is unaffected if we add additional sub classes to the base class.

There are times where we have a reference to a base class, but we know that it is really a sub class, and we want to access it as a sub class. A common example of this can be found in our Graph control. Here all shapes are stored in the generic class ArrayList provided by the .NET Framework. This is very convenient, since it allows us to store all kinds of objects in the list, including WroxShape objects or descendants thereof:

```
        ...
'declaration of shapes collection:
Protected m_WroxShapes As New ArrayList()
...
```

```
'declare line:
Dim bWroxLine As WroxLine = New WroxLine(New Pen(Color.Red, 2))
     '(add points to the line)
...

'add line to shapes collection:
m_WroxShapes.Add(bWroxLine)
...

'The OnPaint method:
Protected Overrides Sub OnPaint(ByVal e As PaintEventArgs)
    MyBase.OnPaint(e)
...
    Dim I As Integer
    For I = 0 To m_WroxShapes.Count - 1
        Dim aWroxShape As WroxShape = CType(m_WroxShapes.Item(I), WroxShape)
        aWroxShape.WroxPaint(Me)
    Next
End Sub
```

In the `OnPaint` method, we now want to iterate the collection and call the `WroxPaint` method of every item. However, since `m_WroxShapes.Item(I)` is of type `Object`, we cannot do this directly. We need to tell the compiler that we are really dealing with an instance of `WroxShape`. The act of 're-typing' an object from one class to another, without changing its representation, is called **casting**. In VB.NET it is accomplished through the `CType` function, as shown in the example above.

It is our responsibility to ensure that the casting is indeed possible. For example, this would be wrong:

```
Dim aPen as New Pen(3,Black)
 Dim aWroxShape As WroxShape = CType(aPen, WroxShape)
```

An object of type `Pen` cannot be cast to `WroxShape`. In this case the runtime system will throw a `System.InvalidCastException` exception. We will see more about exceptions later in this chapter.

Using Delegates

The mechanics of delegates are covered in detail in Chapter 6 on events. They are an excellent supplement to some of the techniques we have already discussed for creating robust reusable designs. So let's end this section with something quite neat. The code below is an extension of our existing graph control, which includes the ability to plot any function:

```
Public Class MyGraph
    Inherits WroxGraph
...
Sub Demo2(ByVal aCoordStart As PointF, ByVal aCoordEnd As PointF,_
          ByVal anXStep As Double, ByVal XTick As Double, _
          ByVal YTick As Double, ByVal aPlotFunction As PlotFunction)

    'clear shapes collection
    m_WroxShapes.Clear()

    'Setup coordinate system
```

```
        SetCoord(aCoordStart, aCoordEnd)
        CreateCoordSystem(XTick, YTick, True)

        'iterate and call the supplied function
        Dim X As Double
        Dim aWroxLine As WroxLine = New WroxLine(New Pen(Color.Green, 2))
        For X = aCoordStart.X To aCoordEnd.X Step anXStep
            Dim aPoint = New PointF(X, aPlotFunction(X))
            aWroxLine.Add(New WroxPoint(aPoint, New Pen(Color.Yellow, 1),_
            WroxPoint.WroxTickType.None))
        Next
        m_WroxShapes.Add(aWroxLine)
        Invalidate()
    End Sub

    Public Delegate Function PlotFunction(ByVal Param As Double) As Double
```

The function takes as input a specification of the coordinate system, what size steps to take, how many tick marks to make on the X and Y axes, and a pointer to a function.

In VB.NET and C#, function pointers are called **delegates**. Compared to function pointers in VB, delegates are type safe. In other words, the compiler will check to make sure that we supply a function with the correct signature.

To use a delegate we must:

- Declare it as a parameter of some type, as we did with '... `ByVal aPlotFunction as PlotFunction)`'.
- Use the parameter within the method as we would have used the method itself, as we did with '... `aPlotFunction(X)`'.
- Define the function signature of the delegate. This is what we did just below the method where the delegate was used. Use the `Delegate` keyword to identify the delegate, and do not provide an implementation for the function or sub.
- Implement a function to be used as the delegate, and pass the delegate to our method. The code for this is shown below:

```
    'the function is defined here
    Public Function MyFunction(ByVal X As Double) As Double
        Return Math.Sin(X) * Math.Sin(50 * X)
    End Function

    'it is used here
    Private Sub MenuGraph_Demo2_Click(ByVal sender As System.Object, _
                                      ByVal e As System.EventArgs) Handles _
                                      MenuGraph_Demo2.Click_        Panel1.Demo2(New
    PointF(-3.14, -1), New PointF(3.14, 1), _
    0.05, 0.628, 0.2, AddressOf MyFunction)
    End Sub
```

And the result is as expected:

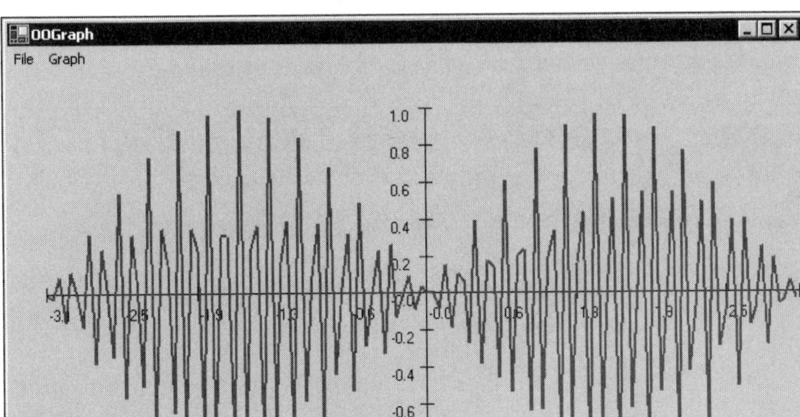

We can, of course, replace `MyFunction` with any other function, as long as it has the same signature.

Visual Forms Inheritance

As we already know, user defined forms are created as sub classes of the generic `Form` class. We change the look of a form by setting its properties, or by adding controls. Further, we can change the form's behavior by overriding methods, and attaching event handlers.

Even if we use the IDE to create the form and add controls, a form's design and behavior is completely defined in code. We can therefore inherit from our own forms, just as we can inherit from the generic `Form` class. We will inherit both the design and the behavior of our base form. This is called Visual Forms Inheritance.

Visual forms inheritance allows us to push generic code up into the base class. It is quite useful when we want to create a number of forms with the same base functionality and a consistent look. In this section we will present a small application that takes advantage of Visual Forms inheritance.

The Test Framework

`WroxTest` is a small application that allows a user to take two types of test. The first is a multiple-choice test, where the user gets points for picking the right answer. The second is a time-based math test, where a question is presented and the user has a certain amount of time to answer. Instead of picking from a list, the user must enter a number; and the faster the user does it, the more points he or she gets. Since these tasks have a lot in common, we will first create a base form with shared appearance and functionality, and then use Visual Forms Inheritance to flesh out the two different test forms.

The Base Form

The Base Form is shown below. At the top, it shows the company logo, the current score, and what question the user is at. At the bottom it has a `Begin` or `Continue` button.

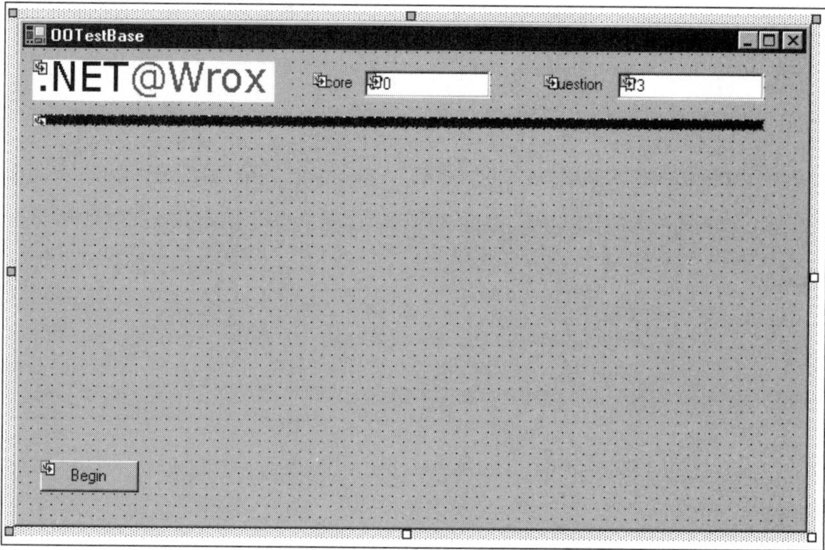

It also has some shared functionality, which is designed to work in concert with functions supplied by sub classes deriving from the form. The code 'behind' the Begin/Continue button is responsible for moving the test along. Each time the user presses the button, the base class:

- Calls `ovrScoreQuestion`, to get the user's score for the question.
- Updates the total score and the question number.
- Calls `ovrPoseQuestion` to present the next question (if any).

In addition, it automatically closes the test window once the test is completed.

```
Public Class OOTestBase
    Inherits System.Windows.Forms.Form
...
    Protected m_QuestionNo As Integer = -1
    Private m_TestScore As Integer

    Shared s_TotalScore As Integer
    Public Shared Property TotalScore()
        Get
            Return s_TotalScore
        End Get
        Set(ByVal Value)
            s_TotalScore = Value
        End Set
    End Property

    Protected Overridable Sub InitializeRemaining()
```

```
        UpdatePanel()
    End Sub

    Protected Overridable Sub UpdatePanel()
        txtScore.Text = m_TestScore.ToString() + "/" + s_TotalScore.ToString()
        txtQuestions.Text = (m_QuestionNo + 2).ToString() + "/" +_
        ovrNoOfQuestions().ToString()
    End Sub

    Protected Overridable Function ovrNoOfQuestions() As Integer
        'dummy implementation

    End Function

    Protected Overridable Sub ovrPoseQuestion()
        'dummy implementation

    End Sub

    Protected Overridable Function ovrScoreQuestion() As Integer
        'dummy implementation

    End Function

    Private Sub btnContinue_Click(ByVal sender As System.Object, _
    ByVal e As System.EventArgs)_
                          Handles btnContinue.Click

        'Called each time the user clicks the begin/continue button
        'It changes the buCalled each time the user clicks the begin/continue
        'button

        Dim QuestionPoints As Integer = 0
        btnContinue.Text = "&Continue"             'Change button text
        If (m_QuestionNo >= 0) Then
            QuestionPoints = ovrScoreQuestion()    'Get points scored by user on
                                                   'this question
        End If
        If QuestionPoints >= 0 Then                'If user has made a selection
                                                   'when button was
                                                   'pressed then
            m_TestScore += QuestionPoints          'Update counters
            TotalScore += QuestionPoints
            UpdatePanel()
            m_QuestionNo += 1                      'continue with next question if
                                                   'not at end
            If m_QuestionNo = ovrNoOfQuestions() Then
                Close()
            Else
                ovrPoseQuestion()
            End If
        End If

End Class
```

`OvrNoOfQuestions`, `ovrScoreQuestion` and `ovrPoseQuestion` will be implemented by the derived classes. Because of polymorphism, a call from the base class of any of these methods will result in a call of the equivalent method in the derived class. This way, the base class can control the flow of the test, and leave the implementation of the specific test to the sub class. This is a very simple example of a **framework**.

Some people may be wondering why we have included dummy implementations of these methods instead of declaring them as `MustInherit`. The reason is that, if `OOTest` is abstract, it cannot be created by the IDE, and then the form cannot be displayed, defeating the purpose of visual forms inheritance.

Using the Inheritance Picker

It's time to create an actual form on the basis of our generic form. This is most easily done using the Inheritance Picker, available from Project, Add Inherited Form...

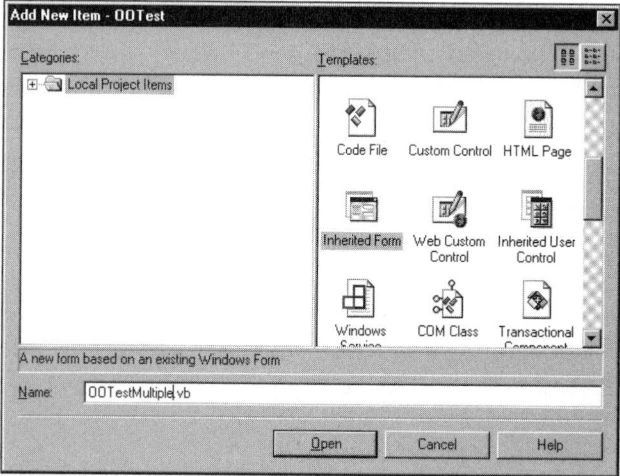

Enter the name of the new form and select Open. We now get a list of all available forms in our project; (we have to have compiled our project once for it to appear):

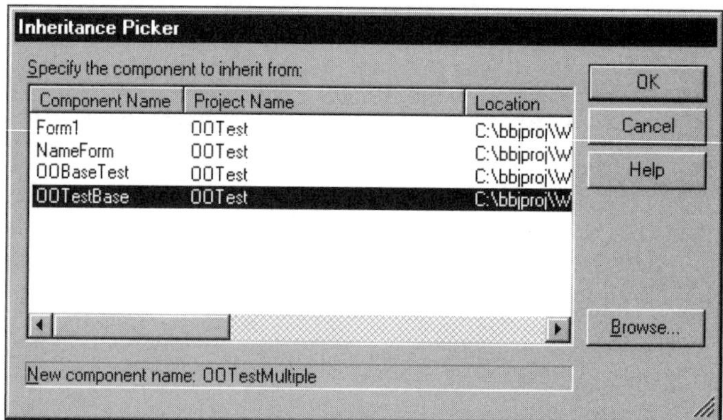

We now get a new form with the specified name. The new form will show all the controls from the base form, but these will be locked and cannot be modified. However, we can add controls. The drawing below shows how we have created two forms on the basis of `OOTest`.

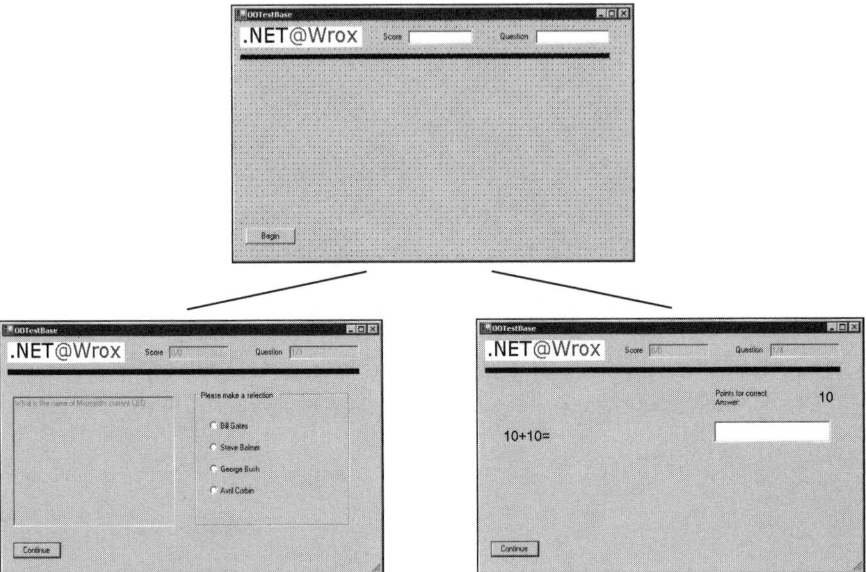

The 'OOMathTest' Form

To prove that we have indeed saved something, let's finally look at the complete code for the MathTest form:

```
Public Class OOTestMath
    Inherits OOTest.OOTestBase

#Region " Windows Form Designer generated code "
#End Region

    Private m_ArrayList As ArrayList
    Private m_Time As Integer

    Protected Overrides Sub InitializeRemaining()
        m_ArrayList = New ArrayList()
        m_ArrayList.Add(New MathQuestion("10+10=", 20, 15))
        m_ArrayList.Add(New MathQuestion("12+13=", 25, 15))
        m_ArrayList.Add(New MathQuestion("119+117=", 236, 25))
        m_ArrayList.Add(New MathQuestion("9*9=", 81, 20))
        MyBase.InitializeRemaining()
    End Sub


    Protected Overrides Function ovrNoOfQuestions() As Integer
        Return m_ArrayList.Count
    End Function
```

```
    Protected Overrides Sub ovrPoseQuestion()
        Dim aQuestion As MathQuestion = _
            CType(m_ArrayList.Item(m_QuestionNo), MathQuestion)

        LblQuestion.Text = aQuestion.m_Question
        m_Time = aQuestion.m_Time
        lblTime.Text = m_Time
        txtAnswer.Text = ""
    End Sub

    Protected Overrides Function ovrScoreQuestion() As Integer
        Dim aQuestion As MathQuestion = _
            CType(m_ArrayList.Item(m_QuestionNo), MathQuestion)
        Dim anAnswer As Integer
        txtAnswer.Text.Trim()
        If IsNumeric(txtAnswer.Text) Then
            anAnswer = CInt(txtAnswer.Text)
        End If
        If anAnswer = aQuestion.m_RightAnswer Then
            Return m_Time
        Else
            Return 0
        End If
    End Function

    Private Sub Timer1_Tick(ByVal sender As System.Object, _
          ByVal e As System.EventArgs) Handles Timer1.Tick
        If m_Time > 0 Then
            m_Time -= 1
            lblTime.Text = m_Time
        End If
    End Sub
End Class
```

It's really very simple. `InitializeRemaining` (declared by us) gets called after `InitializeComponent`, because we put an explicit call to that method into the constructor of `OOTestBase`. `InitializeRemaining` fills an `ArrayList` with all the questions in the test and then calls `InitializeRemaining` in `OOTestBase`. `ovrNoOfQuestions` returns the number of questions, `ovrPoseQuestion` poses the current question, and `ovrScoreQuestion` scores the question, just as expected. Finally the `Timer1_Tick` method is an event handler (more about event handlers in Chapter 6), which gets called every second to decrease the number of points the user gets for a correct answer.

Notice how we did not have to worry about the test flow or the updating of the score. We just had to fill in a couple of functions as 'specified' by the framework.

Another important aspect of visual forms inheritance is that, since all derived forms inherit their looks from the base form, we can very easily update the design of all our forms (colors, font size, etc), just by changing and recompiling the base form. This is especially valuable when visual design changes are made late in the development process.

About Shared Member Variables and Methods

So far we have discussed how each instance of an object holds its own state information. It is, however, possible to define both variables and methods that are shared by all instances of a class. This is often done with variables and methods which are 'global in nature', but closely related to a particular class.

Shared member variables and methods are declared using the `Shared` keyword. In our example we have used a shared variable and property to keep the total score of all tests. If we had kept this as a local object variable, it would 'disappear' each time the object was destroyed (that is, the test was completed). Being declared as shared, the variable is not related to any of the objects in particular. It will exist as a single variable whether there are 0, 1 or 1000 objects instantiated.

A shared variable, property or method can be accessed from any object instance as well as externally:

```
Public Class OOTestBase
    Inherits System.Windows.Forms.Form
...
    Shared s_TotalScore As Integer
    Public Shared Property TotalScore()
        Get
            Return s_TotalScore
        End Get
        Set(ByVal Value)
            s_TotalScore = Value
        End Set
    End Property
...
'when accessed from within any instance of the OOTestBase class:
    s_TotalScore += m_TestScore

'when accessed from 'the outside':
    OOTestBase.TotalScore
```

Interfaces

The support for interface base programming has been formalized in the .NET Framework. We have previously seen that it is possible to define a class where none of the methods or properties is actually implemented in the class. We would do this to declare an interface that others can program to. A more formal approach is to implement an actual interface. This is very similar to what we used to do in COM. It's just a lot simpler. Support is built right into the language and thanks to the common type system (CTS) there is no IDL to struggle with. In this section we will first declare, implement and use a simple interface for a cruise control in a car. We will then show how to create a `MyCar` class, which implements multiple interfaces.

Declaring an Interface

The `Interface` keyword is used in much the same way as the `Class` keyword. The following code declares a simple interface for a cruise control in a car.

```
Public Interface ICruiseControl
    Property IsOn() As Boolean
    ReadOnly Property TargetSpeed() As Integer
```

```
        Sub SetCruise(ByVal Speed As Integer))
    Sub ResetCruise()
        Sub IncreaseSpeed()
        Sub DecreaseSpeed()
    End Interface
```

All properties and methods in an interface are public. Further, they don't provide any implementation and they don't store any member variables.

Implementing an Interface

We can now create a class to implement this interface. In fact, we can either define a class that only implements this interface, or we can define a class that implements the interface while also exposing additional methods and properties. We must, however, implement the complete interface in order to be able to instantiate the class.

The code below shows a class for the `CustomizableCruise` control. It implements the `ICruiseControl` interface, but it also adds an extra function that allows the user to specify how aggressive the controls should be at maintaining the speed:

```
Class CustomizableCruisecontrol
    Implements ICruiseControl
    Private m_IsOn As Boolean = False
    Private m_TargetSpeed = 0

    Property IsOn() As Boolean Implements ICruiseControl.IsOn
        Get
            Return m_IsOn
        End Get
        Set(ByVal Value As Boolean)
            m_IsOn = Value
        End Set
    End Property
    ReadOnly Property TargetSpeed() As Integer Implements
ICruiseControl.TargetSpeed
        Get
            Return m_TargetSpeed
        End Get
    End Property

    Public Sub SetCruise(ByVal Speed As Integer) Implements
ICruiseControl.SetCruise
        m_TargetSpeed = Speed
    End Sub

    Public Sub ResetByAnotherName() Implements ICruiseControl.ResetCruise
        'some implementation

    End Sub

    Public Sub IncreaseSpeed() Implements ICruiseControl.IncreaseSpeed
        'some implementation

    End Sub
```

```
    Public Sub DecreaseSpeed() Implements ICruiseControl.DecreaseSpeed
        'some implementation

    End Sub

    Public Sub SetAggressiveness(ByVal MaxAcc As Integer)
        'some implementation

    End Sub
End Class
```

We use the Implements keyword to specify that the class implements our ICruiseControl interface, just as we would have used Inherits if the class had inherited from another class. We then go on to implement all the properties and methods in the interface. The Implements keyword is also used here to match an implementation in the concrete class with a property or method in the interface. For example the line.

```
Property IsOn As Boolean Implements ICruiseControl.IsOn
```

specifies that this property in the concrete class implements the IsOn property declared in the interface.

While it is good practice, it is not necessary to keep the names the same in the interface and the implementing class. The only requirement is that the function signature is the same. The following line illustrates this:

```
    Public Sub ResetByAnotherName() Implements ICruiseControl.ResetCruise
```

Using an Interface

It's now time to use the customizable cruise control. We can do this directly, or through the interface. Both versions are shown below:

```
Dim aCCC As CustomizableCruisecontrol = New CustomizableCruisecontrol()
Dim aCC As ICruiseControl = aCCC

'Access the class as usual
aCCC.IsOn = True
aCCC.SetCruise(75)
aCCC.ResetByAnotherName()
aCCC.SetAggressiveness(10)

'Access the interface
aCC.IsOn = True
aCC.SetCruise(65)
aCC.ResetCruise()
```

We first create an instance of the object. We then create a reference of the interface type and point it to this object. The following four lines all access the object. Here we use ResetByAnotherName to access the reset method, and we can call SetAggressiveness. The next three lines access the object through the interface. Here we use the name defined by the interface (ResetCruise), and we cannot access the extra SetAggressiveness method.

Implementing Multiple Interfaces

While VB.NET and C# lack support for multiple inheritance, it **is** possible to implement multiple interfaces in the same class. If we, for example, declare a number of interfaces related to different items in a car, such as `IBrake`, `ISpeeder`, `ILights`, etc., we are able to define my car as follows:

```
Public Class MyCar
    Inherits BaseCar
    Implements IBrake, ISpeeder, ISteeringWheel, ILights, IAutomaticShift,
ICruiseControl

    Property IsPushed() As Boolean Implements IBrake.IsPushed
        Get

        End Get
        Set(ByVal Value As Boolean)

        End Set
    End Property
    Property PercentageDown() As Integer Implements ISpeeder.PercentageDown
        Get

        End Get
        Set(ByVal Value As
...
```

This car inherits a lot of functionality from the `BaseCar` class. In addition, it supports all these different interfaces. At first it may seem daunting that we have to provide implementations for each of the methods we inherit from an interface. Remember, however, that we don't have to implement this functionality from scratch. It may already be available in another external class or in a base class. In that case, all we have to do in our implementation methods is to wire it to one of the existing implementations.

We could for example declare an instance of the customizable cruise control:

```
Public Class MyCar
    Inherits BaseCar
    Implements IBrake, ISpeeder, ISteeringWheel, ILights, IAutomaticShift,
ICruiseControl

    Private m_CruiseControl As CustomizableCruisecontrol = New
CustomizableCruisecontrol()
```

And then use it to implement some of the methods pertaining to the `ICruiseControl` interface of the `MyCar` class:

```
    ...
    Public Sub SetCruise(ByVal Speed As Integer) Implements
ICruiseControl.SetCruise
        m_CruiseControl.SetCruise(Speed)
    End Sub
    ...
```

Structured Error Handling

One of the most tedious tasks in professional software development is incorporating good error handling. Until now, the VB programmer has had to contend with rigorously checking function call returns, and incorporating `On Error Goto` or `On Error Resume Next`. VB.NET (and C#) offer a better way, by introducing structured error handling, similar to what is found in C++ and Java.

Consider this function, and focus on what happens if we pass in the number '1':

```
Public Sub Fail(ByVal TriggerError As Integer)
     If TriggerError = 1 Then
        Dim x As Integer = 3 / (TriggerError - 1)
     Else
        Throw New ArgumentOutOfRangeException("TriggerError",
               TriggerError, "OOOPS")
     End If
End Sub
```

In .NET this throws an **exception**. The actual exception class depends on the type of error, but they are all descendants of `System.Exception`. When an exception is thrown, execution leaves the function immediately and propagates up the call stack, until the exception is **caught**.

If you want to experiment with this yourself, you can open up the example from the Wrox web site.

'Try, Catch, Finally'

Structured error handling allows us to insert potentially dangerous code into a `Try`, `Catch`, `Finally` structure. The basic premise is that we will try to execute it, and if it fails we can catch the exception and try to recover gracefully.

Let's try calling our example function:

```
Dim s As String = "It worked"
Try
    Fail(1)
    MessageBox.Show("Executed if there are no exceptions")
Catch
    s = "OOPS an error occurred"
    MessageBox.Show("Executed if there is an exceptions")
Finally
    MessageBox.Show(s,"Always executed")
End Try
```

The daring call to `Fail` is inserted into a `Try`, `Catch`, `Finally` block, and the following applies:

- If `Fail` had succeeded, we would execute all the remaining statements in the `Try` block and everything in the `Finally` block.
- If `Fail` throws an exception, the rest of the `Try` block will not be executed. Instead execution jumps to the `Catch` block followed by the `Finally` block.

If we define a `Try` block, we must also have either a `Catch` or a `Finally` block, or both.

'Throw'ing and Displaying an Exception

The second part of the `Fail` function shows how to throw an exception. This is done using the `Throw` keyword, and by creating an instance of an exception object. `ArgumentOutOfRangeException` is one of many exceptions defined by the .NET framework. Each of these allows us to pass additional information about the problem back to the caller:

```
Throw New ArgumentOutOfRangeException("TriggerError", TriggerError, "OOOPS")
```

'Catch'ing a Specific Exception

We can extend the syntax for the `Catch` block to get access to the exception. In addition, we can have multiple `Catch` blocks to selectively specify which we want to deal with. For example:

```
Try
     Fail(0)
Catch ex As ArgumentOutOfRangeException
    MessageBox.Show(ex.ToString, "AOOR Exception")

Catch ex As Exception
    MessageBox.Show(ex.ToString, "A GenericException")
End Try
```

This results in a message box something like this:

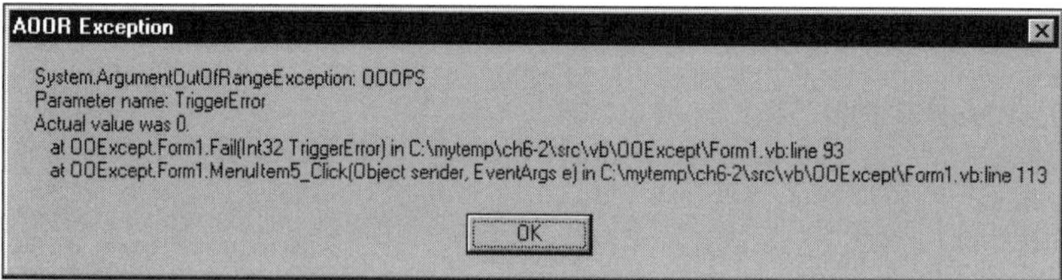

When an exception is caught, the runtime system will try to match the exception with the `Catch` blocks, one `Catch` statement at a time. The first `Catch` statement matching the exception will be executed, and then the program will jump to the `Finally` block, or to the `End Try` statement.

If we have several `Catch` blocks, we should be sure to place the most general at the end. If we switched the order for `Catch Exception` and `Catch ArgumentOutofRangeException` in the code above, the latter would never be executed, since all exceptions match `Exception`.

Summary

This chapter has focused on object-oriented programming, with particular emphasis on inheritance and polymorphism. This greatly enhances our ability to create reusable and manageable code. While the OO paradigm may take a little getting used to, once we have made the leap there is probably no turning back.

Visual Forms Inheritance and the associated IDE support add a new dimension to this. It allows us to create a base form comprising all shared functionality and layout, leaving the specialization to individual forms derived from the base form. This saves time and improves design consistency.

Along the way, we also discussed other powerful additions to our programming toolbox. Function pointers are now type safe, and called Delegates. Garbage collection will be a welcome addition for the C++ programmers – especially the not-quite-expert ones who often spend countless hours trying to find memory leaks. Finally, we looked at structured error handling as an alternative to the infamous `on error goto`.

System.Windows.Forms

Legend: Concrete Class / Abstract class

- System.Object
  - System.MarshalRefObject
    - System.ComponentMode.Component
      - CommonDialog
        - ColorDialog
        - FileDialog
        - FontDialog
        - PageSetupDialog
        - PrintDialog
      - ErrorProvider
      - HelpProvider
      - ImageList
      - Menu
        - ContextMenu
        - MainMenu
        - MenuItem
      - NotifyIcon
      - StatusBarPanel
      - Timer
      - ToolBarButton
      - ToolTip
      - Control
        - ButtonBase
          - Button
          - CheckBox
          - RadioButton
        - DataGrid
        - DateTimePicker
        - GroupBox
        - Label
          - LinkLabel
        - ListControl
          - ComboBox
          - ListBox
            - CheckedListBox
        - ListView
        - MonthCalendar
        - PictureBox
        - PrintReviewControl
        - ProgressBar
        - ScrollableControl
          - ContainerControl
            - Form
              - PrintPreviewDialog
              - ThreadExceptionDialog
            - PropertyGrid
            - UpDownBase
              - DomainUpDown
              - NumericUpDown
            - UserControl
          - Panel
            - TabPage
        - ScrollBar
          - HScrollBar
          - VScrollBar
        - Splitter
        - StatusBar
        - TabControl
        - TextBoxBase
          - RichTextBox
          - Textbox
        - ToolBar
        - TrackBar
        - TreeView
  - ListViewItem
  - TreeNode

4

Introduction to Windows Forms

Forms have always been the standard visual interface for applications on the Windows operating system. We can see the use of forms in the various applications that are used on a daily basis, such as word processing software, spreadsheet software, or any other windows-based application. A form is, roughly speaking, a rectangular area of the screen that is responsible for supplying the user interface to an application. (Although, since Windows 2000 it has been possible to create windows of other shapes. A good example of this is the Office assistant in Office 2000.)

Bear in mind that terminology has recently shifted and is in some cases still somewhat vague. What we now call a **form,** frequently used to be called a **window** (lower-case to distinguish it from the name of the operating system), although the term 'form' has been used specifically in the context of Visual Basic for some years. On the other hand, 'window' has traditionally had a slightly wider meaning in that it can refer to any area of the screen that, as far as the Windows operating system was concerned, was associated with a window handle and represented by a windows class. This includes some controls (items like text boxes or listboxes, which are not capable of existing on their own but need to be placed in another window) as well as forms themselves. Also, the word 'form' tends to imply a dialog box, Single Document Interface (SDI) or Multiple Document Interface (MDI) that primarily contains controls. If an application relied on directly drawing data to the screen using GDI (now replaced by GDI+) or DirectX then we would tend to refer to its main window as a window rather than a form. The sense in which we will use 'form' in this book is that of any window that is capable of existing in its own right.

The new .NET technology, dubbed **Windows Forms**, simply means the set of .NET base classes that make it easy for us to create and manipulate windows and controls. These classes primarily constitute the `System.Windows.Forms` namespace and come in two main varieties: Those that represent forms (that is, main application windows, dialog boxes, etc.) and those that represent controls (that is, items placed in forms, such as textboxes and listboxes). There are also a number of utility classes, and enumerations in the `System.Windows.Forms` namespace, which don't directly represent any form or control, but which assist in working with Windows Forms.

In this chapter, we will discuss the following topics:

- Windows Forms vs. Web Forms
- Types of Form
- Windows Forms in the .NET Framework
- Creating Forms
- Form Class properties
- Adding Forms to an Application

During the course of the chapter we will also build a few applications to help demonstrate different topics – including an editor application called `WroxEdit` that we will build on in the next chapter.

Windows Forms vs. Web Forms

As we saw in Chapter 1, Visual Studio.NET allows us to create two Forms style applications. We can create a Windows Forms application, or a Web Forms application. The difference between the two in simple terms is that Windows Forms allow us to build stand-alone Windows applications, and Web Forms are designed to create applications that will work across the Internet or intranets, using web based technologies. A Windows Form really is a true window, which will be displayed on the local machine on which it was created, while a control created using Windows Forms really is a genuine Windows control. By contrast, a Web Forms control is a .NET class that can generate HTML, XML or client-side JScript code which, when processed and displayed by a web browser, (such as Internet Explorer), will give the same kind of appearance and features as a windows control – such as a textbox or listbox.

If we create a new Windows Forms project in Visual Studio.NET, the project we get will be one that creates and displays windows on the local system. If we create a new Web Forms project, we will get an ASP.NET application that is designed to run in the IIS environment as a web site – able to send out Web Forms to browsers as HTML code.

Web Forms are built with the same IDE used to create Windows Forms, but they use ASP.NET, to provide a platform independent user interface to clients accessing the application across the Internet with a web browser. Keep in mind that this type of application will consume server resources, and places the decision in our hands as to which is the more beneficial to use. However, if we want the application to reach the maximum amount of users, a Web Forms application may be the ticket.

Since we are concentrating on Windows Forms in this book, we will leave Web Forms for the moment, although we will show a practical example of consuming a Web Service with Web Forms and Windows Forms in Chapter 16 on Windows Forms and Web Services.

Features of a Windows Form

Windows Forms are used to present a visual interface to the user for the purposes of interacting with the application, and displaying or accepting input from the user. Windows Forms in the .NET framework still allow us to work with the same type of objects we may already be used to from earlier versions of development tools, such as controls on the forms and form properties, and events and methods.

We can get an idea of the typical features of a form by taking our `WroxEdit` creation as an example. The screenshot shows `WroxEdit` being used to shamelessly promote this book!

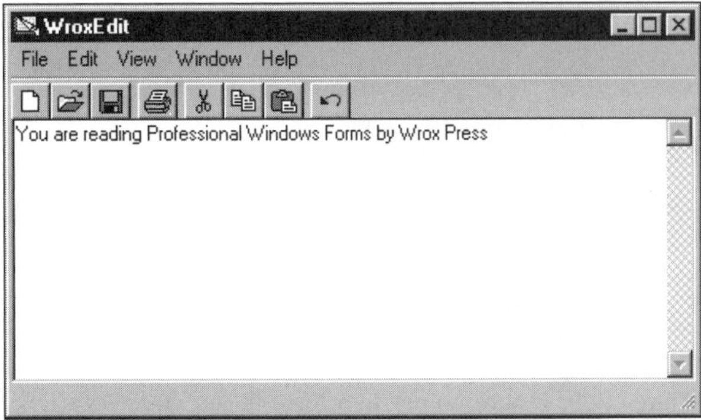

We can see that apart from the basic rectangular shape, a form that's used as the main window of an application, usually has a number of features:

- A title bar with a caption that indicates the purpose of the form: Situated right at the top of the form. To the left of the caption is an icon. Clicking on this icon brings up a standard menu with options to minimize, maximize, restore, move, resize or close the document. In Windows Forms, this menu is supplied by Windows, and is not normally customizable by the developer – it is the same for all applications.
- Maximize/restore: Allows users to minimize and close buttons – at the top right of the form.
- Main menu: Also at the top of the form and located just below the title bar.
- Toolbar: Located below the main menu. This screeenshot shows only one toolbar, but an application may have more, and it is usual for the user to be able to customize which toolbars appear. This facility is not provided by Windows, and is our responsibility to implement it in the code.
- Status bar: Located at the bottom of the form.
- Various controls: Located in the form.
- Borders: These might not look too remarkable, but as we will see later, the style of border (eg. raised or sunken) is normally used to give a visual cue to the user of the nature and purpose of the form.
- Sizegrip: Located at the bottom right of the form, used for resizing with the mouse. (On some forms the user can also resize by clicking and dragging on the borders.)

In fact, the way the Windows Forms object model works, only the title bar (including the icon and maximize/minimize/restore/close, buttons) and the sizegrip are actually considered to be part of the form. The menu, status bar, and other controls (including any scrollbars present) are all treated as separate controls, which we can choose to add to our form if we wish.

> *This model differs from some earlier technologies – for example, in VB6 the main menu was considered part of the form itself. In Windows Forms it is considered a separate control.*

The elements of a form which are not considered to be separate controls are treated in Windows Forms as properties of the `Form` object (the instance of the .NET class derived from `System.Windows.Forms.Form` that represents the form). For example, the caption displayed in the title bar is set using the `Form.Text` property, the code for which would look something like this in VB.NET:

```
' MyForm is an object derived from Form
MyForm.Text = "Hello"    ' set title bar text to "Hello"
```

And like this in C#:

```
// MyForm is an object derived from Form
MyForm.Text = "Hello";
```

This code assumes we already have a reference to a form in our code – we'll soon see how to instantiate and display the form.

Whether the gripper is present is set using the `SizeGripStyle` property in a similar way:

```
MyForm.SizeGripStyle = True    ' displays the sizegrip
```

There are a number of different styles of form available, depending on the situation. For example, if we want a form to be used as a simple dialog box, we would probably want it to have a dialog style border, and would not want it to be **sizeable** or display the maximize/restore and minimize buttons:

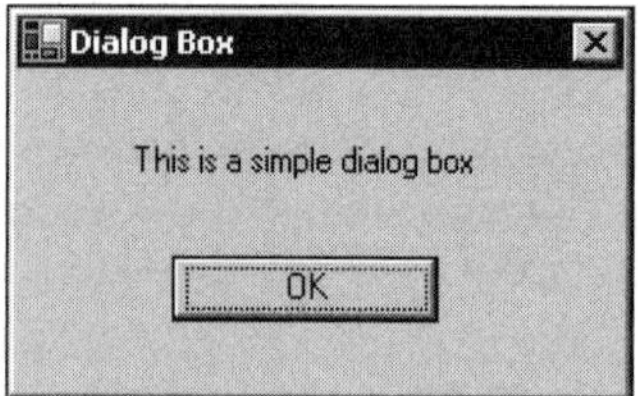

According to the Windows Forms object model, many of these aspects of the form are set using the `Form.FormBorderStyle` property. A number of different border styles are available, that between them control specifically the appearance of the border, whether the title bar is displayed and whether the form is sizeable. We will briefly review the different border styles next.

Types of Form

Borders in Windows Forms differ somewhat from the regular borders used in earlier versions of VB. The `FormBorderStyle` property of Windows Forms determines how the form will behave when resized, as well as how the caption, or title bar, is displayed and what buttons will appear on the border. There are seven border styles to choose from and these are listed here in this table along with descriptions for each.

Border Style	Description
`None`	Contains no border or border elements. This is used mostly for startup forms such as splash screens.
`Fixed 3D`	Creates a 3D effect but does not allow resizing. The border is raised compared to the form body. This style allows the control menu, title bar and the min and max buttons.
`Fixed Dialog`	Use this border style for dialog boxes. The border is not resizable by the user and is recessed in comparison to the form body. This style allows the control menu, title bar and the min and max buttons.
`Fixed Single`	A single line border that is not resizable by the user. This style allows the control menu, title bar and the min and max buttons.
`Fixed Tool Window`	Use this border style for a fixed tool window. This style is not resizable and has a Close button and reduced font size in the title bar. This form will also not appear in the taskbar.
`Sizeable`	The default border style and the one used most often for regular forms. It is resizable and contains a control menu, title bar and min and max buttons.
`Sizeable Tool Window`	The same as the Fixed Tool Window only this one can be resized.

A variety of `Forms` of differing `FormBorderStyle` values are shown below, where the blank rectangle is `FormBorderStyle`, `None`:

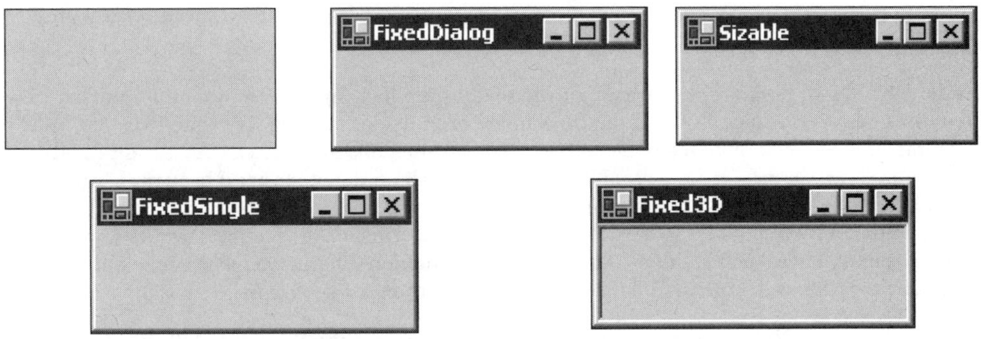

There are a few choices to make concerning the border style for forms. The previous table and screenshots will help you to understand the various differences between each border style, giving you the information to choose the appropriate style for your needs.

Windows Forms and the Windows API

Now we've looked in general terms at what a form is and what features of a form we'd expect to be able to control using Windows Forms code, we'll briefly review the various technolgies that have been used to write forms-based GUI applications on Windows, as well as their relationship to the underlying Windows API.

It should be stressed that when we use Windows Forms, what is happening under the hood is not much different from when a form was created in VB 6.0 or a window in C++ using MFC, or the underlying Windows API functions. Since the earliest days of Windows, forms were instantiated programmatically using the Windows API. The Windows API is a large set of C library functions that are responsible for interacting with the Windows operating system – and form the means by which any application, whether written in C, C++, VB, or C# ultimately calls on the services provided by Windows regardless of whether that is to verify security permissions, access the file system, or create and display a window. Because the API functions were written in C, they were normally only directly accessible from C and C++ code, but they are still what gets called behind the scenes when using other languages (although VB in particular has always shielded the developer from this fact).

For example, to create a window, we'd usually call the function `RegisterClass` (or more recently, `RegisterClassEx`), which informs Windows about the properties of a type of window that we wish to create. Then we'd call `CreateWindow` (or `CreateWindowEx`) to create a window of this type, and `ShowWindow` to show it. Unfortunately, because these were C functions rather than objects, they couldn't really support object-oriented programming. The functions worked by passing windows handles (HWNDs) in their parameter lists in order to indicate which window was being referred to. There was no concept of properties in the sense that .NET and VB 6.0 uses them. For example, to set the caption of a form, we couldn't simply set a property – instead we'd call the `SetWindowText` function, passing in the handle of the relevant window and the new caption. In short, it was monotonous and difficult.

These API functions are still the things that actually do the work in manipulating windows. What's changed is that Microsoft started providing wrappers around them, to make our work in coding up windows applications easier. For example, MFC provided a low level, high performance, C++ class wrapper around the functions. With MFC we get a basic object model, in which C++ class instances wrapped each windows handle, allowing the API functions to be called as member functions of classes instead of passing in windows handles. This also meant that inheritance was supported as well as constructors and destructors.

On the other hand, programming wasn't substantially simplified since there was still, in many cases, a one-to-one correspondence between the C++ member functions and the API functions: An MFC programmer would still quite likely be calling member functions like `RegisterClassEx` and `SetWindowText` on his window. Pre-.NET versions of VB on the other hand brought in an increasingly sophisticated object model, in which many of the underlying API calls were hidden, often wrapped by VB properties, which could be set visually in the VB IDE. This made creating a windows application in VB very simple. However VB did not support implementation inheritance, which made it all but impossible to write well-structured, maintainable, object-oriented programs.

Windows Forms in .NET provides another new wrapper around the Windows API functions, but this time it gives us the best of both worlds. We get the properties, and a visual developer environment, as powerful as that of VB 6.0, but the .NET classes also support implementation inheritance (as well as interface inheritance) thereby enabling true object oriented programming. Not only that, but the list of properties has been extended since VB 6.0, making it easier than ever to manipulate windows. For example, the transparency (on W2K and Windows XP) can be set using the new `Opacity` property, while the `DockStyle` property makes it easy to dock controls or even have a control always automatically fill its containing form or control.

Behind all this we should be aware that the Windows Forms classes are simply very sophisticated wrappers around those old Windows API functions. And just to reinforce the point, there's even a read-only property, `Control.Handle`, available to Windows Forms classes to retrieve the underlying Windows HWND handle, enabling us to manipulate the form with the windows API functions if we so wish (though it's unlikely that we'd need to very often).

Windows Forms support for inheritance is also a time saver when creating applications because we don't have to re-create forms or functionality that already exist, or provide consistency among our forms in the same application. When creating a form for an application, we have the choice of inheriting from the `Form` class that is provided as a part of the .NET framework, or inheriting from an existing form including one that we have created.

Windows Forms in the .NET Framework

The `Form` class is part of the `System.Windows.Forms` namespace, which also contains other controls that can be added to the forms to create the user interface. Let's have a quick look at the `Form` class hierarchy.

'Form' Class Hierarchy

Forms are inherited from the `ContainerControl` and reside in the object model as represented here:

```
Object
    MarshalByRefObject
        Component
            Control
                ScrollableControl
                    ContainerControl
                        Form
```

- As we look at this small inheritance tree for the `Form` object, we can see that the root is the `Object` class. The full component hierarchy for Windows Forms is shown on each chapter divider page.
- The immediate sub class of the `Object` class is `MarshalByRefObject`, which ensures that the object (our form) remains within the application domain in which it was created, and that cross-domain references are handled using proxies. This will only be of concern if we are using multiple application domains and the .NET remoting features in our code.
- The `Component` sub class enables object sharing between applications.
- The next class in the tree is the `Control` class. This is the base class for Windows Forms components that have a visual interface. Note a difference in terminology here from the old ActiveX controls: ActiveX controls didn't necessarily have a user interface, whereas .NET controls are generally understood to be user interface components.
- The `ScrollableControl` class is next in the hierarchy, and implements features that deal with auto-scrolling.
- `ContainerControl` provides functionality needed if a control is to act as a container for other controls (Clearly this applies to forms since almost all forms will contain controls).
- The `Form` class gives us a basic blank form that has the ability to contain controls. However, we should emphasize that the hierarchy does not end here. The main form in a Windows Forms application will almost certainly be a class that is derived from `Form`, and which adds to the basic form those features required by the particular application. We may even derive further classes from that, especially if we have a number of related forms that we wish to specialize.

Creating Forms

In this section, we will see how to add Windows Forms to our C# or VB.NET project. Usually we will add a form to our projects by getting Visual Studio.NET to generate all the code for us, either by creating a new project as a Windows application, or by asking Visual Studio.NET to add a new form to the project by using the Add Item menu option (as we saw in Chapter 2 on Visual Studio.NET). However, in order to understand how the code to create a form works, we are going to start off by coding a basic windows form application by hand. This is because Visual Studio .NET tends to add a lot of extra features to its code, which makes Visual Studio.NET-generated code a lot more complex than required to generate a form. Coding by hand will give code that should make it easier to understand what's going on. Once we've done that, we'll move on to look at the corresponding Visual Studio .NET-generated code.

We'll actually look at two simple Windows Forms programs coded by hand – both of them do no more than display a basic form, which can be maximized, minimized, restored or closed by the normal buttons in the top right corner of the form, but which have no other features. Two programs because we'll look at the C# and the VB.NET versions of the code. In most cases in this book, we simply present code for a given sample in one of the two languages. But since the process of creating a form is such an important operation, it's important to be able to see the code in whatever the preferred language is, hence we will show this in both languages. Remember that all the code is available for download on the Wrox web site.

Coding Up a Form by Hand in C#

Let's look at a small example that displays a GUI window. The code looks like this.

```
using System;
using System.Windows.Forms;

namespace SimpleCSharpHelloWorld
{

    public class SimpleHelloWorldForm : Form
    {
        public SimpleHelloWorldForm()
        {
            this.Text = "Hello World";    // sets the caption
        }
    }

    public class MainEntryPoint
    {
        public static void Main()
        {
            Application.Run(new SimpleHelloWorldForm ());
        }
    }
}
```

Running this code will give the following when executed.

Before we examine the code itself, we'll briefly discuss how to compile it.

As we saw in Chapter 2, we can use the command line to compile our examples. Since we coded this by hand, let's use the C# compiler:

```
C:\test> csc /target:winexe /out:SimpleCSharpForm.exe /reference:System.dll
/reference:System.Windows.Forms.dll SimpleCSharpForm.cs
```

Notice that we use the `/target:winexe` flag to ensure that the compiled code runs as a Windows application. If we do not include this flag, then the code will run as a console application – it will either have to be run from the command line or will cause Windows to create a command prompt window before the form is displayed.

Now let us have a look at the code. The program entry point is as usual the `static Main` method. For a windows application there is no point in `Main` returning a value from or accepting parameters so we define the method as `void Main`. The only statement in the `Main` method:

```
Application.Run(new SimpleHelloWorldForm());
```

does the job of displaying the form. It calls the static method, `Run` of the `System.Windows.Forms.Application` class. This method, when provided with a reference to a form object, displays the form and sets up the message loop that is necessary for the form to be able to accept events. The `Run` method returns when the form gets closed, at which point the program exits.

The form itself requires little explicit code. The fact that a class derives from `System.Windows.Forms.Form` is, by itself, sufficient to provide all the features of a basic form, including the ability to respond to events and, if the form is of the appropriate type, to be resized by the user, and to display a title bar with the usual maximize, minimize and close buttons, and to respond appropriately if the user clicks any of those buttons. We have chosen to add a constructor, but that is only so that we can set the `Text` property of the form (that is, the caption that will be displayed in the title bar) to a suitable string:

```
    public SimpleHelloWorldForm()
        {
            this.Text = "Hello World";
        }
```

Before we examine the code that Visual Studio .NET generates, let us briefly look at the corresponding VB.NET code.

Coding Up a Form by Hand in VB.NET

In the same way as we created a project and typed in the above C# code, we could do the same with VB.NET. In this case the code would look like this:

```
Imports System
Imports System.Windows.Forms

Namespace SimpleVBHelloWorld

    Public Class MainVBForm : Inherits Form
        Public Sub New()
            Me.Text = "Hello World (VB)"
        End Sub
    End Class

    Class MainVBEntryPoint
        Public Shared Sub Main()
            Application.Run(New MainVBForm())
        End Sub
    End Class
End Namespace
```

The procedure for compiling and running this code is the same as for the earlier C# example. If using Visual Studio.NET, then we can create an empty project, add the code in a new file, and ensure that the `System.dll` and `SystemWindows.Forms.dll` libraries are referenced by the project. If compiling from the command line, then the relevant command to type in (assuming the file is called `SimpleVBForm.vb`) is:

```
C:\test> vbc /target:winexe /out:SimpleVBForm.exe /reference:System.dll
/reference:System.Windows.Forms.dll SimpleVBForm.vb
```

However, VB offers an alternative way of compiling that simplifies the code still further: Instead of supplying a shared `Main` function as the program entry point, the VB compiler allows us to specify a class that is derived from `System.Windows.Forms.Form` as the startup object. The VB compiler will arrange for an object of the specified class to be instantiated and passed to the `Application.Run` method automatically. This enables us to compact our VB version to the following code:

```
Imports System
Imports System.Windows.Forms

Namespace SimpleVBHelloWorld

    Class MainVBForm : Inherits Form
        Public Sub New()
```

```
        Me.Text = "Hello World (VB)"
    End Sub
End Class

End Namespace
```

Notice that we have eliminated the Main function and its containing class MainVBEntryPoint. In order for this code to compile and run correctly, we need to specify an additional /Main flag at the command line to indicate the startup object (note that we need to supply the full name including namespace name of this class). Assuming the program is called SimpleVBForm2.vb, this is what we would type at the command line:

```
C:\test> vbc /target:winexe /out:SimpleVBForm2.exe /reference:System.dll
/reference:System.Windows.Forms.dll  /main:SimpleVBHelloWorld SimpleVBForm2.vb
```

At this point we have seen how, in principle, we can code up a program that instantiates and displays a Form in either C# or VB. Notice, that in accordance with .NET's inheritance-based programming model, we have in both cases derived a class from Form, which is used to specialize a generic form into the particular form required by our application. Now we'll look at the (slightly more complex) code that is generated by Visual Studio.NET for the same purpose.

Auto-generating Code for a Form in Visual Studio .NET

We'll start off by looking at the code that Visual Studio.NET generates for us if we create a VB Windows Forms project. The corresponding C# version will be presented later. The following code is what we get if we create a new project in VS.NET as a VB Windows application, and do not make any changes to the VS.NET-generated code.

```
Public Class Form1
    Inherits System.Windows.Forms.Form

#Region " Windows Form Designer generated code "

    Public Sub New()
        MyBase.New()

        ' This call is required by the Windows Form Designer.
        InitializeComponent()

        ' Add any initialization after the InitializeComponent() call

    End Sub

    ' Form overrides dispose to clean up the component list.
    Protected Overloads Overrides Sub Dispose(ByVal disposing As _ Boolean)
        If disposing Then
            If Not (components Is Nothing) Then
                components.Dispose()
            End If
        End If
        MyBase.Dispose(disposing)
```

```
    End Sub

    'Required by the Windows Form Designer
    Private components As System.ComponentModel.Container

' NOTE: The following procedure is required by the Windows Form Designer
    ' It can be modified using the Windows Form Designer.
    ' Do not modify it using the code editor.
    <System.Diagnostics.DebuggerStepThrough()> Private Sub _ InitializeComponent()
        components = New System.ComponentModel.Container()
        Me.Text = "Form1"
    End Sub

#End Region

End Class
```

Although this code looks more complex than our hand-written examples, it essentially does the same thing. Our form class has been given a default name of `Form1`, which we can change to something more appropriate to our project, with the VS.NET properties window (or by doing a find-and-replace-all operation on the source file, as well as changing the name of the startup object in the Project Properties window, to match the new name of the form). The class appears at first not to have been placed in a named namespace. In fact it has been placed in a namespace with the name of the project, but for VB, Visual Studio.NET is able to handle a default project namespace through the project properties.

It is advised that you use the project properties dialog to change the namespace name to something appropriate to your company and project to ensure that the full names of your classes are unique.

Note that since this code is generated by asking Visual Studio.NET for a windows application, Visual Studio.NET automatically ensures that the compilation options are set correctly and all required libraries are referenced.

Let's look at the members of the `Form1` class (generated by Visual Studio.NET) that were not present in our hand-written class.

'InitializeComponent' Method

This method is called from the constructor and is used to set up the initial properties and contained controls for the form. It contains code that, in a hand-generated program, would probably be placed in the constructor itself. As we can see from the above code, the caption of the form `Text` property is set in `InitializeComponent`.

The reason for this method is to assist the design view in displaying the form and allowing us to edit it visually, by dragging and dropping controls, or setting properties in the properties window in Visual Studio.NET. Visual Studio.NET will read and parse the code in `InitializeComponent` to determine the initial values of the properties of the form, and any contained controls, in order to display them correctly in the design view and properties window. This is why this method is surrounded by comments warning us not to manually change any code in it.

In practice, if we know what we're doing, we can modify the code here – and experienced developers will quite likely find themselves doing so. It's a case of being aware that if we're not careful, we could easily prevent the design view from displaying the form correctly, and so prevent ourselves from editing the form visually. This won't, of course, prevent the program from running correctly. On the other hand, we can freely add any code (for example, to make other changes to the Forms's properties) to the constructor, outside the `InitializeComponent` method. However, the design view will not see any such code.

As an example, suppose we wish to change the form's startup caption to 'Simple VS.NET-Generated VB Form'. There are several possible ways.

We could change the text through the properties window in VS.NET. This will cause the code in the `InitializeComponent` method to be automatically changed:

```
' NOTE: The following procedure is required by the Windows Form Designer
    ' It can be modified using the Windows Form Designer.
    ' Do not modify it using the code editor.
    <System.Diagnostics.DebuggerStepThrough()> Private Sub _ InitializeComponent()
        components = New System.ComponentModel.Container()
        Me.Text = "Simple VS.NET-Generated VB Form"
    End Sub
```

Finally, we could add code to the `Form1` constructor:

```
    Public Sub New()
        MyBase.New()

        ' This call is required by the Windows Form Designer.
        InitializeComponent()
        Me.Text = "Simple VS.NET-Generated VB Form"

        ' Add any initialization after the InitializeComponent() call

    End Sub
```

This final way will mean that when the program is run, it will appear with the caption, 'Simple VS.NET-Generated VB Form', but the design view and properties window will still be incorrectly displaying the caption as 'Form1'. This is because Visual Studio.NET is simply reading the text from `InitializeComponent` without noticing that immediately after `InitializeComponent` has been called, the `Text` property gets set to a new value. As it stands this is not the most efficient code – with this code, setting the `Text` property twice will marginally waste processor time. However, if we wanted to do something more sophisticated, such as setting the caption to one of several values based on some other condition, then we'd probably do so by manually editing code in the constructor – the design view isn't capable of coping with that kind of scenario.

'Dispose' Method and 'components' Property

Visual Studio.NET supplies the `Dispose` and `components` members to assist the design view, and also to help the process of disposing the form, and any contained controls when the form is no longer needed. The `components` field is an instance of the class `System.ComponentModel.Container`. Its purpose is simply to provide a convenient, programmatic container, which groups together references to any controls on the form so that all the controls may be conveniently accessed by any code that needs to perform any operations on all the controls. This member is not part of Windows Forms and serves no visual purpose. Whenever we add a control to the form using the design view, part of the generated code in `InitializeComponent` adds the new control to the container collection.

The Dispose method provided ensures that if Dispose is called against the form, then any contained controls that have been placed in the container collection will also be disposed, thus ensuring that resource cleanup takes place at the earliest opportunity. This is important because many Windows Forms controls may hold unmanaged resources, such as windows handles. In our earlier samples of manually created code, we did not supply a Dispose method because the forms we had created in those samples have a lifetime extending until the application shuts down, and do not contain any controls, hence a Dispose method is not really necessary. However, if writing a more complex app manually, we would need to supply one. VS.NET has done that for us in anticipation that it may be needed.

C# Project

We'll quickly present the code that is generated if we create a new C# windows application in VS.NET, for comparison with the VB code.

```
using System;
using System.Drawing;
using System.Collections;
using System.ComponentModel;
using System.Windows.Forms;
using System.Data;

namespace AutoGeneratedCShForm
{
    /// <summary>
    /// Summary description for Form1.
   /// </summary>
   public class Form1 : System.Windows.Forms.Form
   {
      /// <summary>
      /// Required designer variable.
      /// </summary>
      private System.ComponentModel.Container components = null;

      public Form1()
      {
         //
         // Required for Windows Form Designer support
         //
         InitializeComponent();

         //
         // TODO: Add any constructor code after InitializeComponent call
         //
      }

      /// <summary>
      /// Clean up any resources being used.
      /// </summary>
      protected override void Dispose( bool disposing )
      {
         if( disposing )
         {
            if (components != null)
            {
               components.Dispose();
```

```
            }
        }
        base.Dispose( disposing );
    }

    #region Windows Form Designer generated code
    /// <summary>
    /// Required method for Designer support - do not modify
    /// the contents of this method with the code editor.
    /// </summary>
    private void InitializeComponent()
    {
        this.components = new System.ComponentModel.Container();
        this.Size = new System.Drawing.Size(300,300);
        this.Text = "Form1";
    }
    #endregion

    /// <summary>
    /// The main entry point for the application.
    /// </summary>
    [STAThread]
    static void Main()
    {
        Application.Run(new Form1());
    }
  }
}
```

The [STAThread] attribute is present here for compatibility purposes. If we need to call any COM legacy components (ActiveX controls) from our code, it makes calling any such components that live in a COM STA apartment more efficient. It's not there in the VS.NET-generated VB code because that doesn't explicitly show the Main method in the source code.

We can see that the C# code is virtually identical to the VB code, apart from having C# syntax. In particular the `InitializeComponent` method remains, and performs the same purpose, as do the `components` field and the `Dispose` method. The only significant difference in the C# code is the existence of a `static Main` method to start the application off. As remarked earlier, C# requires this method to be explicitly present, whereas the VB compiler is able to rely on setting a startup object instead. In our earlier examples, we defined a separate class to contain the `Main` method, but Visual Studio.NET places `Main` as a static method in the `Form1` class itself. For the simple form here, this makes no difference (except for the largely academic point that using a separate class to start the program off and instantiate the form might be considered technically to be a better illustration of object-oriented principles).

'Form' Class Properties

In this section we'll examine some of the more important properties that are available on the `Windows.Forms.Form` class. In the process, we'll discover how to set many of the aspects of forms that we mentioned earlier were treated as part of the form itself rather than as added controls.

We briefly looked at the properties window in Visual Studio.NET in Chapter 2. Here we will examine the use of this window for a form.

> **The IDE will provide a quick tool tip, in the description pane under the properties list, explaining what a given property is used for.**

It is important to understand that the properties listed for a form in the Properties window are coded into VS.NET – and there are two types of 'property' listed in the Properties window: Most of the listed properties are genuine properties in the sense that they directly correspond to member properties of `System.Windows.Forms.Form`, or of one of its base classes. A few of the 'properties', however, are simply settings used internally by Visual Studio.NET, and do not exist in the `Form` class itself.

We can see the difference by examining this screenshot, in which certain properties for a form have been changed via the Properties window.

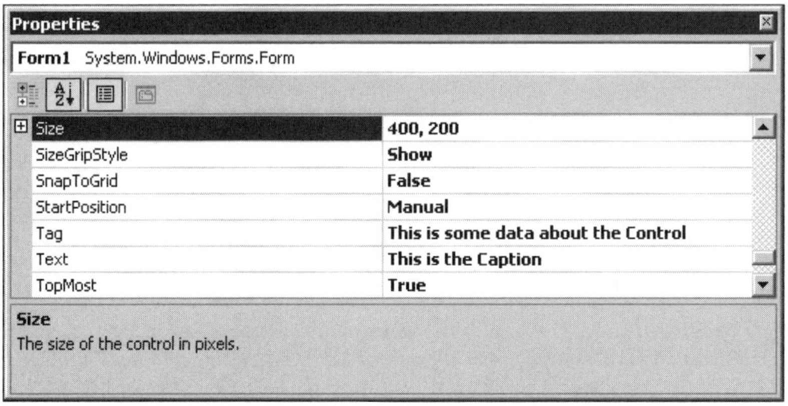

Properties

Form1 System.Windows.Forms.Form

Size	**400, 200**
SizeGripStyle	**Show**
SnapToGrid	**False**
StartPosition	**Manual**
Tag	**This is some data about the Control**
Text	**This is the Caption**
TopMost	**True**

Size
The size of the control in pixels.

This screenshot shows a number of properties. Of these, `Size`, `SizeGripStyle`, `StartPosition`, `Tag`, `Text` and `TopMost` are actual properties that are implemented by `Form` objects (the meaning of these properties will be explained soon). Hence setting these properties in the Properties window results in VS.NET adding this code inside the `InitializeComponent` method (assuming we're using C#).

```
this.ClientSize = new System.Drawing.Size(392, 173);
this.SizeGripStyle = System.Windows.Forms.SizeGripStyle.Show;
this.StartPosition = System.Windows.Forms.FormStartPosition.Manual;
this.Tag = "This is some data about the control";
this.Text = "This is the caption ";
this.TopMost = true;
```

Note that the Size property in the properties window actually maps to the ClientSize property of the form. It indicates the size in pixels of the form.

On the other hand, in the screenshot above, we have also set the `SnapToGrid` property to `False`. `SnapToGrid` does not exist as a property in the Form class, so no code was generated for this. `SnapToGrid` is an internal VS.NET setting, which indicates whether VS.NET will automatically move controls that we place by dragging and dropping onto a grid, thus aligning controls and so making the appearance of the form neater.

One Properties window property falls into both classes. `Name` exists as a property in `System.Windows.Forms.Form`, but is also used by VS.NET to set the name of the variable used to instantiate the control.

It is also important to understand that the **Properties** window does not make available the complete list of member properties of the `Form` class. It allows us to visually modify the most common properties, but there are a number (such as `Form.DesktopLocation`) for which we must modify the code manually if we wish to set them. Full details of these properties can be found in the MSDN documentation.

All of these properties relate to forms, but there are similar properties that span across other controls as well. Many of these properties are implemented not in `Form`, but in the base class, `Control`, and, in many of those cases, we can set the same properties using the Properties window for various Windows Forms controls that are also indirectly derived from `Control`.

WroxEdit

Now that we know how to create forms, let's look at how we make an application by adding controls to them. In this section we will look at how to create a simple text editor called `WroxEdit`, consisting of a form with a text box and a main menu control. (We will cover all controls in detail in Chapters 8, 9, and 10.)

> *Since, we have not yet looked at event handlers, delegates, or event wiring, WroxEdit will have much of its functionality added behind the scenes in the download version. This version will provide a good base from which to build a fully functional editing application.*

To start off, we create a new Visual Basic Windows Application in Visual Studio.NET and call it `WroxEdit`. This will be the basis for our text editor application. Once we have the application open in the IDE, a default form will already be created, just like our earlier samples. We can change the form's `Text` property to `WroxEdit,` and change the Icon to the `note16.ico` icon found in the `Common7/Graphics/Icons/Writing` subfolder of the folder in which Visual Studio.NET was installed. The location of your graphics may differ depending on the type of installation you have performed. With these changes, the form, as displayed in Visual Studio.NET, should look like this:

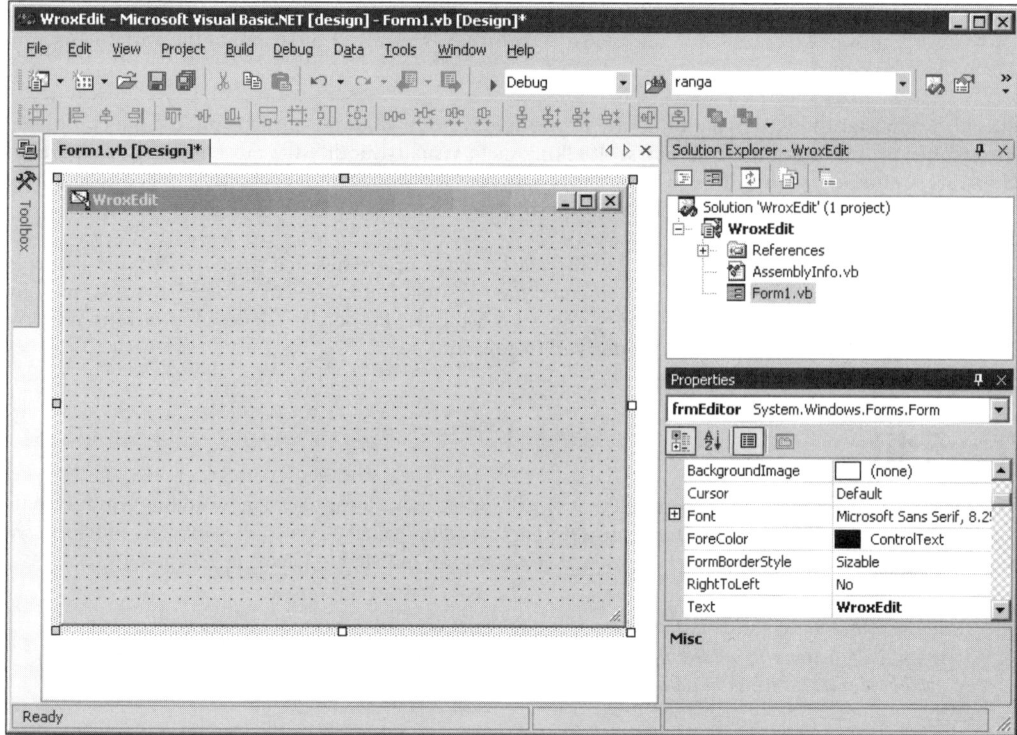

Placing Controls on a Form

Now that we have some of the properties set for the form, it is time to add some controls to the form. We won't go into any depth about the controls we are using, since they will be covered in detail in the relevant controls chapter later in the book.

The first thing we need is, of course, a text box to be used for the text editor. We can now add a `TextBox` control to the form by dragging and dropping from the toolbox. Also, by setting its `Dock` property to `Fill`, we ensure that the text box will always fill the entire window. This is one of the new Windows Forms features that wasn't available in VB 6.0 or in the nearest MFC equivalent, the `CEdit` class. In both MFC and VB 6.0 developers had to set the initial size and location of the control to fill the window, and provide an event handler for the Form's `SizeChange` event (MFC: provide a message handler) to ensure that the textbox resizes whenever the form does. Of course we could do it this way in .NET if we wanted, but just setting the `Dock` property is a lot simpler!

Don't forget we need to set the `Multiline` property to `True` before we can resize the vertical proportion of the textbox. Name this textbox `txtMain`, and change its `Text` property from `TextBox1` to an empty string to ensure that the textbox is empty when first displayed.

Adding some menus to the form will allow us to add functionality to the application, so let's add the `MainMenu` item on the toolbox in Visual Studio.NET by dragging it onto the form. Then we create the following menu structure to begin with. Type '-' in the `Text` property of the menu item to turn it into a separator.

File	**Edit**	**View**	**Help**
New	Undo	Toolbar	Contents
Open	**Separator**	StatusBar	Separator
Separator	Cut	About	
Save	Copy		
Save As	Paste		
Separator	Delete		
Print	**Separator**		
Separator	Find		
Exit			

Creating this menu structure is quite easy and intuitive. By clicking on the menu in the design view in Visual Studio.NET, we are presented with boxes to fill in the names of the menu items, as shown in the following screenshot.

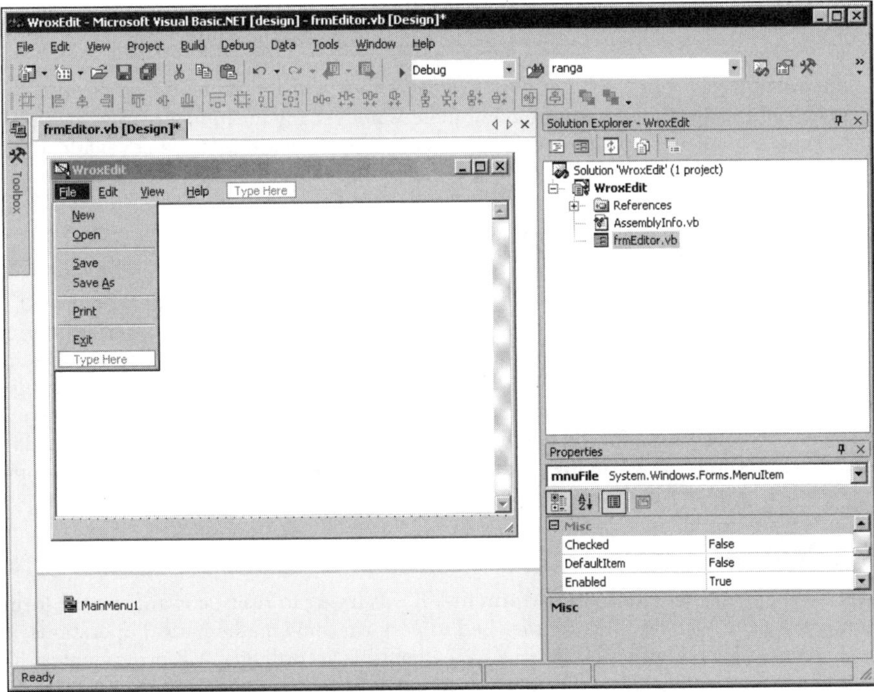

We can add an **accelerator key** to each menu item, and a shortcut key to the most important menu items, as well. This will make our application easier to use and conform to the standard Windows application operations. The accelerator key (also known as the **hot key** and shown underlined in the menu item when the application is running) is added, by prefixing the relevant letter with an '&' symbol.

The **shortcut key** is selected by editing the `Shortcut` property of the menu item in the Properties window. The Properties window will present a `listbox` inviting us to select the shortcut key. Windows Forms will automatically ensure that our chosen shortcut key is indicated in the menu item when the application is running. When this is completed, we should have a form that looks like the one shown below.

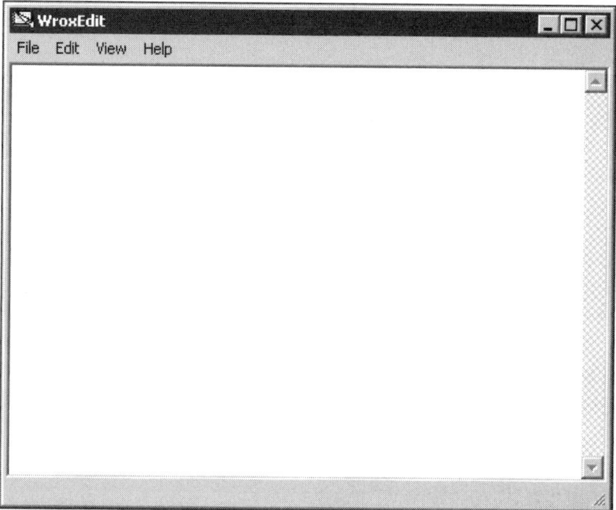

At this point, we now have the base of our text editor form completed. When the application is run, we can type in and edit text within the text box, but there is not yet any functionality to save it, or load other documents. In fact, none of the menu options do anything yet, because we haven't yet added the relevant event handlers. The functionality can be completed later for opening and saving text documents.

Arranging Controls on a Form

Once we have added the controls to our forms that will make up the user interface, our next step is to arrange and size the controls to suit the look and feel we want to convey. User interface design is a big issue when it comes to designing and developing applications (discussed next chapter). The more user-friendly and intuitive an interface is, the better it is for the user of the application and that also makes life easier for the developer in terms of application maintenance and upgrading. It also translates to lower costs in terms of training for the end user of the application. To this end, Visual Studio.NET offers us many different options for arranging controls on our forms either at design time or run time. This and the following sections will discuss those options and show how to use them.

Anchoring Controls

One of the most cumbersome tasks to perform in VB was trying to resize controls on the form when the form itself was resized. The developer either had to perform some mathematical operations, or purchase a third party control that allowed for resizing of the controls accordingly. VB programmers have long wished for this feature to be a part of Visual Basic, and with control anchoring in .NET, it now is (to a certain degree).

Anchoring allows us to specify how we want the control to 'stick' to the parent control. Once we have placed our textbox control on the form and other controls such as toolbars and statusbars, we can then anchor the textbox control to the form. By default, the textbox is anchored to the top and left of the form. We can choose the bottom and right anchor points as well, which will cause the text box to change to the form's size when the user resizes the form itself. The anchor settings can be found under the `Anchor` property as shown in the screenshot below.

> *Notice, that we have added a toolbar with buttons containing icons. We will show how to add images using the `ImageList` control in Chapter 9 on peripheral controls.*

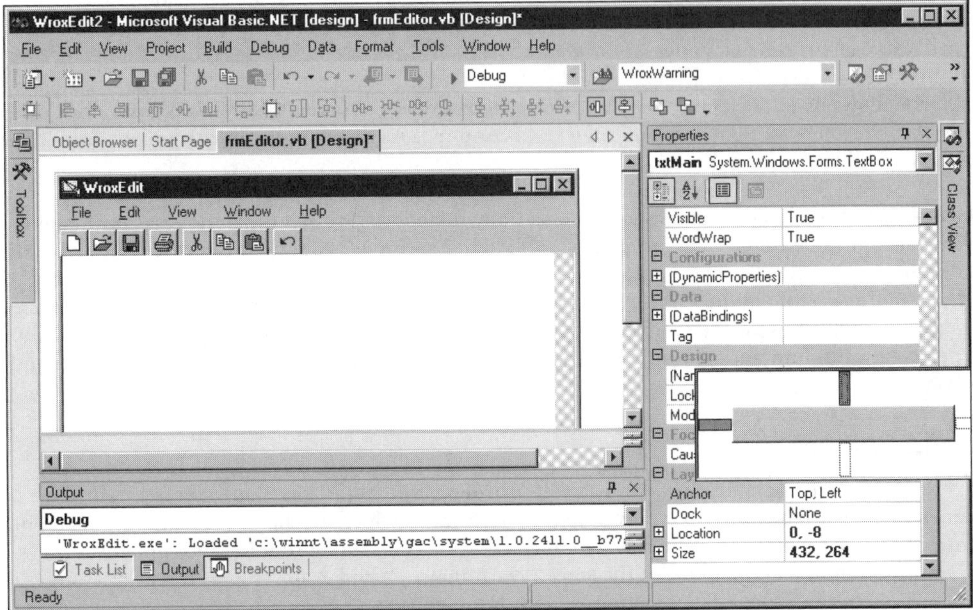

When anchoring, each of the bars that we see can be clicked to select or deselect the appropriate anchor position. For the `TextBox` control, we choose all four. The property will indicate `Top, Left, Right, Bottom`. Once this property is set, run the application and resize the form. The textbox will follow the size of the form on all four sides.

> *For controls that have a size limitation such as the `ComboBox`'s height property, the anchoring will not cause it to exceed that limitation. That means that we cannot anchor the `ComboBox` control to all positions and expect it to take up the entire form.*

One important item to note about anchoring controls is that they are anchored relative to their parent container. As an example of this behavior, create a blank form and add a `GroupBox` control to the form. Set its `Anchor` property to all sides. Add two `RadioButton` controls to the `GroupBox` in the usual manner. Set the `Anchor` property of just one radio button to all sides. Run the application to open the form. Resize the form and note the behavior of the group box control.

Notice that the group box control resizes accordingly with the form, but the two radio buttons will act differently. The one that has its anchor property set to all sides will move within the group box as the form is resized. The one that we didn't set the anchor property for simply remains in its original position (distance from left and top of the group box).

There are some quirks as well in the way that the `Anchor` property works. For example, if we were to create the form that we have for our `WroxEdit` application and set the `Anchor` property prior to placing the tool bar and status bar controls on the form, these last two controls will cover portions of the textbox. Essentially, the form's height property has changed but the `Anchor` property hasn't picked that up.

Docking Controls

Docking of controls on a form allows us to specify which location on the form we want a control to 'glue' to. If we use the Windows Explorer as an example, we will notice that the `treeview` control is docked to the left of the form and the `list view` control is docked to the right side of the form. If we resize the form, the controls will remain docked to their respective sides. This will take place even if they didn't contain resizing code.

VB.NET allows us to dock controls on the form in one of six possible locations. We can dock our control to the left, top, right, bottom, fill (center) or none. As an example, create a blank form and add a button control to the form.

Once we select the left docking option we will immediately notice that the button has now taken up residence at the left edge of the form and has filled the entire left edge. We can resize the width of the button but not the height. This is analogous to the toolbar and statusbar controls that can be docked to the top and/or bottom of the form. As a matter of fact, if we add a toolbar control to a form and don't specify any properties for the toolbar, we can see that it has its dock property set to Top by default. Experiment with different controls and different docking positions to see the effect of docking and resizing the form.

Layering Objects

Layering of objects, or controls, deals with the **z-order** of the objects as placed on the form. The z-order defines which window (form or control) appears in front of which, in the event that more than one control needs to occupy the same space on the screen. It is called z-order because of a three dimensional approach to looking at the screen coordinates. `X` and `Y` are used as the height and width but the `Z` is used to represent a layered approach to the screen.

We change the layer on which the control resides by using the `SendToBack` or `BringToFront` methods. Respectively, these methods will send an object to the back layer and hide it under the top layer or bring the object to the front layer and display it.

To get a feel for how this layering works, create a blank form and, using the double-click method, add two label controls to the form. Using the double-click method will place one label on top of the other. Now add two command buttons to the form as well but place them in the lower center of the form next to each other to obtain a form that looks like this:

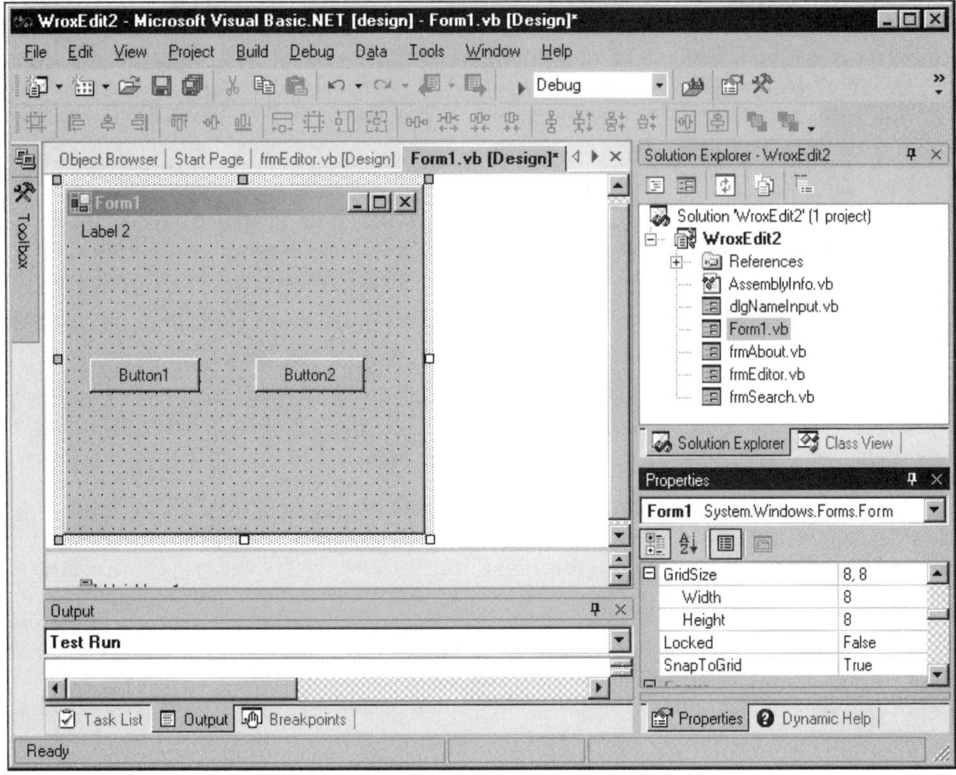

Next, add the following code to the appropriate command button.

```
Private Sub Button1_Click_1(ByVal sender As System.Object, _
ByVal e As System.EventArgs) Handles Button1.Click

    Label1.BringToFront()

End Sub
```

```
Private Sub Button2_Click(ByVal sender As Object, _
ByVal e As System.EventArgs) Handles Button2.Click

    Label2.BringToFront()

End Sub
```

When the user clicks the appropriate button, the corresponding label will be brought to the front of the other label. That's really all there is to layering controls on a form.

A possible use for layering might be if we had multiple controls on a form, tab strip, or container control and there wasn't enough real estate to hold all of the controls comfortably. We could use layering to hide and display the controls as needed.

Positioning Controls

Positioning controls on a form can be accomplished in one of two ways. We can use the designer to drag our controls around to the locations we want, which is of course the easiest way to position the controls. The biggest reason is that we can actually see how the controls will look when we are finished.

> **When we place a control on a form and want to get more precision in positioning it by moving it around, get it as close as possible to the desired location with the mouse and then use the arrow keys on the keyboard for more precise control over the movement. The control can still only be moved in increments equal to the grid spacing if Snap to Grid is turned on.**

The second method is to use the `Location` property of the control. The `Location` property can be set in the designer using the Property window or it can be set in code. Either method involves setting the `X` and `Y` values. The `X` and `Y` values are used to indicate a point at which the top left corner of the control will be positioned.

When positioning controls using code or the `X` and `Y` properties, we have to be aware of the coordinates of the form and other controls on the form. The form or container coordinates start in the upper left corner with `X` and `Y` values of `0` – this is the origin. Incrementing the `X` value causes the control to move to the right and incrementing the `Y` value causes the control to move down in the container.

As mentioned, we can also move the controls around in the parent container by setting the `Location` property in code. When we do so, we have two possible ways of setting the location. We can set the property by specifying the `X` and `Y` values together within parentheses or we can specify each separately. The following code segment shows how to do just that with the two command buttons we have been using all along.

```
Private Sub Form1_Load(ByVal sender As System.Object, ByVal e As _
System.EventArgs) Handles MyBase.Load

    Button1.Location = New Point(50, 75)

    Button2.Left = 75
    Button2.Top = 50

End Sub
```

As we can see, when we run this example and the form loads, the buttons are positioned on the form according to the coordinates specified. Of course, the same rules apply in terms of positioning controls within other container controls too.

Resizing Controls on Forms

For the most part, when we create controls on our form, we size them according to our needs. Very seldom will we need to change the size of the control after we have drawn it on the form. Of course, if we use the double-click method to add a control to the form, it is placed in the form in the default size which may not satisfy our needs. We may also run across an instance where the control's size may interfere with another if the form is sized smaller than the initial design size. We can avoid this by specifying a minimum size for our form with the `MinimumSize` property.

For starters, let's take a look at the easiest way and then move onto resizing in code. Each control that we add to a form or container has selection handles surrounding it. We can resize any control by dragging any of these handles. Drag one of the handles on the sides and we resize the width of the control, drag the top or bottom handles and we resize the height of the control. We can resize the control proportionately by dragging one of the corner handles. We can also hold down the shift key and use the arrow keys to resize the control with more precision.

We can also resize the control in code and there are actually two ways to do this. The first method is to simply change the `Size` property of the control by specifying the `Width` and `Height` properties as shown in this code snippet:

```
Private Sub Button1_Click_1(ByVal sender As System.Object, _
ByVal e As System.EventArgs) Handles Button1.Click

    With Button2
        .Width = 75
        .Height = 15
    End With

End Sub
```

This code will cause the width and height of `Button2` to change according to the values specified in the `Width` and `Height` properties in the click event of `Button1`.

Another way to resize a control in code is to create a rectangle of the size we need and then assign the control's `Bounds` property equal to the dimensions of the rectangle. The code sample provided below demonstrates how to do this:

```
Private Sub Button1_Click_1(ByVal sender As System.Object, _
ByVal e As System.EventArgs) Handles Button1.Click

        Dim rect As New Rectangle(25, 25, 100, 100)
        Button2.Bounds = rect

End Sub
```

The code in this button click event first creates a rectangle that is located at 25 and 25 for the X and Y coordinates. It then specifies the width and height to be 100 pixels each. Once the rectangle is established, we can set the bounds of the button equal to the rectangle and the button will take on the location and size of the rectangle. This, of course, is a round about way of resizing a control.

The familiar Make Same Size option is available in VB.NET as well, so we can resize all buttons on the form to be the same size. Select the button that will be used as the size base first. While holding down the CTRL key, select the remaining controls. When all of the controls are selected, click the Make Same Size button on the toolbar of the IDE to make all the controls the same size.

As can be seen, VB.NET adds some new ways to work with controls on forms as well as keeping some of the mainstay methods as well.

Setting a Form's Location

Locating forms on the user's desktop can be done in a couple of different ways, either on the computer screen, or using the `DesktopLocation` property. Both methods will be discussed in the following sections.

With form positioning, there are issues that will come up with regards to the user's screen resolution. We have to take the position and size into consideration to prevent the form from being displayed off the screen. Once again, we may need to check the user's resolution at startup and set the size accordingly.

Positioning Forms

Forms can be postioned at runtime by setting either one of the `Location` or the `DesktopLocation` properties. The difference between them is that the `Location` gives the coordinates of the top left corner of the form relative to the top left corner of the screen, whereas the `DesktopLocation` gives the coordinates relative to the top left corner of the desktop (ie. the screen excluding the taskbar). For most purposes, `DesktopLocation` is the more appropriate property to use. Both properties are of type `System.Drawing.Point` – a struct that is comprised of an X and Y co-ordinate. Hence we could write:

```
Me.DesktopLocation = New Point (25, 25)
```

or alternatively:

```
Me.Location = New Point (25, 25)
```

These lines of code will respectively place the upper left corner of the form at the desktop (or screen) co-ordinates of 25, 25. This equates to 25 pixels from the left edge of the screen to 25 pixels from the top of the screen.

We can also use the `Left` and `Top` properties of the form to set either the vertical or horizontal position individually. These properties represent screen, not desktop, coordinates.

```
Me.Left = 25
```

If the user is running an application on a system that is using multiple monitors, the co-ordinates of the form will work with the combined co-ordinates of the desktop.

If we wish to set the startup position of the form by setting the `Location` or `DesktopLocation` property in the form's constructor (as opposed to changing the position after the form has already been displayed), then we also need to set the `StartPosition` property:

```
Me.DesktopLocation = New Point(250,250)
Me.StartPosition = StartPosition.Manual
```

If `StartPosition` isn't set, the initial value of `DesktopLocation` will be ignored since Windows will simply use the default Windows starting location for the form.

Keeping a Form on Top

In some instances, we want to be able to keep the forms visible at all times. By default, a form that takes the focus is automatically displayed over the top of all other forms, but it is possible to set a form to stay on top of other forms even when another form takes the focus. This is the behavior exhibited by the task manager for example.

The way to keep a form on top is to set the `TopMost` property to `True`. We can do this in a procedure like handling a user clicking an OnTop menu item on a form, or we can set the property in the initialization code to have the form always on top.

Resizing Forms

Trying to gain good idea of how a form's size will look when the application is running is not always easy, especially when it comes to the variety of screen resolutions that users may be running. In VB 6.0 there was a form layout window that showed the relative size and location of a form in terms of the desktop based on the screen resolution. Visual Studio.NET does not have this feature. Hence there's a little more trial and error guesswork involved in selecting the initial size for the form. But in general, it's not too difficult a task provided we make sure that an appropriate size is set to display the controls in the form.

We will however still need to choose an initial size. By default, if we don't specify a size, the form will be created with a default size of 300 by 300 pixels. To change this, we can either click on a corner or side of the form in the Visual Studio.NET design view and drag to resize it, or set the `Form` class's `Size` property either within the properties window or manually in the code. All these different options obviously have the same programmatic effect – they are effectively just different ways that Visual Studio.NET allows us to edit our code.

The `Size` property takes two parameters like so:

```
Me.Size = New System.Drawing.Size(250, 250)
```

By specifying the size in our code this way, we can check for the screen resolution as the application starts and have the form size be based on the user's resolution.

Adding Forms to an Application

We have two choices when adding a form to an application – we can add a new Windows Form or we can add Inherited Forms.

If there is a form class that has already been created, say one that is used as a base form for company specific applications, then we can reuse that form by adding an inherited form. The inherited form will take its base form from the form that has already been created, but still allows us to customize and add functionality to it.

To add a form to a project, select the Project menu and then choose either Add Windows Form or Add Inherited Form.

Either menu option will open the same dialog box, but will highlight the correct form for us automatically. All we have to do is provide a new name for the form that we are adding.

For more information on creating and saving forms to be inherited from, refer to Chapter 3.

WroxWarnings

In this chapter we've covered a number of topics, and we are now going to work through a sample that puts them together. In particular we are going to demonstrate:

- Creating a control at runtime
- Inheriting controls

- Cross-language interoperability
- Customizing the startup position of a form

The sample is designed to be fun and to illustrate all the above topics rather than to be useful and realistic. It simply displays a small form with a button on it, telling the user not to press the button. The form appears at a specific startup position, 200 pixels across and 300 pixels down from the top left corner of the desktop.

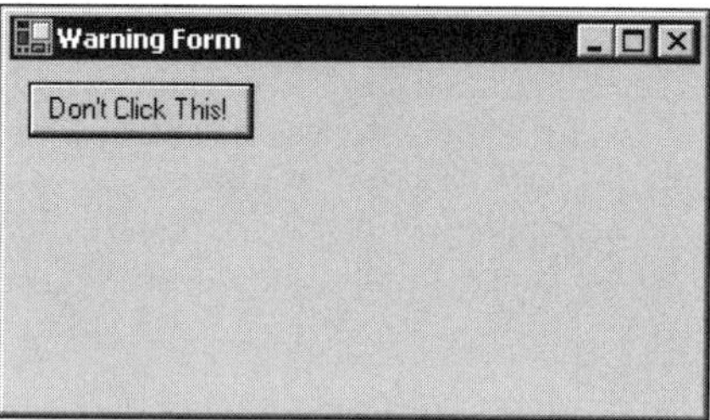

Of course, we know what users are like. Someone's going to want to click the button anyway. If they do, this is what happens:

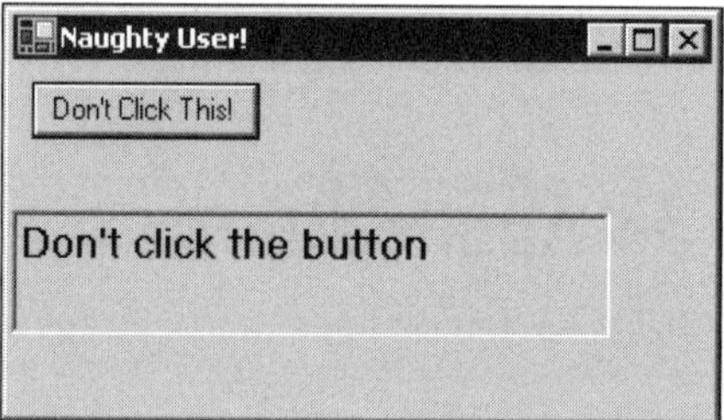

Notice that the caption of the form has changed and, more importantly, that a new control, a read only textbox has appeared on the form. If the user decides to click the button again, the textbox is removed, and a new readonly textbox with a more severe caption appears.

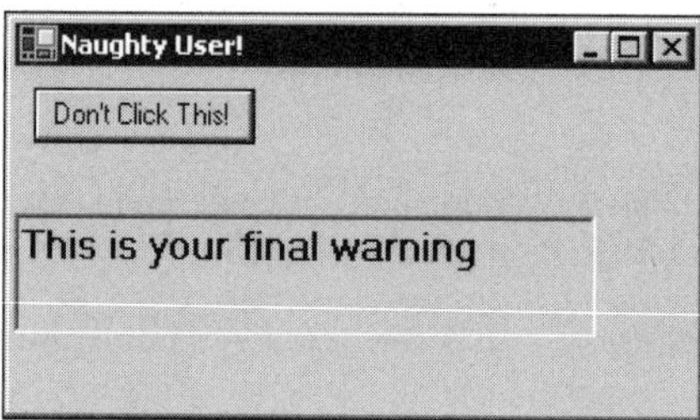

In fact this final stage could be achieved by merely changing the text in the existing textbox, but we've opted for destroying the original textbox and creating a new one in order to illustrate dynamic creation and removal of controls.

Working through the operation of WroxWarnings tells us where the dynamic creation of controls comes in. What about the inheritance and cross-language interoperability? Well they come in through the read only textboxes. Instead of using an ordinary textbox, we've chosen to derive a class from `TextBox`. We will write a derived class, called `WarningBox`, which automatically sets up the font to be displayed for our warnings as well as the fact that the `WarningBox` is read only. We will further derive a class, `SuperWarningBox`, from `WarningBox`, which automatically sets the text to This is your final warning.

And the cross-language interoperability? `WarningBox` is written in VB, `SuperWarningBox` is in C#, and the main form is also in C#.

Since this will be an application consisting of several projects, it's best to create a Visual Studio.NET project with a separate directory for the solution. We'll create the project that holds the `WarningBox` first, a VB Windows control library project, with a solution called `Warnings`.

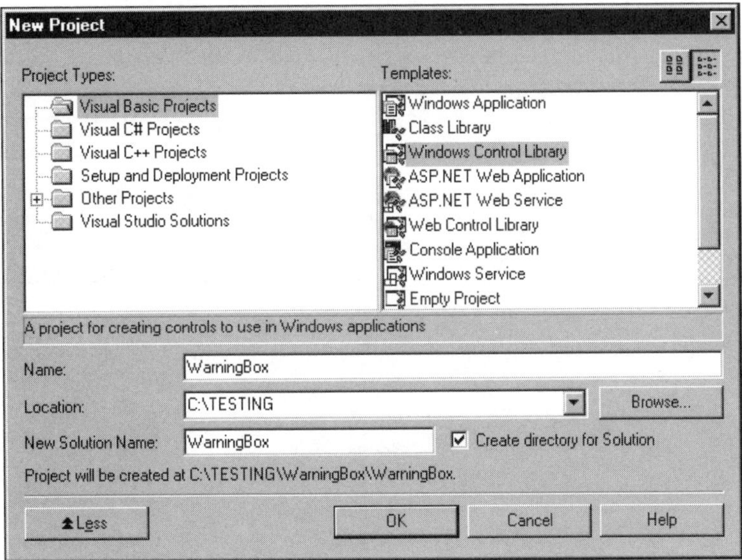

Remember that a Windows Control library contains only the definitions of classes intended to be used in other projects. It won't contain a program entry point.

We will simply take the code that Visual Studio.NET has generated for us and modify it so that `WarningBox` is derived from `TextBox` (by default it's derived from `UserControl`):

```
Public Class WarningBox
    Inherits System.Windows.Forms.TextBox

#Region " Windows Form Designer generated code "

    Public Sub New()
        MyBase.New()

        'This call is required by the Windows Form Designer.
        InitializeComponent()
```

```
        'Add any initialization after the InitializeComponent() call
        Me.Multiline = True
        Me.ReadOnly = True
        Me.Font = New Font("Arial", 12, FontStyle.Bold)

    End Sub
```

With these changes, a `WarningBox` now quite literally is a `TextBox` except that when it is created, it automatically sets itself up to be `Multiline`, `ReadOnly` and to have a large (12pt), bold font suitable for displaying warnings to naughty users!

We have one more change to make. Visual Studio will have given us a default namespace of `WarningBox`. We will change this to a more appropriate namespace name (and to the same namespace as we will be using for the rest of this application):

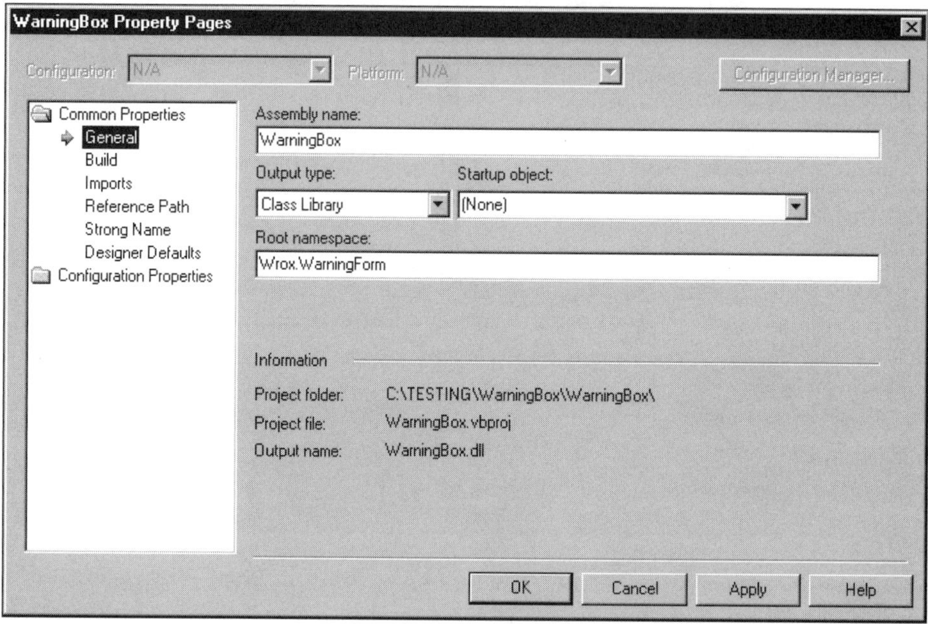

Now let's look at the next derived class, `SuperWarningBox`. This time we'll create a C# class library rather than a C# Windows control library. It doesn't really matter which we choose, since both project types compile to a class library – the only difference is that for a windows control library, Visual Studio.NET writes a bit more code for us.

We create the `SuperWarningBox` project, making sure the project gets added to the current solution rather than having a new solution created, and we modify the code generated as follows.

```
using System;

namespace WarningForm
{
    public class SuperWarningBox : WarningBox
    {
```

```
        public SuperWarningBox()
        {
            this.Text = "This is your final warning";
        }
    }
}
```

This really is two languages working together – we have just derived a class written in C# from a class written in VB.NET. Now, if we instantiate an object of type `SuperWarningBox`, it will be for all practical purposes an ordinary text box, except that its text will be automatically initialized to This is your final warning in the constructor. Note that, as usual for derived classes, the base class constructor will also be executed automatically, so that the `SuperWarningBox` will also be `ReadOnly`, `Multiline` and have a font of bold Ariel 12pt.

We've now created our classes that we need to use. It simply remains to write the main form for the application, which, as remarked, we will do in C#. So we create a new C# Windows Application project in the `Warnings` solution. This time we will call it `WarningForm`. We will add the button to the project using the toolbox, and double-click on the button in the Visual Studio.NET design view to get an `OnClick` event handler added to it. Then we make the following modifications to the Visual Studio.NET generated code.

First we add a member field to the `Form1` class, which will hold a reference to each textbox as it is dynamically created:

```
namespace WarningForm
{
    /// <summary>
    /// Summary description for Form1.
    /// </summary>
    public class Form1 : System.Windows.Forms.Form
    {
        WarningBox dontClickPanel = null;
        private System.Windows.Forms.Button button1;
        /// <summary>
        /// Required designer variable.
        /// </summary>
        private System.ComponentModel.Container components = null;
```

Note that we are adding this code manually, not using the design view. It would be possible to add a `WarningBox` with the design view – we would simply need to add our new `WarningBox` control to the Visual Studio.NET toolbox (by right-clicking on the toolbox and selecting Customize Toolbox from the context menu). However, doing so would generate code that adds the warning box to the form when the form is instantiated. That's not what we want – we only want the `WarningBox` to be instantiated dynamically after the button gets clicked. The design view can't do that for us – we need to write the code to do that by hand.

Now we have our member field, we'll modify the code for the button's `OnClick` event to create the `WarningBox`:

```
private void button1_Click(object sender, System.EventArgs e)
{
    this.Text = "Naughty User!";
```

```
    if (dontClickPanel == null)
    {
       dontClickPanel = new WarningBox();
       dontClickPanel.Text = @"Don't click the button";
       dontClickPanel.Parent = this;
       dontClickPanel.Location = new Point(0,60);
       dontClickPanel.Size = new Size(250,50);
       Controls.Add(dontClickPanel);
       dontClickPanel.Show();
    }
    else
    {
       Controls.Remove(dontClickPanel);
       dontClickPanel.Hide();
       dontClickPanel.Dispose();
       dontClickPanel = new SuperWarningBox();
       dontClickPanel.Parent = this;
       dontClickPanel.Location = new Point(0,60);
       dontClickPanel.Size = new Size(250,50);
       Controls.Add(dontClickPanel);
       dontClickPanel.Show();
    }
}
```

When the user clicks the button, the first thing we do is change the main caption of the form to Naughty User!. Then we examine the `dontClickPanel` field. Since the next thing we will do is set this reference to refer to a new `WarningBox` object, we know that this field is `null` if and only if the user had not clicked the button before. If that's the case, then we instantiate the new `WarningBox`, set its text, location and size and make it visible by calling its `Show` method, which is inherited from `System.Windows.Forms.Control`. We also make sure the `Parent` property of the control is correctly set, and that the control has been added to the form's `ControlsCollection`.

If the user has previously clicked the button, then `dontClickPanel` will refer to the previously created `WarningBox`. Hence we need to destroy this box before we instantiate a new one. After removing it from the form's `ControlsCollection` we call its `Hide` method (inherited from Control) to make the control invisible before destroying it by calling its `Dispose` method. Then we create the new control – in this case a `SuperWarningBox`, which means we don't have to explicitly set its `Text` property because that is set in the `SuperWarningBox` constructor. Setting the `dontClickPanel` reference to refer to a `SuperWarningBox` instance is fine because of the rule that in both C# and VB.NET, a reference variable is allowed to refer to derived class instances.

Notice that in this code, if the user clicks the button a third or fourth time, the `SuperWarningBox` instance will be destroyed and another one created each time. That's not really very efficient but we won't worry about that here because the purpose of the sample is to demonstrate dynamic creation of controls and cross-language inheritance.

Before we finish, we'll make one more change to the `Form1` constructor – just to explicitly illustrate setting the startup position of a form:

```
public Form1()
{
    //
    // Required for Windows Form Designer support
```

```
        //
        InitializeComponent();

        this.StartPosition = FormStartPosition.Manual;
        this.DesktopLocation = new Point(200,300);
    }
```

The solution is almost ready to compile. However, we need to ensure that the project references are set up correctly. The `WarningForm` project needs to reference both the other projects – as usual we set this up in the project references dialog.

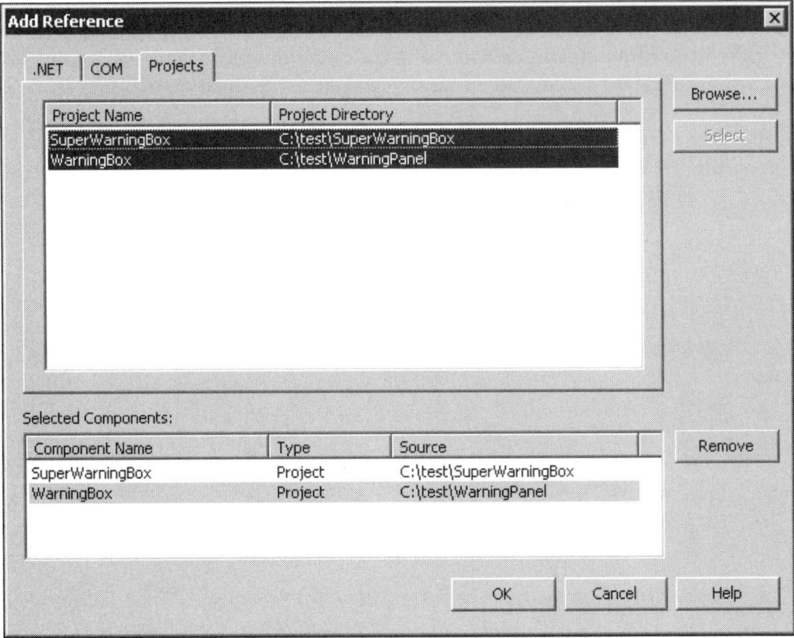

Similarly, the `SuperWarningBox` project needs to refer to `WarningBox`.

Before leaving this sample, we should emphasize that it doesn't really represent a very realistic use of inheritance. In practice, we would probably not write a derived class just to set up a couple of properties in the constructor of a control. For the particular case of the Wrox`Warnings` sample, it would be a good deal easier to just use plain `textbox`es throughout, and set the relevant `TextBox` properties from the `Form1.button1_Click` method. However, if we want to very significantly customize how a control behaves, for example by setting properties, and adding some new methods or adding some event handlers, and want to be able to reuse the customized control then inheritance is a good way to achieve this.

A good example might be if we have one or several applications that require a `TreeView` control that is used to browse the folder system on the local computer. Then the easiest way to do this would be to derive a class from `TreeView`, in which we add methods to add nodes that specifically represent file system folders.

There are several examples that illustrate how to use inheritance of controls in a realistic situation in the WebMate web developer environment case study later in the book.

Summary

This chapter has introduced us to what a Windows Form is and how to create one. For the most part, when we start a Visual Studio.NET application, there is a default form created for us, and we can customize this form to suit our own needs and reflect what our application is designed to do.

We also looked at some elements of Windows Forms such as menu bars and context menus.
We also discussed some form manipulation using the location property to locate the form on the user's screen or desktop as well as looking at some code for resizing forms. Both procedures are important to understand to gain the best use of forms when dealing with various screen resolutions.

The chapter finished up with a look at an example that we called WroxWarnings. This enabled us to drill down a little further into creating a control at runtime, inheriting controls, a quick example of cross-language interoperability, and also customizing the startup position of a form.

With this introductory information, we can now create basic forms with menu bars and context menus and adjust the sizing, location and borders to suite the form's needs.

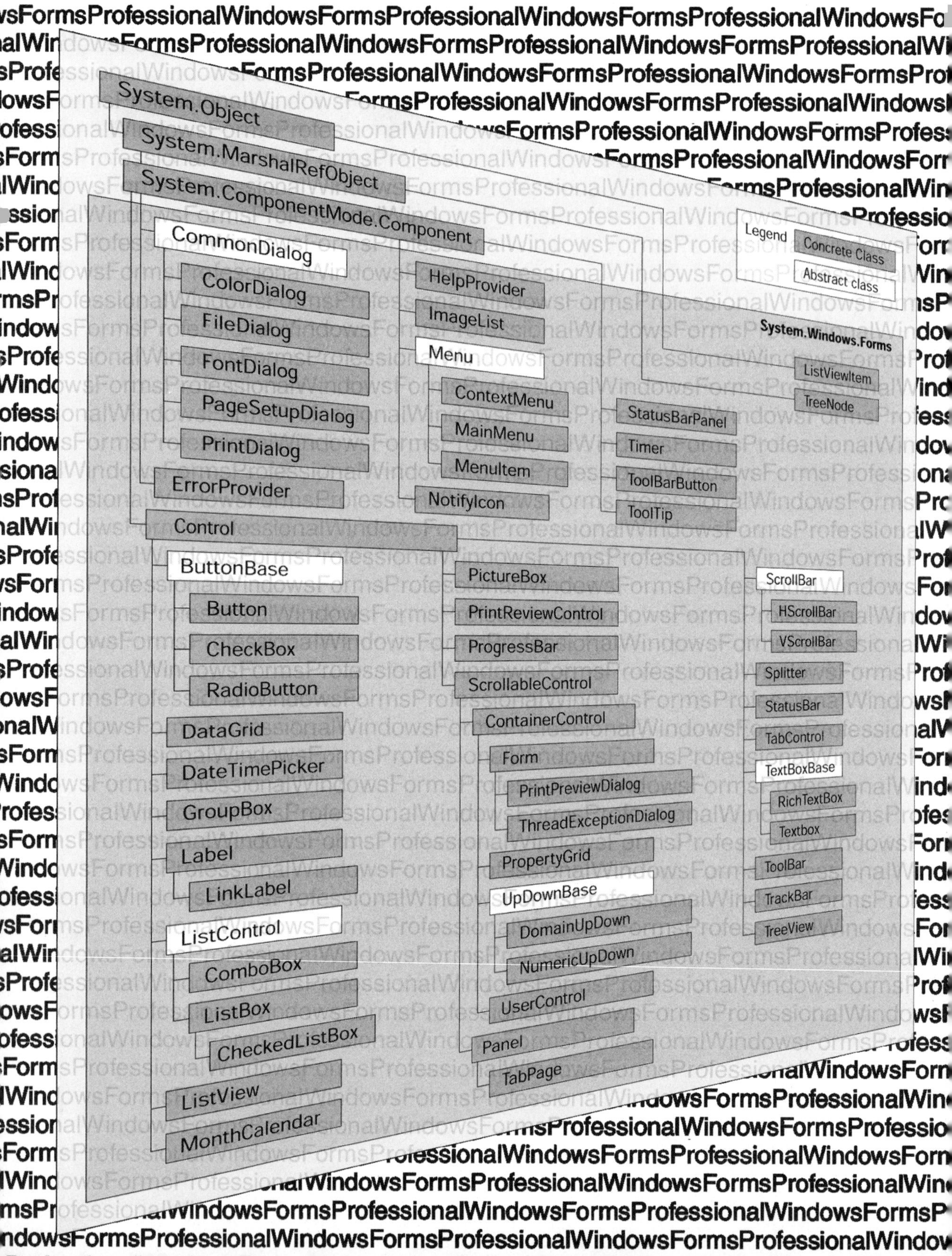
System.Object
System.MarshalRefObject
System.ComponentMode.Component
CommonDialog
ColorDialog
FileDialog
FontDialog
PageSetupDialog
PrintDialog
ErrorProvider
HelpProvider
ImageList
Menu
ContextMenu
MainMenu
MenuItem
NotifyIcon
StatusBarPanel
Timer
ToolBarButton
ToolTip
Legend
Concrete Class
Abstract class
System.Windows.Forms
ListViewItem
TreeNode
Control
ButtonBase
Button
CheckBox
RadioButton
DataGrid
DateTimePicker
GroupBox
Label
LinkLabel
ListControl
ComboBox
ListBox
CheckedListBox
ListView
MonthCalendar
PictureBox
PrintReviewControl
ProgressBar
ScrollableControl
ContainerControl
Form
PrintPreviewDialog
ThreadExceptionDialog
PropertyGrid
UpDownBase
DomainUpDown
NumericUpDown
UserControl
Panel
TabPage
ScrollBar
HScrollBar
VScrollBar
Splitter
StatusBar
TabControl
TextBoxBase
RichTextBox
Textbox
ToolBar
TrackBar
TreeView

5

Windows Forms and Interface Design

In the last chapter we were introduced to our first Windows Form. Now that we know how to create one, and what we might use it for, we can begin to look at some of the more complicated aspects of putting it to use. However, before we dive into more complicated topics like events and data, let's consider how the design and implementation of Windows Forms can influence how we interact with our applications – this is an area of investigation that's referred to as **Human Computer Interaction** (HCI).

Human Computer Interaction is a very large topic, so we shall concentrate specifically on the role played by Windows Forms in HCI as a whole. It's fairly obvious that any good user interface should fulfill certain basic requirements:

- Accurately reflect the functionality of the application.
- Make it as easy and logical as possible for the end user to go about his or her business.

To start off with, we will talk about the philosophies and theories behind how one goes about making a good User Interface (UI). We will then concentrate on how Windows Forms supports these philosophies implicitly with the aid of good Interface programming. Specifically, we will:

- Discuss theoretical concepts of interface design.
- Discuss practical concepts of user interface design.

Following on from this, we will then look at the three main windows styles, namely Single Document Interfaces (SDI), Multiple Document Interfaces (MDI), and Explorer Style windows, and demonstrate how they support good design (code in this chapter is presented in VB.NET). Also, we will see how to create modal and modeless forms to help control the 'flow' of an application. Some of these demonstrations will add their functionality to the `WroxEdit` application that we began in the previous chapter.

Finally, we will have a quick run through of some of the more common controls, pointing out when and where we should use them.

Designing a User Interface

Visual programming languages, for example Visual Basic have become popular because they provide an easy way to design graphical user interfaces (GUIs) and write applications, without having to understand the internals of Windows. Dragging and dropping controls onto the form, and running it, allows us to quickly prototype an application.

Programmers and designers have spent years designing screens and fine-tuning user interfaces. As long as human beings continue to use software applications, user interfaces will always play a critical role in the acceptance of the product.

In this section we will briefly discuss the theoretical points that must be addressed to achieve successful acceptance of the software by the user. The following points should be considered before designing GUIs:

- **Users' skill set**: What experience do they have with Windows (or with computers in general)? Will they prefer to use a mouse or a keyboard? Are they beginners, intermediate users, or advanced users? Are they data entry workers, or business analysts?
- **Expectation of the system**: Is the system intended for beginners or advanced users? Does the system have wizards to guide data entry? Is it expected to have a context-sensitive help system? Is the system expected to provide role based security?
- **Criteria for user acceptance of the application**: What response time is sufficient? What is the availability requirement? Does it address all business functionality?

Once we know the answers to these questions, we need to create a *usable* product. To help us establish exactly what we mean by 'a usable product', let's break 'usability' up into four categories – learnability, effectiveness, flexibility, and robustness – and look at each of these in the context of user interface design.

Learnability

This criterion considers how easy a typical user will find it to learn how to use an interface. Each of the following considerations plays a part in the interface's overall learnability:

- **Predictability**: This refers to the predictability of the software's visual appearance. For example, if the application is designed with forms that follow a standard look and feel, then the users will know how to use the forms consistently. If the application is designed with context menus, the users should be able to predict that a pull-down menu will appear when they right-click on an item. They should be able to predict that the Close button, for example, will appear at the bottom of the form and will close the form when clicked.
- **Consistency**: If users know that the similar objects on the screen have similar meanings, and similar commands will always have a similar effect, they will feel more confident in using the system and will explore the software's features. For example, to make a system consistent, the designer should use consistent terminology for naming captions of labels and forms, and use consistent abbreviations (such as St for State, Zip for Zip Code). Icons should be used to aid in the layout of interfaces to help achieve consistency.

- **Familiarity**: The user interface should be simplified as much as possible, and should be matched with user needs. This should ensure that beginners can learn the system's functionality quickly and easily, and expert users can work extremely rapidly to carry out the tasks and define new features and functions. To make the system familiar to the users, terminology, abbreviations, format and layout of fonts, and display on screen should relate to the user's experience in the real world. For example, if our interface shows a percentage figure that indicates the profit and our users are used to calling it Net Profit, we should use the words 'Net Profit' in the caption of the label. This will help the users recognize it as it relates to their daily business and helps to avoid confusion. Controls should also be intuitive.

  Users should not have to remember the commands, objects, or actions. The interface should provide context sensitive menus and actions that users can choose from, and provide shortcut keys to execute the commands quickly. Wizards should be made available to help complete the frequently performed tasks and to lighten the complexity of data entry.

- **Aesthetics**: Important features for aesthetic layout of interfaces are a sense of balance, regularly spaced and aligned elements, symmetry, predictable patterns, economy of styles, colors, and techniques, sequential arrangement of elements to guide the eye, unity of related ideas, a sense of proportion, simplicity, and grouping related elements together. If several pieces of information need to be displayed and screen space is a premium, then break them and group them using a tab control. Use color judiciously to attract the user's attention.

- **User guide**: A user guide, or help documentation, is very useful. A full-featured user guide should be provided whenever possible. If not, a list of Frequently Asked Questions (FAQs) should be included along with the software. Alternatively, the software could provide a link to a web site that has the user documentation or FAQs.

Effectiveness

This indicates how much the user interface matches the user's needs in terms of reliability, validity, and compatibility. It can be broken down as follows:

- **Reliability**: This refers to the behavior of the system. For example, the same kind of warning/informational messages should be presented to the user for the same kind of actions.

- **Validity**: The user interface must meet all functional, behavioral, and performance requirements. Invalid input should be prevented and reported to the user immediately, using methods such as warning, or error message, dialogs.

- **Compatibility**: The system is suitable for any category of users, and matches with user skills. The user interface should be accessible to users with disabilities. The user interface must provide a good mapping between the business jargon and the programming model.

Flexibility

This refers to the various ways in which the user could interact with the software, as follows:

- **Fixed Response** or **Free Response**: Fixed response means that users are constrained in the response they can make, such as selecting items from a drop-down menu instead of typing input, or selecting only one option from a radio-button group. Free response means the user is less constrained with the interface and can supply different inputs.

- **Granularity**: The interface should permit the user to do various tasks on different levels. The granularity of the application can be explained in terms of depth (fine) and breadth (coarse) of the system – for example, the depth and breadth of the menus. The menu hierarchy should not have too many deep levels (fine), because the users may get lost while navigating through them. However, if the choice of menus is wide (coarse), the users may end up choosing the incorrect menu item. Therefore, it is important to decide upfront how fine or coarse the user interface should be.

Robustness

Robustness applies to the fact that the operating system must be able to protect itself from deliberate or accidental damage, either from internal or external sources, and also be predictable in its responses to such errors. Robustness can be described in terms of Visibility, Recoverability, Responsiveness, and Feedback.

- **Visibility**: The system should provide visual cues to the user about its state. For example, when the user is transferring information, a progress bar should show the progress of the task and the time remaining to complete it. Those who have downloaded data from the Internet will be familiar with 'Downloading 10 minutes remaining' dialog boxes. In applications with a list view or grid, if a row is selected in a grid, that row should be highlighted for reference. Hourglasses should be used to enhance visibility.
- **Recoverability**: The system should allow the user to recover from errors and take corrective action. A good example of this is the Undo/Redo feature in Microsoft Office. If the user tries to delete or exit without saving a file, the system should always inform the user. This usually takes the form of a query, such as 'Are you sure you want to delete this file?' or 'Do you want to save this file before exit?' This ensures that the user does not unintentionally lose important information. The following screenshot shows such a message box:

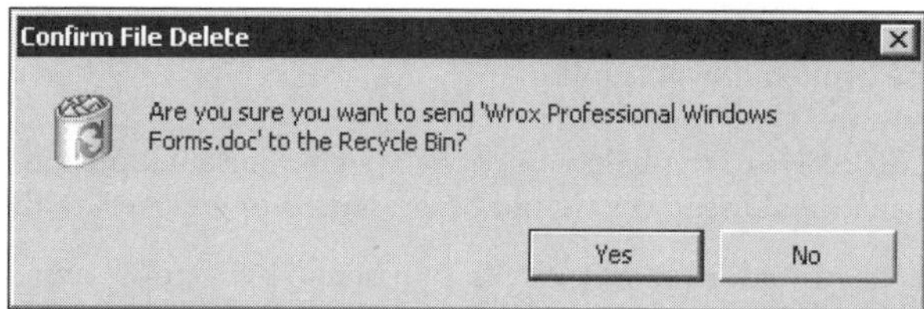

- **Responsiveness**: This refers to the time between the user action and the system response. In desktop applications, the system can respond to the user immediately. In distributed applications, because of network latency, the system cannot obtain an instantaneous response. In this case, the system must inform the user of the progress.
- **Feedback**: Proper feedback must be provided to the user by means of message boxes. For example, if a user encounters errors while using the application, feedback must be provided that is informative and helpful in taking corrective action. The following screenshot shows a totally inadequate feedback message box:

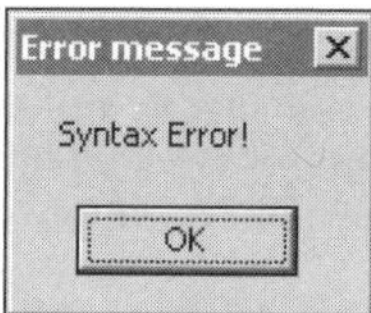

A much more useful feedback message box might look like this:

Each of the concepts mentioned above will have helped to influence the overall design of just about every user interface you are likely to encounter in day-to-day experience. While you may still consider many such UIs to be far from perfect, it's fairly safe to say they'd be a great deal worse had these theoretical issues not been taken into account.

So how can we apply these concepts to our own designs, and produce an interface that fulfils all the conditions detailed above? Let's answer this question by concentrating on some practical design methods.

Practical User Interface Design

Visual Studio.NET provides developers with a wide range of controls and tools that can be used to create a richly functional GUI. These controls can be dragged onto a Windows Form and configured with a few mouse clicks, so it's quite feasible to set out a fully functional form in a matter of minutes. While this certainly makes the mechanics of form building a lot easier, it doesn't guarantee that we'll end up with an *effective* user interface.

As ever, that requires a thorough understanding of what it is we're trying to achieve in any particular situation. Here are a few practical points that we should keep in mind when designing an application interface.

- **Standards**: Set standards for the appearance of a user interface and follow them consistently.

  For example: always use the same terms to describe the same things; decide what to name the program, what captions the windows will have, the captions the message boxes will have, and the names of files and file extensions created by the program; where possible, use terminology that will be familiar to end users.

- **Type of users**: Consider the different types of end users while designing a user interface.

  Can users be categorized as beginners, intermediate, or advanced users? Beginners will not have much experience in Windows, and features like right-clicking may be difficult for them to use. Intermediate users understand the standard Windows elements, including right-clicking and pulling down context menus and using toolbars. Advanced users may use the keyboard shortcuts more than others and concentrate more on the application than on the Windows interface.

  Depending on our user population, we should use appropriate features. Use menu bars, dialog boxes and wizards for beginners to help them understand the interface better. Since beginners tend to make errors in data entry, provide list boxes and combo boxes with pre-filled items. Use the `Monthview` control to accept dates so that users will not make mistakes in entering a date. For intermediate and advanced users, use status bars, toolbars, keyboard shortcuts, and context menus. The user interface should allow a user to transition from a beginner to an advanced user.

- **Prototype**: Prototypes help to envision how a finished product will look and function.

  A prototype will look just like the anticipated application interface, with File | Open and File | Exit menus. Other menu (and sub-menu) items will present appropriate forms when clicked on.

  Once designed, the prototype should be compiled, and an installation program should be created for it. Remember that the installation program has its own GUI, which should also be considered as part of the application's user interface. (The 'U' in GUI does not only refer to users of the application, but also to the users of the installation program, who will expect an easy-to-understand GUI providing different installation options.

- **User-centered design**: Adopt a user-centered design approach from the outset.

  An application's UI will ultimately dictate the comfort level of the people using it – that is, if we have an easy-to-use, consistent, reliable UI, users are going to find it easier to use and so be more comfortable in using it; the opposite also applies. We therefore need to talk to those people and get feedback from them about preliminary designs. Ideally, create a prototype of the interface, let them try it out, and take their comments into account when refining the design.

Having discussed some practical points to consider while designing user interfaces, let us now see how to create the most commonly used interface styles, namely SDI, MDI, and Windows Explorer style applications. Of course, a key part of interface design is the ability to properly control 'how' an application receives input – to this end we shall also look at modal and modeless forms.

SDI Forms

Single Document Interface (SDI) applications are appropriate to use when it makes sense to have only one document open in each instance of the application. Notepad is one familiar example of an SDI application – any instance of Notepad can only hold one text document at a time. To open a new document, we either have to close the current one, or start up a new instance of Notepad. A screenshot of the notepad SDI application is shown below.

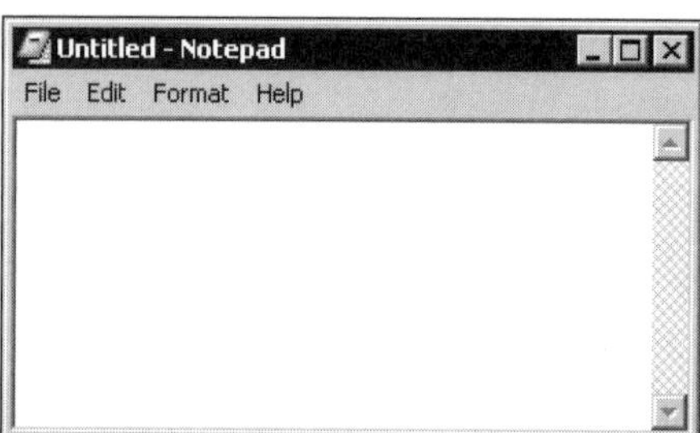

SDI applications can have menus, toolbars, and dialog boxes that can all be opened from menu items. Note that, although they work with single documents, they may consist of several separate forms. However, any functionality those forms expose can still only be applied to the single document currently loaded.

> *If you're building a multiple forms application in VS.NET, remember that you'll need to specify an appropriate startup form in the Project Properties menu.*

Any forms added to a Windows Forms application have a default `IsMDIContainer` property that is set to `False`. If a form has this property set to `True`, it will let us load more than one document at a time.

MDI Forms

Multiple Document Interfaces are appropriate when several documents need to open at the same time. Classic examples of MDI are Microsoft Word and Excel. In these applications, you can have several word or spreadsheet documents open, and are able to cut and paste content from one document to the other.

Within .NET, we can create and use MDI applications by setting the appropriate properties on the forms in our application. This section of the chapter will look at how to create MDI forms, how to create MDI child forms, how to determine which child form is the active form, and how to arrange child forms.

MDI Parent Forms

An MDI application typically has one MDI parent form. The MDI parent form will become the container for the other forms in an MDI application. As with most things in VB.NET, we can create the MDI parent forms in the designer or in code, but, as you will see, there is very little to do in order to make an MDI document, so we will only show the designer method.

Open up a new VB.NET project in the IDE to work with and call it `MDISample`. When the project opens up in the IDE, select the default form and locate the `IsMdiContainer` property in the properties window. Change the value to `True`. Notice that the background changes to a dark gray color.

> *Unlike in VB 6.0 and earlier, there is no indication in the Solution Explorer window that the form is an MDI form.*

It is recommended, but not necessary, to set the `WindowState` property to `Maximize` for this form. The reason behind this recommendation is that it makes it easier to work with the child windows when the parent form has as much real estate as possible.

For any MDI application we will need a menu option to allow us to switch between the open documents. For this reason, we shall create a menu structure for our little MDI program. Drag a `MainMenu` control onto the form and create the following menu structure:

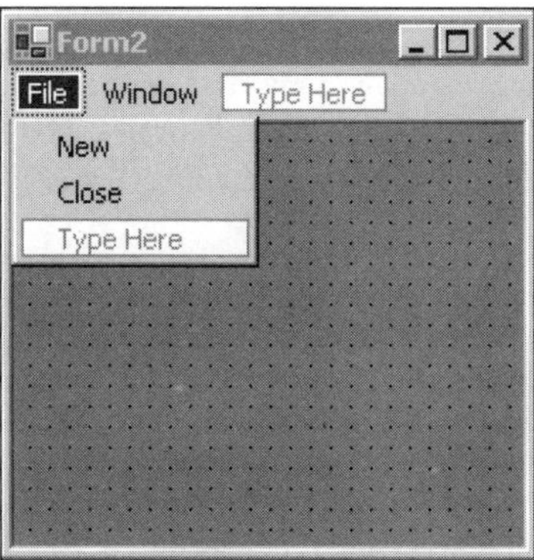

This will provide us with a way to open and close child windows as well as switch between open ones. In order to provide the ability to switch between the open child windows, VB.NET adds a new property to a menu that is known as `MDIList`. This is a Boolean value and when set to `True`, will cause the menu to act as a list for the open child windows. Set the Window menus `MDIList` property to `True`. That is essentially all there is to creating an MDI form using the designer interface.

MDI Child Forms

Once we have created an MDI parent form, we must create at least one MDI child form. We use the child forms to create the interface for our users to interact with. Creating child forms is also a relatively easy task to accomplish.

The first thing we need to do is to add a form to our project. For our purposes we are going to add a simple form to the project and add a `RichTextBox` control to the form. Set the `Anchor` property of the control to all sides, set the `dock` property to `Fill`, and remove the default text from the `Text` property.

Once the form has been created, add the following code in `Form1` to the **File | New** menu click event by double-clicking on that menu item in the designer.

```
Dim NewMDIChildForm As New Form2()
    NewMDIChildForm.MdiParent = Me
    NewMDIChildForm.Show()
```

The first line of code should be familiar by now – we are simply creating a new form object to hold a reference to the form, `Form2`, which we just created. The second line of code tells the form that it is an MDI parent form. Setting the `MdiParent` property to the name of a parent form (in this case, `Me` indicates the MDI form we created because we are calling it from a menu click on that form), will tell the child form that it is a child form and which form is the parent. The last line of code simply shows the form.

Run the program and click the **File | New** menu choice to add the new Child form to our MDI form. Maximize and minimize the child form to see its behavior within the MDI environment.

We can also create menus on the child forms that provide the functionality required for that form. We could, for example, create an **Edit** menu on the form that will contain the necessary **Cut**, **Copy**, and **Paste**. When we open the form in the MDI parent form, the child forms menu will become a part of the MDI form's menu structure.

Arranging Child Forms

When we have multiple child windows open in an MDI application, we should ensure that there are mechanisms in place to allow the user to arrange the forms for easier viewing within the parent form's window. By default, the MDI form will handle the 'minimize' and 'maximize' actions for us, so we don't have to write code to deal with that.

The two most common and well-known styles for arranging windows and MDI child forms are the **Cascade** and **Tile** options. There are methods available in VB.NET that allow us to set these arrangement styles for our MDI applications. Let's take a look at these methods now.

Add a **Cascade** and a **Tile** option to the **Window** menu. Under the **Tile** menu, create two separate submenu items that display **Horizontal** and **Vertical**. This will allow the user to tile the windows in the MDI form horizontally or vertically. Once the menu structure has been created, add the following code to the click events of the `Cascade` and `Tile` | `Horizontal` and `Vertical` menu items.

```
Private Sub mnuWindowCascade_Click(ByVal sender As System.Object, _
        ByVal e As System.EventArgs) Handles mnuWindowCascade.Click

        Me.LayoutMdi(System.Windows.Forms.MdiLayout.Cascade)
```

```
End Sub

Private Sub mnuWindowTileHorizontal_Click(ByVal sender As Object, _
        ByVal e As System.EventArgs) Handles mnuWindowTileHorizontal.Click

        Me.LayoutMdi(System.Windows.Forms.MdiLayout.TileHorizontal)

End Sub

Private Sub mnuWindowTileVertical_Click(ByVal sender As Object, _
        ByVal e As System.EventArgs) Handles mnuWindowTileVertical.Click

        Me.LayoutMdi(System.Windows.Forms.MdiLayout.TileVertical)

End Sub
```

This code provides the necessary functionality to cascade or tile the child windows within the MDI form. Note that the cascade and tile methods are members of the `System.Windows.Forms` namespace. Run the application, open multiple new windows in the MDI form, and see what each setting does to the windows.

Explorer Style Interfaces

You have already seen the Windows Explorer, as most of you use it on a daily basis. .NET allows you to create these interface styles as well. There are many uses for Explorer style interfaces in applications, such as FTP applications for downloading files from FTP servers or even using another interface design, such as the Outlook style interface or a customization dialog form for an application. You will see how to create the customization interface in this section using our `WroxEdit` application.

To start off, open the `WroxEdit` app you have been working with and add a Windows form to the project. Name the form `frmCustomize` and give it a caption of Customize WroxEdit. Follow the steps outlined below to add the necessary controls to the form.

- Add a `TreeView` control to the form and set its `Dock` property to `Left`.
- Add a `Splitter` control to the form. It will automatically dock itself to the `TreeView` control.
- Add a `ListView` control to the form and set its `Dock` property to `Full`.
- Add a couple of buttons, one with `Text` property set to `OK` and one with `Cancel`. You should have a form that looks like that shown here.

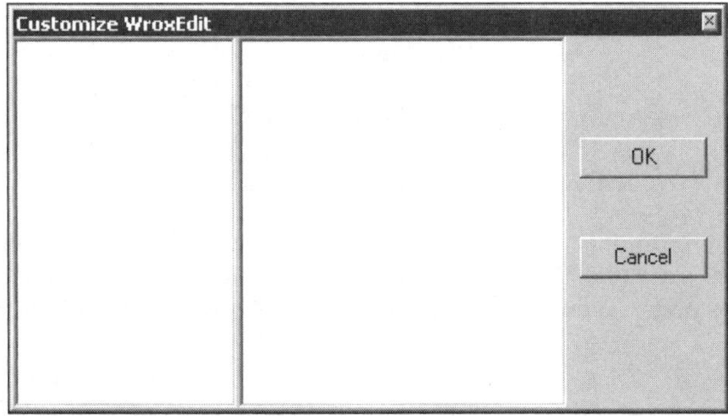

You need to set a few properties of the `ListView` control to get it to behave the way we want. Set the `Alignment` property to `Left` to align the entries along the left edge of the `ListView` control and set the `View` property to `List`. The default alignment is `Top`, which displays your entries such as the following. We prefer to have the list displayed in one column along the left of the control.

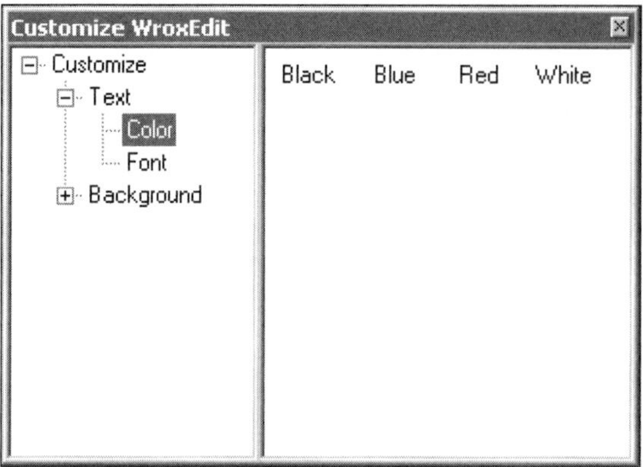

Once you have the necessary controls added, you can begin to add the nodes to the `Treeview` control. To add the nodes, select the `TreeView` control on the form and locate the `Nodes` property in the Properties window. Click the ellipsis button to open the TreeNode Editor dialog box, as shown here.

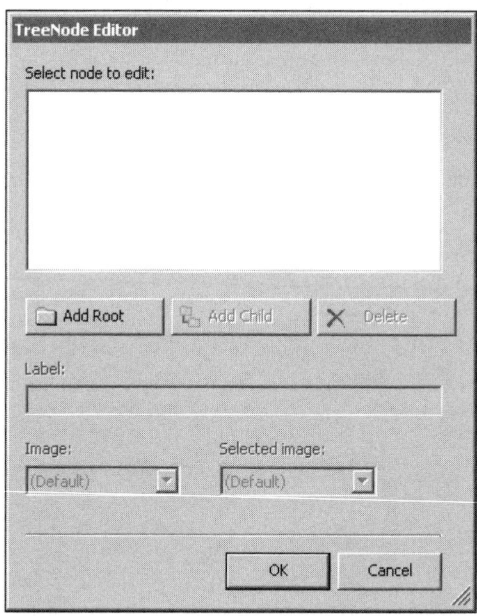

We first need to add a root node, so click the Add Root button and change the label to Customize. This creates a root node for our `TreeView` control. With the root node still selected, click the Add Child two times to add two child nodes: name the first child node Text and the second child node Background.

After you have each child node added and named, select the Text node and add two child nodes to it titled Color and Font. Add one child node to the Background node and call it bgColor. Your nodes should look like the following.

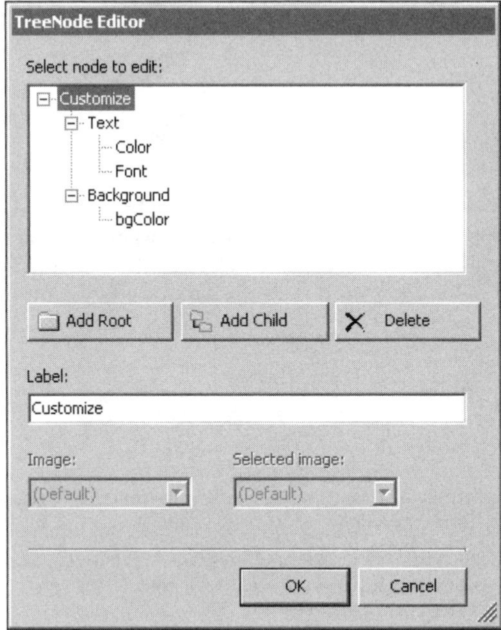

This will form the basis of our Explorer style interface for customizing the text color and font, as well as the background color of the text box control. These values will be written to the registry so that the application can read them on start up and use those values as defaults for new documents until you change them.

The final thing to do is to add an `ImageList` control to the `frmCustomize` form to hold the images that we will use for the `ListView` and `Treeview` controls. Add the `ImageList` and add the following icons, which can be found in the Program Files\Microsoft Visual Studio.Net\Common7 folder. All icons are located in the Writing sub-directory and the wrench icon is located in the Industry subfolder.

- `Font01.ico`
- `Note07.ico`
- `Note08.ico`
- `Pens03.ico`
- `Pencil06.ico`

- ❑ `Pencil07.ico`
- ❑ `Pencil08.ico`
- ❑ `Pencil09.ico`
- ❑ `Wrench.ico`

You can place these in any order that you want in the image list, as VB.NET will allow you to choose the images graphically in the IDE. That is what you will do when you add the images to the `TreeView` control. You can do that now by selecting the `TreeView` control and then choosing the `ImageList` that you added the images to for the control's `ImageList` property. You can also set the `ListView` control to use the same image list.

Enter the following code in the `frmCustomize` class.

```
Imports Microsoft.Win32
```

This `Imports` statement is required to use the registry functions that write our values to the registry.

```
Private Sub TreeView1_AfterSelect(ByVal sender As System.Object,_
        ByVal e As System.Windows.Forms.TreeViewEventArgs) _
        Handles TreeView1.AfterSelect

   If e.Node.Text = 'Color' Then

      With ListView1
         .Clear()
         .Items.Add('Black')
         .Items.Add('Blue')
         .Items.Add('Red')
         .Items.Add('White')
      End With

   ElseIf e.Node.Text = 'Font' Then

      With ListView1
         .Clear()
         .Items.Add('Arial')
         .Items.Add('Times New Roman')
         .Items.Add('Courier New')
      End With

   ElseIf e.Node.Text = 'bgColor' Then

      With ListView1
         .Clear()
         .Items.Add('Black')
         .Items.Add('Blue')
         .Items.Add('Red')
         .Items.Add('White')
```

```
        End With

    End If

End Sub
```

The first subprocedure, `TreeView1_AfterSelect`, determines which node was clicked on the `TreeView` controls and then demonstrates dynamically adding nodes to the `ListView` control. It adds the colors for the text and background color options or font names for the text font selection.

```
Private Sub ListView1_Click(ByVal sender As Object, _
        ByVal e As System.EventArgs) Handles ListView1.Click

    Dim strTreeItem As String
    Dim strListItem As String
    strTreeItem = TreeView1.SelectedNode.Text

    Select Case strTreeItem

        Case "Color"
            strListItem = ListView1.FocusedItem.Text
            WriteValues("Text", "Color", strListItem)

        Case "Font"
            strListItem = ListView1.FocusedItem.Text
            WriteValues("Text", "Font", strListItem)

        Case "bgColor"
            strListItem = ListView1.FocusedItem.Text
            WriteValues("Background", "bgColor", strListItem)


    End Select

End Sub
```

The second subprocedure, the `ListView1_Click` procedure, determines which entry was clicked and calls the `WriteValues` subprocedure with the necessary arguments to create the registry keys and write the values necessary.

```
Private Sub WriteValues(ByVal strSubKey, ByVal strValueKey, _
        ByVal strValue)

    ' Under normal circumstances, this code would
    ' be placed in an install routine to create the
    ' keys once. We are not using an install routine
    ' with this app so we have placed this code here.
    ' Writing to the registry multiple times with the
    ' same values only overwrites the old values with
    ' serious effects on performance on this app.

    Dim rk As RegistryKey = Registry.LocalMachine.OpenSubKey _
```

```
            ('Software\WroxEdit', True)

    Dim newKey As RegistryKey = rk.CreateSubKey(strSubKey)
    rk = Registry.LocalMachine.OpenSubKey('Software\WroxEdit\' + strSubKey, True)

    rk.SetValue(strValueKey, strValue)

End Sub
```

The Explorer style interface is becoming more popular as a means of creating user interfaces for applications. This is a small example that illustrates the use of the common controls that are used in creating an Explorer style interface. You can use other controls in various ways to create Outlook-style interfaces that resemble the Explorer interface.

Modal Forms

One of the nicest features for a programmer, and yet sometimes the most aggravating for users, is the modal form. It is a great way to get the user to respond to the needs of the application without allowing them to wander off to do something else. Some users find modal forms extremely annoying. However, developers know that modal forms are a necessary evil and we will learn how to unleash that 'evil' in this section.

Why Modal?

A modal form is used to force the user to make a selection, or perform a particular action before moving on in the application. This is useful for ensuring that a response is given to a query or that the application is placed into a certain state before the user continues to use it (such as pressing an OK button before being able to move on).

While message boxes called using the `MessageBox.Show` method are modal by design, they are generated by the system and can be thought of as modal dialogs and not modal forms. We can design our own forms and display them modally as discussed in the following section.

Create a Modal Form

In order to see how modal forms work, we will create one here and use it as a learning aid. For our purposes, we will create an 'About' form for our `WroxEdit` application that we created in Chapter 4. Open the `WroxEdit` application in Visual Studio.NET, and add a standard form to the project by choosing Add Windows Form from the Project menu. Add a `PictureBox`, three `Label` controls, a `ProgressBar`, and a `Button` to create the form seen here:

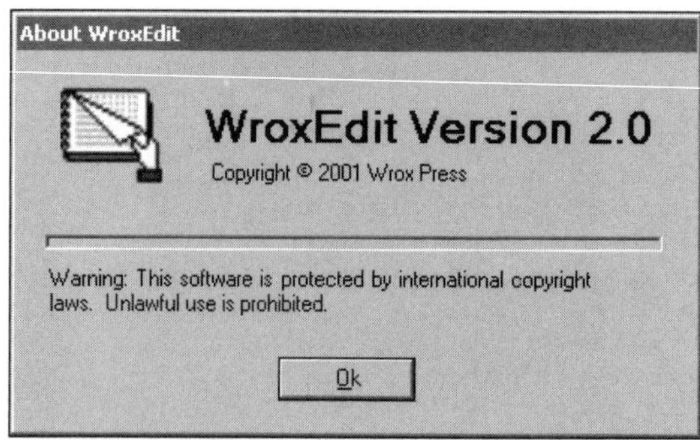

This is the form that we will use to demonstrate the use of modal forms, plus it will serve as a custom **About** form for our text editor application. Like most **About** forms used in Windows applications, this form will be shown in modal format requiring the user to close the form before continuing on.

Once we have created the form, we need to add some code to the command button to unload the form and allow the user to get back to using the program. Add this code here to the `Click` event for the command button, `cmdOk`:

```
Protected Sub cmdOk_Click(ByVal sender As Object, _
        ByVal e As System.EventArgs)Handles cmdOK_Click

   Me.Close()

End Sub
```

This code is simply responsible for closing the **About** form when the user clicks the **Ok** button. What makes this a modal form? Well, once that code is added, we need to create the procedure that will cause this form to display. The most popular place for an **About** box is, of course, under the **Help** menu. We have added the following code under the **Help** menu in the `WroxEdit` application.

```
Public Sub mnuHelpAbout_Click(ByVal sender As Object, ByVal e As System.EventArgs)
Handles mnuHelpAbout.Click

   Dim f As frmAbout = New frmAbout()
   f.ShowDialog()

End Sub
```

The only identifying factor that tells us this is a modal form call is the `showDialog` method of the form object.

> *Unlike in earlier versions of VB where we would call the form's* `show` *method and provide the constant* `vbModal`*, VB.NET does not utilize that. Instead we use the* `Showdialog` *method to display the form modally.*

In terms of application functionality, you should only use modal forms where absolutely necessary – that is, if the application state is of critical importance and an operation requires a user response before it can continue. It's best to avoid over-using modal forms in applications; not only can they be quite annoying if they pop up all over the place, but there may come a time when the system is expecting a response, no-one is there to provide an answer, so the system is left hanging, unable to continue.

Modeless Forms

Modeless forms allow the user to switch between forms within the application. They can either be minimized or left in their normal position before opening the other form. This is the opposite of the modal form that, as we saw earlier, does not allow the focus to be sent back to the previous window until the current window is closed.

Using Modeless Forms

Modeless forms are paramount to provide multitasking in a MDI application. In other words, the user can open several modeless forms, keep them minimized, and bring them up whenever they want. All the open forms appear in the Windows menu item.

In applications where extensive data entry is done, modeless forms will be very useful for the users to switch from one form to another. The Help Window, such as the one displayed in the Microsoft Office Suite of applications, is another example where the users can enter search criteria and move on to perform other tasks.

Create a Modeless Form

We will now create a form that will allow the user to enter a search phrase that would be used to search a help file for relevant information on our `WroxEdit` application. Obviously, the help files will need to be written for there to be any useful returned information, but that can be done later to add that functionality to the application. Our purpose here is to learn how to create and display a modeless form.

So, open the `WroxEdit` application, and add a Windows form to the project. We will set the properties to achieve the look we want next.

Property	Setting
`BackColor`	`255,255,192`
`FormBorderStyle`	`None`
`Location`	`X=575, Y=0`
`ShowInTaskbar`	`False`
`Size`	`232, 136`
`StartPosition`	`Manual`

By setting the properties as listed above, we make the form look like that shown below:

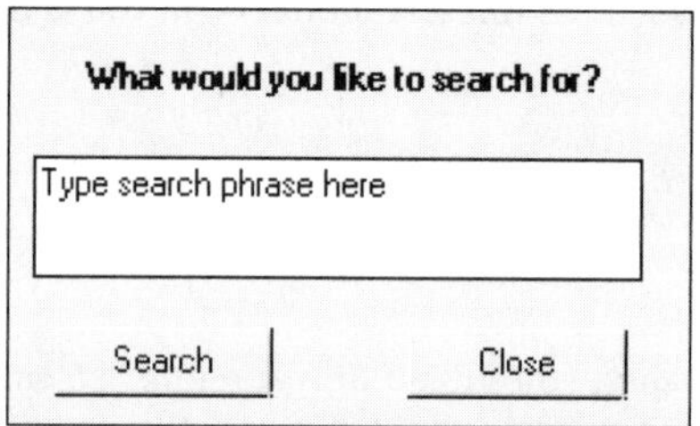

The remaining properties are left at their defaults. By setting the `StartPosition` to manual, we have the ability to locate the form where we want. Experimentation with setting the X and Y locations in code when the form opens to take account of the various screen resolutions is possible, but for our purposes here, we are using a screen resolution of 800X600. This places the form in the top right hand corner by setting the X to 575 and the Y to 0, provided we have set the form's size equal to that in the table.

Once we have created the form, we need to add the code necessary to display the form and to display it in modeless format. That code is shown here.

```
Public Sub mnuHelpSearch_Click(ByVal sender As Object, _
           ByVal e As System.EventArgs) Handles mnuHelpSearch.Click

   Dim frm As frmSearch = New frmSearch()
   frm.Show()

End Sub
```

The only thing to note about this code segment that is different from the modal example is how the form is displayed: the `Show` method is called to display the form in the modeless fashion.

> **If a form is displayed as modal, any code that follows the call to `ShowDialog` will not execute until the form is unloaded or closed. If the form is modeless, the code after the call to the `Show` method will continue to execute, even if the form is open.**

Form Elements

In this section we shall briefly talk about when and where to use controls in order to make an effective and useful interface. Some of the commonly used controls and dialog boxes will be discussed.

- **Buttons, Radio Buttons and CheckBox Buttons**
  A button is a component that the user pushes or clicks in order to trigger a particular action. Buttons come in several varieties, namely command buttons, check box buttons, and radio buttons. Command buttons are normally used for actions such as Save, Close, Yes, No etc,. while radio buttons are normally used where the user must select only one option from a list. Check boxes are used when there are several selections to be made about an item.

- **Text Box, List Box, Combo Box**
  Text boxes are specific areas in which the user can enter text or data. Text boxes are frequently used to ask the user to input some details such as a name, a password etc., as well as to enter numeric values, such as the price of an item.

  A list box contains a set of items from which the user can select one or more items. The user cannot specify any value that is not in the list. A scroll bar is used if the list is long, in order to allow the user to move up and down to view all items in the list. This control is used if the list of items is short, and we want all the items to be visible all the time.

  Combo boxes are used to specify a list of items, but they are hidden in a drop-down box. The user can pull the drop-down and select an item from the list. When the style of the combo box is a drop-down list, the user cannot specify an item that is not in the list. However, when the style is drop-down combo, an item can either be selected from the list, or the user can type an item in the edit box.

- **Message Box**
  Message boxes are used for advice, warning, feedback, or guidance, and don't take user input. They contain icons that indicate the nature of the message such as Critical, Information, Alert, etc.

- **Icons**
  In terms of forms, icons are pictures of objects that relate to a particular action or object. If the icons are intuitive, then users can recognize the object and learn the system quickly. Most applications now use common icons to denote particular tasks, in order to provide a familiar environment to the users. For example, a manila folder is used to denote a file, a trash bin to denote the file deletion action, a printer to denote the printing action, etc. Icons are normally found in toolbars but they can also be placed on buttons.

- **Menu Selection**
  Menus are designed to support ease of use and to eliminate the need to remember complex commands. The menus are constructed with a clear hierarchical structure of all functions or user tasks. Menus provide a number of items or choices, which should use familiar terminology. Users can use a keystroke or mouse click to select their options or items easily. Menus can be categorized and implemented in different ways. There are 'pull-down' menus, popup menus, palette menus, and style sheet menus. For 'pull-down' menus, all items of each group on a menu bar will be pulled down from a top level menu bar, and some items may have a submenu, which will appear at the side of the first menu. Popup menus will appear on the screen whenever an object with an associated menu is selected or clicked.

  The following must be kept in mind while designing menus:

  - Organize structure of items logically into groups, such as File, Edit, View, Tools, etc.
  - Use meaningful titles and familiar terminology for items and groups of items.
  - Keep first level menu item names brief and give longer names to second level menu items.

- **Tree View and List View**
  A tree view control is used to present data that is in a hierarchical form. A popular use of this control can be found in the Windows Explorer: the folder and subfolders system is arranged in a tree view. We can expand and contract a node that has a plus sign against it. If the data conforms to a parent-child format, then the tree view would be a good way to present it.

  The list view can be used in concert with a tree view, or it can be used independently. The list view typically shows the list of files in a folder that was selected in the tree view. The list view can show small icons or large icons, and it can be presented in a Report (or Detail) format with columns of information.

- **Printing**
  Printing should be considered part of the user interface. The standard Windows Print dialog contains several items for printing, such as Page Setup, Print Preview, and Printer Setup, which all play a role in the user interface of the application. Also think about providing the Print Preview feature so that the alignment of text within margins and the format of text can be verified before sending the page to the printer.

Summary

Throughout this chapter we've looked at various form techniques that allow us to add enhanced functionality to our applications. We began by reviewing some important theoretical and practical design aspects. Then we learned how to create SDI, MDI and Explorer style applications. Most of the Windows Forms applications will probably fall under these three categories. Then we saw how to create modal and modeless forms and discussed their use, and finally we discussed the features of some of the commonly used controls.

This information should provide a good solid understanding of User Interface Design techniques that developers can apply to all Windows Forms-based .NET applications.

System.Object
System.MarshalRefObject
System.ComponentMode.Component
Legend
Concrete Class
Abstract class
System.Windows.Forms
CommonDialog
ColorDialog
FileDialog
FontDialog
PageSetupDialog
PrintDialog
ErrorProvider
HelpProvider
ImageList
Menu
ContextMenu
MainMenu
MenuItem
NotifyIcon
StatusBarPanel
Timer
ToolBarButton
ToolTip
ListViewItem
TreeNode
Control
ButtonBase
Button
CheckBox
RadioButton
DataGrid
DateTimePicker
GroupBox
Label
LinkLabel
ListControl
ComboBox
ListBox
CheckedListBox
ListView
MonthCalendar
PictureBox
PrintReviewControl
ProgressBar
ScrollableControl
ContainerControl
Form
PrintPreviewDialog
ThreadExceptionDialog
PropertyGrid
UpDownBase
DomainUpDown
NumericUpDown
UserControl
Panel
TabPage
ScrollBar
HScrollBar
VScrollBar
Splitter
StatusBar
TabControl
TextBoxBase
RichTextBox
Textbox
ToolBar
TrackBar
TreeView

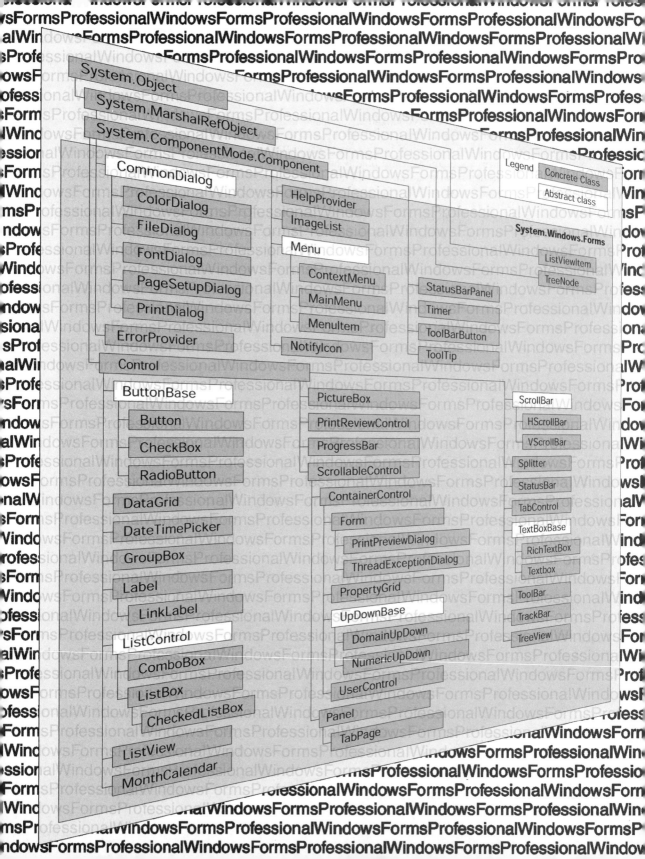

6

Working with Events

A direct consequence of the advent of the modern Graphical User Interface is an event driven programming model. We have put the user in control, and as a consequence, our programs must be ready to respond to one of many possible user actions at any given moment. The older programming model, in which a program was primarily designed to run sequentially from start to finish has been replaced by one in which the main design feature of a program is its ability to react to user events.

Object-oriented programming has embraced this programming model, specifically with the introduction of event handlers implemented as member methods. There have tended to be two approaches used for object-oriented event-driven programming. The first involved deriving a new class, and overriding the virtual method (the default handler) that is called when a given event occurs, adding our code to implement the new event handler. Alternatively, completely new methods may be added, with some arrangements made to ensure that our new method is also called in addition to the default handler when the given event is raised. MFC used message maps to accomplish this, while VB, up to version 6, implemented a model in which event handlers were written by the developer, and the VB6 runtime acted behind the scenes to ensure that each event handler was called at the appropriate time, without the developer having to worry about the details. The .NET framework has introduced the concept of **delegates** for this purpose. Delegates generally provide a clean, simple and intuitive solution for handling events, which combines the ease of use of the VB6 implementation with the flexibility afforded by lower level solutions such as message maps. It is also still possible in .NET to work by overriding virtual methods. Notwithstanding this object-oriented spin on event handling, the fundamental nature of event driven programming has not changed.

As just mentioned, with delegates, the .NET framework adds a couple of new twists to this event driven model. These twists are good. They make our programs easier to develop and maintain. To get the most out of the rest of this book, it is important to understand delegates, and the relationship between delegates and events. We will need to understand the mechanics of event generation, how we write event handlers, and what typical event handling code does.

There are literally hundreds of different events that .NET can generate, and you may wish to add your own custom events too. It is not possible (nor necessary) to cover all these events in this book. Rather, the skills necessary for today's professional developer are to understand the mechanics, understand the capabilities of the system, and know how to use the reference material to get the information necessary to code for the problem at hand.

So, in this chapter, we will:

- Take a look at a number of common events.
- Review delegates in detail in both C# and VB. Because events are implemented using delegates, it is important to understand them fully. We will focus quite heavily on the underlying mechanisms, looking at how delegates operate in general before moving on to how to implement events and event handlers.
- See the implementation details of events. We will write event handlers in both C# and VB. We'll see how Visual Studio helps us in writing event handlers.
- Take a look at the syntax for implementing our own events.

We will, however, first briefly examine some of the more common events you might encounter in Windows Forms programming.

Common Windows Forms Events

Before we examine the principles underlying how events and delegates are implemented in .NET, we'll briefly review some of the events that are available in Windows Forms. There are literally hundreds of events so we can't provide an exhaustive list, but the following list is intended to give you an idea of the events available. The events listed here are defined in the `System.Windows.Forms.Control` class, which means they are available in any control or form (since all control and form classes are directly or indirectly derived from `Control`). However, there are other events that only apply to certain types of control, for example the `TreeView` control defines additional events related to expanding and collapsing nodes in the `TreeView` – clearly these events wouldn't make sense for other controls.

For each event we've provided a rough description of when the event is raised, and made some suggestions for the kind of action that might need to be taken, which we would implement in an event handler. Note that these are only suggestions – obviously whether we write a handler for a given event, and what that handler will do, depends on the application.

Note also that events raised on user actions will only be raised when the control in question has the focus.

Event	When Raised	Possible Action
`BackColorChanged`	The `Control.BackColor` property has changed, for whatever reason.	Change colors of foreground text etc. to make sure text is still visible.
`Click`	The user clicks the main mouse button.	Move the text caret to the location where the user clicked. We would do this if we were writing our own edit control.

Event	When Raised	Possible Action
`DockChanged`	The `DockStyle` of the control has changed.	Possibly move other controls to accommodate this control's new dock style.
`DoubleClick`	The user double-clicks the main mouse button.	Select some item in the control.
`DragDrop`	The user completes a dragdrop operation by releasing the mouse button.	Actually move or copy the data that was being dragged into variables in our application, and update the contents of our controls accordingly.
`DragEnter`	The mouse enters the control while in the middle of a dragdrop operation.	Examine the data being dragged to see if the dragdrop operation should be allowed, and set the cursor accordingly.
`FontChanged`	The font of the control has changed.	Check control sizes and positions to see if any changes need to be made to ensure the text is still entirely visible.
`KeyDown`	A key has been pressed.	Process the key in a game, perhaps to fire a weapon. This event typically would not be used in a business application.
`KeyPress`	A key has been pressed.	Add the character to a string.
`KeyUp`	A key has been released.	Change state that was set when the key went down.
`MouseDown`	The main mouse button has been pressed.	Record that the mouse button is now down (so you can react appropriately if the mouse then moves).
`MouseMove`	The mouse has moved.	If the primary mouse button is currently down, modify the selection according to the mouse movement.
`MouseUp`	The main mouse button has been released.	Take action based on the `MouseDown` and the mouse movement.
`MouseWheel`	The mouse wheel has been moved.	Scroll the text in the control.
`Paint`	The control is to be repainted.	Paint a custom control.
`TextChanged`	The text of the control has changed.	Notify other controls of this.
`Validating`	The contents of the control are to be validated.	Perform custom data validation.

You'll notice from this table that there are some situations in which more than one similar event is raised, which gives us some flexibility of which event we wish to write a handler for. For example if the user presses then immediately releases the main mouse button, the `MouseDown`, `Click` and `MouseUp` events will be raised. Which you handle will depend on precisely what custom action you want taken.

KeyDown and KeyPress differ in the information supplied: KeyPress aggregates the information on what keys were pressed. For example, if the user hits the key h while the SHIFT key is held down, then the information passed to any KeyDown event handler will indicate that this is the situation. The information passed to any KeyPress event handler will indicate simply that uppercase H was pressed. Again, which event is most convenient for your control will depend on exactly what your control needs to do.

Understanding Delegates

Delegates are at the foundation of event handling in .NET. To understand events fully, it is important to understand the semantics of delegates in detail. We will explore here the principles of operation of delegates, as well as the associated syntax in both C# and VB.NET.

Delegates have uses well beyond simply being the mechanism by which the .NET framework implements events. The primary purpose of delegates is that they are the means by which references to methods may be passed around within code. This means that for the first part of this discussion it may appear that we've gone off at a tangent and that the discussion has little to do with Windows Forms events. However, rest assured that the discussion of delegates and method references is important for understanding the event model implemented by .NET and Windows Forms.

We can best understand what a delegate is by seeing an example. Suppose we have some piece of code, and we want a message to be displayed that notifies us when certain error conditions occur. Depending on the context in which the code is run, let us also suppose that there are several ways in which we might want the message displayed – it might be as a message box or it might be written to the console window, or it might even be written to a file. There are a number of approaches we might take to this problem. One approach (not involving delegates) would be to code up a method that checks which output method is required, and writes out the message in the appropriate manner. In C#, the code would be something like this:

```
public void WriteMessage(string message)
{
    switch(desiredOutputMethod)     // desiredOutputMethod is some enum
}
...
```

However, let's assume that the approach we will take is to have different methods that display the message in the appropriate manner (say – WriteMessageToMessageBox, WriteMessageToFile, etc.), and that we will have some variable that has been initialized to refer to whichever method is the correct one to use. We will then display the message by invoking the method *using that variable.* This is a departure from the usual use for variables: We are accustomed to variables being used to store data, but here we are indicating that our variable should store a reference to a method. That is what a delegate is. It's a special type of object that, stores a reference to a method. We will see later that the connection between delegates and events is that in the .NET event model, delegates are used to refer to the event handlers, and the event handlers are actually invoked using delegates.

C and C++ developers will recognize that delegates are very similar to C and C++ pointers to functions. However, there are some important differences. First, delegates can be called in the context of an object. We'll see what this means shortly. Second, we can compose delegates of more than one method. This means that one call to a delegate may actually invoke two or more methods, one after another. This is known as **multi-casting**. We'll look at examples of this later (see the section below entitled *Multi-Casting Using Delegates*).

Another way to think of a delegate is as a mechanism that allows methods to be called anonymously. The caller doesn't need to know anything about the class that contains the method to be called. Also note that using a delegate gives us a way to call a method where the method to be called is determined at run-time rather than at compile-time – it will be whatever method the delegate variable happens to refer to.

Defining, declaring and using a delegate is a three step process:

- We write a delegate definition.
- We declare and instantiate an object of the type of our delegate definition.
- We can then invoke the method that the delegate encapsulates.

A delegate definition is a type, just like a class definition is a type. It allows us to encapsulate a reference to a method. The definition defines the signature of the method that it encapsulates, which consists of the type of the return value (if any – it may be void), as well as the types of all of the arguments to the method. A delegate that refers to a method of a given signature constitutes a type in its own right. This is analogous to declaring a `typedef` for a function pointer in C or C++. It was possible in C and C++ to use pointers to functions without declaring a type. However, in C# and VB.NET, this is not possible. It is mandatory to declare a type in order to use delegates. This restriction ensures greater type safety and prevents some run-time bugs.

We will fully explore delegates in C# first. After finishing exploring all the semantics of delegates in C#, we will present the corresponding syntax in VB.NET.

Delegates in C#

In this section we will develop a short piece of code that implements the scenario of displaying strings we've just mentioned.

We can define a delegate type in C# as follows:

```
delegate void StringOp(string str);
```

All the above statement does is to declare a type, which is a delegate for a function that doesn't return any value, and takes a string as an argument. We've called the type `StringOp` in this example, though obviously the choice of name is up to you.

If we have a method, `WriteStringToMessageBox`, that sends a string to a `MessageBox`:

```
void WriteStringToMessageBox(String message)
{
    MessageBox.Show(message, "Message");
}
```

Then we can declare and instantiate a delegate as follows:

```
StringOp so = new StringOp(MyObject.WriteStringToMessageBox);
```

Where `MyObject` is an instance of whatever class contains the `WriteStringToMessageBox` method.

This code not only declares a (delegate) variable of type StringOp, but also initializes it to refer to the WriteStringToMessageBox method.

Having declared our delegate, we can now invoke it:

```
so("This string will be written in a message box.");
```

The syntax for invoking the delegate is the same as that for invoking a method directly. Invoking the delegate will cause the method to which it refers to be invoked. The difference is that, by going through the delegate, we can change at run-time which method will be invoked by simply reassigning a new value to the delegate variable.

Following is the complete code for a C# console application called StringOps1, which invokes the StringOp delegate. Note that at the moment the sample doesn't look particularly useful, but we will soon develop it further:

```
using System;
using System.Windows.Forms;

namespace StringOps1
{
    class StringOpsExample
    {
        delegate void StringOp(string str);

        static void Main(string[] args)
        {
            StringOpsExample cls = new StringOpsExample ();
            StringOp so = new StringOp(cls.WriteStringToMessageBox);
            so("This string will be written in a message box.");
        }

        void WriteStringToMessageBox(String message)
        {
            MessageBox.Show(message, "Message");
        }
    }
}
```

The delegate above is what we call an instance delegate. This means that the method WriteStringToMessageBox must operate in the context of an instance of the StringOpsExample class. This example implicitly specifies the this object for our delegate. The next two examples will make clear what we mean by this.

Explicitly Specifying an Object for the Delegate

Let's take a look at a minor variation on the above example:

```
using System;
using System.Windows.Forms;

// this sample won't compile. It's deliberately done like that to illustrate
// incorrect use of delegates
```

```
namespace StringOps2
{
    class StringOpsExample
    {
        delegate void StringOp(string str);

        static void Main(string[] args)
        {
            StringOpsExample cls = new StringOpsExample();
            // following line won't compile - we've not specified a context
            // for the delegate
            StringOp so = new StringOp(WriteStringToMessageBox);
            so("This string will be written in a message box.");
        }

        void WriteStringToMessageBox(String message)
        {
            MessageBox.Show(message, "Message");
        }
    }
}
```

This example is almost the same as the first example, except that we've changed the highlighted lines of code. Now it generates an error: An object reference is required for the non-static field, method, or property StringOpsExample.WriteStringToMessageBox(string). This is a similar error to attempting to reference an instance variable from a static method (our static method is `Main` in this case). What this really means is that we did not provide an object, so that the delegate could run in the context of that object.

The point here is that a delegate is not just a pointer to a method. It is in this case a pointer to a method that operates in the context of an instance of a class. It is not even possible to declare and instantiate a delegate that operates on the wrong object, as was the case in C and C++ with function pointers, the C/C++ equivalent of delegates. These types of errors are eliminated at compile time.

Actually, we should have said that a delegate is normally a pointer to a method that operates in the context of an instance of a class. There is an exception to this. Delegates can also encapsulate a reference to a class method (one that is declared as `static` in C#, or `Shared` in VB).

Delegates that Encapsulate Static Methods

Consider the following example: We have added to the code in the StringOps1 example by declaring and invoking a second delegate – but this one prints the message to the console instead of in a message box.

```
using System;
using System.Windows.Forms;

namespace StringOps3
{
    class StringOpsExample
    {
        delegate void StringOp(string str);

        static void Main(string[] args)
```

```
        {
            StringOpsExample cls = new StringOpsExample();
            StringOp so = new StringOp(cls.WriteStringToMessageBox);
            StringOp soConsole;
            soConsole = new StringOp(Console.WriteLine);

            soConsole("This string will be written to the console.");
            so("This string will be written in a message box.");
        }

        void WriteStringToMessageBox(String message)
        {
            MessageBox.Show(message, "Message");
        }
    }
}
```

In this example, we never instantiate an object of type `Console`. The `Console.WriteLine` method is a static method from the Microsoft .NET base classes, and operates in the context of the class, not an instance, so when we declare and instantiate our delegate in the following lines:

```
            StringOp soConsole;
            soConsole = new StringOp(Console.WriteLine);
```

We need not specify an object for the method `WriteStringToMessageBox`. The rule is that, if our delegate encapsulates an instance method, we must specify an object for the delegate. If our delegate encapsulates a class method, we must not explicitly specify an object for the delegate. Modifying the last example, if we attempt to use an object in the instantiation of a delegate that encapsulated a static method, as follows:

```
            StringOp soConsole;
            Console console;
            soConsole = new StringOp(console.WriteLine);
            soConsole("This string will be written to the console.");
```

The compiler would give this error:

"Static member Console.WriteLine `(string)` cannot be accessed with an instance reference; qualify it with a type name instead".

Multi-Casting Using Delegates

Multi-casting is a play on words, based on the term 'broadcasting'. With this construct, we can associate more than one method with a single delegate. A single call to the delegate will then call each of the methods, in order. This will become particularly important when using delegates to implement events. There are many situations where an event is of interest to multiple objects. As an example, we could program a form so that any change to fields on the form would update a local database record. In addition, we could have another object, which tracks whether any changes at all have been made to the record. Using multi-casting, one event handler for each control on the form would validate the TextBox (make sure that the data was valid) and update the database record. Another event handler for each control on the form would tag the record as having been changed. When implementing this second event handler, all controls could use the same event handler.

In C#, the += operator is overloaded for the purpose of adding additional methods to an existing delegate. Consider the following example. In this sample, we have modified the `StringOps3` sample so that one single delegate is used. When this delegate is invoked, the message is written to both the console and a message box:

```
using System;
using System.Windows.Forms;

namespace StringOps4
{
    class StringOpsExample
    {
        delegate void StringOp(string str);

        static void Main(string[] args)
        {
            StringOpsExample cls = new StringOpsExample();
            StringOp so;
            so = new StringOp(Console.WriteLine);
            so += new StringOp(cls.WriteStringToMessageBox);
            String str = "This string will be written both to the console ";
            str += " and in a message box.";
            so(str);
        }

        void WriteStringToMessageBox(String message)
        {
            MessageBox.Show(message, "Message");
        }
    }
}
```

There is a constraint on this technique. All methods used in a multi-cast delegate must return void. If you think about it, if both methods in the delegate returned a value, what would be the return value of this line of code?

```
so("This string will be written both to the console and in a message box.");
```

It doesn't make sense for methods used in a multi-cast delegate to return values, and in fact, it is invalid. Because of this constraint, events in .NET – which are actually implemented as multicast delegates – also cannot return values to their caller. Note that delegates can return values to their caller, but multicast delegates cannot.

We can remove a method from a delegate by using the -= operator:

```
so -= new StringOp(cls.WriteStringToMessageBox);
```

We might need to do this if, for example, we have a Model/View/Controller (MVC) infrastructure in our program. When we add a new view, then we would add a method to a delegate. When we remove a view, we would remove a method from a delegate.

Delegates in VB.NET

We define a delegate type in VB.NET as follows:

```
Delegate Sub StringOp(ByVal str As String)
```

Then we can declare a delegate as follows:

```
Dim so As StringOp = _
New StringOp(AddressOf SomeObjectInstance.WriteStringToMessageBox)
```

Note the use of the `AddressOf` operator. We are not trying to invoke the method, merely indicating which method we wish to refer to. Whereas in C#, this is achieved by giving the name of the method, but omitting the brackets following the name, for example, `Me.WriteStringToMessageBox` instead of `WriteStringToMessageBox("Hello")`. In VB, we just use the `AddressOf` operator.

Having declared our delegate, we can now call it:

```
so("This string will be written to a message box.")
```

The entire example in VB is as follows. This code is the VB equivalent to the `StringOps1` example:

```
Imports System
Imports System.Windows.Forms

Public Class StringOpsExample

    Delegate Sub StringOp(ByVal str As String)

    Shared Sub Main()
        Dim cls As StringOpsExample = New StringOpsExample()
        Dim so As StringOp = New StringOp(AddressOf cls.WriteStringToMessageBox)
        so("This string will be written in a message box.")
    End Sub

    Sub WriteStringToMessageBox(ByVal Message As String)
        MessageBox.Show(Message, "Message")
    End Sub

End Class
```

Note that this code relies on the `System` and `System.Windows.Forms` namespaces being specified using an `Imports` statement.

Delegates that Encapsulate Shared Methods

The following VB.NET example shows a delegate that encapsulates a shared method. It does exactly the same thing as our earlier C# `StringOps3` sample, except that it is written in VB.NET.

```
Imports System
Imports System.Windows.Forms
```

```
Public Class StringOpsExample

    Delegate Sub StringOp(ByVal str As String)

    Shared Sub Main()
        Dim cls As StringOpsExample = New StringOpsExample()
        Dim so As StringOp = New StringOp(AddressOf cls.WriteStringToMessageBox)
        Dim soConsole As StringOp = New StringOp(AddressOf Console.WriteLine)
        soConsole("This will be written to the console.")
        so("This string will be written in a message box.")
    End Sub

    Sub WriteStringToMessageBox(ByVal Message As String)
        MessageBox.Show(Message, "Message")
    End Sub

End Class
```

Multi-Casting in VB.NET

The following VB.NET example shows multi-casting. It is identical to the earlier C# `StringOps4` example, and invokes one multicast delegate to display the same message to the console and a message box:

```
Imports System
Imports System.Windows.Forms

Public Class StringOpsExample

    Delegate Sub StringOp(ByVal str As String)

    Shared Sub Main()
        Dim cls As StringOpsExample = New StringOpsExample()
        Dim so As StringOp = New StringOp(AddressOf Console.WriteLine)
        so = so.Combine(so, New StringOp(AddressOf cls.WriteStringToMessageBox))
        Dim str As String = "This string will be written both to the console "
        str = str & "and in a message box."
        so(str)
    End Sub

    Sub WriteStringToMessageBox(ByVal Message As String)
        MessageBox.Show(Message, "Message")
    End Sub

End Class
```

We note from this code that, whereas in C# we use the += operator to add a method to a multicast delegate, in VB.NET we use the `Delegate.Combine` method to do this.

```
so = so.Combine(so, New StringOp(AddressOf cls.WriteStringToMessageBox))
```

We can remove a method from a delegate using the `Remove` method, as follows:

```
td = td.Remove(td, New TestDelegate(AddressOf vbmde.WriteStringA))
```

Note that the `Combine` and `Remove` methods are not VB specific. We could also use them in C#; however, it is more convenient in C# to use the += and -= operator overloads, which in turn call the `Combine` and `Remove` methods.

When we show multi-casting with events in VB, we will introduce another keyword, namely the `AddHandler` keyword, which simplifies the implementation of multi-casting of events in VB.

Understanding Events

Now that we have seen how delegates are used to refer to methods, we can understand how events are implemented in .NET. Events are simply a special type of multicast delegate. The principle is quite simple, and we'll explain it by using the event of clicking on a control as an example. The `System.Windows.Forms` class contains an event called `Click`. This event is simply a multicast delegate that is there to store references to any event handlers that need to be called when the user clicks on the control.

The internal implementation of the `Control` class, and of its Microsoft-supplied derived classes (`Button`, `TextBox`, `ListBox`, etc.) ensures that whenever the user clicks on the control, this delegate (event) will be invoked. So if we want to add an event handler for this event, we simply write the handler method and add it to the delegate. The handler we write can be a member method of a control class that we've written and which is derived directly or indirectly from `Control`, and in the same class instance as the event. It can also be in a different class, (for example, it might be the class that represents the containing form) – it doesn't matter because when we add a method to a delegate, as we've seen, we indicate the context of the method as well as the method itself.

In this way, when the click event happens, all the handlers for that event will be executed in turn.

We've said that an event is a special type of multicast delegate. It is special in two ways: First, there are some restrictions on the signatures of the event handlers, and second, some .NET languages (including both C# and VB) have additional syntactical constructs to make it particularly easy to use events.

To put this into context let's see how to define an event in C#. The syntax for declaring the event is similar to that for declaring an ordinary delegate except that we use the keyword `event` in the variable declaration.

```
public event EventHandler Click;
```

Here `EventHandler` is the name of the class of delegate.

The developer of a control declares events using this event declaration. This declaration consists of an identifier and a delegate type. The delegate type must not have a return type (it must be declared as `void`). The above is the event declaration for the `Click` event for the `Button` class (the button inherits the `Click` event from the `Control` class):

The definition of `EventHandler` is:

```
public delegate void EventHandler(object sender, EventArgs e);
```

From this, we can see that the `Click` event is declared with a delegate type, `EventHandler`. Events really are delegates. This definition also illustrates the restriction we mentioned on the handler signature. For an event, the handler must return `void` and must take two parameters – an object (which in practice is used to refer to the source that raised the event), and an instance of the class `System.EventArgs`, or of any class derived from `System.EventArgs`. This second parameter is used to pass extra information about the event.

Sometimes when an event requires additional information above and beyond the default information that is in the `EventArgs` object, there will be a different delegate declared that takes a different argument. For example, the handler for the `MouseMove` event is actually defined to be of type `MouseEventHandler`:

```
public delegate void MouseEventHandler(object sender, MouseEventArgs e);
```

with event definition:

```
public event MouseEventHandler MouseMove;
```

The difference is that `MouseEventArgs` implements additional properties that allow retrieval of information concerning the state and location of the mouse.

For most purposes, you don't need to worry about the syntax of declaring events since most of the time you will simply be writing event handlers and adding them to events that have already been defined in the Windows Forms base classes.

We'll now go on to look at how you actually write your own event handlers in both C# and VB.

Writing an Event Handler in C#

For our next exercise, we will go through the process of writing a very simple event handler in Visual Studio, using C#. The handler we will add will respond to the `Click` event on a `Button` control. So, open up Visual Studio, and create a new C# Windows Application project.

There is a shortcut to get VS.NET to add a click event handler for the button (we could double-click on the button), but initially, we won't use this shortcut. We want to understand how we can get to any event handler for any control and the mechanics of how it works. So instead, right-click on the button in your design form, and pick `Properties` from the popup menu. Alternatively, after dragging out the control, while the newly created control is still selected, we can press the *F4* key.

Initially, the property window shows the properties of the control. These are interesting, but not relevant to us at the moment. To see all of the possible events that this control can raise, click on the Events button on the toolbar of the property window. The Events button has the little yellow lightning bolt on it:

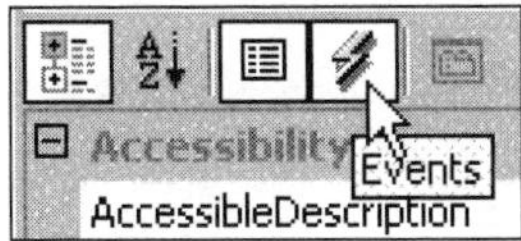

Note that this lightning bolt is not present in VB.NET projects as Visual Studio.NET has alternative means of adding events in VB.NET.

After clicking on this button, we should see this:

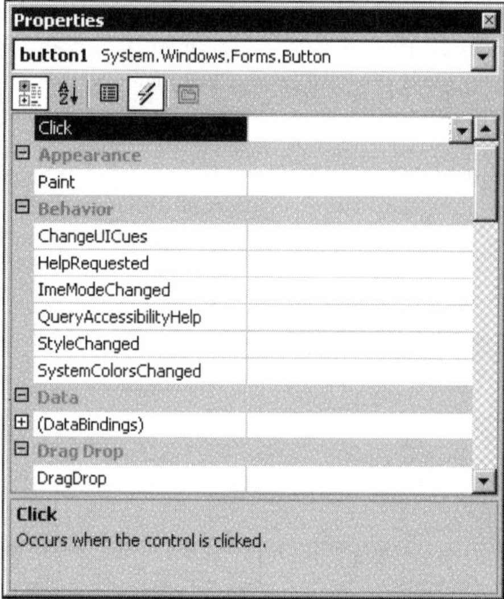

As we can see, this view of the property window is a list that contains two columns. The left column has the name of the event in it. The right column will contain the name of the method that will handle the event. This will be set after we have created an event handler. If we select any event by single-clicking on it, we will normally see a description of that event at the bottom of the property window.

After we have created a new form, and put a button on it, there is not any code for any event handlers in our source file. There are hundreds of potential events, and it would make the source file quite messy if there were empty event handlers for all possible events. In addition, even the existence of empty event handlers would hurt performance, as time would be wasted registering all the handlers with the events at startup time, and these do-nothing handlers would get needlessly called every time an event was raised. So VS.NET doesn't add any event handlers unless we ask it to. There is an easy way that we can get Visual Studio to create an empty event handler for us. This is convenient, because it saves us from having to research the name of the event and the arguments for the event handler.

In this exercise, we want to write an event handler for the `Click` event. We can do this by double-clicking on the `Click` event in the left column of the list, and Visual Studio will automatically bring up the code editor, create an empty event handler called `button1_Click`, and position the insertion point inside of that event handler.

```
    private void button1_Click(object sender, System.EventArgs e)
    {
    }
```

VS.NET has also automatically added the code to add this event handler to the event, though it's presence is not obvious – it's buried away in the `InitializeComponent` method:

```
this.button1.Name = "button1";
this.button1.TabIndex = 0;
this.button1.Text = "button1";
this.button1.Click += new System.EventHandler(this.button1_Click);
```

After double-clicking, you may have to move the properties window to properly see the code editor window. Modify the code so that there is a call to MessageBox.Show, as follows:

```
private void button1_Click(object sender, System.EventArgs e)
{
    MessageBox.Show("Hello there");
}
```

If we look at the property window again, we will see that the Click event now has a method listed in the right-hand column: button1_Click.

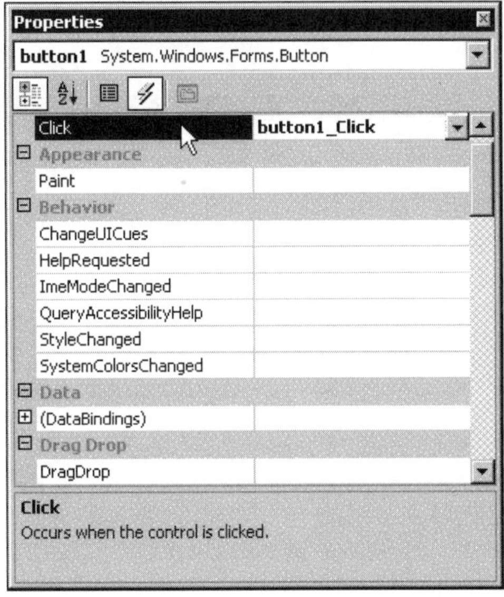

Now, press *F5* to compile and run the application, and click on the button to see the message box.

There is another way to get Visual Studio to create an empty event handler for an event, and this new way has the advantage that we can explicitly name our event handler, rather than taking the default event handler name that Visual Studio assigns. This also means that we can give the same event handler to more than one control – by simply typing in the name of the same method. Rather than double-clicking on the event name in the left column, we can click in the right column. After we have clicked in the right column, we can enter the name for our event handler, and then press the Enter key. Visual Studio will create the empty event handler, add the wiring so that the event handler is registered, and place the insertion point in the new empty event handler, ready for us to enter code. An advantage to this method is that we can give a generic name to the event handler. When Visual Studio automatically assigns an event name for the event handler, it gives it a name such as Button1_Click. If we assign our own name, we can name the event handler something like, btn_Click, then use this event handler for all buttons. This method will be important later, when we are using the same event handler to handle events for more than one control.

Writing an Event Handler in VB.NET

There are some differences in the syntax for handling events in VB when compared to C#. In addition, the user interface for VB.NET in Visual Studio is quite a bit different than for C#. Let's go through the process of implementing an event handler in VB. Primarily the syntax differences and Visual Studio differences are there for backwards compatibility with previous versions of VB.

Open up Visual Studio, and create a new Visual Basic Windows Application project.

Select the `Button` tool, and drag out a button on the form.

Right click on the button, and select **View Code** from the pop-up menu. This brings up the following window:

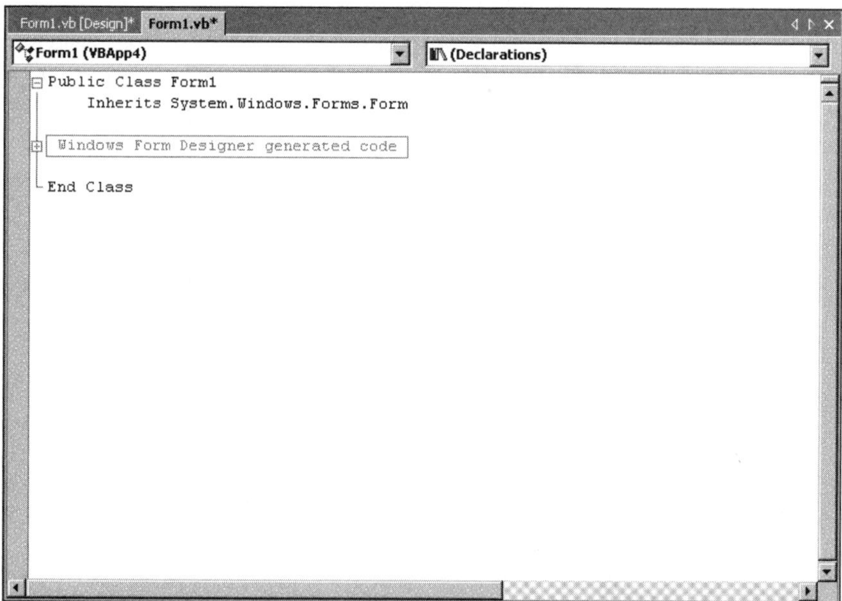

There are drop-down list boxes at the top of the window. The left one allows us to specify the control (class) that we want to work with. Once we have specified a class, the right list box allows us to specify the method that we want to work with. Note that this is different from the C# user interface in that for C# programs you cannot use the left hand listbox to select controls on the form. Hence you can't use these listboxes to add event handlers to controls in C#.

Select **Button1** in the left list box. Then, select **Click** in the right list box. You will notice the same small yellow lightning bolt next to the events in the right list box, marking the events as such. After you have selected **Click** in the right list box, Visual Studio automatically creates an empty event handler and places the insertion point in the newly created event handler.

```
Private Sub Button1_Click(ByVal sender As Object, _
    ByVal e As System.EventArgs) Handles Button1.Click

End Sub
```

The `Handles` clause at the end of the Sub definition is the thing that marks it as being a handler for the `Button1.Click` event and removes the need for a separate line of code that explicitly adds the method to the delegate, as was the case in C#.

We can now add a call to the method `MessageBox.Show` as follows:

```
Private Sub Button1_Click(ByVal sender As Object, _
    ByVal e As System.EventArgs) Handles Button1.Click
    MessageBox.Show("Hello there")
End Sub
```

You can now compile the code and verify that the message box appears when the button is clicked, just as in the C# version of this code.

Static Handling of Events vs. Dynamic Handling of Events

When using Visual Basic .NET, events can be handled in one of two different ways: statically or dynamically. The difference between the two is only syntactic. **Static handling** of events also provides backwards compatibility with previous versions of VB. By default, Visual Studio generates code that handles events statically. Static handling means that the compiler sorts out associating the event handlers with the events. This slightly simplifies the code we write. C# has only dynamic handling.

Static handling of events is simpler, and hides the delegate mechanism from the view of the developer. Static handling of events involves the use of the `WithEvents` and the `Handles` keywords.

When handling an event statically, we declare our event handler with the special keyword `Handles`, followed by the object name and event name. In the example that we've just demonstrated, the method `Button1_Click` is declared to handle the event `Click` for the object `Button1`:

```
Private Sub Button1_Click(ByVal sender As Object, _
ByVal e As System.EventArgs) Handles Button1.Click
```

When the `Button1` object is declared, it is declared using the `WithEvents` keyword. If we expand the Windows Form Designer generated code in the code editor for our form, we will see the declaration of the `Button1` object:

```
Friend WithEvents Button1 As System.Windows.Forms.Button
```

The `WithEvents` keyword signals the compiler to watch for methods that have the `Handles` keyword followed by the object name and the event name. When the compiler finds this, it creates delegates behind the scenes and hooks up the method to the event. Make no doubt about it, delegates are still used at the lowest levels of the system, but the mechanism is hidden from our view.

Now, let's modify this example to not use static handling of events, and instead to use **dynamic handling** of events, which allows us to change event handlers at runtime. Modify the declaration of the `Button1_Click` method so that it does not contain the `Handles` keyword:

```
Private Sub Button1_Click(ByVal sender As Object, _
ByVal e As System.EventArgs)
```

Next, modify the declaration of the `Button1` object, so that it doesn't include the `WithEvents` keyword:

```
Friend Button1 As System.Windows.Forms.Button
```

Finally, modify the `InitializeComponent` method (in the Windows Form Designer generated code), as follows:

```
Me.Button1.Location = New System.Drawing.Point(72, 80)
Me.Button1.Name = "Button1"
Me.Button1.Size = New System.Drawing.Size(120, 32)
Me.Button1.TabIndex = 0
Me.Button1.Text = "Button1"
AddHandler Button1.Click, AddressOf Button1_Click
```

`AddHandler` is a simple way in which we can add a new event handler to the delegate that is associated with the `Button1.Click` event. We can't use `AddHandler` with delegates; we can only use it with events. In other words, the VB statement:

```
AddHandler Button1.Click, AddressOf Button1_Click
```

is completely equivalent to the C# statement:

```
this.button1.Click += new System.EventHandler(this.button1_Click);
```

You can run this application, and it behaves in the same way it used to.

If we were using multi-casting, and we had associated multiple event handlers with the `Click` event, we could remove an event handler using the `RemoveHandler` statement:

```
RemoveHandler Button1.Click, AddressOf Button1_Click
```

As an aside, there are no performance benefits between the two techniques. Either one is equally efficient.

Modification of Windows Form Designer generated code is not necessarily a recommended technique. We did it here for the purposes of illustration of the differences between statically handling events and dynamically handling events, but we should know exactly when we can do it, and why we would want to do it. Don't do it blindly.

Multi-casting when using Static Event Handling

As we mentioned previously, we sometimes want to multicast an event. There is nothing that stops us from declaring two methods as handling the same event. If we go back to our example before we changed the static handling of events to dynamic handling of events, and we add another method (`Button1_Click_AnotherHandler`) to our class:

```
Private Sub Button1_Click(ByVal sender As Object, _
ByVal e As System.EventArgs) Handles Button1.Click
    MessageBox.Show("This is a test")
End Sub

Private Sub Button1_Click_AnotherHandler(ByVal sender As Object, _
```

```
ByVal e As System.EventArgs) Handles Button1.Click
    MessageBox.Show("This is another test")
End Sub
```

both events will fire. It is not defined which event will fire first. It is important that we declare that this method `handles Button1.Click`.

You can also achieve the same effect using dynamic handling, as follows:

Remove the `Handles` keyword from `Button1_Click_AnotherHandler`:

```
Private Sub Button1_Click_AnotherHandler(ByVal sender As Object, _
ByVal e As System.EventArgs)
    MessageBox.Show("This is another test")
End Sub
```

Now, modify the `InitializeComponent` method (it is in the Windows Form Designer generated code), as follows:

```
Me.Button1.Location = New System.Drawing.Point(88, 56)
Me.Button1.Name = "Button1"
Me.Button1.Size = New System.Drawing.Size(104, 48)
Me.Button1.TabIndex = 0
Me.Button1.Text = "Button1"
AddHandler Button1.Click, AddressOf Button1_Click_AnotherHandler
```

If you run it now, again, both methods will fire. This example declares one event statically, and adds another event handler dynamically. This graphically shows that static handling of events really uses delegates – our `AddHandler` statement modified the delegate that Visual Basic had already set up for our event handler that was declared statically.

Note that there is nothing special to VB.NET in this – we can do the same thing in C#, just by adding more events to the event using the += operator. We won't show the code here, however, since it doesn't illustrate any new principles or syntax.

Writing Events for the 'Form' Class

The procedure and user interface in Visual Studio for writing an event handler for the `Form` class in VB.NET is slightly different from the one for writing an event handler for a control (for example, the event that we wrote for a button click). To see this difference, start Visual Studio, and create a new empty Visual Basic Windows Application project, and then view the code. As we have discussed, the code editor window has two list boxes at the top of it. The left list box allows us to select classes and the right list box allows us to select methods and events.

When we look at the drop-down list on the list box, it looks like this:

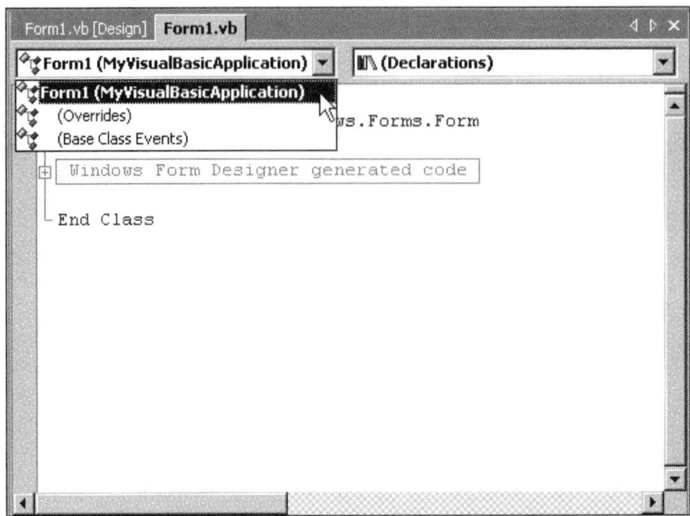

When the first item on the drop-down list is selected, in this case Form1(MyVisualBasicApplication), the right list box will show only the existing methods and events for the form.

When the second item on the list box is selected (Overrides), the right list box shows all possible virtual methods for the form's base classes. Selecting a method in the right list box causes Visual Studio to create an empty overridden method, and places the insertion point in the newly created empty method.

When the third item on the list box is selected, the right list box shows all possible events, both those implemented in the form class itself, and those implemented in the base classes for the form class. Selecting a method in the right list box causes Visual Studio to create an empty event handler, and this empty event handler is declared with the `Handles` clause.

The issue is primarily that there are too many possible methods that can be overridden, and too many events in the `Form` class and its base classes. Visual Studio breaks it up into these three categories to make it much more convenient to deal with large classes.

If you are working in C# then adding events handlers to events in the Form class is no different to the process involved in adding event handlers to controls, which we've already discussed.

Implementing Events by Overriding Methods

Now we've seen how to add event handlers to our code, next we'll look in a bit more detail at the internals of how events are handled in the .NET framework. In the process we'll also point out the alternative way of adding handlers that we mentioned at the beginning of the chapter: Overriding the default handlers instead of adding our own. Doing this is possible in .NET, and it can lead to very slightly more efficient code (though the difference isn't really significant for most applications), but it does mean that we have to write all the code manually – we can't use Visual Studio.NET to auto-generate the handler method definitions for you.

Most of the controls in the Windows Forms class hierarchy are not implemented using the Common Language Runtime (CLR), and the .NET classes. Rather, the developers at Microsoft wrapped existing controls, which were primarily written in C and C++, in managed code that was mostly written in C#. These controls had no notion of delegates. Instead, events were implemented using low-level code known as Windows procedures.

The .NET framework internally wraps these existing controls using virtual methods. For instance, the `Control` class has a protected virtual method `OnClick`. In C#, the signature of this method is:

```
protected virtual void OnClick(EventArgs e);
```

In VB, the signature is:

```
Overridable Protected Sub OnClick(ByVal e As EventArgs)
```

Note that this method has only one parameter, and so is distinguished from any event handler that we add via delegates since all event handlers added using delegates take two parameters, `sender` and `EventArgs`. The `sender` argument is not necessary in this event handler, since the `this` object is the sender object.

This method in the `Control` class is the one that is called internally by Windows in response to the user having clicked the control. It is this method that contains the code that invokes the multicast delegate, `Control.Click`, which will cause any event handlers that we have added to be executed. There are similar virtual methods that are executed whenever any of the other user events occur.

It is this architecture that allows us the alternative means of adding our own event handling code: Instead of adding our own event handler to the event (which is really a delegate), we can inherit a class from the relevant control, and override this method in our class to perform whatever processing we need to be done.

We can do an experiment and see the results of this process for the particular case of a button. If we derive our own `button` class from `System.Windows.Forms.Button`, instantiate it, and register an event handler for the `Click` event, our new button class behaves normally.

Start Visual Studio, and create a new C# Windows Application project.

Add the following class that defines `MyButton` to the `Form1.cs` module. The class `MyButton` derives from `Button`, with an event handler for the `Click` event:

```
public class MyButton : Button
{
    public MyButton()
    {
        this.Click += new System.EventHandler(OnClick);
    }

    public void OnClick(object sender, EventArgs e)
    {
        MessageBox.Show("OnClick event handler called");
    }
}
```

Now, add the following code to the Form1 class.

```
public class Form1 : System.Windows.Forms.Form
{

    MyButton myButton;

    public Form1()
    {
        InitializeComponent();

        myButton = new MyButton();
        myButton.Text = "My Button";
        myButton.Location = new Point(0,0);
        this.components.Add(myButton);
        myButton.Parent = this;
    }
```

If we run this code, it displays a form with a button as expected, and clicking on the button results in the message box being displayed.

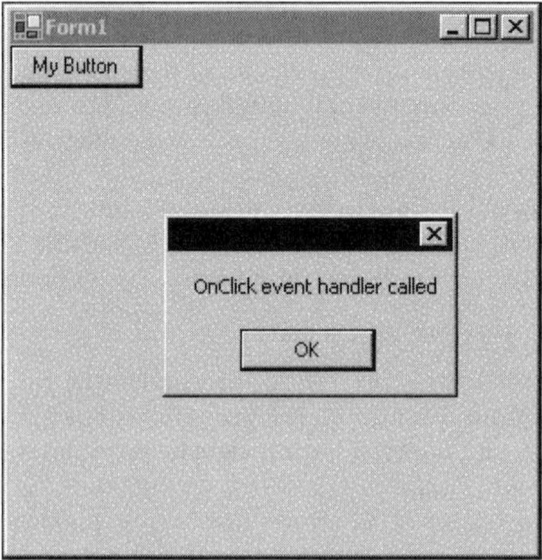

However, if we also override the OnClick method in MyButton, by adding the following code, then we see a change of behavior. Modify the MyButton class as follows:

```
public class MyButton : Button
{
    public MyButton()
    {
        this.Click += new System.EventHandler(OnClick);
    }

    public void OnClick(object sender, EventArgs e)
    {
        MessageBox.Show("OnClick event handler called");
    }
```

```
        protected override void OnClick(EventArgs e)
        {
            MessageBox.Show("OnClick override called");
        }
    }
```

We see the message box put up by the `OnClick` override, but we no longer see our registered event handler, which uses the delegate mechanism, being executed – only the one dialog box gets displayed. If we modify our `OnClick` method, adding a call to `base.OnClick`, as follows:

```
    public class MyButton : System.Windows.Forms.Button
    {
        protected override void OnClick(EventArgs e)
        {
            MessageBox.Show("OnClick override called");
            base.OnClick(e);
        }
    }
```

then we will see our event handler (which uses the delegate mechanism) get executed – so that both message boxes are displayed in turn. In fact, the .NET documentation says: 'Notes to Inheritors: When overriding `OnClick` in a derived class, be sure to call the base class's `OnClick` method so that registered delegates receive the event.'

What we can determine from this exercise is that there are two parallel mechanisms for handling events. The first is based on derivation and overloading of virtual methods. The second is based on delegates. The virtual methods are what actually execute the delegates, and if we derive and override the virtual methods improperly, we will obstruct the event handlers (which are implemented via delegates) from operating correctly.

Which method we choose for handling events is up to us, though in most cases, adding our own event handlers rather than overriding the virtual methods can lead to more robust code.

The Philosophy Behind .NET Events and Delegates

The .NET framework is the one of the first high level programming environments designed from the ground up to accommodate graphical user interfaces, and it shows. Traditional object oriented languages compose classes of members of various types and methods. The .NET languages add two more first class citizens – properties and events.

> *Properties and events have of course existed in previous versions of VB, but without the object oriented facilities of .NET, and the VB6 events weren't as sophisticated as .NET events.*

The value of having properties and events designed directly into the infrastructure of the system is made clearer when using **reflection**. Reflection is the process of using an API to discover the member variables, methods, and other characteristics of classes. Not only can we iterate through the member variables and methods of a class, we can also iterate through its properties and events. This also shows up in the automatic document generation utilities of .NET – the generated documentation explicitly shows the properties and events of a class.

If a class is derived from some other class, then we may need to also look upwards in the class hierarchy for the property or event that we need.

Let's have a look at a couple of event handler examples.

'TextBox' Validation in C#

First, we will write an event handler that validates `TextBox` controls. In this event handler, we will validate that the user has entered a hexadecimal number, that is, the text in the edit control is comprised of only digits 0-9, and letters A-F. If the text is invalid, we will put up an error message, and prohibit the focus from leaving the text box control. This can all be achieved through the `Validating` event supplied by the .NET framework.

Start Visual Studio, and create a new C# Windows Application project. Name this project `CSEventsExample`.

Place two `TextBox` controls and a `Button` control on the form. For both of the `TextBox` controls, set the following properties:

Property Name	Property Value
`CharacterCasing`	`Upper`
`Text`	(nothing)

When finished, the window will look like this:

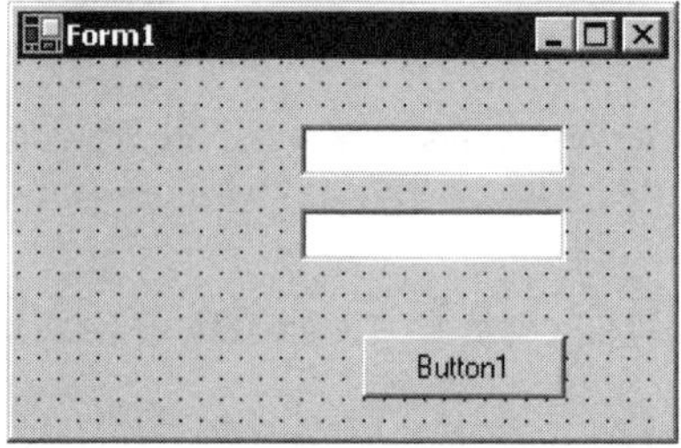

Next we will add an event handler for the `Validating` event for the first `TextBox` control. This time, we will not use the method of double-clicking in the property window on the event name, which would cause Visual Studio to generate an event handler with the default event handler name.

Click on the first `TextBox` control. Press *F4* to bring the focus to the property window, with the properties visible for the first `TextBox` control. Click on the Events button (yellow lightning bolt) on the toolbar in the property window. Find the `Validating` event by scrolling up or down to it in the property window. The `Validating` event fires when the user attempts to leave a `TextBox` control. If the `TextBox` control has invalid data in it, we have the option of forcing the focus to stay in the `TextBox`. Click in the right column, and type `HecDecValidate` and press *Enter*. This will bring up the code editor, with an empty method `HecDecValidate`, with the insertion point positioned inside the function.

Add the following code to the event handler:

```
private void HecDecValidate (object sender,
System.ComponentModel.CancelEventArgs e)
{
    TextBox tb = (TextBox)sender;
    String str = tb.Text;

    for (int si = 0; si < str.Length; ++si)
    {
        if ((str[si] >= 'A' && str[si] <= 'F') ||
            (str[si] >= '0' && str[si] <= '9'))
            continue;
        else
        {
            MessageBox.Show("Invalid hexadecimal number", "Error",
            MessageBoxButtons.OK, MessageBoxIcon.Error);
            tb.Select(0, tb.Text.Length);
            e.Cancel = true;
            return;
        }
    }
}
```

Event handlers have two arguments, the first of which is the sender. Notice that it is passed as type `object`, not as type `TextBox`. This is because an event handler can be used in many different contexts, for many different types of controls, so it can't be declared such that the sender will be only one type of control. We can cast the sender to a `TextBox` and assign it to a local variable in order to use it:

```
TextBox tb = (TextBox)sender;
```

If we were to attempt to cast it to an invalid class, such as a form, the CLR would throw an `InvalidCastException`.

The next item of interest is the following line:

```
e.Cancel = true;
```

The delegate to whom this event was registered is of type `CancelEventHandler`, not `EventHandler`. This is a special type of event handler where we can set the `Cancel` property of `CancelEventArgs` to `true`. This causes the desired validating behavior of our edit control.

Notice that the text box validation behaves properly regardless of whether the focus is moving from the text box via the keyboard or the mouse. If we enter an invalid hexadecimal number and attempt to tab to the push button, or if we enter an invalid hexadecimal number and click on the push button, the validation works properly.

There is a general principle regarding events and user interfaces: the user interface should tell the client code (an event handler) what is going to happen before it happens, and give the event handler the choice as to whether the event will take effect or not.

Using One Event Handler for Two Events

You will notice that our second `TextBox` does not properly validate hexadecimal numbers. Open the design window for the form. Click on the second `TextBox` to select it, and then press *F4* to bring up the property window. If the property window is not currently showing events, click the Events button at the top of the property window. Set the `Validating` event handler to `HecDecValidate`, as shown in the diagram below:

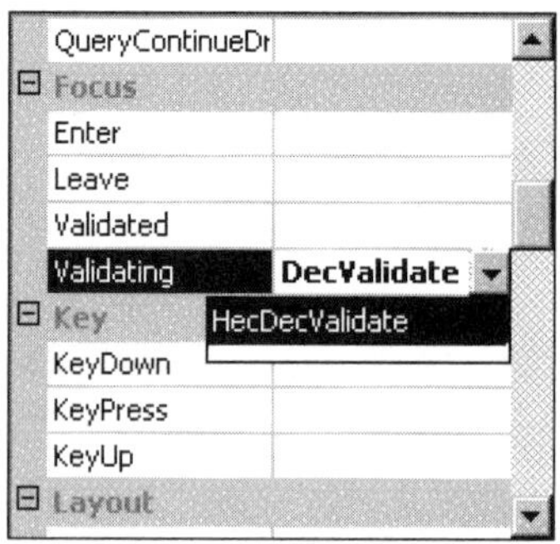

Run the example, and notice that both edit controls now properly validate hexadecimal numbers.

One of the keys to doing this is to refer to the `sender` object in our event handler, rather than explicitly referring to either text box. When the event handler is executed, the `sender` object is set to the `TextBox` control that is currently being validated. We could use this, for example, to display a `Label` control that explicitly tells the user which text box is causing the problem, or to customize the validation behavior according to which text box is being validated.

'TextBox' Validation in VB.NET

Now we will present the same example in Visual Basic.

Start Visual Studio, and create a new C# Windows Application project. Name this project `VBEventsExample`.

As before, place two `TextBox` controls and a `Button` control on the form. For both of the `TextBox` controls, set the following properties:

Property Name	Property Value
`CharacterCasing`	`Upper`
`Text`	(nothing)

The resulting window will look just like the one for the C# example above.

Next we will add an event handler for the `Validating` event for the first `TextBox` control. This time, we will not use Visual Studio to create an empty event handler for us. Instead, we will simply declare our event handler using the `Handles` keyword. We will declare that it handles the `Validating` event for both `TextBox` controls:

```
Private Sub HecDecValidate(ByVal sender As Object, _
            ByVal e As System.ComponentModel.CancelEventArgs) _
            Handles TextBox1.Validating, TextBox2.Validating
    Dim tb As TextBox = CType(sender, TextBox)
    Dim str As String = tb.Text

    Dim si As Integer
    For si = 0 To str.Length - 1
        Dim ss As String = str.Substring(si, 1)
        Dim b As Boolean = (ss >= "A" And ss <= "F") Or _
            (ss >= "0" And ss <= "9")
        If (Not b) Then
            MessageBox.Show("Invalid hexadecimal number", "Error", _
                MessageBoxButtons.OK, MessageBoxIcon.Error)
            tb.Select(0, tb.Text.Length)
            e.Cancel = True
            Return
        End If
    Next
End Sub
```

The declaration of the subroutine specifies that it handle events for both `TextBox` controls:

```
Private Sub HecDecValidate(ByVal sender As Object, _
            ByVal e As System.ComponentModel.CancelEventArgs) _
            Handles TextBox1.Validating, TextBox2.Validating
```

Similar to the C# example, we can cast the sender to a `TextBox` and assign it to a local variable in order to use it:

```
Dim tb As TextBox = CType(sender, TextBox)
```

This example behaves identically to the C# example.

Implementing and Raising Events

When writing custom controls, we would need to implement events. What we mean by implementing events is to write the code so that users of our custom control can write event handlers, and register those event handlers with our custom control. Implementing events actually is not directly tied to writing custom controls, though. Many other types of situations lend themselves to implementation using events. We could write an inventory system, and a re-ordering system could register an event handler to be called when inventory gets too low. Another example is a pharmaceutical application where a security system gets an event when an order for a controlled substance is entered into the system.

In this section, we will see how to implement an event handler, and then raise that event. Our intent is not to show a realistic or even a pseudo-realistic example, but to present the syntax, in both C# and VB, of declaring and implementing a class that contains events.

Events really have nothing intrinsically to do with graphical user interfaces, so for simplicity, we'll make this example a Console application – although the principles are no different for Windows Forms applications.

We have two classes:

- `ImplementsEvent` contains an event called `MyEvent`, as well as methods that, when executed, raise the event.
- `TestEventHandler` is the class that contains the `Main` routine that will be run when the program is executed. `Main` instantiates the `ImplementsEvent` class, adds an event handler to its event, and then calls the method to raise the event.

In C# the code appears as follows:

```
using System;

class ImplementsEvent
{
    public event EventHandler MyEvent;

    // Invoke MyEvent; called from within our class (or perhaps a derived
    // class) whenever we want to raise the event
    protected virtual void InvokeEvent(EventArgs e)
    {
        MyEvent(this, e);
    }

    // this function raises the one and only event in our class
    public void DoSomethingThatRaisesAnEvent()
    {
        EventArgs e = new EventArgs();
        InvokeEvent(e);
    }
}

class TestEvent
{
    // This is our event handler
    private static void MyEventHandler(object sender, EventArgs e)
    {
        Console.WriteLine("The event fired!");
    }

    static void Main(string[] args)
    {
        ImplementsEvent ie = new ImplementsEvent();
        ie.MyEvent += new EventHandler(MyEventHandler);
        ie.DoSomethingThatRaisesAnEvent();
    }
}
```

As we've noted, the first class (`ImplementsEvent`) in our example contains an event, and contains a function that will raise the event. We declare the event with the code:

```
public event EventHandler MyEvent;
```

This member variable is public, so that classes that use our class can register their event handlers, as the class `TestEvent` did with the line:

```
ie.MyEvent += new EventHandler(MyEventHandler);
```

As we have seen previously, the definition of the `EventHandler` class is:

```
public delegate void EventHandler(object sender, EventArgs e);
```

`InvokeEvent` is a protected method. Many of the methods to raise events in the .NET classes are protected. This means that we can raise those events either in the class itself, or in classes that we derive from them. This is a good design decision – external classes should not be able to raise events directly. Our class should explicitly control when events are raised.

The identical example in VB.NET is:

```
Public Class ImplementsEvent
    Public Event MyEvent As EventHandler

    ' Invoke MyEvent; called whenever we want to raise the event
    Protected Overridable Sub InvokeEvent(ByVal e As EventArgs)
        RaiseEvent MyEvent(Me, e)
    End Sub

    ' This function raises the one and only event in our class
    Public Sub DoSomethingThatRaisesAnEvent()
        Dim e As EventArgs = New EventArgs()
        InvokeEvent(e)
    End Sub
End Class

Public Class TestEvent
    ' This is our event handler
    Private Shared Sub MyEventHandler(ByVal sender As Object, _
                                      ByVal e As EventArgs)
        Console.WriteLine("The event fired!")
    End Sub

    Public Shared Sub Main()
        Dim ie As ImplementsEvent = New ImplementsEvent()
        AddHandler ie.MyEvent, AddressOf MyEventHandler
        ie.DoSomethingThatRaisesAnEvent()
    End Sub
End Class
```

Summary

In this chapter, we have seen how event handling is integral to the process of writing graphical user interfaces. We have seen how delegates constitute the primary mechanism for implementing events in the .NET framework. We have explored the semantics of delegates in depth using both C# and VB. We have written event handlers in both C# and VB, and seen how Visual Studio relieves us of much of the burden of the wiring up of event handlers to events. We have seen how events are implemented in the .NET framework. Finally, we have implemented a class that contains a custom event, and seen how to raise that event.

System.Object
System.MarshalRefObject
System.ComponentMode.Component

Legend
Concrete Class
Abstract class

System.Windows.Forms

CommonDialog
ColorDialog
FileDialog
FontDialog
PageSetupDialog
PrintDialog
ErrorProvider
HelpProvider
ImageList
Menu
ContextMenu
MainMenu
MenuItem
NotifyIcon
StatusBarPanel
Timer
ToolBarButton
ToolTip
ListViewItem
TreeNode
Control
ButtonBase
Button
CheckBox
RadioButton
DataGrid
DateTimePicker
GroupBox
Label
LinkLabel
ListControl
ComboBox
ListBox
CheckedListBox
ListView
MonthCalendar
PictureBox
PrintReviewControl
ProgressBar
ScrollableControl
ContainerControl
Form
PrintPreviewDialog
ThreadExceptionDialog
PropertyGrid
UpDownBase
DomainUpDown
NumericUpDown
UserControl
Panel
TabPage
ScrollBar
HScrollBar
VScrollBar
Splitter
StatusBar
TabControl
TextBoxBase
RichTextBox
Textbox
ToolBar
TrackBar
TreeView

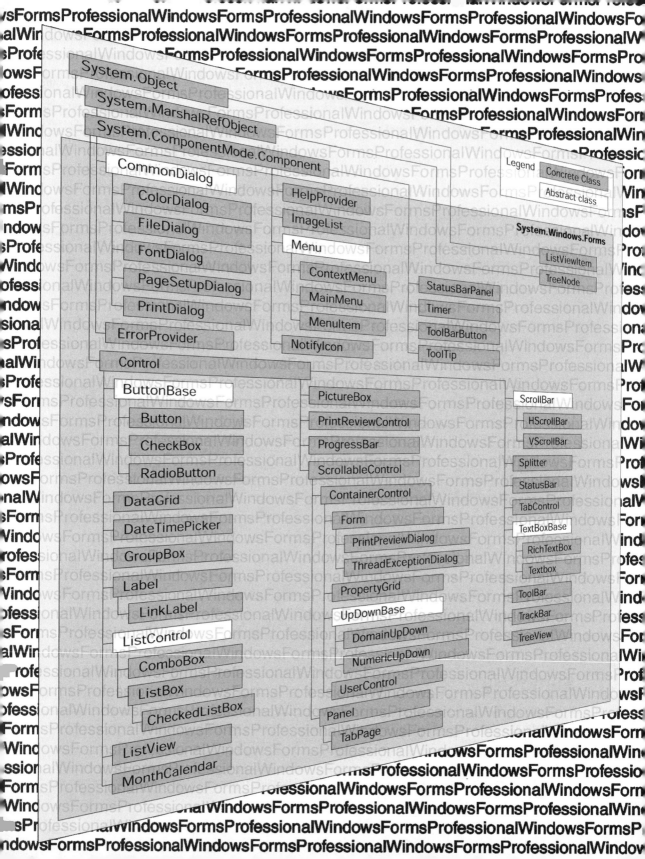

7

Windows Forms and Data

It's a pretty safe bet to say that most of us will need to deal with some sort of data in just about every software application we build today. Database access technologies have been steadily progressing over the past few years beginning with the advent of the Open Database Connectivity (ODBC) standard. Since then, we have seen several different higher-level data access APIs come and go in Visual Basic, including VBSQL, Data Access Objects (DAO), Remote Data Objects (RDO), Active X Data Objects (ADO), and now ADO.NET.

This chapter will focus on how to use the next generation data-access programming model that Microsoft is including as part of the .NET framework – ADO.NET. This new programming model is an important development in this domain of programming. With its focus on disconnected DataSets, ADO.NET gives us powerful tools to build loosely coupled, distributed applications.

In this chapter, we will discuss how we can use the services provided by ADO.NET in our Windows Forms applications to interact with a database. We'll start by looking at the architecture of ADO.NET and how it differs from traditional ADO. Understanding the nuts and bolts of ADO.NET at the lowest level will help us when we make our forms data aware, so we will see a few small console examples that demonstrate ADO.NET in the simplest fashion possible. ADO.NET is a very large, comprehensive class library. It is not possible to cover all of its capabilities in a single chapter, but we will cover enough so that we have a good basic understanding of how it works.

We'll then see an overview of data binding using Windows Forms. We'll start by seeing some of the simplest examples possible. These examples will also introduce some of the extensive facilities in Visual Studio.NET for dealing with data.

After covering these fundamentals, we will see how the wizards in Visual Studio.NET can relieve us from much of the effort to build applications that are data-aware. Once we understand the fundamentals, we are then in a position to use the wizards to lay a framework, which we can then modify for our more specific data needs. This means that we need to understand ADO.NET and how data binding works.

Finally, we will see how we can bind controls to types of data structures (such as arrays and collections) other than those populated from databases. This is an important feature of Windows Forms that can give us a great deal of leverage when building complex applications. Using these features allows us to work smarter.

Examples in this Chapter

Most of the examples in this chapter will involve the 'Northwind' sample database, which is included as part of many of Microsoft's database products. The Microsoft SQL Server Desktop Engine (MSDE) is included with Visual Studio.NET. By default, all of the examples in this chapter use this database engine, but it is also easy to use SQL Server or Access.

To install MSDE, log into an account with Administrator privileges.

- Browse the file `<FrameworkSDK>\Samples\StartSamples.htm`. Typically, this file would be at `C:\Program Files\Microsoft.NET\FrameworkSDK\Samples\StartSamples.htm`, but the location may vary depending on your installation. In this page, there are options to install and configure MSDE.
- Click on the Install the .NET Framework Samples Database link. You will see the file download dialog box. It will indicate that you have chosen to download `InstMSDE.EXE`. There are two radio buttons, giving you the option of what to do with this file. Check the radio button that says Run this program from its current location. Then press the OK button.
- You will be told that the Authenticode signature is not found. Click Yes to install and run the program.
- After running the program, reboot your computer.
- Again browse the file `<FrameworkSDK>\Samples\StartSamples.htm`.
- Click on the Complete the Installation link. Again, you must be logged in using an account with Administrator privileges.
- In the next dialog box, check the radio button that says Run this program from its current location. Then press the OK button.
- You will be told that the Authenticode signature is not found. Click Yes to install and run the program.
- Upon completion of the installation program, you will be told that the samples configuration has completed successfully. If you want to see the QuickStart tutorials, you can click the Launch button in this final dialog box. Otherwise, press the Cancel button. If you press the Cancel button and want to return to the QuickStart tutorials at any point in the future, you can browse the URL http://localhost/quickstart/default.aspx.

As always, all of the code for the sample applications included in this chapter is available for download from the Wrox web site (www.wrox.com).

ADO.NET Architectural Overview

This section will not provide a comprehensive detailed examination of the architecture of ADO.NET as that could fill an entire book on its own, but it will provide an overview.

ADO.NET is the next step in evolution after Microsoft Active X Data Objects (ADO). It is an API for accessing data sources of many kinds, but with a large emphasis on accessing SQL-based relational database engines. The most important new feature is the efficiency and effectiveness with which we can access remote disconnected SQL database engines.

When building n-tier enterprise applications, a typical approach would be to have the business services tier use ADO.NET to talk to the data services tier. By using the disconnected approach, the business services tier can make the least possible demands on the data services tier, using connections to the database engine only when necessary.

Following is a list of the main benefits of ADO.NET:

- **Scalability**: Due to its disconnected approach, ADO.NET can support a much greater number of users. After reading data from the database, we can operate on the data extensively without an active connection to the database. Another disadvantage of a connected approach is the difficulty of dealing with a broken connection.
- **Interoperability**: ADO.NET takes extensive advantage of XML as a format for sending and storing data. Any component that can send or receive XML can be a producer or consumer of data. As an example, using Extensible Stylesheet Language (XSL) and XSL Transformations (XSLT), we can take a DataSet, format it, and display it in a browser. In addition, we could write a module to extract data from a proprietary database, format the data in XML, populate a DataSet from the XML, and bind the data to controls.
- **Ease of Application Redesign**: In the past, changing the number of tiers in an n-tier application has been very difficult, but this may be necessary to reduce demand on limited resources on a particular server. If tiers represent data using XML, it is easier to change the number of tiers – because of the ease with which XML is transmitted over network connections, including over firewalls, any point where data can be represented as XML is a candidate for splitting a tier and creating two tiers. ADO.NET `DataSet` objects convert to and from XML with ease, so this feature expands the number of candidates for splitting a tier.
- **Better Programming Model**: In ADO.NET, we operate on data using the `DataSet` class. When compared to previous implementations of data types that encapsulate database data, such as `Recordset` in ADO, this class better reflects the actual structure of the data, including parent/child and n-to-n relationships. In addition, typed `DataSet` classes give us increased safety and convenience in programming. Visual Studio.NET can provide statement completion for typed classes, providing us with a list of columns in a table when referencing a column.
- **Better performance**: When compared to ADO, elimination of COM marshaling to transmit a `Recordset` among tiers results in significant performance benefits.

ADO.NET Classes

As we mentioned, ADO.NET is built around a disconnected architecture. In other words, a connection to a database is only maintained when actually retrieving or updating data. When not performing these operations, data is maintained in an instance of the central class in ADO.NET – a `DataSet` object. We will be working with and learning more about the `DataSet` class throughout this chapter, but what's important to understand now is that a `DataSet` can really be thought of as an in-memory database. A `DataSet` can include multiple tables, relationships between those tables, and constraints on what data they can contain.

After populating a DataSet with data from a database, you can then add, edit, and delete records in the dataset. However, because a DataSet is essentially a private copy of the data, none of the changes are actually written to the underlying database at the time they take place. Instead, the DataAdapter class is used to both populate a DataSet and write changes back to the actual database. The DataAdapter is the object that encapsulates the actual SQL commands or references to stored procedures used to perform the various database operations. We will have a separate DataAdapter for each table within the DataSet.

As datasets are completely independent of the data source, a DataSet can be populated and then exchanged with other components in an application, or even across the Internet using a technology such as SOAP (Simple Object Access Protocol). The DataSet could then be passed back and synchronized with the back-end database. One of the key aspects of ADO.NET that makes this possible is that XML is one of the fundamental formats for data. Whenever a DataSet is persisted to a file on disk, or a stream for sending to another component, it is automatically done using XML. Any XML file has a certain structure, and this structure can be described using an XML Schema Definition (XSD) file. This file describes the tags, the data types of the tags, acceptable children for a tag, and so on. While the data in a DataSet is persisted as XML, the structure of the data can be loaded from and serialized as an **XSD** file. This will become apparent when we use a wizard in Visual Studio.NET to create DataSet objects. The wizard automatically generates an XSD file and, when the DataSet is instantiated, it has a reference to this XSD file.

Most times, we will not need to be concerned with the XML-based technologies behind ADO.NET since Visual Studio.NET. will be doing most of the work for us. This includes generating and updating schemas based on choices we make in the visual designers. However, you should be aware that ADO.NET does provide the flexibility to interact with these elements directly. We will not be looking much more at the XML aspects of ADO.NET, but you can refer to the Visual Studio.NET documentation for more information.

It should be noted that there might be some instances where it would still be more desirable to work with continuously connected data. In these cases, where having up to the moment data is critical, Microsoft still recommends using traditional ADO in your application. As ADO is a COM based technology, and because .NET works seamlessly with COM, we can certainly write .NET applications that use ADO instead of ADO.NET.

A DataSet is made up of one or more instances of the DataTable class. In other words, unlike Recordset objects, a DataSet does not provide a flat view of the database. It can contain data from multiple tables – because of this, a DataSet can represent structures that were impossible to encapsulate in a Recordset, such as self-relating tables and many-to-many relationships.

Another significant advantage of DataSet involves how we can navigate around the data. In ADO, it was necessary to sequentially iterate through the individual records of a Recordset. In ADO.NET, it now becomes possible to treat a table as any other collection and access particular rows via an ordinal or primary key index. Not only that, but since a DataSet can contain multiple tables, you can even navigate master-detail relationships. For example, while on an order record that shows when an order was placed, you could then navigate from there to the set of order_detail records that show what items were purchased. Later on in this chapter, we'll build an example that shows this.

DataTable objects contain one or more DataColumn objects, which encapsulate a column of data from the database. A DataColumn object contains a reference to a DataType object, which indicates what the type of the column is. For example, we might specify that the column contains string data, integers, or decimals. Properties of the DataColumn class, such as AllowDBNull, Unique, and ReadOnly, constrains data entry and updating of the data, giving us better control over data integrity. There are also automatic data generation features in the DataColumn class, such as AutoIncrement, AutoIncrementSeed, and AutoIncrementStep. We can also create a DataColumn object that contains an expression. This allows us to have DataColumn objects with automatically calculated values, which is a useful feature. A good use for a calculated column would be an Invoice application: in the Invoice Items table, we could have a column that gives us the line item total (quantity * price).

Another capability with the DataColumn class is the ability to register event handlers and watch for the ColumnChanging and ColumnChanged events. Whenever data in the column changes, our event handler gets called, and we can update our display to reflect the new data.

The Model/View/Controller framework is a design pattern based on the listener design pattern, which makes it easier to create an application where we have multiple views of a set of data. If the data changes, we can update all views to reflect the changes in data. If you are not familiar yet with design patterns, there are a number of good books on the subject. Knowledge of design patterns is important for today's object-oriented developer. The ColumnChanging and ColumnChanged events give some of the basic capabilities for implementing an MVC infrastructure.

We can add constraints to a DataTable using the ConstraintCollection class. Two types of constraints are currently implemented: UniqueConstraint and ForeignKeyConstraint. UniqueConstraint ensures that the data in a column is always unique. The ForeignKeyConstraint determines what will happen when data in a parent table is changed. For example, when we delete a parent row, all child rows could be automatically deleted. The options with a ForeignKeyConstraint are:

- Delete all child records
- Set the field(s) in child records to null
- Set the field(s) in child records to a default value
- Raise an exception

The DataSet class automatically provides the functionality that we get with constraints: we don't need to write code to implement it. We simply set the options, and the DataSet class provides the functionality.

A DataSet object can contain one or more DataRelation objects, which relate two DataTable objects together using DataColumn objects. For example, we can create a parent/child relationship, such as an Invoice that contains multiple InvoiceItems. This is similar to a foreign key one-to-many relationship. When we add a DataRelation to a DataSet, both a ForeignKeyConstraint and a UniqueConstraint are created automatically as a side effect of the creation of the DataRelation.

After a DataSet is filled, each DataTable within the set contains zero or more DataRow objects in a DataRowCollection. The DataRow objects contain the actual data read from the database (or some other source).

We can register an event handler with the DataTable class and watch for the RowChanging, RowChanged, OnRowDeleting, and OnRowDeleted events. Similar to the ColumnChanging event, these are some of the basic capabilities for implementing an MVC infrastructure.

We create connections to the database using either OleDbConnection or SqlConnection. The SqlConnection class is optimized for more efficient access to Microsoft SQL Server. The OleDbConnection class can access any native OLE DB provider.

All the OleDbConnection and SqlConnection classes do is open a connection to the database; they don't access any data. As previously mentioned, to populate a DataSet with data using one of these classes, we use a DataAdapter object. A DataAdapter has two subclasses that we will primarily use: SqlDataAdapter and OleDbDataAdapter. The Fill method of the DataAdapter class reads the data source and populates the DataSet with the data. The Update method propagates all changes back to the database.

After populating a DataSet, it is often necessary to have a customized view of a DataTable with different sorting and filtering criteria applied. This allows us to have multiple data bound controls, such as DataGrid controls, each showing a different view into the data. In addition, after making a number of modifications to the data in the DataSet, it would be very inefficient to update the database with the entire DataSet, particularly if we had to send the DataSet to a server at a remote location, possibly using a connection with low bandwidth. It is necessary to have a view into the data of a DataSet that shows just the added, modified, or deleted records. In an area of related functionality, when binding controls to data, it is desirable to keep track of proposed changes to the data, and allow the user to commit the changes all at once, or optionally to cancel making any of the proposed changes. The DataView class provides all of this functionality. It is a customized view of a DataTable that provides for sorting, filtering, and tracking modifications to the data (both permanent modifications, and very temporary modifications made by data bound controls). We use the DataView indexer to get an instance of a DataRowView, which maintains multiple values of the data (Original, Current, and Proposed).

The multiple values of the DataRowView deserve some additional explanation. When the data is initially read from the database using an OleDbConnection or an SqlConnection, the Original and Current values are set to the values as read from the database. The Proposed values are not yet defined.

As we make changes to the DataSet, the Current values are changed, while the Original values remain as they were read from the database. By doing a comparison of the two values throughout the DataSet, we can determine exactly which values need to be updated in the database. After we have updated the database so that it is in sync with the data in the DataSet, we can call the AcceptChanges method on the DataSet. This sets all Original values to the Current values, and prepares the DataSet for another round of changes to the data. Actually, we don't need to do much work to handle this: the DataSet class takes care of all the details for us. We'll understand how later on in this chapter.

The Proposed values are even more transitory. Before the user starts editing any data in a form, we call the BeginEdit method, which sets all Proposed values to the Current values. When the user is editing a record in a form in our application, the Proposed values are set. When the record is as the user wants it and the user commits the changes, we invoke the EndEdit method and the Current values are set from the Proposed values. If the CancelEdit method is invoked, the Proposed values are discarded and all values revert to the Current values.

Don't worry if this seems a little complicated: we'll see some detailed examples of the usage of these classes shortly. The main points to remember are:

- The DataView class provides customized views of a DataTable.
- The customized view can be sorted and filtered by criteria other than the default.

- We can also get DataView objects that show us the modified state of our data (Current values as compared to Original values).
- The modified state of our data includes a Proposed state, which is important for data binding of controls.

Every DataTable always has a DataView object for it. We can get this DataView object using the DefaultView property of the table. This is in addition to any additional DataView objects that we may create.

A DataViewManager contains a collection of DataView objects, one for each table in a DataSet. We can set default sorting and filtering criteria in a DataViewManager, which is convenient in certain circumstances when working with DataView objects. A DataViewManager has the same relationship to a DataSet as a DataView has to a DataTable. If we want to use DataViewManager, we have to put it together in code. There are no facilities to create DataViewManager objects at design time.

All controls actually always bind to a DataView object, not to a DataTable object. When we think that we are binding to the DataTable object, we are actually really binding to the default DataView object.

Following is a tabular summary of the most important classes in ADO.NET. Rather than listing them alphabetically, we list them in a somewhat top-down order. There are a number of auxiliary classes that we don't list, such as those used for raising exceptions, reading directly from the database, etc. Our main intention here is to give an overview of the architecture of the system, so that when we learn about the many other classes in ADO.NET, we can place them in context with the rest of the system.

Class Name	Description
OleDbConnection	Create connections to an OLE DB provider
SqlConnection	Create connections to Microsoft SQL Server 7.0 and 2000
OleDbDataAdapter	Interfaces between a DataSet and an OleDbConnection
SqlDataAdapter	Interfaces between a DataSet and an SqlConnection
DataSet	An in-memory representation of a portion of a database
DataTableCollection	A list of tables in a DataSet
DataTable	An in-memory representation of one table of a DataSet
DataColumnCollection	A list of DataColumn objects in a DataTable
DataColumn	A definition of a column of a DataTable
DataType	Defines the data type of a DataColumn
DataRelationCollection	A list of DataRelation objects in a DataTable
DataRelation	Uses the DataColumn objects to define a relation between two DataTable objects
ConstraintCollection	A list of Constraint objects in a DataTable

Table continued on following page

Class Name	Description
ForeignKeyConstraint	Determines what will happen when data in a parent table changes: delete child, set fields in child records to null, set to default value, or raise an exception
UniqueConstraint	Ensures that the data in a column is always unique
DataRowCollection	A list of DataRow objects in a DataTable
DataRow	An in-memory representation of a single row in a DataTable
DataViewManager	A collection of DataView objects in a DataSet
DataView	A view into a DataTable that can be sorted or filtered; in addition, we can create a DataView to see the Original, Current, Proposed, or Default data for a DataTable
DataRowView	A view into a single DataRow that contains the Original, Current, Proposed, or Default data for the DataRow

Very small examples with as little extra functionality as possible can make the use of these classes clear. To make these examples as simple as possible, we will use the console for output rather than Windows Forms.

Simplest DataSet Example

This example opens a connection to the database, creates a DataAdapter, creates a DataSet, and then fills the DataSet using the DataAdapter. After closing the connection, the example prints the CustomerID field from each record in the DataTable in the DataSet.

Create a new Visual C# Console Application project in Visual Studio.NET. If you are going to use the command line compiler, you must make sure that you include appropriate references to assemblies, otherwise the code will not compile. Enter the following code into class1.cs:

```
using System;
using System.Data;
using System.Data.SqlClient;

public class SimplestDataSetExample
{
   public static void Main()
   {
      // open the connection
      SqlConnection sc = new SqlConnection(
            "server=(local)\\NetSDK;uid=QSUser;pwd=QSPassword;
database=northwind");

      // create a data adapter
      SqlDataAdapter da = new SqlDataAdapter(
            "Select * from Customers", sc);

      // create and fill the DataSet
      DataSet ds = new DataSet();
      da.Fill(ds, "Customers");
```

```
        // close the connection
        sc.Close();

        // print out the DataSet
        DataTable dt = ds.Tables["Customers"];
        foreach (DataRow dr in dt.Rows)
        {
           Console.Write("CustomerID:" + dr["CustomerID"]);
           Console.WriteLine("     CompanyName:" + dr["CompanyName"]);
        }
     }
  }
```

We create the connection using the following line of code:

```
SqlConnection sc = new SqlConnection(
    "server=(local)\\NetSDK;uid=QSUser;pwd=QSPassword;database=northwind");
```

This is one of the simplest ways to create a SQL Connection, where we pass a connection string as an argument to the constructor of the `SqlConnection` class. The connection string consists of name/value pairs separated by semicolons. In this case, we have specified the database server, the user id, the password, and the database name.

If you are using the Microsoft SQL Server Desktop Engine (MSDE) on your development machine, the above line will work to create your connection without modification. We don't even need to explicitly name our own machine: using the text (`local`) will work just fine.

If you are using Microsoft SQL Server 7.0 or 2000 on your development machine, you can use the following line of code to create your connection (changing the `uid` and `pwd` as appropriate, of course):

```
SqlConnection sc = new SqlConnection(
   "server=(local);uid=sa;pwd=sapassword;database=northwind");
```

If you are using Microsoft SQL Server installed on another machine that is available over a network, you can use the following line, changing `ServerName` to the name of the remote machine:

```
SqlConnection sc = new SqlConnection(
   "server=ServerName;uid=sa;pwd=sapassword;database=northwind");
```

Next, we create the `DataAdapter` with the following line of code:

```
SqlDataAdapter da = new SqlDataAdapter(
            "Select * from Customers", sc);
```

We specify the select command and the `SqlConnection` that we just created as arguments to the constructor.

Now, we create a `DataSet` object and fill it with data:

```
DataSet ds = new DataSet();
da.Fill(ds, "Customers");
```

Now that the DataSet has been filled from the database, we can close the connection:

```
sc.Close();
```

Accessing the DataSet after the connection has been closed shows the disconnected nature of the DataSet. We should note that we could leave the connection open if we desire; if we were doing a large amount of processing with small DataSets, this might be more efficient. We print two fields from each row in the table as follows:

```
DataTable dt = ds.Tables["Customers"];
foreach (DataRow dr in dt.Rows)
{
   Console.Write("CustomerID:" + dr["CustomerID"]);
   Console.WriteLine("     CompanyName:" + dr["CompanyName"]);
}
```

This code shows us treating the Rows in the table as a collection and accessing the rows via a primary key index. In other examples, we will see code that demonstrates accessing rows via an ordinal index.

A partial output of the results of this example follows:

```
CustomerID:ALFKI        CompanyName:Alfreds Futterkiste
CustomerID:ANATR        CompanyName:Ana Trujillo Emparedados y helados
CustomerID:ANTON        CompanyName:Antonio Moreno Taquería
CustomerID:AROUT        CompanyName:Around the Horn
CustomerID:BERGS        CompanyName:Berglunds snabbköp
CustomerID:BLAUS        CompanyName:Blauer See Delikatessen
CustomerID:BLONP        CompanyName:Blondesddsl père et fils
CustomerID:BOLID        CompanyName:Bólido Comidas preparadas
CustomerID:BONAP        CompanyName:Bon app'
CustomerID:BOTTM        CompanyName:Bottom-Dollar Markets
CustomerID:BSBEV        CompanyName:B's Beverages
CustomerID:CACTU        CompanyName:Cactus Comidas para llevar
CustomerID:CENTC        CompanyName:Centro comercial Moctezuma
CustomerID:CHOPS        CompanyName:Chop-suey Chinese
CustomerID:COMMI        CompanyName:Comércio Mineiro
CustomerID:CONSH        CompanyName:Consolidated Holdings
```

DataColumn Example

This example opens a connection to the database, creates two DataAdapter objects, creates a DataSet, and then fills the DataSet using both of the DataAdapter objects. As we mentioned previously, we will have a separate DataAdapter for each table within the DataSet. After closing the connection, the example iterates through the DataTable objects in the DataSet, then iterates through the DataColumns in each of the DataTable objects.

Create a new Visual C# Console Application project in Visual Studio.NET. Enter the following code into class1.cs:

```
using System;
using System.Data;
using System.Data.SqlClient;
```

```
public class DataColumnExample
{
   public static void Main()
   {
      // open the connection
      SqlConnection sc = new SqlConnection(
            "server=(local)\\NetSDK;uid=QSUser;pwd=QSPassword;
            database=northwind");

      // set up two data adapters
      SqlDataAdapter daCustomers = new SqlDataAdapter(
            "Select * from Customers", sc);
      SqlDataAdapter daOrders = new SqlDataAdapter(
            "Select * from Orders", sc);

      // create the DataSet and fill it
      DataSet ds = new DataSet();
      daCustomers.Fill(ds, "Customers");
      daOrders.Fill(ds, "Orders");

      // close the connection
      sc.Close();

      // print out the DataSet
      foreach (DataTable dt in ds.Tables)
      {
         Console.WriteLine("Table Name:" + dt);
         foreach (DataColumn dc in dt.Columns)
         {
            Console.Write("  Column Name:" + dc);
            Console.WriteLine("  DataType:" + dc.DataType);
         }
         Console.WriteLine();
      }
   }
}
```

This time, we create two `DataAdapter` objects, one each for the `Customers` and `Orders` tables:

```
SqlDataAdapter daCustomers = new SqlDataAdapter(
   "Select * from Customers", sc);
SqlDataAdapter daOrders = new SqlDataAdapter(
   "Select * from Orders", sc);
```

After declaring the `DataSet`, we execute the `Fill` method on both `DataAdapter` objects:

```
daCustomers.Fill(ds, "Customers");
daOrders.Fill(ds, "Orders");
```

Finally, we can iterate through the tables in the dataset, and all of the columns for each table:

```
foreach (DataTable dt in ds.Tables)
{
   Console.WriteLine("Table Name:" + dt);
   foreach (DataColumn dc in dt.Columns)
   {
      Console.Write("  Column Name:" + dc);
      Console.WriteLine("  DataType:" + dc.DataType);
   }
   Console.WriteLine();
}
```

The example produces the following output:

```
Table Name:Customers
  Column Name:CustomerID  DataType:System.String
  Column Name:CompanyName  DataType:System.String
  Column Name:ContactName  DataType:System.String
  Column Name:ContactTitle  DataType:System.String
  Column Name:Address  DataType:System.String
  Column Name:City  DataType:System.String
  Column Name:Region  DataType:System.String
  Column Name:PostalCode  DataType:System.String
  Column Name:Country  DataType:System.String
  Column Name:Phone  DataType:System.String
  Column Name:Fax  DataType:System.String

Table Name:Orders
  Column Name:OrderID  DataType:System.Int32
  Column Name:CustomerID  DataType:System.String
  Column Name:EmployeeID  DataType:System.Int32
  Column Name:OrderDate  DataType:System.DateTime
  Column Name:RequiredDate  DataType:System.DateTime
  Column Name:ShippedDate  DataType:System.DateTime
  Column Name:ShipVia  DataType:System.Int32
  Column Name:Freight  DataType:System.Decimal
  Column Name:ShipName  DataType:System.String
  Column Name:ShipAddress  DataType:System.String
  Column Name:ShipCity  DataType:System.String
  Column Name:ShipRegion  DataType:System.String
  Column Name:ShipPostalCode  DataType:System.String
  Column Name:ShipCountry  DataType:System.String
```

DataRelation Example

This example enhances the previous example by establishing a relation between the `Customers` table and the `Orders` table. Using the `DataRelation`, the example then prints out every customer, and for every customer, its orders.

Create a new Visual C# Console Application project in Visual Studio.NET. Enter the following code into class1.cs:

```
using System;
using System.Data;
using System.Data.SqlClient;

public class DataRelationExample
{
   public static void Main()
   {
      // open the connection
      SqlConnection sc = new SqlConnection(
            "server=(local)\\NetSDK;uid=QSUser;pwd=QSPassword;
            database=northwind");

      // create two data adapters, fill the DataSet, close connection
      SqlDataAdapter daCustomers = new SqlDataAdapter(
            "Select * from Customers", sc);
      SqlDataAdapter daOrders = new SqlDataAdapter(
            "Select * from Orders", sc);
      DataSet dsCustomersOrders = new DataSet();
      daCustomers.Fill(dsCustomersOrders, "Customers");
      daOrders.Fill(dsCustomersOrders, "Orders");
      sc.Close();

      DataRelation dr;
      DataColumn dc1;
      DataColumn dc2;

      // Get the parent and child columns of the two tables.
      dc1 = dsCustomersOrders.Tables["Customers"].Columns["CustomerID"];
      dc2 = dsCustomersOrders.Tables["Orders"].Columns["CustomerID"];

      // Create a DataRelation using the two columns
      dr = new System.Data.DataRelation("CustomersToOrders", dc1, dc2);

      // Add the DataRelation to the DataSet
      dsCustomersOrders.Relations.Add(dr);

      // Using the DataRelation, print out the DataSet
      DataTable dt = dsCustomersOrders.Tables["Customers"];
      foreach (DataRow drCustomer in dt.Rows)
      {
         Console.Write("CustomerID:" + drCustomer["CustomerID"]);
         Console.WriteLine("     CompanyName:" +
                 drCustomer["CompanyName"]);
         foreach (DataRow drOrder in
                 drCustomer.GetChildRows("CustomersToOrders"))
            Console.WriteLine("  Order ID:" + drOrder["OrderID"]);
            Console.WriteLine();
      }
   }
}
```

The following code sets up the relationship between the two tables:

```
DataRelation dr;
DataColumn dc1;
DataColumn dc2;

// Get the parent and child columns of the two tables.
dc1 = dsCustomersOrders.Tables["Customers"].Columns["CustomerID"];
dc2 = dsCustomersOrders.Tables["Orders"].Columns["CustomerID"];

// Create a DataRelation using the two columns
dr = new System.Data.DataRelation("CustomersToOrders", dc1, dc2);
dsCustomersOrders.Relations.Add(dr);
```

After the relationship has been set up, we iterate through the customers (just like in the first example). Then, for each customer, we use the following code to iterate through the orders:

```
         foreach (DataRow drOrder in
                  drCustomer.GetChildRows("CustomersToOrders"))
            Console.WriteLine("  Order ID:" + drOrder["OrderID"]);
```

A partial output of this example looks like the following:

```
CustomerID:THEBI    CompanyName:The Big Cheese
 Order ID:10310
 Order ID:10708
 Order ID:10805
 Order ID:10992

CustomerID:THECR    CompanyName:The Cracker Box
 Order ID:10624
 Order ID:10775
 Order ID:11003

CustomerID:TOMSP    CompanyName:Toms Spezialitäten
 Order ID:10249
 Order ID:10438
 Order ID:10446
 Order ID:10548
 Order ID:10608
 Order ID:10967
```

In addition to allowing us to iterate through the child records of the customer, the `DataRelation` object would also constrict the `DataSet` so that it could not lose referential integrity. We could not delete a customer without dealing with its orders in some fashion: either they would have to be deleted as a cascading operation, or deleted beforehand. Another possibility is to set the `CustomerID` field in the `Orders` table to null if this were allowable.

DataViewSortFilter Example

This example creates a `DataView` object from a `DataSet` that we read from a database, and establishes sorting and filtering criteria.

Create a new Visual C# Console Application project in Visual Studio.NET. Enter the following code into class1.cs:

```
using System;
using System.Data;
using System.Data.SqlClient;

public class DataViewSortFilterExample
{
   public static void Main()
   {
      // open connection, create data adapters, fill DataSet, close
      // connection
      SqlConnection sc = new SqlConnection(
           "server=(local)\\NetSDK;uid=QSUser;pwd=QSPassword;
           database=northwind");
      SqlDataAdapter da = new SqlDataAdapter(
           "Select * from Customers", sc);
      DataSet ds = new DataSet();
      da.Fill(ds, "Customers");
      sc.Close();

      // get a DataTable from the DataSet
      DataTable dt = ds.Tables["Customers"];

      // create a DataView using the DataTable
      DataView dv = new DataView(dt);

      // Add sort and filter criteria to the DataView
      // The following sorts by the Region field, in DESCENDING order
      // Note: this sort is done in the DataSet, on the client,
      //       not on the server
      dv.Sort = "Region DESC";

      // The following filters by the Region field
      dv.RowFilter = "Region <= 'MA'";

      // now, print out the DataView
      for (int i = 0; i < dv.Count; i++)
         Console.WriteLine( "   " + dv[i]["CustomerID"] + " Region:" +
                dv[i]["Region"]);
   }
}
```

After creating and filling the DataSet, we create and initialize a DataView as follows:

```
// create a DataView using the DataTable
DataView dv = new DataView(dt);

// Add sort and filter criteria to the DataView
// The following sorts by the Region field, in DESCENDING order
dv.Sort = "Region DESC";

// The following filters by the Region field
dv.RowFilter = "Region <= 'MA'";
```

We are then able to iterate through the records in the DataView as follows:

```
for (int i = 0; i < dv.Count; i++)
   Console.WriteLine( "   " + dv[i]["CustomerID"] + " Region:" +
          dv[i]["Region"]);
```

The example creates the following output:

```
LILAS Region:Lara
ISLAT Region:Isle of Wight
SAVEA Region:ID
GROSR Region:DF
HUNGO Region:Co. Cork
LETSS Region:CA
BOTTM Region:BC
LAUGB Region:BC
OLDWO Region:AK
```

TwoDataViews Example

As a variation, this time we create the DataTable and DataView entirely programmatically. In this example, we demonstrate that DataView objects are really just views into the DataTable. Changing the DataTable changes the data as seen by the DataView.

The code for the example is:

```
using System;
using System.Data;

class TwoDataViewsExample
{
   // this method is a more convenient way to add a row to the table
   private void AddRow(DataTable dt, String str)
   {
      DataRow dr = dt.NewRow();
      dr["Item"] = str;
      dt.Rows.Add(dr);
   }

   private void DemoDataViews()
   {
      // Create a DataTable with one column.
      DataTable dt = new DataTable("SimpleTable");
      DataColumn dc = new DataColumn("Item",
                      Type.GetType("System.String"));
      dt.Columns.Add(dc);

      // Add a number of rows into the table
      AddRow(dt, "Apple");
      AddRow(dt, "Banana");
      AddRow(dt, "Peach");
      AddRow(dt, "Grapefruit");
      AddRow(dt, "Jackfruit");
      AddRow(dt, "Orange");
```

```
      AddRow(dt, "Pear");

      // set up two DataView objects, one sorted, the other filtered
      DataView dv1 = new DataView(dt);
      dv1.Sort = "Item DESC";

      DataView dv2 = new DataView(dt);
      dv2.RowFilter = "Item <= 'JZ'";

      // print both views
      PrintView(dv1, "Data View #1");
      PrintView(dv2, "Data View #2");

      // now add a new row that will show up in both views
      AddRow(dt, "Cherry");

      // print both views again
      PrintView(dv1, "Data View #1 (After adding a record)");
      PrintView(dv2, "Data View #2 (After adding a record)");
   }

   private void PrintView(DataView dv, string text)
   {
      Console.WriteLine("\n" + text);
      for(int i = 0; i < dv.Count; i++)
         Console.WriteLine( "\t" + dv[i]["Item"] );
         Console.WriteLine();
   }

   static void Main()
   {
      TwoDataViewsExample tdve = new TwoDataViewsExample();
      tdve.DemoDataViews();
   }
}
```

This time, we did not even create a `DataSet`: we just created a `DataTable`, and then created two `DataView` objects from the `DataTable`. The only new technique in this example is creating the `DataTable` programmatically and adding records to it. Note that this does not create a SQL database: it only creates a `DataTable` in memory.

The `AddRow` method adds the row to the table:

```
private void AddRow(DataTable dt, String str)
{
   DataRow dr = dt.NewRow();
   dr["Item"] = str;
   dt.Rows.Add(dr);
}
```

Running the example gives the following output:

```
Data View #1
    Pear
    Peach
    Orange
    Jackfruit
    Grapefruit
    Banana
    Apple

Data View #2
    Apple
    Banana
    Grapefruit
    Jackfruit

Data View #1 (After adding a record)
    Pear
    Peach
    Orange
    Jackfruit
    Grapefruit
    Cherry
    Banana
    Apple

Data View #2 (After adding a record)
    Apple
    Banana
    Grapefruit
    Jackfruit
    Cherry
```

We can see that after adding the Cherry record to the `DataTable`, it showed up in both `DataView` objects.

DataViewChangesExample

This example demonstrates how the `DataView` class tracks changes made to a `DataSet`. We will first create a `DataTable` programmatically. After creating the `DataTable`, we will add a record, delete a record, and modify a record. We will then create three `DataView` objects that explicitly report these changes. If we were working with a real SQL database, we could send these changes back to the database. It is important to understand this technique, as it is necessary to build database applications using ADO.NET and Windows Forms. We will see examples of this later.

The code for the example is:

```
using System;
using System.Data;

class DataViewChangesExample
{
   // this method is a more convenient way to add a row to the table
```

```
    private void AddRow(DataTable dt, String str)
    {
       DataRow dr = dt.NewRow();
       dr["Item"] = str;
       dt.Rows.Add(dr);
    }

    private void DemoDataViews()
    {
       // Create a DataTable with one column.
       DataTable dt = new DataTable("SimpleTable");
       DataColumn dc = new DataColumn("Item",
                      Type.GetType("System.String"));
       dt.Columns.Add(dc);

       // Add a number of rows into the table
       AddRow(dt, "Apple");
       AddRow(dt, "Banana");
       AddRow(dt, "Peach");
       AddRow(dt, "Grapefruit");
       dt.AcceptChanges();

       // Add a row
       AddRow(dt, "Watermelon");

       // Delete a row
       dt.Rows[1].Delete();

       // Change a row
       dt.Rows[0]["Item"] = "Red Apple";

       // create a view that contains just the added records
       DataView dvAdded = new DataView(dt);
       dvAdded.RowStateFilter = DataViewRowState.Added;

       // create a view that contains just the deleted records
       DataView dvDeleted = new DataView(dt);
       dvDeleted.RowStateFilter = DataViewRowState.Deleted;

       // create a view that contains just the modified records
       DataView dvModifiedCurrent = new DataView(dt);
       dvModifiedCurrent.RowStateFilter = DataViewRowState.ModifiedCurrent;

       // print all of the views
       PrintView(dvAdded, "Data View (Added)");
       PrintView(dvDeleted, "Data View (Deleted)");
       PrintView(dvModifiedCurrent, "Data View (ModifiedCurrent)");
    }

    private void PrintView(DataView dv, string text)
    {
       Console.WriteLine("\n" + text);
       for(int i = 0; i < dv.Count; i++)
          Console.WriteLine( "\t" + dv[i]["Item"] );
    }

    static void Main()
    {
       DataViewChangesExample dvce = new DataViewChangesExample();
       dvce.DemoDataViews();
    }
 }
```

One item of note is where we call the method `AcceptChanges` on the `DataTable` object:

```
AddRow(dt, "Apple");
AddRow(dt, "Banana");
AddRow(dt, "Peach");
AddRow(dt, "Grapefruit");
dt.AcceptChanges();
```

The `AcceptChanges` method commits all the changes made to this table since the last time `AcceptChanges` was called. When we call `AcceptChanges`, all rows marked as Added, Modified, or Deleted will then be marked Original. If we were working with a SQL Database, we would first commit the changes to the underlying database, then call `AcceptChanges`.

We deleted a row as follows:

```
// Delete a row
dt.Rows[1].Delete();
```

We changed a row as follows:

```
// Change a row
dt.Rows[0]["Item"] = "Red Apple";
```

The code to delete and change rows demonstrates accessing rows via an ordinal index.

When we run the example, as we would expect, we see the following output:

```
Data View (Added)
      Watermelon

Data View (Deleted)
      Banana

Data View (ModifiedCurrent)
      Red Apple
```

There are a number of other simple examples that we could see, but these few examples should give a good idea about what is going on when we use wizards to automatically generate code. When we see the code that the wizards generate, it will be familiar.

Data Binding

In Windows Forms, we can bind any property of any control to a data source, and when the data source changes, the property will be set automatically. Traditionally, we would bind the primary display property of the control (such as the `Text` property of a `TextBox` control) to the data source. In Windows Forms, this functionality is extended such that we can bind any property of any control to a data source: we could bind the background color of a `TextBox` so that it changes color based on a status of the underlying record; if we had a real-estate application, we could bind the graphic of an image control so that it automatically displayed the picture of the house that is for sale.

Of course, we can bind to data structures that we have just seen, including such classes as `DataSet`, `DataTable`, and `DataView`. In addition, in Windows Forms we can bind to just about any structure that contains data, such as an array or collection. Towards the end of the chapter, we'll see a couple of examples of this.

There are two types of data binding: simple and complex. We use each type in different situations.

Binding a property of a control to a single data element (such as a value in a record in a `DataSet`) is simple binding.

Complex binding gives us the capability to bind an aggregate data structure to a control that has the capability to display some type of array of data. Examples of such controls are the `DataGrid`, the `ListBox`, and the `ComboBox` controls. For instance, if we bind a `DataTable` to a `ListBox`, the `DataTable` will be displayed in the listbox. Adding a record to the `DataTable` automatically causes the `ListBox` to be updated to reflect the current state of the `DataTable`. Another common example is binding a `DataTable` to a `DataGrid`, which will then display the table in the grid.

We'll take a look at an example of each of these types of data binding.

SimpleDataBound Example

In this example, and from now on, we will use wizards to create our database connections, `DataAdapter` objects, and `DataSet` objects.

Create a new Visual C# Windows Application project in Visual Studio.NET.

In Visual Studio.NET, open the Server Explorer, if it is not already opened. If your Server Explorer doesn't contain a node for the database that you will use, right click on the **Servers** node in the Server Explorer and pick the **Add Server** menu item on the popup menu. This will bring up a dialog box where you can enter a computer name or IP address for the machine that contains your database server.

Expand the tree so that we can see the tables in the Northwind database. After expanding the tree, the Server Explorer will look something like this:

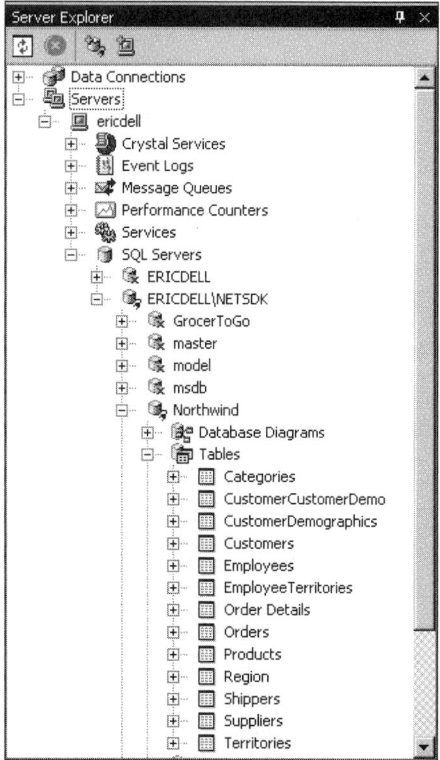

When we created the new project, Visual Studio.NET automatically created a form. Drag the `Customers` table from the Server Explorer to the form. This automatically creates a `SqlConnection` object and a `SqlDataAdapter` object.

Now, we want to have Visual Studio.NET automatically generate a `DataSet` for us to use for data binding. Select the Generate DataSet menu item from the Data menu. This starts a wizard that puts up a dialog box that allows us to change the name of the `DataSet` if we like.

Change the name of the `DataSet` to dsCustomers. Press the OK button. One quick note: the class name for our `DataSet` will be `dsCustomers`. Visual Studio.NET will automatically instantiate an object for our class when we use it in a form, and it automatically appends a number to the end of the class name, so that the instance name will not be identical to the class name. The instance name will be `dsCustomers1`.

If we now look at the Solution Explorer, we will see an entry named dsCustomers.xsd. As we read previously, the structure of the `DataSet` can be loaded from an **XML Schema Definition** (**XSD**) file. The wizard automatically generated an XSD file and, when the `DataSet` is instantiated, it has a reference to this XSD file.

Drag out a `TextBox` control on the form. Change the Text property to "".

Expand the (DataBindings) property. We will see three child properties under it: (Advanced), Tag, and Text. Text is the most common property to which we would bind data. We will see data binding to the Text property shortly. Tag is a property where we can set some type of custom data, so that we can make controls that are data driven. We won't bind data to the Tag property in this chapter. If we desire to bind data to any of the other properties, most of which we would not normally want to bind data to, we could click the (Advanced) child property, and see all possible properties to which we can bind data.

Click in the Text property and we will see a combo box button to the right of the Text property value. When we click the drop-down button, we see a small hierarchical control. Expand the first node that we see, which is dsCustomers1. Expand Customers. Then click on the CustomerID node. The Properties window will look something like this:

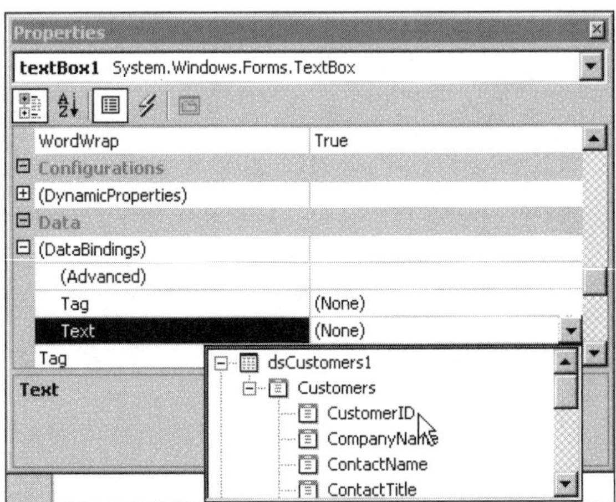

When we are done, the value of the Text property is dsCustomers1 - Customers.CustomerID. Alternatively, rather than using the hierarchical control, we can type the value in directly.

Add a label to the left of the CustomerID `TextBox` control. Set the **Text** property of the label to 'Customer ID:'.

We have one more thing to do: we have a database connection (`sqlConnection1`), we have a `DataAdapter` (`sqlDataAdapter1`), and we have a `DataSet` (the name of the `DataSet` class is `dsCustomers` and the name of the instance of our `DataSet` class is `dsCustomers1`). However, we have not filled our `DataSet` using our `DataAdapter`. Double-click on the form to bring up the form load event handler in the code editor. Modify the event handler to read:

```
private void Form1_Load(object sender, System.EventArgs e)
{
   sqlDataAdapter1.Fill(dsCustomers1, "Customers");
}
```

We have actually finished creating a data bound `TextBox` control. If we run the example, we will see the `CustomerID` for the first customer displayed in the `TextBox`:

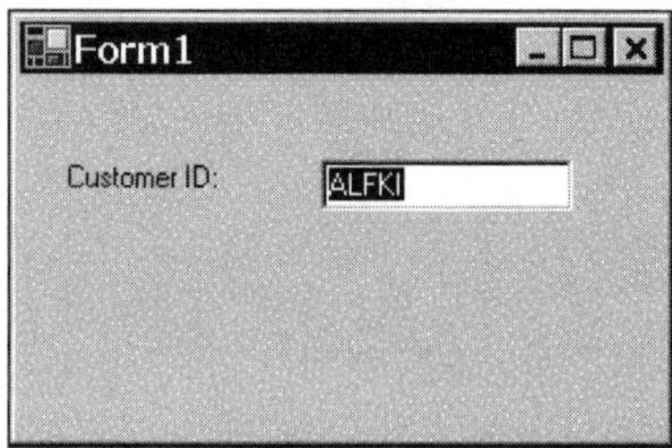

However, there are lots of records in our `DataSet`, and we have no way to navigate to the other records; we only get to see the first record. We'll fix this next.

Add four `Button` controls and a `TextBox`, oriented horizontally below our data bound `TextBox`. Change the **Text** properties of the buttons to '<<', '<', '>', and '>>'. Set the **Text** property of the `TextBox` to ''. Set the **ReadOnly** property of the `TextBox` to **True**.

The resulting window looks like this:

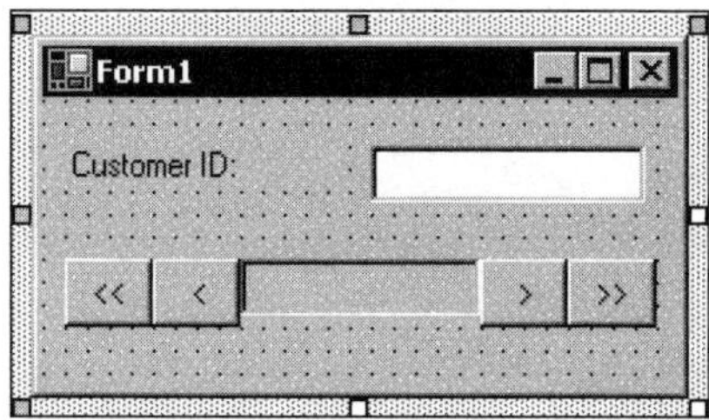

This is often called a 'VCR' control. We need to add some code to make our VCR control functional. Whenever the position of the bound data changes, we want to make the read only `TextBox` control say something like '`Record 3 of 92`'. Add the following method to the form:

```
private void updateVCRControl()
{
   textBox2.Text = "Record " +
```

```
        (BindingContext[dsCustomers1,"Customers"].Position + 1) +
        " of " +
        BindingContext[dsCustomers1,"Customers"].Count;
}
```

Next, modify the form load method, adding a call to `updateVCRControl()` after executing the `Fill` method on the `DataAdapter`.

```
private void Form1_Load(object sender, System.EventArgs e)
{
   sqlDataAdapter1.Fill(dsCustomers1, "Customers");
   updateVCRControl();
}
```

Double-click on the '<<' button in the design window to bring up the event handler. Add the following code:

```
private void button1_Click(object sender, System.EventArgs e)
{
   CurrencyManager cm = (CurrencyManager)
   BindingContext[dsCustomers1,"Customers"];
   cm.Position = 0;
   updateVCRControl();
}
```

Add the following code to the '<' button event handler:

```
private void button2_Click (object sender, System.EventArgs e)
{
   CurrencyManager cm = (CurrencyManager)
   BindingContext[dsCustomers1,"Customers"];
   cm.Position = cm.Position - 1;
   updateVCRControl();
}
```

Add the following code to the '>' button event handler:

```
private void button3_Click(object sender, System.EventArgs e)
{
   CurrencyManager cm = (CurrencyManager)
   BindingContext[dsCustomers1,"Customers"];
   cm.Position = cm.Position + 1;
   updateVCRControl();
}
```

Finally, add the following code to the '>>' button event handler:

```
private void button4_Click(object sender, System.EventArgs e)
{
   CurrencyManager cm = (CurrencyManager)
   BindingContext[dsCustomers1,"Customers"];
   cm.Position = cm.Count - 1;
   updateVCRControl();
}
```

Now, if we run the example, we can navigate through the records. Of course, only having one TextBox control bound to the data provides a limited degree of functionality, but it would be a simple matter to add more data bound controls to allow us to see other columns in the database table.

All of the above functions refer to a property of the form called BindingContext, which deserves some explanation.

When we bind a Windows Forms control to a data source, the data source will have an associated CurrencyManager object. The name CurrencyManager refers to the idea that, for a data source that is bound to controls, there is a current position within the data source. In effect, it is the CurrencyManager that actually does the binding – when the current position changes, it is the CurrencyManager that gets the data from the data source and sets the properties on the controls.

We may have multiple data sources bound to controls in a single form. We could have many TextBox controls bound to a DataSet. In addition we could have a ComboBox bound to an array, and we could have a ListBox bound to a collection. All of these data sources would have their own CurrencyManager, which would maintain the current position in data for the control bound to the data source. The BindingContext object maintains a list of CurrencyManager objects. The BindingContext has an indexer that gives us the CurrencyManager for a particular data source.

```
BindingContext[dsCustomers1,"Customers"]
```

The following diagram shows how there is one BindingContext for a form, which gives access to any number of CurrencyManager objects, each of which manage currency for a data source.

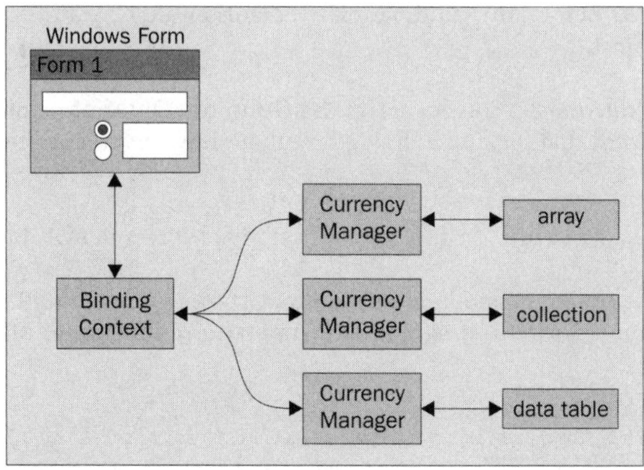

In the code for the button that gets the next record:

```
CurrencyManager cm = (CurrencyManager)
BindingContext[dsCustomers1,"Customers"];
cm.Position = cm.Position + 1;
updateVCRControl();
```

we first take the BindingContext for the form and then index into it to get the CurrencyManager. After we get the CurrencyManager, we can modify the current position within the data source using the Position property.

Note that the CurrencyManager automatically handles boundary conditions. We don't need to worry about setting the Position to an invalid value.

When setting the text for our read only TextBox in our VCR control, we also use the BindingContext and CurrencyManager, but only to retrieve the current position and the total count:

```
textBox2.Text = "Record " +
   (BindingContext[dsCustomers1,"Customers"].Position + 1) +
   " of " +
   BindingContext[dsCustomers1,"Customers"].Count;
```

Later on in this chapter, we will use some wizards to generate all of this automatically for us, but the underlying ideas are the same as in this simple example.

ComplexDataBound Example

In this example we will create the SqlConnection object, the SqlDataAdapter object, and the DataSet in the same way that we did in the last example. We will then bind the DataSet to a DataGrid control, which uses complex data binding instead of simple data binding, because it can display multiple records at once.

Create a new Visual C# Windows Application project in Visual Studio.NET.

In Visual Studio.NET, open the Server Explorer, if it is not already opened. Expand the tree so that we can see the tables in the Northwind database. Drag the Customers table from the Server Explorer to the form. As before, this automatically creates an SqlConnection object and an SqlDataAdapter object.

To automatically generate our DataSet, select the Generate DataSet menu item from the Data menu. This starts a wizard that puts up a dialog box that allows us to change the name of the DataSet if we like.

As before, change the name of the DataSet to dsCustomers. Press the OK button.

We also need to invoke the Fill method on the SqlDataAdapter, to fill the DataSet with data. Double-click on the empty form to bring up the form load event handler. Modify the event handler as follows:

```
private void Form1_Load(object sender, System.EventArgs e)
{
   sqlDataAdapter1.Fill(dsCustomers1, "Customers");
}
```

Using the toolbox, drag out a DataGrid on the form. Set the Anchor property to Top, Left, Bottom, Right, so that we can resize the window and see all of our columns easily.

Set the DataSource property to dsCustomers1. Set the DataMember property to Customers. We can use the drop-down lists in the property editor window to easily set these values.

We can now run the example and see the populated `DataGrid`:

This example doesn't allow us to save any changes to the underlying database. We'll see how to do this shortly.

Wizards

Visual Studio.NET has a couple of wizards that help us build elaborate data bound user interfaces. The two wizards that we will use are the `DataAdapter` wizard and the `DataForm` wizard.

Next, we're going to work through the creation of a simple data-bound form using these two wizards.

DataForm Wizard Example

Before using the `DataForm` wizard, we will use the `DataAdapter` wizard, which will create a data source that we will use in this example.

Create a new Visual C# Windows Application project in Visual Studio.NET.

The DataAdapter Wizard

The Toolbox in Visual Studio.NET has a Data tab, which contains several controls related to data access: DataSet, OleDbDataAdapter, OleDbConnection, OleDbCommand, SqlDataAdapter, SqlConnection, SqlCommand, and DataView. It looks like this:

We could drag these controls onto our form, and use them from that form; however, we are going to use a different approach. Instead of dropping a control on a form, we are going to add a new Component Class to our project so that more than one of our forms can share the same set of data access components.

Select Add New Item from the Project menu. Select the Component Class template in the Add New Item dialog box. We are going to accept the default name for our component class. Press the Open button. Visual Studio.NET will then display a visual designer for our class. Instead of dropping data access controls onto a form, we will drop them onto this visual class designer.

Add an `OleDbDataAdapter` to our component by dragging it from the Data tab of the Toolbox onto our component's designer. This will automatically start the `DataAdapter` Configuration Wizard. The following screenshot shows the Data tab of the Toolbox next to our component's designer:

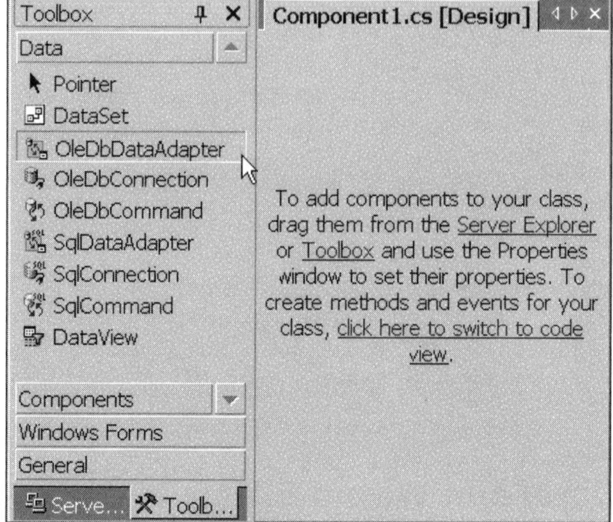

In this case, because we are connecting to a SQL Server database, we could use the `SqlDataAdapter`, which is optimized specifically for SQL Server. However, we will use the `OleDbAdapter` in this case, since it allows more flexibility in the type of database we can use.

Click Next to move past the first page of the wizard. The wizard asks which data connection to use. Click the New Connection button to bring up the Data Link properties dialog box. We need to set up this dialog box with appropriate information. If we were using the MSDE database, values for the dialog box typically would be:

Server Name:	`(local)\NETSDK`
Information to log on to the server:	Use a specific user name and password
User Name:	sa
Password:	password
Select a database on the server:	Northwind

If we were using a local SQL Server connection, values for the dialog box typically would be:

Server Name:	`MyMachineName`
Information to log on to the server:	Use a specific user name and password
User Name:	sa
Password:	password
Select a database on the server:	Northwind

Of course, you will have to replace '`MyMachineName`' with the specific name for your computer.

The dialog box filled out to use MSDE looks like this:

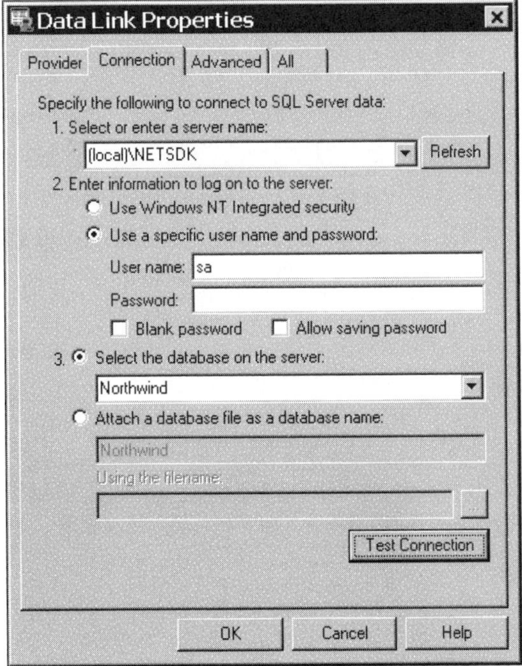

After entering the values for this dialog box, press the Test Connection button. You should see a message box indicating that the test connection succeeded. Press the Next button.

The next dialog box tells us to choose a query type. Make sure that the Use SQL statements radio button is selected. There are other options on this dialog box, which would allow us to use stored procedures. Using stored procedures is beyond the scope of this chapter. Press the Next button.

The next dialog box asks what data the data adapter should load into the dataset. Here, we will specify a Select SQL command that the wizard will use to generate the other SQL statements necessary to support inserts, updates, and deletes. In this case, we will use SELECT * FROM Customers. The window looks like this:

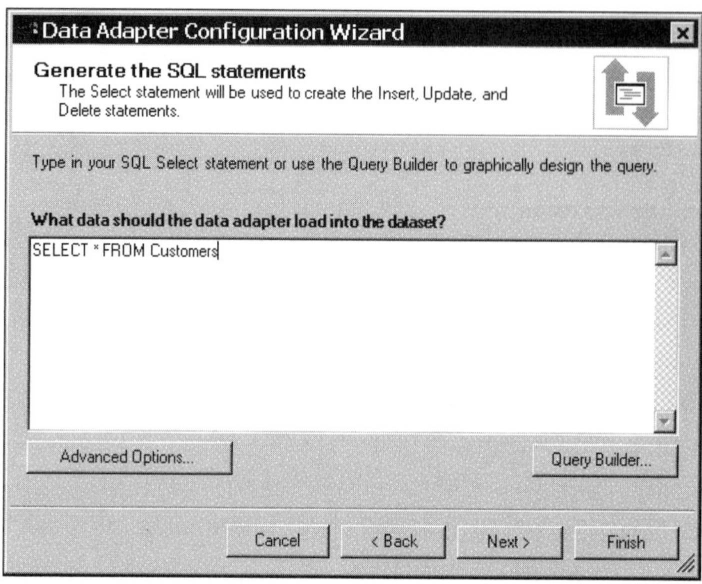

In this dialog box, there are buttons for Advanced Options and Query Builder. The Query Builder allows you to design a more complex query visually in much the same way as Microsoft Access or Enterprise Manager for SQL Server. These buttons are worth exploring.

Press the Next button, and then Finish. The `OleDbDataAdapter` we added earlier is visible and a new `OleDbConnection` component has also been added.

The `OleDbConnection` object is very similar in this case to the old ADO `Connection` object. You can explore the Properties window and you will see values for the Connection String, Database, Server, and others that you have probably seen before. The `OleDbDataAdapter`, on the other hand, is similar to the `Command` object in ADO. However, in this case the `DataAdapter` encapsulates commands for Select, Insert, Update, and Delete. You can explore all of these command properties in the property page for the `DataAdapter`.

Select the Generate DataSet menu item from the Data menu. Change the name of the `DataSet` to dsCustomers. Press the OK button.

Our next step is to add code that will fill our new `DataSet` with actual data. Open up the code view for `Component1` and add the following two methods to the `Component1` class:

```
public dsCustomers FillDataSet()
{
   // declare our DataSet
   dsCustomers ds = new dsCustomers();

   // open our connection, fill it, and close the connection
```

```
        oleDbConnection1.Open();
        oleDbDataAdapter1.Fill(ds);
        oleDbConnection1.Close();

        // return the DataSet
        return ds;
    }

    public void UpdateDataSource(dsCustomers ds)
    {
        // declare three DataSets, to hold the changes to the database
        System.Data.DataSet UpdatedRows;
        System.Data.DataSet InsertedRows;
        System.Data.DataSet DeletedRows;

        // get a DataSet that contains just the modified rows
        UpdatedRows = ds.GetChanges(System.Data.DataRowState.Modified);

        // get a DataSet that contains just the added rows
        InsertedRows = ds.GetChanges(System.Data.DataRowState.Added);

        // get a DataSet that contains just the deleted rows
        DeletedRows = ds.GetChanges(System.Data.DataRowState.Deleted);

        // if any of the operations above returned null, this means that there
        // were no rows modified, added, or deleted.

        // the following lines propagate the changes to the database
        if (UpdatedRows != null)
            oleDbDataAdapter1.Update(UpdatedRows);
        if (InsertedRows != null)
            oleDbDataAdapter1.Update(InsertedRows);
        if (DeletedRows != null)
            oleDbDataAdapter1.Update(DeletedRows);

        // close the connection
        oleDbConnection1.Close();
    }
```

The `FillDataSet` method opens our connection to the database, fills a new `DataSet` object with data and returns that `DataSet` object after closing the connection. The `UpdateDataSource` method is a bit more interesting. It shows that ADO.NET `DataSet` objects are really designed around a disconnected architecture. We can fill our `DataSet` and then make all sorts of changes to it – inserts, updates, and deletes. This method uses `DataSet` methods to retrieve these changes and then update our back-end data source appropriately.

The DataForm Wizard

Next, we will run the `DataForm` wizard to build our data-driven form.

Select Add New Item from the Project menu. Select the Data Form Wizard template in the Add New Item dialog box.

Press the Next button on the first page of the wizard.

The next page of the wizard asks us which dataset we want to use. As there is only one dataset in our new application, this page of the wizard will be filled out correctly by default. The Use the following dataset radio button should be checked and the combo box should contain DataFormWizardExample.dsCustomers, which is the name of our dataset.

Press the Next button. The next page of the wizard asks us to choose the methods to load and update data. If we press the combo box button on the first combo box, we will see our methods that we added to the `Component1` class. Select the `FillDataSet` method.

Next, check the Include an Update Button check box, and select the `UpdateDataSource` method in the second combo box. The window looks like this:

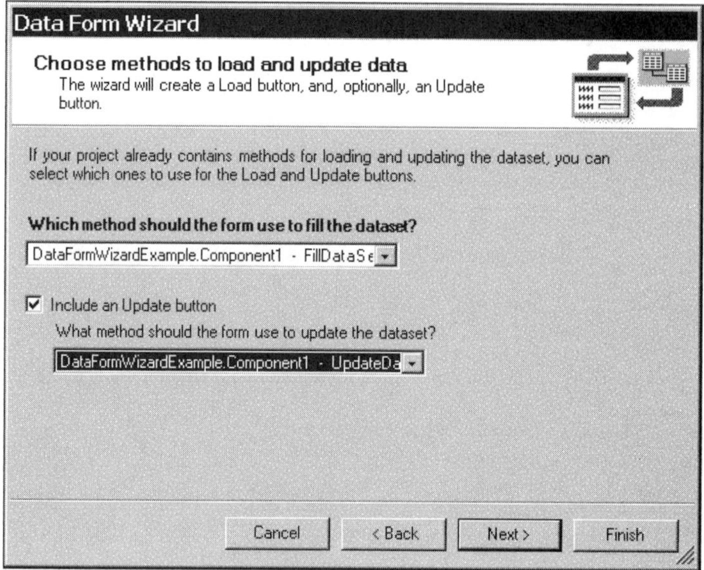

Click Next to bring up the wizard dialog box that allows us to choose which tables and columns to include in our form. We will accept the defaults here.

Press the Next button, which brings us to a dialog box that allows us to choose the display style. For this example, click the Single record in individual controls radio button. After we check this radio button, the rest of the check boxes will all be checked, which is what we want. We want a Cancel All button, as well as Add, Delete, Cancel, and Navigation controls, which are like the VCR controls that we saw previously.

Press the Finish button, and the wizard will create our data-driven form. The results of the wizard look like this:

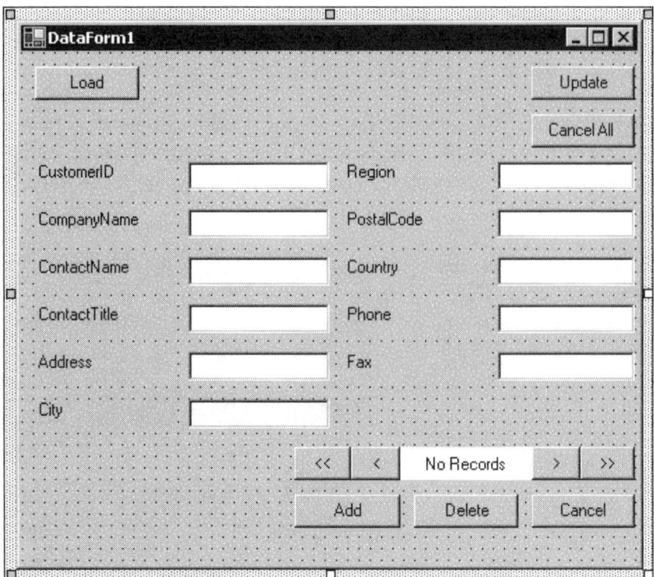

The last thing that we need to do before running our application is set `DataForm1` to be the startup form for our application. Bring up Form1.cs in the code editor. Modify the `Main` method as follows:

```
static void Main()
{
    Application.Run(new DataForm1());
}
```

We can now run our application. When making a commercial application, there would still be a number of details left to attend to, such as making sure that the `CustomerID` field is not null before attempting to add the record. Constraints in the database prohibit adding records with a null `CustomerID` field, and it is better that we detect this problem in the user interface rather than in the database, so that we can give a better error message to the user. However, this application is now a functional database maintenance application.

Creating a DataGrid using the DataForm Wizard

In the same project, we'll run the `DataForm` wizard again, this time creating a `DataGrid` in which we can modify records or add new records. We should note that when we use this wizard to generate a `DataGrid` control that is connected to a `DataSet`, there is no user interface to delete records. If we want that functionality in our application, we would need to add it after we generate the form.

Select Add New Item from the Project menu. Select the Data Form Wizard template in the Add New Item dialog box. Press the Next button on the first page of the wizard.

The next page of the wizard asks us which data set we want to use. Take the default settings. Press the `Next` button.

The next page of the wizard asks us to choose the methods to load and update data. Again, set the first combo box to the `FillDataSet` method. Check the Include an Update Button check box, and select the `UpdateDataSource` method in the second combo box.

Click Next to bring up the wizard dialog box that allows us to choose which tables and columns to include in our form. We will accept the defaults here. Press the Next button, which brings us to a dialog box that allows us to choose the display style. This time, we will accept the default setting. The All records in a grid radio button should be checked.

Press the Finish button, and the wizard will create our data-driven form. The results of the wizard look like this:

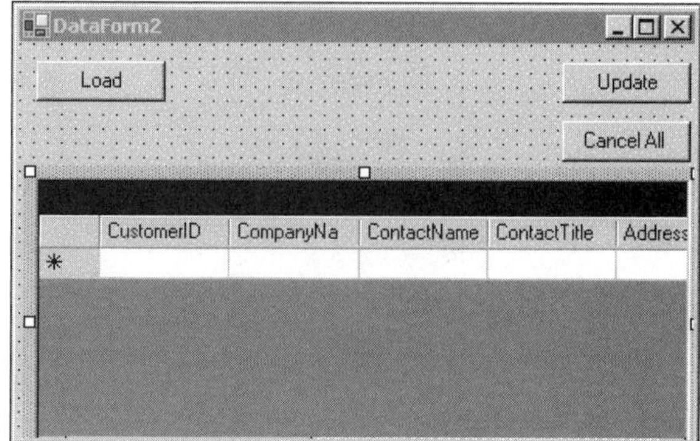

Click on the `DataGrid`, press *F4* to bring up the Properties window, and change the Anchor property to Top, Left, Bottom, Right, so that we can resize the window to see more columns and rows.

The last thing that we need to do before running our application is set `DataForm2` to be the startup form for our application. Bring up Form1.cs in the code editor. Modify the `Main` method as follows:

```
static void Main()
{
   Application.Run(new DataForm2());
}
```

Alternatively, we can modify the application so that we can choose between the two user interfaces, perhaps by adding a menu that allows us to pick between them.

We can now run our application. After running it, press the Load button to load in all of the records from the database. We can modify records and, by scrolling to the bottom of the `DataGrid`, we can add records. Pressing the Update button propagates the changes to the database.

Parent/Child Wizard Example

One of the most common types of database user interfaces are that in which the user can maintain information in two tables, which have a parent/child (sometimes also known as master/detail) relationship. Examples of these types of tables are Invoice/Items, Customer/Orders, etc. There are two common styles of this type of user interface: the first is Form/List, where the parent information is maintained in a form, and the child information is listed in a `DataGrid` below the parent information; the second style is where both the parent and child information are maintained in `DataGrid` controls, where the parent `DataGrid` is above the child `DataGrid`. Clicking on a row in the parent `DataGrid` then shows the appropriate child records for that parent record. In this example, we'll use wizards to create both types of user interfaces.

The DataAdapter Wizard (Again)

Before using the DataForm wizard, we will use the DataAdapter wizard, which will create a data source that we will use in this example. This time, we are going to create a data source that contains two tables. After we create our DataSet, we will create a relationship between the two tables.

Create a new Visual C# Windows Application project in Visual Studio.NET.

Select Add New Item from the Project menu. Select the Component Class template in the Add New Item dialog box. We are going to accept the default name for our component class. Press the Open button: Visual Studio.NET will then display a visual designer for our class.

Add an OleDbDataAdapter to our component by dragging it from the Data tab of the Toolbox onto our component's designer. As before, this will automatically start the DataAdapter Configuration Wizard. Click Next to move past the first page of the wizard.

The wizard will ask which data connection to use. As in the previous example, enter the appropriate information into the dialog box based on the database engine that you will use. If you completed the previous example, Visual Studio.NET will remember the data connection that you previously entered, and make it available as a selection in the combo box in this dialog box. You can select this connection in the combo box, and bypass the step of specifying the information for the connection.

Press the Next button.The next dialog box tells us to choose a query type. Make sure that the Use SQL statements radio button is selected. Press the Next button.The next dialog box asks what data the data adapter should load into the dataset. Enter the SQL command: SELECT * FROM Customers. Press the Next button, and then Finish. The OleDbDataAdapter and OleDbConnection will be visible in the design window for our component.

In the design window, click on the newly created OleDbDataAdapter1 then press *F4* to bring up the properties window. Change the Name property to daCustomers. Again, drag an OleDbDataAdapter from the Data tab of the Toolbox onto the component's design window.

Click Next to move past the first page of the wizard. The wizard will ask which data connection to use. Use the same data connection as before. Press the Next button. The next dialog box tells us to choose a query type. Make sure that the Use SQL statements radio button is selected. Press the Next button.

The next dialog box asks what data the data adapter should load into the DataSet. Enter the SQL command: SELECT * FROM Orders. In the design window, click on the newly created OleDbDataAdapter1, then press *F4* to bring up the properties window. Change the Name property to daOrders.

Select the Generate DataSet menu item from the Data menu. Change the name of the DataSet to dsCustomersOrders. Make sure that both tables have a check box next to them, so that they both will be included in the DataSet. Press the OK button.

When we generate the DataSet, it adds the XML Schema Definition (XSD) file to the Solution Explorer. Right click on the XSD file and select Open on the popup menu. This will bring up the XML Designer window, which lets us edit XML in structured data grid controls. The window looks like this:

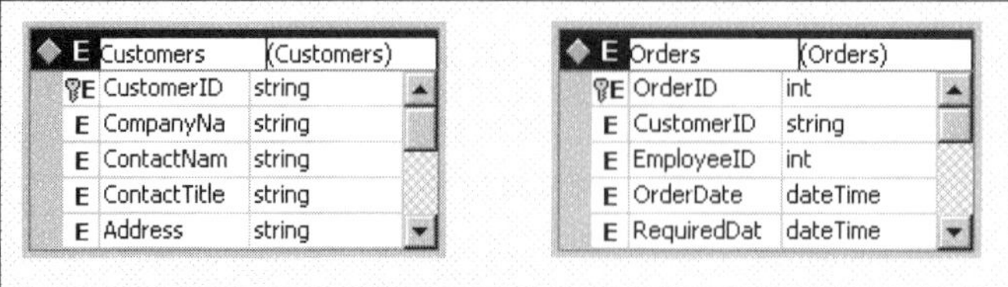

While this does not look like a window that is editing XML, it actually is. In this view, only the actual content of the XML file can be modified, not the tags. For more information about this window, see the section on the Data View in the XML Designer reference in the Visual Studio.NET documentation.

We now need to create the relationship between the two tables. When the XML Designer window has the focus, the Toolbox contains a tab labeled XML Schema. Drag a Relation from the Toolbox onto the Orders grid – you *must* drag the Relation onto the Orders grid, **not** the Customers grid.

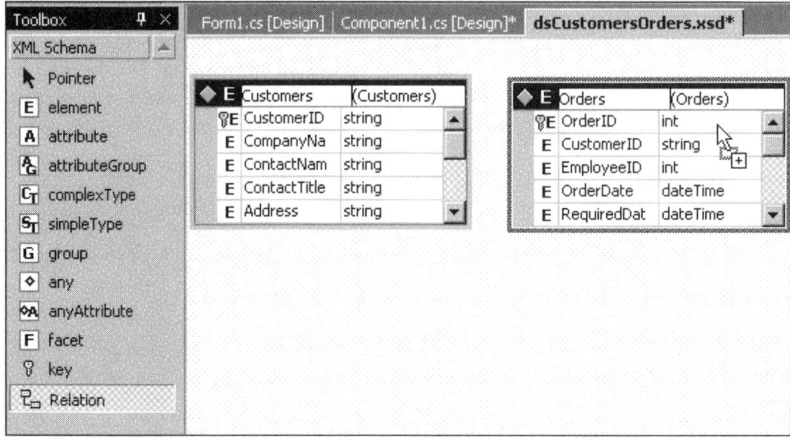

After you drop the Relation on the Orders grid, Visual Studio.NET puts up an Edit Relation dialog box. This dialog box allows us to specify a number of properties of the relation, including the parent element, the child element, how the fields are mapped from one to the other, and the rules for updating, deleting, and accepting/rejecting.

Change the Delete rule to Cascade: this can be done through the combo box at the bottom of the Edit Relation dialog:

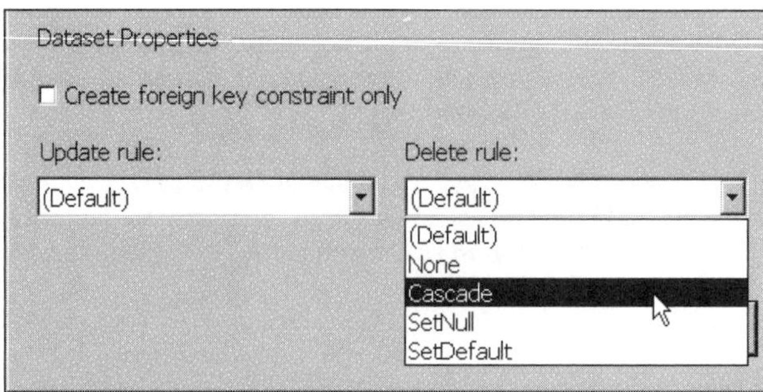

This will modify the behavior of this DataSet so that when we delete a customer in the DataSet, the DataSet will automatically delete all of the customer's orders. Other than this, we don't need to change the default values in this dialog box. Press the OK button.

After we have pressed OK, Visual Studio.NET creates a visual link between the two elements:

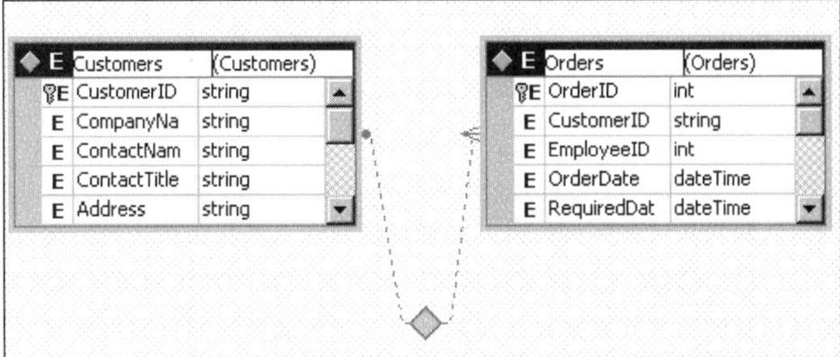

The Customers table has a one-to-many relationship to the Orders table. In this one-to-many relation, the visual link indicates which is the one (indicated by the small solid circle next to the Customers grid), and which is the many (indicated by the three small lines attached to the Orders grid).

There is something about this particular window that could be a bit confusing. The relationship is based on the primary key of the Customers table (Customers.CustomerID), and the foreign key in the Orders table (Orders.CustomerID), yet the screenshot appears to link Customers.CompanyName to Orders.CustomerID: the position of the circle and the three small lines has no significance, except to link the two tables. The positions are not intended to link fields.

If we want to edit the relation between the two tables, we can right-click on the diamond, which is the graphical representation of the relation between the two tables. We can then select Edit Relation from the popup menu, which will bring up the Edit Relation dialog box.

Our next step is to add code that will fill our new dataset with data. Open up the code view for Component1 and add the following two methods to the Component1 class:

```
public dsCustomersOrders FillDataSet()
{
   // declare our DataSet
   dsCustomersOrders ds = new dsCustomersOrders();

   // open our connection, fill it, and close the connection
   oleDbConnection1.Open();
   daCustomers.Fill(ds, "Customers");
   daOrders.Fill(ds, "Orders");
   oleDbConnection1.Close();

   // return the DataSet
   return ds;
}

public void UpdateDataSource(dsCustomersOrders ds)
{
   // declare three DataSets, to hold the changes to the database
   System.Data.DataSet UpdatedRows;
```

```
    System.Data.DataSet InsertedRows;
    System.Data.DataSet DeletedRows;

    // get a DataSet that contains just the modified rows
    UpdatedRows = ds.GetChanges(System.Data.DataRowState.Modified);

    // get a DataSet that contains just the added rows
    InsertedRows = ds.GetChanges(System.Data.DataRowState.Added);

    // get a DataSet that contains just the deleted rows
    DeletedRows = ds.GetChanges(System.Data.DataRowState.Deleted);

    // if any of the operations above returned null, this means that there
    // were no rows modified, added, or deleted.

    // the following lines propagate the changes to the database
    if (UpdatedRows != null)
    {
       daCustomers.Update(UpdatedRows);
       daOrders.Update(UpdatedRows);
    }
    if (InsertedRows != null)
    {
       daCustomers.Update(InsertedRows);
       daOrders.Update(InsertedRows);
    }
    if (DeletedRows != null)
    {
       daOrders.Update(DeletedRows);
       daCustomers.Update(DeletedRows);
    }

    // close the connection
    oleDbConnection1.Close();
}
```

As before, the `FillDataSet` method opens our connection to the database, fills a new `DataSet` object with data, and returns that `DataSet` object after closing the connection. The `UpdateDataSource` uses `DataSet` methods to update our back-end data source appropriately.

There is an interesting point to be made regarding the `UpdateDataSource` method. When we are updating or inserting rows, we propagate the changes to the database for the parent table (`Customers`) first, but when deleting rows, we propagate the changes to the database for the child table (`Orders`) first. This makes sense – we must delete the child rows before we can delete the parent row.

The DataForm Wizard

Next, we will run the DataForm wizard to build our data-driven form.

Before running the wizard, select Save All from the File menu. This is important: we must update the XSD file for our `DataSet`, otherwise the wizard will not run properly.

Select Add New Item from the Project menu. Select the Data Form Wizard template in the Add New Item dialog box. Press the Next button on the first page of the wizard. The next page of the wizard asks us which data set we want to use. Take the default settings. Press the Next button.

The next page of the wizard asks us to choose the methods to load and update data. Again, set the first combo box to the `FillDataSet` method. Check the Include an Update Button check box, and select the `UpdateDataSource` method in the second combo box.

Click Next to bring up the wizard dialog box that allows us to choose which tables and columns to include in our form. The wizard detected that we have a `DataSet` that contains two tables, and that there is a relation between them. It automatically set up the dialog box with the appropriate tables and fields checked for the master and detail table. We will accept the defaults here.

Press the Next button, which brings us to a dialog box that allows us to choose the display style. Check the radio button labeled Single record in individual controls. When we check the radio button, the wizard enables a number of check boxes. These check boxes should be familiar by now and do not require any explanation.

Press the Finish button, and the wizard will create our data-driven form. The results of the wizard look like this:

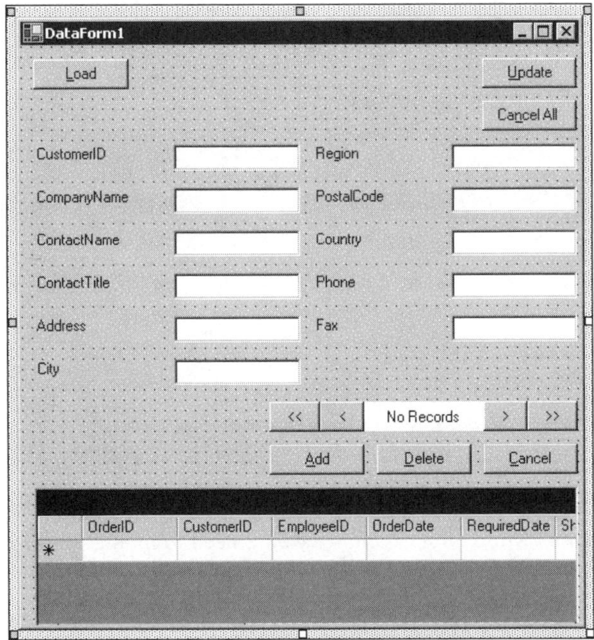

Click on the `DataGrid`, press *F4* to bring up the Properties window, and change the Anchor property to Top, Left, Bottom, Right, so that we can resize the window to see more columns and rows.

The last thing that we need to do before running our application is set `DataForm1` to be the startup form for our application. Bring up Form1.cs in the code editor. Modify the `Main()` method as follows:

```
static void Main()
{
   Application.Run(new DataForm1());
}
```

We can now run our application. After running it, press the **Load** button to load in all of the records from the database. We can modify both parent and child records. We can scroll to the bottom of the `DataGrid` and add child records. Pressing the **Update** button propagates the changes to the database. The completed form looks like this:

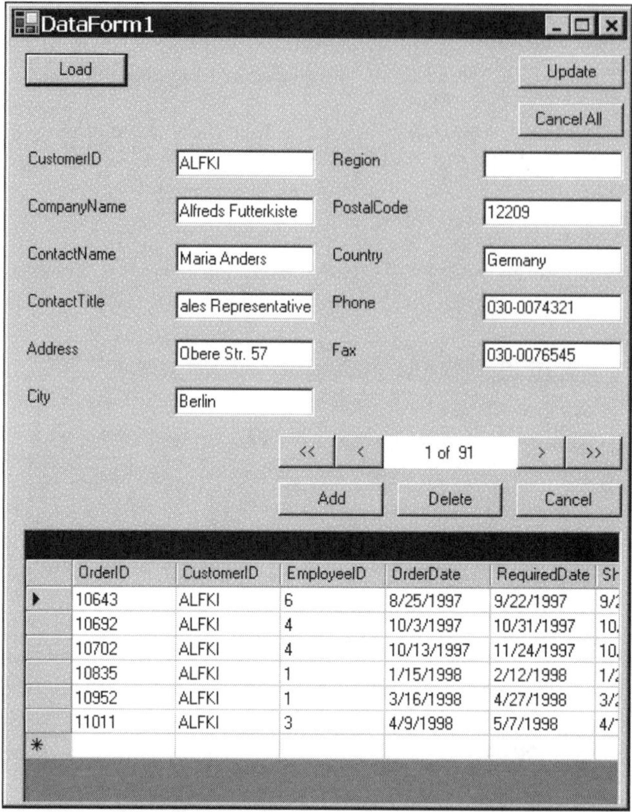

By default, the wizard writes the code for the form such that we can add or modify child records, but we can't delete them. In a real-world application, we would need to modify the resulting code to allow this. There would certainly be other changes that should be made to this application, but this gives us a very good head start.

Parent/Child using Two DataGrid Controls

Let's run the `DataForm` wizard again, but with slightly different parameters. The last time we ran the wizard, we created a user interface with a form on top and a `DataGrid` below. The parent record was in the form, and the child records were in the `DataGrid`. Another style of user interface is one where both the parent and child records are in `DataGrid` controls. This type of interface might be desirable when there are not too many fields in the parent record, and creating a form for the parent record is overkill.

Select **Add New Item** from the **Project** menu. Select the **Data Form Wizard** template in the **Add New Item** dialog box. Press the **Next** button on the first page of the wizard. The next page of the wizard asks us which dataset we want to use. Take the default settings. Press the **Next** button.

The next page of the wizard asks us to choose the methods to load and update data. Again, set the first combo box to the `FillDataSet` method. Check the Include an Update Button check box, and select the `UpdateDataSource` method in the second combo box.

Click Next to bring up the wizard dialog box that allows us to choose which tables and columns to include in our form. We will accept the defaults here. Press the Next button, which brings us to a dialog box that allows us to choose the display style. This time, leave the radio button labeled All records in a grid checked.

Press the Finish button, and the wizard will create our data-driven form. The results of the wizard look like this:

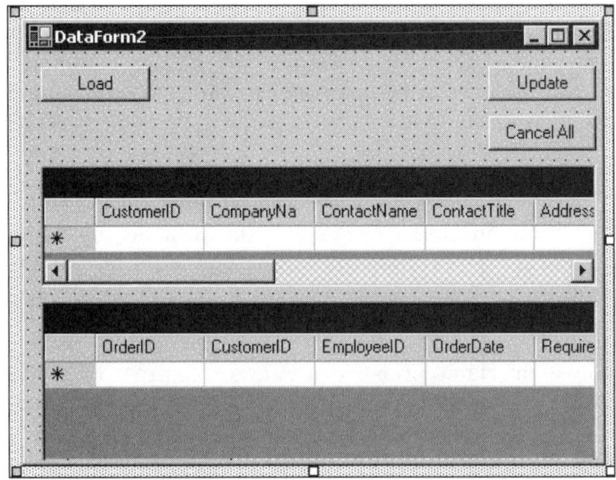

Make the window somewhat larger and move and resize the two `DataGrid` controls. If we like, we can set the Anchor property of the bottom `DataGrid` to Top, Left, Bottom, Right. We can set the Anchor property of the top `DataGrid` to Top, Left, Right.

The last thing that we need to do before running our application is set `DataForm2` to be the startup form for our application. Bring up Form1.cs in the code editor. Modify the `Main` method as follows:

```
static void Main()
{
   Application.Run(new DataForm2());
}
```

Alternatively, you can modify the application so that you can choose between the two user interfaces, perhaps by adding a menu that allows you to pick between them.

We can now run our application. After running it, press the Load button to load in all of the records from the database. We can modify both parent and child records in the `DataGrid` controls. If we put the focus on a particular row in the parent `DataGrid`, the appropriate child records are shown in the child `DataGrid`. Pressing the Update button propagates the changes to the database.

Parameterized Query Example

Often we want to allow users to enter selection criteria into a form. After they have entered the selection criteria, we find all records in the database that match, and then allow the user to browse the records. In this example, we'll create such an interface.

Create a new Visual C# Windows Application project in Visual Studio.NET.

Drag an `OleDbDataAdapter` from the Data tab of the Toolbox onto the form. Click Next to move past the first page of the wizard. The wizard will ask which data connection to use. Use the same data connection as the previous examples. Press the Next button.

The next dialog box tells us to choose a query type. Make sure that the Use SQL statements radio button is selected. Press the Next button. The next dialog box asks what data the data adapter should load into the dataset. Enter the SQL command: SELECT * FROM Customers WHERE Region = ? The question mark (?) is our placeholder for the parameter in our `SELECT` statement. If we were using the `SqlDataAdapter` class, then we could use named variables. Press the Next button, then press the Finish button.

Select the Generate DataSet menu item from the Data menu. Change the name of the `DataSet` to dsCustomers. Press the OK button. Add a `TextBox` to the form. Set the Name property to `txtRegionParameter`. Clear the Text property. Add a `Button` control to the form. This button will fill the `DataSet` based on the value that the user enters in the `txtRegion` `TextBox`. Set the Name property to `btnDoQuery`. Set the Text property to Do Query.

Add a `TextBox` control. Set the Name property to `txtCustomerID`. Clear the Text property. As we have done in previous examples, bind this control to dsCustomers1 - Customers.CustomerID. Click the plus sign to the left of the (DataBindings) property. Click the Text property (below the Tag property). Click the combo box in the right cell of that row. Expand dsCustomers1. Expand Customers and click on CustomerID. As a refresher, the following screenshot shows this operation:

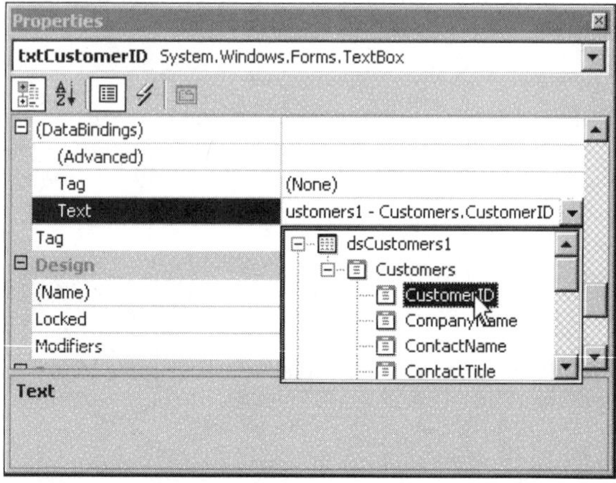

Add a `TextBox` control. Set the Name property to `txtCompanyName`. Clear the Text property. Bind this control to dsCustomers1 - Customers.CompanyName. Add another `TextBox` control, only this time set the Name property to `txtRegion`. Clear the Text property. We normally would not add a control to display the region, but to demonstrate that the query worked properly, we will add it to this example. Bind this control to dsCustomers1 - Customers.Region. Add labels to these `TextBox` controls.

As we did in the first example, add a 'VCR' control for navigating through the records after we do the query. Add four buttons and a `TextBox`, oriented horizontally below our data bound `TextBox`. Change the **Text** properties of the buttons to '<<', '<', '>', and '>>'. Set the **Text** property of the `TextBox` to ''. Set the **Read Only** property of the `TextBox` to **True**.

The resulting window looks like this:

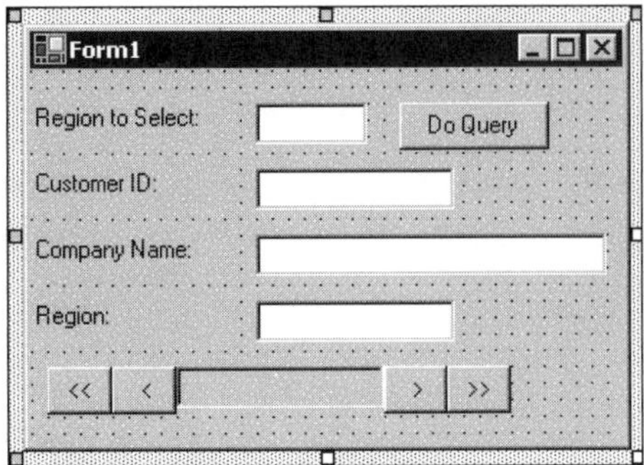

Next, we need to write the event handler for our **Do Query** button. Our code will do the following: first we will set the value of our parameter for our SQL query to whatever the user entered into the `txtRegionParameter TextBox`; we will then call the `Clear` method on the `DataSet` (if we do not clear the `DataSet`, the records returned by our query would be appended to our `DataSet`); finally, we call our data adapter's `Fill` method.

Double-click on the **Do Query** button. Modify the event handler so that it is as follows:

```
private void btnDoQuery_Click(object sender, System.EventArgs e)
{
   oleDbDataAdapter1.SelectCommand.Parameters["Region"].Value =
            txtRegionParameter.Text;
   dsCustomers1.Clear();
   oleDbDataAdapter1.Fill(dsCustomers1);
   updateVCRControl();
}
```

As in the first example, we need to add some code to make our VCR control functional. Whenever the position of the bound data changes, we want to make the read only textbox control say something like 'Record 1 of 16'. Add the following method to the form:

```
private void updateVCRControl()
{
   textBox1.Text = "Record " +
      (BindingContext[dsCustomers1,"Customers"].Position + 1) +
      " of " +
      BindingContext[dsCustomers1,"Customers"].Count;
}
```

Double-click on the '<<' button in the design window to bring up the event handler. Add the following code:

```
private void button1_Click(object sender, System.EventArgs e)
{
   BindingContext[dsCustomers1,"Customers"].Position = 0;
   updateVCRControl();
}
```

Add the following code to the '<' button event handler:

```
private void button2_Click(object sender, System.EventArgs e)
{
   BindingContext[dsCustomers1,"Customers"].Position =
           (BindingContext[dsCustomers1,"Customers"].Position - 1);
   updateVCRControl();
}
```

Add the following code to the '>' button event handler:

```
private void button3_Click(object sender, System.EventArgs e)
{
   BindingContext[dsCustomers1,"Customers"].Position =
           (BindingContext[dsCustomers1,"Customers"].Position + 1);
   updateVCRControl();
}
```

Finally, add the following code to the '>>' button event handler:

```
private void button4_Click(object sender, System.EventArgs e)
{
   BindingContext[dsCustomers1,"Customers"].Position =
           (BindingContext[dsCustomers1,"Customers"].Count - 1);
   updateVCRControl();
}
```

Run the example. Enter OR in the Region to Select textbox and press the Do Query button. Our example will find a few records, and we can navigate through them.

Binding to Arrays and Collections

Our ability to bind controls to data is not limited to binding to `DataSet` objects as the data source: there are many other types of objects to which we can bind. In actuality, binding to `DataSet` objects is a specific case of the more general data binding capabilities of Windows Forms. We can even create our own classes to provide data to data bound controls.

Data sources can have a wide degree of variation in complexity and functionality. They can provide very basic data binding capabilities. Capabilities above and beyond basic data binding include design-time support and structured rollback of changes made to data.

In order to provide data binding, a class needs to implement one of a number of interfaces. We'll take an overview of some of the interfaces that classes can implement, and what data binding functionality they provide.

- **`IList` interface**: Any class that implements the `IList` interface can be used as a data source. We can only bind a class of this type at runtime, not design time. Changes made to the data source are not automatically propagated to the data bound control.
- **`IList` and `IComponent` interfaces**: If a class implements both of these interfaces, it can be bound at design time (and runtime too, of course).
- **`IBindingList` interface**: This interface offers us change notification. Users of a class that implements this interface get notified when the number of items change, or when a particular item changes. This helps support an MVC design.
- **`IEditableObject` interface**: This interface allows the user to control when changes to the underlying data are permanently made. It does this through the `BeginEdit`, `EndEdit`, and `CancelEdit` methods. Similar to transaction processing, these methods allow us to provide the user with the capability to cancel edits that have been partially made. The `DataGrid` uses this type of functionality.
- **`IDataErrorInfo` interface**: This allows our data source to return error information to the bound controls. The `DataGrid` uses this functionality.

In the next example, we will bind a `ListBox` control to a collection.

CollectionListBox Example

Create a new Visual C# Windows Application project in Visual Studio.NET.

Using the ToolBox, drag out a `ListBox` control, then bring up the code editor for the form. Add a `using System.Collections.Specialized` statement at the beginning of the file: this will give us access to the `StringCollection` class:

```
using System;
using System.Drawing;
using System.Collections;
using System.Collections.Specialized;
using System.ComponentModel;
using System.Windows.Forms;
using System.Data;
```

Modify the constructor, as follows:

```
public Form1()
{
    //
    // Required for Windows Form Designer support
    //
    InitializeComponent();

   StringCollection sc = new StringCollection();
   sc.Add("Black");
   sc.Add("Brown");
   sc.Add("Yellow");
   sc.Add("Red");
   sc.Add("Green");
   this.listBox1.DataSource = sc;
}
```

Now, compile and run the application. We can see our listbox populated with the contents of the string collection. However, if we were to change the collection after creating and populating the listbox, our changes to the collection would not be reflected in the listbox.

An interesting approach to solve this problem is to use the `DataTable` class to manage a collection of data. In this case, the `DataTable` is not associated with a `DataSet` object, and it is not read from a database. Instead, we create it, populate it, and link it to our listbox. Then, any subsequent changes to the `DataTable` will be seen in our `ListBox` control.

DataTableListBox Example

Create a new Visual C# Windows Application project in Visual Studio.NET.

Using the ToolBox, create a `ListBox` control. Add a `TextBox` control and two `Button` controls to the form. Clear the Text property of the TextBox control. Change the Text property of the first button to Add Item. Change the Text property of the second button to Delete Item. The resulting user interface looks like this:

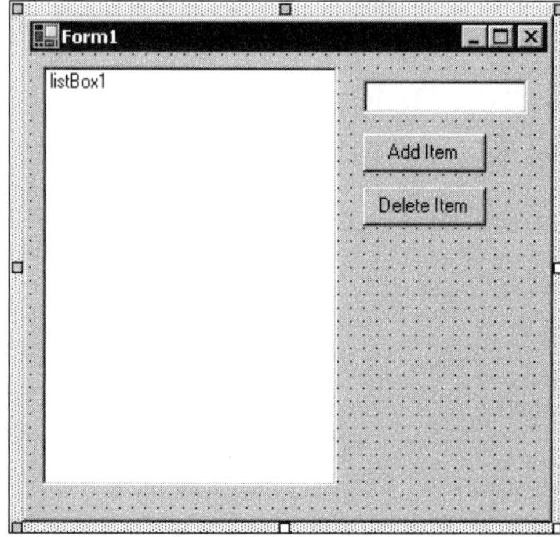

Open the code editor for the form. Declare a private member variable of type `DataTable` in the `Form1` class.

```
public class Form1 : System.Windows.Forms.Form
{
   private System.Windows.Forms.ListBox listBox1;
   private System.Windows.Forms.Button button1;
   private System.Windows.Forms.Button button2;
   /// <summary>
   /// Required designer variable.
   /// </summary>
   private System.ComponentModel.Container components = null;
   private DataTable dt;
```

Next, add the following two methods to the `Form1` class:

```
private void AddRow(DataTable dt, String str)
{
   DataRow dr = dt.NewRow();
   dr["Item"] = str;
   dt.Rows.Add(dr);
}

private void DeleteRow(DataTable dt, String str)
{
   DataView dv = new DataView(dt);
   dv.RowFilter = "Item = '" + str + "'";
   if (dv.Count >= 1)
      dv[0].Delete();
}
```

These methods make it easier to add records to and delete records from our `DataTable`.

Modify the `Form1` constructor as follows:

```
public Form1()
{
   //
   // Required for Windows Form Designer support
   //
   InitializeComponent();

   // Create a DataTable with one column.
   dt = new DataTable("SimpleTable");
   DataColumn dc = new DataColumn("Item", Type.GetType("System.String"));
   dt.Columns.Add(dc);

   // Add a number of rows into the table
   AddRow(dt, "Apple");
   AddRow(dt, "Banana");
   AddRow(dt, "Peach");
   AddRow(dt, "Grapefruit");
   dt.AcceptChanges();

   this.listBox1.DataSource = dt;
   this.listBox1.DisplayMember = "Item";
}
```

In the designer window, double-click on the Add Item button, and modify the click event handler for the button as follows:

```
private void button1_Click(object sender, System.EventArgs e)
{
   if (textBox1.Text != "")
      AddRow(dt, textBox1.Text);
}
```

Modify the click event handler for the Delete Item button as follows:

```
private void button2_Click(object sender, System.EventArgs e)
{
   String str =
         ((DataRowView)(this.listBox1.SelectedValue))["Item"].ToString();
   DeleteRow(dt, str);
}
```

Now, run the application. We can add items to and delete items from the ListBox control. The key point here is that we are manipulating the contents of the ListBox by changing the data in our DataTable object.

Summary

In this chapter, we took a look at ADO.NET at a very high level. We then saw a number of the classes that make up the core of the functionality of ADO.NET. We learned how to create a connection to a database, declare a DataSet, and use a data adapter class to populate the DataSet from the database.

We saw a number of examples that demonstrate the low level capabilities of ADO.NET, including declaring and populating a DataSet, creating relations between tables within a DataSet, and creating DataView objects from DataTable objects. When using wizards to build applications that do data binding, it is very important to understand what is going on at the lowest levels. It is possible that the wizards don't generate exactly the code that we want (sometimes they don't even generate code that works), and after we have generated some forms, it is often desirable to manually modify them to make them do exactly what we want.

We then took a low level look at data binding. We saw that there are two main ways to bind data: simple and complex. We saw two examples that provided the smallest possible example of binding data in these two fashions. We learned what a VCR control is, and how to build one. We learned about the BindingContext class and the CurrencyManager class, and how these classes enable data binding.

We then took a look at the DataForm wizard that is available in Visual Studio.NET to help us to quickly build applications. We saw how to build an application that maintains data in a form, data in a DataGrid, parent/child information in a form and DataGrid, as well as in two DataGrid objects. We saw how to create a DataSet with more than one table and how to graphically create a relation between two DataTable objects.

We built an example that executes a parameterized query, which gives us a Query-By-Example (QBE) capability.

We then looked at some of the interfaces that facilitate data binding, including the IList, IBindingList, IEditableObject, and IDataErrorInfo interfaces. We saw how binding to a DataSet or DataTable is actually a specific case of the more general capability to bind to any class that implements these interfaces. We then built a small example that bound a ListBox control to a collection. We finally built an example that declared and instantiated a DataTable object and bound it to a ListBox control. We saw that the advantage of doing this is that changes to the underlying DataTable object get automatically propagated to the ListBox control.

Data binding is a very important subject when building Windows Forms applications. ADO.NET and the data binding capabilities of Windows Forms give us a powerful tool in our toolbox for building data aware applications.

System.Windows.Forms

Legend: Concrete Class · Abstract class

- System.Object
  - System.MarshalRefObject
    - System.ComponentMode.Component
      - CommonDialog
        - ColorDialog
        - FileDialog
        - FontDialog
        - PageSetupDialog
        - PrintDialog
      - ErrorProvider
      - HelpProvider
      - ImageList
      - Menu
        - ContextMenu
        - MainMenu
        - MenuItem
      - NotifyIcon
      - StatusBarPanel
      - Timer
      - ToolBarButton
      - ToolTip
      - Control
        - ButtonBase
          - Button
          - CheckBox
          - RadioButton
        - DataGrid
        - DateTimePicker
        - GroupBox
        - Label
          - LinkLabel
        - ListControl
          - ComboBox
          - ListBox
            - CheckedListBox
        - ListView
        - MonthCalendar
        - PictureBox
        - PrintReviewControl
        - ProgressBar
        - ScrollableControl
          - ContainerControl
            - Form
              - PrintPreviewDialog
              - ThreadExceptionDialog
            - PropertyGrid
            - UpDownBase
              - DomainUpDown
              - NumericUpDown
            - UserControl
          - Panel
            - TabPage
        - ScrollBar
          - HScrollBar
          - VScrollBar
        - Splitter
        - StatusBar
        - TabControl
        - TextBoxBase
          - RichTextBox
          - Textbox
        - ToolBar
        - TrackBar
        - TreeView
  - ListViewItem
  - TreeNode

8

Basic and Dialog Controls

The mission of the next several chapters is to present a comprehensive overview of the Windows Forms controls deployed initially with Visual Studio.NET. There are approximately three dozen such controls (`TextBox`, `RadioButton`, `Label`, etc.) primarily derived from the `Control` class contained in the System.Windows.Forms namespace. This `Control` base-class exposes half a dozen constructors, over eight properties, a hundred methods, including overridden versions of the same method, and over fifty events.

Each control derived from the `Control` class contains its own constructors, properties, methods, and events. It is derived as follows:

```
Object
    MarshalByRefObject
        Component
            Control
```

This class might be the parent, grandparent, or even great-grandparent class of a standard Windows Forms control. Adding to this complexity is the fact that controls can be created and placed on a form at design time via the user interacting with Visual Studio.NET. Controls can also be placed on a form at run-time by programmatically adding the control to a form.

There are certainly a lot of permutations to discuss with respect to Windows Forms Controls. Those familiar with the 'Mission Impossible' television series and movies recognize this as the point where the recording says, 'This tape will self-destruct in five seconds'. Reviewing every Windows Control is not 'mission impossible'; at least not if a series of 'real-world' Windows applications are developed. Each of these applications contains the six to eight controls being discussed. Over the course of this series of examples, the plethora of properties, methods, events, and basic concepts, which pertain to each control, can be introduced.

It is important, however, to understand that we will not cover every single element of each control since this would lead to a lot of repetition. Instead, we mention the important ones, or ones of specific interest. If you wish to view all the properties, methods, and events, then the documentation is the place to go.

> **Since our aim, in the next few chapters, is to talk about controls specifically, it is recommended that you have the download to view the applications in action since we will not talk at length about the construction of each application.**

In this chapter we will cover the following:

- A C# card counting application (`WroxCount`) containing these controls:
  - `Form`
  - `Panel`
  - `Label`
  - `Checkbox`
  - `TextBox`
  - `Button`
  - `LinkLabel`

The controls mentioned here handle everything from displaying text (`Label`), displaying text in conjunction with a URL (`LinkLabel`), entering text (`TextBox`), or specifying Boolean values (`CheckBox`, checked or unchecked). These controls just so happen to be the controls discussed in this chapter as part of a C# card counting application. This is correct – card counting. This example also demonstrates forms inheritance and the group of controls using the `Panel` class.

- A VB.NET language translation application (`WroxTranslator`), which contains these controls:
  - `RadioButton`
  - `GroupBox`
  - `ListBox`
  - `TrackBar`
  - `PictureBox`
  - `RichTextBox`
  - `H` and `VScrollBar`

This application displays formatted text using the `RichTextBox` control. Traversing this to-be-translated text is augmented using scrollbars as implemented using the `HScrollBar` and `VScrollBar` classes. Group `RadioButtons` are used to select the type of translation (colloquial, technical, formal, etc.) and these `RadioButtons` are grouped using the `GroupBox` class. The source and destination language of the translation are specified (language and dialect) using text displayed in list fashion via a `ListBox`, and by picking the flag of the country where the specific dialect is spoken (for example, `French` is the language, `Canadian` is the dialect). The flag images are displayed using a `PictureBox` instance and these images are traversed using a `TrackBar` instance.

- A C# dialog application (`WroxEditThis`), which covers the following controls:
    - `OpenFileDialog`
    - `SaveFileDialog`
    - `FontDialog`
    - `ColorDialog`
    - `PrintDocument`
    - `PrintPreviewControl`
    - `PageSetupDialog`
    - `PrintPreviewDialog`
    - `PrintDialog`

This application demonstrates the dialogs exposed by Windows Forms. This editor deals with file manipulation such as the opening and saving of files. For this reason, the aptly named `OpenFileDialog` and `SaveFileDialog` dialogs are demonstrated. When editing, the color of text edited can be set using the `ColorDialog`, and the font used in the editor and while printing can also be set using the `FontDialog`. Printing in this mini-editor is the purview of the `PrintDialog` used in conjunction with the document to be printed. The actual document is an instance of the `PrintDocument` class. Both a control and a dialog for displaying a printed preview are addressed: `PrintPreviewControl` and `PrintPreviewDialog` respectively. To add raw and unbridled excitement to this editing application, the `PageSetupDialog` dialog is demonstrated in order to configure the page to be printed.

WroxCount

The first sample Windows Forms application appears as follows (the project is called `WroxCount`):

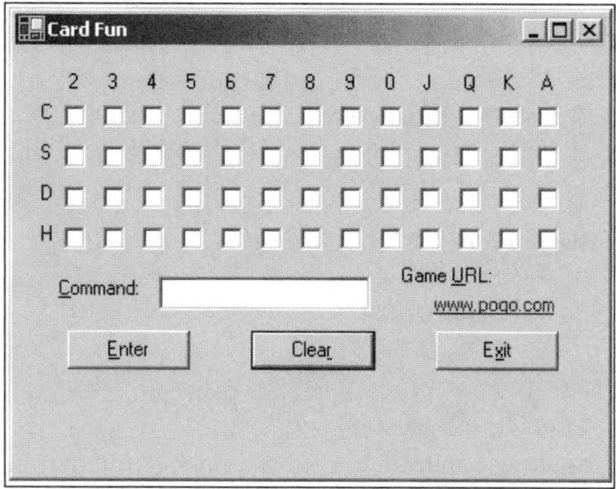

This application is used to count playing cards while engaging in online card games. This chapter will discuss the technical merits of the Windows application, rather than the ethical quandary surrounding card counting!

Each square box in the grid is a CheckBox (control of type CheckBox, that can be checked or unchecked) corresponding to a playing card. Each time a card is played during a game, it can be counted by checking the corresponding box (for example, the CheckBox at grid location C2 corresponds to the 2 of Clubs being played). Using the mouse, each CheckBox corresponding to a card can be clicked individually. The Labels (controls of type Label) to the left of the grid of check boxes correspond to the permissible suits in a deck of cards (C for Clubs, S for Spades, D for Diamonds, and H for Hearts). The Labels above the grid of check-boxes correspond to the permissible face values of cards in a deck of cards (numbers 2 through 10 where 10 is abbreviated to 0, J for Jack, Q for Queen, K for King, and A for Ace).

To the right of the Label containing the text Command: is a TextBox in which the cards played can be typed. For example, typing C2 (2 of Clubs played) in the TextBox followed by clicking the Enter button would check the C2 box in the grid of CheckBoxes. Typing in CJD3 would correspond to seeing the Jack of Clubs (CJ) and the 3 of Diamonds (D3) played. Clicking the Enter button would check grid locations CJ and D3.

A URL (control, LinkLabel), www.pogo.com, is placed on the Form. Clicking on this URL brings up a web browser showing this popular gaming site. Three Buttons (controls of type Button) are available along the bottom of the Form. The Enter Button processes the text in the Textbox labeled, Command:. The Clear Button resets the grid of CheckBoxes to their unchecked state. The Exit Button exits the application.

The empty area at the bottom of the form holds a hidden control (control, Label). If an error is detected in the command text, this Label is made visible and the text of the Label identifies the error. For example, C1 is invalid since there isn't a 1 of Clubs in a conventional deck of cards – the hidden Label would be made visible and this Label would display: Error in Command Text: C1.

The WroxCards class, found in the source file called WroxCards.cs, implements the grid of check boxes and corresponding labels. The remainder of the application is implemented in the WroxParentForm class, derived from WroxCards. The WroxParentForm class is found in the source file called WroxParentForm.cs.

'Form'

We have already seen the general features of a form, but in this section we will look at it in terms of its class properties. When a Windows application is first created, Visual Studio.NET creates a class derived from the Form class.

The Form class itself is derived as follows:

```
Control
    ScrollableControl
        ContainerControl
            Form
```

In the context of the card counting application, the base class, WroxCardBase, is derived from Form:

```
public class WroxCards : System.Windows.Forms.Form
```

A `Form` class contains properties such as:

Property	Description
`AcceptButton`	This `get/set` property specifies the button that is clicked when the user types the enter key while the form is in focus. For our application the Enter button is set as the accept button.
`CancelButton`	This `get/set` property specifies the button that is clicked when the user presses the *Esc* key while the form is in focus. For our application, the Exit button is set as the cancel button.
`DesktopBounds`	`gets/sets` the location and size of the `Form` on the desktop.
`DesktopLocation`	`gets/sets` the location (x and y co-ordinates, in pixels), of the form's top left corner, relative to the upper left corner of the desktop.
`DialogResult`	`gets/sets` the results returned when the `Form` is displayed as a modal dialog (the `ShowDialog` method displays the `Form` as a modal dialog). The `DialogResult` property is of type `DialogResult,` which has as its permissible values: `Abort`, `Cancel`, `Ignore`, `No`, `None`, `OK`, `Retry`, and `Yes`.
`FormBorderStyle`	This `get/set` property of type `FormBorderStyle` specifies the style of border used by the form: `None`, `Fixed3D`, `FixedDialog`, `FixedSingle`, `FixedToolWindow`, `Sizable`, and `SizableToolWindows`.
`Icon`	`gets/sets` the icon displayed for the `Form`.
`Menu`	`gets/sets` the control of type `MainMenu` associated with the `Form`.
`TopMost`	If this `get/set` property is `true` then the `Form` is the top-most form (that is, always shown in front of all the other forms in the application). If this property is `false`, the `Form` does not need to be top-most of all the `Forms` in the application.
`WindowState`	This `get/set` property of type `FormWindowsState` specifies if the `Form` is `Normal`, `Maximized`, or `Minimized`.

The `Form` class is ultimately derived from the `Control` class. The properties exposed by the `Control` class, include (note that there are lot more properties than those listed below):

Control Property	Description
`Height`	`gets/sets` the `Form` height in pixels.
`Text`	`gets/sets` the text displayed in the `Forms` title bar.
`Visible`	This `get/set` property is `true` if the `Form` is visible and `false` if the `Form` is not visible.
`Width`	`gets/sets` the `Form` width in pixels.

The `Form` class exposes methods such as `Close`. This method closes the `Form` and cleans up all resources associated with the `Form`. Once a `Form` is closed it cannot be redisplayed. To hide and then make `Form` visible again, use the `Hide` method. Actually, the `Hide` method is inherited from the `Control` class. The `ShowDialog` method displays the `Form` as a modal dialog.

When displaying a `Form`, rapid updates, such as adding a bunch of child controls, can cause screen flicker, and the constant redrawing can impact performance. For this reason, the `Control` base-class of `Form` exposes the `SuspendLayout` method. This method suspends the layout of the `Form`, and is used when creating and setting up the controls associated with a `Form`. The idea is to create the child controls after `SuspendLayout` is called. Once all the child controls are created and configured, call `ResumeLayout` to resume layout for the `Form` and display the `Form` and its contained controls.

The events exposed by the `Form` include:

Event	Description
`Activated`	Triggered when the `Form` gains focus.
`Closed`	Raised when the `Form` has completed closing (after close).
`Closing`	Raised when the `Form` begins to close (before close).
`Deactivated`	Raised when the `Form` loses focus.
`Load`	Triggered when the `Form` is first loaded.

The `Form` class also exposes events inherited from the `Control` class, such as `Click`, which is triggered when the `Form` is clicked on by the mouse.

This `InitializeComponent` method is used by Visual Studio.NET's Windows Forms Designer to create and set up each control residing on the `Form`. The `InitializeComponent` method is also where Designer sets up the properties and methods associated with the `Form` itself. For the `WroxCount` application, the portion of the `InitializeComponent` method that sets up the `Form` is as follows:

```
// create controls here
this.SuspendLayout();
// setup controls here
this.AcceptButton = buttonEnter;
this.AutoScaleBaseSize = new System.Drawing.Size(5, 13);
this.CancelButton = buttonExit;
this.ClientSize = new System.Drawing.Size(360, 253);
Controls.AddRange(new Control[] {this.buttonExit, this.buttonEnter,
       this.buttonClear, this.linkLabelGames, this.textBoxCommand,
       this.labelCommand, this.labelError});
this.Name = "WroxParentForm";
this.Text = "Card Fun";
this.ResumeLayout(false);
```

A class derived from `Form` can be used as the starting class of an application such as our application, `WroxCount`. The `[STAThread]` attribute must be added before the `Main` method to indicate that the forms will run in a single threaded apartment (STA). STA means that a Windows Form cannot switch between threads after it has been created. To understand this concept, remember that applications can have multiple threads executing within them at any one time (multithreaded applications). Such applications can readily take advantage of multi-CPU machines, because separate threads can execute on separate CPU's. Although multiple CPU's can enhance the performance of a multithreaded application, they are not required in order to utilize threads. Threads are often used to perform a background task, such as downloading a file from the Internet. While a background thread downloads the file, a second thread (dedicated to the GUI) is ensuring that the browser is still responding to user input even as the file is downloading.

An object that must only run inside a single thread is referred to as single threaded. Such an object resides in a single threaded apartment. For a Window Forms application, this means that one thread is responsible for handling all user interaction with the `Form` and the child controls associated with the `Form`. Win32 developers recognize why the `Form`'s code in a Windows Forms application must run as an STA. This is because windows are handled on a per-thread basis, where messages are received by a thread (a message loop receiving messages from message queues) and dispatched to a callback associated with each window (a `WndProc`). The single thread that was used to initially create the window handles all of this.

The `Main` method associated with the `WroxCount` application is as follows:

```
[STAThread]
static void Main()
{
   Application.Run(new WroxParentForm());
}
```

Non Windows Forms applications can use the free threading model by specifying the `[MTAThread]` attribute, which corresponds to a multi-threaded apartment (MTA). Multiple threads can access the objects in such an application. Actually, a Windows Forms application could spawn additional threads to perform such background tasks. These threads would be able to handle any of the processing associated with the `Form` or its child controls. This is because the `Form` was created and run from an STA.

'Panel'

The `Panel` class is used to group controls by serving as a container for these controls. `RadioButtons`, for example, are often grouped and `Panel` can be used to contain and manage this grouping of controls. For our card counting application, the grid of card `CheckBoxes` and their `Labels` are what are grouped on the `Panel`. The lineage from the `Panel` class to the `Control` class is as follows:

```
Control
    ScrollableControl
        Panel
```

When represented in the Windows Forms designer, a `Panel` is just a box outlined with a dashed line:

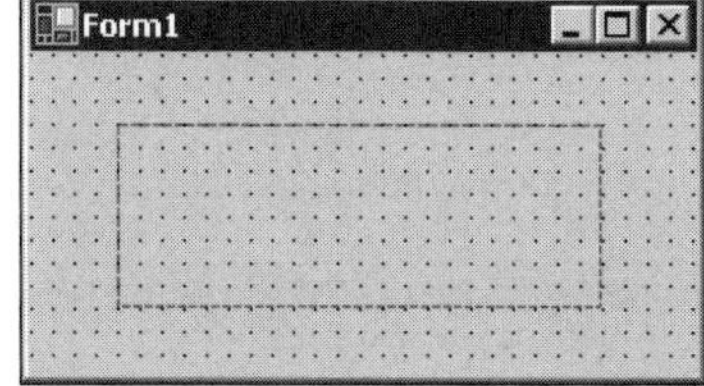

For our example, a `Panel` object, called `panelCurrentHand`, is used to hold the deck of cards. The deck of cards is represented by fifty-two `CheckBox` objects (four rows of thirteen), four `Label` objects represent a card's suit (C, S, H and D), and thirteen `Label` controls represent a card's face value (2 through 0 (ten), J, Q, K, and A).

The only methods and events exposed by the `Panel` class are inherited. The `Panel` class does, however, implement a property of its own:

Property	Description
`BorderStyle`	`gets` and `sets` the `BorderStyle` of the `Panel`. The permissible border style types are `None`, `FixedSingle` (single line), or `Fixed3D` (three-dimensional).

From the `Panel`'s base classes, properties that are of particular interest are also inherited: The `Controls` property (from the base-class `Control`) is a collection that contains the controls associated with the `Panel` (contained by the `Panel`). This collection exposes methods such as `Add`, or `AddRange`, to add controls to the panel, and `Remove` to remove controls from the panel. When the `Visible get/set` property (from the base-class `Control`) is `true`, the `Panel` and all the controls it contains are visible. If `Visible` is `false` then the `Panel`, and the controls it contains, are not visible. The `AutoScroll get/set` property (from the base-class `ScrollableControl`) is of type Boolean. When this property is `true`, the `Panel` will display scrollbars if not all the controls on the panel are completely visible. Specifying the default value of `false` for this parameter causes scrollbars not to be displayed.

The example `Panel` below has its `BorderStyle` property set to `Fixed3D` and the `AutoScroll` property set to `true`:

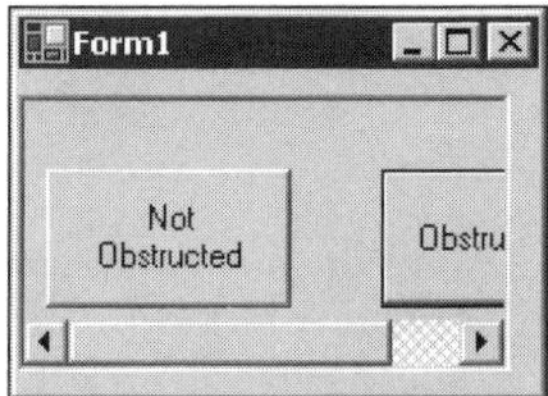

Two buttons reside on the previous panel: one is labeled Not Obstructed, because it is completely visible. The other is labeled Obstructed because it is partially obstructed, as the `Panel` is too small. The horizontal scrollbar is displayed because the `AutoScroll` property is set to `true` and the obstructed button does not quite fit on the `Panel`.

When developing the card counting application, or any other application for that matter, the Windows Forms Designer was used to place the `Panel` control on the `Form`. Each of the `CheckBox` and `Label` controls contained by the `Panel` were created programmatically and then added to the `Panel`'s `Controls` property using the Add method exposed by this property. There is a fair amount of code associated with setting up the `Labels` and `Checkboxes` – rather than jumping into the card playing application just yet, the following code is provided. This code was taken from the application that contains the obstructed button (the project is called `AnAutoScrollPanel`). This code was written entirely by the Windows Forms Designer:

```
this.panelWithAutoScroll = new System.Windows.Forms.Panel();
this.buttonNotObstructed = new System.Windows.Forms.Button();
this.buttonObstructed = new System.Windows.Forms.Button();

this.panelWithAutoScroll.SuspendLayout();
this.SuspendLayout();
this.panelWithAutoScroll.AutoScroll = true;
```

```
this.panelWithAutoScroll.BorderStyle = System.Windows.Forms.BorderStyle.Fixed3D;
this.panelWithAutoScroll.Controls.AddRange(new
        System.Windows.Forms.Control[] {this.buttonNotObstructed,
        this.buttonObstructed});

// ...Rest of setup here...
this.panelWithAutoScroll.ResumeLayout(false);
this.ResumeLayout(false);
```

The basic premise of the previous code snippet is that a `Panel` (`panelWithAutoScroll`) and two `Buttons` (`buttonNotObstructed` and `buttonObstructed`) were created using `new`. After the `Panel`'s `AutoScroll` property was set to `true` and `BorderStyle` set to `Fixed3D`, the buttons were placed on the `Panel`. The `AddRange` method of the `Controls` property was called in order to place `buttonNotObstructed` and `buttonObstructed` on the `Panel`.

Notice the use of the `SuspendLayout` method by both the `Form` (`this.SuspendLayout`), and the `Panel` (`this.panelWithAutoScroll.SuspendLayout;`). This method suspends layout of the controls while wholesale changes are made to the appearance of a control. Adding a bunch of child controls (buttons) to the `Panel`, or adding the `Panel` to the `Form`, equates to wholesale changes. Once the changes are made, the matching `ResumeLayout` methods are called for both the `Form` and the `Panel`.

'Label'

A `Label` control provides descriptive text that is set and retrieved using this control's `Text` property. It is derived as follows:

```
Control
    Label
```

In our card counting example, the labels to the left and above the grid of check boxes are contained in two arrays:

```
private Label [] labelSuitValues;
private Label [] labelFaceValues;
```

The primary lesson learned from these arrays is not Windows Forms related, but pertains to transitioning from C++ to C#, and from C++ to VB.NET. In C++, a single call to `new classname []` will allocate each object in the array and call the default constructor. The same constructor will be called for every element in the array. In C# and VB.NET, dynamic array allocation is a two-step process. In C#, the array is allocated containing `null` pointers. The `WroxGenerateForm` method allocates the arrays of labels (`labelSuitValues` and `labelFaceValues`) using the constants `MaxSuitValue` (value is four, corresponding to the permissible suits C, H, D, and S) and `MaxFaceValue` (value is thirteen, one for each face value in a suit of cards):

```
labelSuitValues = new Label [MaxSuitValue];
labelFaceValues = new Label [MaxFaceValue];
```

Once the arrays are allocated, the individual elements of the arrays must be created using `new Label`, as we see in a code snippet from the `WroxGenerateForm` method, where each `Label` in `labelFaceValues` and `labelSuitValues` is allocated in the relevant line:

```
private void WroxGenerateForm()
{
   int index;

   this.SuspendLayout();
   checkBoxCards = new CheckBox [NumCards];
   labelFaceValues = new Label [MaxFaceValue];
   for (int x = 0; x < MaxFaceValue; x++)
   {
      labelFaceValues[x] = new Label();
      labelFaceValues[x].Size = new Size(18, 18);
      labelFaceValues[x].Location = new Point(22 + x * 24, 6);
      labelFaceValues[x].Text = WroxGetFaceValueString((FaceValue)x);
      panelCurrentHand.Controls.Add(labelFaceValues[x]);
      for (int y = 0; y < MaxSuitValue; y++)
      {
         // setup CheckBoxes for card here
      }
   }

   labelSuitValues = new Label [MaxSuitValue];
   for (int y = 0; y < MaxSuitValue; y++)
   {
      labelSuitValues[y] = new Label();
      labelSuitValues[y].Size = new Size(18, 18);
      labelSuitValues[y].Location = new Point(5, 24 + y * 24);
      labelSuitValues[y].Text = ((SuitValue)y).ToString().Substring(0, 1);
      panelCurrentHand.Controls.Add(labelSuitValues[y]);
   }

   this.ResumeLayout(false);
}
```

Each individual `Label` in the `labelSuitValues` array is created using a separate call to `new`. It would be possible to create separate entries in this array with different constructor values. In our example the same constructor was used (default constructor) for each `Label` created. Before the array of suit and face value labels are created, the `SuspendLayout` method is called for the `Form` (`this.SuspendLayout`). This turns off layout controls on the form until all labels are created. Once each label has been created, the `ResumeLayout` method is called for the `Form` (`this.ResumeLayout(false);`). In the previous code, hints are provided as to how the `CheckBoxes` corresponding to the cards are created (`checkBoxCards = new CheckBox [NumCards];`). In the previous section, the `Panel` class's `Collections` property was discussed. Based on this discussion, calling the `Add` method for the `Panel`'s `Controls` property (`panelCurrentHand.Controls.Add`) should make sense, in that this is how the `Labels` are placed on the `Panel`.

The primary purpose of a `Label` is to provide descriptive text. The `WroxParentForm.cs` source file contains labels that are chock-full of descriptive text, such as:

- `labelCommand`: The `Text` property of this label contains Command:, indicating that the neighboring textbox is where you enter commands.
- `labelURLShortCut`: The `Text` property of this label contains Game URL:, indicating that the neighboring control of type `LinkLabel`, which is `linkLabelGames`, contains the URL associated with the site that provides on line card games.

The labelURLShortCut control appears to be superfluous. Clearly, the text www.pogo.com is a URL, so why label it? A hint as to why this Label object is used can be found in the underscore of this label's Text property, Game URL:. The U is deliberately underlined because the source code text associated with the labelURLShortCut's Text property is "Game &URL:". The ampersand character (&) in this represents a shortcut that is displayed to the user by an underscore. A user selects the shortcut by entering *ALT-U* (where U is the shortcut character). When the user selects the shortcut, the application will move focus to the entry whose tab order property (TabIndex) follows that of Label, which happens to be labelURLShortCut. To demonstrate, consider the following two lines of code extracted from the InitializeComponent method:

```
this.labelURLShortCut.TabIndex = 5;
this.linkLabelGames.TabIndex = 6;
```

A user hits the key sequence *ALT-U* – this causes focus to go to the control that follows labelURLShortCut in the tab ordering. The labelURLShortCut control has a TabIndex property of 5, while the linkLabelGames control has a TabIndex property of 6. The linkLabelGames object is the LinkLabel control that holds the text www.pogo.com, so *ALT-U* sets focus to the URL at which card games are played. labelURLShortCut serves as a keyboard shortcut to accessing this URL via the LinkLabel control.

The labelCommand label contains an underlined C and hence has a shortcut value of *ALT-C*. The TabIndex property of labelCommand is 0, while the value of the TabIndex property for the textbox in which commands are entered (TextBox, textBoxCommand) is 1.

'CheckBox'

The CheckBox is used to represent any two-state variable (for example, yin or yang, male or female, yes or no). The CheckBox class is derived from Control as follows:

```
Control
    ButtonBase
        CheckBox
```

The properties specific to the CheckBox class include:

Property	Description
Appearance	This property (get/set) specifies the appearance of a CheckBox. The default look (Appearance.Normal) is a square that is empty or that contains a check. The Appearance can also be set to Appearance.Button, which displays a standard Windows toggle button (raised for unchecked and depressed for checked).
AutoCheck	If this get/set property is true (default value) the check box contains a check mark when checked (Checked set to true) and no check mark when the box is unchecked (Checked set to false). If the value of AutoCheck is false, then the state of the CheckBox is not marked with a checkmark.

Table continued on following page

Property	Description
CheckAlign	This get/set property, of type ContentAlignment, specifies the CheckBox's horizontal and vertical alignment. The values of this property are self-explanatory and are as follows: BottomCenter, BottomLeft, BottomRight, MiddleCenter, MiddleLeft, MiddleRight, TopCenter, TopLeft, and TopRight.
Checked	If this get/set property is true, the CheckBox is checked; if this value is false, the check box is unchecked. For three state CheckBoxes, this property returns true if the CheckBox is either checked or in an indeterminate state.
CheckState	This get/set property is of type CheckState and represents the state of the check box: checked (Checked), unchecked (Unchecked) and for three state check boxes only, an undetermined state (a grayed-out check box represented by the enumeration value Indeterminate).
ThreeState	If this get/set property is true, the check box is a three state CheckBox (empty, checked, and checked-but-grayed-out). The default for this property is false, representing a two state CheckBox.

Just to get check boxes clear in our minds, here is a recap, with illustrations, of the different properties.

- The following demonstrates both styles of CheckBox appearance (Normal and Button):

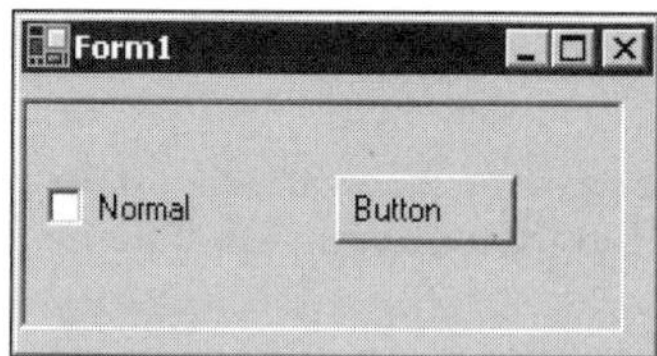

- Below is an example of two CheckBoxes with AutoCheck set to false (the left side has Checked set to true, while the right side has Checked set to false):

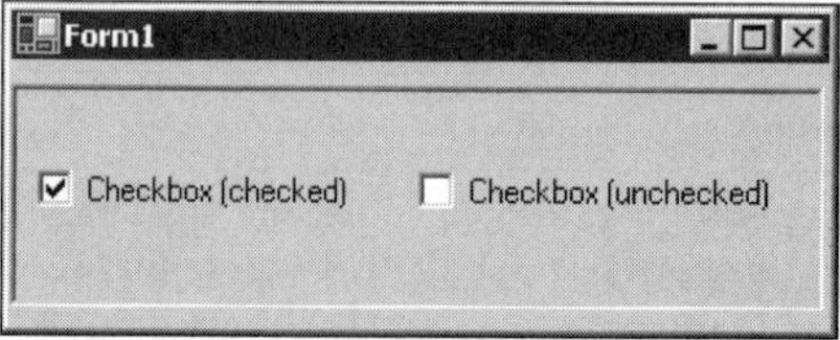

- Here you can see the effect of the different values of the CheckAlign property:

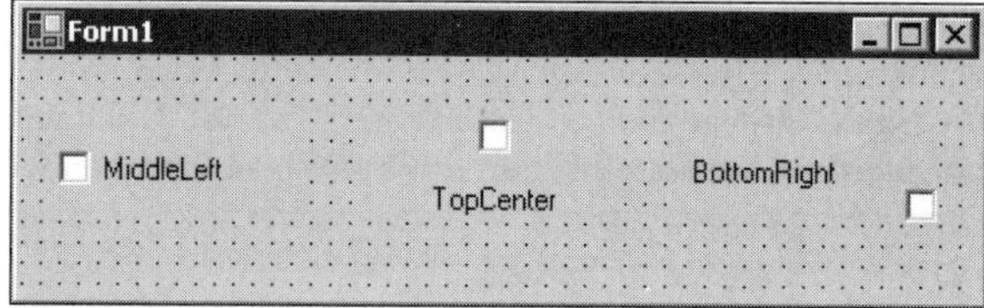

- The following demonstrates each `CheckState`, where the `CheckBoxes` in the top row are set to `Appearance Normal` and the `CheckBoxes` in the bottom row are set to `Appearance Button`:

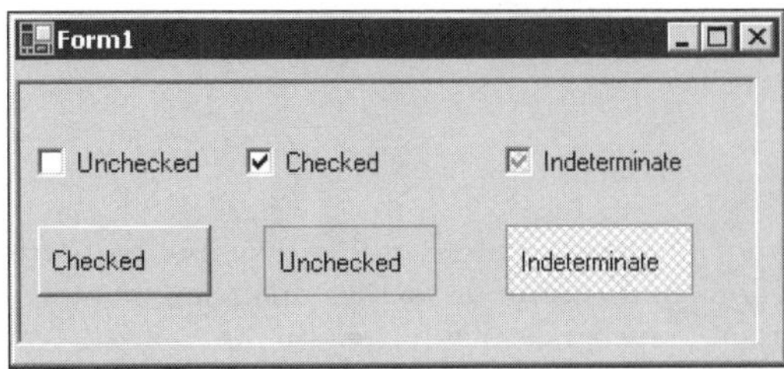

The events implemented by the `CheckBox` class include:

Event	Description
`AppearanceChanged`	Raised when the `Appearance` property's value changes.
`CheckedChanged`	Raised when the value of the `Checked` property changes. For a two-state check box, this means the check box alters from checked to unchecked, or unchecked to checked.
`CheckStateChanged`	Raised when the value of the `CheckState` property changes. For a three-state check box, this event indicates each `CheckState` transition: from unchecked to checked, from checked to indeterminate, and from indeterminate to unchecked.

One `CheckState` property inherited from the `Control` class is worthy of mention: `Size`. This `get/set` property allows the size (x and y length/height) to be set for the `CheckState`. The card counting application has an extremely tight grid of check boxes. The size of each `CheckState` was reduced until there was no overlap between `CheckBox` controls. The `Size` property of `CheckState` does not specify the size of the box, but instead specifies the size of the control. The control actually extends beyond the boundaries of the physical `CheckState` displayed, so reducing the `Size` property serves to ensure that the neighboring controls do not overlap. Overlaps should be avoided, because a click anywhere in the control boundary will result in a change in the check state.

The code in the `WroxGenerateForm` method that creates each `CheckState` is as follows (where `index` is a value from 0 to 51 since there are 52 cards in a deck):

```
checkBoxCards[index] = new CheckBox();
checkBoxCards[index].Text = "";
checkBoxCards[index].Name = "";
checkBoxCards[index].Size = new Size(24, 24);
checkBoxCards[index].Location =
    new Point(22 + x * 24, 22 + y * 24)
checkBoxCards[index].TabStop = false;
panelCurrentHand.Controls.Add(checkBoxCards[index]);
```

The previous code snippet shows each check box being added to the `Panel`, `panelCurrentHand.Controls.Add`. The `TabStop` property of each check box is set to `false`. The check boxes cannot be tabbed through individually: there are fifty-two such controls, so making each a tab stop would just wear out the tab key. The `Size` of the check box was set to `x=24`, `y=24`. The default check box size is `x=104`, `y=24`, so the x dimension was reduced to ensure that the check box controls within the grid do not overlap each other.

'TextBox'

A TextBox controls allows simple text to be entered by a user.

```
Control
    TextBoxBase
        TextBox
```

For basic text entry it is simpler to use TextBox, rather than its more intricate cousin, RichTextBox. The RichTextBox class allows more elaborate text manipulation, but this class is also derived from TextBoxBase. It is important to recognize that the text in the TextBox can be a single line of text, or multiple lines of text. A great many of the TextBox's properties are set based on whether the TextBox is the single-line, or multi-line, variant.

The following properties facilitate the diverse style of text entry supported by TextBox:

Property	Description
AcceptsReturn	A Form can be associated with an AcceptButton. When the *Enter* key is selected, the Accept button on the Form is clicked. If the get/set property for the textbox, AcceptsReturn, is true, then each *Enter* received while the textbox is in focus adds a new line to the text in the textbox. If AcceptsReturn is false, then selecting the *Enter* key activates the Form's default button. The AcceptsReturn property only applies to multi-line textboxes.
AcceptsTab	(From base-class TextBoxBase.)When a tab character is selected in a Form, the focus moves from control to control based on each control's TabIndex property. If this get/set property for the textbox, AcceptsTab, is true, then each tab key hit while the textbox is in focus adds a tab character to the text in the textbox. If Acceptstab is false, then selecting the tab key activates tabbing between controls on the Form.
CharacterCasing	This get/set property, of type CharacterCasing, determines if the textbox does not change case (CharacterCasing value of Normal), makes characters uppercase (value of Upper), or makes characters lower case (value of Lower).
Multiline	(From base-class Control.) If this get/set property is true, then the textbox accepts multiple lines of text. If the Multiline property is false, then the textbox accepts a single line of text.
PasswordChar	When this get/set property is set to zero, text entered into the textbox is displayed as typed. For a single line textbox, when PasswordChar is set to a character value, this character is displayed for each character entered in the textbox. The Text property of the TextBox contains the actual characters typed. If PasswordChar is non-zero, then cut, copy, and paste are disabled for the contents of the TextBox. For multi-line TextBoxes, a non-zero PasswordChar does not change how characters are displayed to the screen, but does disable cut, copy, and paste operations.

Property	Description
ReadOnly	(From base-class TextBoxBase.) – when this get/set parameter is true then the user cannot edit the contents of the TextBox. The default value for property ReadOnly is false, which means the TextBox can be edited.
ScrollBars	This get/set parameter is set to None by default (no scrollbars). If this property is set to Horizontal, then a horizontal scrollbar is visible when the text exceeds the horizontal dimension of the TextBox. Similarly, if the ScrollBars property is set to Vertical, and the TextBox is multi-line, then a vertical scrollbar is visible when the text exceeds the vertical dimension of the TextBox. If a value of Both is specified, then both a vertical and horizontal scrollbar appear when appropriate.
Text	(From base-class TextBoxBase.) This get/set property contains the text entered in the TextBox.
TextAlign	This get/set parameter, of type HorizontalAlignment, specifies the horizontal alignment of the text within the TextBox: Center, Left, and Right.
TextLength	(From base-class TextBoxBase.) Specifies the length of the text in the Text property.

Here are a couple of illustrations of some of the above properties:

- The following is a TextBox containing a PasswordChar of '*'and Text of "Top Secret":

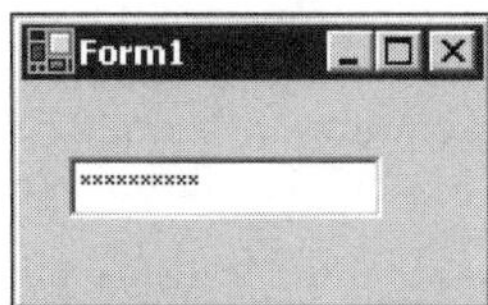

- A multi-line (Multiline set to true) TextBox with ScrollBars set to Vertical is as follows:

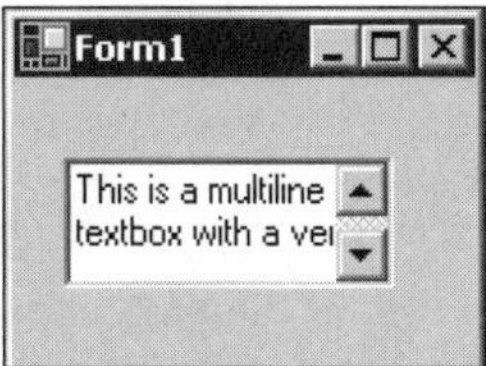

The events of interest associated with a TextBox include several that are derived from Control: KeyUp, KeyPress, KeyDown, MouseUp, and MouseDown. These events are self-explanatory and are useful when manipulating text within an application.

Within the WroxCount application, the Text property of the textBoxCommand TextBox contains the list of cards to be checked off. The Text associated with this TextBox is processed when the button labeled Enter is clicked.

'Button'

The `Button` control is activated by clicking the mouse or, if the `Button` is in focus, hitting the *Enter* key. The basic idea is: click the button, fire a `Click` event, and take action. The `Button` class is derived from `Control` as follows:

```
Control
    ButtonBase
        Button
```

The `Button` control exposes one property and one method of its own:

Property	Description
`DialogResult`	This `get/set` property of type `DialogResult`, retrieves or sets the return value of the parent dialog that contains the button. The permissible values for `DialogResult` include: `Abort`, `Cancel`, `Ignore`, `No`, `None`, `OK`, `Retry`, and `Yes`.

Method	Description
`PerformClick`	This method causes the `Button` to receive a `Click` event.

The `ButtonBase` base-class of `Button` exposes some interesting properties:

ButtonBase Property	Description
`FlatStyle`	This `get/set` property, of type `FlatStyle`, specifies the button style: `Flat`, `Popup` (flat but becomes three-dimensional when mouse hovers over button), `Standard` (three-dimensional style button), or `System` (system defaults dictate look and feel).
`Image`	`gets/sets` the image displayed by the `Button`. For example, the `Button` could display a bitmap.
`ImageList`	This `get/set` property implements a collection of images that can be displayed by the button. The image currently displayed is specified by the `ImageIndex` property.
`ImageIndex`	This `get/set` property specifies which index in the `ImageList` the button displays.

To get more of a feel for buttons, each flavor of the `FlatStyle` property is demonstrated below:

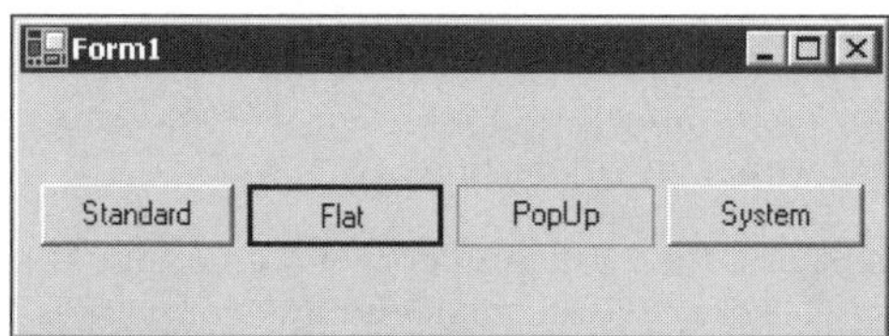

The Button control inherits the Text property from the Control base-class. The Text property is where the Button's text is get/set. The events of interest associated with a Button are also inherited from the Control base-class. These events include:

- Click: A Click event is received when a mouse clicks on the Button, but remember that a Click event is also received when the *Enter* key is pressed while the Button is in focus.
- MouseDown: This event fires when a mouse clicks on the Button, but before the mouse button is released. This event is often used to change how a button is displayed when depressed versus when raised – for example, to show a changed state in a toggle switch.
- MouseUp: This event fires when the mouse button is released after the mouse clicked on a Button. If MouseDown had been used to change a Button's appearance, MouseUp could be used to restore the appearance to the previous version.
- KeyDown: This event is triggered when a key is pressed and the Button is in focus.
- KeyUp: This event is triggered when a key is released (after being pressed while the Button was in focus).

The three buttons associated with the WroxCount application are labeled:

- Enter: Causes the text in the textBoxCommand TextBox to be processed. The details of parsing and handling command text are explained in detail later in this section. The keyboard shortcut *Alt-E* is associated with this button; when this key sequence is entered, the Enter button is clicked.
- Clear: When this button receives the Click event, the check boxes are cleared (all marked as unchecked), any errors displayed are cleared, and the command-text is cleared. A user will typically select Clear when a new hand of cards is dealt. The shortcut *Alt-R* is associated with this button; when this key sequence is entered, the Clear button is clicked.
- Exit: On the Click event, this calls Application.Exit; (the Application class's static method, Exit). The Exit method exits the application. The Exit method causes all the Application class's Run methods to terminate. Depending on how an application is implemented, this will most likely cause the application to exit. The shortcut *Alt-X* is associated with this button; when this key sequence is entered, the Exit button is clicked.

The InitializeComponent method contains three lines of code that make the application usable:

```
this.labelCommand.TabIndex = 0;
this.textBoxCommand.TabIndex = 1;
this.buttonEnter.TabIndex = 2;
```

The labelCommand label has a TabIndex of 0. Recall that when the shortcut of this Label is selected (*Alt-C*), the focus is set to the textBoxCommand TextBox, since the TabIndex of this control has a value of 1. Once text is entered in the textBoxCommand TextBox, the user can hit the tab key and set the focus to the Enter button. This is supported since the TabIndex property of the buttonEnter Button has a value of 2.

The buttonEnter_Click method handles the parsing of the command text in the textBoxCommand TextBox. When an error is encountered while parsing the command text, the Label at the bottom of the Form is made visible and is set to contain an error message:

```
labelError.Text = "Error in command text: " +
                  textBoxCommand.Text;
labelError.Visible = true;
```

The prototype for the `buttonEnter_Click` method is as follows:

```
private void buttonEnter_Click(object sender, System.EventArgs e)
```

The `buttonEnter_Click` method is associated with the `buttonEnter` `Button` by setting the `Button`'s `Click` event inside the `InitializeComponent` method:

```
this.buttonEnter.Click += new System.EventHandler(this.buttonEnter_Click);
```

Creating the `buttonEnter_Click` method and setting the `Click` event for the `Button` was handled by the Windows Forms Designer. In design view of the form, double-clicking on the button generates a method capable of handling the event. This method is named `buttonName_Click`, where `buttonName` is the name of the `Button` control object (`buttonEnter` in our example). Double-clicking on the control in the Windows Forms Designer also creates the setup code inside the `InitializeComponent` method:

```
private void buttonEnter_Click(object sender, System.EventArgs e)
{
}
```

When the text in the `textBoxCommand` `TextBox` is successfully parsed by the `buttonEnter_Click` method, the text is cleared by setting the `Text` property to "" and any error previously displayed is hidden by setting the error label's `Visible` property to `false`. The code from the `buttonEnter_Click` method that performs this is as follows:

```
labelError.Visible = false;
textBoxCommand.Text = "";
textBoxCommand.Focus();
```

The last line of code in the previous snippet sets the focus from the Enter `Button` back to the `TextBox` in which the commands are entered. This makes it extremely efficient to enter the cards seen using only a keyboard. Once focus is set on the `textBoxCommand` `TextBox`, commands can be entered. When the *Enter* key is pressed, the `Form`'s `AcceptButton` property set clicks the Enter button. Once the click has been processed, focus returns quite elegantly to `textBoxCommand`. If the Enter button is clicked using the *Enter* key, the application automatically returns to the control currently in focus. If the Enter `Button` had been clicked manually, the code regarding `textBoxCommand.Focus;` would have ensured the correct behavior. Yes, an actual Windows application that acknowledges that the keyboard is a faster mechanism for inputting information than a mouse, especially when the application properly supports the keyboard!

'LinkLabel'

The `LinkLabel` control handles the display of hyperlinks within a form. This control is derived from the `Label` control and from the `Control` base-class as follows:

```
Control
    Label
        LinkLabel
```

The properties exposed by LinkLabel are:

Property	Description
ActiveLinkColor	Specifies the color of the link when it is active. An active link triggers a LinkClicked event when the link is clicked.
DisabledLinkColor	Specifies the color of the link when it is disabled. A disabled link is a link that does not trigger a LinkClicked event when clicked.
LinkArea	This get/set property is of type LinkArea structure. This property allows a single hyperlink to be specified for a LinkLabel using the LinkArea structure's Start data member (start portion of the hyperlink within the LinkLabel's text) and Length data member (length in characters from the starting point for the link).
LinkColor	This get/set property specifies the color associated with the link.
Links	This collection of Link objects allows a LinkLabel to be associated with a collection of hyperlinks.
LinkVisited	This get/set property is true if the link has been visited and false if the link has not been visited.
VisitedLinkColor	This get/set property specifies the color associated with a hyperlink that has already been visited (LinkVisited property set to true).

The following example shows link text with twenty-four characters, with a Start position of eleven (eleven characters in "Here it is:") and a Length of thirteen (thirteen characters in www.wrox.com):

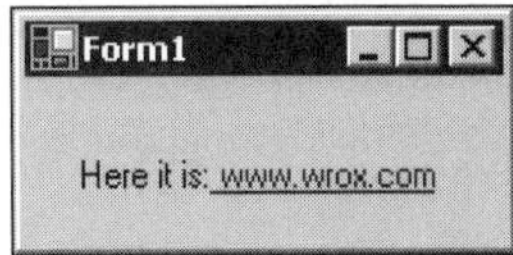

The PointInLink method is implemented by the LinkLabel control. This method is given a set of coordinates (x, y) and returns the Link within a LinkLabel corresponding to these coordinates. A null value is returned if the coordinates do not correspond to the link within the LinkLabel. This method is typically used in conjunction with the MouseEnter event. When the mouse enters (hovers over) a LinkLabel control, it is useful to know if the mouse is hovering over the hyperlink. If the mouse *is* hovering over the actual link, then additional information about the link can be displayed.

The LinkLabel control exposes a number of events, one of which is LinkClicked. This event is fired when the hyperlink is clicked on. In the Windows Forms Designer, if a LinkLabel's hyperlink is double-clicked, a method for handling LinkClicked is created and the setup code associating this method with the LinkLabel is written in InitializeComponent.

The LinkLabel class contains a sub class, Link. The Link class defines each link within the LinkLabel's Links collection. The Link class exposes properties such as:

Link Property	Description
`Enabled`	This `get/set` property is `true` if the link is enabled and `false` if the link is disabled.
`Length`	This `get/set` property, of type `int`, specifies the number of characters of the `LinkLabel`'s `Text` associated with the link. The `Length` property is used in conjunction with the `Start` property.
`LinkData`	This `get/set` property, of type `Object`, specifies data that is associated with the `LinkLabel` that can be accessed when the `LinkClicked` event is triggered.
`Start`	This `get/set` property, of type `int`, specifies where in the `Text` of the `LinkLabel` the URL starts.
Visited	This `get/set` Boolean property is `true` if the link has been visited previously and `false` if the link has yet to be visited.

The link within our example, `linkLabelGames`, is setup within the `InitializeComponent` method as follows:

```
this.linkLabelGames.LinkArea = new System.Windows.Forms.LinkArea(0, 12);
this.linkLabelGames.Location = new System.Drawing.Point(252, 145);
this.linkLabelGames.Name = "linkLabelGames";
this.linkLabelGames.TabIndex = 6;
this.linkLabelGames.TabStop = true;
this.linkLabelGames.Text = "www.pogo.com";
this.linkLabelGames.LinkClicked += new
   System.Windows.Forms.LinkLabelLinkClickedEventHandler(
      this.linklabelCommand_LinkClicked);
```

In the previous code snippet recall that the `TabIndex` property was set to follow the `labelURLShortCut` control's `TabIndex`. The snippet of code shows the `LinkClicked` event being associated with the `linklabelCommand_LinkClicked` method. This method is implemented as follows:

```
private void linklabelCommand_LinkClicked(object sender,
                  System.Windows.Forms.LinkLabelLinkClickedEventArgs e)
{
   System.Diagnostics.Process.Start(linkLabelGames.Text);
}
```

The `Start` method of the `System.Diagnostics.Process` class takes as single parameter the name of a document. The process associated with this document is launched. Our example contains www.pogo.com, which causes a browser to be launched. Specifying `Resume.doc` as the link would launch Microsoft Word and open the file `Resume.doc`. Clicking on a link containing `WorkOnThis.sln` would cause Visual Studio.NET to open using the `WorkOnThis.sln` solution. The `Start` method is not limited to documents alone. The name of an executable could also have been specified and this executable subsequently spawned off as a separate process.

Let's now move on to the WroxTranslator application.

WroxTranslator

The second sample Windows Forms application developed appears as follows:

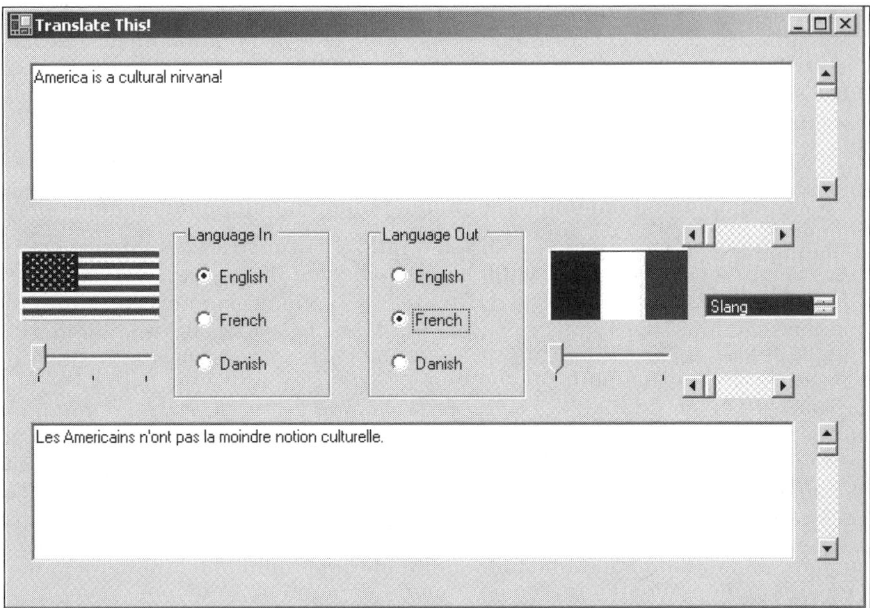

This application could be used to translate text between languages. The window presented in the screen shot behaves as follows:

- The large text entry boxes at the top and bottom of the control are the input (top) and output (bottom) `RichTextBox` objects. Text is entered in either `RichTextBox` and translated in the other. The top entry box contains the string, "America is a cultural nirvana!" and the lower `RichTextBox` contains the verbatim French translation.
- Two sets of `RadioButton` objects (English, French and Danish) are provided in order to define the language input in the left `RichTextBox` (`RadioButtons` labeled Language In) and the right `RichTextBox` (`RadioButtons` labeled Language Out). `RadioButtons` are selected once in each option group so that at most one language in or out can be selected at any time.
- Each triplet of `RadioButton` objects is grouped in a `GroupBox` (Language In and Language Out). The `GroupBox` allows controls to be managed as a group that has a group name label.
- There are two flags displayed on the `Form`: an American flag and a French flag. Each flag is displayed in a `PictureBox` control. The purpose of the flags is to specify which dialect of a language to translate to/from. For example, French could be translated into the dialect of France or Canada (French and Canadian flags respectively) while English could be translated to the American, Canadian, or British version.
- Below each `PictureBox` control is a `TrackBar` control. This track bar can change dialects and hence change the flag displayed in the `PictureBox`. The `TrackBar` for Language In corresponds to English and contains three ticks: American, Canadian, and British English. The `TrackBar` for Language Out corresponds to French and contains two ticks: French or Canadian French.

- The right side of the Form contains a ListBox control with the term Slang visible. This ListBox allows the style of language to be selected: Slang, Formal, or Technical.
- To the right of each RichTextBox is a VScrollBar control. This VScrollBar control allows individual sentences (text ending with a linefeed character) within the corresponding RichTextBox to be traversed. Each time the down arrow of the scrollbar is clicked, the next sentence is highlighted (marked as selected). Each time the up arrow on the scrollbar is clicked, the previous sentence is highlighted (marked as selected). Selecting sentences could be performed in the RichTextBox using a mouse, but the VScrollBar at the top provides a shortcut for selecting individual sentences in the top RichTextBox.
- To the right and below the topmost RichTextBox is an HScrollBar control. This HScrollBar control allows individual words within the topmost RichTextBox to be traversed and selected. To the right and above the bottom RichTextBox is a second HScrollBar control. This HScrollBar control allows individual words within the bottom RichTextBox to be traversed and selected. Each HScrollBar can be clicked once per word in the corresponding RichTextBox. For each click of the right arrow the next word in the document is highlighted and the previous word is no longer highlighted. Clicking the left arrow of the scrollbar causes the previous word to become highlighted.

The algorithm used to translate between languages will not be discussed, as this is a text on Windows Forms development, and not on language translation. The algorithm used to translate depends on language (English, French, and Danish), dialect (American English, Canadian English or British English), and language style (slang, formal, and technical). To be completely candid, the algorithm provided does not perform a completely accurate translation. Readers should feel free to invest several decades of development in creating a complete translation algorithm!

'RadioButton'

A RadioButton is similar to a CheckBox in that it can be checked on/off. When grouped they become modal – that is, at the very most only one RadioButton in a grouping can be selected. For example, if the Danish RadioButton is clicked on and the English RadioButton was previously selected, the English RadioButton is turned off (cleared) and the Danish RadioButton is checked (set). The RadioButton class is derived from Control as follows:

```
Control
    ButtonBase
        RadioButton
```

The properties specific to the RadioButton class include:

Property	Description
Appearance	This property (get/set) specifies the appearance of a RadioButton (Normal or Button).
AutoCheck	If this get/set property is true (default value) the RadioButton automatically changes to be noticeably checked in when control is clicked and the Checked property set to true. If the value of AutoCheck is false, then the clicked state is subtler when the Checked property is true (see illustration below). When AutoCheck is true at most one RadioButton will be checked for a given container (a mutually exclusive grouping of RadioButtons). The containers that can hold RadioButtons in which only one will be checked include Form, Panel, and GroupBox.

Property	Description
CheckAlign	This get/set property of type ContentAlignment specifies the RadioButton's horizontal and vertical alignment. The values of this property of self-explanatory and are as follows: BottomCenter, BottomLeft, BottomRight, MiddleCenter, MiddleLeft, MiddleRight, TopCenter, TopLeft, and TopRight.
Checked	If this get/set property is true the RadioButton is checked and if this value is false then the RadioButton is unchecked.

Just to recap, here are some illustrations of the different properties:

- The following demonstrates both styles of RadioButton appearance (Normal and Button) in both the checked and unchecked state:

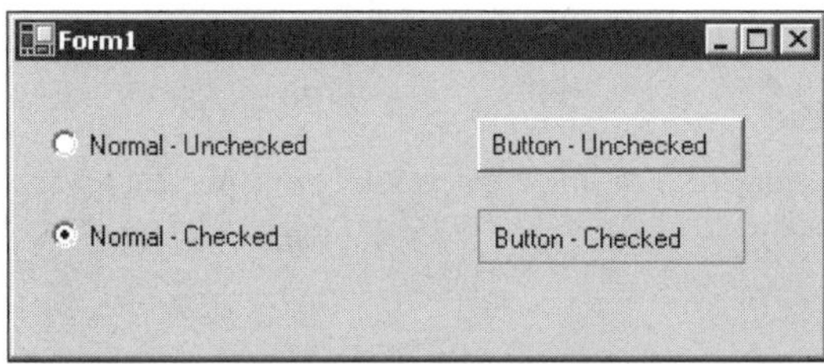

- Below is an example of the style of check for RadioButtons with the AutoCheck property set to false:

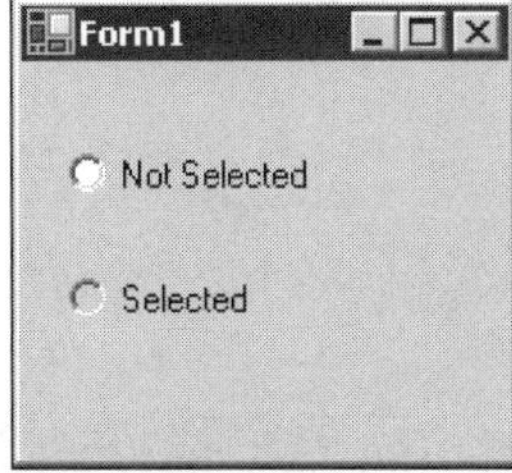

- Here is an illustration of some of the CheckAlign values shown in the designer:

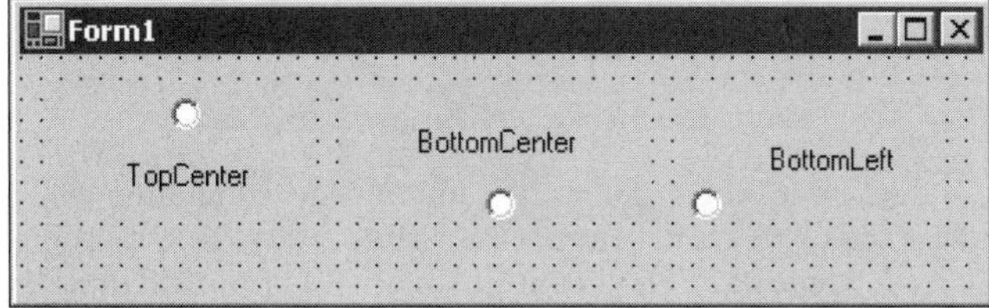

The methods exposed by the RadioButton control include PerformClick. This method causes the RadioButton to receive a Click event. The CheckedChanged event is raised when the value of the Checked property changes for the RadioButton.

The code that creates each RadioButton is generated by the Windows Forms designer and is found in the InitializeComponent method. The code to create the RadioButton that sets the input language to French is as follows:

```
Me.RadioButtonFrenchIn.Location = New System.Drawing.Point(16, 54)
Me.RadioButtonFrenchIn.Name = "RadioButtonFrenchIn"
Me.RadioButtonFrenchIn.Size = New System.Drawing.Size(80, 24)
Me.RadioButtonFrenchIn.TabIndex = 1
Me.RadioButtonFrenchIn.Text = "French"
```

The majority of controls visible on the Form are contained in the Form object itself using the following line of code from the InitializeComponent method:

```
Me.Controls.AddRange(New System.Windows.Forms.Control()_
    {Me.PictureBoxLangOut, Me.PictureBoxLangIn,…
```

The RadioButtons are grouped by using a GroupBox control. The RadioButtons are therefore contained in the Controls collection of a GroupBox object.

'GroupBox'

The GroupBox class is used to group controls by serving as a container for these controls and to provide a label for this grouping of controls. By default, the GroupBox is displayed with no borders, so a GroupBox may not be obvious, or even visible, to a user. The lineage from the GroupBox class to the Control class is as follows:

```
Control
    GroupBox
```

When represented in the Windows Forms designer, a GroupBox is just a box outlined by a line and with a caption at the top left of the box:

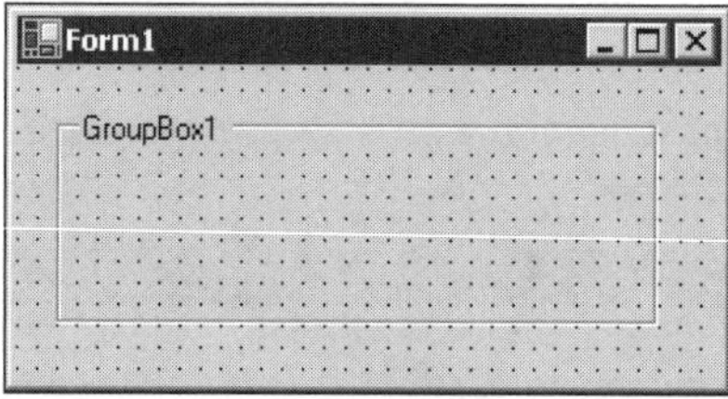

The Text property of the GroupBox is where the caption is stored and the Visible property is used to specify if the GroupBox and all its child controls are visible (true) or not visible (false). The Collections property is where each child control is stored. For our example, two GroupBox objects are used to contain each RadioButton (input language and output language). The portion of the InitializeComponent method that sets up the input language GroupBox and associates each child control (RadioButton) with this GroupBox is as follows:

```
Me.GroupBoxLangIn.Controls.AddRange(New System.Windows.Forms.Control() _
    {Me.RadioButtonFrenchIn, Me.RadioButtonEngIn, Me.RadioButtonDanishIn})
Me.GroupBoxLangIn.Text = "Language In"
```

As with all code in the `InitializeComponent` method, the previous snippet was written by Visual Studio.NET's Windows Forms Designer. There is no mystery as to how the Windows Forms Designer knew to place the `RadioButtons` in the `AddRange` method, which ultimately adds the `RadioButtons` to the `GroupBox`'s `Controls` collection. When each `RadioButton` was dragged and placed inside the line denoting the `GroupBox`, the Windows Forms designer made the `RadioButton` a child of the `GroupBox`. Visually, the previous code snippet creates the following:

The previous `GroupBox` has the ability to display or not display caption text. By default the `GroupBox` is contained in a visible frame. The `Panel` by default does not display a frame and the `Panel` does not have the ability to display caption text. A `Panel` does support scrollbars while a `GroupBox` does not.

'ListBox'

The `ListBox` control displays a list of items that can be selected by a user. Items within the `ListBox` are either selected (highlighted) or not selected (not highlighted). The lineage from the `ListBox` class to the `Control` class is as follows:

```
Control
    ListControl
        ListBox
```

Properties of interest for the `ListBox` include:

Property	Description
`HorizontalScrollbar`	If this `get/set` property is `true` then a horizontal scrollbar is displayed when the width of the items in the `ListBox` extends beyond the right edge of the `ListBox`.
`Items`	This property exposes the `ListBoxItems.ObjectCollection` (a list of all `Items` in the `ListBox`) for a `ListBox`. This collection's methods can be used to set up the items in the `ListBox`: `Add`, `AddRange`, `Clear`, `Insert`, `Remove`, and `RemoveAt`.
`MultiColumn`	If this `get/set` property is `true` then the `ListBox` supports multiple columns. If the `MultiColumn` property is `false`, the `ListBox` supports one column.

Table continued on following page

Property	Description
`SelectedIndex`	This `get/set` property, of type `integer`, specifies which item in the `ListBox` is selected. A value of –1 indicates no item is selected. A value of zero indicates that the zero-positioned item is selected, a value of 1 indicates the first item is selected, and so on. If the `SelectionMode` is set to `MultiExtended` or `MultiSimple`, the index of any selected item can be returned by this property.
`SelectedIndices`	This `get`-only property returns a collection of all the indices selected by the `ListBox` (a property value of type `ListBox.SelectedIndexCollection`).
`SelectedItem`	This `get/set` property, of type `Object`, specifies which item in the `ListBox` is selected. If the `SelectionMode` is set to `MultiExtended` or `MultiSimple`, the value of any selected item can be returned by this property.
`SelectedItems`	This `get`-only property returns a collection of all the items selected by the `ListBox`. This type returned by this property is `ListBox.SelectedObjectCollection`, a collection of type `Object`.
`SelectionMode`	The number of items selected by a `Listbox` is controlled using the `SelectionMode` `get/set` property. This property, of type, `SelectionMode`, is set to `One` in order to allow the `ListBox` to select one item, or is set to `MultiExtended`, or `MultiSimple`, to allow the `ListBox` to select multiple items. `MultiExtended` differs from `MultiSimple` in that the *SHIFT*, *CTRL*, and arrow keys can be used to make selections. These selections are exposed, for example, in Windows Explorer, where *SHIFT* selects a range and *CTRL* toggles individual items. The `SelectionMode` property can also be set to `None`, indicating that no items can be selected.
`Sorted`	If this `get/set` property is `true` then the items in the `ListBox` are sorted alphabetically. If `Sorted` is `false` then the items in the list are not sorted.
`Text`	This `get/set` property specifies the text associated with the currently selected item in the `ListBox`. Setting the `Text` property searches the `ListBox`'s items for an item containing the text specified. If this item is found, it is selected. If the `SelectionMode` property is not set to `None` then the `Text` property returns the text associated with the first item selected within the `ListBox`.

To better understand these properties, consider the following examples:

- When a `ListBox` is in focus in the Windows Forms Designer, the `ListBox`'s `Items` property can be double-clicked (in the Properties window) thus displaying the following dialog, which can be used to add `Items` to a `ListBox`:

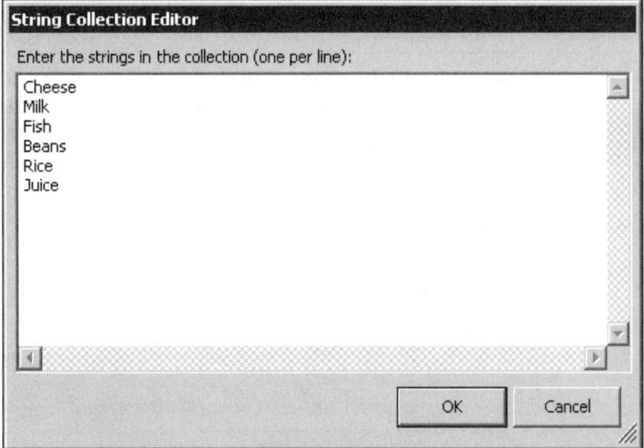

- Below is a ListBox with MultiColumn set to true:

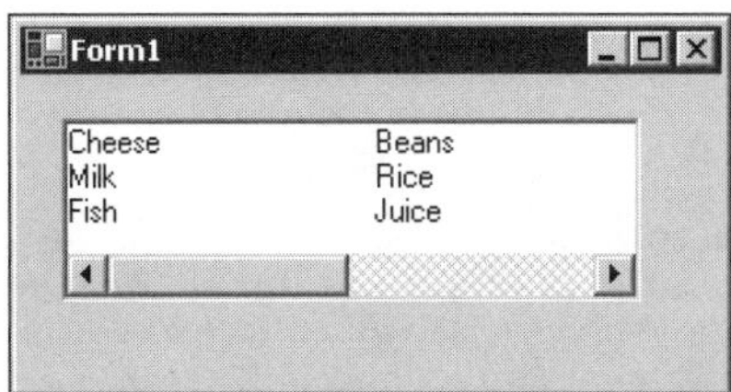

- To demonstrate the Text property's ability to find and select a ListBox item, we will revisit our sample application, WroxTranslator. Recall that in the first screenshot for this application, the item Slang was highlighted in the ListBox. This selected ListBox item is because of the following line of code:

```
ListBoxStyleOfSpeech.Text = "Slang"
```

The ListBox exposes a variety of methods:

Method	Description
ClearSelected	Clears all selected items in the ListBox.
FindString	Returns an integer corresponding to the list entry index where a match is found. The list entry index is zero-based. Finds the first item in the ListBox that matches the string parameter passed to the FindString method. This match is an inexact match with the first entry in the ListBox that starts with the string passed as parameter to the FindString method (for example, parameter "Hello" matches ListBox entry "Hello World"). If no matching string is found, ListBox.NoMatches is returned.

Table continued on following page

Method	Description
FindStringExact	Returns an integer corresponding to the list entry index where a match is found. The list entry index is zero-based. Finds the first item in the ListBox that matches the string specified as the first parameter to FindStringExact. This match is an exact, case-insensitive match where the item's entire string must match the string parameter passed to FindStringExact. If no matching string is found, ListBox.NoMatches is returned.
SetSelected	(integer, bool). Sets or clears the item at the index specified by the integer parameter. If the second parameter (the Boolean) is true then the item is set and if this parameter is false, the item is cleared.
Sort	Causes the items in the ListBox to be sorted alphabetically.

Our application, WroxTranslator, requires that the ListBox, ListBoxStyleOfSpeech, contains a selection. For this reason, the method that handles translation ensures that an item is selected using the following code to detect the number of items selected (the Count property) and if this value is zero, specifies that the zero-positioned item is selected (Item(0)):

```
Dim selectedItem As Object

' In case they have not selected a style of speech we
' assign the default. We did assign a default in the
' constructor but they may have cleared it so we
' need to ensure there is a style of speech selected
If ListBoxStyleOfSpeech.SelectedItems.Count > 0 Then
   selectedItem = ListBoxStyleOfSpeech.SelectedItems(0)
Else
   selectedItem = ListBoxStyleOfSpeech.Items(0)
End If
```

'TrackBar'

The lineage from the TrackBar class to the Control class is as follows:

```
Control
    TrackBar
```

The TrackBar control is the cousin of the ScrollBar in that the TrackBar traverses a range of settings. With a TrackBar, the range traversed is specified (property Minimum to property Maximum). For example, consider a Form that controls an electric guitar where the Minimum setting was zero (off) and the Maximum setting was eleven (loudest music). There would be twelve ticks displayed on such a TrackBar (from 0 to 11).

In our example, the TrackBar displayed for English has three ticks (American, Canadian, and British). Three ticks are facilitated by a Minimum property of zero and a Maximum property of two. When the language is French, the TrackBar has two ticks (corresponding to French and Canadian French). Two ticks are facilitated by a Minimum property of zero and a Maximum property of one.

Some of the properties associated with a `TrackBar` control include:

Property	Description
`Maximum`	This `get/set` property, of type `integer`, specifies the maximum value for a tick mark. Remember if the `Minimum` property is set to zero, the index is zero-based, so ten tick marks correspond to setting `Maximum` to nine.
`Minimum`	This `get/set` property, of type `integer`, specifies the minimum value for a tick mark.
`TickFrequency`	This `get/set` property, of type `integer`, specifies how many actual ticks correspond to a 'tick' drawn on the `TrackBar`. The default value is 1, which is why the English language (US, Canadian and British) contains three tick marks on the `TrackBar`.
`TickStyle`	This `get/set` property, of type `TickStyle`, specifies how the `TrackBar` displays tick marks (`BottomRight`, `TopLeft`, `Both`, and `None`).
`Value`	This `get/set` property, of type `integer`, specifies the current 'tick' of the `TrackBar`. For our application's English language, the zero-positioned tick corresponds to the US flag, the first tick is the Canadian flag, and the second tick is the British flag.

Examples of the appearance of the `TickStyle` property are as follows:

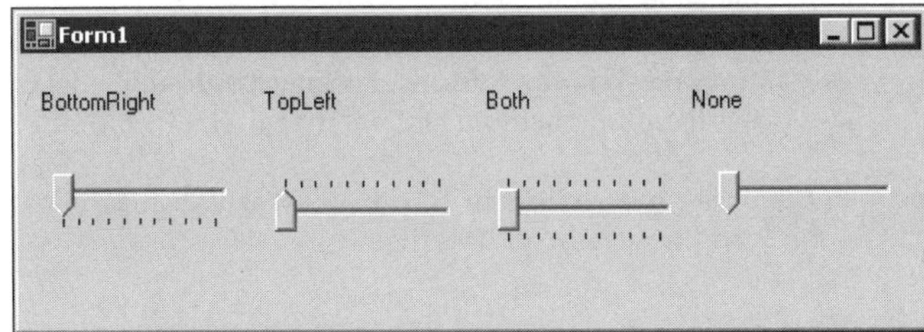

The `TrackBar` supports methods and events, which include:

Method	Description
`OnScroll`	Raises the `Scroll` event as if the mouse slid the `TrackBar`.
`SetRange`	Allows the `Maximum` and `Minimum` property to be set simultaneously.

Event	Description
`Scroll`	Triggered if the `TrackBar` is scrolled (moved via the mouse or programmatically using the `OnScroll` method).
`ValueChanged`	Scrolling causes a change in the `Value` property of the `TrackBar`. This event is raised if the `Value` property changes either by scrolling or by programmatically setting the `Value` property.

Within the WroxTranslator application, the WroxSetFlag method updates the Maximum property of each TrackBar when a new language is selected or if the Scroll event is triggered for a TrackBar. This method is as follows:

```
Private Sub WroxSetFlag(ByVal pictBox As PictureBox, _
                        ByVal trackBarOfFlags As TrackBar, _
                        ByVal language As WroxLanguageType)

   Dim rayConvert() As String

   ' flag pictures for our language
   rayConvert = flagFiles(language)
   trackBarOfFlags.Maximum = rayConvert.Length - 1
   pictBox.Image = Image.FromFile(rayConvert(trackBarOfFlags.Value))
End Sub
```

The flagFiles data member of the class is a two dimensional array of languages in one dimension (English, French and Danish) and .JPG files representing flags in the other dimension (US.jpg, Canada.jpg, and UK.jpg are associated with language English). The array variable rayConvert is used to select the .JPG files for a particular language. The Length property of rayConvert is then used to set the TrackBar's Maximum property. We subtract one because our TrackBar is zero indexed meaning that the Minimum property must be set to zero.

Notice in the previous code snippet that the Value property of the TrackBar is used. If a Scroll event is triggered, a change in the Value has occurred. For our application, the TrackBar for the input language handles the Scroll event using the TrackBarInFlag_Scroll method; the TrackBar for the output language dialect handles the Scroll event using the TrackBarOutFlag_Scroll method. These methods were created using the Windows Forms designer by double-clicking on each TrackBar on the Form. Both of these event-handling methods ultimately call the WroxSetFlag method.

The previous code snippet hints at how our PictureBox object will display flags using the Image class's FromFile method to load the specified .JPG file.

'PictureBox'

The lineage from the PictureBox class to the Control class is as follows:

```
Control
    PictureBox
```

The PictureBox control displays an image as specified by this class's Image property, of type Image. In short, the PictureBox control works hand-in-hand with the Image class found in the System.Drawing namespace.

The properties associated with the PictureBox control include:

Property	Description
BorderStyle	This get/set property, of type BorderStyle, can be set to None, FixedSingle, or Fixed3D.

Property	Description
Image	This get/set property, of type Image, contains the image displayed by the PictureBox.
SizeMode	This get/set property, of type SizeMode, specifies how the PictureBox is sized. The permissible values for this property include: AutoSize (the size of the PictureBox varies to match the size of the image it contains), CenterImage (the picture box is of fixed size; if the centered Image is too large it is cropped accordingly), Normal (the Image is displayed in the upper-left corner of the PictureBox control and if the Image is too large it is cropped accordingly), and StretchImage (the Image is stretched or shrunk to exactly fit the dimension of the PictureBox).

Here we can see the different appearance of each BorderStyle value:

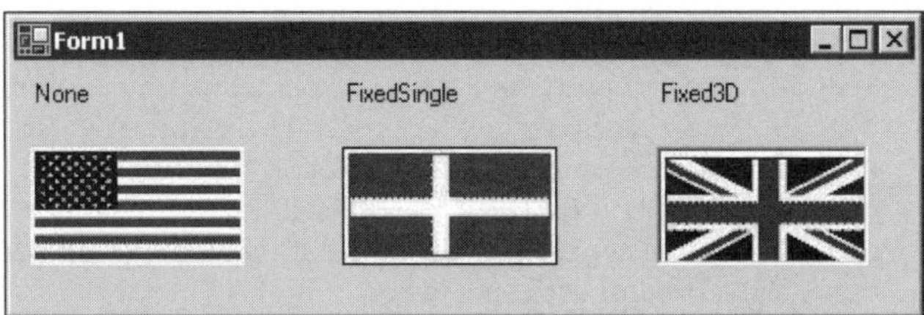

The PictureBox control handles an event that is triggered when the SizeMode changes (the SizeModeChangedEvent). This event can be triggered using the OnSizeModeChanged method. This event and method are of nominal interest but more interesting is the Image class and its methods, such as FromFile. This static method (shared method in VB.NET) creates an Image object using the filename specified. The FromHbitmap method is also static and this method creates an Image object using a Windows bitmap handle. The FromStream method (also static) creates an Image from a Stream instance. Believe it or not Image does exposes methods that are not static in nature such as Save. Living up to its name, the Save method saves an Image object to a file or a stream depending on the parameters passed to this method.

Our application, WroxTranslator, used the Image class's FromFile method to set the Image property of the PictureBox. The specific line of code that handles this is found in the WroxSetFlag method:

```
pictBox.Image = Image.FromFile(rayConvert(trackBarOfFlags.Value))
```

Actually, this line of code is simply specifying a file, such as:

```
pictBox.Image = Image.FromFile("Denmark.jpb")
```

'RichTextBox'

The RichTextBox control is derived from the Control class as follows:

```
Control
    TextBoxBase
        RichTextBox
```

The `RichTextBox` control is the (much bigger) brother of the `TextBox` control. The `RichTextBox` control can be thought of as a mini word-processor, complete with scrollbars, file manipulation (save and load), edit features (select, redo, past, text search), and document formatting (bullets, margins, URL highlight, fonts, colors).

A subset of the properties exposed by the `RichTextBox` control includes:

Property	Description
`BulletIndex`	This `get/set` property, of type `integer`, specifies the number of pixels by which the bullet is indented within the control's text.
`CanRedo`	This `get/set` property is `true` if actions can be undone and `false` if the actions cannot be undone.
`DetectUrls`	This `get/set` property is `true` if URLs are detected when entered in the `RichTextBox` and are formatted accordingly. If this property is `false`, then URL's are not displayed any differently to normal text.
`ScrollBars`	This `get/set` property, of type `RichTextBoxScrollBars`, specifies how and if scrollbars are displayed with the `RichTextBox`. A value of `None` indicates that no scrollbars are displayed, `Vertical` specifies that a vertical scrollbar is displayed if the text exceeds the vertical dimension, and `Horizontal` specifies that a horizontal scrollbar is displayed if the text exceeds the horizontal dimension. Having both specifies that both/either type of scrollbar will be displayed if its corresponding dimension is exceeded by the `RichTextBox`'s text. Values of `ForcedBoth`, `ForcedHorizontal`, and `ForcedVertical` specify that a corresponding type of scrollbar should be displayed, even if the text of the `RichTextBox`'s text does not exceed said dimension display limit.

The methods exposed by the `RichTextBox` control include:

Method	Description
`CanPaste`	Determines if data of a specific format can be pasted to the clipboard.
`Find`	Attempts to find a specific string within the `RichTextBox`'s text.
`LoadFile`	Loads a file into the `RichTextBox` control.
`Paste`	Takes the contents of the clipboard and pastes it into the `RichTextBox` control.
`Redo`	Redoes (reapplies) the last operation performed on the `RichTextBox` control.
`SaveFile`	Saves the contents of the `RichTextBox` control to a file.

A subset of the events exposed by the `RichTextBox` control includes:

Event	Description
`HScroll`	Triggered if the `RichTextBox`'s horizontal scrollbar is clicked or changed via keyboard action.
`VScroll`	Triggered if the `RichTextBox`'s vertical scrollbar is clicked or moved via keyboard action.

Within our sample application, WroxTranslator, the TextChanged event (inherited from Control) was used to initiate language translation. The methods to handle this were initially created by double-clicking on the upper and lower RichTextBox in our application while in the Windows Forms Designer. The methods generated by this were RichTextBoxLangIn_TextChanged and RichTextBoxLangOut_TextChanged. Both of these methods are approximately the same and just operate in different directions with respect to translation. The RichTextBoxLangIn_TextChanged method, is implemented as follows:

```
Private Sub RichTextBoxLangIn_TextChanged(ByVal sender As System.Object, _
        ByVal e As System.EventArgs) Handles RichTextBoxLangIn.TextChanged
   If Not bChangingText Then
      bChangingText = True
      WroxTranslate(RichTextBoxLangIn, TrackBarOutFlag, _
      RichTextBoxLangOut, currentOutLanguage)
      WroxResetScrollBars(RichTextBoxLangIn, _
      VScrollBarParagraphSkipIn, HScrollBarWordSkipIn)
      WroxResetScrollBars(RichTextBoxLangOut, _
      VScrollBarParagraphSkipOut, HScrollBarWordSkipOut)
      bChangingText = False
   End If
End Sub
```

The RichTextBoxLangIn_TextChanged method uses the following private methods:

- WroxTranslate: Performs translation given a language, a dialect, and a language style (formal, slang, or technical).
- WroxResetScrollBars: Resets extra horizontal and vertical scrollbars associated with each RichTextBox. These additional scrollbars facilitate fast per-word and per-line document traversal. These scrollbars must be reset when the text has changed (the TextChanged event) and when translation occurs, because this means text has changed. So, if the input text changes (TextChanged event), its scrollbars are updated. This change is translated to the output text (output RichTextBox) so that the extra scrollbars for the output RichTextBox are reset accordingly.

The RichTextBoxLangIn_TextChanged and RichTextBoxLangOut_TextChanged methods both use the bChangeText data member (variable of type Boolean). In order to understand how this variable is used, consider the following sequence:

- The RichTextBox associated with input language receives a new letter (TextChanged event triggered) and sets the bChangeText data member to true.
- The WroxTranslate method is used to translate this new letter and updates the RichTextBox associated with the output language.
- Updating the text associated with the output language's RichTextBox triggers a TextChanged event. This is a potential infinite recursion, because a TextChanged event ultimately calls WroxTranslate to translate the newly changed text. This recursive blowout of the thread's stack will not take place because WroxTranslate is only called if bChangeText is set to false.

Developers who cut their teeth on Win32 recognize why this takes place. The TextChanged event is really a synchronous Windows message. Such messages are handled synchronously, which results in an infinite recursive loop. The bChangeText data member ensures that only the TextChanged event initiated by user action is translated using the WroxTranslate method.

'HScrollBar' and 'VScrollBar'

The HScrollBar and VScrollBar controls both implement scrollbars, but with a different orientation. These controls are derived from the Control class as follows:

```
Control                          Control
    ScrollBar                        ScrollBar
        HScrollBar                       VScrollBar
```

The HScrollBar and VScrollBar controls implement no properties, methods, or events of their own. Instead, each of these controls inherits their properties, methods, or events from their base-classes: ScrollBar and Control.

With respect to the most interesting properties of the HScrollBar and VScrollBar controls, recall that they are related to the TrackBar control. The difference is that scrollbars do not display tick marks. Keeping this in mind, the following scrollbar-related properties are of interest:

Property	Description
Maximum	This get/set property, of type integer, specifies the maximum increment of the scrollbar. If property Minimum is set to zero, the index is zero-based, so one should be subtracted from the Maximum property to produce the required value.
Minimum	This get/set property, of type integer, specifies the minimum increment value for the scrollbar.
Value	This get/set property, of type integer, specifies the current location (increment value) of the scrollbar.

Each time text is added to a RichTextBox in our application, the Maximum value of the scrollbars may have to be updated. If the Maximum value shrinks and the Value property was set to the Maximum value, the Value also has to be decremented because the Value would otherwise be out of bounds. The WroxResetScrollBars method basically handles this task by counting words for the HScrollBar controls and lines for the VScrollBars controls. The Maximum and Value properties are updated accordingly with the aid of the Max and Min methods exposed by the Math class. The Max and Min methods perform numeric max and min. The scrollbar Value and Maximum property manipulation code found in WroxResetScrollBars is as follows:

```
' Make sure that the value does not go beyond maximum
vScroll.Value = Math.Min(lineCount, vScroll.Value)
hScroll.Value = Math.Min(wordCount, hScroll.Value)
' Make sure both do not go negative (0 is the minimum maximum)
vScroll.Maximum = Math.Max(lineCount, 0)
hScroll.Maximum = Math.Max(wordCount, 0)
```

The events of interest for both flavors of scrollbar control (horizontal and vertical) include Scroll, which is raised if the scrollbar is scrolled either by using a mouse or via keyboard action. Scrolling the scrollbar causes the underlying value of the Value property to change, reflecting the new increment location of the scrollbar. The ValueChanged event is raised if the Value property changes by scrolling using the mouse or by setting the Value property programmatically.

Within our application, WroxTranslator, an HScrollBar control is used to traverse each RichTextBox one word at a time. A VScrollBar control is used to traverse each RichTextBox one sentence at a time, where each sentence is identified by a trailing linefeed character. In the Windows Forms Designer, methods for handling the Scroll events were created by double-clicking on the appropriate scrollbar and letting the Windows Forms Designer implement the shell of the method for handling when this event is triggered. For the VScrollBar associated with the input RichTextBox, the following method is called when the Scroll event is triggered:

```
Private Sub VScrollBarParagraphSkipIn_Scroll(ByVal sender As System.Object,_
ByVal e As System.Windows.Forms.ScrollEventArgs) _
    Handles VScrollBarParagraphSkipIn.Scroll
    WroxSetSelectRange(RichTextBoxLangIn, _
    VScrollBarParagraphSkipIn.Value, True)
End Sub
```

The previous code snippet uses the private WroxSetSelectedRange method to update a region of the selected input RichTextBox control, acting on a per-sentence basis. The HScrollBar and VScrollBar control for both the input and output RichTextBox all use the WroxSetSelectedRange method. The WroxSetSelectedRange method basically counts the words or lines of the appropriate RichTextBox and updates the selected region accordingly (for the n'th word or n'th sentence, where n is specified by the Value of the scrollbar). Once the n'th word or n'th sentence is identified, the SelectionStart property (corresponding to the beginning of the word/sentence) is set for the RichTextBox. The SelectionLength property (corresponding to the end of the selected word/sentence) is set for the RichTextBox. This code is as follows, where startOffset and length are integers calculated by the WroxSetSelectedRange method by counting the words (scrollbar Value words) or lines (scrollbar Value lines):

```
richTextSource.SelectionStart = startOffset
richTextSource.SelectionLength = length
```

That wraps it up for the WroxTranslator application; now let's look at the dialog controls available for Windows Forms.

WroxEditThis

In this section, a simple editing application, WroxEditThis, will be presented. This application is implemented in C#. WroxEditThis will expose a TextBox that supports editing. An instance of a PrintPreviewControl is placed next to the TextBox. This PrintPreviewControl displays what the text in the TextBox will look like when printed. A variety of dialogs (Windows Forms controls categorized as dialogs) will be used by this editor. Specifically we will:

- Load a file into the editor using OpenFileDialog
- Save the contents of the editor to a file with SaveFileDialog
- Change the font of the editor with FontDialog
- Set the colors used by the editor with ColorDialog
- Configure the editor's page setup with PageSetupDialog
- Preview what the editor will print with PrintPreviewDialog
- print the document being edited with PrintDialog

The simple editing application, WroxEditThis, appears as follows:

The editing application consists of a TextBox whose Multiline property has been set to true in order to facilitate text entry (Form's textBoxInData data member). This TextBox has its ScrollBars property set to Vertical. To the right of the TextBox is the PrintPreviewControl (Form's printPreviewControl1data member). The editor exposes a variety of buttons, each of which corresponds to the Windows Forms dialog that will be displayed (Open File button, Save File button, etc.).

Dialogs

The Windows Forms controls implement dialogs that handle everything from file management to printing. A dialog is an encapsulation of controls that perform a specific task. Most non-developers are actually familiar with dialogs. Whether saving a file in Notepad or Word, the SaveFileDialog is displayed by the application. Whether printing a file from WordPerfect or Visual Studio.NET, the PrintDialog is displayed by the application. From a developer's standpoint, the dialog is more than just displayed. The properties, methods, and events associated with the dialog allow tasks such as printing or saving a file to be handled by an application.

Using dialogs to handle commonly performed tasks was a big step forward for Windows (in the mid-1990's) because it gives users a common look-and-feel experience, regardless of the application. Developers benefit because they do not have to reinvent the wheel, save file dialog, or print dialog with each application they develop.

Also included in this discussion of dialogs is a discussion of the PrintPreviewControl. This control resides on the Form, rather than being self-contained like a dialog. The PrintPreviewControl performs functionality exploited by the PrintPreviewDialog, so it makes sense to review both the control and the dialog flavor of print previewing. In a similar vein, the PrintDocument class will also be discussed. With dialogs to set up printed pages, dialogs to print, and dialogs/controls to perform print previewing, an actual document is needed that is to be printed. The PrintDocument class represents this document. The Windows Forms classes presented in this section and the tasks they perform include:

Class	Description
ColorDialog	This dialog displays the colors available and provides controls that allow colors to be customized. Applications from word processors, to drawing programs, to project management software can make use of different colors in order to more clearly present a topic.

Class	Description
FontDialog	This dialog displays a list of fonts available to an application. This dialog is used by any application that displays text in order to specify font, font size, effects (underline, boldface, etc.), and color.
OpenFileDialog	Displays a list of files to be opened for a specific directory. Files of a specific name or extension can be filtered and traversal of directories is supported.
PageSetupDialog	This dialog is used to configure page settings for a page to be printed. The page settings configurable include such things as the page's margins, paper type, orientation (landscape or portrait), and paper source (which paper location the printer uses to retrieve paper).
PrintDialog	The PrintDialog is appropriately named in that it facilitates the printing of a document, including which pages are printed, the number of copies printed, and which printer is used to actually handle the printing.
PrintDocument	Class representing the document to be printed. The PrintDocument class is configured by the PageSetupDialog dialog. The PrintDocument is displayed using the likes of PrintDialog, PrintPreviewControl, and PrintPreviewDialog.
PrintPreviewControl	This control displays what a page or pages will look like when printed (alias a print preview). Differing views of the page can be displayed based on the level of magnification (zoom) specified.
PrintPreviewDialog	This dialog displays what a page will look like when printed.
SaveFileDialog	The SaveFileDialog is used to save a file to disk. The file name and location can be specified using this dialog. The directory structure can be traversed using this dialog in order to select a specific location in which to save the file.

Dialogs do not quite fit into the Windows Forms development model of dragging a control from Visual Studio.NET's ToolBox and placing it on a Form for inclusion in the Form's functionality. A dialog is composed of multiple controls and is displayed in a modal window. Actually, a Form itself can be displayed as a modal dialog by calling the Form class's ShowDialog method.

The remainder of this section covers the Click event associated with each of the buttons that appear in WroxEditThis. Each separate button Click event reveals how the specific dialog was used by our editing application.

'OpenFileDialog'

When the WroxEditThis application was developed, the author chose not to use Visual Studio.NET's Toolbox when setting up the OpenFileDialog class, and instead simply set up this class programmatically. The idea behind this was simply to emphasize that the OpenFileDialog is just a class and there is no need to involve Toolbox every time a Windows Forms related class must be created. The OpenFileDialog class is not derived from Control as are a large number of the Windows Forms controls located in the ToolBox window. Instead, OpenFileDialog is a descendant of the CommonDialog class:

```
CommonDialog
    FileDialog
        OpenFileDialog
```

When the Open File button of the `WroxEditThis` application is clicked, an instance of the `OpenFileDialog` class is created. This all takes place when the `Click` event is handled by the `buttonOpenFile_Click` method. Creating the `OpenFileDialog` instance is as follows:

```
OpenFileDialog openFileDialog = new OpenFileDialog();
```

The constructor used in the previous code snippet was the default constructor, the only constructor exposed by this dialog. The `OpenFileDialog` class's `ShowDialog` method is called within the button click handler, the `buttonOpenFile_Click` method, and the following is displayed:

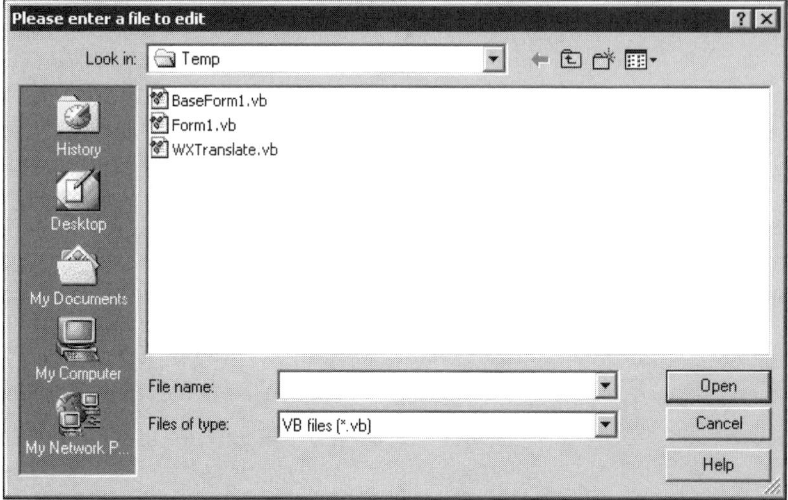

Both the `OpenFileDialog` and `SaveFileDialog` classes are derived from `FileDialog`. A common base-class is an indication (which turns out to be true) that these dialogs share a large amount of functionality. For this reason, these two classes have a large number of methods, properties, and events in common. You will read more about the properties, methods, and events in this section, but here is a quick reference to those we will cover:

Property	**Description**
`AddExtension`	This property, if `true`, automatically adds the `DefaultExt` to the filename entered by the user if they hadn't already specified an extension.
`CheckFileExists`	This property, if set to `true` (the default value), causes the open file dialog to display a warning if the OK button of the open file dialog is selected and the filename specified by the user is not found.
`CheckPathExists`	This property, if set to `true` (the default value), will warn if the path does not exist when OK is selected from the open file dialog.

Property	Description
DefaultExt	This property specifies a default extension value: if we were programming in VB.NET, it would make sense to set this property to 'vb', which would then be added to the filename entered by the user if they hadn't already specified an extension.
FileName (or FileNames)	This property allows the filename (or filenames) mentioned to be retrieved.
Filter	This property, of type string, specifies which files display in the dialog, according to its value (for example, '.cs' for C# files).
FilterIndex	This property is used in conjunction with the Filter property in order to specify which filter is initially displayed when the OpenFileDialog is launched.
InitialDirectory	Setting this property specifies from which directory the 'files to open' list will be generated.
Multiselect	This property, when set to false (the default value), indicates that only one file at a time can be returned.
RestoreDirectory	When this property is set to true, the OpenFileDialog instance resets the current directory to its original value after the dialog is closed, provided the OK button is not selected, in order to open a file.
ShowHelp	This property is set to true when an actual Help button is to be displayed on the OpenFileDialog.
Title	This property gets/sets the Title.
ValidateNames	When this property is set to true, each filename entered is validated to ensure that it is a well-formed filename based on the underlying file system.

Method	Description
OpenFile	This method returns a Stream that contains the file specified by FileName, opened as read-only.
ShowDialog	Allows the dialog to be displayed.

Event	Description
HelpRequest	Inherited from the CommonDialog base-class.

For example, both the save and open flavors of the FileDialog can get and set the dialog box's title via the property. Within the WroxEditThis application, this property is set as follows for the open file dialog:

```
openFileDialog.Title = "Please enter a file to edit";
```

The open file dialog box will not be displayed until the ShowDialog method is called. The appearance and behavior of the OpenFileDialog instance can be specified using properties from when this object is instantiated until ShowDialog is called. When the dialog box is displayed, the user has an opportunity to enter a filename (or filenames) that can be retrieved using the FileName (or FileNames) property. The basic form in which the OpenFileDialog is used is as follows:

```
OpenFileDialog openFileDialog = new OpenFileDialog(); // create instance

// Configure dialog box appearance and behavior using properties

// Block while dialog is shown
if (openFileDialog.ShowDialog() == DialogResult.OK)
{
    // Process results here using the FileName property,
    // the FileNames property or the OpenFile method
}
```

The properties exploited in the WroxEditThis application include setting the CheckFileExists property to true. Actually, this is the default setting for the property. The CheckFileExists property causes the open file dialog to display a warning if the OK button of the open file dialog is selected and the filename specified by the user is not found. The dialog will still close (since OK was selected) but a warning will be displayed. An example of the warning generated by this property is as follows:

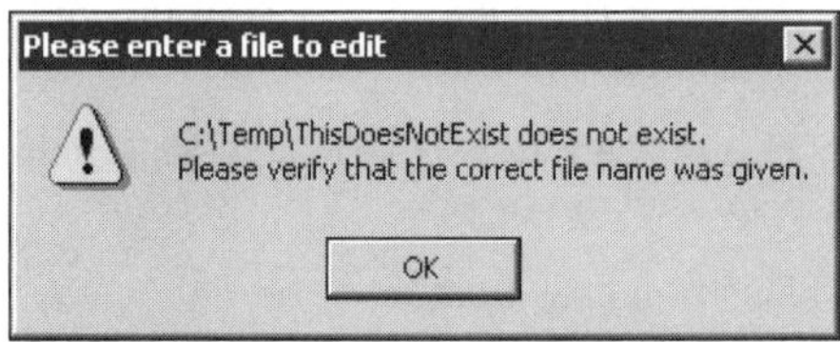

The previous warning was generated because the path existed, but the file did not. The CheckPathExists property can also be set to true. This property will warn if the path does not exist when OK is selected from the open file dialog. Once again, the dialog will still be closed, but a warning generated. By default, CheckPathExists is set to true. An example of the warning generated by this property is as follows:

The difference between these two properties is a matter of precision. If CheckPathExists is false and CheckFileExists is true, then a warning will be displayed if an invalid path or file is encountered. The warning will indicate that the filename was invalid, even if the invalid portion of the full file path was a directory within the file's path. Setting CheckPathExists to true would display a specific warning if the path were invalid rather than the more generic file invalid warning. Hopefully it is intuitive what happens when both CheckFileExists and CheckPathExists are set to false: no check is made of either the file's existence or the path's validity.

The OpenFileDialog Windows Forms control provides yet another property that checks the validity of the file specified: ValidateNames. When this property is set to true, each filename entered is validated to ensure that it is a well-formed filename based on the underlying file system. For example, if the filename prt: is specified, the following will be displayed:

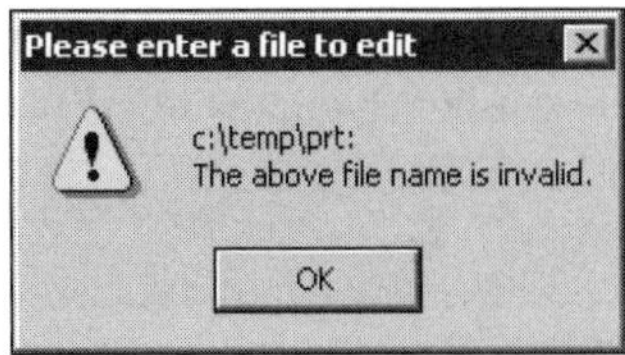

Notice in the previous screenshot that the precision has been enhanced with respect to validating the FileName property. prt: is an invalid Win32 filename, but is actually a file that exists (it is a filename used and reserved by the operating system). The check related properties are set up as follows:

```
openFileDialog.CheckFileExists = true;
openFileDialog.CheckPathExists = true;
openFileDialog.ValidateNames = true;
```

For the WroxEditThis application, the DefaultExt property is set to "vb" and the AddExtension property is set to true, which is the default value for this property. This combination of properties means that if the user does not provide an extension, the OpenFileDialog control will automatically append this extension based on the default extension provided (DefaultExt, "vb"). If AddExtension has been set to false, this adding of the extension would not have taken place. These parameters are set up as follows; notice that there is no period '.' specified before the DefaultExt:

```
openFileDialog.AddExtension = true;
openFileDialog.DefaultExt = "vb";
```

When the open file dialog is displayed, the files contained in the dialog are determined using a filter. For example, a filter of '*.txt' would only display files such as power.txt, corruption.txt, and lies.txt. A '*.cs' filter would display only C# source files, '*.vb' would display only VB source files, and '*.*' would display every file, regardless of extension. The filters provided to the open file dialog are get and set using the Filter property. This property, of type string, is set by specifying a string of the following form (where items in rounded brackets are required and items in square brackets are optional):

```
(info text | file filter) [| info text | file filter]
```

The 'info text' is simply informative text describing what the filter does. For example, specifying 'typical C++ file' as info text indicates to the user that the filter contains extension such as *.cpp and *.h. The 'file filters' follow a '|' character. Each 'file filter' is separated from the next by semicolons, ';'. The file filter can contain wild cards, such as '*.cs' for all C# source files and '*.vb' for all VB source files. More specific file filters are permissible, such as files starting with 'si' would be filtered through the use of 'si*.*'. The FilterIndex property is used in conjunction with the Filter property in order to specify which filter is initially displayed when the OpenFileDialog is launched. The filter index runs from 1 (the first filter in the series) to N (where there are N total filters specified). The filters for the WroxEditThis application are specified as follows:

```
openFileDialog.Filter = "typical C++ files |*.cpp;*.h;*.inl|" +
                        "C# files (*.cs)|*.cs|" +
                        "VB files (*.vb)|*.vb";
openFileDialog.FilterIndex = 3; // point to *.vb filter (3rd filter)
```

When the FileOpenDialog is displayed, the filters are next to the **Files of type:** label. The following excerpt from a FileOpenDialog screenshot shows the filters in action:

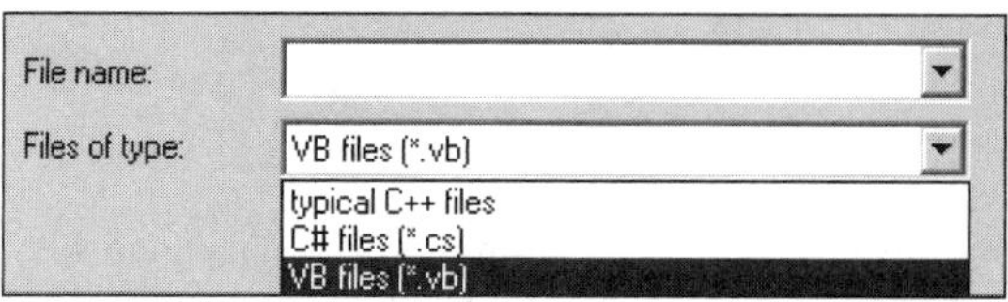

Based on the previous filters, the primary purpose of our editor should be clear. This simple editing application is designed for working with source files, such as files with extensions of the following form: *.vb, *.cs, and *.cpp. Clearly, these filters do not prevent users from displaying and editing text (as is demonstrated in this section).

When the OpenFileDialog is displayed, help features are built right into the dialog. For example, when the cursor is placed in the OpenFileDialog's **File name:** TextBox and the F1 key is pressed, the following help text is displayed:

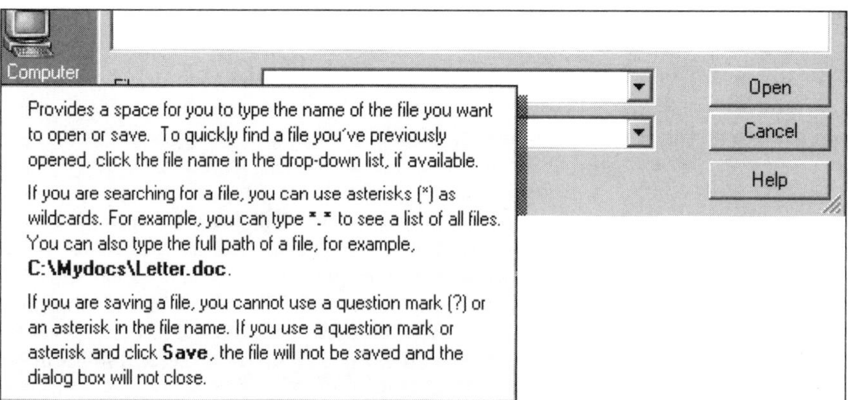

The previous help text was provided by the dialog and was displayed because the ShowHelp property of the OpenFileDialog was set to false (the default setting). This is not as counterintuitive as it might seem. The ShowHelp property is set to true when an actual **Help** button is to be displayed on the OpenFileDialog. This **Help** button can be associated with developer-provided help. This property is inherited from the FileDialog base-class. Setting this property does not mandate that help information be displayed via the **Help** button; rather, it enables help information to be displayed in this manner. The HelpRequest event is inherited from the base-class, CommonDialog. In order to set help up, an EventHandler class will be added to the common file dialog. The basic setup required to support help is as follows:

```
openFileDialog.ShowHelp = true;
openFileDialog.HelpRequest +=
      new System.EventHandler(this.openFileDialog_Help);
```

The openFileDialog_Help method is the callback that will handle the HelpRequest event. Do not confuse this method with the callback called when the **Open File** button is clicked. The openFileDialog_Help method is called when the **Help** button on the OpenFileDialog is clicked. This method is implemented as follows:

```
private void openFileDialog_Help(object sender, System.EventArgs e)
{
    MessageBox.Show("Help Text Here", "Help Title Here");
}
```

With respect to help, only a meager MessageBox is displayed, but at least you weren't charged hourly for this tech support! In the real world, help could be as simple as a MessageBox. A separate help application might be launched. A browser window might be opened to a specific URL. Help could also be implemented by launching a separate dialog (created using the Form class) that contains help information.

For the WroxEditThis application, the InitialDirectory property of the open file dialog is set to "c:\temp". It is recognized that c:\temp is not the standard location used by Windows 2000 or Windows XP. This directory was set for demonstration purposes, since most machines still contain a c:\temp directory. Setting this property specifies from which directory the 'files to open' list will be generated. Our application also sets the Multiselect property to false (the default value), indicating that only one file at a time can be returned. WroxEditThis implements a simple editor that can only edit a single file at a time, so setting Multiselect to false makes intuitive sense. Applications that can process multiple files should specify true for the value of Multiselect. The filename retrieved by the OpenFileDialog is returned using the FileName property. If Multiselect is true then the FileNames property returns an array of filenames selected by the open file dialog. The type returned by FileNames in VB.NET is string , in C# is string [], and in C++ is string*. The code used to specify the initial directory (property, InitialDirectory) and the multi-select (property, Multiselect) is as follows:

```
openFileDialog.InitialDirectory = "c:\\temp";
openFileDialog.Multiselect = false;
```

The WroxEditThis application does not rely on either the FileName or FileNames property in order to retrieves its files. Instead, it calls the OpenFile method of OpenFileDialog. The OpenFile method returns a Stream that contains the file specified by FileName opened as read-only. In the buttonOpenFile_Click method, this Stream is passed to a constructor, of type StreamReader (variable, readStream). The StreamReader class reads a file as a stream. This class is found in the System.IO namespace, so the appropriate using directive (or imports directive in VB.NET) must be specified. The StreamReader class exposes the ReadToEnd method, which reads every character in a stream (the file specified) and returns it as type string. This string is returned and assigned to the Text property of the TextBox used by our editor application (variable, textBoxInData). The code that displays the open file dialog box and opens the file returned is as follows:

```
if (openFileDialog.ShowDialog() == DialogResult.OK)
{
    StreamReader readStream = new StreamReader(openFileDialog.OpenFile());

    textBoxInData.Text = readStream.ReadToEnd();
    readStream.Close();
}
```

In the previous code snippet the return code of the ShowDialog method was examined. This return code is of type DialogResult. When an open file dialog closes it can return either OK (the **OK** button was selected) or Cancel (the **Cancel** button was selected). Other types of dialog boxes can return different types depending on the buttons exposed in the dialog box. The other permissible values of the DialogResult enumeration include Abort, Ignore, No, None, Retry, and Yes. No code was included in the previous example to handle any exceptions raised by the StreamReader class (file not found, access denied, file opened exclusively by another application, etc.). Error handling is an exercise left to the reader.

The buttonOpenFile_Click method is implemented as follows:

```
private void buttonOpenFile_Click(object sender, System.EventArgs e)
{
    OpenFileDialog openFileDialog = new OpenFileDialog();

    openFileDialog.ShowHelp = true;
    openFileDialog.HelpRequest +=
    new System.EventHandler(this.openFileDialog_Help);
    openFileDialog.Title = "Please enter a file to edit";
    openFileDialog.AddExtension = true;
    openFileDialog.DefaultExt = "vb";
    openFileDialog.CheckFileExists = true;
    openFileDialog.CheckPathExists = true;
    openFileDialog.ValidateNames = true;

    // Okay under Windows 2K and XP this is not the default temp but most
    // machines have c:\\temp
    openFileDialog.Filter = "typical C++ files |*.cpp;*.h;*.inl|" +
                            "C# files (*.cs)|*.cs|" +
                            "VB files (*.vb)|*.vb";
    openFileDialog.FilterIndex = 3; // point to *.vb filter (3rd filter)
    openFileDialog.RestoreDirectory = false;
    openFileDialog.InitialDirectory = "c:\\temp";
    openFileDialog.Multiselect = true;
    if (openFileDialog.ShowDialog() == DialogResult.OK)
    {
        StreamReader readStream = new
        StreamReader(openFileDialog.OpenFile());
        textBoxInData.Text = readStream.ReadToEnd();
        readStream.Close();
    }
}
```

When the RestoreDirectory property is set to true the OpenFileDialog instance resets the current directory to its original value after the dialog is closed, provided the **OK** button is not selected, in order to open a file. To understand this, consider a case where the RestoreDirectory property is set to true and the OpenFileDialog was used to traverse the directory, C:\DontComeBack. No attempt was made to open a file in C:\DontComeBack because the **Cancel** button was clicked. The next time the OpenFileDialog class is instantiated, the path will be restored to C:\temp. Had **OK** been clicked, the current path would be set to C:\temp. The default setting for the RestoreDirectory property is false. In the WroxEditThis application, each time the **Open File** button is selected, a new instance of an OpenFileDialog object is created. For this reason it made no sense to set the open file dialog's RestoreDirectory. This property only applies to an instance of an OpenFileDialog that is used multiple times by the same application.

In order for the current directory associated with the OpenFileDialog to be retained, the ShowDialog method has to be called multiple times for a single instance of this class. For the WroxEditThis application, this could be accomplished if the openFileDialog variable was made a data member of the Form, rather than a local variable of the buttonOpenFile_Click method. The remainder of the dialogs used in this chapter will be data members of the Form, rather than being created on the fly in the click handling method.

The OpenFileDialog exposes other properties not used by the WroxEditThis application. This class exposes a Boolean property, DereferenceLinks. When this property is true, the file's path is returned by the dialog rather than shortcut to the file (the *.lnk). The ReadOnlyChecked property returns true if the open file dialog's read-only check box was checked and false if it was not checked. The read-only check box is displayed if OpenFileDialog's ShowReadOnly property is set to true. If ShowReadOnly is false then the read-only check box is not displayed. The ReadOnlyChecked and ShowReadOnly properties are used so that the user opening the file can specify if they would like the file opened as read-write or read-only.

'SaveFileDialog'

The SaveFileDialog is the first cousin of the OpenFileDialog Windows Forms control.

```
CommonDialog
    FileDialog
       SaveFileDialog
```

One difference in these first cousins is that the file opened by the OpenFile method of OpenFileDialog is read-only, while the OpenFile method for SaveFileDialog opens the file as read-write. Clearly, when saving, a file must be writeable, so this difference makes sense.

The approach taken with respect to demonstrating using SaveFileDialog will be to add this dialog to the WroxEditThis application using Visual Studio.NET's Toolbox. Just like a Windows Forms control, the Toolbox icon for SaveFileDialog can be dragged from the Toolbox and dropped on the Windows Forms Form control. Where this differs from using a Windows Forms control (derived from the Control class) is that the SaveFileDialog does not reside on the Form itself. See the following screenshot where the saveFileDialog1 at the bottom of the screen is the instance of the SaveFileDialog class dragged and dropped onto the Windows Forms Form class:

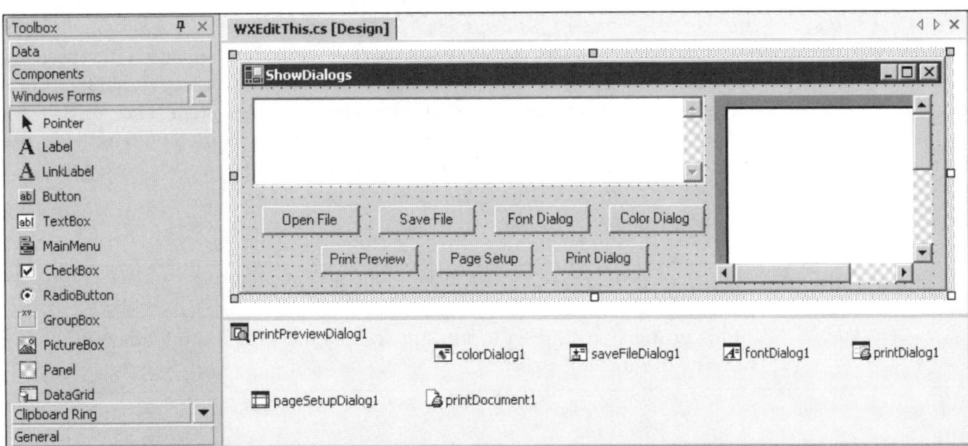

As it turns out, saveFileDialog1 is a data member of the Form. This means that the SaveFileDialog needs only to be set up once (created once and having properties set up a single time). Each time the SaveFileDialog is needed, its ShowDialog method can be called to display the dialog. The properties of the SaveFileDialog will be configured using the Properties window of Visual Studio.NET. This is opposed to programmatically, as was the case with OpenFileDialog.

By selecting the saveFileDialog1 displayed under the Form in Visual Studio.NET, the properties of this dialog can be configured. The Properties window for the SaveFileDialog class appears as follows:

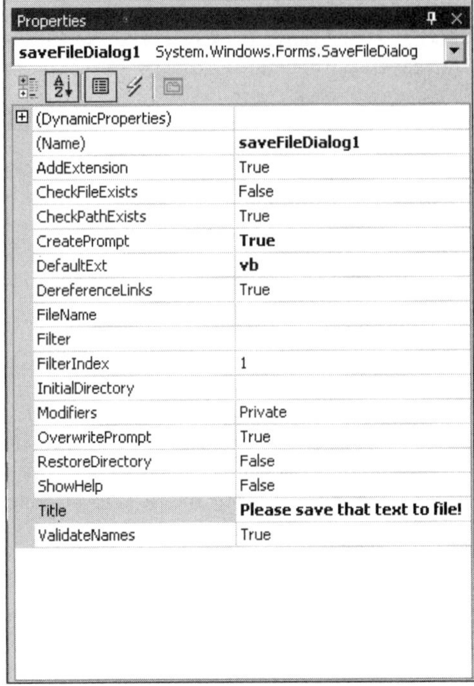

The SaveFileDialog shares properties such as AddExtension, CheckFileExists, CheckPathExists, DefaultExt, DereferenceLinks, FileName, Filter, FilterIndex, InitialDirectory, RestoreDirectory, ShowHelp, Title, and ValidateNames with its cousin class, OpenFileDialog. The difference is that these properties affect how the filename is interpreted when it is used in conjunction with the save operation. For example, ValidateNames ensures that the user entered a filename to save that is valid within the context of the underlying file system. The CheckFileExists, when set to true, will display an error if the filename specified does not exist. Rather than calling this property CheckFileExists, it might be better to call it 'must overwrite existing'.

There is, however, at least one property pertinent only to SaveFileDialog:

Property	Description
CreatePrompt	This property, when set to true, prompts the user if the filename they are saving to does not exist.

When the ShowDialog method of the saveFileDialog1 data member is executed, the following modal dialog is displayed:

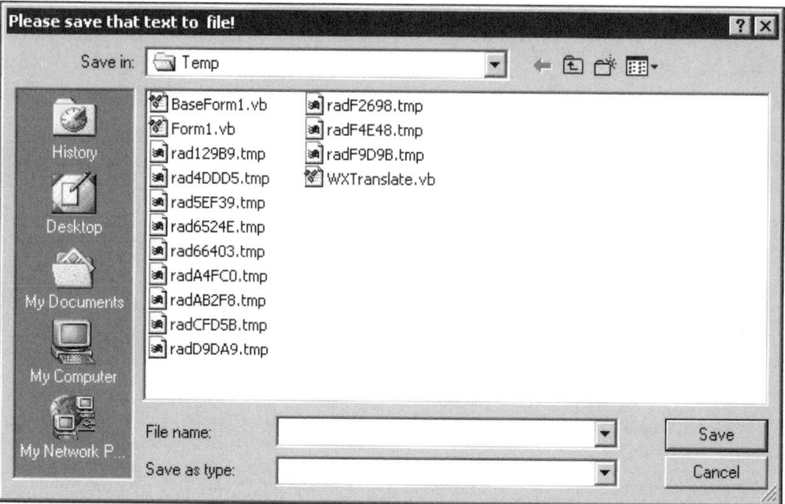

The property of saveFileDialog1 was set to true in the Properties window. By setting this to true, the user is prompted if the filename they are saving to does not exist. Under this circumstance, the user is given the opportunity to create this file. The following dialog is displayed if the file does not exist, CreatePrompt is true, and the Save button was selected:

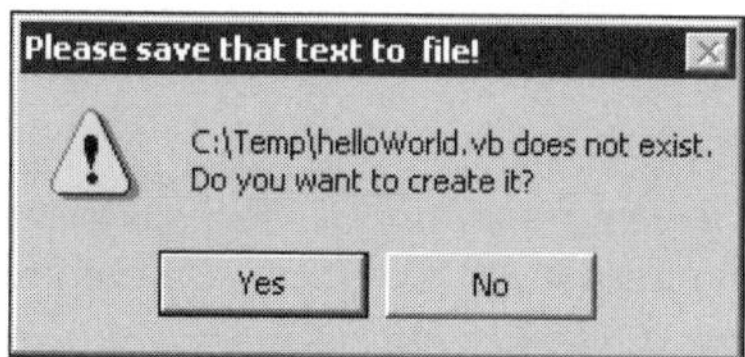

Once the Save button is selected, the OpenFile method of saveFileDialog1 can be executed. This method opens the file for read-write access and returns an instance of a Stream class. The one caveat related to CreatePrompt is that the file opened by the OpenFile method will be created, even it does not exist before OpenFile is called.

This file creation takes place, even if the user was never prompted to create the file, or if the user was prompted and they declined to create the file. This behavior appears to be a bit contradictory. Developers who rely on the exact behavior of the CreatePrompt property and OpenFile method should take the time to verify how it works for the exact version of the .NET Framework their product will ship with. The contradictory behavior discussed is just the kind of thing that may be changed by Microsoft in a later version of .NET. The beautiful thing about .NET is that an application can be shipped to run on a specific version of .NET and hence the exact behavior exposed can be guaranteed. Mentioning that this behavior may change is just a topic of discussion and does not represent any foreknowledge of Microsoft's intentions!

The SaveFileDialog is displayed using ShowDialog when the Save File button of WroxEditThis is selected. When the Save File button is clicked, the buttonSaveFile_Click method is called courtesy of the Click event. The code that saves a file does not bother reading the FileName property exposed by the OpenFileDialog. Instead, the OpenFile method is returned. This method opens the file specified and returns a class of type Stream. This Stream is passed into an instance of the StreamWriter class. The StreamWriter (instance, writeStream) uses its WriteLine method to write all the text contained in the textBoxInData textbox, to the destination file (the file opened for saving). Once the contents of the editor's TextBox are saved, the StreamWriter is closed using this class's Close method. The code that displays the save file dialog box and subsequently saves the file returned is as follows:

```
private void buttonSaveFile_Click(object sender, System.EventArgs e)
{
    if (saveFileDialog1.ShowDialog() == DialogResult.OK)
    {
        StreamWriter writeStream =
        new StreamWriter(saveFileDialog1.OpenFile());

        writeStream.WriteLine(textBoxInData.Text);
        writeStream.Close();
    }
}
```

'FontDialog'

The FontDialog class is a descendant of the CommonDialog class.

```
CommonDialog
    FontDialog
```

When the Font Dialog button of WroxEditThis is clicked, an instance of the FontDialog is displayed. The instance of the FontDialog (fontDialog1) was created using the Toolbox in order to drag a FontDialog icon from the Toolbox to the Form associated with the WroxEditThis application.

The properties and methods associated with FontDialog are as follows:

Property	Description
AllowScriptChange	If the property is false, the script cannot be changed. If this property is true, then scripts such as Western, Hebrew, Arabic, and Cyrillic can be selected.
AllowVectorFonts	This property, when set to true (the default value), displays vector fonts.
AllowVerticalFonts	This property, when set to true (default value is true), displays vertical fonts (as opposed to the horizontal fonts that Westerners are used to).
AllSimulations	This property, when set to true (default value is true), displays simulation fonts.
Color	This property returns the color selected (type, Color).

Property	Description
FixedPitchedOnly	When displaying source code, fixed width (pitch) fonts are preferable and FixedPitchOnly set to true ensures that only these will be displayed. The default value for the FixedPitchOnly property is false.
Font	This property returns the font selected (type, Font).
MaxSize	This property allows the maximum point size displayed by the dialog to be specified.
MinSize	This property allows the minimum point size displayed by the dialog to be specified.
ScriptOnly	If this property is true, then non-ANSI scripts can be displayed (OEM or symbol). Setting this property to false (the default value) displays all types of scripts.
ShowApply	Determines whether an Apply button is shown or not.
ShowColor	The default value for this property is false. Specifying a color dictates the color of the characters typed with the selected font.
ShowEffects	Determines whether special font effects are shown or not.

Method	Description
ShowDialog	Displays the dialog, when set to true.
Reset	This method resets the FontDialog boxes settings to their defaults, so that when the dialog is subsequently displayed it contains no legacy user settings.

The dialog displayed when the Font Dialog button is clicked (Click event triggering the buttonFontDialog_Click method) is as follows:

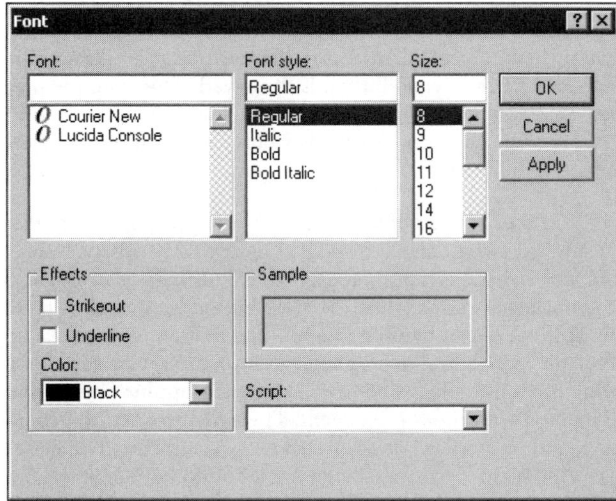

The font dialog is broken down into sets of grouped controls. Each grouping is configured by different properties of the `FontDialog` class. For example, under the Font: label is a textbox where a font can be entered and a listbox containing permissible fonts displays entries such as Courier New and Lucida Console. The fonts displayed seem quite sparse – the sparseness can be attributed to the `FontDialog`'s `FixedPitchedOnly` property being set to `true`.

The Effects group box contains a Strikeout and an Underline check box. These check boxes are displayed when the `FontDialog`'s `ShowEffects` property is set to `true`. These check boxes dictate if the font selected utilizes special effects, such as all text being struck out, or underlined, or possibly both, could be selected. Setting the `ShowEffects` property to `false` would cause these check boxes not to be displayed. In the same vein, the listbox labeled Color: is displayed only because the `FontDialog`'s `ShowColor` property is set to `true`. Note, this book is not printed in color so it is up to the reader to imagine that an example of blue, red and magenta characters were displayed in order to demonstrate fonts of different colors!

The Font style: portion of the dialog is where a choice can be made between Regular, **Bold**, *Italic*, or ***Bold Italic***. The Size: portion of the dialog allows the size (in points) of the font to be selected. Permissible selections include:

8
10
12
14

The `FontDialog`'s `MinSize` and `MaxSize` properties govern the range of sizes available. The Sample group box contains a read-only textbox in which a sample of the font selected will be displayed. The Script: listbox displays the various script types in which a font can be displayed. Below is a set of samples (from the Sample textbox) that demonstrates a script of type Turkish (left), Greek (right), and Cyrillic (bottom).

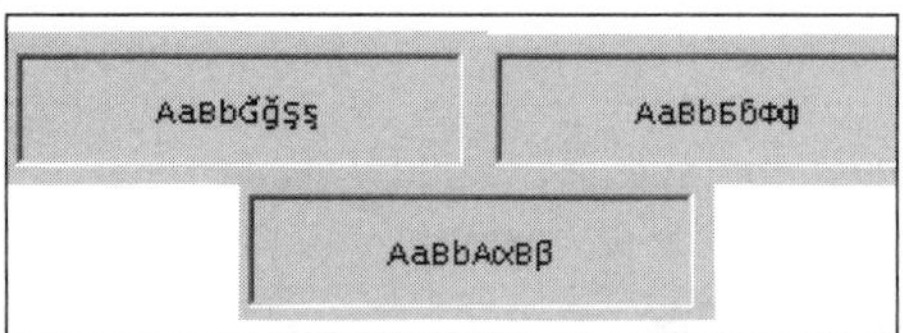

Just like `OpenFileDialog` and `SaveFileDialog`, the `FontDialog` class contains a `ShowHelp` property. When this is set to `true`, a Help button is displayed. The example presented for `OpenFileDialog` demonstrated how to set help up for a dialog. The `FontMustExist` property, when set to `true`, verifies that the font the user entered is valid (exists) on the user's system. If the font does not exist then a warning is displayed.

Underneath the OK and Cancel buttons of the `FontDialog`, it is possible to display an Apply button. The Apply button is displayed if the `FontDialog`'s `ShowApply` property is set to `true`. When the Apply button is clicked, the `FontDialog` remains visible, but the `Apply` event is raised. This is similar to the `HelpRequest` event being raised when the Help button is clicked. A method can be associated with the `Apply` event. This event can be used to apply the font changes to the application while leaving the `FontDialog` still displayed. This allows the end-user to audition a variety of font configurations before ultimately closing the font dialog. The `WroxEditThis` application associates the `fontDialog_Apply` method with the `Apply` event. This code was set up using the Properties window and hence this code is found in the `InitializeComponent` method. The code to set up displaying the Apply button (property, `ShowApply`) and to assign a method to handle when the Apply button is selected (method, `fontDialog_Apply`) is performed as follows:

```
this.fontDialog1.ShowApply = true;
this.fontDialog1.Apply += new System.EventHandler(this.fontDialog_Apply);
```

These properties are used by the `fontDialog_Apply` method in order to set the font. The textbox's font (`TextBox` property, `Font`) is set using the font returned by `FontDialog` (property, `Font`). The `fontDialog_Apply` method also sets the font color of the textbox (`Textbox` property, `ForeColor`) to the color returned by `FontDialog` (property, `Color`). The code that implements the `fontDialog_Apply` method is as follows:

```
private void fontDialog_Apply(object sender, System.EventArgs e)
{
    textBoxInData.Font = fontDialog1.Font;
    textBoxInData.ForeColor = fontDialog1.Color;
}
```

Specifying a `Font` and `ForeColor` in the previous code changes the font and fore color of all text in the `textBoxInData TextBox`. Using a `RichTextBox` control, it would have been possible to set the font and color of specific text ranges. Although the previous code snippet shows the `ForeColor` property of the `TextBox` being set, this color is not used when printing the contents of the `textbox`. When the various print and print preview dialogs and controls are presented in this section, they will only focus on the `Text` and `Font` properties of the `textBoxInData TextBox`. Setting the `TextBox`'s fore color allows the user to make the text entry aesthetically pleasing.

The following code snippet from the `WroxEditThis` application demonstrates the `FontDialog` being displayed (method, `ShowDialog`). This code is contained in the click handling code contained in the `buttonFontDialog_Click` method that is associated with the Font Dialog button's `Click` event. The `buttonFontDialog_Click` method calls the `fontDialog_Apply` method in order to set the actual font and color values of the textbox. This approach sets the font and color when the OK button is selected and not just when the Apply button is selected on the `FontDialog`. The `buttonFontDialog_Click` method is implemented as follows:

```
private void buttonFontDialog_Click(object sender, System.EventArgs e)
{
    if (fontDialog1.ShowDialog() == DialogResult.OK)
    {
        fontDialog_Apply(this, System.EventArgs.Empty);
    }
}
```

'ColorDialog'

Clicking the Color Dialog button of the `WroxEditThis` application causes an instance of a `ColorDialog` to be displayed (with the help of this class's `ShowDialog` method).

```
CommonDialog
    ColorDialog
```

The `ColorDialog` class is closely related (same base-class) to the Windows Forms classes `FileDialog`, `FontDialog`, `PageSetupDialog`, and `PrintDialog`. In spite of this familial relationship, `ColorDialog` does not share a significant number of properties, methods, and events with its cousins. This commonality includes the `ShowHelp` property, `Reset` method, and the `ShowDialog` method. Here are some others:

Property	Description
AllowFullOpen	This property, when set to true, determines that the Define Custom Colors box should be displayed (non-grayed out).
AnyColor	If this property is true then all available colors are displayed by the dialog. If the value of the AnyColor property is false then a set of basic colors is made available to the color dialog box.
Color	This property returns a structure of type Color. The Color structure exposes methods that are useful in interpreting the array of integers returned by the CustomColors property. Specifically, the Color structure's FromArgb method returns an instance of a Color structure based on the RBG value (type, integer) specified. The ToArgb method of the Color structure returns an integer value corresponding to the Color object represented as an RGB value.
CustomColors	This property is a get and set using an array of integers. Each integer in the array corresponds to a color in RBG form. The color specified by the user is returned or set using the Color property.
FullOpen	Displaying the full color dialog is achieved by setting this property to true and is disabled by setting this property to false (default value).
SolidColorOnly	If SolidColorOnly is true then the user can select only solid colors; if this property is false then non-solid colors can be selected.

The ColorDialog instance, colorDialog1, used by the WroxEditThis application was created with Visual Studio.NET's Toolbox. When the Color Dialog button is clicked, the ShowDialog method of the instance colorDialog1 is called. The number of colors displayed by this dialog depends in part on the AnyColor and SolidColorOnly properties.

The ColorDialog is displayed when the Color Dialog button is aware of the color capabilities specified for the display. Keeping this in mind, the following ColorDialog is displayed when the Color Dialog button is clicked for the WroxEditThis application:

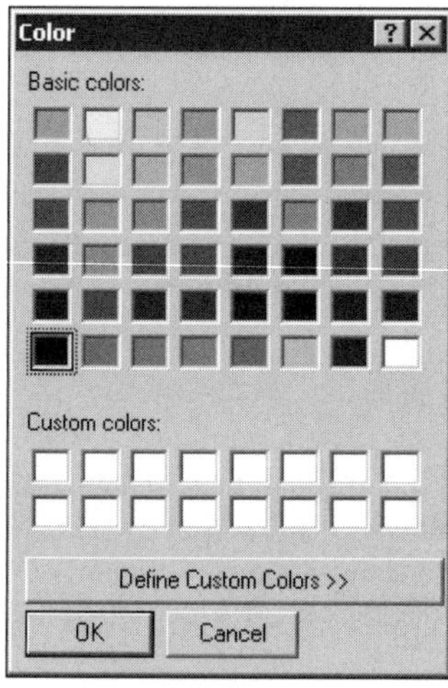

Notice that vibrant colors are displayed in each square underneath the Basic Colors: label. Okay, maybe recognizing colors in a black-and-white-printed book is a stretch, but notice that the bottom left square under the Basic Colors: is highlighted. When the OK button on the color dialog is selected, the highlighted color is returned as the `Color` property of the `ColorDialog` instance. The highlighted color just so happens to be black.

The Define Custom Colors >> button in the color dialog display makes additional controls visible to the right side of the color dialog. These additional controls allow custom colors to be specified, based on hue, saturation, and luminance or by setting red, green, and blue values (RGB). The color dialog box displayed when Define Custom Colors >> is selected is as follows:

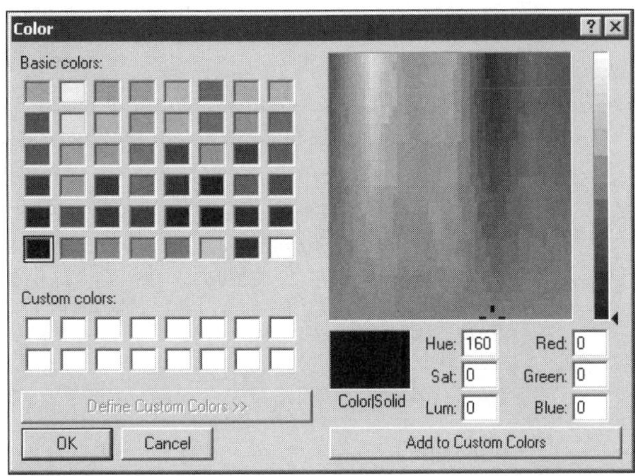

The previous version of the dialog could be displayed automatically when the dialog is displayed using the `ShowDialog` method. Displaying the full color dialog is achieved by setting the `FullOpen` property to `true`. The custom colors displayed in the dialog are set and retrieved using the `CustomColors` property.

Clicking the Color Dialog button of the `WroxEditThis` application triggers the `buttonColorDialog_Click` method. The code associated with the `buttonColorDialog_Click` method is as follows:

```
private void buttonColorDialog_Click(object sender, System.EventArgs e)
{
   if (colorDialog1.ShowDialog() == DialogResult.OK)
   {
      textBoxInData.ForeColor = colorDialog1.Color;
   }
}
```

'PrintDocument'

The `PrintDocument` class is included on Visual Studio.NET's Toolbox under the Windows Forms category, even though an instance of this class displays nothing directly on the screen. The `PrintDocument` class is found in the `System.Drawing.Printing` namespace. The purpose of this class's inclusion on the Toolbox is so it can be dragged onto a `Form`, where it will become a data member of the `Form` (data member, `printDocument1`, for the `WroxEditThis` application). This instance of `PrintDocument` is used by the dialogs and controls affiliated with printing, and the `PrintDocument`'s `Print` method is exposed – and with printing comes configuration, and lots of it.

Here are some properties and methods associated with PrintDocument:

Property	Description
DefaultPageSettings	This property, of type PageSettings, corresponds to the default page settings for the document. This property configures the settings corresponding to how a page will be printed by a printer. The properties of the PageSettings class are beyond the scope of this chapter and are for the most part self-documenting (Bounds, Color, Landscape, Margins, PaperSize, PaperSource, PrinterResolution, and PrinterSettings).
DocumentName	This property (type, string) gets and sets the document's name.
PrintController	This property is of type PrintController. This property specifies the manner in which a document will be guided through the print process.
PrinterSettings	This property is of type PrinterSettings. This property specifies how an entire document will be printed. The PrinterSettings class exposes properties such as Collate, Copies, Duplex, MaximumCopies, MaximumPage, MinimumPage, PaperSizes, PaperSources, PrinterResolutions, PrintRange, and PrintToFile.

Method	Description
Print	Initiates printing by raising PrintPage events.

Event	Description
PrintPage	Each time a PrintPage event is handled by the PrintDocument, a page is printed. The events get raised until the document is fully printed.

The following object hierarchy specifies three classes that serve to control the print process because they are all derived from PrintController:

```
Object
    PrintController
        PreviewPrintController
        StandardPrintController
        PrintControllerWithStatusDialog
```

An instance of type PreviewPrintController can be assigned to a PrintDocument's PrintController property. The PreviewPrintController will display the pages of the document to the screen (a print preview). Displaying a status dialog while printing is permissible using an instance of the PrintControllerWithStatusDialog class. This instance would be assigned to PrintDocument's PrintController property. Standard printing (no status dialog, no preview) is possible by assigning an instance of type StandardPrintController to PrintDocument's PrintController property.

The WroxEditThis application code for handling the PrintPage event is actually written by the Windows Forms Designer and can therefore be found in the InitializeComponent method of the Form. The following code snippet from this method demonstrates the PrintPage event being handled by associating a method (printDocument1_PrintPage) with this event:

```
this.printDocument1.PrintPage +=
new System.Drawing.Printing.PrintPageEventHandler
(this.printDocument1_PrintPage);
```

The prototype for the printDocument1_PrintPage method takes an object as the first parameter and a PrintPagesEventArgs class (from the System.Drawing.Printing namespace) as the second argument. The prototype for the printDocument1_PrintPage method is as follows:

```
private void printDocument1_PrintPage(object sender,
System.Drawing.Printing.PrintPageEventArgs e)
```

The actual printing of the document, and status as to how much of the document has been printed, is coordinated using the parameter of type PrintPagesEventArgs. WroxEditThis allows text to be edited, so when it comes to printing, the discussion of PrintPagesEventArgs pertains to the printing of text. This class exposes the following useful properties and methods:

Property	Description
Graphics	This property is of type Graphics and corresponds to the surface on which printing will be performed. This property can be used in conjunction with a Font object in order to determine the height (Font.GetHeight) and width (Font.Size) of the font within the graphics context specified by Graphics.
Graphics.DrawString	The DrawString method draws a line of text.
HasMorePages	This property, of type Boolean, allows the method handling the PrintPage event to communicate back to the printing process. If all pages have been printed then the PrintPage event handling method sets HasMorePages to false. If more pages are available to be printed then HasMorePages is set to true by the method handling the PrintPage event.
MarginBounds	This property is of type Rectangle. The rectangular region specified by the MarginBounds corresponds to the area of the print document that resides inside the margins.
MarginBounds.Height	This property can be used when handling a PrintPage event in order to determine how many lines are contained on a page. The basic algorithm for determining the per-page line count is to take the height of the page (Height property) and divide it by the height of the font used to display the document.
MarginBounds.Left	The distance from the left side of a page to where the body of the page (what is printed) starts. This property is passed to the DrawString method in order to specify the left-side boundary at which DrawString should draw the string.

Table continued on following page

Property	Description
MarginBounds.Top	The distance from the top of the page to where the body of the page (what is printed) starts.
MarginBounds.Width	Corresponds to the size of the horizontal dimension of a page. The Width is useful in determining how many characters can be displayed on a line. The good news is that the fonts displayed for the WroxEditThis application are fixed-width. This makes determining the number of characters per-line a matter of division (the width of the page divided by the size of the font used to display the document).

Let's look more closely at some of these properties:

- Here we see how to use the Graphics property to calculate the lines-per-page and characters-per-line:

```
int linesOnAPage = (int)(e.MarginBounds.Height /
textBoxInData.Font.GetHeight(e.Graphics));
int charactersOnALine = (int)(e.MarginBounds.Width /
textBoxInData.Font.Size);
```

- When computing at what offset to print a line of text, the MarginBounds.Top property must be taken into account, as follows:

```
yOffset = lineCount * textBoxInData.Font.GetHeight(e.Graphics) +
e.MarginBounds.Top;
```

- The MarginBounds.Left property, used to set the left hand boundary of the page, is demonstrated as follows:

```
e.Graphics.DrawString(outputLine, textBoxInData.Font, Brushes.Black,
e.MarginBounds.Left, yOffset, new StringFormat());
```

Most of the issues pertinent to printing have been presented (lines-per-page, characters-per-line, offset from left margin, offset from top margin, and the drawing of text), but what happens if the line of text is longer than the horizontal margin of the document being printed? A wrapping algorithm is needed to address this problem. Before we can determine how to wrap, we must also discuss how to retrieve the text to display. The Form of the WroxEditThis application contains a data member, strReader, of type StringReader. This data member is declared as follows:

```
private StringReader strReader;
```

The StringReader data member is used to traverse the text associated with the editor application's TextBox, textBoxInData. The StringReader instance is created the first time that the PrintPage event is handled. Determining if it is the first time is achieved by checking if the value of the strReader data member is null or not. If it is null then the instance of the StringReader class has to be instantiated as follows, where the text to print is passed in as a parameter to the StringReader instance's constructor:

```
if (strReader == null)
{
    strReader = new StringReader(textBoxInData.Text);
}
```

Each line displayed by calling `DrawString` is retrieved from the `StringReader` instance using this instance's `ReadLine` method. The return value of this method is assigned to a data member of the `Form`. This data member, `residue`, is of type `string` and is assigned a line of text as follows:

```
residue = strReader.ReadLine();
```

So, each line from the `StringReader` is read into an instance of a `string` named `residue`. This is a rather odd name for the line of text to be printed. Actually, the line read from the `StreamReader` may be one or more lines of text printed. Recall that the characters-per-line were computed and placed in the `charactersOnALine` variable. The number of characters-per-line was computed to be seventy-eight for this application. If the string returned from `StringReader`'s `ReadLine` contained two hundred characters, then three lines would be printed (78 characters, 78 characters, and the remainder, 44 characters). The word wrap algorithm is simply a wrap at the end-of-line boundary. In a true word processor, the word wrap boundary would be computed based on where spaces or dashes occurred between words.

The `WroxAssignOutput` method was implemented as part of the `WroxEditThis` application in order to whittle the residue string down `charactersOnALine` characters at a time. The characters removed from `residue` are returned in the `outputLine` parameter. The following implementation of `WroxAssignOutput` relies on the string manipulation learned in everyone's first computer science course at university:

```
private void WroxAssignOutput(ref string residue, ref string outputLine,
int charactersOnALine)
{
    if (residue.Length < charactersOnALine)
    {
        outputLine = residue;
        residue = null;
    }

    else
    {
        outputLine = residue.Substring(0, charactersOnALine);
        residue =  residue.Remove(0, charactersOnALine);
    }
}
```

The `residue` string must be a data member of the `Form` in case the string spans multiple pages. Spanning multiple pages means that the first part of the string will be printed on one page (during the handling of a `PrintPage` Event) and the remainder of the string will be printed during the next `PrintPage` Event. The code that checks to see if there is `residue` and if not performs `StringReader`'s `Readline` is as follows:

```
if ((residue == null) || (residue.Length == 0))
{
    residue = strReader.ReadLine();
```

```
        if (residue == null)
        {
            break;
        }

        WroxAssignOutput(ref residue, ref outputLine, charactersOnALine);
    }
    else
    {
        WroxAssignOutput(ref residue, ref outputLine, charactersOnALine);
    }
```

Once the last page has been displayed, the `StringReader` instance, `strReader`, can be set to `null`. The next time the document is printed, the `StringReader` can be recreated and reassigned to the text exposed by the editor's textbox. Setting the `StringReader` to `null` coincides with ending the printing process by setting the `PrintPagesEventArgs` class's `HasMorePages` property to `false`. An example of this is as follows:

```
    if (outputLine == null) // End of buffer so HasMorePages=false
    {
        e.HasMorePages = false;
        strReader = null;
    }
```

The code within the `WroxEditThis` application that uses these methods and properties of the `PrintPagesEventArgs` parameter to print is as follows:

```
private string residue = "";
private StringReader strReader;

private void printDocument1_PrintPage(object sender,
    System.Drawing.Printing.PrintPageEventArgs e)
{
    int lineCount = 0;
    int linesOnAPage = 0;
    int charactersOnALine = 0;
    float yOffset = 0.0F;
    string outputLine = null;

    if (strReader == null)
    {
        strReader = new StringReader(textBoxInData.Text);
    }

    linesOnAPage = (int)(e.MarginBounds.Height /
    textBoxInData.Font.GetHeight(e.Graphics));
    charactersOnALine = (int)(e.MarginBounds.Width /
        textBoxInData.Font.Size);
    while (linesOnAPage > 0)
    {
        if ((residue == null) || (residue.Length == 0))
        {
            residue = strReader.ReadLine();
```

```
            if (residue == null)
            {
               break;
            }

         WroxAssignOutput(ref residue, ref outputLine, charactersOnALine);
      }
      else
      {
         WroxAssignOutput(ref residue, ref outputLine, charactersOnALine);
      }

      yOffset = lineCount * textBoxInData.Font.GetHeight(e.Graphics) +
      e.MarginBounds.Top;
      e.Graphics.DrawString(outputLine, textBoxInData.Font, Brushes.Black,
      e.MarginBounds.Left, yOffset, new StringFormat());
      lineCount++;
      linesOnAPage--;
      }

      if (outputLine == null) // End of buffer so HasMorePages=false
      {
         e.HasMorePages = false;
         strReader = null;
      }
      else // print more pages since more text exists
      {
         e.HasMorePages = true;
      }
   }
```

The other events handled by the `PrintDocument` class include `BeginPrint` (event raised when printing is initiated), `EndPrint` (event raised when printing is complete), and `QueryPageSettings` (event raised when the page settings are queried). The `PrintDocument` class exposes methods that can manually raise these events. The `OnBeginPage` method raises the `BeginPage` event, `OnEndPage` method raises the `EndPage` event, the `OnPrintPage` method raises the `PrintPage` event, and the `OnPageQueryPageSettings` method raises the `QueryPageSettings` event.

'PrintPreviewControl'

Thus far, a variety of classes have been introduced that reside on Visual Studio.NET's Windows Forms Toolbox, but do not actually appear on the `Form` associated with the application. Bucking this trend is the `PrintPreviewControl` that resides on Visual Studio.NET's Toolbox and, when dragged and dropped accordingly, resides on the `Form` associated with a Windows Forms application.

The purpose of the `PrintPreviewControl` is to display a preview of what is to be printed on the `Form` itself. For the simple editing application, `WroxEditThis`, when text is typed into the textbox, it is immediately displayed in the `PrintPreviewControl` on the right side of the `Form`. The `PrintPreviewControl` is associated with an instance of a `PrintDocument` (the document to be printed).

Properties, methods, and events pertinent to `PrintPreviewControl` include:

Property	Description
Document	This property (type, PrintDocument) can be set to the document to be printed.
AutoZoom	This property, when set to true, alters the magnification of the print preview (the zoom) to ensure that all pages are displayed. This property struts its stuff after the print preview control is resized or if the number of pages displayed is changed. In the latter case, the zoom will be adjusted to show the number of pages requested for display.
Column	This property (default value of one) retrieves the number of pages displayed by the control in the horizontal direction.
Rows	This property specifies the number of pages displayed vertically by the control (default value of zero).
Zoom	This property specifies the level of magnification used when displaying a document This value is of type double and a value of 1.0 (the default value) represents 100% magnification, 2.0 represents 200%, and 0.75 represents 75%.
UseAntiAliasing	This property (type, Boolean), when true, causes anti-aliasing to be used when displaying the print preview. The default value for this property is false.
StartPage	This property is an integer that specifies the start page displayed in the control (the upper left page in the grid of pages previewed). This property's default value is zero.

Method	Description
InvalidatePreview	This method invalidates the present print preview and forces it to be redrawn. The print preview is redrawn because InvalidatePreview causes PrintPage events to be fired off until printing is completed.
OnStartPageChanged	When this method is called, a StartPageChanged event is triggered.

Event	Description
StartPageChanged	This event is fired when the value of the StartPage property is altered.
TextChanged	This event informs the PrintPreviewControl that new data is available.

Recall that the WroxEditThis application contains a textbox, textBoxInData. When the contents of this textbox are modified, these changes are reflected in the PrintPreviewControl instance that resides on the application's form (instance, printPreviewControl1). The delegate for the handling event is set up in the Form's InitializeComponent method. The textBoxInData_TextChanged method is as follows:

```
private void textBoxInData_TextChanged(object sender, System.EventArgs e)
{
  printPreviewControl1.InvalidatePreview();
}
```

The previous event handling method calls the PrintPreviewControl's InvalidatePreview method. It is important to note that updating the print preview each time a character is added or deleted is not terribly efficient. For large documents, this could greatly impact the performance of our editor. The previous sentence was just a polite way to say, 'this is an example application and if you use this in the real world DO NOT call InvalidatePreview for every character typed on the screen'!

The PrintPreviewControl control is derived from the Control class and hence exposes the methods, properties, and events of Control. In addition, the WroxEditThis application uses the default values of Column and Row, so that only a single page is displayed at a time.

'PageSetupDialog'

When a page is printed, the paper size (letter or legal size for an American printer), orientation (landscape or portrait), and margins (distance of print from top, left, right and bottom of paper) can be specified using the Windows Forms dialog called PageSetupDialog. This dialog is derived from the CommonDialog class, so it exposes methods such as Reset and properties such as ShowHelp. For the WroxEditThis application, a PageSetupDialog is displayed when the Page Setup button is clicked. The dialog displayed by this action is as follows:

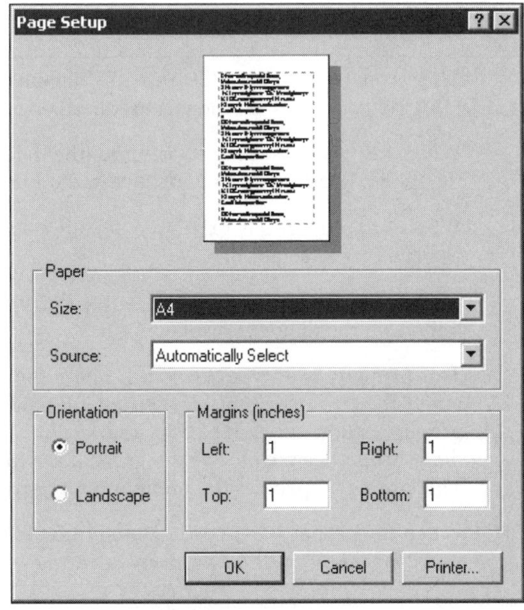

The PageSetupDialog is a data member, pageSetupDialog1, of the Form associated with the WroxEditThis application. This data member was added to the Form using Visual Studio.NET's Toolbox, by dragging the icon representing a PageSetupDialog onto the Form.

The mechanism used to display the `PageSetupDialog` was this class's `ShowDialog` method being called from the method of the `Form` used to handle when the **Page Setup** button is clicked. The `buttonPageSetup_Click` method handles when **Page Setup** is clicked and is implemented as follows:

```
private void buttonPageSetup_Click(object sender, System.EventArgs e)
{
   if (pageSetupDialog1.ShowDialog() == DialogResult.OK)
   {
      printPreviewControl1.InvalidatePreview();
   }
}
```

The previous bit of code shows that if the **OK** button on the `PageSetupDialog` is clicked, the `InvalidatePreview` method is called for the `PrintPreviewControl`. The `PageSetupDialog` changes the page's appearance (portrait versus landscape and margins). If the appearance of the page is changed then the actively displayed print preview is invalid, hence the `InvalidatePreview` method is called.

In Visual Studio.NET's **Properties** window, the `Document` property of the `PageSetupDialog`, `pageSetupDialog1`, was set to `printDocument1`. What a surprise! We associated the document to be printed with the dialog used to set up printing. This way, the settings specified by the `PageSetupDialog` are associated with the document to be printed. This setup was handled in the `Form`'s `InitializeComponent` method.

Here are some of the properties particularly useful to `PageSetupDialog`:

Property	Description
`AllowMargins`	This property, when set to `true` (the default value), displays the **Margins** group box on the page setup dialog as non-grayed out.
`AllowOrientation`	When `AllowOrientation` is `true` (the default value) the controls in this group (**Portrait** and **Landscape** radio buttons) are not grayed out.
`AllowPaper`	When `AllowPaper` is `true` (the default value), both paper **Size** and **Source** can be selected.
`AllowPrinter`	When this property is set to `true` (the default value), the **Printer** button on the dialog is displayed.
`MinMargins`	This property is of type `Margins`, where the `Margins` class is found under the `System.Drawing.Printing` namespace, and exposes the properties `Bottom`, `Left`, `Top`, and `Right`. The values specified for these properties are of type integer and are in hundredths of inches. This property specifies the minimum margins to be printed.
`ShowHelp`	When the property is `true`, a **Help** button is displayed. The default value for the `ShowHelp` property is `false`.

In the previous discussion of what the properties do, the simplicity of the `PageSetupDialog` may have been lost. To understand the simplicity, consider the following:

- The `PrintPreviewControl` instance is associated with the `Form`'s data member, `printDocument1`, through its `Document` property.

- The PageSetupDialog instance is also associated with the Form's data member, printDocument1, through its Document property.

The PrintDocument instance, printDocument1, is the only connection between the PageSetupDialog and PrintPreviewControl. So, the PageSetupDialog is used to set the right margin to 5.5 inches (a document width of an inch). When the PrintPreviewControl is invalidated (method, InvalidatePreview) it automatically redraws itself with a text width of an inch. Below is an example (on the left) of the original PrintPreviewControl (text width, 6.5 inches) and an example (on the right) of the print preview control displaying text with a width of a single inch:

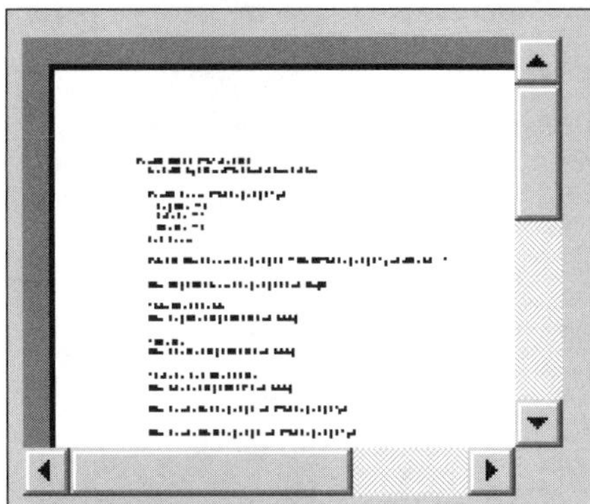

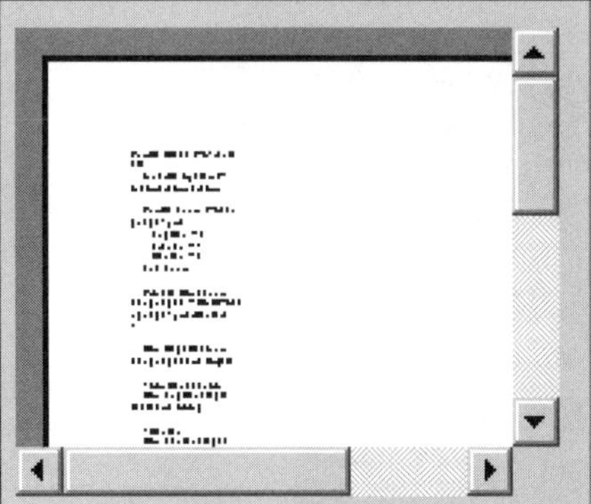

The PrintDocument instance is also what is shared in common with the PrintPreviewDialog and PageSetupDialog. This is also the relationship between PageSetupDialog and the PrintDialog. It is just that simple.

'PrintPreviewDialog'

The PrintPreviewDialog class displays an instance of the PrintPreviewControl class along with some additional controls that manage the PrintPreviewControl. The class, PrintPreviewControl, generates a preview of what a document (PrintDocument) will look like when printed by a printer. The PrintPreviewDialog class is derived directly from the Form base-class. This makes intuitive sense, since this dialog is simply a container for a variety of child controls. Since PrintPreviewDialog is derived from Form, it exposes the dozens and dozens of methods, properties, and events of the Form class.

An example of the PrintPreviewDialog can be displayed using the Print Preview button of the WroxEditThis application. The PrintPreviewDialog instance, printPreviewDialog1, was associated with WroxEditThis's form using Visual Studio.NET's Toolbox. The Click handling method of the Print Preview button simply calls the ShowDialog method of printPreviewDialog1 in order to display this dialog. This code is as follows:

```
private void buttonPrintPreview_Click(object sender, System.EventArgs e)
{
   printPreviewDialog1.ShowDialog();
}
```

The printPreviewDialog1 data member contains a Document property. The Windows Forms designer in the InitializeComponent method sets the value of the Document property. The value of the Document property has been set to the PrintDocument data member of the WroxEditThis application, namely printDocument1. When ShowDialog is used to display the PrintPreviewDialog instance, the PrintPage event is sent to the PrintDocument. In simple English, 'You show the dialog and the document knows to print because of the PrintPage event'. The instance of a PrintPreviewDialog displayed by the Print Preview button being clicked (executing the printPreviewDialog1.ShowDialog method) is as follows:

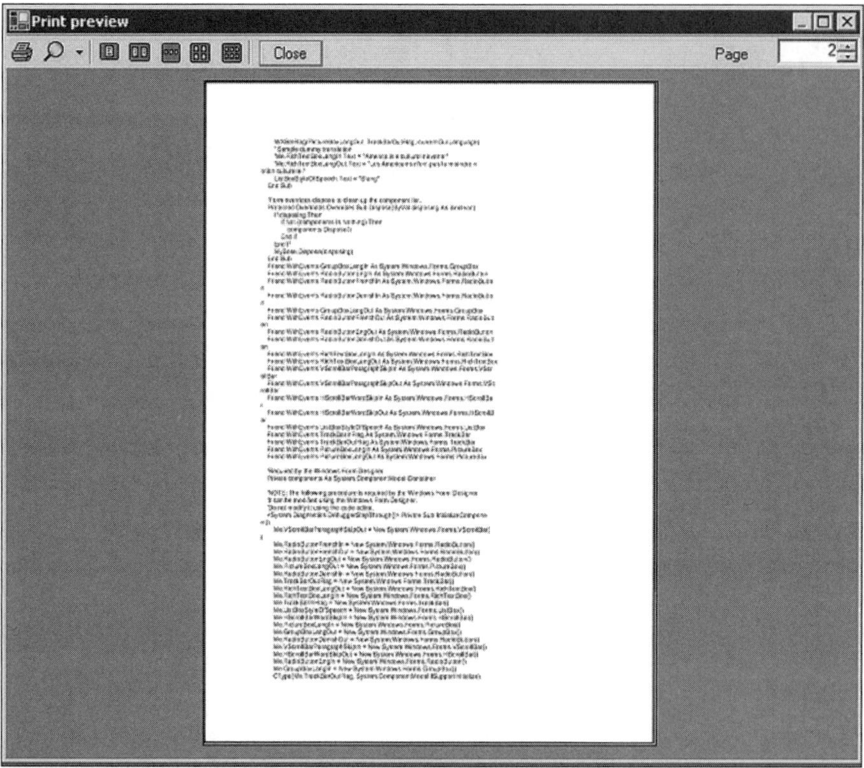

The printDocument1_PrintPage traverses the text associated with the editor and streams this text to the graphic context (Graphics property) provided by the parameter of type PrintPagesEventArgs.

The toolbar exposed by the PrintPreviewDialog is directly controllable using methods and properties exposed by this class. The icons on the toolbar, including an icon for printing, an icon for zooming the image in and out (the magnify glass icon), an icon for setting the page layout, and a button for closing the dialog, clearly map to properties associated with the PrintPreviewControl control that resides on the dialog. A series of icons are even provided that control the Row and Column property of PrintPreviewControl (icons to display single page, two pages, three pages, etc.).

The properties exposed directly by PrintPreviewDialog (as opposed to the properties inherited by this class) include the UseAntiAliasing Boolean, which performs the same function as the UseAntiAlias property of the PrintPreviewControl. The actual PrintPreviewControl associated with the dialog can be accessed using the PrintPreviewControl property.

'PrintDialog'

Fonts, print preview, and page settings are nifty, but the point of this exercise is to print what has previously been configured. The PrintDialog is what handles this task. This dialog is derived from CommonDialog. The modus operandi in order to take advantage of a PrintDialog is standard (drag it from Visual Studio.NET's Toolbox and bingo, we have a data member in the form). Once a PrintDialog data member is instantiated, ShowDialog can be called and the dialog itself is displayed. The PrintDialog contains a member, Document, of type PrintDocument. This is the document to be printed and since it is of type PrintDocument it exposes a Print method.

For the WroxEditThis application, the Print Dialog button is what triggers PrintDialog and its method, ShowDialog. The print dialog displayed by this action is as follows:

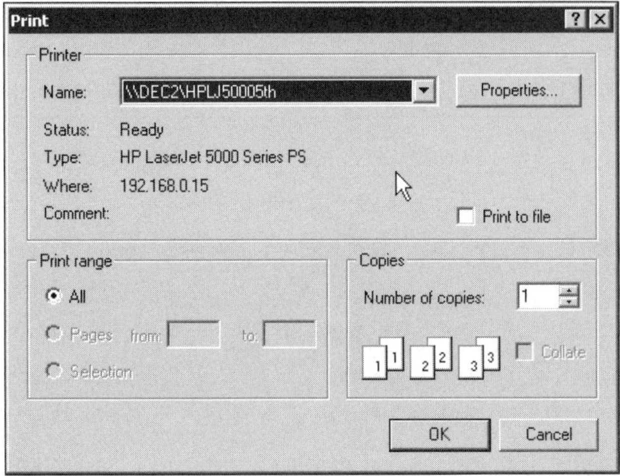

As always, we'll take a look at some of the properties, methods, and events that PrintDialog exposes:

Property	Description
AllowPrintToFile	If this property is set to true (the default setting), the check box labeled Print to file is available. Setting this check box directs the printed output to a file rather than a printer.
AllowSelection	When this property is set to true, the radio check box labeled Selection will not be grayed out. Not being grayed out means that the user selected a region of text to display. The default value for this property is false.
AllowSomePages	If this property is set to true, the Pages radio button within the Selection group is also not grayed out.
PrinterSettings	This property is of type PrinterSettings and is used to contain settings for the printer, including such things as whether the printer is duplex capable, is the print job to be collated, how many copies are to be printed, and what paper sizes are supported.

Table continued on following page

Property	Description
PrintToFile	When the Print to file check box is checked, this property returns true; when the check box is not checked this property returns false.
ShowHelp	When the property is set to true, a help button is displayed; if this value is false (the default value), no help button is displayed.

Method	Description
Reset	This method resets the PrintDialog to its default setting (typically print all of the document and only print a single copy).

Event	Description
Click	Fires when the Print Dialog button is clicked.

The buttonPrintDialog_Click method is implemented as follows (where ShowDialog displays the PrintDialog):

```
private void buttonPrintDialog_Click(object sender, System.EventArgs e)
{
   if (printDialog1.ShowDialog() == DialogResult.OK)
   {
      printDialog1.Document.Print();
   }
}
```

The previous code snippet demonstrates that after the PrintDialog is displayed, printing is initiated by calling the Print method of the PrintDocument associated with the Document property. Once Print is called, so began the PrintPages events that are handled by the method, printDocument1_PrintPage. This in turn prints the document to the location specified by the PrintDialog (to a specific printer or to file). This printing is based on the configuration dictated by the PrintDialog (ranges of text within the document, numbers of copies and other properties). Developers in no way have to manipulate the print drivers to specify number of copies, etc. The PrintDialog does all the hard work behind the scenes.

Summary

The graphical elements exposed by the Toolbox are quite diverse – as we saw demonstrated via a card counting application, language translator, and a lightweight editor. The latter application showed a variety of dialogs common across Windows Forms.

The card counting application, `WroxCount`, utilized a variety of the simplest Windows Forms controls to create a fairly sophisticated application. The `CheckBox` and `Label` are two of the most basic controls, but these controls were not merely dragged and dropped onto a form. The `CheckBox` and `Label` controls were generated as part of a card counting grid that resided on a `Panel`. This `Panel` was the core portion of the `WroxChild` base-class, used by the card counting application.

Inheriting from the base-class simplified the development of the card counting application. A `TextBox` was used in order to enter commands and a `LinkLabel` was added in order to jump to a gaming web site. Buttons were provided to enter cards, clear the grid of cards, and exit the application. The card counting application paid particular attention to the speed of text entry. This was achieved by logically specifying the `TabIndex` property of the controls in order to provide quick form traversal using the tab key. Sensible shortcuts were used in order to quickly access elements on the form without having to slow down by clicking a mouse.

The language translation application was built around two `RichTextBox` controls: source (pre-translation text) and destination (post-translation text). These text entry controls served as editors for entering the text to be translated. The `GroupBox` class was used in conjunction with `RadioButtons` in order to specify the language to translate from and to. Further refining the translation was a `ListBox` that allowed the style of language to be specified and a `PictureBox` class used in conjunction with a `TrackBar`. These last two controls (`TrackBar` and `PictureBox`) were used to specify the dialect of a language to translate to/from (French from France, French from Canada, etc.).

The final example, `WroxEditThis`, demonstrated the use of the various controls that implement dialogs by creating a simple text editing application. These dialogs give the developer the ability to create applications with increased functionality, using encapsulated controls that can simply be dropped into a form and configured to suit the application. The dialogs give an application a standard Windows look and feel, and save the developer from having to spend time setting up his or her own Print Preview or Save File dialogs.

The two-dozen classes reviewed in this section represent less than half of the controls initially provided on the Visual Studio.NET's Toolbox. The next chapter will review menus in detail and the third chapter in this series will cover controls such as `TreeView`, `ListView`, and `TabControl`.

Legend: Concrete Class / Abstract class

System.Windows.Forms

- System.Object
  - System.MarshalRefObject
    - System.ComponentMode.Component
      - CommonDialog
        - ColorDialog
        - FileDialog
        - FontDialog
        - PageSetupDialog
        - PrintDialog
      - ErrorProvider
      - HelpProvider
      - ImageList
      - Menu
        - ContextMenu
        - MainMenu
        - MenuItem
      - NotifyIcon
      - StatusBarPanel
      - Timer
      - ToolBarButton
      - ToolTip
      - Control
        - ButtonBase
          - Button
          - CheckBox
          - RadioButton
        - DataGrid
        - DateTimePicker
        - GroupBox
        - Label
          - LinkLabel
        - ListControl
          - ComboBox
          - ListBox
            - CheckedListBox
        - ListView
        - MonthCalendar
        - PictureBox
        - PrintReviewControl
        - ProgressBar
        - ScrollableControl
          - ContainerControl
            - Form
              - PrintPreviewDialog
              - ThreadExceptionDialog
            - PropertyGrid
            - UpDownBase
              - DomainUpDown
              - NumericUpDown
            - UserControl
          - Panel
            - TabPage
        - ScrollBar
          - HScrollBar
          - VScrollBar
        - Splitter
        - StatusBar
        - TabControl
        - TextBoxBase
          - RichTextBox
          - Textbox
        - ToolBar
        - TrackBar
        - TreeView
  - ListViewItem
  - TreeNode

9

Peripheral and ActiveX Controls

In this chapter, we'll continue our quest through the myriad of controls within Windows Forms. This time, we will focus on controls that normally reside at the edges of the form, and which help navigate the application. Specifically, we will look at:

- Menus and `MenuItems`
- `ContextMenus`
- `ToolBars` and `ToolBarButtons`
- `Tooltips`
- `StatusBars` and `StatusPanels`

We will also discuss a couple of 'invisible' controls, which are often used when creating a navigation system:

- `Timer`
- `ImageList`

The equivalent icons on the toolbox are shown below:

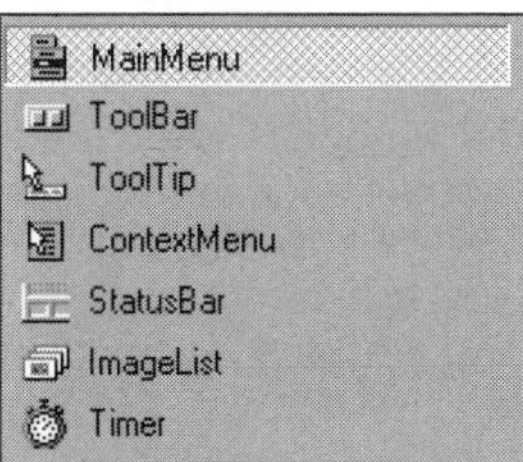

Building on the convention started in Chapter 8, we will begin by introducing a sample application, where all the controls are demonstrated. This is then followed by a discussion of each group of controls.

Finally, we will look at how to add an ActiveX control to the list of available controls on the ToolBox, and how to use the control on a form. This is very easy to do, so rest assured that any investment made in customized controls is retained when you move to Windows Forms.

WroxMenu

When creating a typical navigational system in Windows Forms, we will probably spend 80% of our time configuring properties using the IDE and only 20% adding code manually. Often, the code we need to write is pretty straightforward.

We have created a sample application called `WroxMenu` to demonstrate many of the features that we will be discussing throughout the chapter. We'll also be examining how many of the controls used to create this application were created so we can see how to work with each control, and what it produces.

The sample application is shown below in a somewhat exploded view:

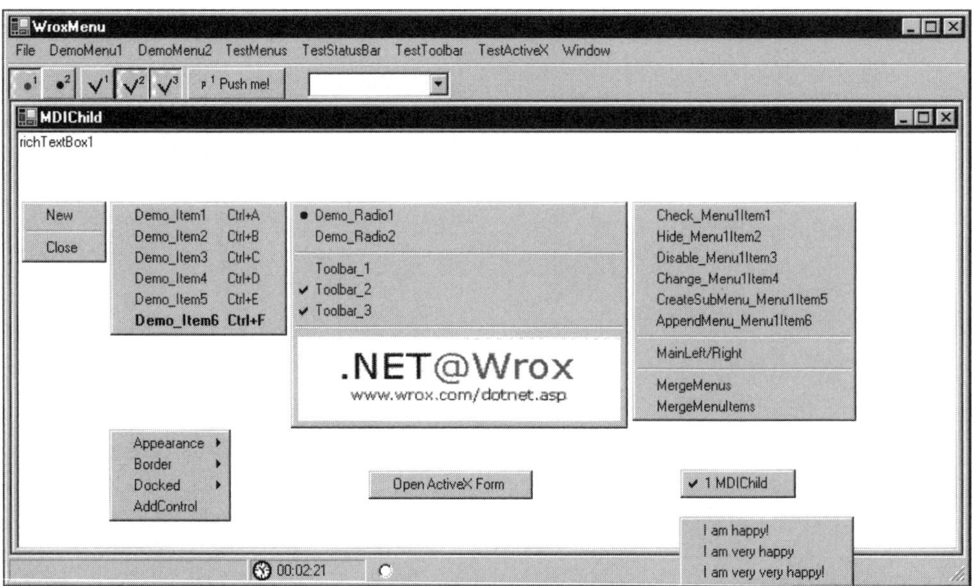

At the top you can see a number of menus. They are shown in their pulled-down state further down on the application screenshot.

The File | New menu creates a new MDI window; Close closes the application. Creating MDI windows and adding them to the main form allows us to demonstrate the purpose of the `MDIList` property on the Window menu. Window is a standard Window menu. It keeps a list of all open MDI windows, and allows the user to select between them.

DemoMenu1 is just a 'passive' menu. The items on this menu are changed by the commands initiated from the TestMenus menu. For example the first item on this menu is checked and unchecked when you check and uncheck the first menu item on the TestMenus menu. DemoMenu1 is also used to show how to merge two menus. The MergingMenu item and the items MM_11 to MM_23 (that are discussed later in this chapter) are all created using menu merge. The MergingMenu is created when you select the MergeMenus item on the TestMenus menu, and MM_11 to MM_23 are created when you select MergeMenuItems on that menu.

DemoMenu2 is created mainly to demonstrate coordination between a menu and the toolbar. Demo_Radio1, and Demo_Radio2 correspond to the two first radio buttons on the toolbar. Toolbar_1,2,3 correspond to the 3 check buttons on the toolbar. The menu also demonstrates how to make a so-called owner drawn menu item. Owner drawn menu items give the programmer the freedom **and responsibility** to write the code used to render the menu item. In this application, we will just show a bitmap. We could however also have shown text in other fonts or colors along with any type of shape that can be rendered using GDI+. Selecting this item has the same effect as pressing the Push Me toolbar button.

The TestMenus menu is mostly used to manipulate DemoMenu1 and DemoMenu2.

Finally, TestStatusBar makes changes to the statusbar, while TestToolbar makes changes to the toolbar, and TestActiveX opens up a new form hosting an ActiveX control. We have also attached a context menu (ContextMenu) to the toolbar, which appears when we right-click on the toolbar.

The `ToolBar` has one `ToolBarButton` for each of the `MenuItems` on DemoMenu2. In addition, we have inserted a combo box to show that a toolbar can host any kind of control.

The `StatusBar` is located at the bottom of the screen. It has two `StatusBarPanels`. The first panel shows which item on DemoMenu1 or the ContextMenu has been selected. The second panel shows the time. We have again inserted a radio button, just to show that a `StatusBar` can host any kind of control.

Terminology

It is prudent to agree on some of the terminology that pertains to menus, since it has changed slightly from the pre- .NET days. For example, what were previously called accelerator keys, are now called shortcut keys. Here are two diagrams to reaffirm or introduce the terminology we'll be using here:

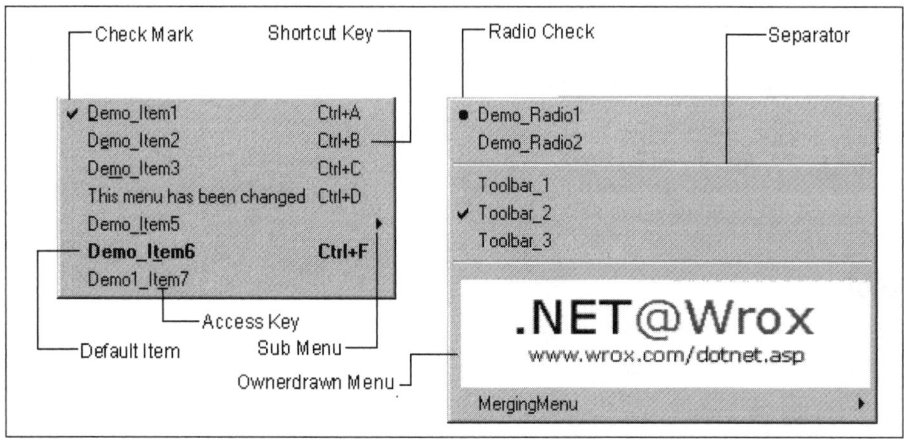

A check mark or a radio check is placed to the left of the menu item text, to indicate that an option related to the menu item is selected – or checked.

An item can be marked as the **default item**. A default item will appear in bold. In addition, if the default item appears in a sub-menu, double-clicking on that submenu will automatically select the default item.

We can also assign a shortcut key to a menu item. We used these in the last chapter, but to re-cap: shortcut keys allow the user to select the item, simply by pressing the shortcut key combination (for example *Ctrl-A* for Demo_item1). Similar to shortcut keys are access keys, which are identified by one letter being underlined on the menu item. Again, we touched on this in the last chapter, but to re-cap: if the access key is associated with a top-level menu, we can activate the menu by pressing *Alt-somekey*, where *somekey* is the letter that is underlined. If the access key is on a sub menu (like Demo_Item2), we must first open the menu (that is click on DemoMenu1 or press *Alt-1*),. Then select the menu item just by pressing the letter (in this case, e).

'MainMenu' and 'MenuItem'

We can very quickly get to experiment with menus and menu items. Firstly, we create a new application.

As we saw in Chapter 4, to add a menu system, we simply select the `MainMenu` icon from the Toolbox and drag it onto the Form. The menu will appear at the top of the form, and expand as you start to fill it out.

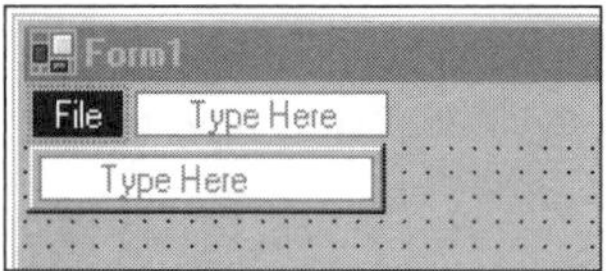

At the same time the IDE will have assigned the form's `MainMenu` property to `MainMenu1`.

MaximizeBox	True
⊞ Menu	**MainMenu1**
MinimizeBox	True

The purpose of the `MainMenu` class is to serve as the root for a complete menu system. Its most important property is its `MenuItems` collection. This contains a collection of `MenuItems`, and these can again contain collections of (sub) `MenuItems`. Each time the menu is expanded on the screen using the IDE, it will automatically generate code to create additional instances of the `MenuItem` class and add these to the appropriate `MenuItems` collection.

The `MainMenu` class only has one Boolean property: `RightToLeft`. This may be used to specify if the text in the whole menu system should be shown from right to left, as is custom in Arabic languages.

In the following, we will concentrate the discussion on the `MenuItem` class.

'MenuItem'

`MenuItem` is derived from `Menu`, as shown below:

Object
  MarshalByRefObject

Componenet
  Menu
    MainMenu
      MenuItem

Properties

MenuItem has a number of properties; some of the more interesting ones are listed below:

Property	Description
Checked	This get/set property is True if the MenuItem is checked and False if the item is not checked.
RadioCheck	This get/set property determines the icon to display for a **checked** MenuItem. If set to True, a checked MenuItem will be adorned with the RadioCheck icon.
DefaultItem	If this get/set property is True, this menu item will be the default item (it is possible to mark more than one item on a menu as the default, should you need to).
Shortcut	This get/set property can be set to a shortcut key combination for the MenuItem, or 'none' if no shortcut is desired (if the same shortcut key is assigned to several MenuItems, the Windows Forms library will just pick the first item).
ShowShortcut	If a shortcut key is assigned, this get/set property determines if the key will be displayed on the menu.
OwnerDraw	If this get/set property is True, the menuItem is considered to be owner drawn (we discuss owner drawn menus in more detail a little later in this chapter).
Text	This get/set property contains the text actually displayed on the menu.
MDIList	Setting this get/set property to True, will cause Windows Forms to use it as the root for creating a list of MDI windows hosted by the form, where this menu resides.
MenuItems	This property is used to store a list of submenu items.

Let's take a closer look at three of these.

Text: If you assign the Text property a single hyphen (-) the MenuItem will become a separator. Further, if you put an ampersand in front of a letter in the text, that letter becomes the access key for the menu item, and the letter will be shown underlined (as we saw in the last chapter). For example the menu entry Demo_Item2 is defined by setting the text property to D&emo_Item2.

MDIList: This property is illustrated in our sample application. If we open two MDIChild windows in our application, we can use the Window MenuItem to select which window appears on top. All we had to do was to create the top-level Window MenuItem and set its MDIList property to True. Windows Forms takes care of updating the list as more MDI children are created or deleted. Further clicking on a menu item causes the corresponding child window to be activated. To experiment with this using the sample application, you may create MDI child windows by selecting File|New.

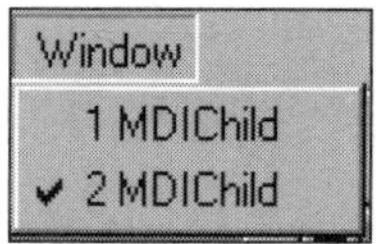

MenuItems: A complete menu system comprises a MainMenu, with its MenuItems collection containing instances of the MenuItem class for each of the top-level menus. Each of these top-level menus will again have a MenuItems collection, which may again be populated with MenuItem objects representing individual menu items, etc. We will often want to work with the MenuItems collection programmatically to access an individual menu item, or to add or remove items from the collection.

MenuItems are instances of the class MenuItemCollection, which has two properties:

Property	Description
Count	The total number of MenuItem objects in the collection
Item	A property used to access a specific MenuItem within the collection

Like other collections in the .NET Framework, the MenuItemCollection is zero-based, so the first menu item will be MenuItems.Item(0).

MenuItemCollection also implements the following methods (in addition to the standard methods inherited from Object):

Method	Description
Add	Add a MenuItem to the collection
AddRange	Add an array of MenuItems to the collection; (if we investigate the code created by the visual designer, we find that it uses successive calls to AddRange to build the complete menu system)
Clear	Remove all MenuItems from the collection
Contains	Returns True if a given MenuItem, supplied as parameter, exists in the collection
IndexOf	Returns the index of a given MenuItem, supplied as parameter, in the collection
MergeOrder and MergeType	These two get/set properties are used to determine how MenuItems on two menus are combined, if the two menus are merged
Remove	Remove a MenuItem, supplied as parameter, from the collection
RemoveAt	Remove a MenuItem, specified by a supplied index, from the collection

In relation to the pair of methods dealing with merging, we can merge two menus by using the Menu.MergeMenu or the MenuItem.MergeMenu method. If two menus are merged using Menu.MergeMenu, and the MergeOrders of the two menus are different, the .NET Framework will order the items, so that the ones with the lower MergeOrder will be placed first. If the MergeOrder is the same, the .NET Framework will use the MergeType to determine how to perform the merge. The value of MergeType may be one of the following:

- `Add`: The `MenuItem` is simply added to the collection of existing `MenuItems` in the Menu.
- `MergeItems`: All submenu items of this `MenuItem` will be merged with those of the existing `MenuItem` at the same position in a merged menu.
- `Remove`: The `MenuItem` is not included when menus are merged.
- `Replace`: The `MenuItem` replaces an existing `MenuItem` at the same position on a merged menu.

Menu merging is quite convenient when we have an application where the available menu items change with the application state. In this case, we can create the main menu to contain the minimum set of `MenuItems` that are always available. We can then use the IDE to create a number of extra `MainMenus` and programmatically add or remove them at the appropriate time. We'll see an example of this later in the chapter.

Methods

`MenuItem` implements the following methods:

Method	Description
`CloneMenu`	Creates a clone of the menu or `MenuItem`. The most common use for cloning is to create a number of menus that are similar to a 'base' menu, but with different sets of additional `MenuItems`.
`GetContextMenu`	Retrieves the context menu of which this `MenuItem` is part.
`GetMainMenu`	Retrieves the `MainMenu` of which this `MenuItem` is part.
`MergeMenu`	Merges two `MenuItems`, as discussed above.
`OnClick`	Raises the `Click` event, see below.
`OnDrawItem`	Raises the `DrawItem` event, see below.
`OnMeasureItem`	Raises the `MeasureItem` event, see below.
`OnPopup`	Raises the `Popup` event, see below.
`OnSelect`	Raises the `Select` event, see below.
`PerformClick`	Generates a `Click` event on the `MenuItem`; that is the equivalent of the user manually clicking the menu.
`PerformSelect`	Generates a `Select` event on the `MenuItem`; that is the equivalent of the user manually selecting the menu.

`PerformClick` can be useful when we want a toolbar button to have the same function as a MenuItem. Let's see how we can implement this:

```
private void Toolbar_1_ButtonClick(object sender,
   System.Windows.Forms.ToolBarButtonClickEventArgs e)
{
   if (e.Button.Tag.ToString()=="R1")
      menuDemoMenu2_Demo_Radio1.PerformClick();
...
```

First, need to create the required functionality in the `Menu_Click` event handler, and simply have the Toolbar `ButtonClick eventhandler` call `PerformClick` on the `MenuItem`. This is shown in the code section above.

Events

`MenuItem` employs the following events:

Event	Description
`Click`	This event occurs when the MenuItem is clicked or selected, using the associated access key or shortcut key
`DrawItem`	This event occurs when an owner drawn `MenuItem` is **actually** drawn. See the '*Ownerdrawn Menus*' section below for further details
`MeasureItem`	This event occurs **just before** an owner drawn `MenuItem` is to be drawn. See the Ownerdrawn Menus section below for further discussion of this event
`Popup`	If a MenuItem has an associated list of sub MenuItems, the Popup event will occur just before the sub menu items are made visible
`Select`	This event occurs when the user places the cursor on the menu item

Let's take a closer look at the `Click`, `Select` and `Popup` events.

Click: A sample generic Click event handler is shown below (you can see that we can easily assign more than one MenuItem to the same event handler):

```
Private Sub WroxGenericClick(ByVal sender As System.Object, _
      ByVal e As System.EventArgs) Handles _
                 menuDemoMenu1_Demo_Item1.Click, _
                 menuDemoMenu1_Demo_Item2.Click, _
                 menuDemoMenu1_Demo_Item3.Click, …

    Dim aMenuItem As MenuItem = CType(sender, MenuItem)
    StatusBar_1.Panels(0).Text = "You selected: " + aMenuItem.Text
End Sub
```

This event handler casts the sender object into a `MenuItem` object. It now has access to all the properties of the `MenuItem` that was clicked, including the text. In the example, the menu text is assigned to a panel in the `Statusbar`, which we will discuss later.

Notice the use of the `Handles` keyword in VB to specify which events are handled. When using VB, the easiest way to add additional events is probably to add them manually in the code as shown here.

Using the IDE and coding in C# it's probably easier to select all the menus for which we want to assign the same menu handler, then open up the property inspector, click on the lightning icon and finally, select the event handler of choice.

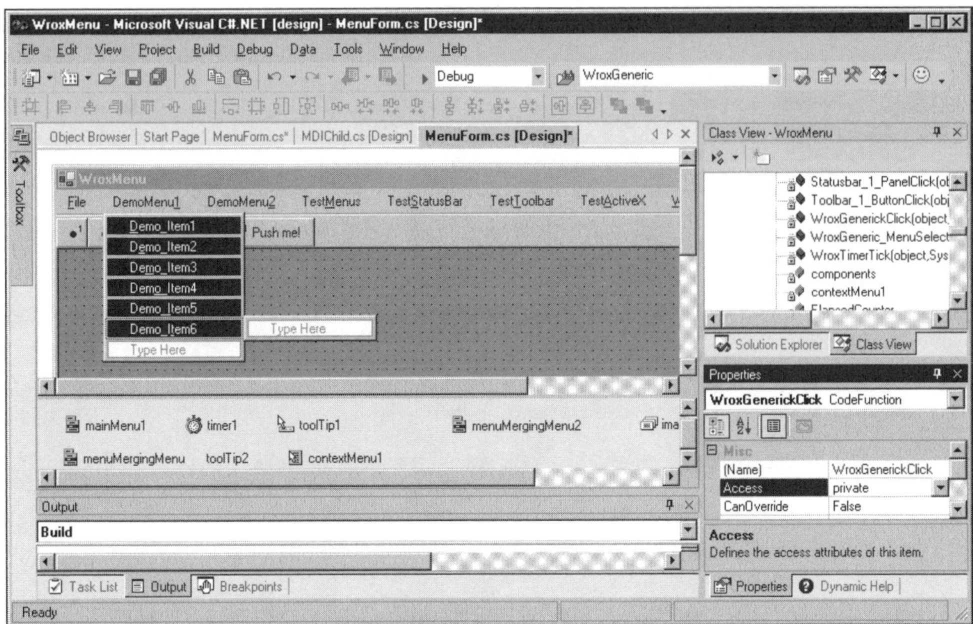

`Select`: A `MenuItem` is typically selected when we place the mouse cursor over the `MenuItem`, or when the `MenuItem` is highlighted by scrolling over it using the arrow keys. We have included an example of how to use this event in a later section of the chapter discussing the `StatusBar`.

`Popup`: If we have a (sub)menu with content that changes often depending on application state, we may postpone actually updating the (sub)menu until you receive the `Popup` event. Consider a situation where the contents of the submenu would change each time the user clicks on a new object on the screen. If the user clicks on 100 objects, the submenu would change 100 times. But the user may only open the submenu once. By postponing the task of updating the submenu's `MenuItems` collection until the user actually opens the menu, we have just saved 99 menu updates.

Simple Menu Manipulation

Let's briefly look at a few ways that we can dynamically change a menu. The code snippets (in VB) shown below represent some of the event handlers implemented for the `MenuItems` under menu TestMenus. They all change the contents of the menu DemoMenu1.

```
Private Sub menuTestMenus_CheckMenu1item1_Click(ByVal sender As System.Object,_
   ByVal e As System.EventArgs) Handles menuTestMenus_CheckMenu1item1.Click

   Dim aMenuItem As MenuItem = CType(sender, MenuItem)
   aMenuItem.Checked = Not aMenuItem.Checked

   menuDemoMenu1_Demo_Item1.Checked = aMenuItem.Checked
End Sub
```

As you can probably guess from the highlighted line, this event handler checks or unchecks the first item on the DemoMenu1. After the first two lines, the sender object is cast into a `MenuItem` object, thus giving us full access to the menu item that was just clicked. The second line then toggles the checked state of the `MenuItem` being clicked.

The following lines change the `Visible`, and `Enabled` properties of `MenuItems` in **DemoMenu1**:

```
Private Sub menuTestMenus_HideMenu1item2_Click(ByVal sender As System.Object,_
ByVal e As System.EventArgs) Handles menuTestMenus_HideMenu1item2.Click

   Dim aMenuItem As MenuItem = CType(sender, MenuItem)
   aMenuItem.Checked = Not aMenuItem.Checked

   menuDemoMenu1_Demo_Item2.Visible = Not aMenuItem.Checked
End Sub

Private Sub menuTestMenus_Disable_Menu1Item3_Click(ByVal sender As System.Object,_
ByVal e As System.EventArgs) Handles menuTestMenus_Disable_Menu1Item3.Click

Dim aMenuItem As MenuItem = CType(sender, MenuItem)
   aMenuItem.Checked = Not aMenuItem.Checked

menuDemoMenu1_Demo_Item3.Enabled = Not aMenuItem.Checked
End Sub
```

This event handler changes the text of a `MenuItem` in the **DemoMenu1** menu:

```
Private Sub menuTestMenus_ChangeMenu1item4_Click(ByVal sender As System.Object,_
ByVal e As System.EventArgs) Handles menuTestMenus_ChangeMenu1item4.Click

Dim aMenuItem As MenuItem = CType(sender, MenuItem)
   aMenuItem.Checked = Not aMenuItem.Checked
      If (aMenuItem.Checked) Then
         menuDemoMenu1_Demo_Item4.Text = "This menu has been changed"
      Else
         menuDemoMenu1_Demo_Item4.Text = "Demo_Item4"
      End If
End Sub
```

And here is the code to add and remove a complete submenu under `Item_5` of the **DemoMenu1** menu:

```
Private Sub menuTestMenus_CreateSubMenu_Menu1Item5_Click(ByVal sender As _
System.Object, ByVal e As System.EventArgs) Handles _
menuTestMenus_CreateSubMenu_Menu1Item5.Click

Dim aMenuItem As MenuItem = CType(sender, MenuItem)
aMenuItem.Checked = Not aMenuItem.Checked

   If aMenuItem.Checked Then
      Dim I As Integer
      For I = 0 To 9
         Dim aSubMenu As MenuItem = _
         New MenuItem("Demo Item5_SubMenu_" + _
         I.ToString(), AddressOf WroxGenericClick)
         menuDemoMenu1_Demo_Item5.MenuItems.Add(aSubMenu)
      Next
   Else
      menuDemoMenu1_Demo_Item5.MenuItems.Clear()
   End If
End Sub
```

To create and add the submenu, simply create `MenuItems` and add them to the `MenuItems` collection of the parent `MenuItem`. Notice how we can specify both the text on the menu item, as well as the desired event handler (`WroxGenericClick`) in the constructor.

To remove the submenu, call the `Clear` method on the `MenuItems` collection as discussed earlier under *`MenuItem` methods.*

Menu Merging

As mentioned earlier we can use `MergeMenu to` modify menus or menu items in our menu system, depending on the application state.

For the following discussion, we have created two extra `MainMenus` using the IDE, `menuMergingMenu` and `menuMergingMenuII`.

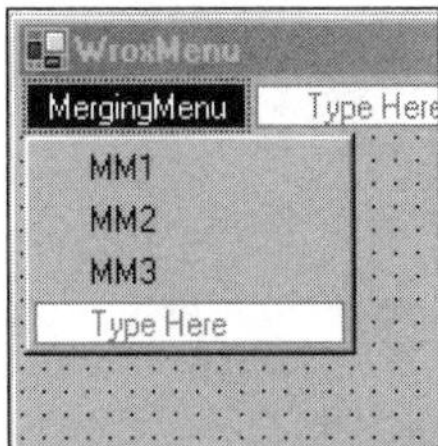

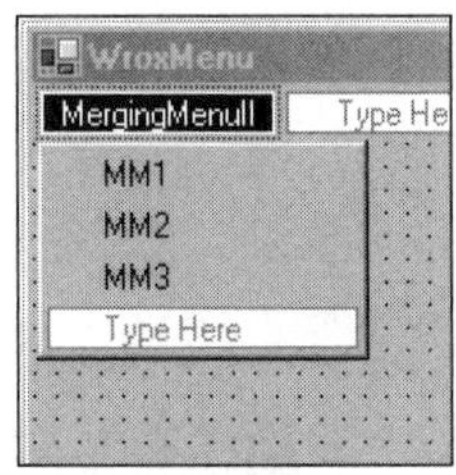

When merging menus, the result of the merge will depend on a combination of the following:

- The relative `MergeOrder` of the `menu items` in the two menus we're merging (the item with the lowest `MergeOrder` will appear first in the resultant menu).
- If two `MenuItems` have the same `MergeOrder` the outcome will be determined by the `MergeType` as discussed above under *MenuItem Properties.*
- Finally, it is important to consider the 'menu level' of the menu being merged in. Remember that a `Menu` is really a collection of `MenuItems`, which again may contain collections of `MenuItems`.

In this example, `menuMergingMenu` is simply the starting point for the first of the two menus, `menuMergingMenu.MenuItems(0)` is the only top level `MenuItem` in the menu (in other words is equivalent to the item labeled MergingMenu), and `menuMergingMenu.MenuItems(0).MenuItems(0)` is the first menu under MergingMenu, that is the item labeled MM1_1).

Merging a Top Level Menu: The following code adds an additional menu item to the bottom of DemoMenu1. The additional item will be the whole `menuMergingMenu`:

```
Private Sub menuTestMenus_MergeMenus_Click(ByVal sender As System.Object, _
ByVal e As System.EventArgs) Handles menuTestMenus_MergeMenus.Click


Dim aMenuItem As MenuItem = CType(sender, MenuItem)
aMenuItem.Checked = Not aMenuItem.Checked

If (aMenuItem.Checked) Then
   menuDemoMenu1.MergeMenu(menuMergingMenu)
```

```
    Else
       Dim I As Integer
          For I = menuDemoMenu1.MenuItems.Count - 1 To 0 Step -1
             If (menuDemoMenu1.MenuItems(I).Text.StartsWith("MergingMenu")) Then
                menuDemoMenu1.MenuItems.RemoveAt(I)
             End If
          Next
       End If
    End Sub
```

To add the menu we simply call menuDemoMenu1.MergeMenu, passing in the menu we want to merge in. Since the MergeOrder of menuMergingMenu is set to 2 in this example, and all items in menuDemoMenu1 have a MergeOrder of 0 the menuMergingMenu will be inserted at the end, as shown.

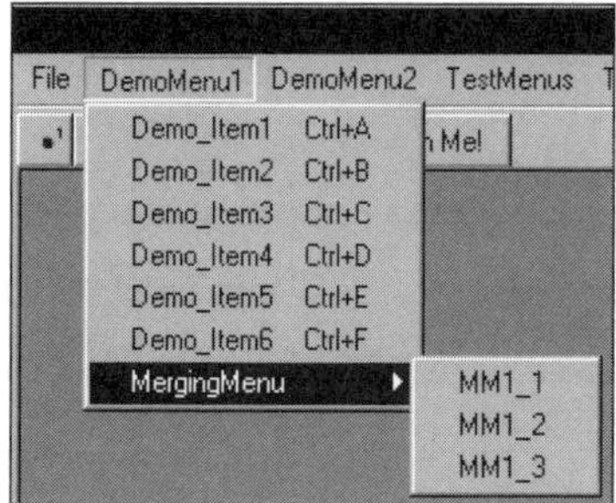

The part of the code that removes the menu when the command is unchecked is a little complicated. Since there are several functions that may modify DemoMenu1 we can't know what position our extra menu was inserted into. We have therefore coded a For-loop to iterate all items and remove the one with the text MergingMenu.

Merging 2 MenuItems collections: The following example is a little more elaborate. It shows how to combine the two extra menus and then add all the items at the end of DemoMenu1, to get the result shown below.

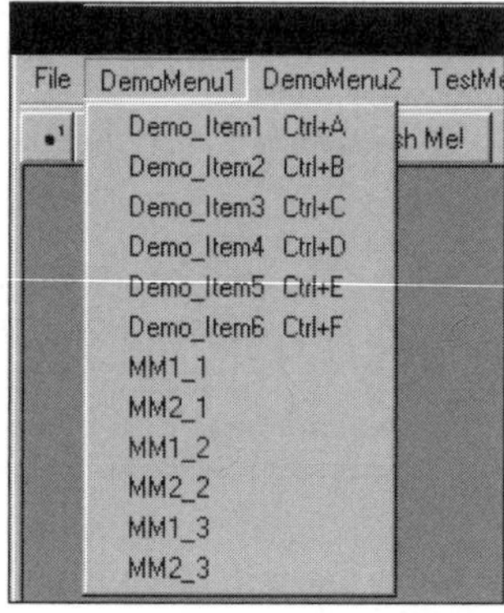

First, we create a copy of the menuMergingMenus MenuItems collection using the CloneMenu method. Then we merge in the items from the menuMergingMenu2.MenuItems collection. Finally, we merge the combined menu into menuDemo1:

```
Private Sub menuTestMenus_MergeMenuItems_Click(ByVal sender As System.Object,_
   ByVal e As System.EventArgs) Handles _
   menuTestMenus_MergeMenuItems.Click
      Dim aMenuItem As MenuItem = CType(sender, MenuItem)
      aMenuItem.Checked = Not aMenuItem.Checked

   Dim aNewMenuItem As MenuItem
   aNewMenuItem = menuMergingMenu.MenuItems(0).CloneMenu()
   aNewMenuItem.MergeMenu(menuMergingMenu2.MenuItems(0))

   If aMenuItem.Checked Then
      menuDemoMenu1.MergeMenu(aNewMenuItem)
         Else
      ...
         End If
   End Sub
```

Looking at the application, notice how we had to merge the `MenuItems` collections of the two extra menus rather than just the menus, to include the 'MM' items at the top level. Also notice the order in which they are merged. When creating the two extra MainMenu objects using the IDE we set the `MergeOrder` of MM1_X to 5, 15 and 25, while we set the `MergeOrder` of MM2_X to 10, 20 and 30. Consequently the menu items have been interleaved.

'Ownerdrawn' Menus

So far we have only discussed menus that display text. As we've seen, they are very easy to specify using the IDE. In fact, all we have to do is to enter the text for each menu item, and the .NET library takes care of displaying them.

However, since a picture is sometimes worth 1000 words, there are times where we may not be satisfied with displaying pure textual menus. If that's the case, we can specify that a menu item should be owner drawn. This informs Windows that you do not want it to render the menu item, but rather call code supplied by you to undertake the rendering. There is a little programming involved in doing this, but it gives you complete flexibility to display bitmaps, graphs and or text in different fonts and colors. Our sample application shows this menu:

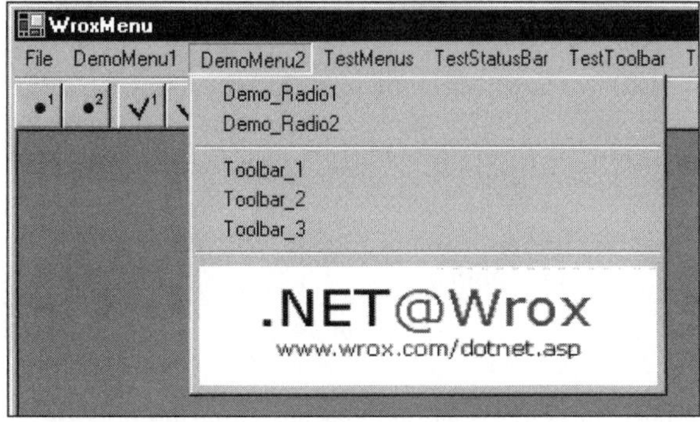

Implementing an 'Ownerdrawn MenuItem': To make a `MenuItem` 'ownerdrawn' we must set its `Ownerdrawn` property to `True`. The .NET Framework will now send two events that we must provide handlers for:

1. The `MeasureItem` event is sent before the menu item is displayed. The called event handler will receive a `MeasureItemEventArgs` object, which amongst others contains the members `ItemHeight` and `ItemWidth`. The purpose of this event handler is to specify how much space in pixels the drawing of the menu item is going to require. The .NET Framework will first send this event to all ownerdrawn menu items to get the size requirements for each item.

Once the Framework knows the desired size for all menu items, it will decide how much space it will actually allocate for each item; an item may not be allocated the same amount of space that it had specified in the `MeasureItem` event handler. Consider two menu items. One item specifies `ItemWidth=100` pixels and the other Item specifies `ItemWidth=200` pixels. Since all Menu items obviously have to be equally wide, it's very likely that both will be asked to draw themselves to a width of 200 pixels.

2. The `DrawItem` event is then sent when the menu item is drawn. The event handler receives a `DrawItemEventArgs` object. A partial specification for this is listed as follows:

Property	Description
`BackColor`	A suggested background color: either `SystemColors.Window` or `SystemColors.HighlightText`, depending on whether this item is selected. In a normal setup `SystemColors.Windows` will be the gray color on Windows menus, toolbars, etc. `SystemColors.HighlightText` is the blue color used to identify selected items.
`Bounds`	The rectangle outlining the area in which the painting should be done.
`Font`	A suggested font, usually the parent control's `Font` property.
`ForeColor`	A suggested foreground color: either `SystemColors.WindowText` or `SystemColors.HighlightText`, depending on whether this item is selected.
`Graphics`	The `Graphics` object with which painting should be done.
`Index`	The index of the item that should be painted.
`State`	Miscellaneous state information, such as whether the item is 'selected', 'focused', or some other such information.

Method	Description
`DrawBackground`	Draws the background of the given rectangle with default Windows control colors.
`DrawFocusRectangle`	Draws a handy focus rectangle in the given rectangle. The focus rectangle is a dashed rectangle around an item to indicate that it is selected.

So let's look at the implementation for the ownerdrawn menu item on the DemoMenu2 menu.

The event handler for the MeasureItem event is simple. It just returns the size of the image we want to draw, together with a little space. We add the extra space to give us room to draw a blue background around the item, if it is selected.

```
Private Sub menuDemoMenu2_OwnerDrawn_MeasureItem(ByVal sender As Object, _
ByVal e As System.Windows.Forms.MeasureItemEventArgs) Handles _
menuDemoMenu2_OwnerDrawn.MeasureItem

    e.ItemHeight = ImageList2.Images(0).Height + 4
    e.ItemWidth = ImageList2.Images(0).Width + 4
End Sub
```

The image is stored in an ImageList object called ImageList2. We will discuss ImageList later in this chapter.

The code for the DrawItem event is shown below:

```
Private Sub menuDemoMenu2_OwnerDrawn_DrawItem(ByVal sender As Object, _
ByVal e As System.Windows.Forms.DrawItemEventArgs) Handles _
menuDemoMenu2_OwnerDrawn.DrawItem
    'Draw the owner drawn menu item
      Dim R As Rectangle
      Dim aPen As Pen = New Pen(e.BackColor, 2)
      R = e.Bounds
    'Since the rectangle was inflated in the MesaureItem event handler
    'We can now deflate it to leave a little extra space around it.
    'This is used to mark if the item is selected or not.
      R.Inflate(-4, -4)
      e.Graphics.DrawRectangle(aPen, R)
      e.Graphics.DrawImage(ImageList2.Images(0), R)
    End Sub
```

First, we create a pen in the appropriate background color. The suitable color is quite conveniently made available in the DrawItemEventArgs parameter. Then we draw the rectangle around the image, and finally we draw the image.

Context Menus

Context menus are usually provided to give the user access to functions that relate to a specific set of controls on a form. The user will place the mouse over the control, and right-click to make the context menu appear. There are often different context menus for different parts of the application. For example, right-clicking in the document area in Word brings up a context menu with commands like Cut, Copy, Paste, Font, etc. Right-clicking on the toolbar brings up a list of available toolbars such as: Standard, Formatting, AutoText, etc.

In our sample application we have attached a context menu to the toolbar control:

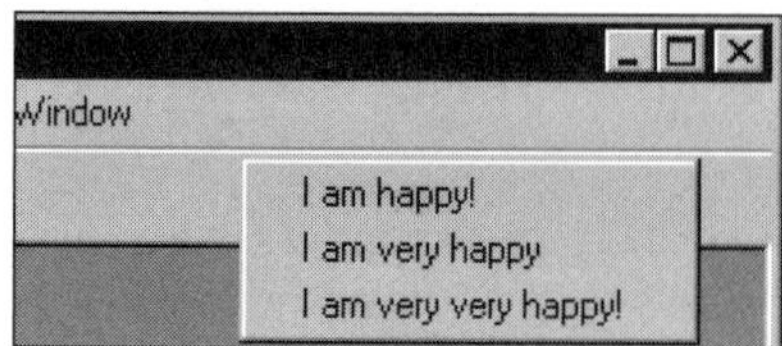

'ContextMenu'

The `ContextMenu` control inherits from the Menu class:

```
Object
    MarshalByRefObject
        Component
            Menu
                ContextMenu
```

It's easy to create a `ContextMenu` programmatically or using the IDE. Either way, the process is almost identical to creating a `MainMenu`. Using the IDE, pick the `ContextMenu` tool from the Toolbox and drag it onto the form. The icon for the `ContextMenu` will appear in the component tray, and the menu designer will appear at the top of the form, just like when we were designing the `MainMenu`.

While `ContextMenu` is a control in itself, with properties, methods and events, here, we are referring to it as a property of other controls, so a list of its properties, methods and events has been omitted.

Once a context menu is created, we attach it to one or more controls by setting the controls `ContextMenu` property. As soon as we've assigned the `ContextMenu` of a control, the Windows Forms library takes care of the rest. There is not additional code to write to get the menu to appear when the user right-clicks the control.

If we decide that we want to invoke a context menu programmatically, for example in response to the user simply hovering over a control, we can call the context menus `Show` method. This will pop up the menu at a specified position. The method does not return until the menu is dismissed.

And that's it. Just like a `Menu`, a `ContextMenu` contains a collection of `MenuItems`, so all the things we discussed above for `MainMenus` and `MenuItems` can also be applied to `ContextMenus`, including dynamic construction and modification of the menus' contents.

'ToolBar' and 'ToolBarButton'

A toolbar provides the user with an easy access to the most commonly used functions. In the past, toolbars only contained buttons, which mirrored the function of certain menu items. Nowadays the concept is extended. A toolbar can include all kinds of controls including combo boxes, which are used very often to allow quick selection of key property value. For example, Word, in its standard layout, includes combo boxes for the paragraph type, text font name and size and the desired zoom factor.

In this section we will discuss how to create a simple toolbar for our sample application using the IDE. Initially the toolbar contains only buttons, but we will then add a combo box programmatically. The sample toolbar is shown below:

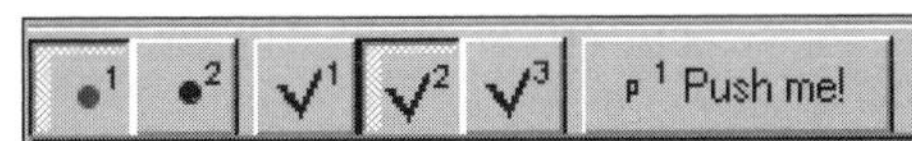

Adding a 'Toolbar'

To add a toolbar to a form simply pick the toolbar control from the toolbox and place it on the form. Initially it will be docked to the top of the form. We can change that by changing the value of the `Dock` property using the property inspector.

But, perhaps most importantly, a `ToolBar` keeps a `Buttons` collection of `ToolBarButton` objects. Let's look at the `ToolBarButton` class first.

'ToolBarButton'

The `ToolBarButton` class comes from the `Component` class:

```
Object
    MarshalByRefObject
        Component
            ToolBarButton
```

Properties

Some of the main properties of `ToolBarButton` are described below:

Property	Description
`DropDown`	Places a 'down' button on the toolbar. If we assign a `MenuItem` or `ContextMenu` to the button's `DropDownMenu` property, this menu will be displayed when the button is pressed.
`ImageIndex`	This `get/set` property determines which graphic (if any) is displayed on the `ToolBarButton`. If set, this number is an index into an `ImageList` object, which is associated with the parent `ToolBar` (see later). The drop-down list in the editor allows the user to quickly select between all the images available in the `ImageList`.
`PartialPush`	This `get/set` property determines the appearance of a non-pushed button if the button `Style` is set to `ToggleButton`. If `PartialPush` is true, the button will appear grayed or 'dimmed'.

Table continued on following page

Property	Description
Pushed	This get/set property is True if a button is in its 'pushed' state and False if the button is not pushed.
Separator	This is a separator between two buttons. The width of the separator is fixed.
Style	This get/set property determines the style of the ToolBarButton. Possible values are PushButton (the button will depress when the user clicks with the mouse, but bounce back when the mouse button is lifted) and ToggleButton (the button can be either 'in' or 'out' depending on the value of its Pushed property).
Tag	This get/set property is intended to store 'user data' which relates to the button.
Text	This get/set property specifies any text that may appear on the ToolBarButton. If we specify image and text, these two items will be positioned next to each other on the button. Whether the image or the text is shown furthest to the left is determined by the TextAlign property of the ToolBar.
ToolTipText	This get/set property specifies which tooltip text should be shown for the button.

Let's take a closer look at the Tag property.

The value of Tag does not affect the appearance or functionality of the ToolBarButton. Tag is very convenient when writing code to handle events from all buttons on a toolbar. When we receive the ToolBarButtonClickEventArgs object, we can inspect the Tag value to determine which button was actually clicked. For example:

```
private void Toolbar_1_ButtonClick(object sender,
                System.Windows.Forms.ToolBarButtonClickEventArgs e)
{
   if (e.Button.Tag.ToString()=="R1")
      menuDemoMenu2_Demo_Radio1.PerformClick();
   if (e.Button.Tag.ToString()=="R2")
...
```

ToolBarButtons can be added to a toolbar using the ToolBarButton Collection Editor. To access this, find the Buttons property in the property inspector for the Toolbar.

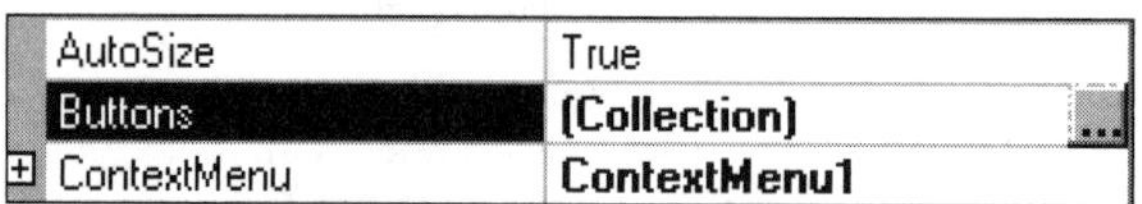

Click the ... ellipses to open up the Toolbarbutton Collection Editor.

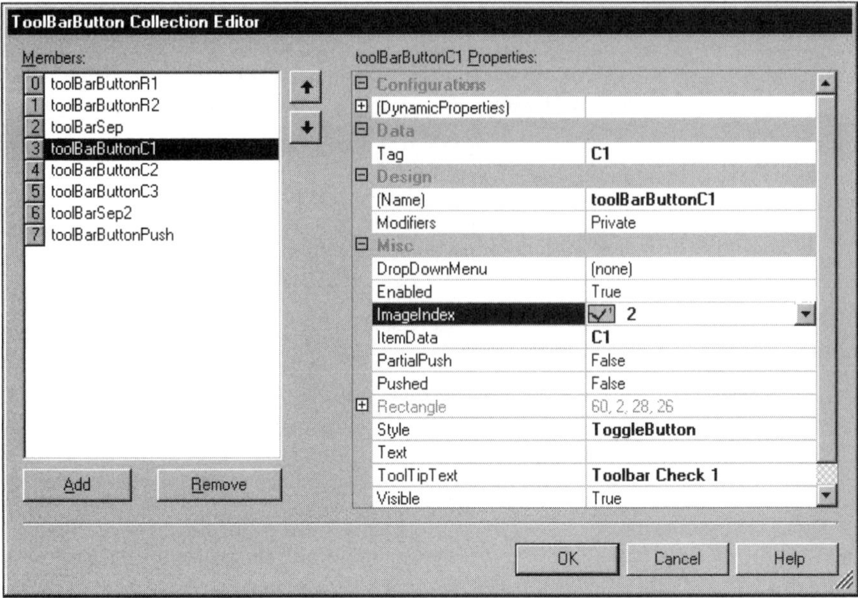

Use Add and Remove to add or remove the buttons, use the up and down arrows to change their order, and use the properties editor to set the properties of each `ToolBarButton`.

'ToolBar'

`ToolBar` is derived from `Control` as follows:

```
Object
    MarshalByRefObject
        Component
            Control
                ToolBar
```

Properties

Some of the properties unique to the `ToolBar` control are listed below:

Property	Description
`Appearance`	A `get/set` property that determines the appearance of the toolbar. Possible values are `Normal` and `Flat` (if `Appearance` is `Flat`, the buttons appear to be flat, but become three dimensional, when you move the mouse over them).
`AutoSize`	If this `get/set` property is `True`, the `ToolBar` will automatically resize to match the size of the `ToolBar` buttons and the size of the form in which the `ToolBar` is embedded.
`BorderStyle`	This `get/set` property determines the style of the toolbar's border. Possible values include `None`, `FixedSingle` and `Fixed3D`.

Table continued on following page

Property	Description
`Buttons`	This `get/set` property keeps the collection of `ToolBarButtons` (as discussed above).
`ButtonSize`	If we `get` this `get/set` property, it will return the size of the largest button on the `ToolBar`.
`Divider`	This `get/set` property determines if there should be a visible divider at the top of the toolbar (to separate it from the menu).
`Dock`	This get/set property determines where the `ToolBar` will be docked. Possible values (of type `DockStyle`) include: `Bottom`, `Fill`, `Left`, `None`, `Right` and `Top`.
`DropDownArrows`	This `get/set` property determines if a drop down button should display a drop down arrow. If `DropDownArrows` is `True` the button will show a down arrow, and the user must press that in order to invoke the menu. If `DropDownArrows` is `False`, no down arrow is shown and the user just presses the button to invoke the menu.
`ImageList`	This is a `get/set` property that holds the collection of images, which can be used on the `ToolBarButtons`.
`ShowToolTips`	This `get/set` property determines if assigned `ToolTips` will be shown. `ToolTips` will be shown if `ShowToolTips` is set to `True`.
`TextAlign`	This `get/set` property determines the order of appearance from left to right of an image and text if both are specified for a button. Possible values are: `Right` or `Underneath`.
`Wrappable`	This `get/set` property determines if the toolbar can wrap buttons to the next line, if the screen becomes too small to display all toolbar buttons on one line.

Let's take a closer look at the `ButtonSize` property.

`ButtonSize` will have been automatically calculated as buttons are added to the `ToolBar`. However, if you set this property, the value assigned to `ButtonSize` will become the size for all buttons.

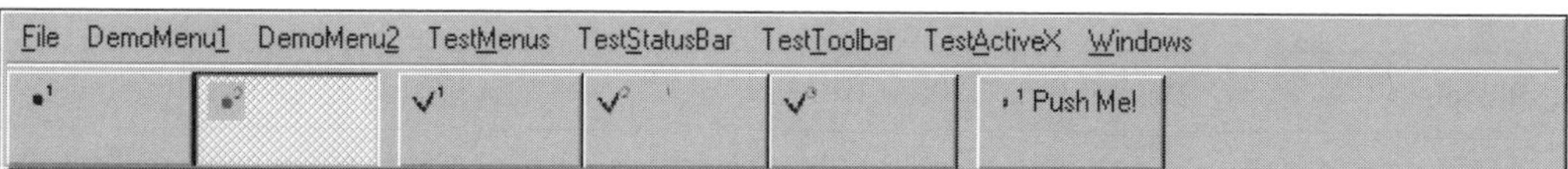

This is the new appearance of the toolbar after `ButtonSize` was assigned to 80*40 using the IDE.

If, for some reason, you want to go back to the previous layout, where buttons are sized according to the required size, you can just delete the contents of the `ButtonSize` property field, and the sizes will be recalculated:

Simple Programming with 'ToolBar' and 'ToolBarButton'

When a `ToolBarButton` is clicked, the `Click` event is routed to an event handler, which is shared for all buttons on the toolbar. This is different from what we've seen with `MenuItems`, where by default, we get a new event handler for each menu item click.

The shared toolbar event handler receives a `ToolBarButtonClickEventArgs` object, which has a `Button` property of type `ToolBarButton`. We can use the value of the `Button.Tag` member to find out which button was pressed, **provided of course, you have previously initialized it**.

Since buttons on a toolbar often replicate an existing menu function, we will probably want to share code for handling the toolbar click and the menu click. This is most easily done by keeping all the functionality in the `MenuItems` `Click` event handler method, and then simply calling the `MenuItem.PerformClick` method from the `ToolBarButton` click event handler.

```
Private Sub ToolBar1_ButtonClick(ByVal sender As System.Object, _
ByVal e As System.Windows.Forms.ToolBarButtonClickEventArgs) _
Handles ToolBar1.ButtonClick
        If (e.Button.ItemData = "R1") Then
            menuDemoMenu2_Demo_Radio1.PerformClick()
        ElseIf e.Button.ItemData = "R2" Then
            menuDemoMenu2_Demo_Radio2.PerformClick()
        ElseIf e.Button.ItemData = "C1" Then
            menuDemoMenu2_Toolbar_1.PerformClick()
        ElseIf e.Button.ItemData = "C2" Then
            menuDemoMenu2_Toolbar_2.PerformClick()
        ElseIf e.Button.ItemData = "C3" Then
            menuDemoMenu2_Toolbar_3.PerformClick()
        ElseIf e.Button.ItemData = "BP" Then
            menuDemoMenu2_OwnerDrawn.PerformClick()
        End If
End Sub
```

Setting 'ToolBarButton' Properties Programmatically

The code below is called when the user selects the first item on the DemoMenu2 menu, or if they press the first toolbar button.

```
Private Sub menuDemoMenu2_Demo_Radio1_Click(ByVal sender As System.Object, _
   ByVal e As System.EventArgs) _
   Handles menuDemoMenu2_Demo_Radio1.Click
   menuDemoMenu2_Demo_Radio1.Checked = True
   menuDemoMenu2_Demo_Radio2.Checked = False
   ToolBar1.Buttons(0).ImageIndex = 6
   ToolBar1.Buttons(0).Pushed = True
   ToolBar1.Buttons(1).ImageIndex = 1
   ToolBar1.Buttons(1).Pushed = False
End Sub
```

In addition to setting the correct check state for the menu, the event handler also updates the toolbar. The first toolbar button (index 0) is set to its 'down' state (`Pushed=true`) and assigned a red radio button graphic (`ImageIndex=6`). (This, of course, assumes that the ImageList has a red radio button graphic at location 6.) The second `ToolBarButton` (index 1) is set to its 'up' state (`Pushed=false`) and assigned a blue radio button graphic (`ImageIndex=1`).

Assigning another Control

While it is not possible to use the IDE to place a control on the `ToolBar`, it's easy to do so programmatically. The code below would add a combo box with three entries:

```
ComboBox aComboBox= new ComboBox();
aComboBox.Left=250;
aComboBox.Top=5;
aComboBox.Items.Add("Green");
aComboBox.Items.Add("Blue");
aComboBox.Items.Add("Red");
Toolbar_1.Controls.Add(aComboBox);
```

The code is straightforward. Instead of accessing the `Buttons` collection, which is particular to the `ToolBar` class, it accesses the `Controls` collection, which is shared by all descendants of `Control`.

And the result would look like this:

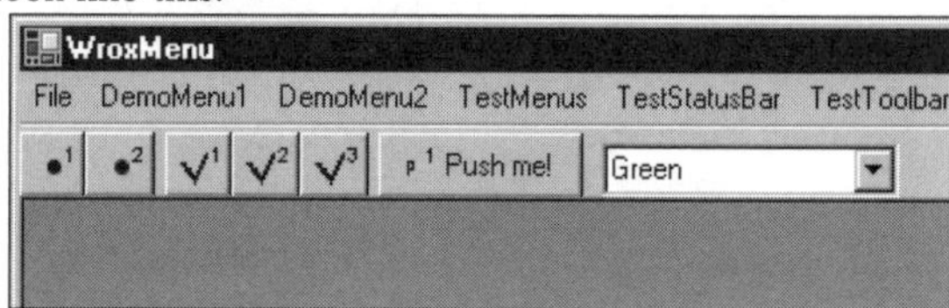

Tooltips

Tooltips are the small helpful windows that often appear if a mouse is left over a control for a second or two. The tooltip is intended to provide an additional hint. You can associate one or more tooltips with any control on a form.

To enable tooltips using the IDE, drag the `ToolTip` tool from the ToolBox onto the Form. The `ToolTip` icon will appear in the component tray. The `ToolTip` control is responsible for displaying the tooltip, and you can set its properties to specify the exact tooltip behavior. Once the tooltip is defined, you can associate it with the different controls.

'ToolTip'

The `ToolTip` control is derived from the `Component` class:

```
Object
    MarshalByRefObject
        Component
            ToolTip
```

Properties

The `ToolTip` properties mostly deal with how quickly and for how long the tooltip should appear:

Property	Description
`Active`	This `get/set` property is `True` if the `ToolTip` control is active and will display a tooltip. If it is `False`, the tooltips will not be displayed.
`AutomaticDelay`	This `get/set` property determines the number of milliseconds before a tooltip appears for the first time. When you set `AutomaticDelay`, the values of `AutoPopDelay`, `InitialDelay` and `ReShowDelay` will also be set to appropriate values (although they may be changed individually afterwards).
`AutoPopDelay`	This `get/set` property specifies the time (in ms) that the tooltip will remain visible if the mouse stays over the control. As a default `AutoPopDelay` is set to 10 times the value assigned to `AutomaticDelay`.
`InitialDelay`	This `get/set` property specifies the time (in ms) that the mouse must be over the same tooltip region in order for the tooltip to appear. As a default `InitialDelay` is set to the same value as `AutomaticDelay`.
`ReshowDelay`	This `get/set` property determines the time before a tooltip appears, if you move the mouse directly from one tooltip region to another. As a default `ReshowDelay` is set to 1/5th the value of `AutomaticDelay`.
`ShowAlways`	If this `get/set` property is true, the tooltip will be displayed even if the control with which it is associated is not enabled and active. If `ShowAlways` is `False`, a tooltip will only be shown if the control is enabled and in an active window.

Assigning 'ToolTip's to Controls

`ToolTips` can be assigned programmatically or by using the IDE. Once we've have placed one or several `ToolTip` controls in the component tray, the IDE will add one line for each `ToolTip` control in any other controls property inspector. In our test application, we have created two `ToolTip` controls, and we get the ability to set texts for both `ToolTip` controls in the property inspector for the `ToolBar` control.

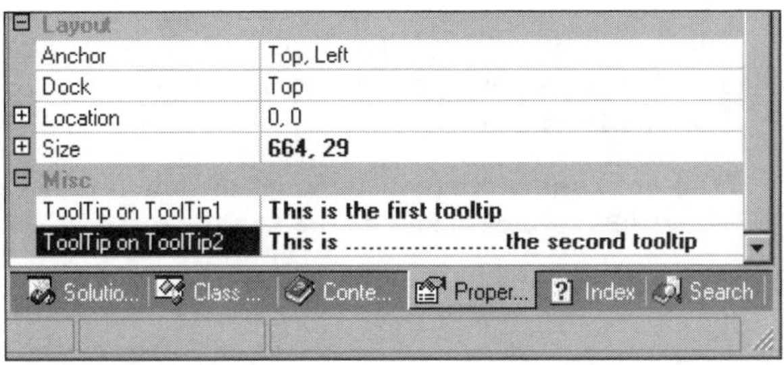

Since we have set the `AutomaticDelay` property for `toolTip1` to 500 ms and to 2000 ms for `toolTip2`, you will first see `toolTip1` appear, followed by `toolTip2`, when you place the mouse over the Toolbar.

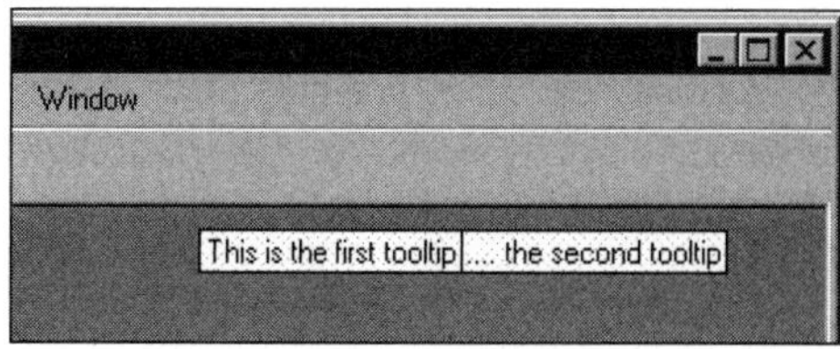

If you prefer to assign the tooltips programmatically, you can use the SetToolTip method. The lines shown below represent the code generated by the IDE to associate the two tooltips without ToolBar.

```
Me.ToolTip1.SetToolTip(Me.ToolBar1, "This is the first tooltip")
Me.ToolTip2.SetToolTip(Me.ToolBar1, "This is the second tooltip")
```

'StatusBar' and 'StatusBarPanel'

A StatusBar provides the user with pertinent state information. From a programming perspective, there's a lot of similarity between a StatusBar and a ToolBar. Just like the ToolBar keeps a collection of ToolBarButtons, the StatusBar keeps a collection of StatusBarPanels.

'StatusBar'

Also, like the ToolBar, a StatusBar is derived from Control, and can therefore host any other control:

```
Object
    MarshalByRefObject
        Component
            Control
                StatusBar
```

Properties

Some properties unique to the StatusBar are discussed below:

Property	Description
Dock	This get/set property determines where the StatusBar will be docked. Possible values (of type DockStyle) include: Bottom, Fill, Left, None, Right and Top.
Font	This get/set property determines the font used on all StatusBarPanels, and on the StatusBar itself.
Panels	This get/set property holds the collection of StatusBarPanels (discussed below).
ShowPanels	This get/set property determines if the StatusBar should show the panels (ShowPanels=true), or it should show the text, assigned to its Text property (ShowPanels=false).

Property	Description
`SizingGrip`	This `get/set` property determines if the sizing grip graphic should be displayed.
`TabStop`	This `get/set` property determines if the user can navigate to the `StatusBar`.
`Text`	This determines the text to be displayed, when the `ShowPanels` property is false.

Depending on the value of the `StatusBars` `ShowPanels` property, the `StatusBar` will either show all status bar panels, or just text associated with the `StatusBar` itself.

Programming `StatusBar` to show the `StatusPanels`, and using a `SizingGrip` at the far right looks like this:

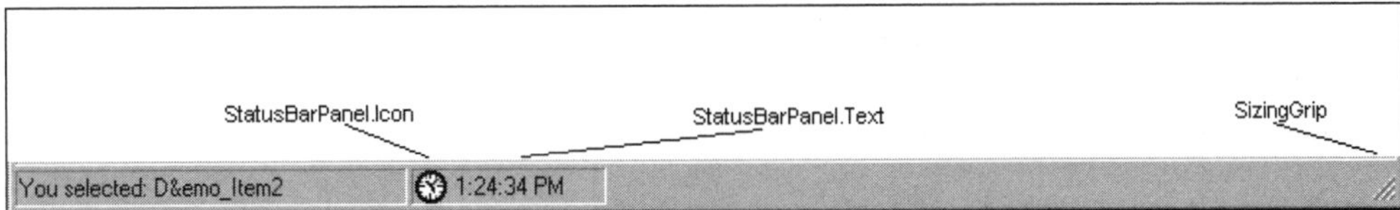

Programming `StatusBar` with `ShowPanels` set to `False` looks like this:

De&mo_Item3

Instead of showing the status panels, it now shows the StatusBar's own `Text` property.

In addition to all the methods and events `StatusBar` inherits from `Control`, it implements an extra `PanelClick` event. This event is fired if the user clicks inside a `StatusBarPanel` (discussed below).

The event handler will receive a `StatusBarPanelClickEventArgs` object, which, amongst others, includes a `Button` property, specifying which mouse button was used to click the panel, and `StatusBarPanel`, which is a reference to the panel itself.

With the following sample implementation:

```
Private Sub StatusBar_1_PanelClick(ByVal sender As System.Object, _
       ByVal e As System.Windows.Forms.StatusBarPanelClickEventArgs)_
       Handles StatusBar_1.PanelClick
        MessageBox.Show("You clicked:" + e.StatusBarPanel.ToString() + _
        " using the " + e.Button.ToString() + _
        " mouse button", "Hello from the StatusBar")
End Sub
```

you will get this message box when you click the `StatusBarPanel`, which shows the time the application has been running.

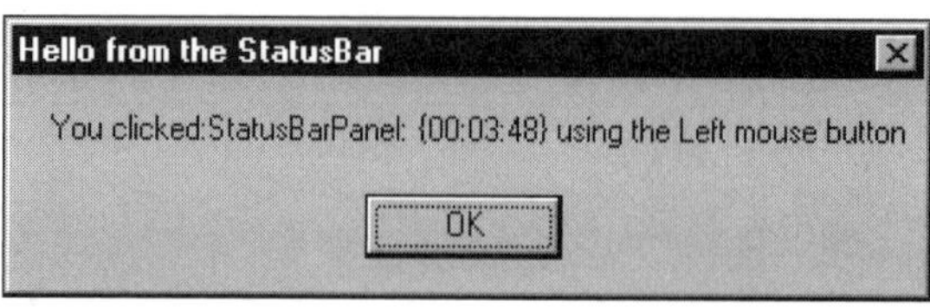

'StatusBarPanel'

The `StatusBarPanel` control derives from the `Component` class:

```
Object
    MarshalByRefObject
        Component
            StatusBarPanel
```

Properties

`StatusBarPanels` properties include:

Property	Description
`Alignment`	This `get/set` property determines how the text or image displayed in the `StatusBarPanel` is aligned. Possible values are `Left`, `Center` or `Right`.
`AutoSize`	This `get/set` property determines how a `StatusBarPanel` is resized if the width of the whole `StatusBar` changes, or if the contents of the `StatusBarPanel` changes (see below for possible values).
`BorderStyle`	This `get/set` property determines the style of the border around the `StatusPanel`.
`Icon`	This `get/set` property allows you to associate an icon with a `StatusBarPanel`. You may use the IDE to point to the icon you want displayed.
`MinWidth`	This `get/set` property determines the minimum width to which the `StatusBarPanel` can be resized.
`Style`	Set this `get/set` property to `text`, if the `StatusBarPanel` is a regular panel that displays an icon and some text. Set the property to `OwnerDraw`, if the `StatusPanel` should be drawn by methods provided by you. Unlike owner drawn `MenuItems`, you do **not** have to create event handlers for `MeasureItem` and `DrawItem` events. Instead, you must override the `Paint` method of the parent `StatusBar` control.
`Text`	This `get/set` property specifies the text to be displayed in the `StatusBarPanel`.
`ToolTipText`	This `get/set` property specifies the tooltip text to be shown. The text will be shown even if you have not created any tooltip controls.
`Width`	This `get/set` property determines the width of the `StatusBarPanel` control.

Let's look at some possible values of the `AutoSize` property:

- `Contents`: The panel will be resized to match the size of the contents in the `StatusBarPanel`.
- `None`: as the name suggests, no resizing takes place.
- `Spring`: The `StatusBarPanel` will try to take up 'as much space as possible'; observing the space already allocated to other `StatusBarPanels`. If there is more than one `StatusBarPanel` with the `AutoSize` property set to `Spring`, these panels will share the remaining available space.

We can experiment with these values using the TestStatusBar|AutoSize menu items in our sample application.

`StatusBarPanels` can be added to the `StatusBar` using the `StatusBarPanels` Editor. This can be invoked by clicking on the ellipses button … next to the `Panels` property.

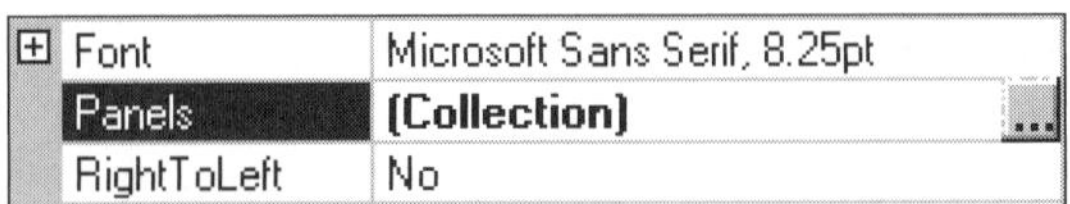

As we can see, it's very similar to the ToolBar Button Collection Editor discussed earlier.

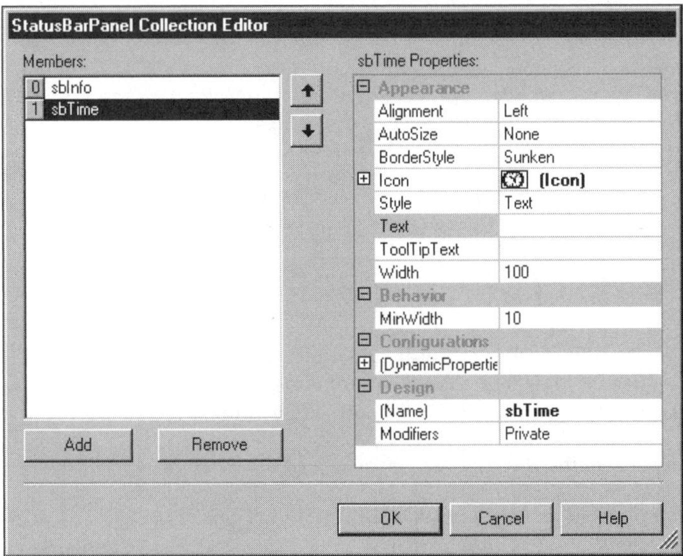

Use Add and Remove to add or remove the panels, use the up and down arrows to change their order, and use the properties editor to set the properties of each `StatusBarPanel`.

Simple Programming with 'StatusBar' and 'StatusBarPanel'

Here we will look at how to display the time in a status panel, and how to use the whole status bar to show 'extended' menu information. Finally we'll look at how a `StatusBar` can also host controls.

Displaying Elapsed Time

Unlike VB6, there is **not** a property on the `StatusBarPanel`, which will automatically show a running clock. To do that, we must add a timer to the form (timers are discussed in the next section). When the timer triggers, we must get the time and update the `Text` property for the status panel accordingly. The code below increments a counter every second. The value counter is converted to a `TimeSpan` object for formatting purposes and displayed to show the amount of time the application has been running:

```
Private Sub Timer1_Tick(ByVal sender As System.Object, _
ByVal e As System.EventArgs) Handles Timer1.Tick
      ElapsedCounter = ElapsedCounter + 1
      Dim aTimeSpan As TimeSpan = New TimeSpan()
      aTimeSpan = TimeSpan.FromSeconds(ElapsedCounter)
      sbTime.Text = aTimeSpan.ToString()
End Sub
```

`sbTime` is the name of the `StatusBarPanel`, where the text should be displayed.

Showing Extended Menu Information

In many applications, the `StatusBar` switches between showing the panels, when the user works with the main part of the form, and showing extended information about menu items, when the user scrolls through the menu system.

To implement this behavior, we must implement a couple of event handlers pertaining to the `Form` itself:

```
Private Sub Form1_MenuStart(ByVal sender As Object, ByVal e As System.EventArgs) _
Handles MyBase.MenuStart
'Disable display of panels, so we can show which menu is being displayed
   StatusBar_1.ShowPanels = False
End Sub

Private Sub Form1_MenuComplete(ByVal sender As Object, ByVal e As _
System.EventArgs) Handles MyBase.MenuComplete
'(Re)enable display of panels…
   StatusBar_1.ShowPanels = True
End Sub
```

The `MenuStart` event is fired when the user starts opening the menu system, and `MenuComplete` is fired when the user 'leaves' the menu system, and the menus are retracted. These events are fired both when a user works with the form's main menu and with a context menu.

We use these events to set the `ShowPanels` property of the `StatusBar`.

Finally, we must implement an event handler for the `MenuItem.MenuSelect` event and assign it to every menu item's `MenuSelect` event property. In our case, the event handler is very simple. It just assigns the `MenuItem's Text` property to that of the `StatusBar`. In a more advanced implementation, this handler could look up an appropriately longer explanation to be displayed on the `StatusBar`.

```
Private Sub menuFile_Select(ByVal sender As System.Object, _
ByVal e As System.EventArgs) Handles menuFile.Select, menuContextHappy.Select,…

     ' Generic handler for almost all "Menu Select" events.
     ' Updates status bar to show latest selected event...
    Dim aMenuItem As MenuItem = CType(sender, MenuItem)
```

```
    StatusBar_1.Text = aMenuItem.Text
End Sub
```

Controls on the 'StatusBar'

For completeness, let's just show the code necessary to add a `RadioButton` control to the status bar. Again we just create the control, and add it to the `StatusBars Control` collection:

```
Private Sub menuTestStatusBar_AddControl_Click(ByVal sender As System.Object,_
    ByVal e As System.EventArgs) Handles _
    menuTestStatusBar_AddControl.Click
        If StatusBar_1.Controls.Count = 0 Then
            Dim aRadioButton As RadioButton = New RadioButton()
                aRadioButton.Left = 310
                aRadioButton.Width = 200
                aRadioButton.Text = "A RadioButton on the StatusBar"
                StatusBar_1.Controls.Add(aRadioButton)

            Else
                StatusBar_1.Controls.RemoveAt(0)
            End If
        End Sub
```

The value of 310 assigned to the `Left` property is the number of pixels from the left of the `StatusBar` to the start of the `RadioButton` control. `Width` is the width of the control.

'Timer'

The `Timer` is an invisible control. Once you drag it from the ToolBox onto the form it will reside in the Component Tray. If enabled, the `Timer` will fire `Tick` events at regular intervals.

Timer derives from the `Component` class:

```
Object
    MarshalByRefObject
        Component
            Timer
```

Properties

Properties include:

Property	Description
`Enabled`	This `get/set` property determines if the `Timer` is enabled or not. The `Timer` will fire events if `Enabled` is `True`, and `Interval` is greater than zero. We can also set this property by calling the `Start` and `Stop` methods on the `Timer`.
`Interval`	This `get/set` property represents the interval (in ms) between two `Tick` events.

Events

The 'lonely' event is:

Event	Description
Tick	Triggered at regular intervals specified by the value of Interval, if Enabled is True.

The event handler will receive the generic EventArgs object along with the Sender object. The Sender can be used to identify which Timer triggered the event, if more timers are wired to the same event handler.

We have already seen one used for the Timer object:

```
Private Sub Timer1_Tick(ByVal sender As System.Object, _
ByVal e As System.EventArgs) Handles Timer1.Tick
    ElapsedCounter = ElapsedCounter + 1
    Dim aTimeSpan As TimeSpan = New TimeSpan()
    aTimeSpan = TimeSpan.FromSeconds(ElapsedCounter)
    sbTime.Text = aTimeSpan.ToString()
End Sub
```

'ImageList'

ImageList, as another invisible control, is derived from Component:

```
Object
   MarshalByRefObject
      Component
         ImageList
```

As the name implies, an ImageList keeps a list of images. All images in the list must share certain characteristics, such as size, and color depth. In addition to keeping the list, ImageList also has a Draw method that draws a selected image onto a supplied Graphics object. This makes ImageList a convenient helper class for other classes like ToolBar, ListView and TreeView. As we have already seen, we assigned an ImageList to the ToolBar and we could then use images from that list for display on the individual buttons.

An additional minor benefit of using an ImageList is that it allows us to import images into the applications resource repository using the IDE very easily. We took advantage of this, when we implemented the ownerdrawn MenuItem.

```
e.Graphics.DrawImage(ImageList2.Images(0), R)
```

Alternatively we would have had to either add the bitmap to the solution using Solution Explorer, or programmatically instantiate an instance of the bitmap.

Properties

ImageList exposes the following properties:

Property	Description
ColorDepth	This get/set property specifies the number of colors used to display an image. Possible values include: Depth4Bit (default), Depth8Bit, Depth16Bit, Depth24Bit and Depth32Bit.
Images	This get/set property holds the collection of Images.
ImageSize	This get/set property specifies the size in pixels of the images in the ImageList.
TransparentCol or	This get/set property specifies a color that will not be rendered when the image is drawn.

ColorDepth, ImageSize and TransparentColor don't affect how the individual image is stored in the application resource. It only defines the properties that will be used for all images, when they are drawn on ToolBars, ListViews, etc.

Methods

ImageList only exposes one public method that is not derived from Component.

Method	Description
Draw	A method that will draw one of the images in the list, identified by an index supplied as parameter into a Graphics object, also specified as a parameter.

The Draw method is overloaded, and it is also possible to include a so called 'raster op code', which specifies how the rendering is to be done. For a detailed description of how drawing works in Windows Forms please refer to Chapter 12, which covers GDI+.

The Images Collection

Images are added using the Image Collection Editor.

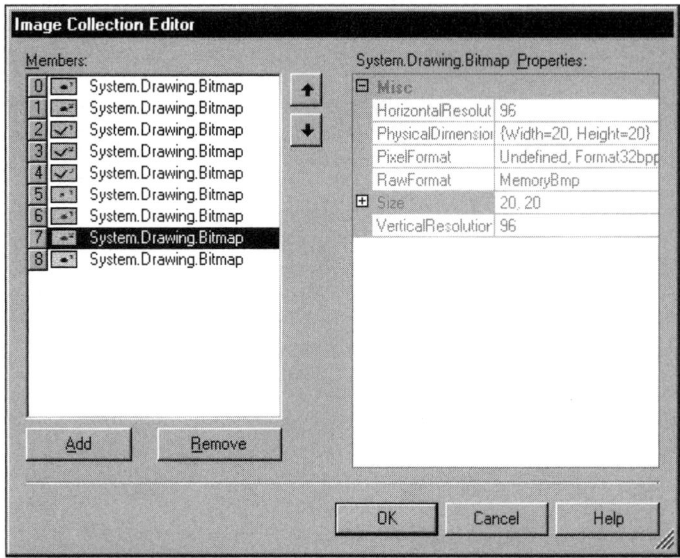

When an image is added, the right side of the editor will show information pertaining to the image, but we can't modify this.

Since images are described in a subsequent chapter covering GDI+, we'll concentrate on the `ImageList` control itself.

Programming with 'ImageList'

To get a flavor for how you can work with `ImageLists` programmatically, we'll show you how to create and initialize a new `ImageList`, and then display one of the images in the list on a Form. The sample code is available in VB and C# in a solution called `TestImageList` located in the vb folder under the chapter directory.

To declare an instance of an `ImageList` in the Form, the code is as follows:

```
Protected aImageList As ImageList = New ImageList()
```

Then you can specify a `Sub` routine (like `InitializeImageList`) to initialize it like this:

```
Sub InitializeImageList()
        Try
            aImageList.Images.Add(New Bitmap("radio1.bmp"))
            aImageList.Images.Add(New Bitmap("radio2.bmp"))
            aImageList.Images.Add(New Bitmap("radio1selected.bmp"))
            aImageList.Images.Add(New Bitmap("radio2selected.bmp"))
        Catch
            MessageBox.Show("Error loading images. Please make sure they are _
            located in the default directory")
        End Try
End Sub
```

This subroutine adds four images to the list. Notice that we have enclosed the calls to `Add` within a `Try Catch` block to catch exceptions if the images cannot be found.

Make sure you insert a call to the `InitializeImageList` subroutine in the forms constructor as follows:

```
Public Sub New()
    MyBase.New()

    ' This call is required by the Windows Form Designer.
    InitializeComponent()
    InitializeImageList()
    ' Add any initialization after the InitializeComponent() call
End Sub
```

Finally, you can create an event handler for the `Paint` method for the form as follows:

```
Private Sub Form1_Paint(ByVal sender As System.Object,_
    ByVal e As System.Windows.Forms.PaintEventArgs) _ Handles MyBase.Paint
        If (aImageList.Images.Count > 0 And SelectedImage >= 0) Then _
            aImageList.Draw(e.Graphics, New Point(10, 10), SelectedImage)
        End If
End Sub
```

This will draw the selected image (between 0 and 3) on the Form at location 10,10 (distance in pixels from the upper left corner). Notice the notation; we use `aImageList.Draw`... to actively draw the image on the supplied Graphics. Alternatively, we would have written:

```
e.Graphics.DrawImage(aImageList.Images(2), 10, 10)
```

The result is the same. In this case the image list only serves as a passive container for storing images, and the `Graphics` object is the one responsible for performing the rendering.

Using an ActiveX Control

While Windows Forms offers a comprehensive set of controls right out of the box, there are times where we may want to add to the collection. Perhaps a marketing person may prefer a slightly un-standard implementation of something to 'differentiate our product'. Perhaps you are already using or have developed controls with special visual representation and functionality.

Fortunately, it is very easy to incorporate and use any of the ActiveX controls that we may already be using. In this section, we'll quickly show how to add an existing ActiveX control to the toolbox. We'll then continue to move it to a form. The control we will add is the `Calendar` control, which comes with Microsoft Office. In 'real life' there's probably little reason why anybody would include this particular control, since Windows Forms supplies a similar `MonthCalendar` control. However, picking an existing control allows us to focus on the task at hand – using an existing ActiveX control rather than building a new one.

Adding an ActiveX Control to the ToolBox

It's probably nice to keep all the ActiveX controls grouped logically in the ToolBox. Let's therefore start by creating a new tab for our controls. Right-click on the ToolBox and choose the Add Tab menu option. This will add a new tab with the cursor placed in the name field. Enter a name for the tab – for example ActiveX controls – and click on the tab to open it.

It's almost equally simple to add the new control. Right-click on the ToolBox and choose the Customize Toolbox menu option. When the Customize Toolbox dialog appears, click the COM Components tab. Then check the control you want to import, in this case the `Calendar` Control.

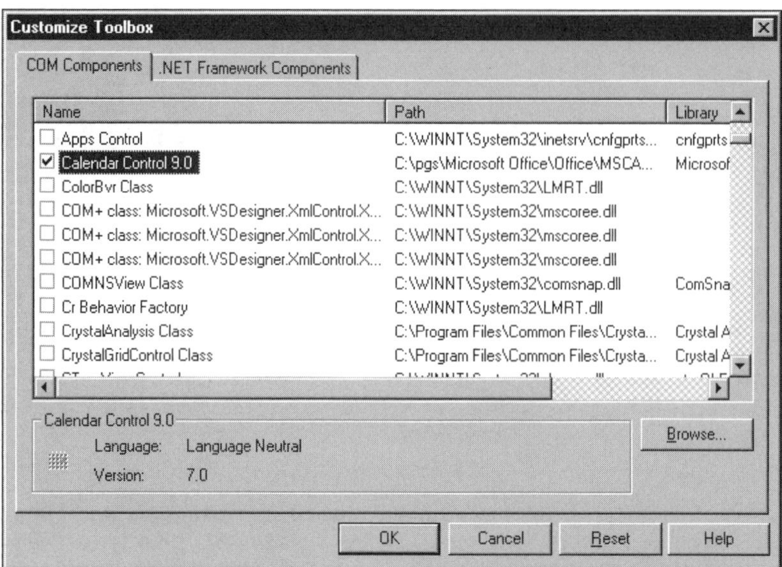

When you press OK, the wizard will automatically generate a .NET wrapper around the ActiveX control. The wrapper simulates an ActiveX container for the control to run in. At the same time, it uses COM interoperability to access the control. There are performance issues with this, since all property and method calls are marshaled between the .NET and the COM environment. It is of course still preferable to the alternative; not being able to reuse ActiveX controls!

Adding the ActiveX Control to the Form

The control is now available on the ToolBox for you to add to the form. In our sample application we have created a new Form (ActiveXForm) and dragged the `Calendar` control onto it. In the following screenshot, we can see the ActiveX control being available on the ToolBox to the left. In the middle we can see the control on the form. We have set the `Dock` property to `Full` so the control fills up the complete form. Finally, we can see the properties that the ActiveX control exposes to the right in the property inspector. From then on we can use it as we would any other control.

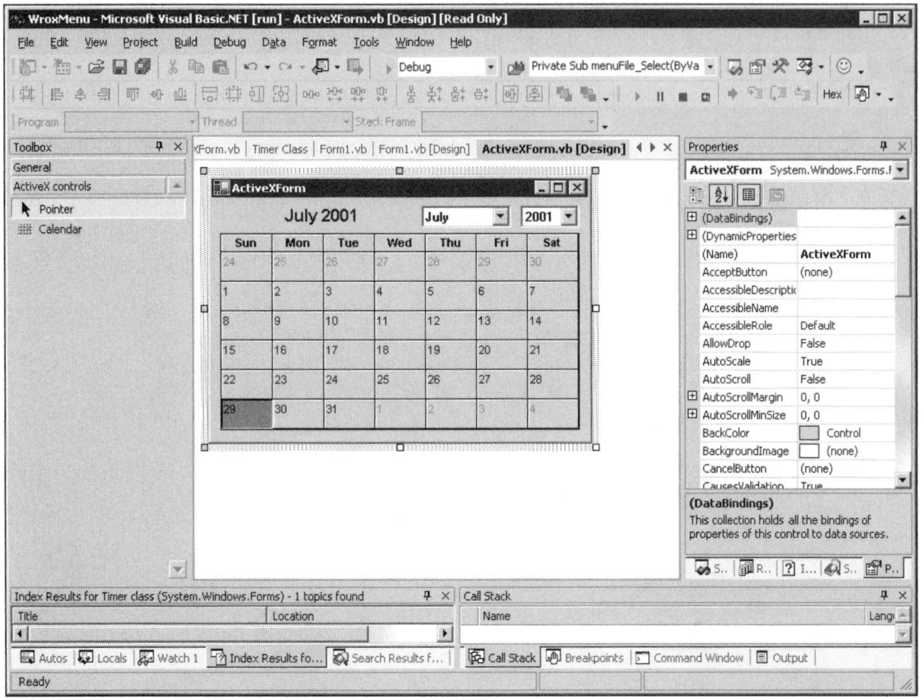

Summary

This chapter has covered the controls needed to create a professional navigation system. We have discussed how to create menus, toolbars and status bars using the IDE. We have also shown how to modify or extend them programmatically in response to user actions.

We have touched on how we can tie these controls together. For example, when a menu is selected (checked), the related toolbar button will also be depressed. Looking back to the good old MFC days, the MFC ClassWizard actually had more built in support for this kind of interaction. However, as we have demonstrated here, it's possible to implement most of what we need with just a few lines of code. And since Windows Forms supports Visual Forms inheritance, we only need to implement this code once; in the base form.

Finally, we looked at how to use existing ActiveX controls. This proved to be very simple, since the IDE does most of the work. It is easy to reuse all of your existing controls, if you cannot find a suitable .NET equivalent. But maybe you should wait a little while before making that decision. There are more controls to come in the next chapter!

System.Object
System.MarshalRefObject
System.ComponentMode.Component
Legend
Concrete Class
Abstract class
CommonDialog
ColorDialog
FileDialog
FontDialog
PageSetupDialog
PrintDialog
ErrorProvider
HelpProvider
ImageList
Menu
ContextMenu
MainMenu
MenuItem
NotifyIcon
System.Windows.Forms
ListViewItem
TreeNode
StatusBarPanel
Timer
ToolBarButton
ToolTip
Control
ButtonBase
Button
CheckBox
RadioButton
DataGrid
DateTimePicker
GroupBox
Label
LinkLabel
ListControl
ComboBox
ListBox
CheckedListBox
ListView
MonthCalendar
PictureBox
PrintReviewControl
ProgressBar
ScrollableControl
ContainerControl
Form
PrintPreviewDialog
ThreadExceptionDialog
PropertyGrid
UpDownBase
DomainUpDown
NumericUpDown
UserControl
Panel
TabPage
ScrollBar
HScrollBar
VScrollBar
Splitter
StatusBar
TabControl
TextBoxBase
RichTextBox
Textbox
ToolBar
TrackBar
TreeView

10

Advanced Controls

This chapter looks at the final fourteen Windows Forms controls. We will look at three of the most complex controls, namely:

- `TreeView`
- `ListView`
- `TabControl`

As well as this, we discuss a control that displays an icon on the Windows System Tray, a control that associates help with controls, a control that associates error information with controls, and a control that allows docked controls on a form to be resized at runtime. They are, respectively:

- `NotifyIcon`
- `HelpProvider`
- `ErrorProvider`
- `Splitter`

Also presented are controls that allow the input of dates and times:

- `DateTimePicker`
- `MonthCalendar`

The remainder of the controls introduced are:

- `CheckedListBox`
- `ProgressBar`
- `DomainUpDown`
- `NumericUpDown`
- `ComboBox`.

A Scheduling Application

Our scheduling application (available in the download) is composed of two separate executables:

- `WroxScheduleClient01`: This Windows Forms C# application creates, deletes, and modifies appointments stored in the schedule application. When appointments are modified, the results are sent to a file containing a persisted version of the appointment data.
- `WroxScheduleSrv`: This VB.NET service runs in the background and informs the user when an appointment must be attended. This service monitors a file used to persist appoints in order to determine when the appointments data store has been changed.

The basic architecture of this dual-executable application is as follows:

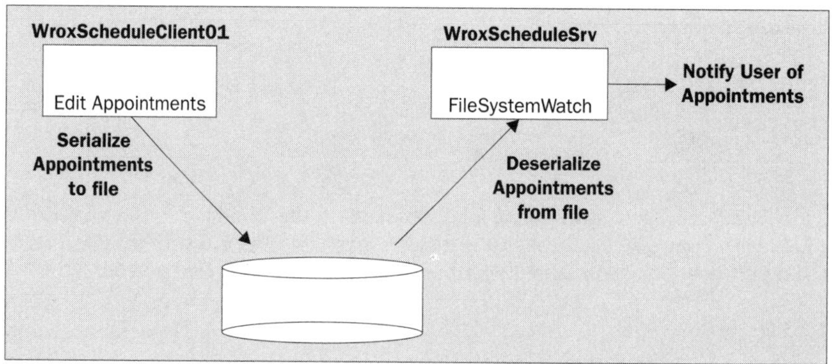

The `WroxScheduleClient01` application manipulates appointments, and at the same time demonstrates a large variety of controls (`DateTimePicker`, `MonthCalendar`, `CheckedListBox`, `ComboBox`, `ListView`, `TreeView`, `TabControl`, `Splitter`, `DomainUpDown`, `NumericUpDown`, `ProgressBar`, `HelpProvider`, and `ErrorProvider`). The serialization of the appointments to a file will not be presented in this section, as it isn't relevant to Windows Forms. This code is included in the downloadable examples.

The `WroxScheduleSrv` application displays an icon on the Windows System Tray. This can be used to manage the service (a Windows service), `WroxScheduleSrv`. Actually, making `WroxScheduleSrv` a service, and having it monitor the persisted store of appointments using `FileSystemWatcher`, is implemented as part of the downloadable example. This code is not reviewed in this section, as it does not contain code specific to Windows Forms development. Although, if you wish to learn more about `FileSystemWatcher`, it is discussed in Chapter 11 on components.

'NotifyIcon'

The NotifyIcon class is derived from the Component base class.

```
Object
    MarshalByRefObject
        Component
            NotifyIcon
```

In Visual Studio.NET's Toolbox, the NotifyIcon component is represented by an icon and can be dragged-and-dropped onto a Form. The NotifyIcon control sits in the component tray, which resides below the Form displayed in Visual Studio.NET. Other classes that are contained in the component tray include OpenFileDialog, PrintDialog, FontDialog, and other non-control components.

To understand what a NotifyIcon is, recall that on most Windows machines, the taskbar runs along the bottom of the screen. The taskbar is what holds, amongst other things, the Start menu. At the opposite end of the taskbar to the Start menu is the Windows System Tray, or Notification Area. This tray contains a set of icons that manage applications running in the background. The Windows Forms class used to place such an icon on the system tray is the NotifyIcon class. An example of the system tray is shown here:

At the right side of the list of icons is an icon represented by a W above an X. This is the icon used to control the server run in conjunction with the scheduling application (executable, WroxScheduleSrv), and this icon is actually just a property, the Icon property, of an instance of type NotifyIcon. This quite stylish icon was added using Visual Studio.NET (File | New | File | Icon File).

Above the W/X icon is the text 'Scheduler Controller Icon'. This tool tip text is displayed when the mouse hovers over the Wrox icon. The origins of this tool tip text are not mysterious. This text is simply the Text property of the NotifyIcon instance. The Text property was assigned the value of the tool tip text displayed in the previous screenshot.

Below is an example from the WroxScheduleSrv application in the Windows Forms Designer that contains an instance of the NotifyIcon class, SchedulerControlNotifyIcon. The NotifyIcon exposes two constructors. One constructor takes no parameters, and the other is as follows, where the parameter to the constructor is of type IContainer:

C#:

```
public NotifyIcon(IContainer container);
```

VB.NET:

```
Public Sub New(ByVal container As IContainer)
```

The following VB.NET snippet from the WroxScheduleSrv project's Windows Forms Designer generated code (method, InitializeComponent), demonstrates this component in action:

```
Me.components = New System.ComponentModel.Container()
Me.SchedulerControlNotifyIcon = _
                New System.Windows.Forms.NotifyIcon(Me.components)
```

The Form contains a collection of components (property, components) of type Container. This property exposes the IContainer interface. When the SchedulerControlNotifyIcon instance of type NotifyIcon is created, the components data member of the Form is passed to the constructor (Me.components). The IContainer interface implemented by the components data member exposes properties and methods relevant to the manipulation of a collection of objects. The property exposed by this interface is Components, which contains the collection of components. The methods exposed are Add (add component to the collection) and Remove (remove component from the collection).

Thus far, the Icon and Text properties of the NotifyIcon class have been presented. The Visible property (type, Boolean) of the NotifyIcon class is set to True to display the icon in the system tray. When Visible is set to False, the icon is not displayed in the system tray. The ContextMenu property is of type ContextMenu. This context menu is displayed when the icon within the system tray is right-mouse-clicked.

The events associated with the NotifyIcon class include Click, DoubleClick, MouseDown, MouseMove, and MouseUp. The NotifyIcon class only exposes methods inherited from the Component base class.

'TabControl' and 'TabPage'

These are derived as follows:

```
Object
    MarshalByRefObject
        Component
            Control
                TabControl
```

```
Object
    MarshalByRefObject
        Component
            Control
                ScrollableControl
                    Panel
                        TabPage
```

An instance of the TabControl class is a bit like a personal organizer – a small book with a set of index tabs along one side. Each tab is represented by an instance of a TabPage class. With respect to the tab control, by default the tabs run along the top of the control, but they can also be aligned to the bottom, left, or right. The tab control contains multiple pages that are selected using a tab. The selected tab is the only page displayed. This page contains controls, and the tabs are a way to categorize the functionality of these controls.

The TabControl class is placed onto a Form using either the tried and true 'drag from the Toolbox' technique, or by double-clicking. An example of a TabControl residing on a Form is shown below, where the TabControl is the rather mundane empty square that takes up the majority of the Form:

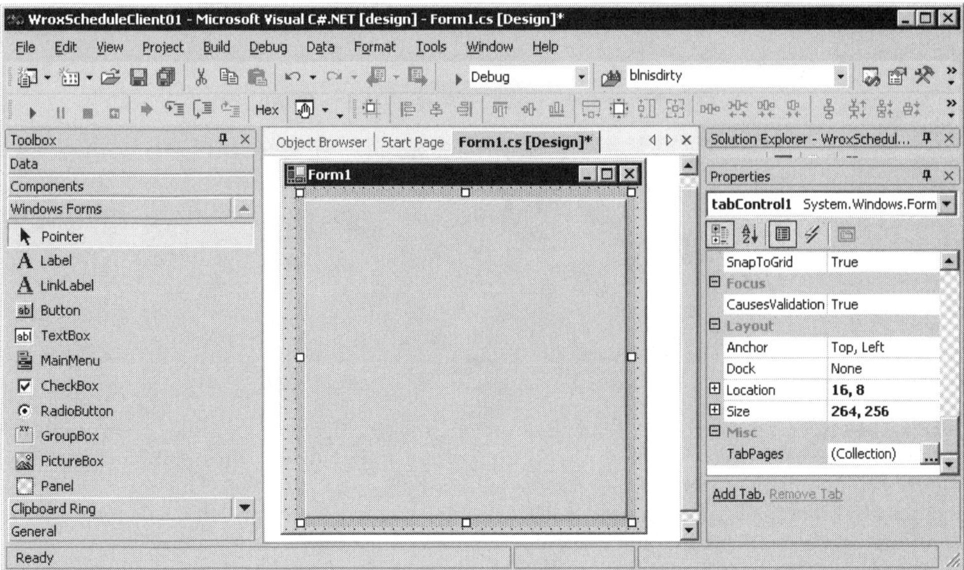

The Properties window on the right side of the screenshot is where the real action takes place. The `TabPages` property is the key that makes the `TabControl` work. This property contains a collection of `TabPage` instances (one instance per panel/page on the `TabControl`). Clicking the left mouse button on the '...' next to the `TabPage`'s value displays the TabPage Collection Editor dialog. This dialog contains an Add button that allows pages to be added to the `TabControl`, and a Remove button to remove pages from the `TabControl`. When there are no `TabPages` on the tab control, the Remove button is grayed out and cannot be selected.

After the Add button has been selected three times, the `TabControl` contains three tabs. The text displayed at the top of each page can be edited (the Text property), as can the name of each TabPage instance (the Name property). The TabPage Collection Editor appears as in the following screenshot, corresponding to the `TabPages` exposed by the `WroxScheduleClient01` application:

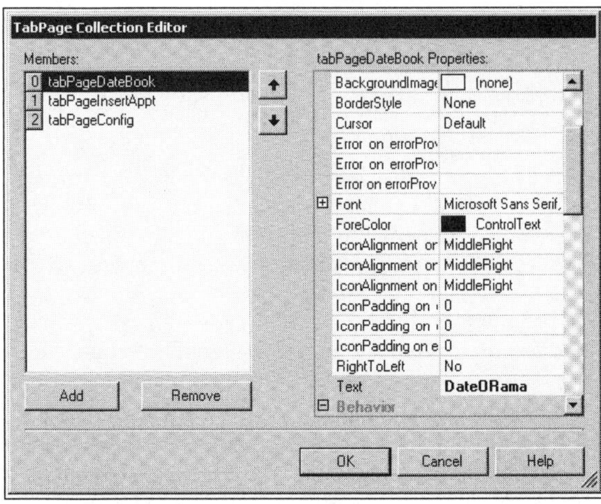

Three instances of the TabPage class have been created, and thus the Windows Forms Designer appears as follows:

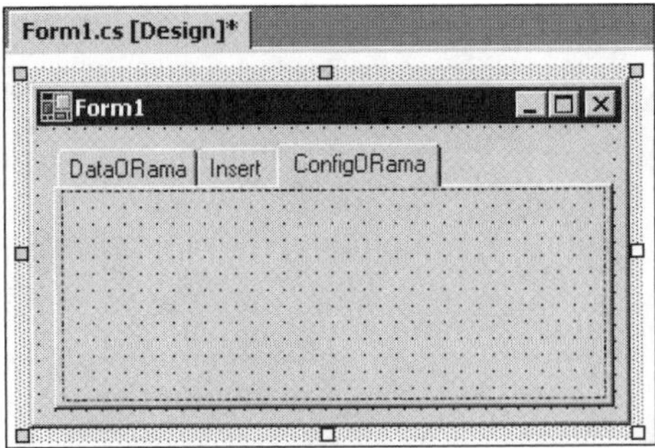

Notice in the screenshot that there are three tabs along the top of the TabControl. Windows Forms controls can now be dragged from the Toolbox and dropped onto the top-most TabPage. A developer can select a particular page on which to drop Windows Forms controls by clicking on the page's tab. When the application is running, a user can select which TabPage is displayed by clicking on the page's tab. At this stage, all the 'programming' required to manage the tab pages for the WroxScheduleClient01 application has been completed. The developer has yet to write a line of actual code.

It is possible to work more intricately with both the TabControl and TabPage classes. The TabPage class exposes a Text property, which contains the text displayed in the TabPage's tab. The ToString method for this class has been overridden to return the value of the Text property when the ToString method is executed. Tool tip text can also be associated with a TabPage via the ToolTipText property. The ImageIndex property allows an image to be associated with the TabPage. The list of images is actually contained in the TabControl that contains said TabPage. The TabControl property, ImageList, contains a list of images that can be associated with TabPages.

Given a control, it is possible to retrieve the TabPage on which the control resides. The GetTabPageOfComponent method provides this functionality. The prototype for this method is as follows:

C#:

```
public static TabPage GetTabPageOfComponent(object comp); // C#
```

VB.NET:

```
Public Shared Function GetTabPageOfComponent(_
      ByVal comp As Object) As TabPage
```

The component is specified as this method's lone parameter. The return value is the TabPage on which the component resides.

The number of TabPages contained on a TabControl is retrievable using the TabControl's TabCount property. The TabPages property (type, TabPageCollection) of the TabControl class contains the list of TabPages associated with the TabControl. The TabPageCollection collection exposes methods and properties including:

Property	Description
`Count`	This property, of type `integer`, specifies the number of pages in the collection.
`IsReadOnly`	This Boolean property returns `True` if the collection is read-only and `False` if the collection can be updated.
`Item`	This property returns a `TabPage` object for the index specified (first parameter, type `integer`). The index is zero based (from zero to `Count-1`).

Method	Description
`Add`	This method takes a single parameter of type `TabPage`. The `TabPage` instance specified by this parameter is added to the collection.
`AddRange`	This method adds a set page to the `TabPage` collection in one fell swoop. The `TabPages` added are specified using a parameter of type `TabPage[]`.
`Clear`	This method removes all `TabPages` from the collection.
`Contains`	This method returns `True` if the `TabPage` passed to it via its first parameter exists in the collection. `False` is returned if the `TabPage` does not reside in the collection.
`IndexOf`	This method returns the index corresponding to where a specific `TabPage` resides in the collection. A `TabPage` instance is passed as the lone parameter to this method and the index corresponding to the `TabPage` is returned. A value of -1 is returned if the `TabPage` specified is not contained in the collection.
`Remove`	This method takes a `TabPage` instance as a parameter and removes this entry from the collection.
`RemoveAt`	This method takes an index instance as a parameter and removes the `TabPage` from the collection that resides at this index location.

Determining which `TabPage` is presently selected (the foremost `TabPage`) is accomplished using the `TabControl`'s `SelectedTab` property (type, `TabPage`). The index of the presently selected `TabPage` can be retrieved using the `TabControl`'s `SelectedIndex` property. The following excerpt from `WroxScheduleClient01` demonstrates a portion of the setup code generated by Visual Studio.NET:

```
// tabControl1 is the TabControl that contains TabPage's
//    0) tabPageDateBook, 1) tabPageInsertAppt, 2) tabPageConfig

tabControl1.Controls.AddRange(new System.Windows.Forms.Control[] {
          tabPageDateBook, tabPageInsertAppt, tabPageConfig});
this.tabControl1.SelectedIndex = 0;    // a.k.a. tabPageDateBook
```

The code demonstrates the `Controls` property's `AddRange` method being called to add three pages to the `TabControl` instance, `tabControl1`. Notice that the `TabPage` currently selected resides at index zero (the first page in the collection).

It should be clear from the code snippet that three TabPages are contained on the TabControl (tabPageDateBook, tabPageInsertAppt, and tabPageConfig). Multiple rows of TabPages can be displayed, provided that the Multiline property (type, Boolean) of TabControl is set to true. The snippet did not set the MultiLine property and hence the default value (False) applies, which means the tab pages are displayed in a single row. The RowCount property of TabControl retrieves and sets the number of rows of TabPages currently displayed. The RowCount property is not relevant to the previous code snippet since MultiLine is set to its default value, False.

The appearance of the TabPages can be fine-tuned using the Appearance property (type, TabAppearance) of the TabControl. This property can be set to show tabs that appear as three-dimensional buttons, flat buttons, or regular tab pages:

The alignment of the tabs is not confined to the top of the TabControl. The Alignment property (type, TabAlign) allows the tab alignment to be specified as Bottom, Left, Right, and Top, which is the default value. The HotTrack property (type, Boolean) is set to True if the appearance of a TabPage changes when the mouse hovers over said TabPage. By default, the appearance change causes a TabPage's text to change from black to blue.

The most drastic method exposed by the TabControl is RemoveAll. This method removes all TabPages from the tab control, essentially purging the TabPages property. The events exposed by the TabControl include SelectedIndexChanged. This event indicates that a different TabPage has been selected. The DrawItem event can also be triggered. This event fires for owner-drawn tabs when it is time to draw such tabs. Owner-drawn controls are beyond the scope of this chapter. Using the OnSelectedIndexChanged method, it is possible to raise a SelectedIndexChanged event, and using the OnDrawItem method it is possible to raise a DrawItem event.

'Splitter'

The Splitter class is derived as follows:

```
Object
    MarshalByRefObject
        Component
            Control
                Splitter
```

The Splitter class supports the resizing of docked controls at runtime. To better understand the previous rather obfuscated sentence, consider the following screenshot:

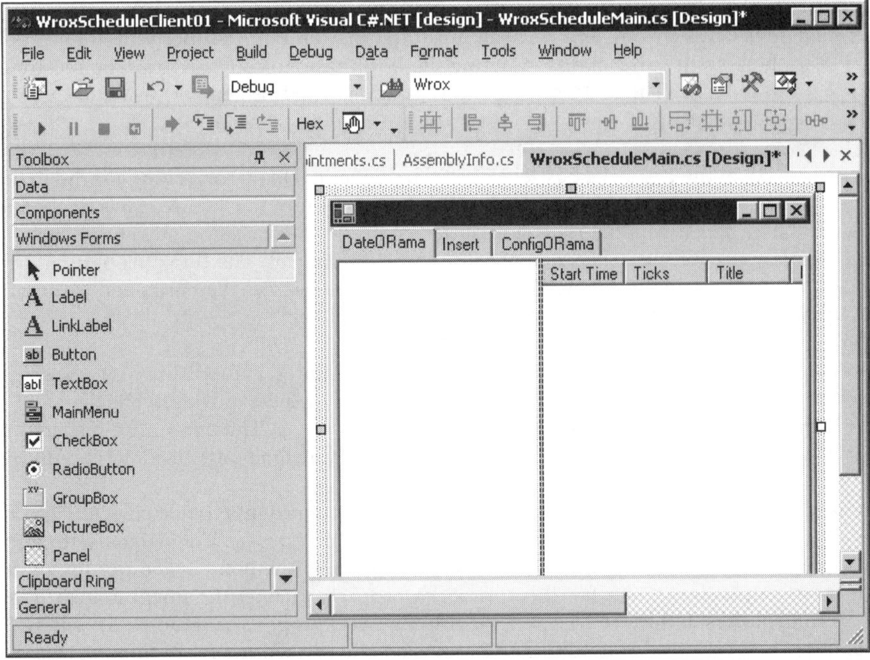

Screenshot shows Visual Studio.NET's Toolbox, which contains an icon for the Splitter. The right side of the screenshot contains the Windows Forms Designer opened for the `WroxScheduleClient01` application. The two empty squares within the Designer window are a `TreeView` control (left-hand square) and a `ListView` control (the right-hand square). A `Splitter`, when dragged from Visual Studio.NET's Toolbox, is placed on a docked **control** (a control whose `Dock` property is not set to `None`.

In the screenshot, there is a double-dotted line between the `TreeView` and `ListView` control. This line is an instance of a `Splitter` class, `splitterTreeFromList`. This class allows the size of the `TreeView` and `ListView` to be changed at runtime. By left-clicking on the Splitter and dragging it towards the right, the `TreeView` gets larger while the `ListView` gets smaller. The `Splitter` can also be dragged to the left (`ListView` gets larger at the expense of the `TreeView`).

In order to support the `Splitter`, a bit of configuration needs to be performed on the `TreeView` and the `ListView` controls. The `Dock` property of the `TreeView` is set to `Left`, indicating that this control is docked to the left side of the `Form`. Visual Studio.NET's Properties window displays the following when the `Dock` property is changed for `TreeView`:

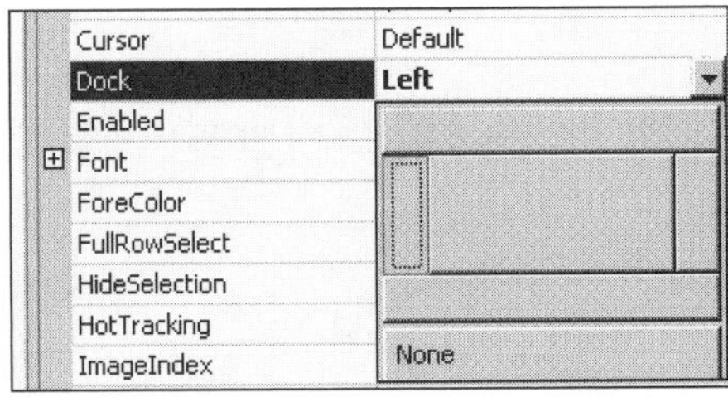

Each rectangle in the screenshot corresponds to a specific Dock setting of type DockStyle. The very bottom rectangle is labeled None and corresponds to setting the Dock property to None. The second rectangle from the bottom corresponds to setting the Dock property to Bottom. The rectangle in the middle sets Dock to Fill. The Fill setting is discussed later in this chapter, when the settings for the ListView are presented.

The Dock property of the Splitter is set to Left by default. This Dock setting for the Splitter instance – splitterTreeFromList – is set to this value because the TreeView is docked left. The Splitter instance appears on the right side of the TreeView because the Splitter is designed to grow and shrink along the undocked side of the TreeView control. The Dock property of the ListView is set to Fill. As the TreeView grows and shrinks across the horizontal plane of the Form, the ListView will grow and shrink to fill in the Form completely.

The events associated with the Splitter class are SplitterMoved and SplitterMoving. The SplitterMoved event is triggered once the Splitter has completed moving, while the SplitterMoving event is triggered when the Splitter is moving. The OnSplitterMoved method raises a SplitterMoved event, and the OnSplitterMoving method raises the SplitterMoving event.

The BorderStyle property of the Splitter control is a property of type BorderStyle. This property can be set to Fixed3D, FixedSingle, and None (no border). The default setting for BorderStyle is None. The MinExtra property sets the size of the non-docked portion of the splitter area. For the example shown thus far, the MinExtra property dictates the smallest horizontal size of the ListView control. Recall that the ListView control's Dock property is set to Fill, where fill corresponds to the extra needed to fill in the Form. The MinSize property of the Splitter specifies the minimum size of the docked control managed by the Splitter. For the example shown thus far, the TreeView control is docked left. This control can be shrunk to a minimum horizontal size as specified by the MinSize property of the Splitter.

The Splitter's Cursor property is inherited from the Control base class. For the example presented thus far, Splitter is docked left. For this reason, the Cursor property is set to VSplit (see below where VSplit corresponds to vertical split). If the Splitter has been docked right, the cursor also would have been set to VSplit. If the Splitter were docked as Top or Bottom then the Cursor property would be set to HSplit (where HSplit corresponds to horizontal split). Examples of the HSplit and VSplit cursors are as follows:

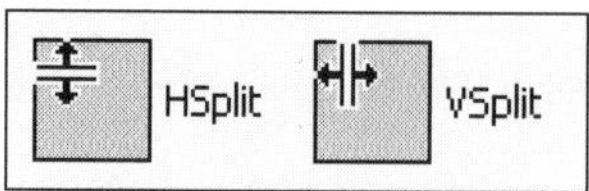

So far, there is still no user-written code associated with the WroxScheduleClient01 application. All code pertinent to the Splitter is generated by Visual Studio.NET's Windows Forms Designer.

'MonthCalendar'

The MonthCalendar class is a control that displays a calendar and allows a specific date to be selected. It is derived as follows:

```
Object
    MarshalByRefObject
        Component
            Control
                MonthCalendar
```

This class is derived directly from the `Control` class. An example of the `MonthControl` is as follows:

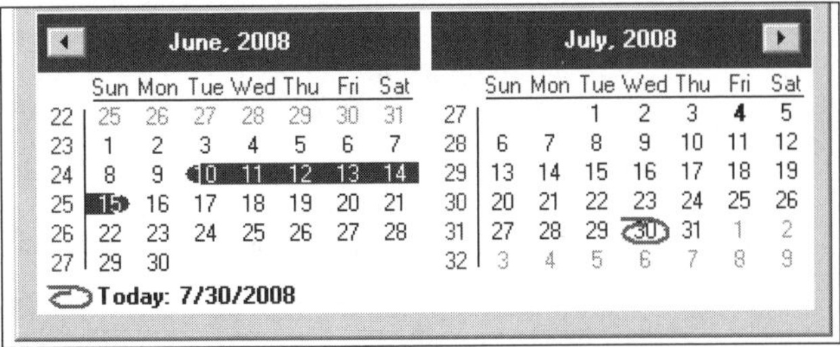

Various properties of the `MonthCalendar` class are as follows:

Property	Description
`AnnuallyBoldedDates`	This property contains an array of `DateTime` structures. Each date in this collection will be displayed as bold face in the monthly calendar. These dates are recurring, meaning that they will bolded from year to year (birthdays, holidays, etc.). In the screenshot above of a `MonthCalendar`, the date July 4, 2008 was marked using boldface. This boldface is because this date is specified as a member of the `AnnuallyBoldedDates` property's `DateTime` collection. Dates recurring on a monthly basis are contained in the `MonthlyBoldedDates` (type, `DateTime []`). Non-recurring dates are contained in the `BoldedDates` property (also of type `DateTime []`.
`CalendarDimensions`	Allows multiple months within the same year to be displayed at one time. The `Width` data member of the `Size` structure represents the number of months displayed in the X-dimension and the `Height` data member of the `Size` structure represents the number of months displayed in the Y-dimensions. All months displayed are within the same year. Twelve months in a year means that `Height` multiplied by `Width` must be less than or equal to twelve.
`DefaultSize`	This property specifies the size in pixels (height and width) of the calendar. This size includes the text at the bottom of this control where the current date is displayed. The size of a single month displayed within the `MonthCalendar` is specified using the `SingleMonthSize` property.
`FirstDayOfWeek`	This property specifies the first day of the week displayed in the calendar. This property can be set to any day of the week (`Sunday`, `Monday`, etc.) or `Default`. Most Western cultures use Sunday as the first day of the week.
`MaxDate`	This property specifies the upper bound on the date displayed by the control. The default values for this property are January 1, 1753 (minimum) and December 31, 9998 (maximum).

Table continued on following page

Property	Description
`MaxSelectionCount`	This property specifies the maximum number of days that can be selected in the control. The default value for this parameter is seven, meaning a span of an entire week can be selected at once.
`MinDate`	This property specifies the lower bound on the data displayed by the control. The default values for this property are January 1, 1753 (minimum) and December 31, 9998 (maximum).
`ScrollChange`	This property of the `MonthCalendar` control specifies the number of months incremented each time the scroll-forward button is clicked (the right arrow) or decremented each time the scroll-backward button is clicked (the left arrow). Setting this value to less than zero or greater than 20,000 generates an exception of type `ArgumentException`.
`SelectionEnd`	This property (type, `DateTime`) retrieves the last date of the selected range.
`SelectionRange`	This property shows the selected dates. In the screenshot of the `MonthCalendar` control, June 10 through June 15 is selected.
`SelectionStart`	This property (type, `DateTime`) retrieves the first date of the selected range.
`ShowTodayCircle`	This property of the `MonthControl` is set to `True` in the previous screenshot, so the current date (July 30, 2008) is circled. Specifying `false` for this property causes the circling line not to be displayed for the current date. This circling line would also not be displayed in the text at the bottom of the control. Even when the `ShowTodayCircle` property is set to `false`, the current date is displayed at the bottom of the control; it is just not circled.
`ShowWeekNumbers`	When this property is set to `True`, the week numbers are displayed alongside each month, as in the previous screenshot. Setting this property to `False` would cause these numbers not to be displayed.
`TitleBackColor`	Sets the background color of the month's title.
`TitleForeColor`	Sets the foreground color of the month's title.
`TodayDate`	This property specifies the current date of the `MonthCalendar` control. The `TodayDateSet` property returns `True` if the user has set today's date explicitly.
`TrailingForColor`	This property sets the color of trailing days – days displayed in months other than the month currently in focus (for example, if the month shown is June, May 25 through May 31 were displayed as trailing days).

The `MonthCalendar` class exposes methods for managing the various flavors of dates displayed in boldface:

- `AddAnnuallyBoldedDate`

- AddBoldedDate
- RemoveAllAnnuallyBoldedDates
- RemoveAllBoldedDates
- RemoveAnnuallyBoldedDate
- RemoveMonthlyBoldedDate
- UpdatedBoldedDates

When the MonthCalendar control is displayed in the WroxScheduleClient01 application, all current appointments for the application are represented as bolded dates. These dates are set for each appointment using AddBoldedDate, and removed when an appointment is deleted using RemoveBoldedDate. For example, when the current appointments are loaded, the instance of the MonthCalendar, monthCalendarAppt, is updated as using the collection of appointments contained as a data member of the Form. This data member, appointments, is of type WroxAppointments. The code that traverses the appointments collection and updates monthCalendarAppt, using AddBoldedDate, is as follows:

```
// WroxAppointments appointments data member already set up in
// WroxSetupTreeView() so we can traverse the existing appoints
// in the application

WroxAppointment appt;

// foreach was failing in an early version of .NET so just use
// a counter and GetByIndex

for (int count = 0; count < appointments.Count; count++)
{
   DateTime traverseDate;

   appt = (WroxAppointment)appointments.GetByIndex(count);
   for (traverseDate = appt.StartDate;
        traverseDate < appt.EndDate;
       )
   {
      monthCalendarAppt.AddBoldedDate(traverseDate);
      traverseDate = traverseDate.AddDays(1);
   }
}
```

Some other methods include:

Method	Description
GetDisplayRange	This method retrieves the range of dates displayed by the control, and has a return type of SelectionRange.
HitTest	Takes a position as input (either a Point structure or two integers corresponding to X and Y) and returns information with respect to what location on the calendar was 'clicked'. This method allows a developer to determine the type of region on the MonthCalendar where the mouse was clicked (on a next month button, on a date, on a day of the week, etc.). The return value of the HitTest method is a nested class found within MonthCalendar, the HitTestInfo class. The Time property of HitTestInfo specifies the date within the calendar that was hit. The HitArea data member of the HitTestInfo class is an enumeration (type, MonthCalendar.HitArea) that specifies the precise location on the MonthCalendar where the mouse was clicked, for instance CalendarBackground, Date, DayOfWeek, NextMonthButton, etc.
SetCalendarDimenions	Sets the dimensions of the calendar in pixels (X and Y coordinates).
SetDate	This method sets the current date of the MonthCalendar class. This method takes one parameter, of type DateTime. This parameter corresponds to the current date to be set.
SetSelectionRange	Specifies the range of dates selected. This method takes, as input, a start time (type, DateTime) and end time (type, DateTime).

The MonthCalendar class exposes methods that fire off events. These methods include:

- OnDateChanged: Event fired when the present date changes.
- OnDateSelected: Event fired when the selected range of dates changes.

The data received by a method handling either the DateChanged and DateSelected events includes a parameter of type DateRangeEventHandler class. The DateRangeEventHandler class exposes the following properties:

- Start: This property (type, DateTime) corresponds to the start time of the action that triggered the event.
- End: This property (type, DateTime) corresponds to the end time of the action that triggered the event.

Within the WroxScheduleClient01 application, the TabPage instance labeled Insert contains an instance of the MonthCalendar. This is used to specify the date of the appointment created. The entire TabPage labeled Insert (including the MonthCalendar instance) is as follows:

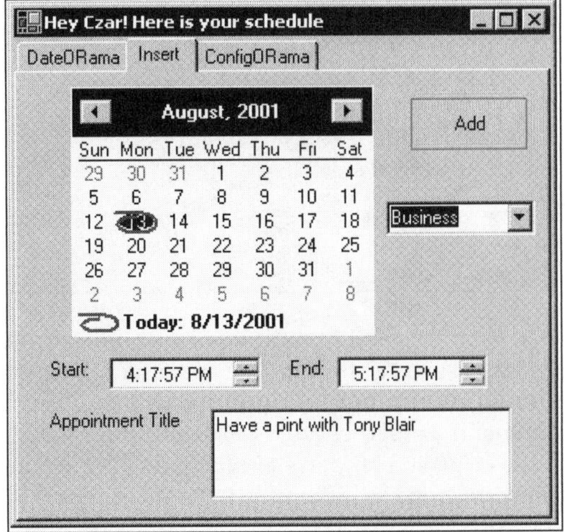

The rectangular region in the screenshot, labeled Add, is simply a Button. The non-standard representation is because the `FlatStyle` property of the `Button` is set to `Popup`.

'DateTimePicker'

The `DateTimePicker` class allows a date and/or time to be selected. This `DateTimePicker` is derived directly from the `Control` class.

```
Object
    MarshalByRefObject
        Component
            Control
                DateTimePicker
```

The physical appearance of this control is quite malleable. Two specific visual flavors of this control are as follows:

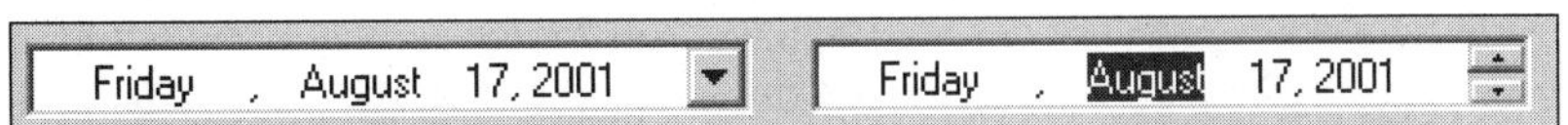

The `DateTimePicker` on the left is displayed with the `ShowUpDown` property set to `False`. The `DateTimePicker` on the right is displayed with the `ShowUpDown` property set to `True`. There is a significant difference in how these instances behave. The instance on the right contains up/down arrows. Notice that in the right instance of the `DateTimePicker`, the month August is highlighted. The up/down arrows are used to change the value of the highlighted item (month, day or year). The left instance of the `DateTimePicker`, when selected (left mouse click), displays the month associated with the presently displayed date. An example of this is as follows:

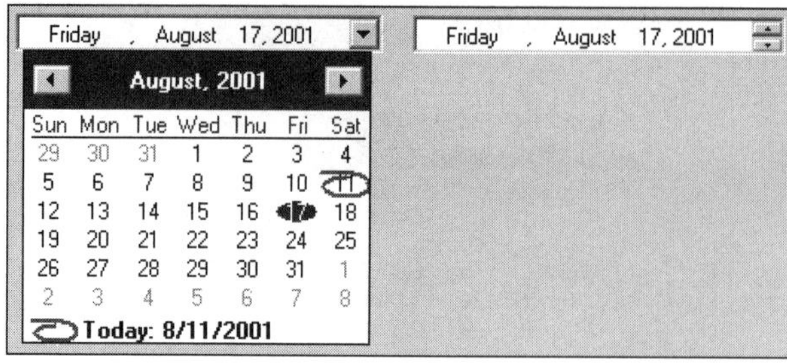

In screenshot, the highlighted date (August 17, 2001) and current date (August 11, 2001) are just like their counterparts in the MonthCalendar control. The appearance of the DateTimePicker displays a MonthCalendar class, provided the ShowUpDown property is set to True. For this reason, the DateTimePicker control contains properties also associated with the MonthControl class. Both these classes contain a MaxDate and MinDate property of type, DateTime. The properties exposed by the DateTimePicker class that correspond to differently named properties in MonthControl include:

Property	Description
CalendarFont	Specifies the font used when displaying the calendar's dates.
CalendarForeColor	The colors of the DateTimePicker's calendar are specified using this property and the CalendarMonthBackground property.
CalendarTitleBackColor	Corresponds to the MonthCalendar's TitleBackColor property.
CalendarTitleForeColor	Corresponds to the MonthCalendar's TitleForeColor property.
CalendarTrailingForeColor	Corresponds to the MonthCalendar's TrailingForeColor property.

Readers should recall from a previous screenshot that there were two DateTimePicker instances associated with the WroxScheduleClient01 application's Insert TabPage. These DateTimePicker instances (dateTimePickerApptStart and dateTimePickerApptEnd) are displayed as follows:

Based on the previous screenshot, it should be clear why this class is called the DateTimePicker and not the OnlyADatePicker. That's right! It can be used to select times as well as dates. The key to this epic mystery is the Format property. The Format property is of type DateTimePickerFormat enumeration. The permissible values for this enumeration are Long, Short, Time, and Custom. The previous two instances of DateTimePicker had their Format property set to Time. The code in the WroxScheduleClient01 application that specifies this is generated by the Visual Studio.NET Designer and is as follows:

```
dateTimePickerApptEnd.Format = System.Windows.Forms.DateTimePickerFormat.Time;
dateTimePickerApptStart.Format = System.Windows.Forms.DateTimePickerFormat.Time;
```

For the `Format` property, the difference between `Short` (see left `DateTimePicker`) and `Long` (see right `DateTimePicker`) is as follows:

When the `Format` property is set to `Custom`, the `CustomFormat` property must be set. To give an idea as to how the `CustomFormat` string is specified, consider the following custom format settings that specify how a day is displayed:

- d: A single `d` in the `CustomFormat` string displays day as a one or two-digit number.
- dd: This `CustomFormat` string displays the day as a two-digit number. Single digit days (1 though 9) have the digit prefixed by zero (01 through 09).
- ddd: The day of the date is displayed as a three-character corresponding to the day name (Sun, Mon, etc.).
- dddd: Displays the name of day in full (Sunday, Monday, etc.).

An example of a `DateTimePicker` instance where `Format` is set to `Custom` and `CustomFormat` is set to `'d dd ddd dddd'` is as follows:

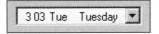

The previous example is a bit contrived, but serves to demonstrate these formats. Custom format settings are also available for displaying hours, minutes, seconds, months, and years, and can even address how AM and PM are displayed.

The `DropDownAlign` property (type, `LeftRightAlignment`) specifies how the drop down calendar will be aligned. The permissible values for the `DropDownAlign` property are `Left` and `Right`. The latter setting means that the behavior is inherited. The differences between `Left` (see the left `DateTimePicker` below) and `Right` (see the right `DateTimePicker` below) are best demonstrated visually, and are as follows:

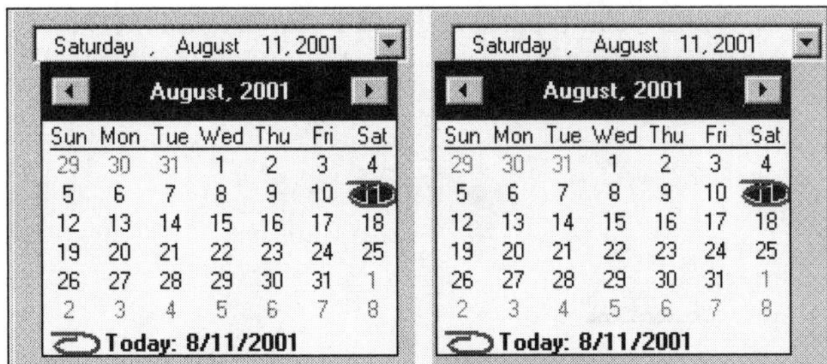

Other properties that influence the DateTimePicker's appearance include PreferredHeight and ShowCheckBox. The PreferredHeight property (type, integer) is a read-only property that specifies the preferred height of the control in pixels. When the ShowCheckBox property is set to True, the date displayed contains a check box. The default value for this property is False, which corresponds to no check box being displayed. A DateTimePicker with Format set to Time and ShowCheckBox set to True is as follows:

The specific date/time displayed by the DateTimePicker can be retrieved and set using the Value property (type, DateTime). The text version of the date/time can be set and retrieved using the Text property. When the Checked property is True, the value of the DateTimePicker (the Value property) has been set and it is possible to update this value. Correspondingly the CheckBox displayed will contain a check. When this property is False, the Value property cannot be updated and the CheckBox will not contain a check.

The DateTimePicker exposes a variety of read-only fields that are static in C# terminology, or Shared in VB.NET terminology. These fields retrieve certain default values for all DateTimePicker instances for an application. The fields exposed by the DateTimePicker are self-explanatory, in that they all correspond to non-static properties previously reviewed: DefaultMonthBackColor, DefaultTitleBackColor, DefaultTitleForeColor, DefaultTrailingForeColor, MaxDateTime, and MinDateTime.

The CloseUp event is raised when the calendar is dismissed or disappears. This event is only pertinent if the ShowUpDown property is set to False. The OnCloseUp method allows the CloseUp event to be triggered programmatically. The month has to be displayed before CloseUp can be raised. When the month is displayed, the DropDown event is triggered. The OnDropDown method can trigger this event using programmatic intervention. Again, the ShowUpDown property must be set to True in order for DropDown to be raised. When the format changes (property, Format) the DateTimePicker's FormatChanged event is raised. The OnFormatChanged method also causes this event to be triggered. When the value (property, Value) of the DateTimePicker is changed, the ValueChanged event is raised. A program can use the OnValueChanged method to raise the ValueChanged event.

'ComboBox'

The ComboBox sounds like a style of Latin dance, but in reality it is a control that displays a textbox for editing in conjunction with a listbox of permissible values. The ComboBox, like the ListBox, is derived directly from the ListControl class. It is represented by an icon on the ToolBox, and can be deposited on a Form via drag-and-drop.

```
Object
    MarshalByRefObject
        Component
            Control
                ListControl
                    Combobox
```

The items in the drop down list of the ComboBox are contained in the Items property (type, ComboBox.ObjectCollections). Items can be added to this collection programmatically. At design time, a developer can add items to the collection by selecting the Items property for the ComboBox from Visual Studio.NET's **Properties** window. This action displays the **String Collection Editor** dialog. This dialog is a great way to add items to the drop-down list associated with the ComboBox. The **String Collection Editor** dialog for the WroxScheduleClient01 application's ComboBox, comboBoxReason, is as follows:

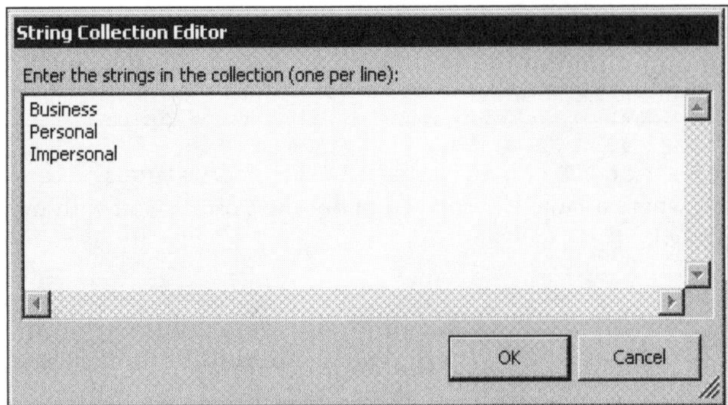

The screenshot contains the reasons for scheduling an appointment in the oft-discussed scheduling application. When displayed, the comboBoxReason instance appears in the form displayed on the left in the following illustration (the drop-down list is not displayed by default), and when the drop down list is selected it appears as the form on the right (drop-down list displayed):

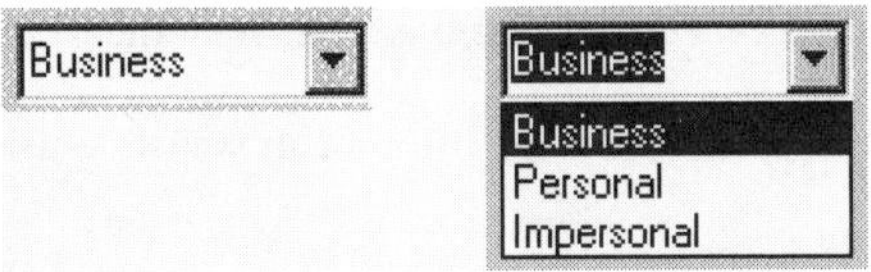

Some of the properties of ComboBox include:

Property	Description
Focused	This property returns True if the ComboBox is the control currently in focus.
SelectedIndex	This property retrieves the index of the selected item within the list. When the selected item is specified, the Text property is updated to reflect the selected item.
SelectedText	This property contains the selected text from within an editable portion of the ComboBox. A portion of the text in the editable region (Text property) of the ComboBox can be selected, or all the text in the editable region can be selected.
SelectionLength	This property specifies the length of the selected region within the Text property.

Table continued on following page

Property	Description
SelectionStart	This property specifies where in the Text property the selected text begins, if only a portion has been selected.
SelectItem	This property retrieves the SelectedItem within the list.
Sorted	This property specifies if the list of items is sorted (true) or not (false).
Text	This property contains the text in the editable portion of the ComboBox.

An example of Text, SelectedText, SelectionStart, and SelectionLength in action is shown in the next screenshot, where a label is displayed under the ComboxBox with the values for each of these properties displayed:

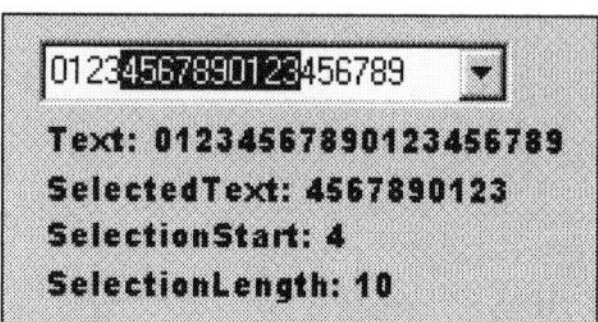

The size and appearance of the ComboBox can be fine-tuned using properties such as DrawMode, DropDownWidth, IntegralHeight, ItemHeight, MaxDropDownItems, MaxLength, and PreferredHeight. The style of the ComboBox's drop-down list is specified using the DropDownStyle property (type, ComboxBoxStyle). The permissible styles include:

- The text portion can be edited, and the list portion is visible using arrow keys up/down (style, Simple).
- The text portion is editable, but an arrow button must be used to make the list portion viewable (style, DropDown).
- The text portion cannot be edited, and the user must select an arrow button to make the list portion viewable (style, DropDownList).

The Items property is a collection and exposes properties such as Count and methods such as Add, AddRange, Clear, Insert, and Remove. The AddRange method is used by the Windows Forms Designer to add the developer-specified items to the ComboBox as follows:

```
this.comboBoxReason.Items.AddRange(new object[] {
                    "Business", "Personal", "Impersonal"});
```

More ComboBox methods are as follows:

Method	Description
AddItemsCore	This method allows multiple items to be added to the ComboBox.
BeginUpdate	This method disables all screen updates for the ComboBox control and should be called before multiple additions are made to a ComboBox.

Method	Description
EndUpdate	This method should be called to re-enable screen updates for the ComboBox once the contents of the ComboBox have been updated. BeginUpdate and EndUpdate in tandem reduce flicker when a large number of update, are made to a ComboBox.
FindString	This method finds strings in the ComboBox.
FindStringExact	This method finds exact matches for strings in the ComboBox. The ListBox class also exposes these variations of the find method. FindString and FindStringExact were reviewed in detail in the chapter where the ListBox was introduced.
Select	Selects a range of items within the ComboBox.
SelectAll	Selects all items within the ComboBox.

The most common used events exposed by the ComboBox include:

Event	Description
DropDown	This event is raised when the drop-down list of the ComboBox is displayed.
SelectedIndexChanged	This event is raised when the index of a selected item changes.
SelectionChangedCommitted	This event is raised when the selected item is modified and this change is reflected in the ComboBox.

'CheckedListBox'

The CheckedListBox control displays a listbox where each item in the listbox is prefixed by a checkbox. It doesn't take a psychic to predict that the class, CheckedListBox, is derived directly from the ListBox class.

```
Object
    MarshalByRefObject
        Component
            Control
                ListControl
                    ListBox
                        CheckedListBox
```

An example of a CheckedListBox control is found on the ConfigORama TabPage of the WroxScheduleClient01 application. The purpose of this CheckedListBox is described by a Label, whose Text property is set to Select default appointment:. This instance of CheckedListBox that specifies the default text associated with an appointment is as follows:

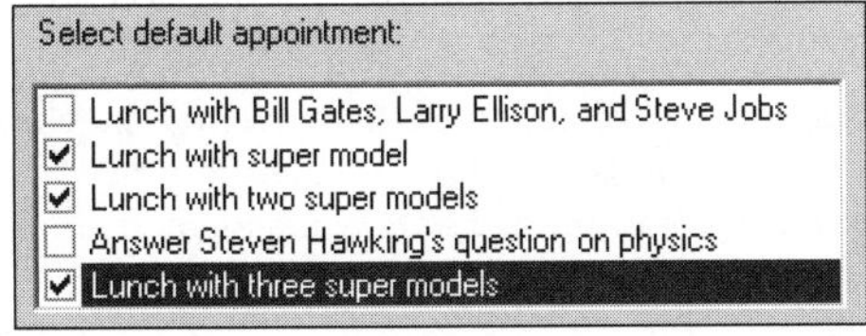

The CheckedListBox class exposes a collection of the items displayed with Items property. This property is of type, CheckedListBox.ObjectCollection. The ObjectCollection property is a collection of objects. Every .NET object implements a ToString method, which is why, regardless of object type, the item can be displayed in the CheckedListBox instance. Even though Items exposes a collection of objects, this collection can be traversed as if it were a collection of strings. To demonstrate this consider the following example where CheckedListBox instance clb is traversed:

C#:

```
foreach (string str in clb.Items) {}
```

VB.NET:

```
Dim str As String
For Each str In clb.Items
Next
```

Each item displayed in the CheckedListBox can be selected, but this does not mean that the item's check box is checked. By default, the check box associated with each item must be clicked.

Some of the properties of CheckedListBox include:

Property	Description
CheckOnClick	This property, when set to True, causes the check box corresponding to each item clicked on to be toggled (checked if clear, and cleared if checked) if the item itself is clicked on. The default value for this property is False, which means that the check box must be manually checked.
SelectionMode	This property controls how many items within the CheckedListBox can be selected. The permissible, self-documenting values for this property include None and One. The SelectionMode enumeration includes values for specifying multiple selections – MultiSimple and MultiExtended. It is not permissible to select multiple values with a CheckedListBox, so specifying MultiSimple or MultiExtended for the SelectionMode property results in an ArgumentException exception being raised. The selected value is only the item highlighted. It is possible to have multiple items with checked check boxes, even though One item can be selected. Even though the SelectMode is One, multiple check boxes can be set. If None is specified for a SelectionMode then no check boxes can be checked.
ThreeDCheckBoxes	This property should be set to True (default value) if three-dimensional check boxes are to be displayed by the CheckedListBox control. If this property is set to False then two-dimensional check boxes are displayed.

The CheckedListBox class exposes a collection of the currently checked indices through the CheckedIndices property. This property is of type CheckedIndexCollection. This collection could be traversed as follows, for the CheckedListBox instance, clb:

C#:

```
foreach (int index in clb.CheckedIndices) {}
```

VB.NET:

```
Dim index As Integer
For Each index In clb.CheckedIndices
Next
```

The CheckedListBox class also exposes a collection of the currently checked items through the CheckedItems property. This property is of type CheckedItemCollection. The items in the collections CheckedIndexCollection and CheckedItemCollection correspond to values within the CheckedListBox that are of either a CheckState of Checked or Indeterminate.

Two properties inherited by CheckedListBox from ListBox are of particular interest: Sorted and HorizontalScrollbar. These properties were documented in the section discussing the ListBox, but through the magic of inheritance they are available to the CheckedListBox.

Determining if a particular CheckedListBox item is checked within the collection exposed by the Items property is handled by the GetItemChecked method. The concept is simple: provide an index as a parameter (type, integer) and return a Boolean as True if the item is checked and False if not checked. The SetItemChecked method causes an item displayed at an index within the Items collection to be checked or unchecked. An integer parameter specifies the index and a Boolean parameter specifies checked (True) or unchecked (False). In C# and VB.NET the prototypes for GetItemChecked and SetItemChecked are as follows:

C#:

```
public bool GetItemChecked(int index);
```

```
public void SetItemChecked(int index, bool value);
```

VB.NET:

```
Public Function GetItemChecked(ByVal index As Integer) As Boolean
```

```
Public Sub SetItemChecked(ByVal index As Integer, _
                          ByVal value As Boolean)
```

The specific check state of an item in the Items property can be get and set using the methods GetItemCheckState and SetItemCheckState respectively. Each of these items takes an index as a parameter (type, integer). The GetItemCheckState method returns a value of type CheckState (permissible values Checked, Unchecked, and Indeterminate). The SetItemCheckState method takes a second parameter of type CheckState and uses the value of this parameter to specify the check state of the item found and the index specified. The prototypes for these methods are as follows:

C#:

```
public CheckState GetItemCheckState (int index);
```

```
public void SetItemCheckState(int index, CheckState value);
```

VB.NET:

```
Public Function GetItemCheckState(ByVal index As Integer) As CheckState
```

```
Public Sub SetItemCheckState(ByVal index As Integer, ByVal value As CheckState)
```

The CheckedListBox directly exposes the ItemCheck event. This event is fired when the state of a check box within the CheckedListBox is to be changed, before the state of the check box changes. The prototype in C# and VB.NET for this event's handler is as follows:

C#:

```
private void clb_ItemCheck(object sender, ItemCheckEventArgs e)
```

VB.NET:

```
Private Sub clb_ItemCheck(ByVal sender As System.Object, _
            ByVal e As ItemCheckEventArgs) Handles clb.ItemCheck
```

The second parameter for this method, of type ItemCheckEventArgs, identifies what action took place. The properties of this class are Index, indicating which item's check state is changed, CurrentValue (type, CheckState), the current value of the item's check state, and NewValue (type, CheckState), the value of the check state that the item is changing to. It is important to recognize that the values contained in the CheckedListBox CheckedIndices property represent the checked items at the time of ItemCheck event and not the items after the ItemCheck event has been processed. This subtly caused a bug in an early version of the WroxScheduleClient01 application. To understand this behavior, consider the following change in state that triggers an ItemCheck event:

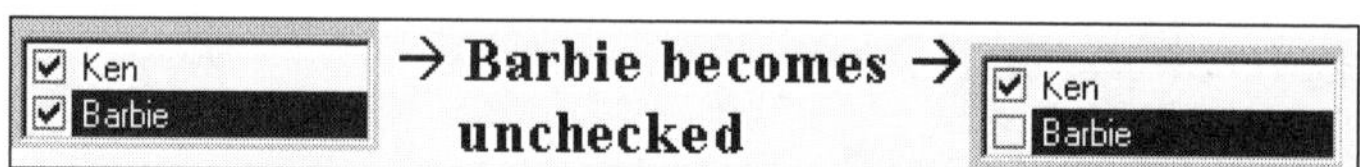

When the method for handling the ItemCheck event is fired, the state of the major players is as follows:

- CheckedListBox's CheckedIndices property: Contains values for 0 (Ken checked) and 1 (Barbie checked). This is the state before the ItemCheck was handled.
- Parameter ItemCheckEventArgs's Index property: 1, indicating Barbie's value has changed.
- Parameter ItemCheckEventArgs's CurrentValue property: Set to Checked since Barbie was checked before ItemCheck was triggered.
- Parameter ItemCheckEventArgs's NewValue property: Set to Unchecked since Barbie will become unchecked after the ItemCheck event is handled.

'CheckedListBox' in the 'WroxScheduleClient01' Application

The `WroxScheduleClient01` application used a data member, `checkedListBoxDefaultTitle`, of type `CheckedListBox`. Each value in this `CheckedListBox` instance is concatenated to create the title associated with an appointment. Recall that in a previous screenshot the items in the `CheckedListBox` instance were checked as follows:

Select default appointment:

☐ Lunch with Bill Gates, Larry Ellison, and Steve Jobs
☑ Lunch with super model
☑ Lunch with two super models
☐ Answer Steven Hawking's question on physics
☑ Lunch with three super models

Concatenating the three entries in the default appointments `ComboBox` would create the following default appointment title when the Insert `TabPage` of the `WroxScheduleClient01` application is selected:

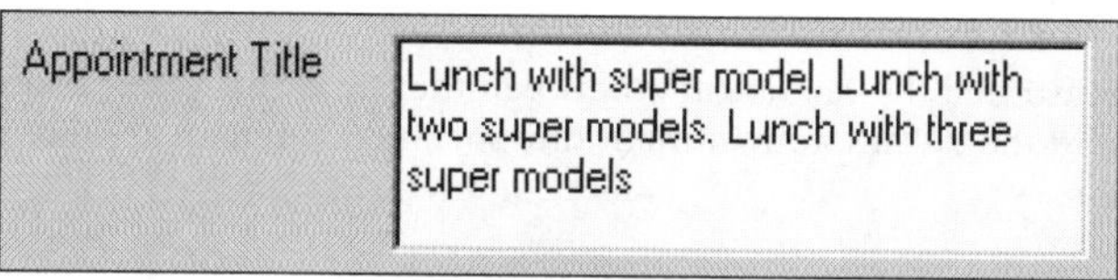

The code that takes the checked items within the instance `checkedListBoxDefaultTitle`, of type `CheckedListBox`, is found in the `clgDefaultTitle_SelectedIndexChanged` method. This method handles the time when a `SelectedIndexChanged` event is raised by the `CheckedListBox` instance, `checkedListBoxDefaultTitle`. This event is inherited by the `CheckedListBox` class via the base-class, `ListBox`. This event-handling method iterates through the collection of checked indices within the `CheckedListBox`:

```
foreach (string str in checkedListBoxDefaultTitle.CheckedItems)
```

Each selected item from within the `CheckedListBox` is concatenated with a variable, `defaultTitle`, of type `string`:

```
    defaultTitle += str;
```

Once each selected item has been added to the variable, `defaultTitle`, the `Text` associated with the `TextBox` used to hold the title when a new appointment is created is set:

```
textBoxTitle.Text = defaultTitle;
```

The `clgDefaultTitle_SelectedIndexChanged` method ensures that a period and a space are placed between each item added to the `defaultTitle` variable. The `bIsFirst` variable, is used in order to facilitate this functionality. The body of this event-handling method is as follows:

```
private void clbDefaultTitle_SelectedIndexChanged(object sender,
             System.EventArgs e)
{
   string defaultTitle = "";
```

```
    bool bIsFirst = true;

    foreach (string str in checkedListBoxDefaultTitle.CheckedItems)
    {
        if (bIsFirst)
        {
            bIsFirst = false;
        }

        else // period comes before 2nd, 3rd, 4th element
        {
            defaultTitle += ". ";
        }

        defaultTitle += str;
    }

    textBoxTitle.Text = defaultTitle;
}
```

So, this section demonstrated the relationship between the `ComboListBox` that contained default appointments titles and the default appointment title specified when an appointment is added to the scheduling application.

'TreeView'

The `TreeView` class is derived as follows:

```
Object
    MarshalByRefObject
        Component
           Control
               TreeView
```

The left pane of Windows Explorer is a classic example of an instance of a `TreeView` control. For Windows Explorer, the tree view contains a hierarchical list of folders. The left pane of `RegEdit.exe` also contains a `TreeView` control. For `RegEdit.exe`, the tree view contains a hierarchical list of registry keys:

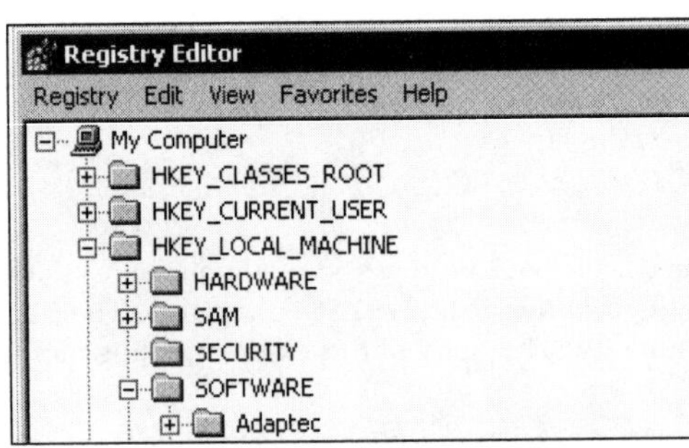

The Windows Forms variant of the `TreeView` control is a direct descendant of the `Control` base-class, and contains a multitude of methods and properties. These properties include:

Property	Description
`CheckBoxes`	When this Boolean property (default value, `false`) is `True`, check boxes are displayed next to each node with-in the `TreeView`'s tree.
`HideSelection`	When this Boolean property is set to `True`, then the selected node of the `TreeView` remains selected even after the `TreeView` loses focus.
`HotTracking`	When this Boolean property (default value, `False`) is set to `true` then each node the mouse pointer passes over appears to be a hyperlink.
`ImageIndex`	This property indicates which image within `ImageList` is the default image displayed by a node.
`ImageList`	This property (date type, `ImageList`) contains a collection of images that can be used by nodes within `TreeView`. Nodes of the tree can be associated with images. Consider Windows Explorer, which uses various icons to represent each folder. One of the most common images used to represent a folder in Windows Explorer is an icon that looks like a manila folder (a standard folder).
`Indent`	This property represents the number of pixels each child node is indented within the hierarchy of the tree view.
`LabelEdit`	When this property is `True` then the label associated with nodes of the tree can be edited. Windows Explorer has this property set to `true` for most folders, indicating that the folders can be renamed (non-read-only folders).
`Scrollable`	When this property is `True` then scrollbars are displayed when all the nodes of the tree cannot be contained in either the vertical or horizontal dimension.
`SelectedImageIndex`	This property specifies the image associated with the node when said node is selected.
`ShowLines`	This property, when set to `True` (default value), displays lines between the nodes in the `TreeView`.
`ShowPlusMinus`	When this property is `True` (default value) then a minus sign is displayed next to nodes with no children and a plus sign is displayed next to nodes with children.
`ShowRootLines`	This property specifies that lines should be displayed between the nodes at the `TreeView`'s root. By default this property is set to `true`.
`VisibleCount`	This property returns the total number of nodes that can be displayed at once for the `TreeView`. This count of each node visible within the hierarchy is a read-only property.

Node Management, 'TreeNodeCollection', and 'TreeNodes'

The bulk of the TreeView's complexity is associated with the management of nodes within the hierarchy. The list of all nodes within an instance of a TreeView control is contained in the Nodes property with data type TreeNodeCollection. The TreeNodeCollection exposes interfaces that include IList, ICollection, and IEnumerable. The elements contained in the TreeNodeCollection are of type TreeNode. Each TreeNode contains a property, Nodes, of type TreeNodeCollection. The TreeNode's Nodes property is used to contain each level within the hierarchy (the children's children). An example of the relationship between a TreeView control and TreeNodes is as follows:

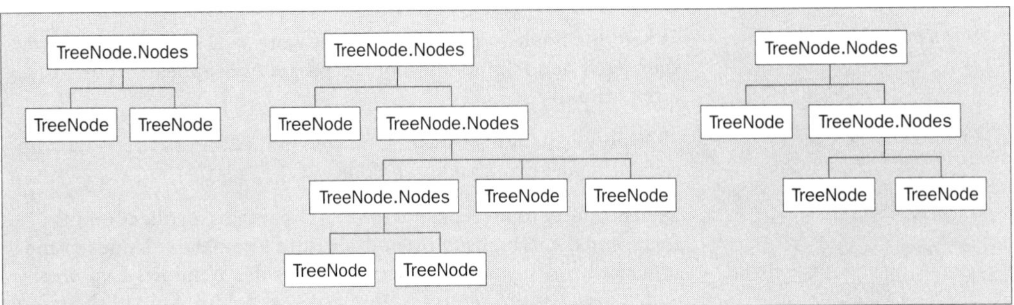

The SelectedNode property of TreeView specifies the currently selected node within the hierarchy. If no node is presently selected, the value of the SelectedNode property is set to null in C# and nothing in VB.NET. The TopNode property retrieves the topmost node visible within the tree. The value of TopNode is completely dependent on what nodes are visible. In theory, if only nodes ten levels deep were visible on the Form, then a top node that is ten levels deep would be returned.

To understand the concepts of TreeNodes and TreeNodeCollections, consider the following screenshot from the WroxScheduleClient01 application:

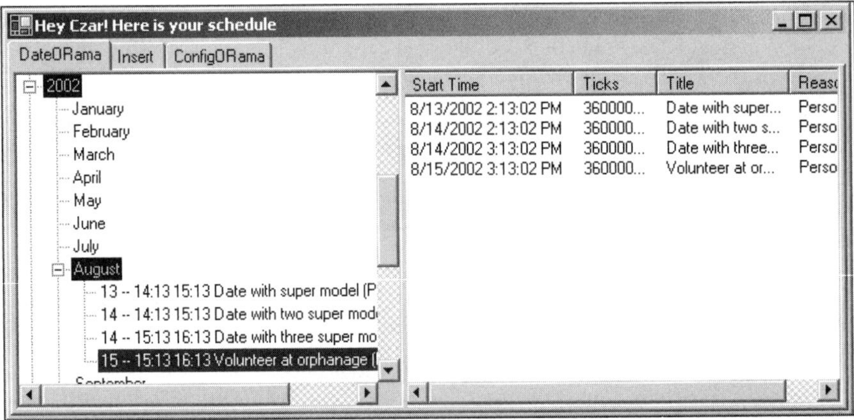

The root of the TreeView instance, treeViewScheduler, contains a Nodes collection. Each element in the Nodes collection corresponds to a year (2001, 2002, etc). Each year is actually a TreeNode instance. The code within the WroxScheduleClient01 application's WroxSetupTreeView method sets up this top level of the TreeView hierarchy as follows:

```
int yearCount;
TreeNode tempYearNode;

appointments = new WroxAppointments();
treeViewScheduler.BeginUpdate();
for (yearCount = (int)numericUpDownMinYear.Value;
     yearCount <= (int)numericUpDownMaxYear.Value;
     yearCount++)
{
   tempYearNode = new TreeNode(yearCount.ToString());
   treeViewScheduler.Nodes.Add(tempYearNode);

   // Loop here and setup months using tempMonthNode

}

treeViewScheduler.EndUpdate();
```

In this code snippet, the `appointments` data member is assigned to be `new WroxAppointments`. The `WroxAppointments` class is a quick representation of appointments and is far from complete. Remember that the topic of this chapter is Windows Forms controls and not efficient .NET appointment data management! The `yearCount` integer is used to iterate between the first year to display and the last year to display. The `NumericUpDown` controls, `numericUpDownMinYear` and `numericUpDownMaxYear`, specify the application's minimum and maximum years, respectively.

Within the code snippet, two rather important methods of the `TreeView` class are demonstrated, `BeginUpdate` and `EndUpdate`. These methods were already discussed in the context of the `ComboxBox` control. With respect to the `TreeView`, the reasons for calling `BeginUpdate` and `EndUpdate` are the same – to reduce flicker when a large number of updates are made to a `TreeView`.

The `Nodes` property of each year-level `TreeNode` instance contains twelve entries (corresponding to the months of the year). Each month within a year is actually a `TreeNode`. This `TreeNode` contains the appointments that take place within a given month. In the previous screenshot from the `WroxScheduleClient01` application there are four appointments for the year 2002: one on August 13, two on August 14, and one on August 15. The code to set up the `TreeNode` instances corresponding to months is found in the previous code snippet in the line documented as '`loop here and setup months using tempMonthNode`'. This code to set up months is as follows:

```
DateTimeFormatInfo dateTimeInfo = new DateTimeFormatInfo();
int monthCount;

monthCount = 1;
foreach (string monthName in dateTimeInfo.MonthNames)
{
   TreeNode tempMonthNode;

   tempMonthNode = new TreeNode(monthName);
   tempYearNode.Nodes.Add(tempMonthNode);
   monthCount++;
}
```

This code is not quite verbatim from the WroxScheduleClient01 application. The local variables were shuffled to make the example clearer. The idea of the code snippet is to create an instance of a DateTimeFormatInfo class, dateTimeInfo. The MonthNames property for this instance is called. The MonthNames property returns the name of each month with the calendar specific to the current locale. On an English machine this would be January, February, etc. On a machine set to a German locale, MonthNames would return Januar, Februar, etc. Each month name is added as a TreeNode to the Node's property:

```
tempMonthNode = new TreeNode(monthName);
```

of the year in which the month falls:

```
tempYearNode.Nodes.Add(tempMonthNode);
```

Recall from previously demonstrated code that the tempYearNode variable corresponded to the year node added to the Nodes property of the TreeView control. The tempMonthNode variable will be used to add appointments that take place within a certain month. The monthCount variable in the previous code snippet is used in conjunction with the yearCount variable to match which appointments should be added to a given month node of a given year node within the TreeView.

The code that manages the adding of appointments for display within a month is fairly complex. Additionally, this code is not particularly Windows Forms-specific. Once an appointment is found to reside in a given month of a given year, it is added to the month's Nodes property using the Add method, as follows:

```
TreeNode leaf = new TreeNode(appointment.ToString());

leaf.Tag = appointment;
tempMonthNode.Nodes.Add(leaf);
tempMonthNode.ForeColor = this.BackColor;
tempMonthNode.BackColor = this.ForeColor;
tempYearNode.ForeColor = this.BackColor;
tempYearNode.BackColor = this.ForeColor;
appointment = null;
appointmentIndex++;
```

The appointment variable in this code snippet is of type WroxAppointment. The year and month of the appointment variable match the month and year of the node added to the tree. The appointmentIndex variable is used to traverse the appointments managed by the application. When an appointment is found for a month of a year, an instance of a TreeNode, leaf, is created:

```
TreeNode leaf = new TreeNode(appointment.ToString());
```

Also, the Tag property for the leaf instance is set to the appointment. This allows the leaf to access its corresponding appointment if an operation such as delete is performed on the leaf node representing the appointment (delete the leaf instance and the leaf deletes the actual appointment).

This leaf node of type TreeNode is added to the month's Nodes property using the Add method, tempMonthNode.Nodes.Add(leaf);. When a month contains an appointment, the foreground and background colors of the month's TreeNode are reversed. For example, the foreground color is changed as follows:

```
tempMonthNode.ForeColor = this.BackColor;
```

Similarly, the foreground color and background color of the TreeNode of the year in which the appointment resides is also toggled. This toggling is achieved using the foreground and background colors of the Form, this.ForeColor and this.BackColor. This swapping of colors is performed so that users of the application can quickly determine which years/months have appointments scheduled for them.

To view the code within the WroxScheduleClient01 application's WroxSetupTreeView method in its entirety, see the source file, WroxScheduleMain.cs. Also not presented in this section is a rigorous dissection of the TreeNode and TreeNodeCollection classes. These infrastructure classes of the TreeView class are critical to the setup of a tree view.

Appointments can be removed from the TreeView and from the store of appointments (data member, WroxAppointments appointments). The KeyPress event exposed by TreeView is inherited from the Control base-class. The KeyPress event is part of three key-related events: KeyPress, KeyUp, and KeyDown. The KeyPress event is handled for the WroxScheduleClient01 application via the treeViewScheduler_KeyPress method. This method ultimately handles deleting a specific appointment (the Tag property found in the corresponding TreeNode). Deletion is not applicable to year or month nodes, only appointment nodes.

Two parameters are passed to the treeViewScheduler_KeyPress method:

- object sender: This first parameter corresponds to the control (the TreeView instance treeViewScheduler) that caused the event to be triggered.
- KeyPressEventArgs e: This second parameter (type, KeyPressEventArg) contains a property, KeyChar, (type, char), which specifies the key pressed. Another property contained in the KeyPressEventArg is Handled (type, Boolean). The method handling the KeyPress event should set Handled to False if Windows should handle the key pressed event as part of default processing. Setting this value to True indicates that the method handling KeyPress took responsibility for handling the particular key pressed.

The scheduling application deletes appointments (leaf nodes from the TreeView) when the backspace or delete keys are selected. Other keys are ignored. In order to handle this, the System.Windows.Forms Keys enumeration is used. This enumeration provides values for the backspace key (Keys.Back) and the delete key (Keys.Delete). These values are compared against the key pressed (the KeyChar property of the KeyPressEventArgs class) as follows:

```
private void treeViewScheduler_KeyPress(object sender,
             System.Windows.Forms.KeyPressEventArgs e)
{
    if (((int)e.KeyChar == (int)Keys.Back) ||
        ((int)e.KeyChar == (int)Keys.Delete))
    {
        e.Handled = true;
        // handle delete here since we are backspace or delete key
    }
    else
    {
        e.Handled = false;
    }
}
```

Notice in this code snippet that if the key that raised the `KeyPress` event is `Back` or `Delete` then `e.Handled` is set to `True`, indicating that the method took responsibility for handing this event. If another key is specified then Windows will handle this event as part of its default processing.

When a delete or backspace key is pressed, the node presently selected has to be determined by the `treeViewScheduler_KeyPress` method. This is the node marked for deletion. The node presently selected is determined using the `SelectedNode` property of the `TreeView` class. If no node is selected, the method exits. The code for determining the selected node is as follows:

```
TreeNode treeNode = ((TreeView)sender).SelectedNode;

if (null == treeNode)
{
    return; // nothing selected
}
```

Once the selected node to be deleted has been determined, the level of this node must be computed. A `TreeNode` with a parent of `null` is at the root. The `Parent` of a `TreeNode` is determined using the `Parent` property. Such nodes in the `WroxScheduleClient01` application correspond to years. This node type cannot be deleted. Nodes whose grandparent is `null` correspond to month nodes. Such nodes can also not be deleted (although it might be nice to delete months in the real world when your credit card bill is exceptionally high!). This leaves only appointments that can be deleted. Appointments have a great-grandparent of `null`. The code in the `treeViewScheduler_KeyPress` method for determining year, month, or appointment node is as follows:

```
TreeNode treeNode = ((TreeView)sender).SelectedNode;
int level = 0;

while (true)
{
    treeNode = treeNode.Parent;
    if (null == treeNode)
    {
        break;
    }

level++;
}

if ((level == 0) || //year level
    (level == 1)) // month level
{
    return ;
}
```

Actually, a simpler approach to the same problem would be to simply test to see if the selected `TreeNode`'s `Tag` property was non-null (an appointment). If, in the future, the `Tag` property of a year or month `TreeNode` is set to a value, then this method for detecting the type of `TreeNode` (year, month or appointment) would become invalid. Once a node has been identified to be an appointment, it can be removed from the `TreeView` using the leaf `TreeNode`'s own `Remove` method and from the list of appointments using the `Remove` method exposed by `WroxAppointments`:

```
TreeNode monthTreeNode, yearTreeNode;

treeNode = ((TreeView)sender).SelectedNode;
monthTreeNode = treeNode.Parent;
appointments.Remove((WroxAppointment)treeNode.Tag);
treeNode.Remove();
```

There appears to be some superfluous code in this snippet, namely that the parent (a month `TreeNode`) of the appointment tree node was saved. Remember that months and years that contain an appointment are specially highlighted. If there are no more appointments for the month, its colors are returned to normal. If there are no more appointments for the year, its colors are returned to normal.

```
// If month contains no more appointments, reset the colors
// back to normal (toggle foreground and background colors)

if (monthTreeNode.Nodes.Count == 0)
{
    bool allAreEmpty = true;

    monthTreeNode.ForeColor = this.ForeColor;
    monthTreeNode.BackColor = this.BackColor;
    yearTreeNode = monthTreeNode.Parent;

    // Traverse each month in the year to see if the
    // month contains an appointments (month.Nodes.Count > 0)

    foreach (TreeNode month in yearTreeNode.Nodes)
    {
        if (month.Nodes.Count > 0)
        {
            allAreEmpty = false;
            break;
        }
    }

    if (allAreEmpty)
    {
        yearTreeNode.ForeColor = this.ForeColor;
        yearTreeNode.BackColor = this.BackColor;
    }
}
```

The `treeViewScheduler_KeyPress` method in its entirety is as follows:

```
private void treeViewScheduler_KeyPress(object sender,
            System.Windows.Forms.KeyPressEventArgs e)
{
    if (((int)e.KeyChar == (int)Keys.Back) ||
        ((int)e.KeyChar == (int)Keys.Delete))
    {
        DateTimeFormatInfo dateTimeInfo = new DateTimeFormatInfo();
        TreeNode treeNode = ((TreeView)sender).SelectedNode;

        if (null == treeNode)
```

```
    {
        return; // nothing selected
    }

    int level = 0;

    while (true)
    {
        treeNode = treeNode.Parent;
        if (null == treeNode)
        {
            break;
        }

    level++;
    }

    if ((level == 0) ||   //year level
       (level == 1))     // month level
    {
        return ;
    }

    TreeNode monthTreeNode, yearTreeNode;

    treeNode = ((TreeView)sender).SelectedNode;
    monthTreeNode = treeNode.Parent;
    appointments.Remove((WroxAppointment)treeNode.Tag);
    treeNode.Remove();

    // If month contains no more appointments, reset the colors
    // back to normal (toggle foreground and background colors)

    if (monthTreeNode.Nodes.Count == 0)
    {
        bool allAreEmpty = true;

        monthTreeNode.ForeColor = this.ForeColor;
        monthTreeNode.BackColor = this.BackColor;
        yearTreeNode = monthTreeNode.Parent;

        // Traverse each month in the year to see if the
        // month contains an appointments (month.Nodes.Count > 0)

        foreach (TreeNode month in yearTreeNode.Nodes)
        {
            if (month.Nodes.Count > 0)
            {
                allAreEmpty = false;
                break;
            }
        }

        if (allAreEmpty)
        {
```

```
                yearTreeNode.ForeColor = this.ForeColor;
                yearTreeNode.BackColor = this.BackColor;
            }
        }
    }
}
```

'TreeView' Methods and Events

The `CollapseAll` method collapses all expanded nodes within the `TreeView`. The antithesis of this method is `ExpandAll`. The `GetNodeCount` method takes a single parameter of type Boolean. This method returns the count of all nodes at the root of the `TreeView` if the parameter is specified as `False`. Specifying `True` for the `GetNodeCount` parameter returns the count of nodes including nodes in sub-trees.

The `GetNodeAt` retrieves a node (return value, `TreeNode`) by specifying its location with respect to the form. This overloaded method takes either a `Point` as a parameter or two integer values as parameters, where the two integers correspond to the X and Y location of the node to be retrieved. Using Visual Studio.NET, it would be possible to generate a method that handled the `MouseDown` event. The prototype for this method, including some code that detects which tree node was selected, is as follows:

```
private void treeViewScheduler_MouseDown(object sender,
            System.Windows.Forms.MouseEventArgs e)
{
    TreeNode treeNode;

    treeNode = ((TreeView)sender).GetNodeAt(e.X, e.Y);
    MessageBox.Show(treeNode.ToString(),
            "Show using MouseEventArgs X and Y Property");
}
```

In the code snippet, the `MouseEventArgs` parameter specifies the X and Y coordinates (in terms of client coordinates) where the mouse click occurred. These coordinates can be passed to the `TreeView`'s `GetNodeAt` method. This method, in turn, returned the `TreeNode` that was sitting beneath the mouse down click. A `MessageBox` is displayed, indicating which `TreeNode` was clicked on.

The `MouseDown` event previously discussed is inherited by the `TreeView` class. The `Control` base-class is what actually exposes the `MouseDown` event. The events exposed directly by `TreeView` include the following:

Event	Description
`BeforeCheck`, `AfterCheck`	These events fire before and after a node containing a check box is checked. The `OnCheck` method programmatically triggers the `AfterCheck` event.
`BeforeCollapse`, `AfterCollapse`	These events fire before and after a node is collapsed. The `OnCollapse` method programmatically triggers the `AfterCollapse` event.

Table continued on following page

Event	Description
BeforeExand, AfterExpand	These events fire before and after a node is expanded. The OnExpand method programmatically triggers the AfterExpand event.
BeforeLabelEdit, AfterLabelEdit	These events fire before and after a node's label is edited. The OnLabelEdit method programmatically triggers the AfterLabelEdit event.
BeforeSelect, AfterSelect	These events fire before and after a node is selected. The OnSelect method programmatically triggers the AfterSelect event.

However, probably the most intriguing event of TreeView is the ItemDrag event. This event is fired when an item is dragged. The prototype for a method that handles the ItemDrag event is as follows:

```
private void treeView_ItemDrag(object sender,
                System.Windows.Forms.ItemDragEventArgs e){}
```

The ItemDragEventsArgs class is passed to the event handler indicating just what is up with this dragging process. The properties associated with the ItemDragEventsArgs class include:

- Button (type, MouseButtons): The specific mouse button clicked when dragging was instigated.
- Item (type, object): The specific item (TreeNode) being dragged.

The OnItemDrag method can programmatically trigger the ItemDrag event.

'ListView'

The ListView class displays a list of items. These items are displayed in one of four views. The ListView most commonly recognized in the world of Windows is the right side of Windows Explorer. Inside the right pane of Windows Explorer files can be viewed as:

- File names displayed as list
- File names plus details displayed as list
- File names with small icons
- File names with large icons.

In the .NET context the ListView class is derived directly from the Control class.

```
Object
    MarshalByRefObject
        Component
            Control
                ListView
```

The ListView is rather typically dragged from the Toolbox and dropped onto the Form that is to contain the ListView instance. The View property of the ListView is used to specify which view of the list is displayed. The permissible values for this property's type are not quantum physics: List, Details, SmallIcon, and LargeIcon. Examples of a ListView with the View property set to LargeIcon (left side) and SmallIcon (right side) is found in the following screenshot from the VB.NET application WroxFlauntListView (a quick application that just demonstrates the ListView class):

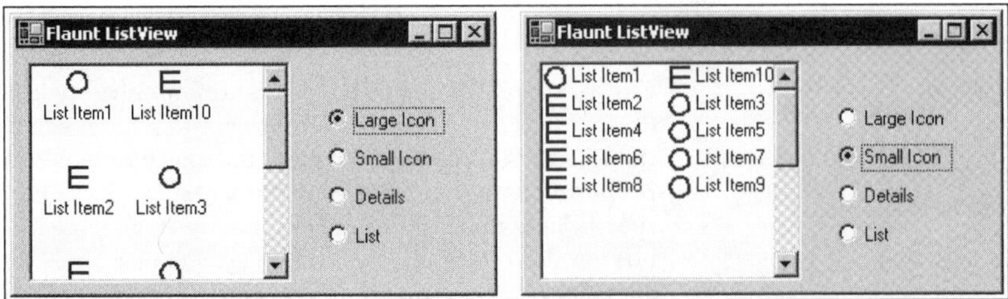

Examples of a ListView with the View property set to List (left side) and Details (right side) are found in the following screenshot, also from the application WroxFlauntListView:

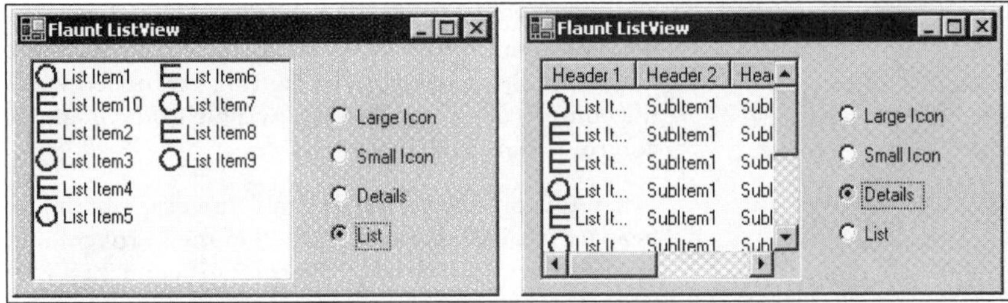

The basic premise of a ListView is that it contains a list of items. Potentially, multiple columns can represent said items (see View set to Details in previous screenshot). This behavior is just like in Windows Explorer, where the file name, size, date, and type is contained in separate columns. The Columns property (type, ColumnHeaderCollection) contains a list of the columns associated with the ListView control. When a ListView instance is selected in the Windows Forms Designer, the Properties window of Visual Studio.NET lists the properties associated with the ListView. Double-clicking on the Columns property displays the ColumnHeader Collection Editor dialog (see below):

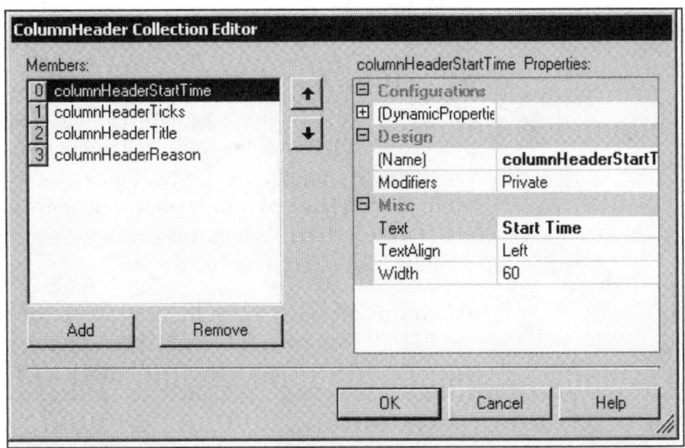

The entries displayed in the screenshot are the columns displayed by the WroxScheduleClient01 application. The ListView for this application displays each appointment for a given month in a ListView with columns corresponding to the appointments Title, Reason, StartDate, and Ticks (where ticks are the number of clock ticks in the appointment).

Some of the properties of ListView are as follows:

Property	Description
Activation	This property facilitates the activation of entries within the list (for example, in Windows Explorer, when an executable file in the ListView pane is activated, the executable is run). This property can be set to OneClick or TwoClick. These values specify how many mouse clicks it takes to activate an item. For both of these settings, the item's text changes color when the cursor hovers over the item. A value of Standard can also be specified for the Activation property. When Standard is specified, the item does not change color and a double-click is required to activate the list item.
AlignmentProperty	This property specifies the behavior of any elements being moved. Items moved can remain where they were dropped, be aligned to the left side of the control, be aligned with the top of the control, or can snap to an invisible grid contained in the control (value, SnapToGrid).
AllowColumnReordering	When this property is set to True, the user can drag column headers to different positions within the list of columns. This user intervention reorders the columns contained in the ListView.
AutoArrange	When this property is set to True then items are automatically arranged based on the value of the Alignment property.
FullRowSelect	This property specifies if the entire row of an item is highlighted when the user selects the item or if only the item selected will be highlighted.
GridLines	This property specifies whether or not grid lines are displayed. By default GridLines are not displayed.
HeaderStyle	This property is as much substance as style. When the value of this property is set to Clickable then the column headers of the ListView items act as buttons that allow an action to take place. Within Windows Explorer the action is 'sort', where files are sorted by name, date, type, and size. When this property is set to Nonclickable the column headers are displayed but do not act as buttons. When this property is set to None, then column headers are not displayed.
HideSelection	When this property is set to True, then the selected items of the ListView are hidden when the ListView is no longer in focus.

Property	Description
HoverSelection	This property specifies, if set to True, that items within the list view can be selected by merely hovering the cursor over the item.
LabelEdit	If this property is True then the labels in the ListView can be user edited.
LabelWrap	If this property is True then the labels wrap if the horizontal dimension of the ListView control is exceeded.
MultiSelect	If this property is True then multiple items within the ListView can be selected. This is the same behavior as in Windows Explorer when multiple files can be dragged in the list view pane.
Scrollable	If this property is True then scrollbars are visible for the ListView control.
FocusedItem	This property denotes the item currently in focus within the ListView.
TopItem	This property denotes the top item in the ListView. The top item within the list view is also indicated using the property (type, ListViewItem).
Sorting	The property of ListView specifies the order used to sort the items. The permissible values for the SortOrder enumerator are None, Ascending, and Descending. The default setting for the Sorting property is None.

Display related properties are also exposed by the ListView control, including BackColor, ForeColor, DefaultSize, and BorderStyle. CheckBoxes can be displayed for each item within the ListView list. The properties related to the manipulation of these CheckBoxes are as follows:

- CheckBoxes: When this property is set to True then CheckBoxes are displayed for each element in the ListView list.
- CheckedItems: This property contains a list of the items whose check boxes are checked.
- CheckIndices: This property contains a list of the indices of the items whose check boxes are checked.

Both of the CheckedItems and CheckIndices properties exposed by ListView behave identically to their like-named counterparts previously discussed with respect to the CheckedListBox class.

'ListView' Collection Properties

The ListView class appears complicated but can be set up in a quite straightforward manner using the ListView's collection properties:

- Set up each column in the Columns property (the columns displayed when View is set to Details).

- Set up a list of images to display when `View` is set to `LargeIcon`. The collection property containing the list of images is `LargeImageList`.
- Set up a list of images to display when `View` is set to `SmallIcon`. The collection property containing the list of images is `SmallImageList`.
- Create each list item displayed in the `ListView` by adding entries to the `Items` property.

Code that programmatically sets up the `Columns` property can be found in the `WroxFlauntListView` application, where `ListViewDemo` is a data member of type `ListView`:

```
Dim j As Integer
Dim columnHeader As ColumnHeader

For j = 1 To 5
    columnHeader = New ColumnHeader()
    columnHeader.Text = "Header " & j
    ListViewDemo.Columns.Add(columnHeader)
Next
```

The sample `ListView`, `ListViewDemo`, now contains five columns. Two images can now be added to the `LargeImageList` and the `SmallImageList` properties:

```
Dim imageList As ImageList = New ImageList()

imageList.Images.Add(New Icon("odd.ico"))
imageList.Images.Add(New Icon("even.ico"))
ListViewDemo.SmallImageList = imageList
ListViewDemo.LargeImageList = imageList
```

In this code snippet both the small and large image lists are set to the same `ImageList` instance. In most real-world applications, the contents of `SmallImageList` and `LargeImageList` are likely to be different.

Thus far, the infrastructure (column headers and lists of images) for a `ListView` has been set up. This leaves the individual list items to be set up. Each element in the `ListViewItemCollection` is of type `ListViewItem` class. Each `ListView` item created should have its `Text` property set to the text to display for the item (for example, the file name displayed in Windows Explorer). If five columns were created for the `ListView` then the `Text` property corresponds to the first column. The `ListViewItem` class exposes the `Tag` property (type, object). Data associated with the list item can be specified using the `Tag` property. Data to display for the other columns (besides the first column) still needs to be set up. Specifying the data associated with other columns is the sole duty of the `ListViewItem`'s `SubItems` property.

If an image is to be associated with the `ListViewItem`, the `ImageIndex` property should be set to an index value, with corresponding images in the `ListView`'s `SmallImageList` and `LargeImageList` properties. The following code snippet from the `WroxFlauntListView` application performs all of the steps previously discussed for the `ListView` instance, `ListViewDemo`:

```
Dim i As Integer
Dim listViewItem As ListViewItem

For i = 1 To 10
```

```
        listViewItem = New ListViewItem()
        listViewItem.Text = "List Item" & i
        listViewItem.ImageIndex = i Mod 2
        For j = 1 To 4 ' j defined at top of method
            listViewItem.SubItems.Add("SubItem" & j)
        Next
        ListViewDemo.Items.Add(listViewItem)
    Next
```

The `ImageIndex` property is set in this code snippet to either 0 or 1. There are two images in the image list: a large E (for even) and O (for odd). The image displayed for each item in the list is the image corresponding to even or odd (the position of the item within the list with respect to being even or odd).

Recall that at the beginning of this section four screenshots were displayed corresponding to setting the `View` property of `ListView` respectively to `LargeIcon`, `SmallIcon`, `List`, and `Details`. Nowhere in the previous setup code that handled `Column`, `SmallImageList`, `LargeImageList`, and `Items`, was `View` mentioned. This is not an oversight. There was no need to mention how the `List` is displayed versus `Details` versus `SmallIcon`. The `ListView` just displays the items (the .NET Framework does the work for you) based on the value set for the `View` property.

The small application dedicated to showing off the `ListView` – `WroxFlauntListView` – contained four radio buttons that corresponded to `List`, `Details`, `SmallIcon`, and `LargeIcon`. The methods that handle when the radio button's checked status changes contains the code that changes the `ListView`'s `View` property. Two of the methods that handle the `CheckStatusChanged` event for the `LargeIcon` and `SmallIcon` radio buttons are as follows:

```
Private Sub RadioButtonLargeIcon_CheckedChanged(_
            ByVal sender As System.Object, ByVal e As System.EventArgs) _
            Handles RadioButtonLargeIcon.CheckedChanged
    ListViewDemo.View = View.LargeIcon
End Sub

Private Sub RadioButtonSmallIcon_CheckedChanged(_
            ByVal sender As System.Object, ByVal e As System.EventArgs) _
            Handles RadioButtonSmallIcon.CheckedChanged
    ListViewDemo.View = View.SmallIcon
End Sub
```

Notice in these two reviewed methods, the one extremely powerful line of code in each (`ListViewDemo.View = ...`). The code used to implement the `WroxFlauntListView` application can be found (in its entirety) in the `WroxFlauntListView.vb` source file.

'ListView' Methods and Events

The methods exposed by `ListView` include:

Method	Description
`ArrangeIcon`	Triggers the programmatic arrangement of the icons (for small and large icon views).
`BeginUpdate`	Identical to the `BeginUpdate` method of the `TreeView` class.

Table continued on following page

Method	Description
`Clear`	This method is provided to completely empty the list of items in the `ListView`.
`EndUpdate`	Identical to the `EndUpdate` method of the `TreeView` class.
`EnsureVisible`	This method makes sure that the item is visible and takes a parameter, of type `integer`. This parameter corresponds to the index value of an item in the `Items` property. The displayed list view is scrolled if necessary to ensure that the item specified is visible.

The events exposed by `ListView` are:

Event	Description
`AfterLabelEdit`	Event fired after a label is edited.
`BeforeLabelEdit`	Event fired before a label is edited.
`ColumnClick`	Event fired when a column header is clicked.
`ItemActivated`	Event fired when an item is activated.
`ItemCheck`	Event fired when an item is checked. This pertains only to `ListViews` containing check boxes.
`ItemDrag`	Event fired when an item is dragged using the mouse.
`SelectedIndexChange`	Event fired when the item selected changes.

Methods are provided to raise these events programmatically: `OnAfterLabelEdit`, `OnBeforeLabelEdit`, `OnColumnClick`, `OnItemActivate`, `OnItemDrag`, and `OnSelectedIndexChanged`.

'ListView' in 'WroxScheduleClient01'

An instance of a `ListView` class is featured on the DateORama `TabPage` of the `WroxScheduleClient01` application. This `ListView` is only populated when a month in the `TreeView` is selected and the said month contains appointments. The method that handles the event triggered when a new node in the `TreeView` is selected is `treeViewScheduler_AfterSelect`. This method ensures that the node selected contains appointments (code previously reviewed). At the tail end of this method is the code that populates the `ListView` pane of the DateORama `TabPage`.

Before the `ListView` is updated, the `BeginUpdate` method is called and, once the `ListView` has been updated, the `EndUpdate` method is called. Recall that this sequence was called to reduce flicker when substantially updating the contents of the `ListView`. Traversing the `Nodes` collection of a `TreeNode` corresponding to a month populates the `ListView`. This `Nodes` collection contains the `TreeNode`'s representing the appointments occurring that month. This traversal code is as follows (where `treeNode.Nodes` in the list of appointments for a month):

```
foreach (TreeNode travTreeNodes in treeNode.Nodes)
```

Each appointment TreeNode contains a Tag property that is associated with a reference to an appointment (an instance of type WroxAppointment). This Tag property's value is used to set up each ListViewItem. The Text of the ListViewItem is set to the appointment's start date (property, StartDate). The ListView contains columns corresponding to properties exposed by the WroxAppointment class: StartDate, Ticks, Title, and Reason. The first column displays the Text property of the ListViewItem, so adding to the ListViewItem's SubItems fills in the remaining three columns. The Add method exposed by SubItems is called to fill in the text associated with Ticks, Title, and Reason.

The portion of the code within the treeViewScheduler_AfterSelect method that sets up the ListView is as follows:

```
ListViewItem listViewItem;
WroxAppointment appt;

listViewAppointments.BeginUpdate();
foreach (TreeNode travTreeNodes in treeNode.Nodes)
{
    listViewItem = new ListViewItem();
    appt = (WroxAppointment)travTreeNodes.Tag;
    listViewItem.Text = appt.StartDate.ToString();
    listViewItem.SubItems.Add(appt.Ticks.ToString());
    listViewItem.SubItems.Add(appt.Title);
    listViewItem.SubItems.Add(appt.Reason);
    listViewAppointments.Items.Add(listViewItem);
}

listViewAppointments.EndUpdate();
```

'NumericUpDown'

The NumericUpDown control class is a Windows Forms control derived from the Control class. This style of class is placed on a Form using the tried and true method of drag from the Toolbox window and drop on the Form. The lineage from the NumericUpDown class to the Control class as follows:

```
Object
    MarshalByRefObject
        Component
            Control
                ScrollableControl
                    ContainerControl
                        UpDownBase
                            NumericUpDown
```

The NumericUpDown control class allows a number to be displayed. The value of the number can be incremented or decremented by scrolling the value up or down. Up/down buttons are provided in support of scrolling up and down. At most one numeric value at a time is displayed by this control (see below):

Some of the properties of NumericUpDown include:

Property	Description
DecimalPlaces	This property represents the number of decimal digits displayed by the control (default value, 0).
Hexadecimal	Specifying a value of True for this property means that the values of the NumericUpDown control will be displayed as hexadecimal.
Increment	This property represents the amount to increment the NumericUpDown control each time it is clicked. The default value is 1.
Maximum	This property specifies the upper bound scrollable. The default value is 100.
Minimum	This property specifies the lower bound scrollable. The default value is 0.
ReadOnly	This property is set by default to False. Setting this property to False allows the user to enter a number manually rather than only relying on the up/down buttons provided by the NumericUpDown control. Only numeric characters can be entered into the value displayed by the control. What is legally a numeric character is based on whether or not the control displays decimal or hexadecimal (the Hexadecimal property). Specifying a value of True for ReadOnly means that the up/down buttons are the only mechanism that can be used to modify the value displayed by the NumericUpDown control.
ThousandsSeparator	Setting the property to True displays a separator every three digits. When False is specified (default value) for this parameter then no thousands separator is specified. The actual character representation of the thousands separator is locale-specific, where the locale corresponds to the cultural location of the machine. In most of Europe, when ThousandsSeparator is True, a period will be displayed, while in the United States a comma will be displayed.
Value	The value displayed by the control is accessed via this property (type, Decimal with default value, 0).

These properties are all exposed directly by the NumericUpDown class. Other properties are exposed via the UpDownBase class. These properties of note include:

- UpDownAlign: By default this property is set to Right, specifying that the up/down arrows appear on the right side of the control. Specifying a value of Left causes the up/down arrows to appear on the left side of the control (see below where Right is right and Left is left):

- InterceptArrowKeys: When this property is True (the default) then the up/down arrow keys on the keyboard can be used to increment/decrement the control, provided the control is in focus. It is an exercise left to the reader to determine the behavior when the InterceptArrowKeys property is set to False.

As for methods, take a look at these:

Method	Description
`DownButton`	This method decrements the `Value` of the control by the value specified in the `Increment` property.
`UpButton`	This method embraces logic and hence, when called, increments the `Value` of the control by the value specified in the `Increment` property.
`ValueChanged`	This event is raised if the value of a `NumericUpDown` control is changed. This event can be fired programmatically by calling the `OnValueChanged` method.

In the `WroxScheduleClient01` application, the `NumericUpDown` control is used to specify the first year specified in the `TreeView` of appointments and the last year specified in the `TreeView` of appointments. The upper-bound and lower-bound specifying `NumericUpDown` control instances are contained on the ConfigORama `TabPage` and are as follows:

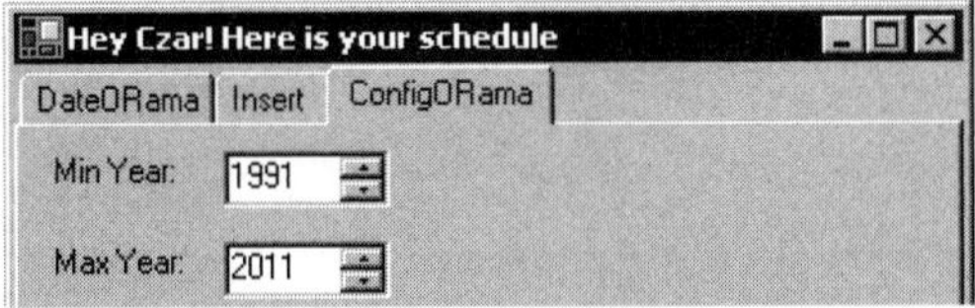

In this screenshot it makes sense that the value in the Min Year `NumericUpDown` control is less than the Max Year. The `ValueChanged` method of each of these controls is handled in order to ensure that the minimum value is less than the maximum value. When the value of the Min Year `NumericUpDown` control changes, the `numericUpDownMinYear_ValueChanged` method is called as follows:

```
private void
    numericUpDownMinYear_ValueChanged(object sender, System.EventArgs e)
{
    if (numericUpDownMinYear.Value >= numericUpDownMaxYear.Value)
    {
        numericUpDownMinYear.Value = numericUpDownMaxYear.Value - 1;
    }
}
```

The basic premise of this method is to ensure that the minimum year is always at least one less than the maximum year. The `numericUpDownMaxYear_ValueChanged` method is called when the value of the Max Year control changes. This method ensures that the maximum year is always at least one greater than the minimum year. An alternate approach to fixing this user error would be to permit the said error to occur and to use instances of type `ErrorProvider` to display error information for each control of type `NumericUpDown`. The use of `ErrorProvider` to identify per-control errors is discussed in a later section of this chapter.

'DomainUpDown'

The DomainUpDown class is first cousin of the NumericUpDown class.

```
Object
    MarshalByRefObject
        Component
            Control
                ScrollableControl
                    ContainerControl
                        UpDownBase
                            DomainUpDown
```

This familial relationship is specified because both of the aforementioned classes are derived directly from the UpDownBase class. While the NumericUpDown class scrolled though lists of numbers, the DomainUpDown class scrolls through a list of text strings. One string at time is displayed and up/down buttons are provided to facilitate the scrolling up and down. These strings are specified programmatically using the DomainUpDown class's Item property.

The DomainUpDown class is a Windows Forms control in the classic style: drag from Toolbox and drop onto the Form. The Item property for this class can be selected from the Properties window. When selected, the Item property causes the String Collection Editor dialog to be displayed, as follows:

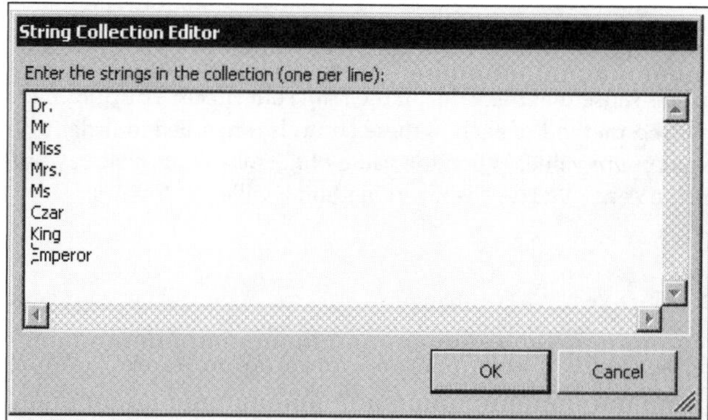

This screenshot is actually from the WroxScheduleClient01 application. Within this application, a DomainUpDown instance is used to determine the title displayed for the user of the scheduling application (Mr, Mrs, etc.).

The other properties exposed by the DomainUpDown class include:

Property	Description
SelectedIndex	This property returns the numeric index value for the selected item in the domain list. Initially this value is set to -1 indicating that a value has yet to be selected.
SelectedItem	This property returns the value of the string presently selected. In C# the default initial value for this property is null.

Property	Description
Sorted	When True, the strings in the Items property are sorted. When False (the default) the strings are displayed in order of their position within the Items collection.
Wrap	When this property is True, the string collection displayed wraps around after the last string has been accessed (returning back to the first string). When True, if the string before the first string is selected, then the next value displayed is the last string in the Items collection. The default value for this property is False, representing no wrapping.

For the DomainUpDown class the SelectedItemChanged event is raised when the item selected is changed. The OnSelectedItemChanged method programmatically raises this event. The DownButton and UpButton methods programmatically trigger the down button and the up button respectively. The DomainUpDown class inherits the UpDownAlign and InterceptArrowKeys properties from the UpDownBase class. The NumericUpDown class also inherits these properties. These properties behave identically for both the DomainUpDown and the NumericUpDown classes.

The DomainUpDown class also inherits properties from the UpDownBase class:

- ReadOnly: The ReadOnly property causes the same behavior for a DomainUpDown control as it does for a NumericUpDown control.
- Text: This property contains the text entered by the user. When the ReadOnly property is false then the text contained in the Text property is not added to the Items collection. Whether an entry from the Items collection, or a user-entered value, is displayed, the Text property contains the string displayed by the DomainUpDown control.
- RightToLeft: When the RightToLeft property is Yes, the text is aligned with the right side of the control. When this property is set to No (the default), the text is aligned along the left side of the control.

Within the WroxScheduleClient01 application, a DomainUpDown control is contained on the ConfigORama TabPage (see the following):

The text, Title:, is associated with a label while the text, Czar, is associated with the DomainUpDown instance, domainUpDownTitle. The value selected for this DomainUpDown instance is displayed as part of the title of the Form for the WroxScheduleClient01 application. Specifically, the title of the application is displayed as "Hey *titlehere*! Here is your schedule". To ensure this text displays correctly, the DomainUpDown instance, domainUpDownTitle, initially has its SelectedItem property set using the value currently displayed by the DomainUpDown control (the Text property). The SelectedItem property is set up as follows:

```
domainUpDownTitle.SelectedItem = domainUpDownTitle.Text;
```

Each time the selected text is changed (event, `OnSelectedItemChanged`), the `domainUpDownTitle_SelectedItemChanged` method is called as part of the `WroxScheduleClient01` application. The code for this method was associated with the `OnSelectedItemChanged` event by double-clicking on the `DomainUpDown` control when it was displayed in the Windows Forms Designer. Visual Studio.NET created the shell for the `domainUpDownTitle_SelectedItemChanged` method. This method is implemented as follows:

```
private void domainUpDownTitle_SelectedItemChanged(object sender,
                                                   System.EventArgs e)
{
    this.Text = "Hey " + domainUpDownTitle.Text +
                "! Here is your schedule";
}
```

In this code, the `Text` property is used instead of the `SelectedItem` property. This allows the user to manually enter text into the `DomainUpDown` control, rather than simply relying on the contents of the `Items` collection. The user is able to enter any text they wanted, because the `ReadOnly` property is set to the default value, `False`.

'ErrorProvider'

The `ErrorProvider` control is a direct descendant of the `Control` class.

```
Object
    MarshalByRefObject
        Component
            Control
                ErrorProvider
```

The `ErrorProvider` control identifies a control that contains an error. A flashing icon is placed next to the control that is in error, represented by the `Icon` property of type `Icon`). When the mouse hovers over this error-identifying icon, text can be displayed specifying information regarding the error (this is, tool tip text). To demonstrate the `ErrorProvider` in action, consider the following screenshot from the `WroxScheduleClient01` application (just be aware that there is a bug in the `Icon` property of the `ErrorInfo` class, which means that the icon does not display: however, this is what it *should* look like!):

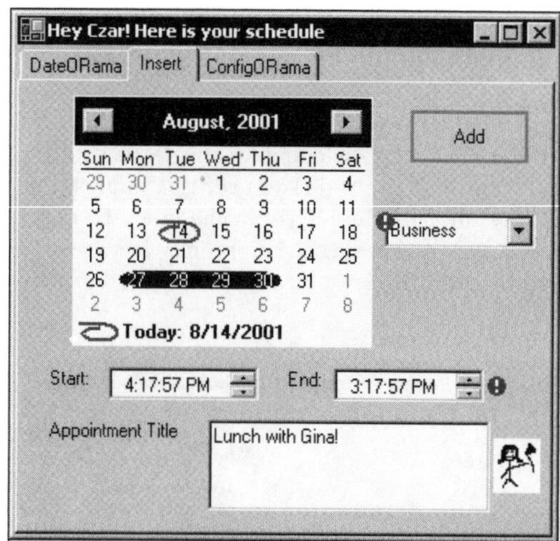

In the screenshot it is illegal to:

- Select an appointment that spans multiple days: August 27 through August 30 is selected for the `MonthCalendar` control, so a flashing exclamation point is displayed next to this control. Actually, the exclamation point icon indicating this error appears to the right of the `MonthCalendar` control. A better placement should be implemented, because it could be misconstrued as being associated with the `ComboBox` containing the text, Business.
- Specify an end time that is before the start time: The `DateTimePicker` control corresponding to the end time of the appointment is in error and is so denoted by a flashing exclamation point next to this control.
- Go to any appointment with your ex, Gina: The `TextBox` control specifies "Lunch with Gina" which is clearly an error (horrendous mistake!). This is why a flashing icon containing her likeness is displayed next to the `TextBox` control.

The screenshot was created by dragging an `ErrorProvider` icon from Visual Studio.NET's **Toolbox** and dropping it on the `Form`. This process was performed three times, thus creating three data members for the `Form` of type `ErrorProvider` (`errorProviderMonthCalendar`, `errorProviderDateTimePicker`, and `errorProviderTitle`). This did not create controls on the `Form`, but data members contained in the `Form`. The three `ErrorProvider` instances correspond to three separate controls on the `Form`, for which error information will be displayed.

Thus far, the `Icon` property of the `ErrorProvider` has already been discussed. Icons can be retrieved from a variety of locations including an application's resources or loaded directly from a file. An example of loading an icon from a file is as follows:

```
errorProviderTitle.Icon = new Icon("TheEx.ico");
```

An example of the text associated with the `SetError` method being displayed is as follows:

The `BlinkRate` property specifies the rate in milliseconds at which the `Icon` and the corresponding error text will blink. The `BlinkStyle` property can be set to `NeverBlink`, `AlwaysBlink`, or to blink only when the icon is already displayed and a new text string is specified (`BlinkIfDifferentError`). The default setting for this property is `BlinkIfDifferentError`). Another way to achieve `NeverBlink` behavior is to set the `BlinkRate` property to zero.

The `ContainerControl` property specifies the parent of the `ErrorProvider` instance. This parent can also be specified using a constructor that takes a single parameter of type `ContainerControl`.

The `ErrorProvider` has the ability to track errors related to `DateBound` controls. In support of this feature, the `DataSource` property can be associated with a `DataSet`. This `DataSet` contains tables whose fields are associated with a control. The `DataMember` property allows more explicit identification of the element in error. The `DataMember`'s string specifies a data table within the `DataSource`'s `DataSet` that is to be monitored. The `BindToDataAndErrors` method allows the data source (first parameter) and data member (second parameter) to be specified by a single method call. Once `BindToDataAndErrors` has been called, the `UpdateBinding` method can be called to ensure that the `DataSource` and `DataMember` properties are updated.

The CanExtend method is used to determine if a particular control can be used with the ErrorProvider. CanExtend takes as a parameter an object (a control) and returns a Boolean value. If the Boolean value is True then the control can be extended (typically this will be a control derived from the Control class). If the Boolean return value is False then the control cannot be extended (typically the control specified was a Form or a ToolBar).

A variety of methods exist for ErrorProvider that handle getting and setting the look and feel of how the ErrorProvider is displayed, with respect to the control it is associated with. These methods include specifying where the error icon will be displayed, with respect to the control (the GetIconAlignment and SetIconAlignment methods). The space between the error icon and the control can also be configured using the GetIconPadding and SetIconPadding methods.

The key method to the ErrorProvider is the SetError method. This method takes two parameters: a Control and a string. The control is hence in error and the string is ultimately what is displayed when the mouse hovers over the error icon. The error text associated with the control can be retrieved using the GetError method, which contains a single parameter of type Control (the control whose error text is to be retrieved). The return value for the GetError method is of type string. The prototypes for SetError and GetError are as follows:

C#:

```
public string GetError(Control control);
public void SetError(Control control, string value);
```

VB.NET:

```
Public Function GetError(ByVal control As Control) As String
Public Sub SetError(ByVal control As Control, ByVal value As String)
```

There are no events associated with the ErrorProvider class.

'ErrorProvider' in 'WroxScheduleClient01'

The screenshot at the start of this section presented three instances of the ErrorProvider being displayed on the Insert TabPage of the WroxScheduleClient01 application. These ErrorProvider instances were errorProviderMonthCalendar, errorProviderDateTimePicker, and errorProviderTitle. Each of these ErrorProvider instances is associated with a particular control when the Add button on the Insert TabPage is clicked. The method for handling this button being clicked is buttonAdd_Click.

Within the buttonAdd_Click method, the errorProviderMonthCalendar ErrorProvider instance is associated with the MonthCalendar if the range of days selected spans more than one day. The SetError method is used to associate error text with the MonthCalendar instance, monthCalendarAppt.

```
if (monthCalendarAppt.SelectionStart.Day !=
    monthCalendarAppt.SelectionEnd.Day)
{
   errorProviderMonthCalendar.SetError(monthCalendarAppt,
             "Only one day at a time can be selected");
    bIsError = true;
}
```

This code snippet is a bit contrived. The `MonthCalendar` class contains a property, `MaxSelectionCount`. This property specifies the maximum number of days that can be selected at a time. If this property were set to one then there would be no need to associate an `ErrorProvider` with the instance, `monthCalendarAppt`.

The `SetError` method is called in a similar manner for the `errorProviderDateTimePicker` `ErrorProvider` instance. `SetError` is called when the `DateTimePicker` instances that specify when an appointment starts and ends are in error (start time occurring after or equal to end time):

```
if (dateTimePickerApptStart.Value >= dateTimePickerApptEnd.Value)
{
    errorProviderDateTimePicker.SetError(dateTimePickerApptEnd,
        "Start date must be less than the End date ");
    bIsError = true;
}
```

The title of the appointment is specified by the `textBoxTitle` `TextBox`. The `CompareInfo` class is used to search the `Text` associated with this `TextBox` for a string indicating invalid data. The string that indicates invalid data is 'Gina'. Developers are free to specify the name of their own ex, thus indicating who an appointment should not be made with!

```
CompareInfo compareInfo = CompareInfo.GetCompareInfo("en-Us");

if ((-1) != compareInfo.LastIndexOf(textBoxTitle.Text, "Gina"))
{
    errorProviderTitle.SetError(textBoxTitle,
        "Fool! Do not go out with your exgirlfriend!");
    bIsError = true;
}
```

If the `bIsError` Boolean was set to `True` in each of the previous code snippets then the `buttonAdd_Click` method returns and does not attempt to add the appointment to the list of appointments maintained. The error-detecting portion of the `buttonAdd_Click` method is displayed below:

```
private void buttonAdd_Click(object sender, System.EventArgs e)
{
    bool bIsError = false;

    // Our scheduling application is lazy and only allows appoints
    // to be booked on single day. For this reason the selection
    // range has to occur in the same day

    if (monthCalendarAppt.SelectionStart.Day !=
        monthCalendarAppt.SelectionEnd.Day)
    {
        errorProviderMonthCalendar.SetError(monthCalendarAppt,
                "Only one day at a time can be selected");
        bIsError = true;
    }

    // the start date must be less than the end date
    if (dateTimePickerApptStart.Value >= dateTimePickerApptEnd.Value)
    {
        errorProviderDateTimePicker.SetError(dateTimePickerApptEnd,
```

```
            "Start date must be less than the End date ");
        bIsError = true;
    }

    // System.Globalization
    CompareInfo compareInfo = CompareInfo.GetCompareInfo("en-Us");

    if ((-1) != compareInfo.LastIndexOf(textBoxTitle.Text, "Gina"))
    {
        errorProviderTitle.SetError(textBoxTitle,
            "Fool! Do not go out with your exgirlfriend!");
        bIsError = true;
    }

    if (bIsError)
    {
        return ;
    }

    // Add WroxAppointment to WroxAppointments collection (appointments) here
}
```

This code snippet did not bother to show how an appointment is actually added to the list of appointments maintained by the application. This manipulation is pertinent to an examination of the `System.Collections` namespace, and not the `System.Windows.Forms` namespace.

'HelpProvider'

Per-control help can be displayed courtesy of the `HelpProvider` class. This class is derived directly from `Component` and is similar in some respects to the `ErrorProvider` class.

```
Object
    MarshalByRefObject
        Component
            HelpProvider
```

The `ErrorProvider` class displayed text and an icon associated with the control. The `HelpProvider` displays help information specific to a control when the *F1* key is pressed. An example of just the style of help that can be displayed is as follows:

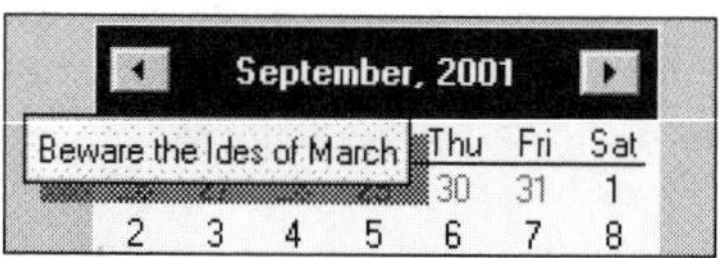

The help text displayed is 'Beware the Ides of March'. This text was displayed when the `MonthCalendar` control in the screenshot was in focus and the *F1* key was pressed. Associating this help text was simply a matter of creating an instance of a `HelpProvider` (instance, `helpProvider`) and then calling the `SetHelpString` exposed by the `HelpProvider` class:

```
helpProvider.SetHelpString(monthCalendarAppt, "Beware the Ides of March");
```

In this code snippet, the variable `monthCalendarAppt` is the instance, type `MonthCalendar` class, for which help was displayed. Creating the `HelpProvider` is achieved using the well-traveled road of Toolbox to `Form` and abracadabra a data member is associated with the `Form`. This new data member is of type `HelpProvider`. Once this `HelpProvider` data member is created, individual controls on the `Form` can have help associated with them.

The `HelpProvider` class implements a single property of its own, `HelpNameSpace`. The `HelpNameSpace` property corresponds to a file name that contains help text. This file name should be either a raw HTML file or a compiled help file (`*.chm`).

It was already demonstrated that the help text associated with a control could be specified using the `HelpProvider's SetHelpString` method. The `GetHelpString` method provides an ability to retrieve the help text associated with a particular control. These methods support help displayed via programmatic text, rather than help retrieved from a file.

The help contained in a file uses keywords to look up a particular help topic. A control for which help is available is associated with a keyword. Behind the scenes, this keyword is used to retrieve the control's help information as it is contained in the help file. The keyword for a control is specified using the `SetHelpKeyword` method (parameter one of type `Control` and parameter two of type `string` corresponding to the keyword). The keyword for a control can be retrieved using the `GetHelpKeyword` method (return value `string` corresponding to the keyword).

Each control for which help is provided can have its ability to show help enabled or disabled. The `SetShowHelp` method takes a `Control` as a parameter and a Boolean as a parameter. If the Boolean value is `True` then help is enabled for the specified `Control`. If `False` is specified then help is disabled for the `Control`. The default setting for this Boolean is `True`. The value of this Boolean can be retrieved using the `GetShowHelp` method.

URL-based help is ultimately supported since the `HelpNamespace` property specifies a URL. The `help keyword` is used to jump to a specific location within this help-URL. The specific form with which this help navigation will take place is set using the `SetHelpNavigator` method and retrieved using the `GetHelpNavigator` method. The prototype for the `SetHelpNavigator` method is as follows:

C#:

```
public virtual void SetHelpNavigator(Control ctl,
                                     HelpNavigator navigator);
```

VB.NET:

```
Overridable Public Sub SetHelpNavigator(ByVal ctl As Control, _
                                        ByVal navigator As HelpNavigator)
```

The first parameter (the `ctl Control`) corresponds to the control whose help navigation is to be specified. The second parameter specifies how help will be navigated be specifying a value of type `HelpNavigator`. The permissible values for the `HelpNavigator` enumeration are `Topic`, `TableOfContents`, `KeywordIndex`, `Find`, and `AssociatedIndex`. Each of these keywords corresponds to a specific way in which to search for and locate a URL, or the contents of information found at a URL.

'ProgressBar'

The ProgressBar control is used to track the progress of some activity.

```
Object
    MarshalByRefObject
        Component
            Control
                ProgressBar
```

In the following screenshot, the ProgressBar is forty percent filled:

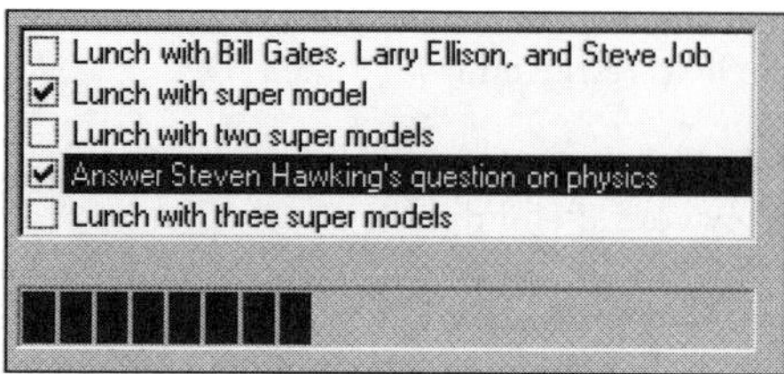

The ProgressBar is forty percent filled because it is tracking the number of items checked in the CheckedListBox instance – the CheckedListBox contains five items and two are checked, hence the ProgressBar is forty percent filled. This is a rather contrived use of a ProgressBar; more typical uses include the status of web download, or the status of a program install.

Some properties of ProgressBar include:

Property	Description
Maximum	This property specifies the upper bound represented by the progress bar. The default value is 100.
Minimum	This property of the ProgressBar specifies the lower bound represented by the progress bar. The default value is 0.
Step	This property specifies the amount to increment the Value property each time the PerformStep method is called. The default value of this property is 10. If the Step increments Value above Maximum then the value is reset to Minimum.
Value	This property specifies the current value of the progress (the amount of progress made).

Recall in the previous screenshot that the ProgressBar is used to track the number of items checked in a CheckedListBox instance. The code that sets up the progressBarCheckedListBox instance of a ProgressBar makes use of the number of items in the checkedListBoxDefaultTitle instance of CheckedListBox. This setup code is as follows:

```
progressBarCheckedListBox.Minimum = 0;
progressBarCheckedListBox.Maximum =
         checkedListBoxDefaultTitle.Items.Count;
progressBarCheckedListBox.Value = 0;
```

The code snippet sets the Maximum property of the ProgressBar to reflect the number of values in the CheckedListBox. The Minimum property is set to zero and the Value property is set to its initial progress (zero). Each time a check box in the CheckedListBox is checked or unchecked, the clbDefaultTitle_SelectedIndexChanged method is called. This method updates the Value of the ProgressBar using the number of checked items in the CheckedListBox:

```
progressBarCheckedListBox.Value =
    checkedListBoxDefaultTitle.CheckedIndices.Count;
```

The Increment method advances the Value of the ProgressBar by specifying a parameter of type integer. The underlying Value of the ProgressBar is incremented by the number passed as the parameter to Increment. The PerformStep method increments the underlying Value of the ProgressBar by the amount specified in the Step property. The ProgressBar exposes no events directly. Since this class is derived from Control, it inherits a plethora of events (KeyUp, KeyDown, DoubleClick, etc.).

Summary

Over the past three chapters, dozens of Windows Forms Controls have been introduced. These controls are the genes that make up the complex genetic structure of a Windows Forms application. From the humble Button, Label, and TextBox, to the more intricate ListView, TreeView, PageControl, and Splitter, these controls make up the vast majority of Windows Forms related classes used by most client-side applications. Resizing the TreeView and ListView controls was achieved using Splitter. Dates and times were manipulated using DateTimePicker and MonthCalendar. A variety of interesting text and numeric input controls were presented (ComboBox, CheckListBox, NumericUpDown, and DomainUpDown). Even help and errors were addressed (HelpProvider and ErrorProvider).

There may appear to be a certain amount of overlap with respect to the functionality exposed by each type of control. Text, for example, can be entered in a dozen different ways. The art of Windows Forms development is usability. By exploring the subtleties of each control, usability can only be enhanced.

Legend: Concrete Class / Abstract class

System.Windows.Forms

- System.Object
  - System.MarshalRefObject
    - System.ComponentMode.Component
      - CommonDialog
        - ColorDialog
        - FileDialog
        - FontDialog
        - PageSetupDialog
        - PrintDialog
      - ErrorProvider
      - HelpProvider
      - ImageList
      - Menu
        - ContextMenu
        - MainMenu
        - MenuItem
      - NotifyIcon
      - StatusBarPanel
      - Timer
      - ToolBarButton
      - ToolTip
      - Control
        - ButtonBase
          - Button
          - CheckBox
          - RadioButton
        - DataGrid
        - DateTimePicker
        - GroupBox
        - Label
          - LinkLabel
        - ListControl
          - ComboBox
          - ListBox
            - CheckedListBox
        - ListView
        - MonthCalendar
        - PictureBox
        - PrintReviewControl
        - ProgressBar
        - ScrollableControl
          - ContainerControl
            - Form
              - PrintPreviewDialog
              - ThreadExceptionDialog
            - PropertyGrid
            - UpDownBase
              - DomainUpDown
              - NumericUpDown
            - UserControl
          - Panel
            - TabPage
        - ScrollBar
          - HScrollBar
          - VScrollBar
        - Splitter
        - StatusBar
        - TabControl
        - TextBoxBase
          - RichTextBox
          - Textbox
        - ToolBar
        - TrackBar
        - TreeView
  - ListViewItem
  - TreeNode

11

Components and Reports

Windows Forms Components can be used to perform a wide variety of tasks, such as monitoring file-system changes, getting process information, starting and stopping Windows Services, and monitoring the performance of a system. They are different from most Windows Forms Controls in that they do not have a visual interface, and they are derived from the `Component` class. The `Component` class implements the `IComponent` interface that describes the behavior of Windows Forms components.

VS.NET ships with the following components, all of which can be accessed from the toolbox:

- `FileSystemWatcher`
- `EventLog`
- `MessageQueue`
- `PerformanceCounter`
- `Process`
- `ServiceController`
- `Timer`
- `ReportDocument`
- `DirectoryEntry`
- `DirectorySearcher`

During the course of this chapter we will learn how to use all the components except the `Timer`, which has already been covered in Chapter 9 on controls.

At the end of the chapter, we will look at the `CrystalReportViewer` control and the `ReportDocument` component, which allow us to include high quality presentation material in our forms.

WroxAdmin

`WroxAdmin` is a VB.NET project that was developed to demonstrate the use of components in the toolbox, and can be used as an administration tool. Components are not strictly part of the 'Windows Forms world', but they are important and can really enhance our Windows Forms applications.

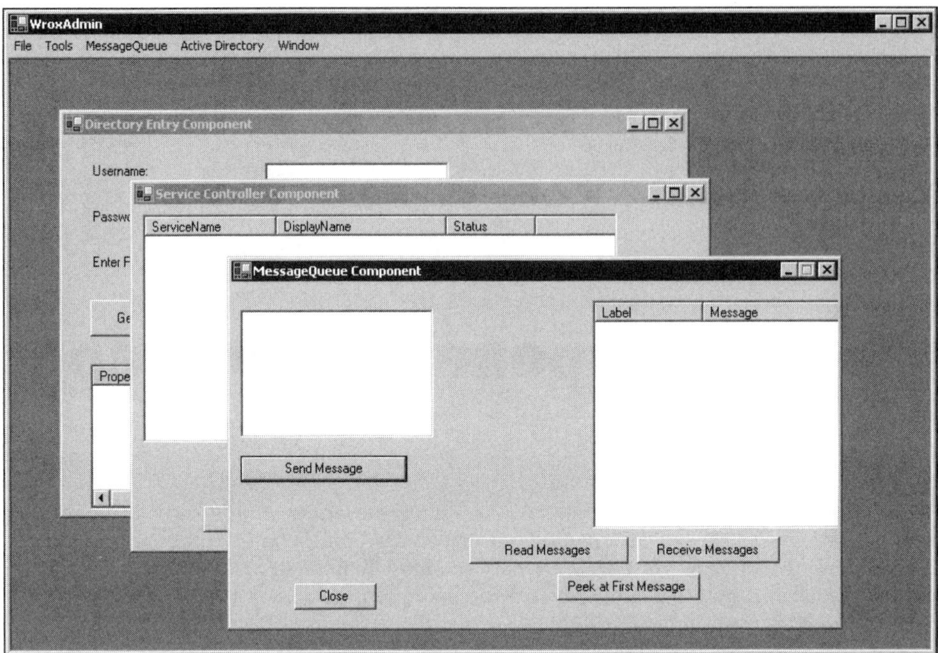

The screenshot above shows WroxAdmin with a few of its child windows open. This tool will help in understanding how to incorporate components into our applications. We will begin with the `MessageQueue` component since it is required for some of the other components in our `WroxAdmin` tool to function.

'MessageQueue' Component

The `MessageQueue` component is used to build messaging functionality in our application. Using this, we can connect to existing queues and send and receive messages. Messages can be as simple as strings, and as complex as objects with properties. The `MessageQueue` class belongs to the `System.Messaging` namespace, and is derived as follows:

```
Object
    MarshalByRefObject
        Component
            MessageQueue
```

Refer to the MSDN for a list of its members.

In WroxAdmin, the MessageQueue component is used to demonstrate sending complex messages to a queue. After sending messages, the sample will demonstrate how to read the queue without removing messages from it, as well as how to receive messages from a queue. This screenshot shows the MessageQueue component form in WroxAdmin:

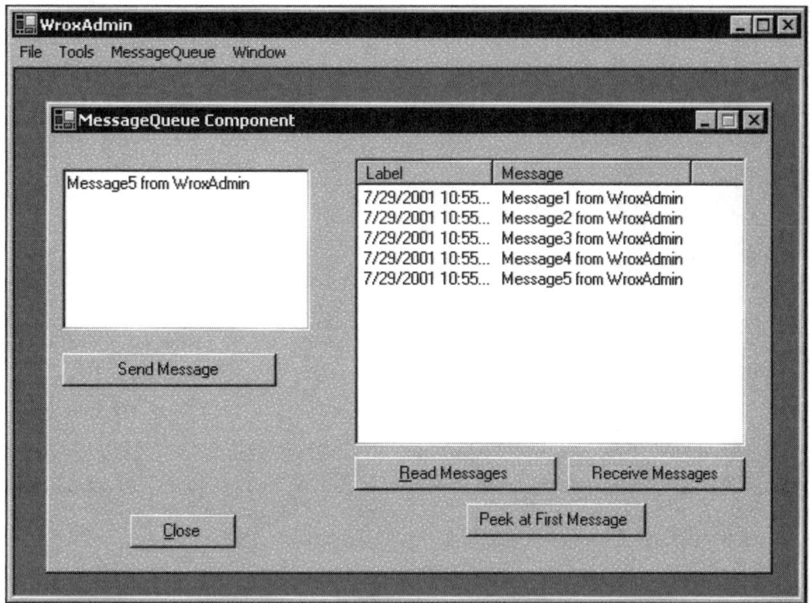

Using WroxAdmin, we can type a message and send it to a queue. We can then read all the messages without removing them from a queue by clicking the Read Messages button. We can remove all the messages by clicking the Receive Messages button. After sending several messages to the queue, we can peek at the first message by clicking the Peek at First Message button.

Setting Up a Message Queue

To set up a message queue to store and process messages, we must first install the MSMQ software. This can be done when the OS is installed, or it can be added later from the Windows NT/2000 Installation CD. For more information on this, check out http://www.microsoft.com/msmq/.

After installing the MSMQ software, we can right-click on MyComputer and select Manage to see the Message Queuing node. We can add a new public queue by right-clicking on the Message Queue node and then selecting Add | Public Queue. In the dialog box that opens up, specify Inbox as the name of the queue. The following screenshot shows how to create a new queue:

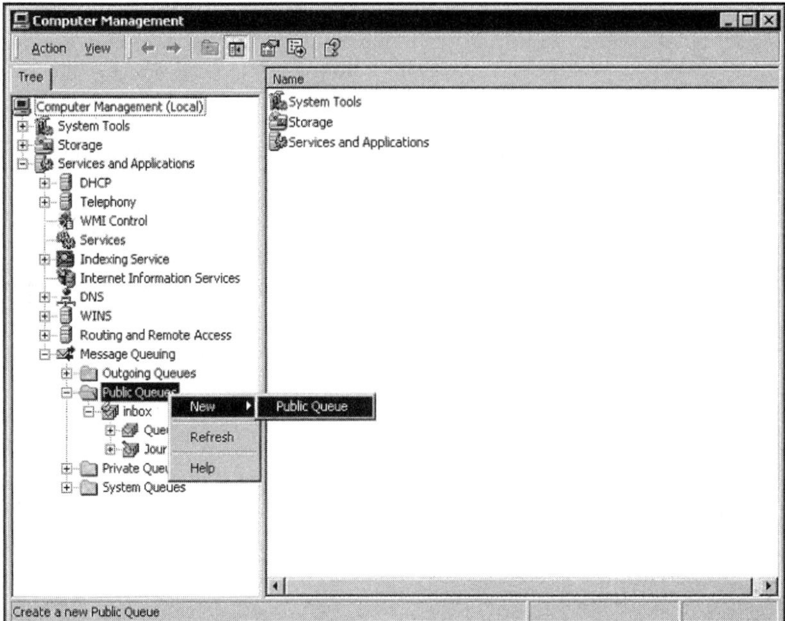

Adding an Instance of 'MessageQueue' Component

We can add a `MessageQueue` component in one of several ways:

- Use the toolbox and drag a `MessageQueue` component to the Windows Form. It will appear in the component tray, ready for configuration.
- Use the Server Explorer and identify the queue we want to send and receive messages. Then right-click on the queue and Add to Designer, or drag and drop it into the Windows Form. It will be configured for us. Following is a screenshot of the properties window of a MessageQueue component, added from the server explorer:

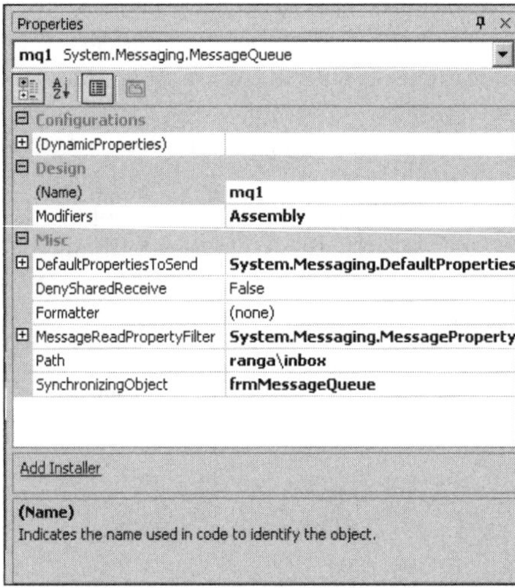

- Create a MessageQueue Component and bind it to the existing Inbox queue in code, as follows:

```
Dim mq1 As New System.Messaging.MessageQueue(".\Inbox")
```

Configuring a 'MessageQueue' Component

We use the `Path` property to specify which queue our component references. If we created the component from the toolbox, then when we click on the path field in the properties window, we will be presented with a dialog box like the one shown in the following screenshot, where we can select the queue that we want:

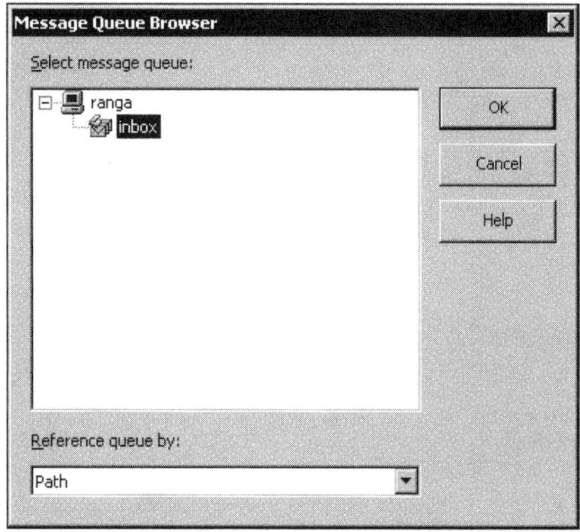

The `Formatter` property determines how the message content will be serialized before being sent to a queue, and also how it will be extracted from a message after its reception. The available options are `ActiveXMessageFormatter`, `BinaryMessageFormatter` and `XMLMessageFormatter`, which is the default.

When `DenySharedReceive` is set to `True`, only one component at a time can look at the messages in a queue.

Sending Simple Messages

Using the `MessageQueue` component, we can send a message to a queue very easily. We first create and configure a component to point to the queue that we want to send messages to. Then we call the `Send` method as follows:

```
Mq1.Send("message")
```

Sending Complex Messages

In real-world situations, we will want to send more complex messages and have more control over the messages that we send. For this we can use the `Message` object to construct our message, and then send the `Message` object to the queue. In WroxAdmin, the following code does this:

```
Dim mq1 As New System.Messaging.MessageQueue (".\Inbox")
Dim message1 As System.Messaging.Message("Message1 from WroxAdmin")
Message1.Label = "WroxAdmin"
Mq1.Send(message1)
```

So, we type the message text in a textbox and click on the send button. The message will be sent to a queue called `Inbox`. After sending a couple of messages we can view the queue (MyComputer | Manage | MessageQueue node), as shown here:

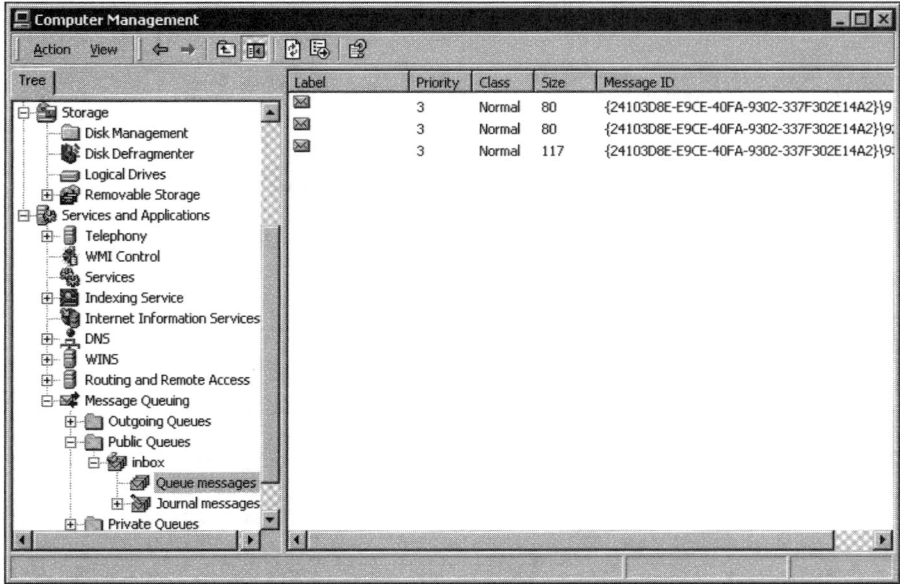

We can view the message text by selecting a message and viewing its properties (right-click, and select Properties), as shown in the following screenshot. We can see the words Message1 from WroxAdmin:

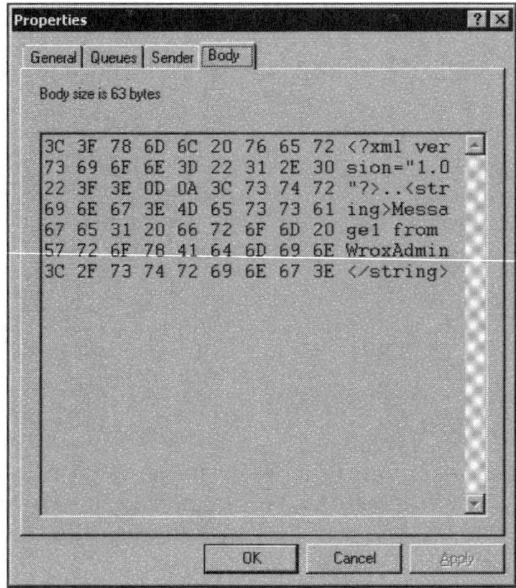

We can also see the message text from the Server Explorer itself. To do this, we navigate to the queue and select the message we want to view. In the properties window, select the `BodyStream` property. We will see the message body in XML format:

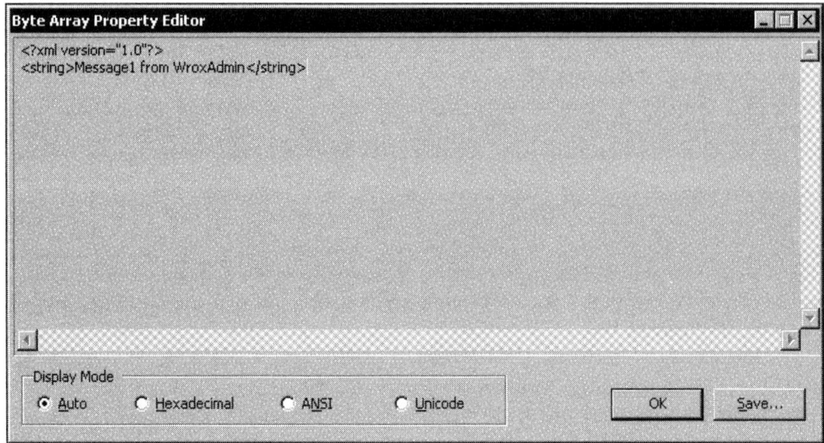

Retrieving Messages from a Queue Without Removing

Once messages are sent to a queue, they can either be read for processing without removing them from the queue, or they can be removed and then processed. Use the `GetAllMessages` method of the `MessageQueue` component to get an array of all messages in the queue. In WroxAdmin, the code to read the messages from a queue is as follows:

```
Private Sub cmdReadMessages_Click(ByVal sender As System.Object, _
ByVal e As System.EventArgs) Handles cmdReadMessages.Click

        ' Clear the listview
        lvwMsgs.Items.Clear()

        ' Create a queue object and connect it the Inbox queue
        Dim mq3 As New System.Messaging.MessageQueue()
        mq3.Path = ".\Inbox"

        ' Create a formatter of type xmlmessageformatter
        Dim fmt As System.Messaging.XmlMessageFormatter = CType(mq3.Formatter, _
        System.Messaging.XmlMessageFormatter)
        fmt.TargetTypeNames = New String() {"System.String"}

        ' Declare an array of message objects
        Dim Msg() As System.Messaging.Message 'array of message objects
        Dim i As Integer

        ' Retrieve a snapshot of all messages
        Msg = mq3.GetAllMessages()

        ' Clear the current contents of the list.
        lvwMsgs.Items.Clear()

        'Display the label and the body of the message
```

```
        For i = 0 To Msg.Length - 1
            lvwMsgs.Items.Add(Msg(i).Label)
            lvwMsgs.Items(i).SubItems.Add(Msg(i).Body)
        Next
    End Sub
```

Removing Messages From a Queue

We can remove the messages from a queue and process them. We can use the `Receive` method of the `MessageQueue` component to retrieve the message one at a time, as follows:

```
    mq1.Receive()
```

Alternatively, we can use the `MessageEnumerator` to retrieve and remove all the messages. In WroxAdmin, when we click on the **Receive Messages** button, all the messages are retrieved, displayed, and then removed.

```
Private Sub cmdReceiveMessages_Click(ByVal sender As System.Object, _
ByVal e As System.EventArgs) Handles cmdReceiveMessages.Click

    ' Clear the list
    lvwMsgs.Items.Clear()

    Dim i As Integer

    ' Declare and configure a queue component
    Dim mq2 As New System.Messaging.MessageQueue()
    mq2.Path = ".\Inbox"

    ' Declare a formatter
    Dim fmt As System.Messaging.XmlMessageFormatter =  CType(mq2.Formatter, _
    System.Messaging.XmlMessageFormatter)
    fmt.TargetTypeNames = New String() {"System.String"}

    ' Declare a MessageEnumerator
    Dim msgEnum As System.Messaging.MessageEnumerator

    ' Use GetEnumerator to enumerate the messages in the queue
    ' Convert it into the System.Message.MessageEnumerator type
    msgEnum = CType(mq2.GetEnumerator, System.Messaging.MessageEnumerator)

Try

    ' Move to the first message in the enumerator
    ' Using Current property, display the label and body
    ' Use the TimeSpan object to specify a delay of 3 seconds
    msgEnum.MoveNext(New TimeSpan(0, 0, 3))
    Dim lvwItem As ListViewItem
    lvwItem = lvwMsgs.Items.Add(msgEnum.Current.Label.ToString)
    lvwItem.SubItems.Add(msgEnum.Current.Body.ToString)

    ' Remove the message from the queue using RemoveCurrent()
    msgEnum.RemoveCurrent()
        Catch ex As Exception
        MessageBox.Show("No messages in queue")
        End Try
    End Sub
```

The enumerator is, by default, positioned before the first message. When MoveNext is used for the first time, it moves to the first message in the enumerator.

It is important to note that using the GetEnumerator method does not automatically remove messages from a queue. It is only when we use the msgEnum.RemoveCurrent method that the message is removed. If we do not use the RemoveCurrent method, then the message will not be removed. In that case, the GetEnumerator method provides a dynamic connection to the queue – that is, as messages are added to the queue, they are instantly made available to the enumerator after we reset the pointer by using the Reset method (for more on this method, consult the documentation).

Peeking at Messages

Using the Peek method, we can peek at the first message in the queue, without removing the message from the queue. We can use the Peek method to ascertain if a message has arrived in a queue. In WroxAdmin, the peek method is used as follows:

```
Private Sub cmdPeek_Click(ByVal sender As System.Object, _
ByVal e As System.EventArgs) Handles cmdPeek.Click
    lvwMsgs.Items.Clear()
    Try
        Dim lvwItem As ListViewItem
        Dim mq4 As New System.Messaging.MessageQueue(".\Inbox")

        Dim fmt As System.Messaging.XmlMessageFormatter = CType(mq4.Formatter, _
        System.Messaging.XmlMessageFormatter)
        fmt.TargetTypeNames = New String() {"System.String"}

        Dim msgFirst As System.Messaging.Message
        msgFirst = mq4.Peek(New TimeSpan(0, 0, 3))

        lvwItem = lvwMsgs.Items.Add(msgFirst.Label)
        lvwItem.SubItems.Add(msgFirst.Body)
    Catch
        MessageBox.Show("no message in the queue")
    End Try
End Sub
```

'FileSystemWatcher' Component

The FileSystemWatcher class belongs to the System.IO namespace and is derived as follows:

```
Object
    MarshalByRefObject
        Component
            FileSystemWatcher
```

The main purpose of this component is to monitor the file system for changes to files, directories, and their attributes, and take action based on the changes. The component can monitor changes to either the local or a remote file system. For example, if we have a file that is shared by several users. We can set up a watch to monitor the changes to the file and send e-mail to a concerned few, or send a message to a message queue. This component will be very useful in applications where we need to take action after users upload files to their folders (as in bulletin-board systems). It can also be used so that instead of constantly polling the directory for new files, we can wait for notifications indicating that a new file has been created.

Essentially, we can capture any change to the file system, such as when files are created or deleted, or if files of a particular type are created or changed. This component can be used both in Windows Forms and ASP.NET applications, but it works only in Windows NT/2000/XP systems, and will not work in Windows 9X series systems.

The `FileSystemWatcher` component form is demonstrated in the `WroxAdmin` tool in the Tools | FileSystemWatcher menu item, as shown in the screenshot below. In this form, we specify the directory to watch in the textbox, and then click on Watch to begin to watch the file system. When we make changes or create files in the file system, the component is notified of the events and a message is sent to the message queue.

The labels indicate that changes have been made to a file, and a new file has been created. Notice that, while the directory being watched is `c:\`, the `FileSystem` activities in the subdirectory of `c:\` have been captured. We will, of course, need to set up a message queue and configure its path correctly before attempting to test this section.

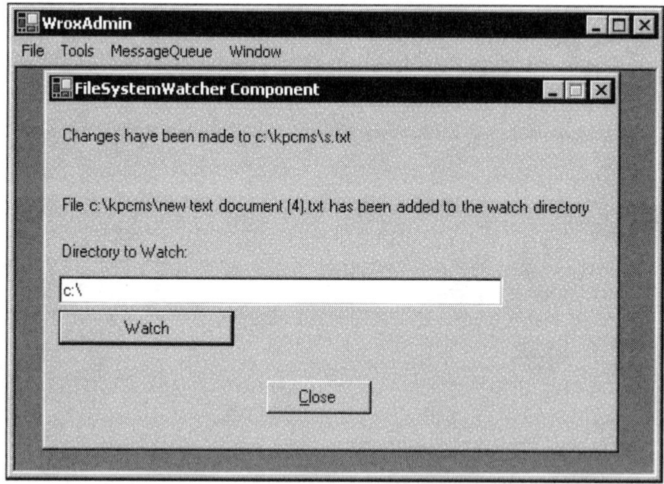

Adding a 'FileSystemWatcher' Component

A `FileSystemWatcher` component instance can be added to a Windows Form in two ways.

We can add it in the usual way, by dragging and dropping from the toolbox to the Windows Form. This will add an instance of the component to the form and will appear in the bottom of the form in the component tray. A screenshot from `WroxAdmin` is shown below, with a file system watcher component (`fswatcher1`), in the component tray. A message queue component (`mq1`) has also been added to the tray.

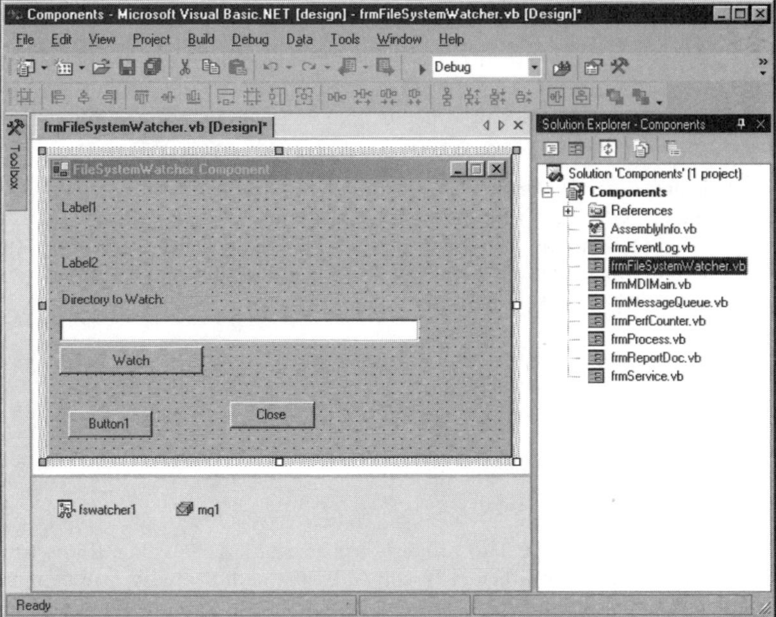

Alternatively, we can add the component instance directly in code as follows:

```
Dim fsWatcher1 As New System.IO.FileSystemWatcher ()
```

The above code is equivalent to adding a `FileSystemWatcher` component from the toolbox. If we do not use the designer, we have to supply all properties and methods by coding it ourselves. Refer to the MSDN documentation for a list of properties and methods of the `FileSystemWatcher` component.

Configuring the 'FileSystemWatcher' Component

If we add an instance of `FileSystemWatcher` from the toolbox, then we can click on the instance and set the properties in the properties window that appear as shown below:

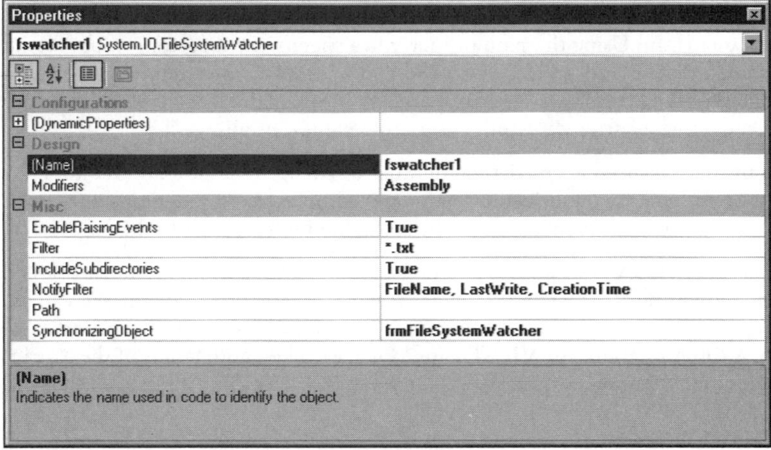

Let's take a quick look at these properties:

- `EnableRaisingEvents`: Set this to `True` for the component to be able to raise events. This is set to `False` if we do not want the component to raise events. This will be useful, when we want to turn-off raising events for a specific time interval. In WroxAdmin, this property has been set to `True` at design time.

- `Path`: This property specifies the fully qualified path to the directory that is to be watched. For example `c:\test`, or even `\\server1\test` for a directory on the network. In `WroxAdmin`, we will not set it in the properties window, because the user will type in a desired path of the folder to watch in the text box (`txtDir`) and this path is supplied to the `fswatcher1` component's path property as follows:

```
Private Sub cmdWatch_Click(ByVal sender As System.Object, _
ByVal e As System.EventArgs) Handles cmdWatch.Click

    fswatcher1.Path = txtDir.Text

End Sub
```

- `IncludeSubdirectories`: This property has a `True/False` value. If it is `True`, sub-directories within the root directory (specified by the path property) will be monitored. The same changes in the subdirectories are watched, as are those in the main directory. In `WroxAdmin`, this is set to `True` in the IDE.

- `Filter`: Use this property to watch for changes to a specific file, specific file type, or specific directory name in the directory to be watched (specified by path property). For example, to watch only the text files in the path directory, use `*.txt`. To watch changes to only a file called `test.txt`, specify `test.txt` in the `Filter` property. In `WroxAdmin`, this has been set to `*.txt` at design time. This could be done in code as well, as follows:

```
fswatcher1.Filter="*.txt"
```

  Or, if we want to watch more than one file type, for example `.doc` as well, then:

```
fswatcher1.Filter="*.doc, *.txt"
```

- `NotifyFilter`: Using the path property, we specify the directory to be watched. But what are the changes that need to be watched and notified to the component? These changes are specified in the `NotifyFilter` property. We can set the `NotifyFilter` property to watch for changes to security, directory names, file names, or all.

  This property is used to restrict the number of changes that are notified to the component instance. If too many notifications are received by the component instance, it may run out of buffer space. For more information on sizing the buffers, refer to the VS.NET documentation.

  The component can be configured to raise events only when a file or directory is created, or when a file or directory name changes, or when a file's size changes. We can set multiple changes to watch for by separating the values with a comma in the properties window, or by using a BitOr operator for VB.NET (or | for C#). The valid values of the `NotifyFilters` enumeration that are used to specify the `NotifyFilter` property are listed below:

Notify Enumerator	Description
Attributes	The attributes of the file or folder – such as read only, hidden, etc
CreationTime	The time the file or folder was created
DirectoryName	Changes to the name of directories
FileName	Changes to name of files
LastAccess	The date the file or folder was last opened
LastWrite	The date the file or folder was last edited
Security	The security settings of the file or folder
Size	Changes to the size of the file or folder

In code, we can specify NotifyFilters as follows:

```
fswatcher1.Notifyfilter = IO.NotifyFilters.FileName BitOr
IO.NotifyFilters.LastWrite BitOr IO.NotifyFilters.CreationTime
```

Events

Based on the values provided for the Path, IncludeSubDirectories, Filter, and NotifyFilter properties, the component will receive event notifications from the system. These events must be handled to take appropriate action. The FileSystemWatcher component can handle the following events:

- Created: Raised whenever a directory or file is created.
- Deleted: Raised whenever a directory or file is deleted.
- Renamed: Raised whenever the name of a directory or file is changed.
- Changed: Raised whenever changes are made to the size, system attributes, last write time, last access time, or security permissions of a directory or file.

Copying and moving operations in the file system also raise events. When a file is copied, the system raises a Created event in the directory to which the file was copied, but no event is raised in the original directory. When a file is moved, a Deleted event is raised in the source directory and a Created event in the target directory.

Each change to a file in a directory raises a separate event. If a user makes multiple changes to a single file, the application raises a separate event for each change. For example, if we are watching a directory that contains three files that are all changed, three Changed events will be raised. If a file is renamed, both a renamed and a changed event will be raised, because the renaming will cause the last access time to change.

Event handlers can be written for each event (Created, Deleted, Renamed, Changed). As we saw from Chapter 6, an event handler is a method that is bound to an event for a component, form, or control. Each event handler provides two parameters that are useful to handle the event. Firstly, the sender, which provides an object reference to the object responsible for the event, and secondly, the e parameter, which provides an object for representing the event and its information. In WroxAdmin, the changed event is handled as follows:

```
Private Sub fswatcher1_Changed(ByVal sender As System.Object, _
ByVal e As System.IO.FileSystemEventArgs) Handles fswatcher1.Changed
        Label1.Text = "Changes have been made to " & e.FullPath
        mq1.Send(Label1.Text)
        MessageBox.Show("message sent successfully")
    End Sub
```

The `FileSystemEventArgs` object provides information about the event that has been raised – in this case, the `FullPath` of the file that was changed. This is used to display the `FullPath` of the file in the label. Then using the `MessageQueue` instance, the `FullPath` of the file is sent to the `MessageQueue` in the system.

Similarly, the created event has been trapped and used as follows:

```
Private Sub fswatcher1_Created(ByVal sender As Object, _
ByVal e As System.IO.FileSystemEventArgs) Handles fswatcher1.Created

    Label2.Text = "File " & e.FullPath & " has been added to the watch directory"
        mq1.Send(Label2.Text)
        MessageBox.Show("message sent successfully")
    End Sub
```

Whenever a file is created, it is displayed in the label, and a message is sent to the queue. In `WroxAdmin`, when a file was created in `c:\kpcms` (a subdirectory of `c:\`), the `Created` event is triggered. This sends the name of the file to a message queue. This is because, although the folder that is under watch is `c:\`, the component has its `IncludeSubDirectories` property set to `True`.

The `FileSystemWatcher` component is a welcome addition to the programmer's toolbox. It can be programmed to monitor both local and remote file systems, and execute business processes based on `FileSystem` activities.

'EventLog' Component

The `EventLog` component, an instance of the `EventLog` class in the `System.Diagnostics` namespace, is derived as follows:

```
Object
    MarshalByRefObject
        Component
            EventLog
```

It provides a convenient method to read from and write to event logs in any computer in the network. It also can be used to add custom event logs to the system and also write to them. Logging errors and other useful information to the event logs is in keeping with good system management practice. In Windows 2000, right-clicking on MyComputer, and selecting Manage will invoke the event viewer. Once open, the event viewer displays several event logs. The screenshot below shows a sample event viewer window with several event logs:

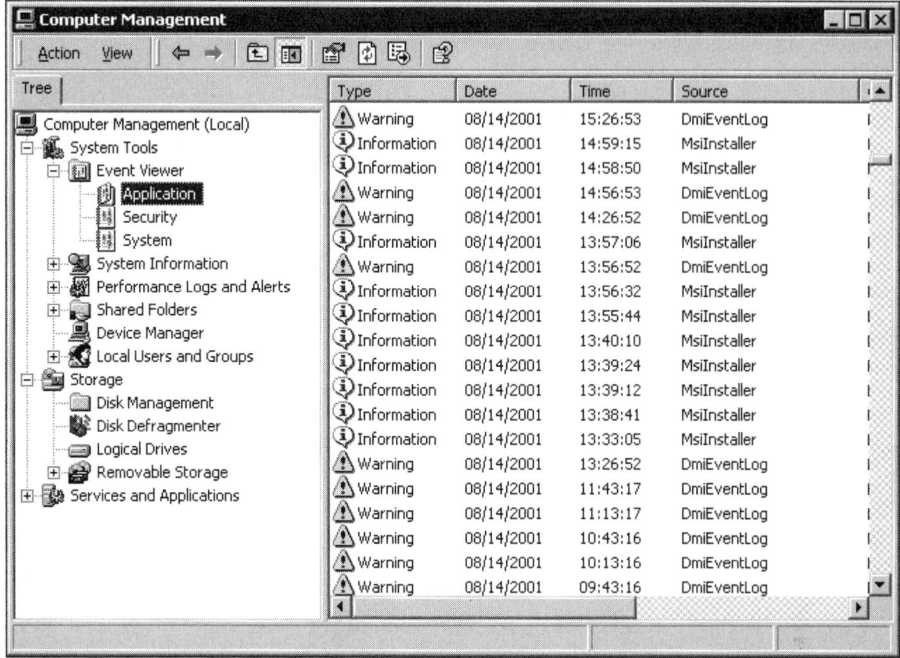

The `EventLog` component form in `WroxAdmin` can be seen by selecting the Tools/EventLog menu item and is shown below. In this form, we can query all the entries from the Application Log and write an entry into it using .NET as the source. A source is used to identify the application that made an entry in the `EventLog`. After writing an entry, we can verify it by querying the contents of the log. We can also clear the `EventLog`. While this is a simple example, it will provide the foundation for further customization and incorporation into our own applications.

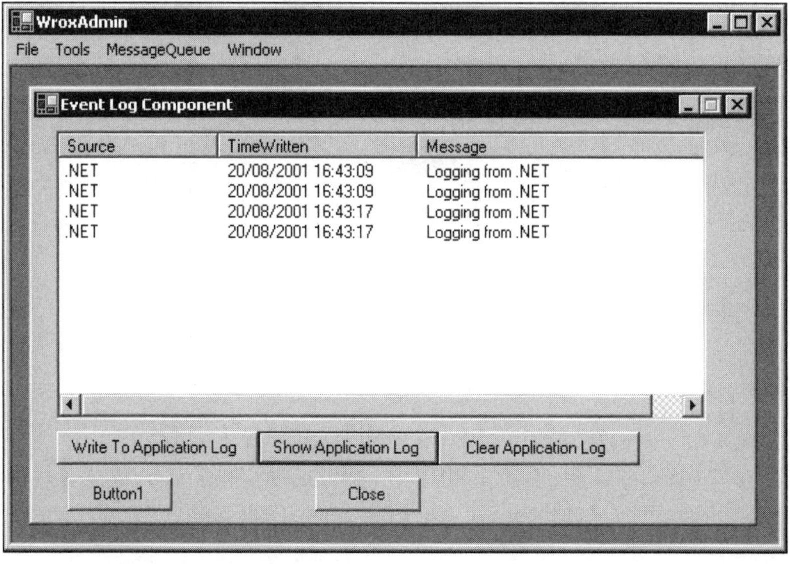

Before exploring the `EventLog` component that comes with Windows Forms, we should note some basic information about event logs in general, and the `EventLog` component that ships with the .NET Framework.

An event is an important activity in either the software or hardware of the system that is logged into one of the event logs. An event in a log is represented by an `EventLogEntry` object in .NET, and can be classified into one of the following event types – Errors, Warnings, Information, Success audits, and Failure Audits. Several applications can write entries to the same log. An application that writes entries to an `EventLog` is called a Source.

There are three event logs available by default on computers running Windows 2000 or Windows NT 4.0:

- System Log: Used to register events that occur on system hardware components, such as device drivers not working properly.
- Security Log: Used to register events related to security changes and violations.
- Application Log: Used to track events that occur in an application.

Apart from the default event logs, programs such as DNS Server, File Replication Service, and Active Directory may create their own custom logs. Event logs can be used from Windows Forms as well as ASP.NET applications.

The `EventLog` component in the toolbox can be used to connect to event logs on both local and remote computers, and these logs can be read and written to, provided the necessary permissions are available.

Adding an 'EventLog' to a Windows Form

An `EventLog` component instance can be added to a Windows Form in three ways. Apart from dragging and dropping, and adding the component by hand, we can also open the Server Explorer from the View menu and expand the EventLog node. We should see a screen similar to the one shown below:

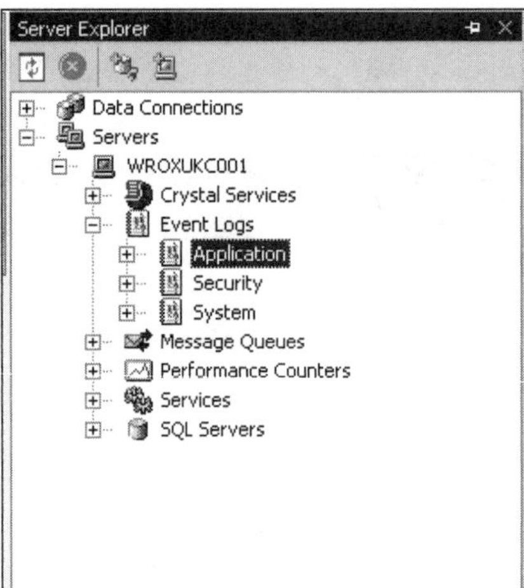

Select the required log, and drag and drop it into the Windows Form. We should see the `EventLog` component instance in the component tray in the form and the properties of the component are configured for us, as shown below:

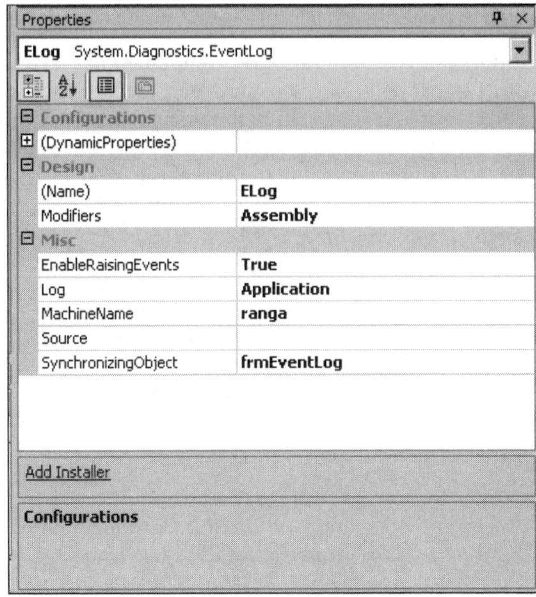

We can see that the `MachineName` has been set, and the `Log` has been set to `Application`.

Configuring an 'EventLog' Component

Let's take a look at the more important properties of an `EventLog` component. Of course, these can be set in the properties box and the code:

- `MachineName`: This is the name of the machine that has the log that we want to read from or write to. We can set this in code, using:

```
EventLog1.MachineName = "machinename"
```

- `Log`: This is the name of the log that we want to read from or write to. Set this in code using:

```
EventLog1.Log = "NameOfLog".
```

- `Source`: This is the name of the source of the `EventLogEntry` (or Entries) that we want to query. Set this in code using:

```
EventLog1.Source = "SourceName"
```

- `EnableRaisingEvents`: Set this to `True` to enable the `EventLog` component to raise events. When entries are written to the log, an `EntryWritten` event is raised that we can write a handler for. Set this in code using:

```
EventLog1.EnableRaisingEvents = True
```

Once we have created the `EventLog` component instance and configured it to point to a specific log, we can read from and write to the log.

Reading From an Event Log

Reading from a log is straightforward. The EventLog component has a collection called Entries that is referenced using the Entries property of the component. Each entry in an EventLog corresponds to an EventLogEntry object. We simply iterate through the collection and read each entry's source, timewritten, and message properties. In WroxAdmin, the EventLog instance is called Elog. lvwElog is the name of the ListView control that displays the details of each entry:

```
' Dimension a eventlogentry object
    Dim Entry As EventLogEntry
    Dim lvwItem As ListViewItem

' Loop thru the Entries collection and get the properties
For Each Entry In ELog.Entries
    lvwItem = lvwElog.Items.Add(Entry.Source)
    lvwItem.SubItems.Add(Entry.TimeWritten)
    lvwItem.SubItems.Add(Entry.Message)
Next
```

We can query the EventLogEntry object to get more information about each entry. Use the IntelliSense or the MSDN to find a list of properties of this object.

Writing to an Event Log

Entries can be written to an EventLog in two different ways, as detailed below.

Firstly, we specify the Source property of the EventLog component. This can be any string value, but it is preferable to give a meaningful value, such as the name of the application, so that the problem can be easily identified. In WroxAdmin, the Source property is set to ".NET" (ELog.Source = ".NET"). We set the source only once. From then on, whenever an EventLogEntry is written from this specific component instance, the source is assumed to be the one that was registered originally.

We must set the Source property on the EventLog component before we can write entries to a log. When a component writes an entry, the system automatically checks to see if the source we specified is registered with the event log that it is writing to, and calls the CreateEventSource method if it has not been created already.

Next, we should specify the message that we want to write to the EventLog. This is a string value. We should construct the message string with useful information that can help in interpreting and correcting the problem.

Next, call the WriteEntry method of the EventLog component instance, and specify the message and the EventEntryType. In WroxAdmin, the following code was used to enter a log to the application log:

```
ELog.WriteEntry("Logging from NET", EventLogEntryType.Information)
```

The message specified has a restriction of 16K bytes. Also, the application writing to the log must have write access to the log.

We can specify several parameters when we write an entry, including the type of entry we're making, an ID that identifies the event, a category, and any binary data we want to append to the entry. For more information on the properties associated with an entry, see EventLog members in MSDN.

The second way of writing an event to an event log uses the `EventLog.CreateEventSource` method to register an event source with the log to which we want to write an entry. We specify the source string as the first parameter and specify the log that we want to write to as the second parameter. For example, to register the `".NET"` source in the application log of our app, we use the following code:

```
If Not EventLog.SourceExists(".NET") Then _
    EventLog.CreateEventSource(".NET", "Application")
End If
```

Then we instantiate an `EventLog` component directly in code using the following syntax:

```
Dim EventLog1 as new System.Diagnostics.EventLog()
```

The `Source` property for the component is set to the source that we registered:

```
EventLog1.Source = ".NET"
```

Call the `WriteEntry` method to specify the entry to be written to the log along with the message:

```
EventLog1.WriteEntry("Logging from .NET")
```

We can specify the entry type (Error, Information, etc) in the overloaded parameters of the `WriteEntry` method.

Clearing an Event Log

To clear an event log of all existing entries, and allow it to start recording events again, we use the `Clear` method:

```
Elog.Clear()
```

where `Elog` is an `EventLog` component instance. Administrator permission is required on the computer on which the log resides in order to clear event log entries.

Creating a Custom Log

Apart from reading and writing entries to the standard existing logs, the `EventLog` component can be used to create custom logs, and write `EventLog` entries to them. After writing entries to a custom log, it is possible to read the entries back. We will see how to do this in the following section.

To create a custom log, we use the `SourceExists` method first, to verify that the source we are using does not already exist, and then call the `CreateEventSource` method with the name of a log that does not exist. Because this log does not exist, the system will create a custom log for us when this code is run. The following snippet shows how to create a custom `EventLog` called `CustomLog`:

```
If Not EventLog.SourceExists(".NET") Then
    EventLog.CreateEventSource(".NET", "CustomLog")
End If
```

Deleting a Custom Log

We can use the EventLog.Delete method to delete an entire event log. Use this method with caution, as deleting a log will also delete any sources registered in it:

```
EventLog.Delete("CustomLog")
```

Writing Entries to a Custom Log

Writing entries to a custom log is the same as writing entries to any other log. Set the Source property for the component, and then call the WriteEntry method and specify a text message:

```
ELog.Source = ".NET"
ELog.WriteEntry("Message from .NET")
```

'EventLog' Methods

There are several other methods of the EventLog component. These include:

- Exists("<LogName>"): This returns True or False depending on whether a given log exists.
- SourceExists("<SourceName>"): Verifies whether a given source exists.
- DeleteEventSource("<SourceName>"): Deletes a source (first check if one exists) as shown below:

```
If EventLog.SourceExists(".NET") Then
    EventLog.DeleteEventSource(".NET")
End If
```

To get a list of all event logs on a particular machine, use the EventLog.GetEventLogs method. This method will return an array of all the logs in the machine.

Events

The EventLog component raises an event called EntryWritten event, whenever an entry is written to the log we are interested in. We can define a handler for this event, as follows:

```
Private Sub Elog_EntryWritten(ByVal sender As System.Object, ByVal e As
System.Diagnostics.EntryWrittenEventArgs) Handles Elog.EntryWritten

    If e.Entry.Source = ".NET" Then
       MessageBox.Show("Entry written to application log. Source: " & _
           e.Entry.Source)
    Else
        MessageBox.Show("Entry written to by another source")
    End If
End Sub
```

'PerformanceCounter' Component

The `PerformanceCounter` component, which belongs to the `System.Diagonostics` namespace, is used to read from performance monitors and write performance information to custom monitors. For example, we can record the number of transactions committed by our application and take action to fine tune the performance based on that information. We can use the component to connect to performance counters in both local and remote machines. We can even write values to existing custom counters, and also create our own custom counters. The class is derived as follows:

```
Object
    MarshalByRefObject
        Component
            PerformanceCounter
```

Before we explore the programming elements behind the `PerformanceCounter` component, it is important to understand some basic elements of a performance counter. The performance counter of the system can be accessed from Control Panel | Administrative Tools. It typically appears as shown below:

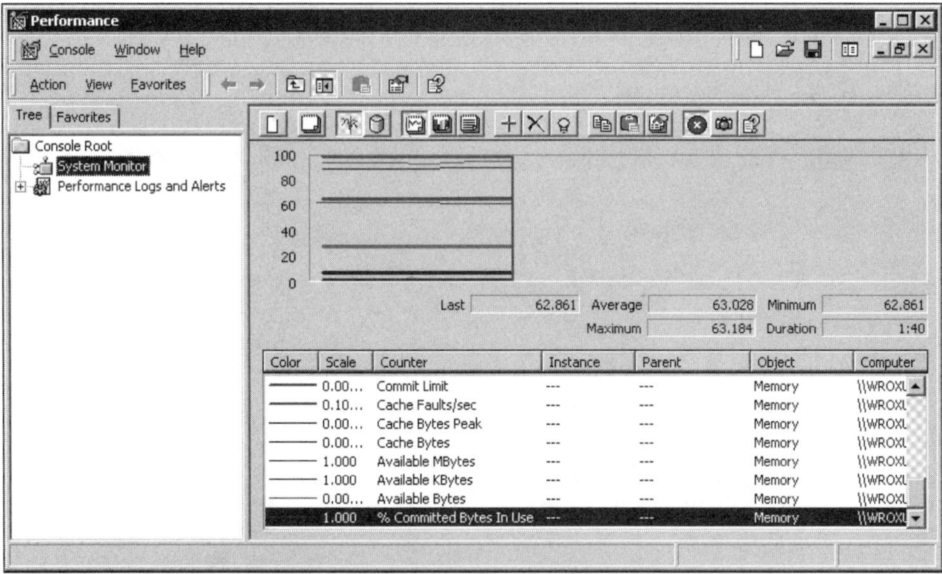

Performance counters are classified into categories. There are predefined categories such as memory, distributed transaction coordinator etc. Each category has several counters in it. For example, in the screenshot above, the counters of the memory category are displayed under the `Counter` column. Each counter measures a certain aspect of the system or the application.

Categories are further broken down into instances. When we right-click on the performance monitor and add a counter, we will see a dialog box similar to the one shown overleaf:

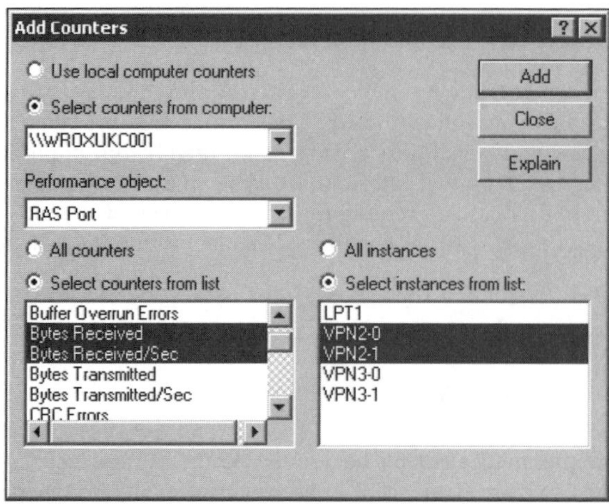

Here we can see the RAS Port category (a category is also called a performance object) and a list of counters in the list box on the left. On the right hand-side, we can see a list of instances. In the above screenshot the Bytes Received and the Bytes Received/Sec counters were selected, and VPN2-0 and VPN2-1 were selected as the instances to monitor. After making the above selections, the performance monitor looks something like this:

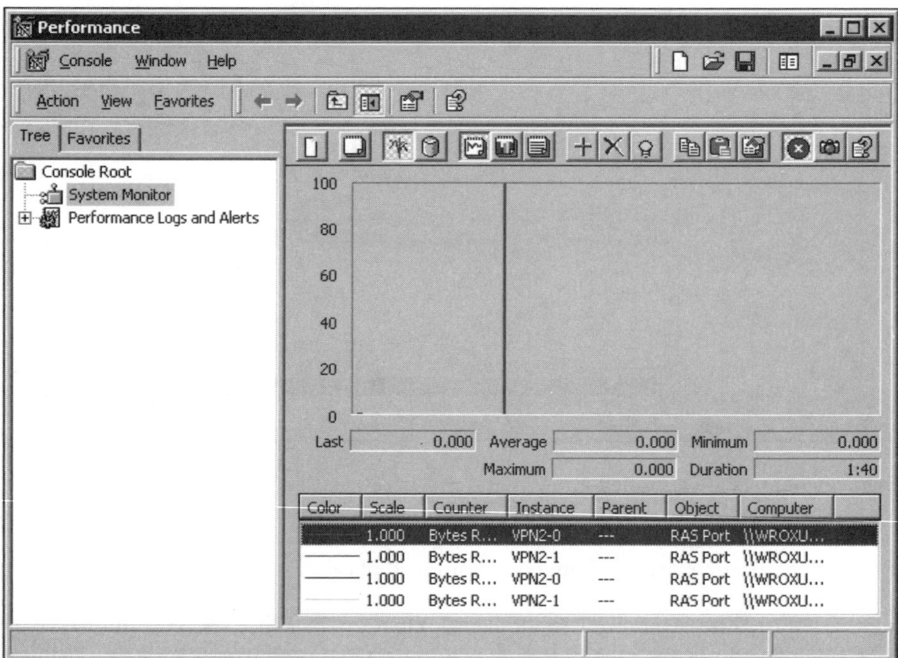

So, the two instances (VPN2-0 and VPN2-1) have been added for each counter (Bytes Received and Bytes Received/Sec).

WroxAdmin tool uses the component to get a list of categories, and then gets a list of counters and their values for each category. The WroxAdmin tool's PerformanceCounter form can be opened from Tools | PerformanceCounter, and is shown below:

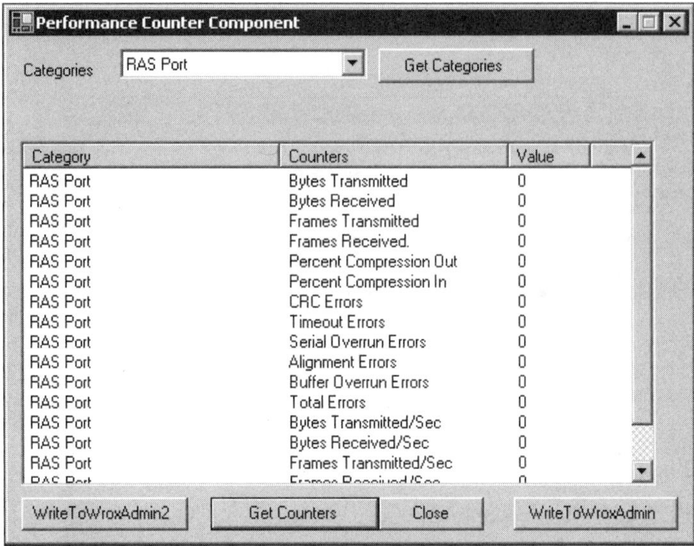

Adding an Instance of 'PerformanceCounter'

A PerformanceCounter component can be added in several ways:

- From the Server Explorer, expand the performance counters node and navigate to the desired counter and instance. The screenshot below shows the performance counter node in the server explorer:

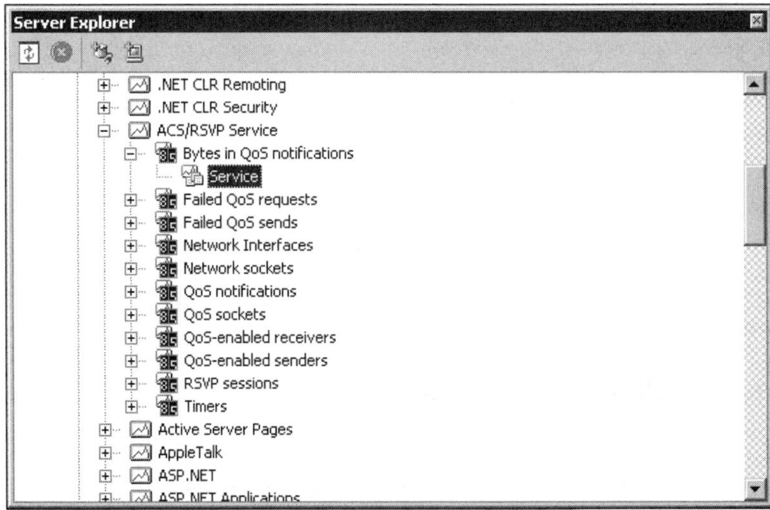

Select the desired counter or instance and drag and drop it into the form or right-click on the item and select Add to Designer. A performance counter component will automatically be created and configured. The Properties window of the component is shown below:

Notice the category name, the counter name, and instance name – these are the properties that we selected in the server explorer above.

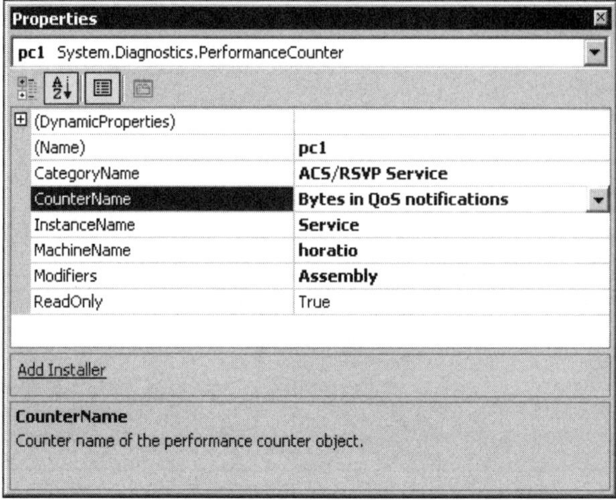

- Add the component to the form directly from the toolbox and then use the properties window to configure it.
- Create an instance of the `PerformanceCounter` component directly in code as follows:

```
Dim c As New System.Diagnostics.PerformanceCounter("CategoryName","CounterName")
```

There are several constructors with variations in the parameters that we can supply. If we do not supply any parameters when we create the component, then we can supply the `CategoryName`, `CounterName`, and `InstanceName` separately, as shown in this example code below:

```
c.MachineName="machinename"
c.CategoryName="RAS Port"
c.CounterName="Bytes Received/Sec"
c.InstanceName="COM1"
c.ReadOnly=True
```

The `ReadOnly` property indicates that the component can be used only to read values from counters and not to write values to counters.

Programming the 'Performance Counter'

The `PerformanceCounter` is the base-class for other components. `PerformanceCounterCategory` in the `System.Diagnostics` namespace is used to provide access to the categories for which performance counters exist. We can use the methods in this class to create new categories and custom counters, to verify that categories and counters exist, and to read the existing counters in a category.

The Create method of the PerformanceCounterCategory class is used to define a new category containing one or more counters. Similarly, the Delete method removes a user-defined category and the counters it contains. We can use the Exists method on the PeformanceCounterCategory class to determine if a category of counters already exists. Use the Increment or IncrementBy methods on the PerformanceCounter class to increment a counter value by one or by the specified integer and to return the new value of the counter. Similarly, we can use the Decrement method to reduce a counter's value. Use the NextValue method of the PerformanceCounter class to return the next calculated value for the sample. Use the GetCounters method of the PerformanceCounterCategory class to return an array of counters in a category.

Getting a List of Categories

We can use the GetCategories method of the PerformanceCounterCategory class to get a list of categories registered in the system. In WroxAdmin, this is done using the code shown below:

```
        Dim cat() As PerformanceCounterCategory
        cat = PerformanceCounterCategory.GetCategories()
```

GetCategories returns an array of PerformanceCounterCategory objects – this array is stored in a variable called cat. We can then walk through each item category in the array, get its name, and show it in the combo box called cboCats:

```
    For i = 0 To cat.Length - 1
        cboCats.Items.Add(cat(i).CategoryName)
    Next
```

Reading from Counters

We can connect to an existing category and get a list of counters in it. Then we can query each counter and read its values. In WroxAdmin, the category is first obtained and shown in a combo box. We can then pick a category and click on the Get Counters button to get a list of counters and their values. The code snippet in WroxAdmin is shown below:

```
        ' Connect to the chosen category object
        Dim cat As New PerformanceCounterCategory("categoryname", "machinename")

        ' Dimension a performance counter array to store the counters
        Dim pc() As PerformanceCounter, i As Integer

    ' Use GetCounters to get an array of counters
    pc = cat.GetCounters()

    ' Loop through the array and read the counter name and its value
    ' Show the name and value in the listview
    For i = 0 To pc.Length - 1
        lvwPerfItem = lvwPerf.Items.Add(cboCats.Text)
        lvwPerfItem.SubItems.Add(pc(i).CounterName)
        lvwPerfItem.SubItems.Add(pc(i).NextValue.ToString)
    Next
```

Custom Counters

We can create custom counters in the following ways, but we can only create a new custom counter in a new category – we cannot add a new counter to an existing category:

- In Server Explorer, right-click on performance counters and select Create New Category. The dialog box, shown in the screenshot below will appear. Specify the category name, a description of the category, a counter name and the counter type:

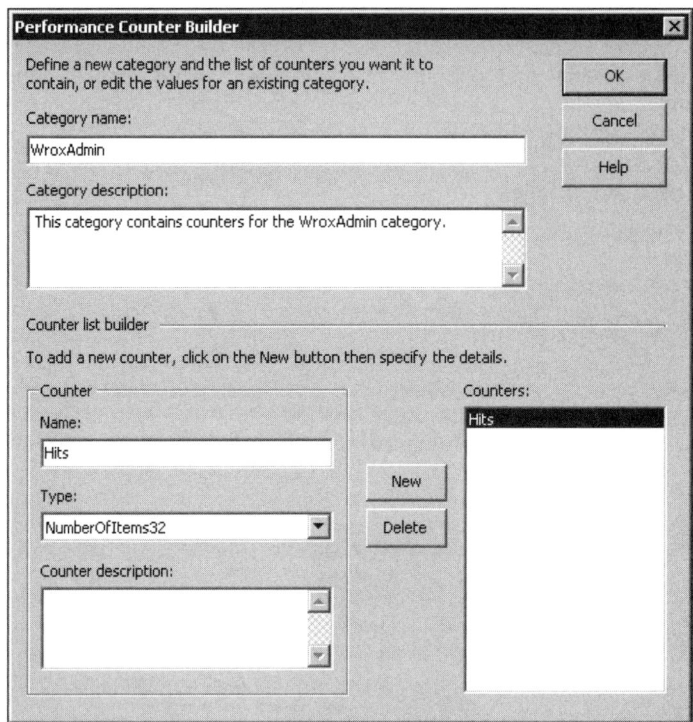

While specifying counter types, to maintain a simple count, use `NumberOfItems32`. This stores the counter's value as a 32-bit number. If we want to keep track of large numbers, then we can use `NumberOfItems64`. Use `RateOfCountsPerSecond32` to keep track of the counter values per second that are nominal. For high frequency counts, use `RateOfCountsPerSecond64`. To calculate the average of the counter values, use `AverageTimer32`.

- Alternatively, we can create a counter in code and configure it like this:

```
Dim perfCounter As New System.Diagnostics.PerformanceCounter()
```

Writing Values to 'Performance Counters'

We can write a value to the counter using one of several methods. One is to use `IncrementBy` of the `PerformanceCounter` class, and give it a positive or a negative value. For example, incrementing with a value of `5` will increase the counter's raw value by five, and incrementing it with a value of `-5` will decrease the counter's raw value by five. Use the `Increment` and `Decrement` methods to increase or decrease the counter's raw value by one. If we want to set the counter's raw value to a specific number, then we can use the `RawValue` property.

Only custom counters can be written to (using `Increment`, `Decrement`). Before we do this, we should set the `ReadOnly` to `False`. We cannot write to the system provided counters. Sample code snippets are shown below:

```
    ' So we can write a value to the counter
    perfCounter.Readonly = false

    ' Increase by the value in text box
    perfCounter.IncrementBy(CLng(txtIncrement.text))

    ' Decrease the counter value by one
    perfCounter.Decrement()

    ' Set the raw value to the value on text box
    perfCounter.RawValue = CLng(txtRawValue.Text)
```

'ServiceController' Component

As the name implies, the `ServiceController` component, which is in the `System.ServiceProcess` namespace, is used to connect to an existing service in the local or remote machine, and issue commands to that service. For example, we may want to make absolutely sure that the Distributed Transaction Coordinator service has been started before executing a transaction. We can check this easily by connecting the Service Controller component to the DTC service, and checking its status. If it has a Stopped status, we can start it up and then execute our transaction. We can also use a timer control along with this component to check the status of a service once a while. Essentially, we can control the Windows Services in the local and remote computers. We cannot, however, create or delete Windows Services by using the `ServiceController` component.

The `ServiceController` class is derived as follows:

```
Object
    MarshalByRefObject
        Component
            ServiceController
```

A list of available non-device driver services (such as the www service) can be retrieved by clicking on the Get Services button in the `WroxAdmin` tool. Then we can select any service and start it or stop it. We can incorporate the service controlling features of the component. A screenshot of the `ServiceController` form used in `WroxAdmin` is shown below:

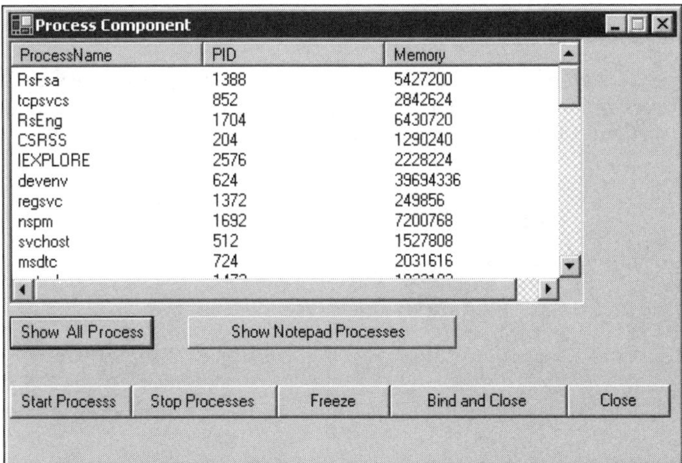

Adding an Instance of the 'ServiceController' Component

There are three ways to add an instance of a `ServiceController` component to our Windows Form:

- **Using the Server Explorer**: First, add the Server whose services we want to connect to by right-clicking on the Server's node and selecting Add Server. Then expand the Services node, and locate the service that you want to control. Then right-click on the service, and click `Add To Designer`. A `ServiceController` component will be added to your form and configured to interact with the selected service.

  In the screenshot shown below, the machine name and service name have been set. Note that the `ServiceName` is `W32Time`, whereas in the Server Explorer it is listed as Windows Time. The name in the Server Explorer is the display name. The component needs the `ServiceName` of the service, not the display name. In the `WroxAdmin` tool, all the services are shown with both their display names and service names.

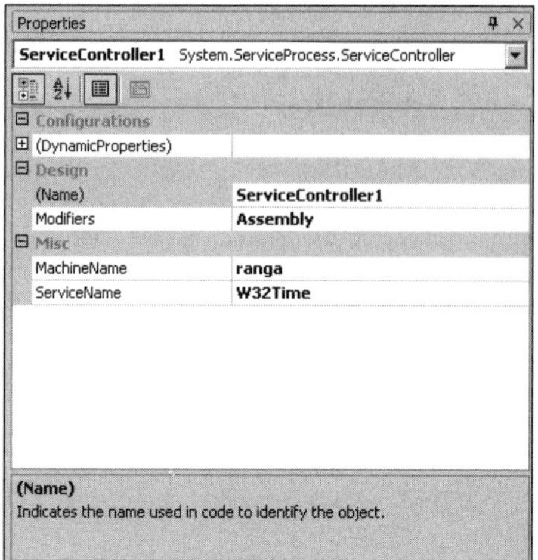

- **Using the toolbox**: Add a service controller component to the form and set the `MachineName` and `ServiceName` properties.

- **In code**: Create a `ServiceController` component in code and configure it as follows:

```
Dim Controller1 As New System.ServiceProcess.ServiceController()
Controller1.MachineName="."   ' The period refers to the local machine
Controller1.ServiceName="W32Time"
```

Retrieving Lists of Services

Use the `GetServices` method to get an array of `ServiceController` objects, each representing one non-device driver service in the computer. To retrieve the services associated with device drivers use the `GetDevices` method. In `WroxAdmin` a list of services is obtained as follows:

```
'Clear the listview
lvwService.Items.Clear()

'Dim an array of type ServiceController

Dim myServiceControllers() As ServiceController

'Dim ServiceController that will be used to iterate through the array
```

```
        Dim objService As ServiceController
        Dim lvwServiceItem As ListViewItem

        Try

            'Call GetServices on the ServiceController class
            'GetServices returns an array of ServiceController objects

            myServiceControllers = ServiceController.GetServices()
            For Each objService In myServiceControllers
                lvwServiceItem = lvwService.Items.Add(objService.ServiceName)
                lvwServiceItem.SubItems.Add(objService.DisplayName)
            lvwServiceItem.SubItems.Add(objService.Status)
            Next

    Catch ex As Exception
       Message.Show("Exception is : " & ex.ToString())
       End Try
```

In `WroxAdmin`, we can select a service and start it or stop it. First, we get the selected service's `ServiceName` from the `ListView`:

```
        ' Get the selected service
        Dim lvwSelItem As ListViewItem
        lvwSelItem = lvwService.SelectedItems(0)
```

Then, we create a new `ServiceController` object and pass the `ServiceName` to its constructor. The machine is assumed to be the local machine by default, so it need not be specified:

```
   Dim objService As New ServiceController(lvwSelItem.SubItems(0).Text)
```

Now we check to see whether the process is already running using the `ServiceController` object's `Status` property which returns a value from the `ServiceControllerStatus` enumeration. If the process is not running, we start the service using the `Start` method.

```
        If objService.Status = ServiceControllerStatus.Running Then
            MessageBox.Show("Service is already running")
        Else
            objService.Start()

        End If
```

'Process' Component

The `Process` component, which belongs to the `System.Diagnostics` namespace, can be used to connect to existing processes, start a new process, stop an existing process, and find information about a process such as memory utilized, etc. The `Process` component can be used in Windows 95, Windows 98, Windows Me, Windows NT 4.0, and Windows 2000. While all the functionality of a process component is available on the local computer, we can only read process information from a remote computer. We cannot start or stop processes in a remote computer.

The class is derived as follows:

```
Object
    MarshalByRefObject
        Component
            Process
```

In WroxAdmin, various features of the Process component are demonstrated. A list of all the processes are retrieved and displayed with memory occupied by the process. Notepad instances are created and the processes specific to those instances are displayed with their memory information. Process components are created and bound to the running processes and then those processes are terminated.

Adding a 'Process' Component

As usual, we can:

- Add a process component directly from the toolbox.
- Using the server explorer, identify the process and drag it into the form.
- Add a process component programmatically as follows:

```
Dim p As New System.Diagnostics.Process()
```

Configuring a 'Process' Component

If we add the Process component directly from the toolbox, we can configure it from the properties window. The screenshot on the right shows the Properties window:

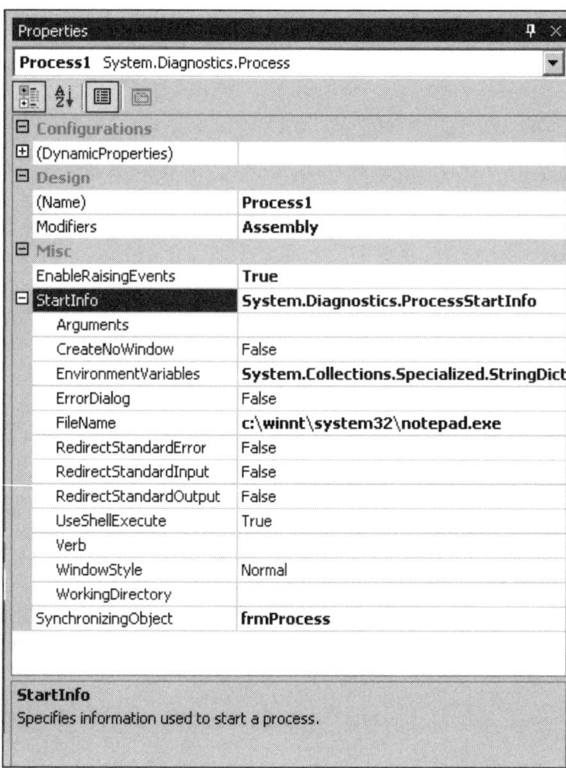

The EnableRaisingEvents property is set to either True or False. If True, the process component will raise an Exited event if the process is stopped.

The StartInfo property returns a ProcessStartInfo object that has a set of properties that are used to specify information about the process that needs to be started. The Filename property specifies the full path to the name of the file that will be executed to start the process. WindowStyle can be set to start the process in a maximized or minimized or normal window.

If the Process component is created in code, then it can be configured in code as follows:

```
Dim p As New System.Diagnostics.Process()
p.StartInfo.FileName = "c:\winnt\system32\notepad.exe"
p.StartInfo.WindowStyle = ProcessWindowStyle.Normal
p.EnableRaisingEvents = True
```

Once we have created a Process component and configured it, we can add code to start and stop it as follows:

```
p.Start()
p.Stop()
```

There are other variations of the Start method where we can supply the filename to the start method, if we have not already done so. For example, we can write code like this to start the notepad from the Start method:

```
    p.Start("c:\winnt\sytem32\notepad.exe")
```

Before we learn how to stop a running process, let's see how to bind to a running process.

Binding to a Running Process

There are three methods that can be used to bind to a running process:

- GetProcessById(<ProcessId>): Returns a Process component for a specific process ID. If the process is running on a remote computer, we must supply the remote computer name as the second parameter.
- GetProcesses: Returns an array of Process components, one for each process in the local computer. We supply the remote computer name as a parameter to get a list of Process components from a remote machine.
- GetProcessesByName(<ProcessName>): This is used if we know the name of the process that we want to bind to. This method will return an array of process components that all have the specified process name. In WroxAdmin, several notepad instances are made to run by clicking on the start button. Then, to bind to each notepad process only, we use this method, as follows:

```
Dim notepadproc() As Process
notepadproc = System.Diagnostics.Process.GetProcessesByName("notepad").
```

Stopping a Process

To stop a running process, we first bind a `Process` component to the running process using one of the methods described in the preceding section. Then, depending on the process that is running, there are two ways to stop a running process. If the process has a graphical user interface, we use the `CloseMainWindow` method to it. If not, we use the `Kill` method.

`CloseMainWindow` will prompt the user to save any unsaved data and then stop the process. The `Kill` method will not prompt the user to save the data. So, calling the `Kill` method on a process that has a graphical user interface will result in loss of unsaved data. In `WroxAdmin`, when several instances of Notepad are running, they are all fetched into an array and then their process is terminated using the `CloseMainWindows` method, as shown below:

```
Dim notepadproc() As Process, i As Integer
notepadproc = System.Diagnostics.Process.GetProcessesByName("notepad")

        For i = 0 To notepadproc.Length - 1
            notepadproc(i).CloseMainWindow()
        Next
```

'WaitForInputIdle' and 'WaitForExit'

We can use the `WaitForInputIdle` method to instruct the component to wait until the process we are managing enters an idle state, but can be called only for processes that have a graphical user interface. `WaitForInputIdle` is useful if we want to make sure that a process is not taking input, before issuing a command to stop it. We can also supply, as a parameter, the number of milliseconds that we want the component to wait before it issues the next command:

```
Dim p As New process()
p.Start("c:\winnt\system32\Notepad.exe")
p.WaitForInputIdle()
```

The `WaitForExit` method is used to set a delay for a process before it exits. This freezes the thread of execution for the specified duration. In `WroxAdmin`, when the `Freeze` and `Close` button is clicked, the component freezes for 2 seconds, and then closes:

```
For Each proc In myprocesses
   proc.WaitForExit(2000) 'wait for 2 seconds
   proc.CloseMainWindow()
Next
```

'DirectoryEntry' Component

The `DirectoryEntry` component is used to access a directory service. A directory service is a hierarchical data store where objects can be stored. The Windows 2000 Active Directory is such a hierarchical directory service, where object types of User, Printer, Computer, etc, are stored.

The assembly `System.DirectoryServices` where the component `DirectoryEntry` resides has some classes that use ADSI (Active Directory Service Interface) COM interfaces to make it easy for .NET to access directory services. The name ADSI is somewhat misleading in that this programming interface can not only be used to access the Active Directory, but also every directory service that has an ADSI provider, such as the Internet Information Server (IIS) Metabase to configure the IIS, the Exchange Server, Novell Directory Services, and the Windows NT 4 domain. For more information on Active Directory, see *Professional ADSI Programming* by Wrox Press (*ISBN 1861002262*). Alternatively, go to Control Panel | Configure Your Server and let the Active Directory Installation Wizard guide you through the setup.

The `DirectoryEntry` component is used to access an object in the directory store, and to read and write the properties of this object, and it is derived as follows:

```
Object
    MarshalByRefObject
        Component
            DirectoryEntry
```

With the WroxAdmin tool, we can enter a username and a password to authenticate with the directory service and enter a path to an object. Pressing the Get Properties button lists all the properties of the selected object, in the list view below this button. Pressing the Get Children button lists the name of all children of the selected object in the list view.

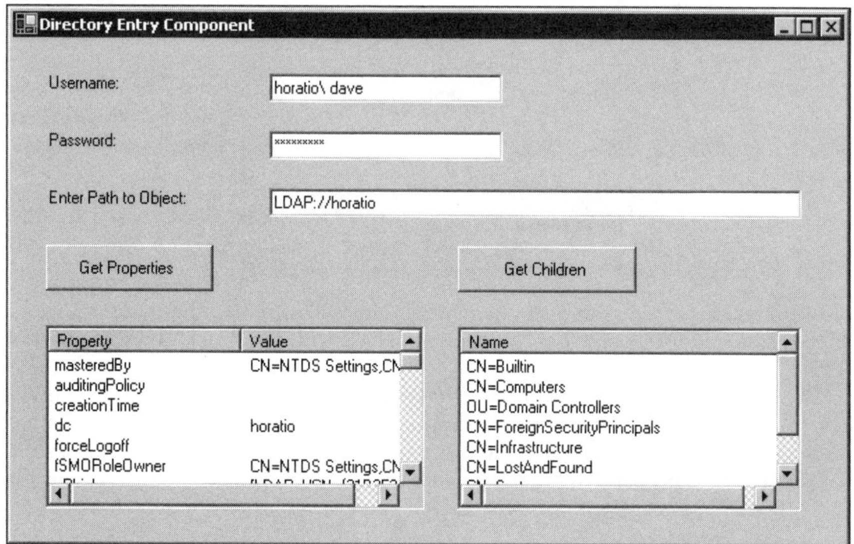

Adding a 'DirectoryEntry' Component

There are two ways to add a `DirectoryEntry` component to the Windows Form:

- Drag and drop a `DirectoryEntry` component from the toolbox to the Windows Form
- Create an instance of the class `DirectoryEntry`, as shown in the following code:

```
Dim entry As New DirectoryServices.DirectoryEntry()
```

It is also possible to specify the path of an object when creating a new instance:

```
Dim entry As New DirectoryServices.DirectoryEntry("LDAP://OU=Authors, _
DC=WroxPress, DC=local")
```

If we drop the component from the toolbox, a reference to the assembly `System.DirectoryServices` is done automatically. If we create an instance, we have to do this ourselves.

Configuring the 'DirectoryEntry' Component

If we drop the component to the Windows Form using the toolbox, the properties of this component can be configured with the toolbox as we see in the picture below:

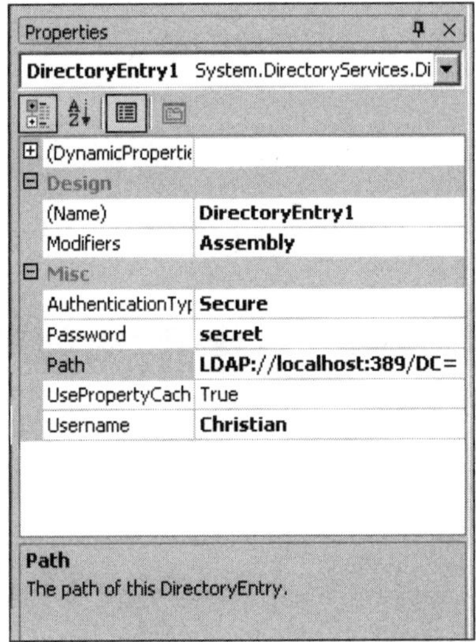

Usually, we will set most properties programmatically, instead of setting them in this dialog, as the values will be requested from the user. This is also the case with the WroxAdmin application.

If the properties `Username` and `Password` are not set, the user identifier of the currently logged on user will be used. So setting this property isn't normally required. To use a different user and password from the one that currently is logged on to access the directory service we can set the `Username` and `Password` properties. If property values should not only be read but also written, it's necessary to change the `AuthenticationType` from the default value `None`, as can be seen in the picture above.

'Path'

The most important part to set is the `Path` property. It defines the unique name of the object in the directory service that is used to access this object. The syntax of this entry depends on the ADSI provider that is used. An example of how to set the `Path` property:

```
DirectoryEntry1.Path = "LDAP://localhost:389/OU=Wrox Press, _
DC=eichkogelstrasse, DC=local
```

Similar to all providers is this notation to set the path:

```
protocol://server name:port number/distinguished name
```

The first part of this string defines the protocol that should be used. With the protocol, the ADSI provider can be selected. The following table shows the possible values for the protocol and the provider.

Protocol	Description
LDAP:	LDAP Server such as the Exchange Server and the Windows 2000 Active Directory Service. LDAP is the short name for Lightweight Directory Access Protocol.
GC:	The Global Catalog of the Active Directory can be accessed for fast read-only queries.
IIS:	The IIS metadata directory is selected to read and configure the Internet Information Server.
WinNT:	With this protocol it's possible to access Windows NT 4 domains with very limited capabilities compared to the Active Directory.
NDS:	To access the Novell Directory Service, NDS can be used.
NWCOMPAT:	The old version of Novell's directory service, Novel Netware 3.x requires this protocol.

The second part of the `Path` property defines the server name and the port number of the server. Using the Active Directory as the provider, the server name is optional, as **serverless binding** can be used to access the objects. With serverless binding, the server answering fastest is used automatically. The specification of the port number is only necessary if the Server is configured to listen to a port other than the default port. This is the case if both an Active Directory Domain Controller and an Exchange Server are installed on the same machine. The default port number for LDAP is 389 where the LDAP server of the Active Directory listens to incoming requests.

An example path string using serverless binding is shown in the following code segment. Here we use the LDAP protocol to access the Active Directory, the object specified is, for example, the domain `eichkogelstrasse.local` using the LDAP syntax.

```
DirectoryEntry1.Path = "LDAP://DC=eichkogelstrasse, DC=local"
```

The last part of the `Path` property specifies the distinguished name of the object in the directory service. The specification of this name is different depending on the provider used.

Property Cache

The property `UsePropertyCache` specifies whether or not the properties of the object we access from the directory service should be cached on the client. The first time we read a property from a `DirectoryEntry` object, all the properties of the object are cached in the client. This means that when we access additional properties, the server isn't contacted to get the values, as all the properties are stored in the memory of the client.

Methods and Properties of the 'DirectoryEntry' Component

Besides the properties to configure the DirectoryEntry component that we have already seen, this component has some more properties, as listed in the table below:

Property	Description
Children	If the object accessed is a container object that has children, a collection of type DirectoryEntries is returned from the property Children. We can walk through all the children objects, as can be seen later in the WroxAdmin application.
NativeObject	Because the classes of the namespace System.DirectoryServices put a layer above ADSI, we can get direct access to the ADSI object with the property NativeObject.
Parent	With the property Parent, we go up the hierarchical tree to access the container object of the current DirectoryEntry.
Properties	Properties returns a PropertyCollection of all the properties of the DirectoryEntry object. Each of these has a name and a value that can be accessed with properties of this collection class: PropertyNames and Values. We will have a look at how to access the properties with the WroxAdmin application.
SchemaClassName	With VB.NET, the behavior and attributes of objects are defined with classes. The attributes of a directory object are defined in the schema. The property SchemaClassName returns the name of the schema class that defines the properties for a directory object.
SchemaEntry	We can use the SchemaEntry object to get more information about the attributes of a directory object. The property SchemaEntry returns an instance of DirectoryEntry as the schema objects itself are stored within the directory service.

The methods of the DirectoryEntry class are listed in the table below.

DirectoryEntry Methods	Description
Close	The method Close frees resources held by the DirectoryEntry instance.
CommitChanges	If we change the values of properties, only the data of the cache is changed. To update the properties of the directory object in the directory service, CommitChanges must be called after changing the values.
DeleteTree	DeleteTree deletes the directory object that DirectoryEntry points to, and all its child objects.

Method	Description
MoveTo	MoveTo moves the entry to a new parent object in the tree. As with Rename, CommitChanges must be called to make the change permanent.
RefreshCache	If the cache is used with the default configuration UsePropertyCache = True, the cache is filled when the first property of the directory object is read. With the method RefreshCache the properties of the directory object are read again.
Rename	With Rename, the name of the entry gets changed. CommitChanges must be called to make the change permanent if the cache is used.

Accessing the Properties of a Directory Object

Let us look at the source code of the WroxAdmin tool. First we will talk about the event handler of the click event for the Get Properties button.

We set the Username and Password properties of the DirectoryEntry component to the values received from the textbox, so that the user can authenticate with the directory service. Then the Path property is set to the value specified in the textbox txtPath.

```
Private Sub btnProperties_Click(ByVal sender As System.Object, _
ByVal e As System.EventArgs) Handles btnProperties.Click
    Try
        DirectoryEntry1.Username = txtUsername.Text
        DirectoryEntry1.Password = txtPassword.Text
        DirectoryEntry1.Path = txtPath.Text
```

The Properties property of the DirectoryEntry component returns a PropertyCollection. To get to all property names of the object that was selected with the Path property, we use the property PropertyNames, which returns a collection.

```
        ' Access the directory service to get the properties
        ' of the selected object
        Dim coll As System.DirectoryServices.PropertyCollection = _
        DirectoryEntry1.Properties

        ' Get all property names of the object
        Dim propNames As ICollection = coll.PropertyNames
```

In the For Each loop, every property name is displayed as the leftmost item in the list view lvwProperties. Every item in the propNames collection is a string that is referenced with the propName variable.

```
        Dim propName As String
        Dim i As Integer = 0

        lvwProperties.Items.Clear()
```

```
            For Each propName In propNames

                ' Display the property name in the list view
                lvwProperties.Items.Add(propName)
```

Using the `Item` property of the `PropertyCollection` class to pass a property name, returns a `PropertyValueCollection`, because a single property of a directory entry object may have multiple values. For example, the `Phone` property of a user may have multiple phone numbers. In this case, we ignore that fact, as most properties are single-valued, and access only the first value with `coll.Item(propName)(0)`. Because not all property values of a directory object can be represented in a string, we check if the value is a string to display it in the list view. All other property values are not displayed.

```
                ' Display property values of type String
                If TypeOf coll.Item(propName)(0) Is String Then
                    Dim val As String
                    val = coll.Item(propName)(0)
                    lvwProperties.Items(i).SubItems.Add(val)
                End If

                i += 1
            Next
```

If the wrong user name was entered or the object cannot be found in the directory service, an exception occurs. We catch all exceptions in the handler to display the error message to the user.

```
        Catch ex As Exception
            MessageBox.Show(ex.Message)
        Finally
            DirectoryEntry1.Close()
        End Try
    End Sub
```

Accessing the Children of a Directory Object

In the second handler of the WroxAdmin application, we display all children objects of the selected directory object. As with the previous code example we set again the `Username`, `Password`, and `Path` property of the `DirectoryEntry` object.

```
    Private Sub btnChildren_Click(ByVal sender As System.Object, _
    ByVal e As System.EventArgs) Handles btnChildren.Click
        Try
            DirectoryEntry1.Username = txtUsername.Text
            DirectoryEntry1.Password = txtPassword.Text
            DirectoryEntry1.Path = txtPath.Text
```

Using the `Children` property of the `DirectoryEntry` class we get a collection of type `DirectoryEntries`. As the name says, this is a collection of `DirectoryEntry` objects.

```
            ' Get all children of the selected object
            Dim children As System.DirectoryServices.DirectoryEntries
            children = DirectoryEntry1.Children
```

With the `For Each` statement, we enumerate all `DirectoryEntry` objects in the `DirectoryEntries` collection to display the value of the `Name` property in the list view.

```
            Dim child As System.DirectoryServices.DirectoryEntry

            ' Write the name of every child object to the list view
            lvwChildren.Items.Clear()
            For Each child In children
                lvwChildren.Items.Add(child.Name)
            Next
        Catch ex As Exception
            MessageBox.Show(ex.Message)
        Finally
            DirectoryEntry1.Close()
        End Try
    End Sub
```

'DirectorySearcher' Component

The `DirectorySearcher` component is used to find objects in a directory service. Using the `DirectorySearcher` class in the `System.DirectoryServices` namespace, we define a filter to specify the objects we want to find, and to get a collection of objects returned where the filter matches.

The `DirectorySearcher` component is an instance of the `DirectorySearcher` class, which is derived as follows:

```
Object
    MarshalByRefObject
        Component
            DirectorySearcher
```

With the WroxAdmin tool we can enter a username and a password to authenticate with the directory service, like we did before with the `DirectoryEntry` component. In the textbox for the search root we define the entry point in the directory service, where the search for objects should start. With the filter string the search query is specified to find objects. In the screenshot below, we search for all objects of type User. After the Start Search button is clicked the path of all objects found is displayed in the list view.

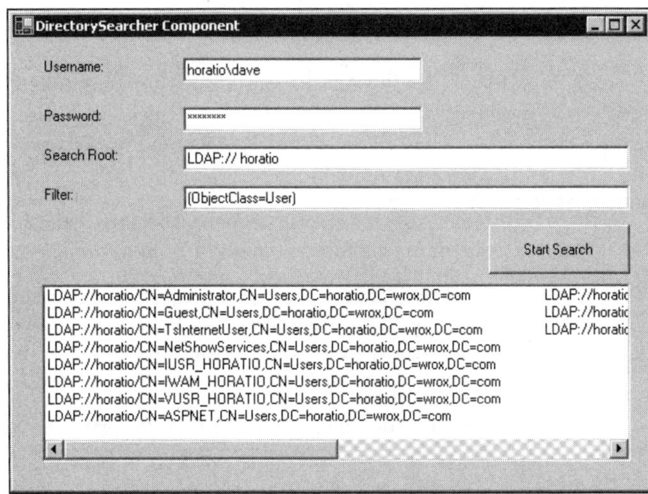

Adding a 'DirectorySearcher' Component

As with the `DirectoryEntry` component, there are two ways to add this component to a Windows Form application. We can drag and drop the component from the toolbox to the form, or create it programmatically. In most cases, we will also add a `DirectoryEntry` component when adding a `DirectorySearcher` component, because we have to define where the search should start with the `DirectoryEntry` component.

Configuring the 'DirectorySearcher' Component

If we add the `DirectorySearcher` component with the help of the toolbox to the Windows application, the component can be configured using the Properties window, as can be seen in the following screenshot:

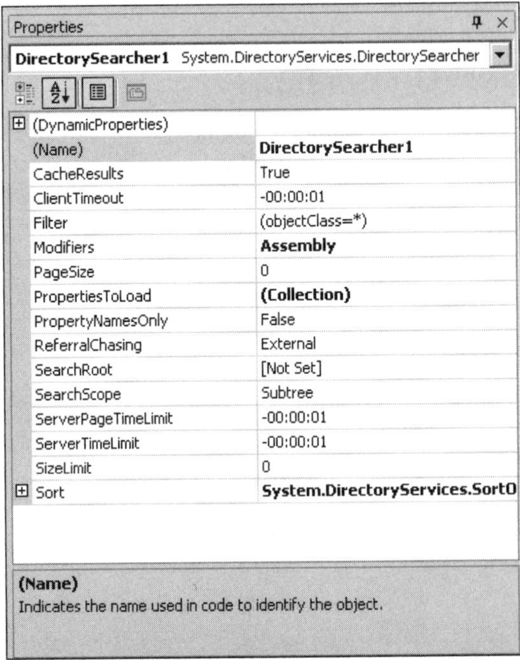

As we can see, there are a lot of properties that can be configured for this component. The properties are listed in this table:

Property	Description
`CacheResults`	The `CacheResults` property specifies if the returned objects of the query should be stored in a client cache.
`ClientTimeout`	With the `ClientTimeout` property we can define how long the client waits for the server to return the requested search to the client. If the timeout is reached before the search is finished, no records are returned. The default value –1 means that the search continues indefinitely.

Property	Description
`Filter`	The most important property of the `DirectorySearcher` component is the `Filter` property, as it defines the query to search for objects. Next, we will look more closely at the syntax of the filter.
`PageSize`	If our search should return a larger number of objects, we should think of splitting the results. With a **paged search** interim, results of already found objects are returned to the client. The number of objects that should be returned is specified with the `PageSize` property. The next search that is started is continued where the previous search left off, so with every search a page is returned.
`PropertiesToLoad`	An object in the directory can have a lot of properties assigned. For example, a user object can have a first name and last name, department, e-mail address, phone numbers, address, and many more. We may not be interested in all these properties with a query for an object. The `PropertiesToLoad` property specifies the properties we are interested in, and ensures that just these properties are written to the client query cache. The default value for `PropertiesToLoad`, if nothing is set, makes just the values for `Path` and `Name` available in the result set.
`PropertyNamesOnly`	If we are just interested in the properties that are available to specific objects, but not the value of these properties, we can set the `PropertyNamesOnly` property to `True`.
`SearchRoot`	The `SearchRoot` property defines the root object in the hierarchy of the directory service where the search should start. The property type of the `SearchRoot` is the `DirectoryEntry` class, so we can define an instance of the `DirectoryEntry`, as we saw in the last section, to specify the root of the search. If the `SearchRoot` is not set, the search starts at the root object of the domain where we are logged in.
`SearchScope`	With `SearchScope` we define how deep the search should go. Setting this property to `SearchScope.Base` just checks a single object that's defined with `SearchRoot` if it applies to the selected filter. Setting the property to `SearchScope.OneLevel` checks all immediate children objects of the root object in the tree. The default value `SearchScope.Subtree` searches the complete tree starting with the root object.
`ServerPageTimeLimit`	For paged searches we can also set the time the search may take to fill the objects in a single page. The default value –1 means that the search continues for as long as the `ServerTimeLimit` property is set.

Table continued on following page

Property	Description
ServerTimeLimit	The ServerTimeLimit property defines how long the server should search. If the timeout is reached with ServerTimeLimit all objects found up to this point are returned to the client, unlike the ClientTimeout property. A default value of -1 means that a server-determined default of 120 seconds is used.
SizeLimit	The search can be limited by the time the search takes, but also by the number of objects returned. With the SizeLimit property we can set how many objects should be returned with a single search. The default value is 1000 if nothing is specified.
Sort	The result can be sorted by specifying a Sort property, which is an instance of the class SortOption. Not only can the direction of the sort be set (SortDirection.Ascending, SortDirection.Descending), but also the property name of the directory object that should be used for sorting can be specified.

Setting the Filter

The filter uses the LDAP syntax to specify the query to find the objects in the directory service. In the filter we can specify property names and the corresponding values we are looking for.

If we don't set a value for the Filter property, the default Filter is (objectClass=*), which means that we search for objects that have an objectClass property where the value doesn't matter. As every object has a property objectClass, every object of the directory service will be returned in the result of this query (as long as no other limit like size limits or timeouts of the search applies).

The following code shows an example of how we can specify that we are only interested in objects of a certain type:

```
DirectorySearcher1.Filter = "(objectClass=user)"
```

Setting the filter to (objectClass=user) means that we are only looking for objects of type user.

With the filter, it's also possible to define compound statements where multiple expressions are merged with & or | operators. The operators for the compound statements must be prefixed to the expressions where the operators apply. & is the LDAP syntax for AND, which means that all expressions that follow must match. | is the OR operator, indicating that only one of the expressions that follow must match.

```
DirectorySearcher1.Filter = "(&(objectClass=user)(lastName=Nagel*))"
```

The Filter property set above means that we are looking for objects of type user where the property lastName starts with Nagel.

Methods of the 'DirectorySearcher' Component

Just setting the filter of the DirectorySearcher component doesn't start the search. We have to call one of the methods that are listed in the following table.

Method	Description
FindAll	With FindAll, all occurrences of the filtered objects are returned in a SearchResultCollection.
FindOne	FindOne just returns the first instance that is found in the directory service where the specified Filter is a hit.

Searching the Active Directory

In the WroxAdmin tool we have the whole code that deals with the DirectorySearcher object in the handler of the click event of the search button.

We set the Username, Password, and the Path property of the DirectoryEntry1 object. This object is assigned to the SearchRoot property of the DirectorySearcher component so that the search starts here. The Filter property is set to the text of the filter textbox.

```
Private Sub btnSearch_Click(ByVal sender As System.Object, _
ByVal e As System.EventArgs) Handles btnSearch.Click
    Try
        DirectoryEntry1.Username = txtUsername.Text
        DirectoryEntry1.Password = txtPassword.Text
        DirectoryEntry1.Path = txtSearchRoot.Text
        DirectorySearcher1.SearchRoot = DirectoryEntry1
        DirectorySearcher1.Filter = txtFilter.Text
```

Calling the FindAll method of the DirectorySearcher component returns an object of type SearchResultCollection. The SearchResultCollection contains SearchResult objects that can be used to open the corresponding directory object.

```
        ' Get all objects in the directory where the filter matches
        Dim coll As DirectoryServices.SearchResultCollection
        coll = DirectorySearcher1.FindAll()

        ' Set the Path of the returned objects to the listview
        lvwSearch.Clear()
        Dim entry As System.DirectoryServices.SearchResult
        For Each entry In coll
            lvwSearch.Items.Add(entry.Path)
        Next

    Catch ex As Exception
        MessageBox.Show(ex.Message)
    Finally
```

```
            DirectoryEntry1.Close()
            DirectorySearcher1.Dispose()
        End Try
    End Sub
```

'CrystalReportViewer' and 'ReportDocument'

Windows Forms comes with a `CrystalReportViewer` control and a `ReportDocument` component. Since these two are mostly used in concert with each other, we will discuss them in a combined section. In WroxAdmin, we will demonstrate how we can display reports on demand in a `CrystalReportViewer` control, and how to create **untyped** and **typed** `ReportDocument` objects and bind them to a `CrystalReportViewer` control (we will talk about untyped and typed objects a little later in the section on the `ReportDocument` component).

'CrystalReportViewer' Control

The `CrystalReportViewer` control corresponds to a `CrystalReportViewer` class, which belongs to the `CrystalDecisions.Windows.Forms` namespace. It will work in Windows 98/ME/NT/2000 and above platforms. The class provided properties, methods, and events that allow us to control how the viewer appears and functions.

The `CrystalReportViewer` control is derived as follows:

```
MarshalByRefObject
    Component
        Control
            ScrollableControl
                ContainerControl
                    UserControl
                        CrystalReportViewer
```

Adding a 'CrystalReportViewer' Control to the Windows Form

We can add a `CrystalReportViewer` control by double-clicking the control, or by dragging and dropping the control on to the Windows Form. The following screenshot shows a Windows Form with the control added. We can see a list of icons on the top of the form. These icons are used to print a report, export a report, find a text in a report, etc. On the left of the control is a column of white space. When a report has group sections, the group headers will appear here. Clicking a group header will take us directly to the group information.

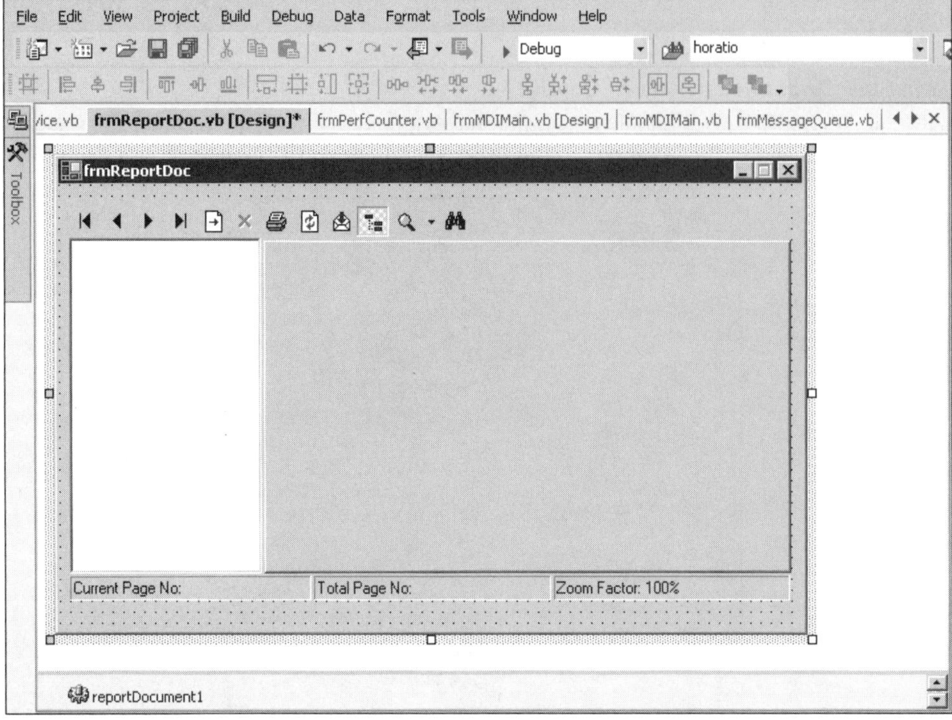

Creating a Crystal Report

Since the `CrystalReportViewer` control needs a crystal report file as the report source, we need to create a report first. We can create a crystal report from within the IDE. Right-click on the solution node and select Add | New Item from the File menu. Select Crystal Report and click on Open. This will open a wizard that will help in creating the report. The wizard options are shown in the screenshot on the right:

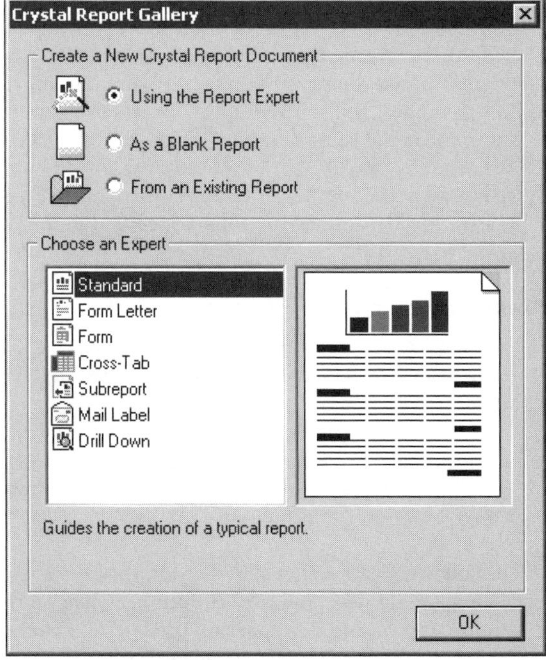

For more information on how to create your own Crystal Reports, take a look at the MSDN documentation.

Configuring the 'CrystalReportViewer' Control

Once a viewer control has been added, its properties can be set in the IDE, or they can be set in code. The following screenshot shows the properties window of the `CrystalReportViewer` control.

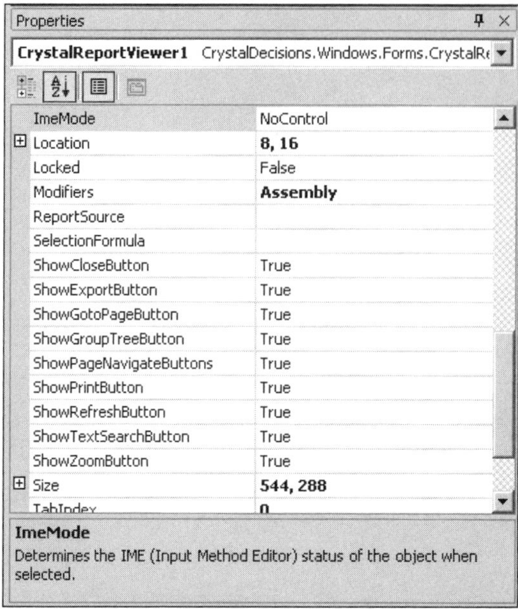

The `ReportSource` property is used to specify the full path to the report to be viewed. Once this property is set, the report will be displayed in the viewer. We can also set several properties that control how the report is displayed in the form. For example, we can hide the export button, show the print button, hide the refresh button, and so on, by setting the properties beginning with `Show`.

In WroxAdmin, the `ReportSource` property of the control is not set in the properties window. Instead it is set in code, so that any report specified in the textbox can be displayed in the `CrystalReportViewer` control.

Viewing the Report

Viewing a report is simple – just specify the path to the report as the report source. In WroxAdmin the report path is specified at runtime in the textbox. The following code binds the report file to the control:

```
Private Sub cmdView_Click(ByVal sender As System.Object, _
ByVal e As System.EventArgs) Handles cmdView.Click
        CrystalReportViewer1.ReportSource = txtReport.Text
End Sub
```

The following screenshot shows a sample Crystal Report inside the control on the form. Experiment by clicking on the print and export buttons. Click on the Toggle Group Tree button and observe the group window appear and disappear on the left. Click on the groups and see how the report scrolls to display information about the selected group.

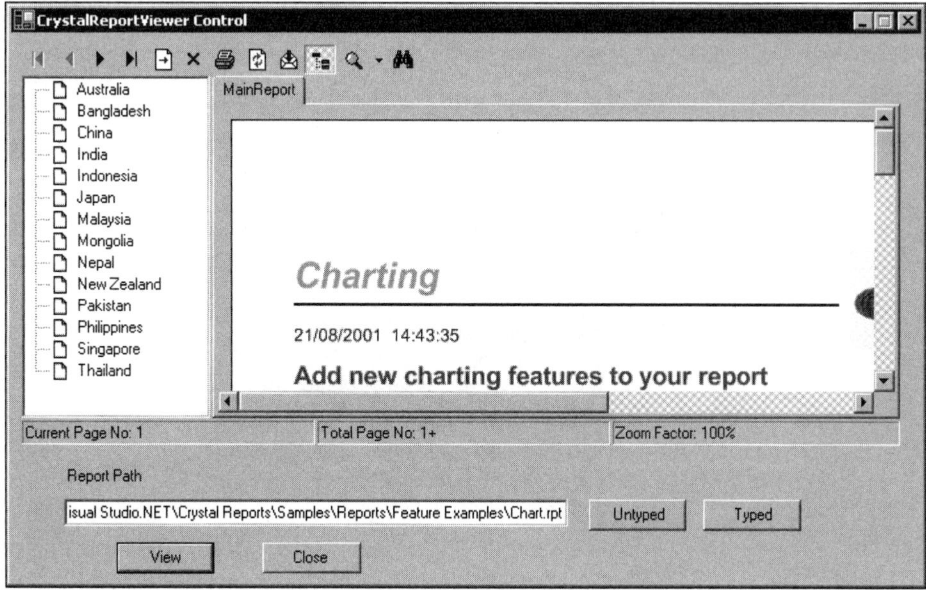

The concept described above can be extended to provide a very robust user interface for the users. For example, a list of all reports can be classified into groups (like sales, accounting, etc.) and then displayed in a `TreeView` control. Then, as the user double-clicks on a report, the report can be specified as the `ReportSource` and displayed in the `CrystalReportViewer` control.

Next, we will discuss the `ReportDocument` component and see how it can be used to gain more control over the reporting functionality.

The 'ReportDocument' Component

The `ReportDocument` component is represented by a `ReportDocument` class, which is a member of the `CrystalDecisions.CrystalReports.Engine` namespace. The class is derived as follows:

```
Object
    MarshalByRefObject
        Component
            ReportDocument
```

It contains properties and methods to specify, format, load, export, and print a Crystal Report. `ReportDocument` components can be classified as untyped and typed. Typed components are also referred to as **strongly-typed** components.

Untyped components are those that are associated with a specific report only at runtime, and not during design time. No specific `ReportDocument` class is created for it at design time. A typed report component, on the other hand, is one for which a class is created at design time. A specific report must exist and is specified at design time to create a typed component. In WroxAdmin we will see how to create one of each type and use them.

Adding an Untyped/Typed 'ReportDocument' Component

A `ReportDocument` component (typed or untyped) can be added by dragging and dropping a `ReportDocument` component into the Windows Form, or it can be created in code. While adding the component from the toolbox, a dialog pops up, as shown below, where we can specify that we want an untyped component. In WroxAdmin, two `ReportDocument` components have been added to the Windows Form – one untyped and one typed.

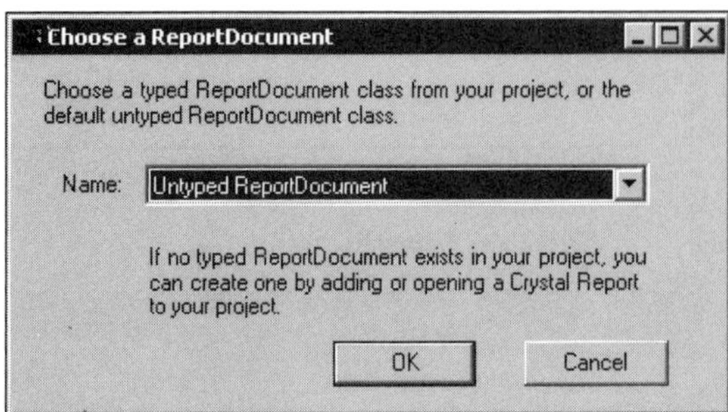

While adding a typed `ReportDocument`, we specify `Components.CrystalReport1` from the combobox, as shown in the following screenshot, to specify that we want a class that represents the `CrystalReport1.rpt` file that is already in the project.

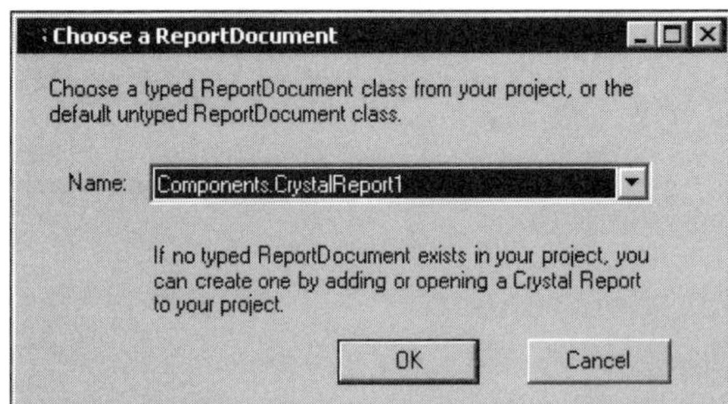

After the component is added to the Windows Form, we can change the name of the components and specify the print options in the properties window. In WroxAdmin, these have been named as `rptDocTyped` and `rptDocUntyped`. The properties of these components can also be set in code.

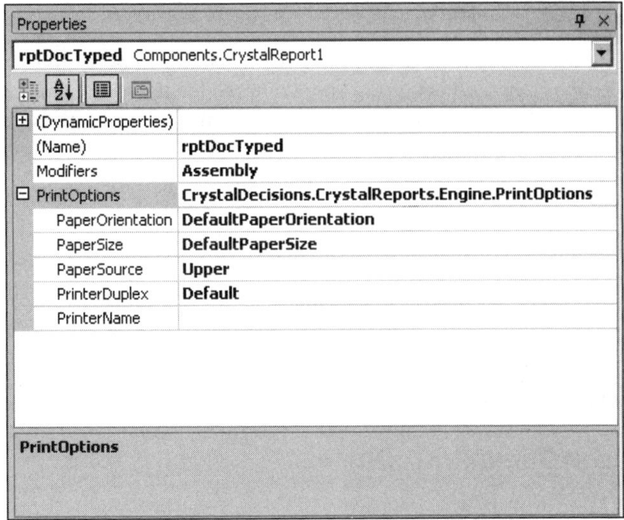

Typed and untyped `ReportDocument` components can also be added directly in code, using the `ReportDocument` class of the `CrystalDecisions.CrystalReports.Engine` namespace. For example, the following code will create an untyped `ReportDocument` object, `rptDocUntyped`:

```
Dim rptDocUntyped As New CrystalDecisions.CrystalReports.Engine.ReportDocument()
```

The following code will create a typed `ReportDocument` object, `rptDocTyped`, which represents the specific report file named `CrystalReport1.rpt` that already exists in the project:

```
Dim rptDocTyped As New CrystalReport1
```

Loading a 'ReportDocument' Component with a Crystal Report

We can load an untyped report component with a specific report, by using the `Load` method of the `ReportDocument` object. This can be done after the call to `InitializeComponent`, or elsewhere. In WroxAdmin, the `rptDocUntyped` object is loaded with a specific report, `CrystalReport1.rpt`, as follows:

```
#Region " Windows Form Designer generated code "

    Public Sub New()
        MyBase.New()

        'This call is required by the Windows Form Designer.
        InitializeComponent()

        'Add any initialization after the InitializeComponent() call
        rptDocUntyped.Load("c:\data\netprojects\components\crystalreport1.rpt")
End Sub
```

We do not have to load a typed `ReportDocument` component, because it was already created with reference to a specific report.

Binding a 'ReportDocument'

A ReportDocument must be bound to a Windows Forms viewer in order to display it. This is done by specifying the ReportDocument object as the report source for the viewer control. The syntax is the same for both typed and untyped components. In WroxAdmin, the rptDocTyped and rptDocUntyped components are bound to the CrystalReportViewer control as follows:

```
Private Sub cmdBindUntyped_Click(ByVal sender As System.Object, _
ByVal e As System.EventArgs) Handles cmdBindUntyped.Click

        CrystalReportViewer1.ReportSource = rptDocUntyped
End Sub
```

When the buttons marked Typed and Untyped are clicked, we can see that the typed and untyped documents are bound and displayed in the CrystalReportViewer control.

Scripting the 'ReportDocument' Object

The ReportDocument class provides a rich set of public properties, methods, and events that can be used to customize the way reports are created and presented to the users. For example, we can use the RecordSelectFormula property to filter out specific records that need to be displayed. The IsSubReport property can be used to find out if the report is a sub report. The Export method can be used to export a report to a file, and the PrintToPrinter method can be used to control the printing options. Refer to the documentation or IntelliSense in the IDE for a comprehensive list of members.

Summary

In this chapter we have seen how to use the components provided by Visual Studio.NET to enhance our applications. We began by showing the WroxAdmin application, which contains all the components and the CrystalReportViewer control. Then we discussed how to add each component to a form, and showed their individual uses.

We can now perform a wide variety of tasks from within our Windows Forms applications, including:

- Send, remove, peek at, and receive messages from a queue
- Monitor files and directories
- Read and write to event logs
- Retrieve lists of services
- Bind to running processes
- Access properties of directories, and search the Active Directory
- View crystal reports from our forms

- System.Object
  - System.MarshalRefObject
    - System.ComponentMode.Component
      - CommonDialog
        - ColorDialog
        - FileDialog
        - FontDialog
        - PageSetupDialog
        - PrintDialog
      - ErrorProvider
      - HelpProvider
      - ImageList
      - Menu
        - ContextMenu
        - MainMenu
        - MenuItem
      - NotifyIcon
      - StatusBarPanel
      - Timer
      - ToolBarButton
      - ToolTip
      - Control
        - ButtonBase
          - Button
          - CheckBox
          - RadioButton
        - DataGrid
        - DateTimePicker
        - GroupBox
        - Label
          - LinkLabel
        - ListControl
          - ComboBox
          - ListBox
            - CheckedListBox
        - ListView
        - MonthCalendar
        - PictureBox
        - PrintReviewControl
        - ProgressBar
        - ScrollableControl
          - ContainerControl
            - Form
              - PrintPreviewDialog
              - ThreadExceptionDialog
            - PropertyGrid
            - UpDownBase
              - DomainUpDown
              - NumericUpDown
            - UserControl
          - Panel
            - TabPage
        - ScrollBar
          - HScrollBar
          - VScrollBar
        - Splitter
        - StatusBar
        - TabControl
        - TextBoxBase
          - RichTextBox
          - Textbox
        - ToolBar
        - TrackBar
        - TreeView
  - ListViewItem
  - TreeNode

Legend: Concrete Class; Abstract class

System.Windows.Forms

12

Introduction to GDI+

There are many reasons why Windows Forms developers need to write graphics code. Many types of applications, including Computer Aided Design / Computer Aided Manufacture (CAD/CAM), games, and charting programs require that we write graphics code in our Windows Forms application. Many commercial business applications benefit from custom controls, which give their application a unique appearance and increased usability. Writing custom controls in Windows Forms requires GDI+ programming.

It is enjoyable to write graphics code. We can change our code and see the results immediately on the screen. By writing a new custom control that gives our application a better appearance and a new level of usability, we can add significant value to our applications.

In this chapter, we will first explain the semantics of drawing using GDI+. After going through these semantics, we will take an overview of the main classes that we will use to build graphical windows and custom controls.

Throughout this chapter, we will build a moderately complex example program to display a bar chart. As we cover the classes of GDI+, we will add capabilities to our bar chart that use the features of the classes. We will build eight progressively more advanced versions of our bar chart example, as follows:

- `BarChart1`: A bar chart using line drawing functions
- `BarChart2`: Add color to our bars using brushes
- `BarChart3`: Add legends using text and fonts
- `BarChart4`: Add bitmaps to the bars by drawing images
- `BarChart5`: Add a watermark, demonstrating coordinate system transforms and the Alpha value of colors

- `BarChart6`: Add horizontal and vertical scrolling
- `BarChart7`: Add printing capability
- `BarChart8`: Add print preview capability

The purpose of the `BarChart` examples is to demonstrate a number of drawing techniques. For the purposes of this chapter, we want to minimize the issues that are peripheral to drawing, so we will not make this example as elaborate as we would if we were making a general purpose commercial charting library. For example, if we were making a commercial library, we would sub-class our bar chart from `System.Windows.Forms.UserControl`, so that the control could be embedded in other windows, instead of from `System.Windows.Forms.Form`, and we would develop this control so that we could use the design facilities in Visual Studio to interactively layout the chart. We also might make a much more sophisticated data model, and we might separate the data model into a different namespace from the bar chart drawing code. However, all of these points are peripheral to learning the technology of drawing graphics, so we will not discuss them further.

In addition to the bar chart example, we'll build a few other small examples to demonstrate some specific features of GDI+. Then we will take a look at a high level at some of the extensive capabilities of GDI+, including:

- Clipping
- The Drawing2D namespace
- The Imaging namespace

After the overview on each of the above topics, we'll look at what classes are used to implement the features, and where to go for further reading. Knowing what we can do, and understanding the class hierarchy is half the battle.

Overview of Graphical Drawing

As you might be aware from programming using other graphical toolkits, one of the fundamental ideas behind drawing graphics in windowing applications is that the operating system does not keep a bitmap of each window if it is not visible. Instead, using an event based programming model, the operating system requests each window to re-draw itself when it becomes visible. If only a portion of the window becomes visible, when the operating system asks for the window to be re-drawn, it will tell the window exactly what it expects to be drawn.

When we are writing a program that draws into a window, we create a class that derives from `System.Windows.Forms.Form`. When we are writing a custom control, we derive a class from `System.Windows.Forms.UserControl`. In both of these situations, we write an event handler for the `Paint` event. This event handler will be called by the operating system whenever the window needs redrawn.

Windows Forms passes a `PaintEventArgs` object as an argument to the `Paint` event. The `PaintEventArgs` contains a `Graphics` object and a `ClipRectangle`.

The `Graphics` class, in the `System.Drawing` namespace, contains many methods to do the actual drawing, including methods for drawing lines, rectangles, ellipses, arcs, and more. Used in conjunction with these methods are classes that encapsulate drawing tools that will be familiar to programmers who have used other graphics class libraries: `Pen`, `Brush`, `Font`, and `Image`. We will discuss the classes in the following order:

- Graphics
- Coordinate system classes, including Point, Size, Rectangle, GraphicsPath, and Region
- Color
- Pen
- Brush
- Font
- Image

The ClipRectangle tells our Paint event the rectangle that needs to be painted. We don't need to draw anything outside of this rectangle, and in fact, even if we try to draw outside of this rectangle, our drawing has no effect on our window.

The 'Graphics' Class

There are three types of objects onto which we can draw. We can draw to windows and controls in windows. We can draw to pages that are being sent to the printer. We can draw to images and bitmaps in memory.

The Graphics class encapsulates a GDI+ 'drawing surface', and provides us with functions so that we can draw on any of these drawing surfaces. Among other capabilities, we can use it to draw arcs, curves, bezier curves (special types of curves that make smoothly flowing graphics), ellipses, images, lines, rectangles, and text. It is possible to write one set of code that does drawing to all three types of surfaces. We'll examine this further on in the chapter.

There are a couple of different ways that we can get a Graphics object for a window. If we write a method to handle the Paint event, we will get a Graphics object as an argument to the event. In addition, we can get a Graphics object on demand for any window, so that we can do drawing operations while handling a character event, a mouse event, or any other type of event. We saw the Paint event, and discussed event handlers in Chapter 6, but it would be useful to briefly cover it here, by showing how to create an event handler for the Paint event.

Start Visual Studio, and create an empty Visual Basic Windows Application project. Right-click on the Design window for the newly created form, and select View Code from the popup menu. At the top of the window, there are two combo boxes. The left combo box allows us to select a class, and after selecting a class, the right combo box allows us to select a specific method to override, or an event to implement.

The Form class has many methods that can be overridden, and even more events that can be implemented. When looking at the drop-down list for the left combo box, we see the following items:

- Form1 (YourAppName)
- (Overrides)
- (Base Class Events)

If we select the first item (Form1), the second combo box will show just the methods and events that have already been implemented for the form. It will not show any of the methods and events that potentially could be implemented.

If we select the second item, the second combo box will show all of the methods that are declared as `Virtual` in base classes of our `Form` class. We are interested in writing a new event handler, so we are not currently interested in this selection.

If we select the third item, the second combo box will show all of the instances for which we could write an event. When we select an item in the second combo box, Visual Studio creates an empty event handler, automatically generates the code to do the wiring for our event handler, and places the insertion point in our empty event handler.

Select **Base Class Events** in the left combo box. Select **Paint** in the right combo box. Visual Studio will create an event handler that looks like this:

```
Private Sub Form1_Paint(ByVal sender As Object, _
ByVal e As System.Windows.Forms.PaintEventArgs) Handles MyBase.Paint

End Sub
```

Okay, that's the end of the digression. Let's get on with our discussion of the `Graphics` class.

We'll get the `Graphics` object from the `PaintEventArgs` that is passed in with the event:

```
Private Sub Form1_Paint(ByVal sender As Object, _
ByVal e As System.Windows.Forms.PaintEventArgs) Handles MyBase.Paint
    Dim g As Graphics
    g = e.Graphics
    ' do our drawing here
End Sub
```

At other times, we may want to draw directly into our window without waiting for the `Paint` event. This would be the case if we are writing code for selecting some graphical object on the window (similar to selecting icons in Windows Explorer), or dragging some object with the mouse. The second way to get a `Graphics` object, is by calling the `CreateGraphics` method on the form, which is another method that `Form` inherits from `RichControl`:

```
Protected Sub Form1_Click(ByVal sender As Object, ByVal e As System.EventArgs)
    Dim g As Graphics
    g = Me.CreateGraphics
    ' do our drawing here
    g.Dispose()
End Sub
```

However, this is a less common technique. Primarily, we will do almost all of our drawing in response to a `Paint` event. Windows will generate these `Paint` events for a variety of reasons, including creation of the window, resizing the window, exposing the window from underneath another window, and programmatic invalidation of the window. This event based infrastructure actually helps minimize window repainting – if multiple areas of a window get invalidated due to any of the above reasons, Windows will coalesce the exposures, and our window will only repaint once.

For more information on `Paint`*, and other events, please see Chapter 6.*

Call 'Dispose' on 'Graphics' Objects

You have probably seen what happens with Windows when it runs out of resources. Sometimes it runs slowly, and sometimes it will not draw applications properly. A well-written application will free up resources when it is done with the resources.

There are several data types in .NET that implement the `IDisposable` interface. This interface defines a `Dispose` method that should be called to free up resources. `Dispose` should be called as soon as the application is done with the object, so that the resources can be freed as soon as possible. The `Graphics` class is one of the classes that implement this interface. One point to note: it is important to only call `Dispose` if we created the `Graphics` object ourselves. If we got the `Graphics` object as an argument to a `Paint` event, we did not create the `Graphics` object, so we should not call the `Dispose` method on it.

The `IDisposable` interface defines that the `Dispose` method should be called in the destructor of a class that implements the interface. This means that eventually, the `Dispose` method will be called. However, this does not alleviate our responsibility to call it in a timely fashion. Here is the reason: The garbage collector is what calls the destructor, and the semantics of the garbage collector define that we don't know when it is going to run. There are no guarantees. When we are running on a Windows 9X operating system with a lot of memory, the garbage collector may run very infrequently. Windows 9X operating systems are particularly sensitive to running out of resources, and may run out before the garbage collector runs. Windows 2000 and later versions of Windows do not have this problem, but it is better coding practice to free resources as soon as we are done with them.

There is a new keyword and construct in C# in the .NET framework. The `using` keyword automatically calls the `Dispose` method when an object goes out of scope. The following C# code shows the correct use of the `using` keyword:

```
using (Graphics g = this.CreateGraphics())
{
    g.DrawLine(Pens.Black, new Point(0, 0), new Point(3, 5));
}
```

According to the .NET documentation the above code is the same as:

```
Graphics g = this.CreateGraphics();
try {
    g.DrawLine(Pens.Black, new Point(0, 0), new Point(3, 5));
}
finally {
    if (g != null)
        ((IDisposable)g).Dispose();
}
```

It should be noted that there are two uses of the `using` keyword. One is as above. The other is the `using` directive that allows us to use the types in a namespace without needing to fully qualify the names in the namespace. This is a separate use of the `using` keyword.

There is no equivalent keyword and construct for Visual Basic, so VB developers must call `Dispose` explicitly. Examples in this chapter are written in VB, so we won't be using the `using` construct here.

Before we get into our first example, we need to examine coordinates and colors.

Coordinate System

It is important to have a programming model such that given a drawing operation, we can know exactly what pixels will be affected. When building custom controls, we would typically draw lots of rectangles, and horizontal and vertical lines. Having a line that runs one pixel too short or too far is very noticeable.

The coordinate system in GDI+ is based on imaginary mathematical lines that run through the center of each pixel. The origin of this coordinate system is the upper left corner of the window. We often refer to an intersection of these mathematical lines as an X-Y pair, as in X = 2, Y = 3. A shorthand notation for this same point is point (2,3).

Because controls within windows are actually in child windows, each control has its own coordinate space. The upper-left corner of the control is at coordinate (0, 0), regardless of where the control is placed in its containing window.

The default behavior for GDI+ when drawing a line is to center the line on the mathematical line that we specify. When drawing a horizontal line using integer coordinates, we could think of the pixels as being half above the mathematical line, and half below the mathematical line. If we were to draw a horizontal line that is one pixel wide from point (1, 1) to point (5, 1), the following pixels will be drawn:

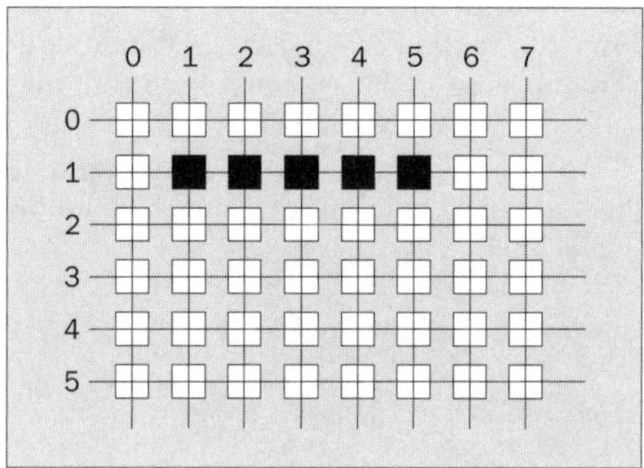

When we draw a diagonal line from point 1, 0 to point 4, 3, the following pixels will be drawn:

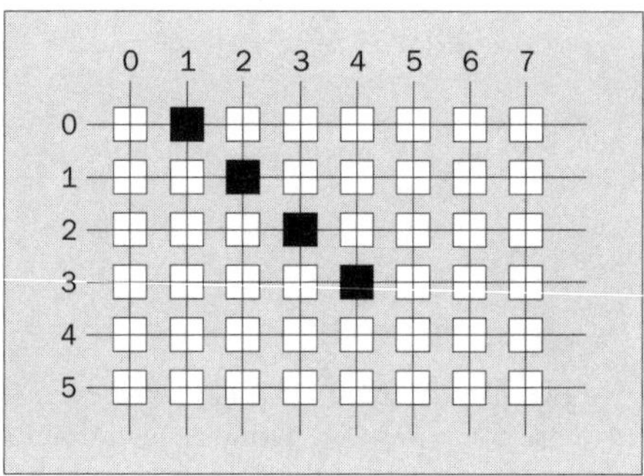

When we draw a rectangle with the upper left corner at 1, 0 and a size of 5, 4, it looks like this:

This distance is 5 pixels

It is important to note something about the above figure. We specified a width of 5, yet there are 6 pixels drawn in the horizontal direction. We specified a height of 4, yet there are 5 pixels drawn in the vertical direction. If we consider the mathematical lines that run through the pixels, then the mathematical rectangle is exactly 5 pixels wide and 4 pixels high – the pixels falls a half pixel outside the mathematical line, and a half pixel inside the mathematical line.

When we consider anti-aliasing, the model gets somewhat more complicated. Some of the pixels will be 'half' colored in. This has the effect of creating the appearance of a smoother line, which will partially avoid the stair step appearance of a diagonal line.

Following is a line without anti-aliasing:

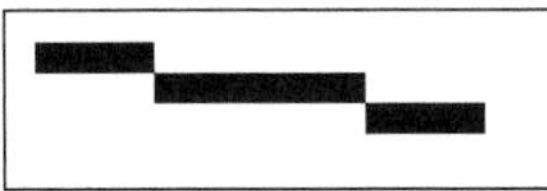

The same line drawn with anti-aliasing appears as follows:

If we were to view the anti-aliased line at a high resolution, it would have the appearance of a much smoother line. It will not have as much of a stair-stepped appearance.

'Point', 'Size', and 'Rectangle'

There are three structures that we will often use to specify coordinates when drawing: `Point`, `Size`, and `Rectangle`.

We use the `Point` structure to represent a single point in our coordinate space. We will use this structure as an argument to many GDI+ methods, such as `DrawLine`. We declare and construct a `Point` structure as follows:

```
Dim p As Point = New Point(1, 1)
```

After we have constructed a Point structure, we can get and set the X and Y coordinates using public properties.

The Point structure uses Integer precision. There is a corresponding structure, PointF, which uses single precision floating-point precision. When drawing complex graphics, it is often more accurate to store interim calculations in floating-point variables instead of integer variables. Many of the drawing methods take instances of the PointF structure instead of instances of the Point structure. GDI+ will then do appropriate rounding operations to determine which pixels are colored. It will also use anti-aliasing to create the appearance of graphics that more closely approximate the coordinates as specified by the floating-point coordinates. We should note that if we are drawing graphics that never use anti-aliasing, and all of our coordinates can be expressed in integers, it is more efficient to use the Point structure rather than the PointF structure.

We use the Size structure to represent sizes in pixels. The Size structure contains a width and a height. We declare and construct a Size structure as follows:

```
Dim s As Size = New Size(5, 5)
```

After we have constructed a Size structure, we can get and set the width and height of it using public properties.

Just as with the Point structure, there is a corresponding SizeF structure that uses floating-point precision.

We use the Rectangle structure to specify the coordinates of a rectangle. In essence, a rectangle consists of a Point structure (which defines the upper left corner of it) and a Size structure. There are two constructors for a Rectangle. One takes four arguments: the X position, the Y position, the width, and the height:

```
Dim r1 As Rectangle = New Rectangle(1, 1, 5, 5)
```

The other takes a Point and a Size structure:

```
Dim p As Point = New Point(1, 1)
Dim s As Size = New Size(5, 5)
Dim r2 As Rectangle = New Rectangle(p, s)
```

We can set and get all aspects of the location and size of a rectangle using public properties. In addition, there are other useful methods to test if a rectangle is empty, and take the intersection and union of two rectangles.

There is also a RectangleF structure that uses floating-point precision.

'GraphicsPath'

As a convenience when dealing with more complicated graphics drawing operations, we can use the GraphicsPath class to draw a series of connected lines, bezier curves, arcs, pie shapes, polygons, rectangles, and more. We can draw the path with a single call to the method DrawPath. We can fill the path with a call to the method FillPath.

We should note that this will not optimize drawing time. This class is only a convenience to the programmer – it provides an additional layer of abstraction.

We also use GraphicsPath objects when constructing a PathGradientBrush, which are used for creating special shading effects. We'll see more details on PathGradientBrush when we discuss drawing shapes.

To construct a GraphicsPath, we pass as arguments to the constructor an array of points and an array of PathTypes. The PathTypes array is a byte array. Each element in the PathTypes array corresponds to an element in the array of points, and tells the class how the path is to be constructed. For the point at the beginning of the path, we use a path type for that point of PathPointType.Start. If the point is a junction between two lines, we use a path type for that point of PathPointType.Line. If the point is to be used to construct a bezier curve, we use a path type for that point of PathPointType.Bezier.

Following is code to create a GraphicsPath with four line segments:

```
Dim path As GraphicsPath
path = New GraphicsPath(New Point() { _
New Point(10, 10), _
New Point(100, 100), _
New Point(10, 120), _
New Point(100, 10), _
New Point(130, 40) _
}, New Byte() { _
CType(PathPointType.Start, Byte), _
CType(PathPointType.Line, Byte), _
CType(PathPointType.Line, Byte), _
CType(PathPointType.Line, Byte), _
CType(PathPointType.Line, Byte) _
})
e.Graphics.DrawPath(Pens.Black, path)
```

Following is the line that is drawn using the path:

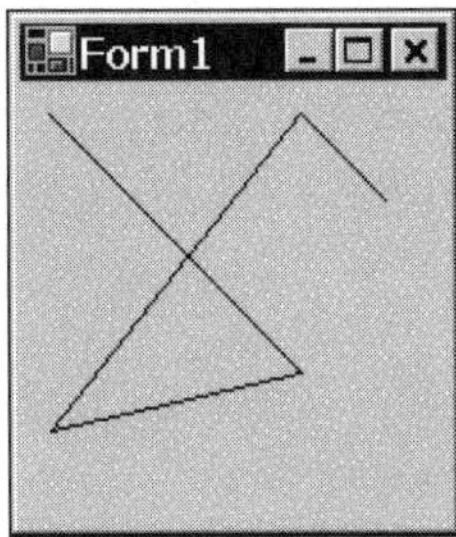

Let's take a closer look at the constructor for this GraphicsPath object. The constructor takes two arguments. The first is an array of points that we construct in place:

```
New Point() { _
  New Point(10, 10), _
  New Point(100, 100), _
  New Point(10, 120), _
  New Point(100, 10), _
  New Point(130, 40) _
}
```

The second argument is an array of bytes that we construct in place:

```
New Byte() { _
   CType(PathPointType.Start, Byte), _
   CType(PathPointType.Line, Byte), _
   CType(PathPointType.Line, Byte), _
   CType(PathPointType.Line, Byte), _
   CType(PathPointType.Line, Byte) _
}
```

Finally, in the above example, we call the `DrawPath` method:

```
e.Graphics.DrawPath(Pens.Black, path)
```

'Region'

The `Region` class is a complex graphical shape that is comprised of rectangles and paths. The constructor for the `Region` class is overloaded, and can take a `GraphicsPath` or `Rectangle` as an argument. When using a `GraphicsPath` to construct a region, the path is closed. The ending point is connected to the beginning point for the purposes of constructing the region. After constructing a region, we can add additional area to the region using the `Union` method, we can subtract from the region using the `Exclude` method, or we can intersect the region with another region or rectangle using the `Intersect` method. After constructing a `Region`, we can draw that region using the method `FillRegion`. There are other uses of regions, including clipping operations, which we will discuss later.

The following code creates a region, excludes a `Rectangle` to it, adds a `GraphicsPath` to it, and then fills that region with the color red:

```
Dim r1 As Rectangle = New Rectangle(10, 10, 100, 100)
Dim r2 As Rectangle = New Rectangle(40, 40, 50, 50)
Dim r As [Region] = New [Region](r1)
r.Exclude(r2)

Dim path As GraphicsPath = New GraphicsPath(New Point() { _
New Point(45, 45), _
New Point(145, 55), _
New Point(200, 150), _
New Point(75, 150), _
New Point(45, 45) _
}, New Byte() { _
CType(PathPointType.Start, Byte), _
CType(PathPointType.Bezier, Byte), _
CType(PathPointType.Bezier, Byte), _
CType(PathPointType.Bezier, Byte), _
CType(PathPointType.Line, Byte) _
})
r.Union(path)
e.Graphics.FillRegion(Brushes.Red, r)
```

The above path being added to the region is a closed path. The code draws the following shape:

> *Of course, you will need the code download from Wrox in order to see the color versions of the code examples in this chapter.*

'Color'

Colors are an integral part of graphical drawing operations. When we draw, we must specify what color to draw in.

We use the `Color` structure to encapsulate colors. We can create a color by passing red, green, and blue (RGB) values into a method in the `Color` structure, but we rarely would need to do this. Instead, we can use about 150 properties of the `Color` structure to get pre-made colors. We can declare a variable of type `Color` and initialize it as follows:

```
Dim lightGoldenrodYellow As Color = Color.LightGoldenrodYellow
Dim redColor As Color = Color.Red
```

There are two different forms in which any color can be represented. The first is RGB. We can also break the color down into three components: hue, saturation, and brightness. We can use methods in the `Color` structure to do this. Those methods are `GetBrightness`, `GetHue`, and `GetSaturation`.

We can draw semi-transparently in GDI+. The means by which we accomplish this is the Alpha component in the `Color` structure. The Alpha component is a value between 0 and 255, with 0 being completely transparent, and 255 being completely opaque. Using this facility in colors allows us to create fade-in/out effects, such as the menu effects in Windows 2000. We can also create watermark effects, where we draw over other graphics semi-transparently. We will see an example of this technique further on in this chapter.

Drawing Using Pens

We use the Pen class to draw lines. The Pen object defines the color, width, and pattern of the line. The pattern of the line can either be solid, or composed of dashes and/or dots.

We'll start by creating a bar chart that is made up of only lines.

Our bar chart project initially will have two modules. One module will contain the data for the bar chart. We'll name this module `GraphData.vb`. The other module will contain the code to draw the bar chart. For simplicities sake, we will put this code in the default form that Visual Studio creates when we create a new project. As previously mentioned, in a commercial project, we would put this drawing code into its own module, and use it from the form, but for the purpose of learning to write graphics code, we'll keep it simple and put it into the form itself.

'BarChart1'

Start Visual Studio.NET, and create a new Visual Basic Windows Forms project. Name this project `BarChart1`.

Before we add any code to Form1, we will add another set of classes that will contain the data for the bar chart. From the Project menu, select Add Class. Name the file for the class `GraphData.vb`. After you click the Open button, Visual Studio creates a new file and opens an editor window for that file. We will define four classes in this file:

```
' this class encapsulates the appearance of each bar
Public Class BarStyle
    Public Enum BarTypeEnum
        Solid
        LinearGradient
        PathGradient
    End Enum
    Public BarType As BarTypeEnum
    Public Color1 As Color
    Public Color2 As Color  ' only used if barType == LinearGradient
End Class

' this class contains the data for one bar
Public Class GraphDataElement
    Public Value As Double
    Public BarStyle As BarStyle
    Public XAxisLabel As String
    Public ImageName As String
    Public Sub New(ByVal val As Double, ByVal xal As String, _
    ByVal imname As String, ByVal bs As BarStyle)
        Me.Value = val
        Me.XAxisLabel = xal
        Me.ImageName = imname
        Me.BarStyle = bs
    End Sub
End Class

' this class contains information for the bar chart as a whole
Public Class GraphData
    Public Data As ArrayList
    Public MaximumY As Double
    Public Title As String
    Public Sub New()
        Me.Data = New ArrayList()
    End Sub
End Class

' This class contains metrics for drawing the bar chart.
' The metrics for displaying on the screen can be different
' than metrics for drawing to the printer.
Public Class GraphMetrics
    Public Size As Size
    Public XAxisDelta As Integer
    Public YAxisDelta As Integer
    Public BarSpacing As Integer
    Public BarWidth As Integer
    Public PenWidth As Integer
End Class
```

The above classes allow us to specify the data and metrics for drawing the bar chart. The data consists of multiple data values, along with information on how to draw the bar. Ideally, these classes would have private data members, and have properties to get and set them. For brevity, we are implementing it in as simple a fashion as possible.

The above classes contain references for defining bar types of `LinearGradient` and `PathGradient`. We will not use certain features of these data structures in the first example, but rather than re-visiting them to add features when we need them for subsequent examples, they are presented in their final form. We will use the `LinearGradient` and `PathGradient` bar types in examples further on in the chapter, and at that time, their meaning will be made clear.

Add the following private data members to the `Form1` class:

```
Private gd As GraphData
Private dgm As GraphMetrics  'GraphMetrics for graphs displayed in a window
```

These variables will hold the data and metrics for our graph. The variable `dgm` contains the display graph metrics. Later, when we are going to print the graph, we will also declare a variable for the printer graph metrics. These graph metrics data structures contain information that abstracts the differences between drawing on the screen and drawing to the printer. For instance, there may be a different pixel resolution between the two devices, so encapsulating the graph metrics in this fashion allows us to have one set of code that draws to both devices. The bars would be a different width, and the spacing between the bars would be different.

Next, add a constructor to the `Form1` class, as follows:

```
Public Sub New(ByVal rect As Rectangle, ByVal gd As GraphData)
    MyBase.New()

    'This call is required by the Win Form Designer.
    InitializeComponent()

    'The initialization goes after the InitializeComponent() call
    Me.gd = gd
    Me.Bounds = rect    'set the size of the window

    'these are the graph metrics for drawing on the screen
    dgm = New GraphMetrics()
    dgm.XAxisDelta = 30
    dgm.YAxisDelta = 40
    dgm.BarSpacing = 30
    dgm.BarWidth = 40
    dgm.PenWidth = 1
    dgm.Size = New Size(400, 300)
End Sub
```

The constructor initializes our data members, and sets the size of the window.

Next, add a `Shared Main` method to `Form1`:

```
Shared Sub Main()
    Dim gd As GraphData = New GraphData()
    gd.MaximumY = 100
    gd.Title = "Transportation"
```

```
    Dim bs As BarStyle = New BarStyle()
    bs.BarType = BarStyle.BarTypeEnum.Solid
    bs.Color1 = Color.Blue
    gd.Data.Add(New GraphDataElement(25, "Cars", "car.bmp", bs))

    bs = New BarStyle()
    bs.BarType = BarStyle.BarTypeEnum.LinearGradient
    bs.Color1 = Color.Blue
    bs.Color2 = Color.White
    gd.Data.Add(New GraphDataElement(35, "Trains", "train.bmp", bs))

    bs = New BarStyle()
    bs.BarType = BarStyle.BarTypeEnum.LinearGradient
    bs.Color1 = Color.Red
    bs.Color2 = Color.White
    gd.Data.Add(New GraphDataElement(65, "Boats", "boat.bmp", bs))

    bs = New BarStyle()
    bs.BarType = BarStyle.BarTypeEnum.PathGradient
    bs.Color1 = Color.Green
    gd.Data.Add(New GraphDataElement(85, "Planes", "plane.bmp", bs))

    ' Set initial size of the window rectangle
    Dim windowRectangle As Rectangle = New Rectangle(0, 0, 420, 332)
    System.Windows.Forms.Application.Run(New Form1(windowRectangle, gd))
End Sub
```

Here, we declare and initialize the GraphData. In this first example, we are only going to draw lines for our bars, so we will not be using the colors, text, or bitmaps yet. We will use them in the more advanced examples. Even though we will initially not be using all of the data in these data structures, we will not need to make any further changes to them as we make our bar chart more and more elaborate.

Now add the following methods to our Form1 class:

```
Private Sub DrawAxes(ByVal g As Graphics, ByVal gm As GraphMetrics)
    Dim pen As Pen = New Pen(Color.Black, gm.PenWidth)

    ' Draw the X axis
    g.DrawLine(pen, New Point(0, gm.Size.Height - gm.XAxisDelta), _
    New Point(gm.Size.Width, gm.Size.Height - gm.XAxisDelta))

    ' Draw the Y axis
    g.DrawLine(pen, New Point(gm.YAxisDelta, 0), _
    New Point(gm.YAxisDelta, gm.Size.Height))

    pen.Dispose()
End Sub

Private Sub DrawBars(ByVal g As Graphics, ByVal gm As GraphMetrics)

    ' x contains the x position of the next bar to be drawn
    Dim x As Integer = gm.YAxisDelta + gm.BarSpacing

    Dim pen As Pen = New Pen(Color.Black, gm.PenWidth)
```

```
    Dim gde As GraphDataElement

    ' the GraphDataElements are the bars - the following iterates through the
    ' bars.
    For Each gde In gd.Data

        ' draw the black line for each bar
        ' calculate the bar height
        Dim barHeight As Integer = CType(gde.Value / gd.MaximumY * _
       (gm.Size.Height - 2 * gm.XAxisDelta), Integer)

        ' calculate the rectangle for the bar
        Dim r As Rectangle = New Rectangle(x, _
        gm.Size.Height - gm.XAxisDelta - barHeight, gm.BarWidth, _
        barHeight)

        ' draw the bar
        g.DrawRectangle(pen, r)
        ' calculate the x position of the next bar

        x = x + gm.BarWidth + gm.BarSpacing
    Next
    pen.Dispose()
End Sub

Public Sub DrawToGraphics(ByVal g As Graphics, ByVal gm As GraphMetrics)
    DrawAxes(g, gm)
    DrawBars(g, gm)
End Sub
```

Next, add a `Paint` event for the form. We reviewed how to add this event earlier in this chapter. Modify the `Paint` event so that it contains the following code:

```
Private Sub Form1_Paint(ByVal sender As Object, _
ByVal e As System.Windows.Forms.PaintEventArgs) Handles MyBase.Paint

    Dim g As Graphics = e.Graphics
    DrawToGraphics(g, dgm)

End Sub
```

The first thing that we do in the `Paint` event is declare a variable of the `Graphics` class. We then initialize that variable from the `PaintEventArgs` class. We then call the method `DrawToGraphics` to draw the bar chart to the drawing surface that is encapsulated by the `Graphics` object. We separate this functionality because later, when printing the bar chart, we will use this same function for drawing to other drawing surfaces. The methods `DrawAxes` and `DrawBars` do the actual drawing. When we construct the pen, we pass as parameters to the constructor a color and a width of the pen. In this example, the color is black, and the width is based on our `GraphMetrics` class.

Now compile and run the code. When you run it, it will create this window:

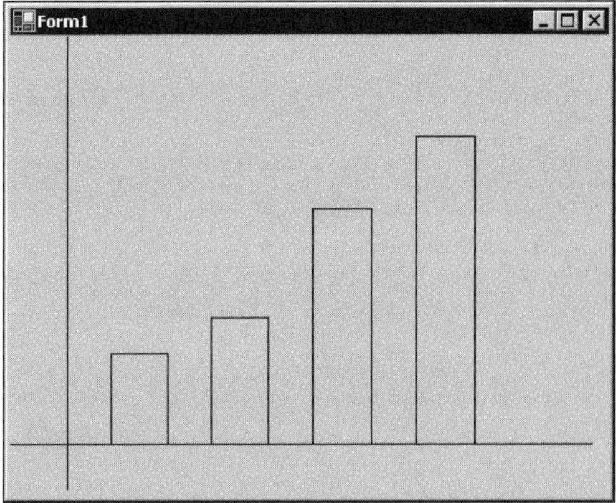

When we draw each line, as in the following code:

```
g.DrawLine(pen, New Point(0, gm.Size.Height - gm.XAxisDelta), _
    New Point(gm.Size.Width, gm.Size.Height - gm.XAxisDelta))
```

we pass the Pen object that we just created, along with the starting point and ending point of the line.

Just as for Graphics objects, it is important to either call Dispose on Pen objects when we are finished with them (or in C# use the using construct), otherwise our application may deplete the Windows resources.

In this example, we constructed a Pen object. However, there is an easier way to get a Pen object. The Pens class contains properties for getting approximately 150 pens, one for each of the pre-defined colors that we learned about previously. These pens all have a width of one, and are a solid line (not a dashed line). The following code shows how to get a pen from the Pens class:

```
Private Sub Form1_Paint(ByVal sender As Object, _
ByVal e As System.Windows.Forms.PaintEventArgs) Handles MyBase.Paint

    Dim g As Graphics = e.Graphics
    g.DrawLine(Pens.red, New Point(0, 0), New Point(10, 10))

End Sub
```

In this case, we did not create the Pen, so it is not necessary to call Dispose.

There are many more features of the Pen class. We could create a pen to draw a dashed line. We can create a pen with a width thicker than one pixel. There is an Alignment property of the Pen class that allows us to define whether the pen is drawn to the left or right (or above/below) of the line that we specify. By setting the StartCap and EndCap properties, we can specify that our lines are ended with an arrow, a diamond, a square, or rounded off. We can even program a custom start cap and end cap using the CustomStartCap and CustomEndCap properties. After learning about images, we will see how to specify a Brush with a Pen, so that we can draw the line using a bitmap instead of a solid color. For more information, see the Pen class in the .NET Framework Reference.

Drawing Using Brushes

The next version of our bar chart will use the `Brush` class to fill in our bars with colors. In this application, we will only be filling rectangles, but in other applications, we could use this class to draw many other types of shapes, such as ellipses, pies, and polygons. The `Brush` class is an abstract base class. To instantiate a `Brush` object, we use classes derived from `Brush`, such as `SolidBrush`, `TextureBrush`, `LinearGradientBrush`, and `PathGradientBrush`.

We use a `SolidBrush` to fill a shape with a solid color.

A `TextureBrush` object represents a brush constructed using a bitmap. When constructing it, we also specify a bounding rectangle and a wrap mode. Using the bounding rectangle, we can construct our brush using just a portion of the bitmap. We don't need to use the whole bitmap if we don't want to. The wrap mode has a number of options, including `Clamp`, which clamps the texture to the object boundary, `Tile`, which tiles the texture, and `TileFlipX`, `TileFlipY`, and `TileFlipXY`, which tile while flipping the image for successive tiles.

If we want to draw a gradient of two colors, we use the `LinearGradientBrush` class. The first color transitions to the second color at a specified angle.

`PathGradientBrush` creates an elaborate shading effect, where the shading runs from the center of the path to the edge of the path.

Call `Dispose` on `Brush` objects. Just as for `Graphics` and `Pen` objects, it is important to call `Dispose` on `Brush` objects when we are finished with them (or in C#, use the `using` construct), otherwise our application may deplete the Windows resources.

'BarChart2'

With each successive example, we will see only the changes between the previous example and the one that we are building. After we complete one example and get it working, we can close the solution in Visual Studio, make a copy of the directory, open the solution in the new directory, and make all changes in the new project.

Right-click on the form, and select View Code from the popup menu.

At the top of the file, add an `Imports` statement, as follows:

```
Imports System.Drawing.Drawing2D
```

In this example, we will be using the `LinearGradientBrush` and `PathGradientBrush`, which are in the `Drawing2D` namespace. It is more convenient to add the `Imports` statement, so that we don't need to fully qualify the names of the brushes.

Find the constructor for the `Form1` class, and add a call to `SetStyle` after the call to `InitializeComponent`. The modified constructor is as follows:

```
Public Sub New(ByVal rect As Rectangle, ByVal gd As GraphData)
    MyBase.New()

    'This call is required by the Win Form Designer.
    InitializeComponent()
```

```
        'The initialization goes after the InitializeComponent() call
        SetStyle(ControlStyles.Opaque, True)
        Me.gd = gd
        Me.Bounds = rect    'set the size of the window

        'these are the graph metrics for drawing on the screen
        dgm = New GraphMetrics()
        dgm.XAxisDelta = 30
        dgm.YAxisDelta = 40
        dgm.BarSpacing = 30
        dgm.BarWidth = 40
        dgm.PenWidth = 1
        dgm.Size = New Size(400, 300)
    End Sub
```

The call to SetStyle above changes the behavior of the Form class, so that it will not draw the background of our form. To improve the appearance, we want to draw a white background, and to prevent the Windows Forms class library from first drawing the background as gray, we add the call to the SetStyle method. The term opaque refers to the idea that our window will draw everything in the window – we won't leave any pixels undrawn, therefore our window could be said to be opaque to everything underneath it.

Now, modify the DrawBars method as follows:

```
    Private Sub DrawBars(ByVal g As Graphics, ByVal gm As GraphMetrics)

    ' x contains the x position of the next bar to be drawn
    Dim x As Integer = gm.YAxisDelta + gm.BarSpacing

    Dim pen As Pen = New Pen(Color.Black, gm.PenWidth)
    Dim gde As GraphDataElement

    ' the GraphDataElements are the bars - the following iterates through the
    ' bars.
    For Each gde In gd.Data

    ' draw the black line for each bar
    ' calculate the bar height
    Dim barHeight As Integer = CType(gde.Value / gd.MaximumY * _
    (gm.Size.Height - 2 * gm.XAxisDelta), Integer)

          ' calculate the rectangle for the bar
          Dim r As Rectangle = New Rectangle(x, _
          gm.Size.Height - gm.XAxisDelta - barHeight, gm.BarWidth, _
          barHeight)

          ' draw the bar
          g.DrawRectangle(pen, r)

          ' calculate the x position of the next bar
          x = x + gm.BarWidth + gm.BarSpacing

          ' draw the interior of each bar
```

```
        ' calculate the interior rectangle of the bar
        Dim r2 As Rectangle = New Rectangle(r.X + 1, r.Y + 1, r.Width - 1, _
        r.Height - 1)
        Select Case gde.BarStyle.BarType
           Case BarStyle.BarTypeEnum.Solid
               Dim sBrush As SolidBrush = _
                  New SolidBrush(gde.BarStyle.Color1)
               g.FillRectangle(sBrush, r2)
               sBrush.Dispose()

            Case BarStyle.BarTypeEnum.LinearGradient
               Dim r3 As Rectangle = New Rectangle(r2.Left - 5, r2.Top, _
               r2.Width + 10, r2.Height)
               Dim lBrush As LinearGradientBrush = _
               New LinearGradientBrush(r3, gde.BarStyle.Color1, _
               gde.BarStyle.Color2, 0F)
               g.FillRectangle(lBrush, r2)
               lBrush.Dispose()

            Case BarStyle.BarTypeEnum.PathGradient
               Dim path As GraphicsPath = New GraphicsPath(New Point() { _
               New Point(r2.Left, r2.Top), _
               New Point(r2.Right, r2.Top), _
               New Point(r2.Right, r2.Bottom), _
               New Point(r2.Left, r2.Bottom) _
               }, New Byte() { _
               CType(PathPointType.Start, Byte), _
               CType(PathPointType.Line, Byte), _
               CType(PathPointType.Line, Byte), _
               CType(PathPointType.Line, Byte) _
               })
                   Dim pgb As PathGradientBrush = New PathGradientBrush(path)
                  pgb.SurroundColors = New Color() { _
                  gde.BarStyle.Color1 _
                  }
               g.FillPath(pgb, path)
               pgb.Dispose()
            End Select
      Next
      pen.Dispose()
   End Sub
```

This time we create an instance of a `SolidBrush`, a `LinearGradientBrush`, and a `PathGradientBrush`. Note the disposal of the brushes after we are done with them.

When constructing the `LinearGradientBrush` object, if the angle (the last argument to the constructor) is specified as zero, then the first color will transition to the second color from left to right. The angle is specified in degrees, moving in the clockwise direction, so if we had used 45 degrees, then we would have drawn a gradient starting with blue at the upper left corner, and transitioning to white at the lower right corner. Because we specified the same bounding rectangle when constructing our brush as when we drew the rectangle, we only see one instance of the transition of the brush from one color to the other. If we drew a larger rectangle but kept the gradient rectangle the same, we would see the transition pattern repeated. The following screenshot shows a gradient brush where the angle is 45 degrees. In this case, the gradient rectangle is small (40x40 pixels), and the rectangle drawn is much larger, so we see many instances of the transition of the brush from one color to the other.

Bear in mind that with PathGradientBrush, we do not repeat the beginning point at the end of the list of points. If we repeat the beginning point at the end, the algorithm to compute the center of the gradient gives a heavier weight to the point that was repeated, and the center is offset towards that direction.

Finally, modify the Paint event as follows:

```
Private Sub Form1_Paint(ByVal sender As Object, _
ByVal e As System.Windows.Forms.PaintEventArgs) Handles MyBase.Paint
    Dim g As Graphics = e.Graphics
    g.FillRectangle(Brushes.White, ClientRectangle)
    DrawToGraphics(g, dgm)
End Sub
```

This is the code to draw the background of the window in white, as we planned to do when we added the call to the SetStyle method in the constructor. Just as with the Pens class, there is a Brushes class that contains properties for getting approximately 150 brushes, one for each pre-defined color. These are solid brushes. The above code uses a white brush obtained from the Brushes class.

Compile and run the code. When you run it, it will create this window:

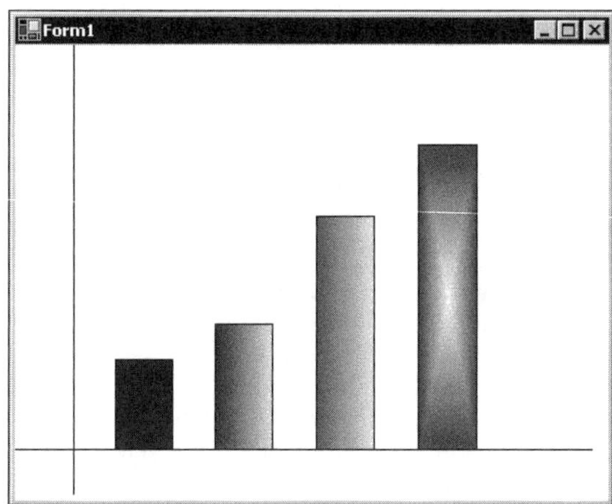

Drawing Text Using Fonts

Next, we want to add text to our bar chart. We use the `Font` class to draw text. Using the `Font` class, we can specify the three main characteristics of a font. They are the font family, the font size, and the font style.

A font family is a set of fonts having a similar basic design, but having variations in styles. For instance, we could have a font family of Times New Roman, which would be comprised of the unadorned font, a bold variation, an italic variation, and a bold, italic variation. Other examples of font families are Courier and Arial.

Call `Dispose` on `Font` objects. It is important to call `Dispose` on `Font` objects when we are finished with them (or in C#, use the `using` construct), otherwise our application may deplete the Windows resources.

When we draw text, we specify a bounding rectangle of the text to draw. Normally, this rectangle should be at least the height of the font. The width of the rectangle normally should be wide enough to accommodate our text. We would only vary from this rule if we were drawing clipped text.

The `StringFormat` class allows us to modify the text layout, including right, left, or center alignment, and line spacing. In addition, it has capabilities to affect other display characteristics, such as ellipsis insertion, right justification of text, line spacing, and national digit substitution. For more information, see the `StringFormat` class in the .NET Framework Reference. Our next bar chart example draws centered text using the `StringFormat` class.

'BarChart3'

We are now ready to modify the last example, printing the label for the X-axis centered below each bar. In addition, we will print the value for each bar above the bar. Finally, we will add a title for the bar chart above the bars, and draw a rectangle around the title.

Add a new method `DrawLabels` as follows:

```
Private Sub DrawLabels(ByVal g As Graphics, ByVal gm As GraphMetrics)
    Dim x As Integer = gm.YAxisDelta + gm.BarSpacing
    Dim gde As GraphDataElement
    For Each gde In gd.Data
        Dim barHeight As Integer = CType(gde.Value / gd.MaximumY * _
        (gm.Size.Height - 2 * gm.XAxisDelta), Integer)
        Dim r As Rectangle = New Rectangle(x, _
        gm.Size.Height - gm.XAxisDelta - barHeight, gm.BarWidth, _
        barHeight)
        x = x + gm.BarWidth + gm.BarSpacing

        ' draw the value for the bar
        Dim valueRect As Rectangle = New Rectangle(r.Left, _
        r.Top - Font.Height, r.Width, Font.Height)
        Dim s As String = gde.Value & "%"
        Dim sf As StringFormat = New StringFormat()
        sf.Alignment = StringAlignment.Center
        g.DrawString(s, Font, Brushes.Black, _
        New RectangleF(valueRect.Left, valueRect.Top, valueRect.Width, _
        valueRect.Height), sf)
```

```
            ' draw the label for the bar
            Dim labelRect As Rectangle = New Rectangle( _
            CType(r.Left - gm.BarSpacing / 2, Integer), _
            gm.Size.Height - gm.XAxisDelta, r.Width + gm.BarSpacing, _
            Font.Height)
            g.DrawString(gde.XAxisLabel, Font, Brushes.Black, _
            New RectangleF(labelRect.Left, labelRect.Top, labelRect.Width, _
            labelRect.Height), sf)
        Next
    End Sub
```

This method shows the calculation of the appropriate rectangle for some text and then drawing it.

It uses the `Brushes` class to get a black brush for drawing the text. Because the particular overloaded `DrawString` method that we wished to use takes a `RectangleF` as an argument instead of a `Rectangle`, we declare and initialize the `RectangleF` object in the call to the `DrawString` method.

In the above method, we use the default font for the form. This is a font that is already instantiated, which we can get by accessing the `Font` property of the form.

Add a new method called `DrawTitle`, as follows:

```
    Private Sub DrawTitle(ByVal g As Graphics, ByVal gm As GraphMetrics)
        ' draw the title for the bar chart
        Dim titleFont As Font = New Font("Times New Roman", 18, _
        FontStyle.Bold Or FontStyle.Italic)

        ' calculate the width and height of the title string
        Dim titleSizeF As SizeF = g.MeasureString(gd.Title, titleFont)

        ' calculate the rectangle for the title
        Dim titleRect As Rectangle = New Rectangle(gm.YAxisDelta * 2, _
        gm.XAxisDelta, titleSizeF.Width, titleSizeF.Height)

        ' inflate it by one, and draw the black border
        titleRect.Inflate(1, 1)
        g.DrawRectangle(Pens.Black, titleRect)

        ' deflate by one, and draw the white interior
        titleRect.Inflate(-1, -1)
        g.FillRectangle(Brushes.White, titleRect)

        ' now draw the string
        g.DrawString(gd.Title, titleFont, Brushes.Blue, titleRect.Left, _
        titleRect.Top)

       ' and dispose
       titleFont.Dispose()
    End Sub
```

The `DrawTitle` method shows the instantiation of a font where we specify the font family, the size of the font, and the style of the font.

```
Dim titleFont As Font = New Font("Times New Roman", 18, _
FontStyle.Bold Or FontStyle.Italic)
```

Because we instantiated it, it is our responsibility to call `Dispose` on the `Font`.

```
titleFont.Dispose()
```

One of the common activities when drawing text is determining the width in pixels of a given string of text. We have to determine this width based on the string, the font in which we will draw the text, and the drawing surface on which we will draw. The variation of the pixel resolution of the various drawing surfaces means that the text width for a given string will be different on each drawing surface. Screens typically have 72 pixels per inch. Printers can be 300, 600, 1200, or even more pixels per inch. We can use the MeasureString method of the Graphics class to calculate this pixel width. Following is some VB code that demonstrates the use of this method:

```
Dim str As String = "This is a string"
Dim size As SizeF = e.Graphics.MeasureString(str, Font)
e.Graphics.DrawRectangle(Pens.Black, 0, 0, size.Width, size.Height)
e.Graphics.DrawString(str, Font, Brushes.Blue, New RectangleF(0, 0, _
    size.Width, size.Height))
```

When drawing the text, we calculate the bounding rectangle for our text. We get the height of the font using the `Height` property. For illustrative purposes, we draw this rectangle in black, so that the bounding rectangle of our text is very clear.

Back to our example, modify the method `DrawToGraphics` as follows:

```
Public Sub DrawToGraphics(ByVal g As Graphics, ByVal gm As GraphMetrics)
    DrawAxes(g, gm)
    DrawBars(g, gm)
    DrawLabels(g, gm)
    DrawTitle(g, gm)
End Sub
```

Now compile and run the code. When you run it, it will create this window:

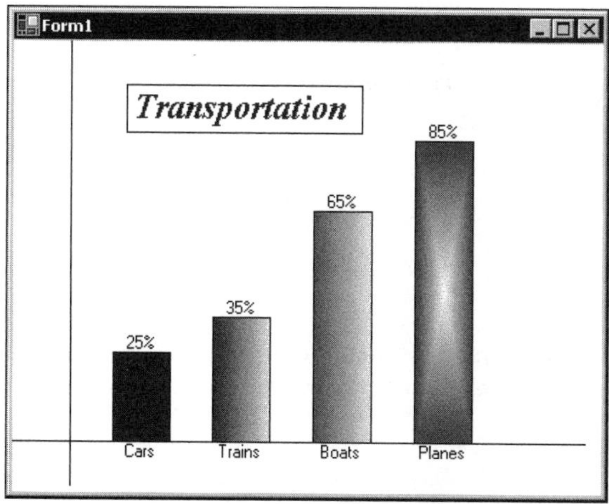

We only specify the rectangle in which the text will go. The baseline of a font is the imaginary line that most of the characters of the font 'sit' on. GDI+ and the font determine where the actual baseline will go. We have no control of that.

When we draw the text, we pass a brush to the `DrawString` method. In this example, we only passed brushes that have a solid color to the `DrawString` method. We could just as easily have passed other types of brushes, such as a `LinearGradientBrush` or `TextureBrush`.

One area of functionality in this example that we did not touch on is drawing multi-line text. Using GDI+, it could not be easier. All we need to do is to specify a rectangle when calling `DrawString` where the width is less than the length of the string (in pixels), and the height is sufficient to draw multiple lines.

Drawing Using Images

There are many uses for images in GDI+. Naturally, we can draw images into a window, but there are other uses. We can create a brush (TextureBrush) from an image, and then use that brush in any method that takes a brush, such as drawing a shape. We can also create a pen using a TextureBrush, and use that pen to draw lines.

Another important usage of images is the technique of double buffering. In this technique, instead of drawing to a window, we make all of our graphical drawing operations into an image. After the image is exactly as we want it, we draw the image to the window with a single operation. Some graphical drawing tasks take an extraordinary amount of processing power. The elapsed time can be noticeable. Drawing a three dimensional scene is one example. One technique for drawing a three dimensional scene consists of drawing the objects that are farthest from the point of view first. Then we would successively draw closer and closer objects. This creates the appearance where near objects obscure objects that are farther away. However, this technique, if drawn directly to the screen, creates a flickering effect. We could see the objects farther away for a very short amount of time before they are obscured by near objects.

A better technique is to draw the scene to an image in memory, then draw the image to the window when the image is completed.

GDI+ will handle the mechanics of double buffering automatically for us. However, it is useful to understand the mechanism, and occasionally, it is advantageous to manually do the double buffering ourselves.

The `Image` class is an abstract class. There are two subclasses of `Image` that we are concerned with: `Bitmap` and `Metafile`.

The `Bitmap` class is the one that we will use most often. It is a general-purpose image, with a height, width, and color depth. Color depth refers to the precision with which colors are represented in the image.

When we extend the bar chart, we will use the `Bitmap` class to load images from files and draw them onto the bars.

Call `Dispose` on `Image` objects. It is important to call `Dispose` on them when we are finished (or in C#, use the `using` construct), otherwise our application may deplete the Windows resources.

We can create an `Image` object from one of several possible sources. One of the most common sources would be to load the image from a file, which can be in the JPG, GIF, or BMP format. We can also download an image from a location on the Internet. After we have read the image, there are no differences required to our code that depend on the different types of images. We can also create an empty image, and then draw into it.

'BarChart4'

Let's now modify the last example, drawing a small image onto each bar, near the top of the bar. Add the following method to our `Form1` class:

```
Private Sub DrawImages(ByVal g As Graphics, ByVal gm As GraphMetrics)
    Dim x As Integer = gm.YAxisDelta + gm.BarSpacing
    Dim gde As GraphDataElement
    For Each gde In gd.Data
        Dim barHeight As Integer = CType(gde.Value / gd.MaximumY * _
        (gm.Size.Height - 2 * gm.XAxisDelta), Integer)
        Dim interiorRect As Rectangle = New Rectangle(x + 1, _
        gm.Size.Height - gm.XAxisDelta - barHeight + 1, _
        gm.BarWidth - 2, barHeight - 2)
        x = x + gm.BarWidth + gm.BarSpacing

        ' draw the image on the bar
        Dim theImage As Image = New Bitmap(gde.ImageName)
        Dim delta As Integer = (interiorRect.Width - theImage.Width) / 2
        Dim imageRect As Rectangle = New Rectangle( _
        interiorRect.Left + delta, interiorRect.Top + delta, _
        theImage.Width, theImage.Height)
        g.DrawImage(theImage, imageRect)
        theImage.Dispose()
    Next
End Sub
```

When we draw the image, we pass a `Rectangle` as one of the arguments to the `DrawImage` method. If the image is not the same size as the rectangle that we pass to `DrawImage`, GDI+ automatically resizes the image to fit in the specified rectangle. In this case, however, we pass a rectangle where the height and width are identical to the image, so GDI+ will not do any resizing.

In this simple example, if the value of the bar were small enough, there would not be room to fit the image on the bar. A real-world application would need to take this into consideration, perhaps drawing the image above the bar in that case.

Modify the method `DrawToGraphics` as follows:

```
Public Sub DrawToGraphics(ByVal g As Graphics, ByVal gm As GraphMetrics)
    DrawAxes(g, gm)
    DrawBars(g, gm)
    DrawLabels(g, gm)
    DrawTitle(g, gm)
    DrawImages(g, gm)
End Sub
```

Before running this version of the bar chart, you must get the images from the Wrox web site, and place them in the same directory as the built executable. By default, this directory is a subdirectory of the directory where your Visual Studio project is. For example, if you built this example in a directory named `BarChart4`, the executable will be built in `BarChart4\bin`. This is where you should put the BMP files.

Now compile and run the code. When you run it, it will create this window:

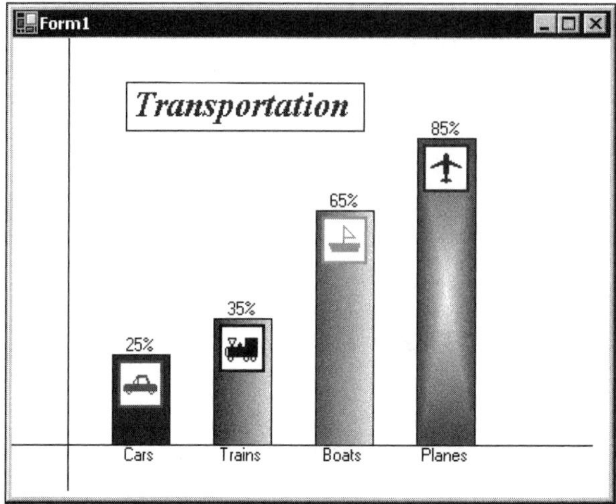

Drawing with a Texture Brush

We'll digress from our bar chart example now to demonstrate some techniques using the `TextureBrush` class. We will load an image from a JPG file, create a new image that is a smaller version of the image that was read, create a texture brush from the small image, and draw an ellipse with the brush.

'TextureBrushExample1'

Start Visual Studio.NET, and create a new VB Windows Forms project. Right-click on the form, and select View Code from the popup menu. We need to declare a private variable in our `Form1` class to hold the image after we read it from a file. After declaring the `Form1` component, add two declarations as follows:

```
Public Class Form1
    Inherits System.Windows.Forms.Form

    Private theImage As Image
```

Modify the constructor as follows:

```
Public Sub New()
    MyBase.New()

    'This call is required by the Windows Form Designer.
```

```
        InitializeComponent()

        'Add any initialization after the InitializeComponent() call
        SetStyle(ControlStyles.Opaque, True)
        theImage = New Bitmap("blurplane.jpg")

    End Sub
```

In the constructor, we create `theImage` from the `blurplane.jpg` file in the `Bin` directory of the example code.

Finally, add a `Paint` event, and modify it as follows:

```
    Private Sub Form1_Paint(ByVal sender As Object, _
    ByVal e As System.Windows.Forms.PaintEventArgs) Handles MyBase.Paint

        Dim g As Graphics = e.Graphics
        g.FillRectangle(Brushes.White, ClientRectangle)

        Dim tBrush As Brush = New TextureBrush(theImage, New Rectangle(0, 0, _
          theImage.Width, theImage.Height))
        g.FillEllipse(tBrush, ClientRectangle)

    End Sub
```

Before compiling, make sure to copy the JPG file to the directory where the executable is built. To get the JPG file, see the introduction, where instructions on getting all examples and associated images can be found. When we run this application, the window looks like this:

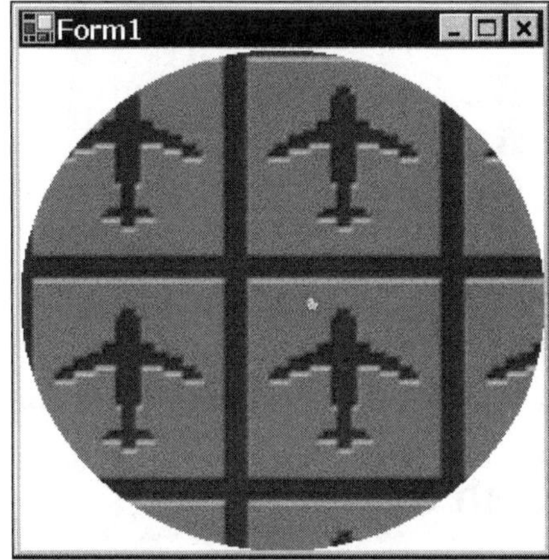

When we create the `TextureBrush`, we pass a rectangle to the constructor to specify what part of the image will be used for the brush. In this case, we specify that we will use the entire image. Whatever is drawn using the `TextureBrush` is drawn with the bitmap instead of a solid color.

Drawing with a Pen that Uses 'TextureBrush'

The next example shows a different use of a TextureBrush. In this example, after creating the TextureBrush, we create a Pen object from that TextureBrush. Then, whatever we draw with that pen will be drawn using the bitmap in the TextureBrush. If the pen has a width of only one pixel, this is not a very interesting technique. However, if the pen has a width much greater than one, this is an interesting way to draw a bitmap in a very carefully controlled area.

'TextureBrushExample2'

Starting with the TextureBrushExample1, change the Paint event so that it appears as follows:

```
Private Sub Form1_Paint(ByVal sender As Object, _
ByVal e As System.Windows.Forms.PaintEventArgs) Handles MyBase.Paint
    Dim g As Graphics = e.Graphics
    g.FillRectangle(Brushes.White, ClientRectangle)

    Dim tBrush As Brush = New TextureBrush(theImage, New Rectangle(0, 0, _
      theImage.Width, theImage.Height))
    Dim tPen As Pen = New Pen(tBrush, 15)
    g.DrawRectangle(tPen, 20, 20, 240, 240)
End Sub
```

This is an example of drawing with a pen that we created using a brush that we created using an image.

Drawing Text Using an Image

We can also use a TextureBrush when drawing text. In this technique, the text is not drawn with a solid color, but instead, the bitmap that is associated with the TextureBrush is used to draw the text. With very small fonts, this is not a very interesting technique, but with large fonts, this can give a unique appearance to text.

'TextureBrushExample3'

Modify the `paint` event as follows:

```
Private Sub Form1_Paint(ByVal sender As Object, _
ByVal e As System.Windows.Forms.PaintEventArgs) Handles MyBase.Paint

    Dim g As Graphics = e.Graphics
    g.FillRectangle(Brushes.White, ClientRectangle)

    Dim tBrush As Brush = New TextureBrush(theImage, New Rectangle(0, 0, _
      theImage.Width, theImage.Height))
    Dim trFont As Font = New Font("Times New Roman", 148, FontStyle.Bold)
    g.DrawString("HI!", trFont, tBrush, _
      New RectangleF(ClientRectangle.Left, ClientRectangle.Top, _
      ClientRectangle.Width, ClientRectangle.Height))
End Sub
```

When we run it, it appears as follows:

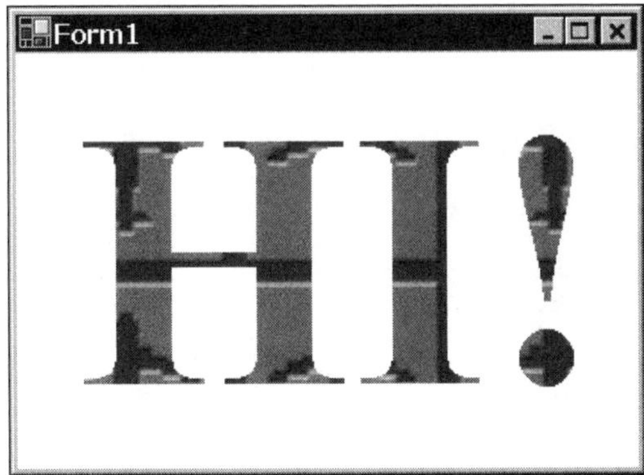

Geometric Transformation and the Alpha Component

GDI+ has the capability to do geometric transformations. This capability allows us to automatically change the scale and rotation of all of our drawing operations. These transformations are specified through a 3 X 3 affine matrix. An affine matrix is one that involves transformations of translation, rotation and reflection in an axis. Setting up this matrix directly is beyond the scope of this book. However, it is not necessary to set it up directly. There are methods that make it very easy to do scaling and transformations, so that we do not need to interact directly with the affine matrix. The `ScaleTransform` method of the `Graphics` class allows us to automatically scale drawing operations. Scaling can be done independently in the X and Y directions. The `RotateTransform` method allows us to automatically rotate our drawing operations.

The Alpha component of colors allows us to draw semi-transparent graphics over the existing contents of a drawing surface. When combined with timer events, using the Alpha component of colors allows us to create fade in / out effects. Another use is to create a watermark effect.

We will use a combination of geometric transformation and the Alpha component to add a 'Draft' watermark over our bar chart.

'BarChart5'

Now, back to our `BarChart` example. Open the example in Visual Studio. Add the following method to our `Form1` class:

```
Private Sub DrawWatermark(ByVal g As Graphics)

    ' We are going to rotate our text 20 degrees counter clockwise
    g.RotateTransform(-20)

    ' Create a very large, bold font
    Dim draftFont As Font = New Font("Arial", 64, FontStyle.Bold)

    ' Create a color that is semi-transparent
    Dim alphaColor As Color = Color.FromArgb(100, Color.Black)

    ' Now create a brush from our semi-transparent color
    Dim alphaBrush As SolidBrush = New SolidBrush(alphaColor)

    ' Calculate the rectangle where our watermark text will go
    Dim alphaRectangle As Rectangle = New Rectangle(ClientRectangle.Left, _
    ClientRectangle.Top, ClientRectangle.Width, ClientRectangle.Height)

    ' Move our rectangle down 150 pixels
    alphaRectangle.Offset(0, 150)

    ' Draw the text that will be the watermark
    g.DrawString("Draft", draftFont, alphaBrush, _
    New RectangleF(alphaRectangle.Left, alphaRectangle.Top, _
    alphaRectangle.Width, alphaRectangle.Height))

    ' Dispose of the font that we created
    draftFont.Dispose()
End Sub
```

The call to `RotateTransform` takes a single-precision floating point number as an argument. This number is expressed in degrees. There is no option to specify the angle in radians. Some programmers prefer to work in radians, and will need to convert the radians to degrees to use `RotateTransform`. The coordinate space rotates in a clockwise direction and the origin of the coordinate space is the center of rotation.

The following line declares a variable of type `Color` and instantiates it using the `FromArgb` method of the `Color` structure:

```
Dim alphaColor As Color = Color.FromArgb(100, Color.Black)
```

The first argument (the Alpha argument) of the method `FromArgb` is an integer between 0 and 255. If this argument is 0, anything drawn in the color will be completely transparent, and if the argument is 255, anything drawn will be completely opaque. It is interesting to experiment with this value and see the resulting behavior.

Modify the `DrawToGraphics` method as follows:

```
Public Sub DrawToGraphics(ByVal g As Graphics, ByVal gm As GraphMetrics)
    DrawAxes(g, gm)
    DrawBars(g, gm)
    DrawLabels(g, gm)
    DrawTitle(g, gm)
    DrawImages(g, gm)
    DrawWatermark(g)
End Sub
```

We can now compile and run the code. When we run it, it will create this window:

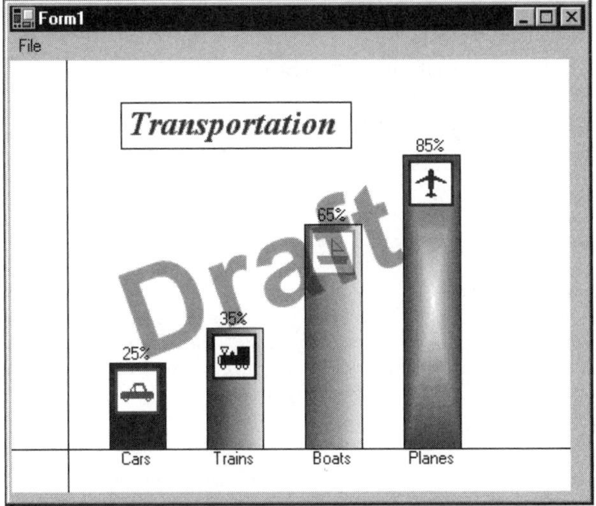

Horizontal and Vertical Scrolling

Sometimes graphics may be too big to display in a window, in which case it is convenient to add horizontal and vertical scrolling capabilities for the user. Sometimes this feature is called a 'virtual space' or a 'view port'.

One easy way to implement this functionality is as follows:

- Draw the graphics into an `Image` instead of directly to the screen.
- Add a `Panel` to our window, anchoring the panel to all four sides of the window, and setting the `AutoScroll` property of the panel to true.
- Add a `Picturebox` of an appropriate size to the panel.
- Place our image into the `Picturebox`.

'BarChart6'

We'll now go through this process:

- Open up the designer window for Form1.

- Drag out a panel on the form, and make it a little bit smaller than the size of the window.
- Change the `Anchor` property so that the panel is anchored to all four sizes of the window.
- Change the `AutoScroll` property to `True`.
- Change the `Location` property to 0, 0.
- Change the `Size` property to 288, 272.
- Drag out a **PictureBox** within the panel. Make sure that you drag within the boundaries of the **Panel** so that the **PictureBox** will be contained within the **Panel**. It doesn't matter what size you make it, as we will manually adjust the size using the **Properties** window.
- Change the `Location` property of the **PictureBox** to 0, 0.
- Change the `Size` property of the **PictureBox** to 400, 300.

This is all that we need to do in the design window. Now, add an `Image` member variable named `displayImage` to the `Form1` class:

```
Public Class Form1
    Inherits System.Windows.Forms.Form

    Private gd As GraphData
    Friend WithEvents Panel1 As System.Windows.Forms.Panel
    Friend WithEvents PictureBox1 As System.Windows.Forms.PictureBox
    Private dgm As GraphMetrics  'GraphMetrics for graphs displayed in a window

    Private displayImage As Image
```

Next, modify the constructor for the `Form1` class. There are two modifications to this method. First, delete or comment out the call to the `SetStyle` method. Because we are using the `PictureBox` and the `Panel` controls, we will not be doing the drawing directly. We no longer need this option to be set for the form. Second, modify the method to create and initialize the bitmap, and set the `Image` property of the `PictureBox` to our image:

```
Public Sub New(ByVal rect As Rectangle, ByVal gd As GraphData)
    MyBase.New()

    'This call is required by the Win Form Designer.
    InitializeComponent()

    'The initialization goes after the InitializeComponent() call

    'The following call to SetStyle should be commented out
    'SetStyle(ControlStyles.Opaque, True)
    Me.gd = gd
    Me.Bounds = rect    'set the size of the window

    'these are the graph metrics for drawing on the screen
    dgm = New GraphMetrics()
    dgm.XAxisDelta = 30
    dgm.YAxisDelta = 40
    dgm.BarSpacing = 30
    dgm.BarWidth = 40
    dgm.PenWidth = 1
```

```
    dgm.Size = New Size(400, 300)

    ' create the image that will go into the PictureBox
    displayImage = New Bitmap(dgm.Size.Width, dgm.Size.Height)
    DrawToImage()
    PictureBox1.Image = displayImage
End Sub
```

Add a new method, DrawToImage, as follows:

```
Private Sub DrawToImage()
    Dim g As Graphics = Graphics.FromImage(displayImage)
    g.FillRectangle(Brushes.White, New Rectangle(New Point(0, 0), _
    displayImage.Size))
    DrawToGraphics(g, dgm)
End Sub
```

DrawToImage uses the FromImage method of the Graphics class to get an instance of the Graphics class. By drawing using this Graphics object, we are using the Image as a drawing surface.

Delete the Paint event, as we no longer need it. The following is the listing of the paint event, which you need to delete.

```
Private Sub Form1_Paint(ByVal sender As Object, _
ByVal e As System.Windows.Forms.PaintEventArgs) Handles MyBase.Paint
    Dim g As Graphics = e.Graphics
    g.FillRectangle(Brushes.White, ClientRectangle)
    DrawToGraphics(g, dgm)
End Sub
```

Because Visual Basic uses static event handling (refer to Chapter 6 on events for details on this), we don't need to remove any wiring of the code, viz. the registration of an event handler with a delegate.

Once again, we can compile and run the code. When we run it, it will create this window:

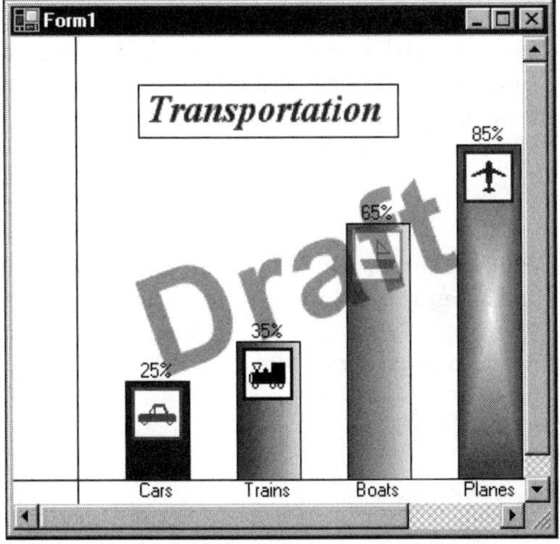

If we resize the window, the scroll bars will adjust to reflect the proportion of the bar chart that is visible. If the window is made large enough, the Panel control will make the scroll bars invisible. If the window is small enough that the scroll bars are visible, the user can operate the scroll bars to see all of the bar chart.

We also could have accomplished a similar behavior by setting the Form's `AutoScroll` property. However, this technique is somewhat more flexible, because it could allow us to combine our scrolling area with other controls in the form.

This example also demonstrates double buffering. It's possible to notice the order of drawing in the previous examples if the computer is not too fast. However, after these modifications, our application displays the bar chart all at once.

Printing

Next, we will modify our bar chart application so that we can print to the printer.

The mechanics of printing are:

- Declare a class that is a subclass of the `PrintDocument` class.
- In this class, if we need to do any initialization before starting the print job, we can override the method `OnBeginPrint`.
- In this class, override the method `OnPrintPage`. The functionality that we need to implement in this method is described below.
- When we want to print, perhaps in response to the user picking an item on a menu, we create an instance of our `PrintDocument` class. We put up the printer selection dialog, and if the user clicks OK in response to this dialog, we call the `Print` method on our print document.

The `OnPrintPage` method will be invoked once for each page that we will print. In this method, we can get a `Graphics` object from the event object. Drawing to this `Graphics` object actually draws on the printed page. Each time that we print a page, before returning from this method, we set a variable in the event object that indicates whether this is the last page, or if there are more pages to print.

We will also modify our bar chart application so that we have a different set of `GraphMetrics` for the printer. This demonstrates a common technique of abstracting the differences in metrics between the screen and the printer, encapsulating them in a class, and using the appropriate version when drawing, so that we can have only one set of code for drawing, and this code is capable of drawing in an intelligent fashion to either the screen or the printer.

'BarChart7'

Before we add any code to Form1, we will add another file that will contain the class derived from `PrintDocument`. This class enables us to print the bar chart. From the Project menu, select Add Class. Name the file for the class `GraphPrintDocument.vb`. After we have clicked the Open button, Visual Studio creates a new file and opens an editor window for that file. We will define one class in this file:

```
Imports System.Drawing.Printing

Public Class GraphPrintDocument
    Inherits PrintDocument
```

```
    Private form As Form1

    Public Sub New(ByVal form As System.Windows.Forms.form)
        MyBase.New()
        Me.form = form
    End Sub

    'If we wanted to do any initialization for printing, we could override
    'the OnBeginPrint method

    'Override the OnPrintPage to provide the printing logic for the document
    Protected Overrides Sub OnPrintPage(ByVal ev As PrintPageEventArgs)
        MyBase.OnPrintPage(ev)
        form.DrawToGraphics(ev.Graphics, form.PrintGraphMetrics)
        ev.HasMorePages = False
    End Sub

End Class
```

We modified the constructor for this class to take our form as an argument. We need a reference to the form so that we can invoke the `DrawToGraphics` method on it, and so that we can get the `PrintGraphMetrics` from it when we invoke the `DrawToGraphics` method. All the code to do the actual drawing will remain in our form – in fact we have already written it.

In the method `OnPrintPage`, the first thing that we do is to call up to the base-class. The documentation for the printing classes state that we must have this behavior. After calling up to the base-class, we invoke the `DrawToGraphics` method on our form. We pass the `Graphics` object that we got from the event, and we get and pass the `PrintGraphMetrics` to the method, thereby drawing the graphics with the correct metrics for the printer. Finally, because in this application we know that our bar chart will only take one page, we unconditionally set `ev.HasMorePages` to `False`. If this were an application where we were printing a large file, then we would determine algorithmically whether to set `HasMorePages` to `True` or `False`.

For this version of the bar chart, we want a menu with items on it for printing and previewing.

- Open up the designer for Form1.
- Using the toolbox, select the MainMenu control and drag and drop it on the form.
- Change the text of the menu to File.
- Add an item to the File menu, and change the text of the item to Print.
- Change the `Name` property of the Print menu item to Menu_Print.
- Add another item to the File menu, and change the text of the item to Preview.
- Change its `Name` to Menu_Preview.

Add the following code to the event to the Print menu item:

```
Private Sub Menu_Print_Click(ByVal sender As System.Object, _
ByVal e As System.EventArgs) Handles Menu_Print.Click
```

```
    Try
        Dim pd As GraphPrintDocument = New GraphPrintDocument(Me)
        Dim dlg As New PrintDialog()
        dlg.Document = pd
        Dim result As DialogResult = dlg.ShowDialog()
        If (result = System.Windows.Forms.DialogResult.OK) Then pd.Print()
        End If
    Catch ex As Exception
        MessageBox.Show("An error occurred printing the file - " + ex.Message)
    End Try

End Sub
```

First, we declare and instantiate a GraphPrintDocument object. We then put up the PrintDialog, and get back the results from it. If the user pressed the Ok button, then we call the Print method on the print document.

We need to declare and initialize the graph metrics for the printer. Add a variable declaration for our form class as follows:

```
Public Class Form1
    Inherits System.Windows.Forms.Form

    Private gd As GraphData
    Friend WithEvents Panel1 As System.Windows.Forms.Panel
    Friend WithEvents PictureBox1 As System.Windows.Forms.PictureBox
    Private dgm As GraphMetrics  'GraphMetrics for graphs displayed in a
                                 'window
    Private pgm As GraphMetrics  'GraphMetrics for graphs printed to the
                                 'printer
    Friend WithEvents MainMenu1 As System.Windows.Forms.MainMenu
    Friend WithEvents Menu_File As System.Windows.Forms.MenuItem
    Friend WithEvents Menu_Print As System.Windows.Forms.MenuItem
    Friend WithEvents Menu_Preview As System.Windows.Forms.MenuItem
    Private displayImage As Image
```

Modify the constructor for the Form class to create and initialize the printer GraphMetrics variable:

```
Public Sub New(ByVal rect As Rectangle, ByVal gd As GraphData)
    MyBase.New()

    'This call is required by the Win Form Designer.
    InitializeComponent()

    'The initialization goes after the InitializeComponent() call
    'SetStyle(ControlStyles.Opaque, True)
    Me.gd = gd
    Me.Bounds = rect    'set the size of the window

    'these are the graph metrics for drawing on the screen
    dgm = New GraphMetrics()
    dgm.XAxisDelta = 30
    dgm.YAxisDelta = 40
    dgm.BarSpacing = 30
```

```
        dgm.BarWidth = 40
        dgm.PenWidth = 1
        dgm.Size = New Size(400, 300)

        ' these are the graph metrics for drawing to the printer
        pgm = New GraphMetrics()
        pgm.XAxisDelta = 30
        pgm.YAxisDelta = 40
        pgm.BarSpacing = 30
        pgm.BarWidth = 40
        pgm.PenWidth = 1
        pgm.Size = New Size(400, 300)

        ' create the image that will go into the PictureBox
        displayImage = New Bitmap(dgm.Size.Width, dgm.Size.Height)
        DrawToImage()
        PictureBox1.Image = displayImage
    End Sub
```

Finally, we need to add a `PrintGraphMetrics` property to our form class:

```
    Public ReadOnly Property PrintGraphMetrics () As GraphMetrics
        Get
            Return pgm
        End Get
    End Property
```

The `GraphMetrics` class, which was defined early on in this chapter, defines the physical characteristics of the bar chart, including its size, the space allocated to the X and Y axes, the bar width, the space between the bars, and the width of the pen that draws the bars.

Now compile and run the code. When we run it, we can select File/Print from the menu and it will print the bar chart.

Finally, we will modify our bar chart application to add print preview capabilities.

'BarChart8'

We don't need to modify any of the code that implements the mechanics of printing – neither the drawing code, nor our implementation of `GraphPrintDocument`. All we need to do is to initiate printing in a different fashion.

Open up the designer for Form1. Double-click on the Preview menu item. Visual Studio will bring up the code-editing window with the insertion point in the event for that menu item. Add the following code to the event:

```
    Private Sub Menu_Preview_Click(ByVal sender As System.Object, _
    ByVal e As System.EventArgs) Handles Menu_Preview.Click
        Try
            Dim pd As GraphPrintDocument = New GraphPrintDocument(Me)
            Dim dlg As New PrintPreviewDialog()
            dlg.Document = pd
            dlg.ShowDialog()
```

```
        Catch ex As Exception
            MessageBox.Show("An error occurred - " + ex.Message)
        End Try
    End Sub
```

First, we declare and instantiate a `GraphPrintDocument` object. We then create the `PrintPreviewDialog`, and call the `ShowDialog` method. The `PrintPreviewDialog` is a standard dialog box. It is supplied by the .NET framework.

Now we can compile and run the code. When we run the code, File/Preview is selectable from the menu. The preview window looks like this:

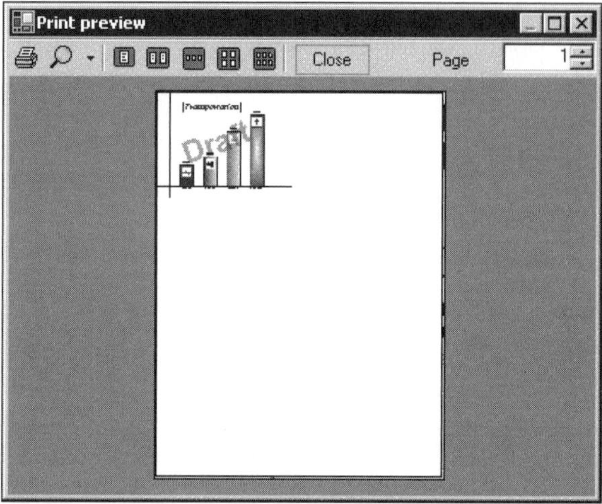

The user can manipulate the print preview window in a variety of ways. They can zoom in or out, change the number of pages concurrently displayed, change which page is currently displayed, and press the printer button to directly print the document.

Advanced Capabilities of GDI+

There are many more capabilities of GDI+. Next, we will introduce a few of these areas starting with **clipping**. There are three contexts where clipping is important.

When the `Paint` event gets called, in addition to the `Graphics` object, the event is passed a clipping rectangle. For simple drawing routines, we don't need to pay much attention to this clipping rectangle, but if we have a very elaborate drawing routine that takes a lot of time, we can reduce this drawing time by testing against this clipping rectangle before we draw. We know the bounding rectangle of whatever graphic or figure that we need to draw. If this bounding rectangle does not intersect with the clipping rectangle, then we can skip the drawing operation.

The following screenshot shows one window containing a bar chart that is partially obscured by another window:

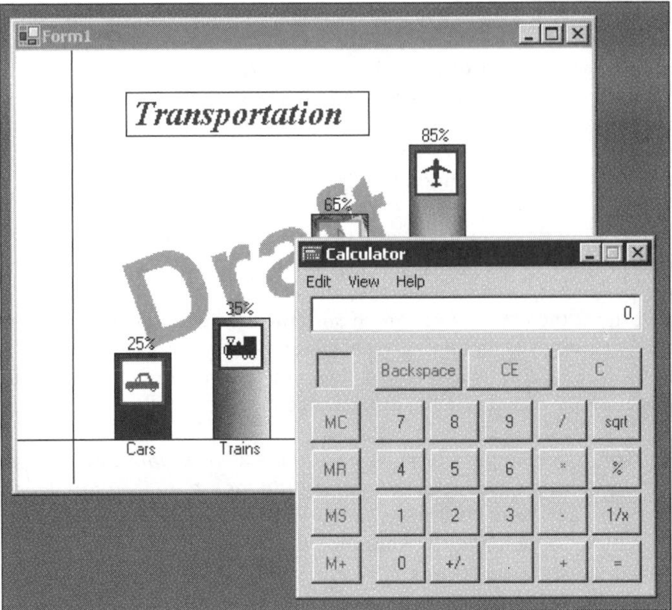

After the calculator has been closed, and after the Windows operating system has drawn the border of the window, the bar chart window would look like this:

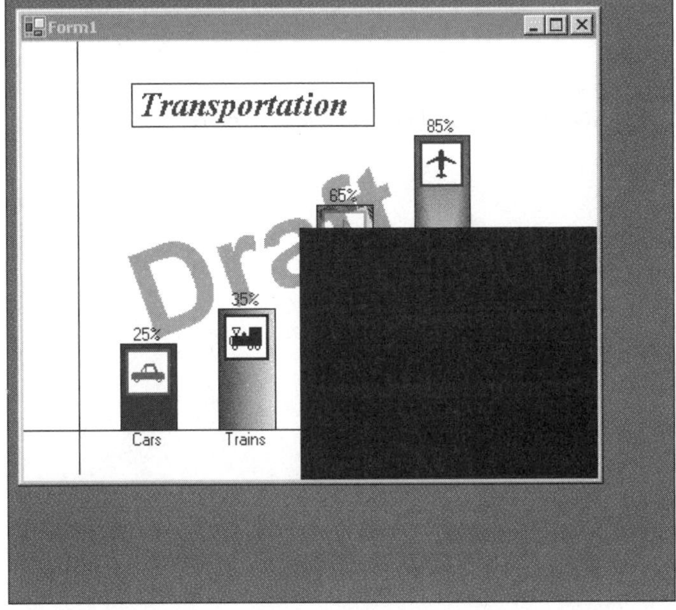

At this point, the `Paint` event for the bar chart window would be called, with the clipping region set to the exposed area. The bar chart would now need to draw the portions of its window that were exposed. It would not need to redraw the car or trains bars, and in fact, even if the `Paint` event tried to draw into the window in an area other than the exposed area, it could not. Any drawing that it did would be ignored. The bar chart window knows the bounding rectangle for the cars bar, and can determine if this rectangle intersects with the exposed portion of the window. Having determined that it does not intersect, the drawing routine can abandon the drawing of the bar.

It may be that if we need to draw only part of a figure or graphic, it turns out to be more convenient to draw the entire figure, and clip the drawing to just what we want to see. We may have an image, and want to draw just a portion of that image. Rather than create a new image that is just a portion of the original image, we can set the clipping rectangle, and then draw the image such that just the portion that we want to see 'shows through' the clipping area. When creating a marquee (scrolling text), this is the technique that we would use. By successively changing where we draw the text, and at the same time setting a clipping region, we can create the appearance of horizontally moving text.

Finally, there is a graphics technique where we can create a 'view port' into a larger graphic. The user can move this view port around, perhaps by dragging the mouse on the graphic, or manipulating scroll bars. The view port also may be moved programmatically based on other actions that the user takes. In this case, setting a clipping region and drawing such that only what we want to see shows through is a good technique.

See the `Clip` property of the `Graphics` class in the .NET documentation for more information.

The final topic we will look at is the `System.Drawing.Imaging namespace.` The classes in this namespace provide advanced imaging support. Two main areas of functionality are metafiles and the `Encoder/Decoder` classes. A metafile describes a sequence of graphics operations that can be recorded and later played back. The `Encoder` and `Decoder` classes enable us to extend GDI+ to support any image format.

See `System.Drawing.Imaging` in the documentation for more details.

Summary

In this chapter, we covered some of the classes in the `System.Drawing` namespace. We saw how the `Graphics` class encapsulates a drawing surface. We reviewed the mechanics of drawing, where the `Paint` event is invoked whenever our window needs to be redrawn.

We explored colors and coordinate systems. We covered the `Point`, `Size`, and `Rectangle` structures that we use to specify positions and sizes on our drawing surface. We explored the `GraphicsPath` and `Region` classes that facilitate printing complex images.

Next, we saw some examples of drawing lines, shapes, text, and images, and then discussed printing and print previewing.

We learned that it is very important to call `Dispose` on certain classes when we are done with them. Those classes are:

- `Graphics`
- `Pen`
- `Brush`
- `Font`
- `Image`

Finally, we got an overview of additional graphical capabilities in the .NET framework, and we saw where we could go in the .NET Reference Documentation for more detail on these additional capabilities.

System.Object
System.MarshalRefObject
System.ComponentMode.Component

Legend
Concrete Class
Abstract class

System.Windows.Forms

CommonDialog
ColorDialog
FileDialog
FontDialog
PageSetupDialog
PrintDialog
ErrorProvider
HelpProvider
ImageList
Menu
ContextMenu
MainMenu
MenuItem
NotifyIcon
StatusBarPanel
Timer
ToolBarButton
ToolTip
ListViewItem
TreeNode

Control
ButtonBase
Button
CheckBox
RadioButton
DataGrid
DateTimePicker
GroupBox
Label
LinkLabel
ListControl
ComboBox
ListBox
CheckedListBox
ListView
MonthCalendar
PictureBox
PrintReviewControl
ProgressBar
ScrollableControl
ContainerControl
Form
PrintPreviewDialog
ThreadExceptionDialog
PropertyGrid
UpDownBase
DomainUpDown
NumericUpDown
UserControl
Panel
TabPage
ScrollBar
HScrollBar
VScrollBar
Splitter
StatusBar
TabControl
TextBoxBase
RichTextBox
Textbox
ToolBar
TrackBar
TreeView

13

Internationalization

Internationalization is a topic very often overlooked when developing an application. Two common responses are: 'We don't have time for all of that extra work' and 'We can't afford to translate all of our UI into another language'. This is an age where the Internet provides us with the ability to deliver software to anyone in the world at virtually no cost, and yet it's easy to overlook the fact that only about 10% of the world's population has English as its primary language.

Building an application that can support an international array of users involves two distinct processes, namely **globalization** and **localization**. Therefore, this chapter has been notionally divided into two halves, one to examine each of these topics. In general, these terms can be thought of as follows:

- **Globalization**: The system appropriately formats a piece of data based on the cultural identity of the user. For example, using a comma instead of a decimal point (when displaying numbers) for a user in Germany.
- **Localization**: The system chooses the appropriate version of a piece of data based on the cultural identity of the user. For example, displaying the Japanese version of a particular message box for a user in Japan.

Fortunately, Microsoft has provided extensive support both in Windows and in the .NET Framework for these two concepts. In this chapter, we will be covering:

- The new concept of cultures and how they are used.
- The aspects of an application that are sensitive to changes in culture.
- Overriding some of the globalization services provided by .NET.
- Creating and using custom resources in our applications.
- Using Visual Studio, and the WinRes tool, to visually build localized versions of a form.

In the first few sections of this chapter, we will be building a simple Windows Forms application that will serve as the starting point for many of the examples in subsequent sections. This is necessary because the current culture of an application is normally set automatically, based on settings in the user's operating system. This first example, on the other hand, demonstrates how to dynamically change the culture of an application at runtime. This is a capability we will need in most of the other examples.

Globalization

The term globalization is defined in the .NET SDK Documentation as: 'the process of creating a core application that supports localized user interfaces and regional data for all users'. What this really means is that our application will be aware of the system's culture and will be able to alter its UI through the use of classes in the `System.Globalization` namespace, which we will be examining throughout the rest of this section. However, what we'll see is that most of the process of globalization happens for us automatically, without any extra code on our part. We just need to understand what aspects of our application will be affected, and when we may want to prevent certain behavior from occurring.

Introduction to Culture

What exactly does the term 'culture' mean in the context of a software application? In .NET, this term is used to represent information about the language to use, the writing system, the calendar used, and methods for common operations such as printing dates and sorting strings.

A culture is always identified using the format: `<language code>-<country/region code>`. The **language code** is a lowercase two-letter code. These codes are listed in the ISO 639-1 standard, while the country or region code is from the ISO 3166 standard (more information and news regarding this standard can be obtained at http://lcweb.loc.gov/standards/iso639-2/iso639jac.html).

The table below is a small subset of the nearly 200 culture names recognized by the .NET Framework. We will retrieve the complete list of supported cultures when we build our first example application in the next section.

Culture Name	Language-Country/Region
En	English
en-AU	English – Australia
en-CA	English – Canada
en-GB	English – United Kingdom
en-US	English – United States
Fr	French
fr-FR	French – France
fr-CA	French – Canada
De	German
de-AT	German – Austria
de-DE	German – Germany

It is noticeable that some cultures listed in the table above do not include a country/region code. These cultures are referred to as **neutral cultures** and are only used for resource selection. We will talk more about resource selection in the section on localization later in this chapter. Cultures that do include both a language code and a country/region code are referred to as **specific cultures.** A specific culture can be used both for resource selection, and for the other globalization features that we will be examining.

> *Culture in the .NET Framework takes the place of the national language support (NLS) locale, which used a system of locale ID (LCID) codes. The LCID property of the `CultureInfo` class provides interoperability and eases integration with NLS-based software. A good reference for information on building pre-.NET international applications is "International Programming for Microsoft Windows" published by Microsoft Press (ISBN 1572319569).*

Changing Cultures

Before diving into all the details of what's available in the .NET Framework to support globalization, let's start by building a simple Windows Forms application that demonstrates how much things can change just by running our application under a different culture. This application will also introduce how we can change the current culture at runtime and will therefore serve as a starting point for examples in upcoming sections.

Start by creating a new VB.NET Windows Application and dropping a `ComboBox` and a `TextBox` control onto the new form. For the `ComboBox`, we want to rename it to `ComboCulture` and clear out the `Text` property. It would also be helpful to set the `Sorted` property of the `ComboBox` to `True` to make items easier to find when running the example. For the `TextBox`, we want to rename it to `TextCulture` and clear out the `Text` property for it as well. Then, go ahead and increase the width of the `TextBox` so the form looks something like this after compilation:

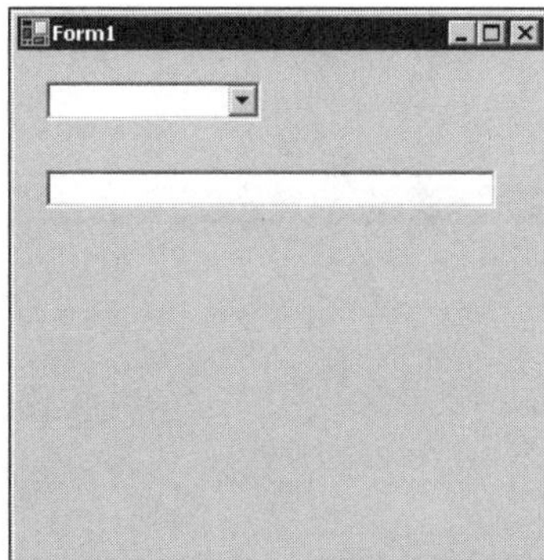

We will now add the code that will populate our `ComboBox` with a list of cultures. First, double-click the blank portion of the form to bring up the `Form1_Load` event handler. However, before we can add the code in the Load event, we will add a pair of `Import` statements to the top of our code:

```
Imports System.Globalization
Imports System.Threading
```

The need for the `Globalization` namespace may have been expected, since it was mentioned in one of the previous sections. However, the inclusion of the `Threading` namespace requires a brief explanation.

Although a culture is identified using the two-part format described in the previous section, the entity used in the framework to represent a culture is the `CultureInfo` class. We will examine this class in more detail later. However, it's necessary to mention it now because there are two properties of `System.Threading.Thread.CurrentThread` that are of type `CultureInfo`. These two properties are used to identify the application's current culture and are named `CurrentCulture` and `CurrentUICulture`. These two properties are also available as static members of the `CultureInfo` class in the `Globalization` namespace. However, these properties are read-only. If we wish to change the culture programmatically, we must access the properties through the current thread. This also means that culture can be controlled on a per-thread basis if desired. Once again, this will usually only be for debugging purposes, as the current culture is set automatically based on the user's OS. We will be using the `ComboBox` on our form to change the value of `CurrentCulture`, while the `CurrentUICulture` property will be discussed in the section on localization later in this chapter.

We can now add the code in the `Form1_Load` event handler to populate our `ComboBox`:

```
Dim CultureX As CultureInfo

For Each CultureX In CultureInfo.GetCultures(CultureTypes.SpecificCultures)
    ComboCulture.Items.Add(CultureX)
Next

TextCulture.Text = Thread.CurrentThread.CurrentCulture.Name + "     " _
+ Thread.CurrentThread.CurrentCulture.DisplayName
```

If we run the application now, the `TextBox` should display the ID for the application's current culture, followed by a few spaces and then the full name of the culture. This should look something like the following:

en-US   English (United States)

If we then click to expand the `ComboBox`, we should see a list of IDs for every specific culture that the framework will recognize:

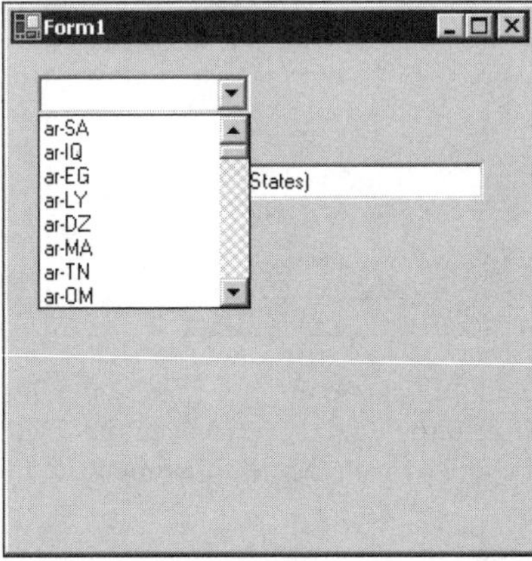

The next step is to setup our application so that selecting a culture ID from the `ComboBox` will change the current culture of the application. Bring up the `cmbCulture_SelectedIndexChanged` event handler by double-clicking on the `ComboBox` in the form designer, and then add the following code:

```
Thread.CurrentThread.CurrentCulture = ComboCulture.SelectedItem

TextCulture.Text = Thread.CurrentThread.CurrentCulture.Name + "     " _
+ Thread.CurrentThread.CurrentCulture.DisplayName
```

As is probably obvious, this code just changes our application's current culture to whatever culture was selected from the `ComboBox` and updates our `TextBox` to display the same.

So far, our application isn't very exciting. What we will do next is add some other controls to our form that will allow us to see what kinds of things can be affected just by running in a different culture.

Let's add three `Label` controls to our form so things look something like that shown below:

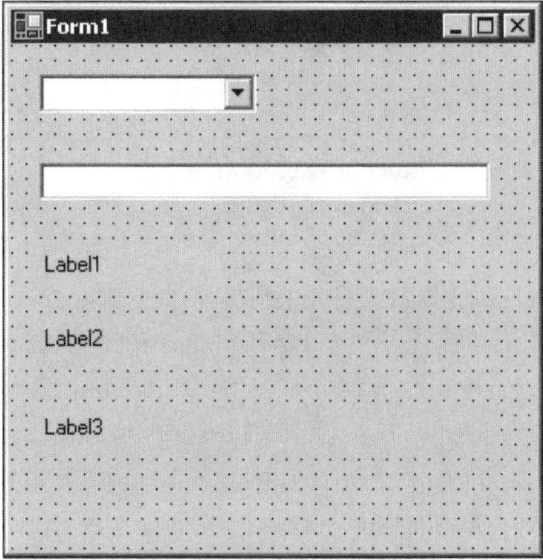

We'll now add a routine to supply a value for each of these `Labels`:

```
Private Sub SetLabels()
    Label1.Text = Format(1000000, "Standard")
    Label2.Text = Format(5250.95, "Currency")
    Label3.Text = Now()
End Sub
```

Notice that we are using the `Format` function here to change how our two numeric values will appear. The formats '`Standard`' and '`Currency`' are both predefined formats in VB.NET, but the function has many others, as well as the ability to specify custom formats. You can refer to Help in Visual Studio for more information on using `Format`.

Then, we'll be sure and call this function when the form is first loaded, and whenever a different culture is selected. The complete code should now appear as follows:

```
Imports System.Globalization
Imports System.Threading

Public Class Form1
    Inherits System.Windows.Forms.Form
```

```
'Windows Form Designer generated code

   Private Sub Form1_Load(ByVal sender As System.Object, _
   ByVal e As System.EventArgs) Handles MyBase.Load
      Dim CultureX As CultureInfo

      For Each CultureX In _
      CultureInfo.GetCultures(CultureTypes.SpecificCultures)
         ComboCulture.Items.Add(CultureX)
      Next

      TextCulture.Text = Thread.CurrentThread.CurrentCulture.Name + "    " _
      + Thread.CurrentThread.CurrentCulture.DisplayName

      SetLabels()
   End Sub

   Private Sub ComboCulture_SelectedIndexChanged(ByVal sender As _
   System.Object, ByVal e As System.EventArgs) _
   Handles cmbCulture.SelectedIndexChanged
      Thread.CurrentThread.CurrentCulture = cmbCulture.SelectedItem

      TextCulture.Text = Thread.CurrentThread.CurrentCulture.Name + "    " _
      + Thread.CurrentThread.CurrentCulture.DisplayName

      SetLabels()
   End Sub

   Private Sub SetLabels()
     Label1.Text = Format(1000000, "Standard")
     Label2.Text = Format(5250.95, "Currency")
     Label3.Text = Now()
   End Sub
End Class
```

Our application is now a little more exciting. If we run the application now and change the culture, the data for our three labels will automatically be formatted in a manner appropriate for the culture selected. For example, if we switch between 'en-US', 'en-GB', and 'de-DE', we should notice the following differences in the formatting of the data:

Culture	Number	Currency	DateTime
English (United Stated)	n,nnn,nnn.nn	$n,nnn.nn	mm/dd/yyyy hh:mm:ss
English (United Kingdom)	n,nnn,nnn.nn	£n,nnn.nn	dd/mm/yyyy hh:mm:ss
German (Germany)	n.nnn.nnn,nn	n.nnn,nn €	dd.mm.yyyy hh:mm:ss

Notice that although the appropriate currency symbol is used when the culture is changed, no currency conversion is being performed. In certain cases, we may not want the symbol to change. We can prevent this from happening by overriding this particular globalization behavior. This will be demonstrated later in the section titled 'Currency'.

For developers already familiar with the formatting used by different cultures, it can be an interesting exercise to experiment with different culture values to see the effect it has on these types of information. We will take a closer look at which types of data are 'culture-aware', and when we may want to prevent certain formatting behavior a little later in the section titled *Culture-Sensitive Data.*

'CultureInfo' Class

As we saw when building the sample application, an instance of a `CultureInfo` class is used in the framework to actually hold culture-specific information, such as the associated language, sublanguage country/region, calendar, and cultural conventions. This class also provides the information required for culture-specific operations, such as formatting dates and numbers, sorting and comparing strings, and determining character type information.

We dynamically changed the current culture in the previous example by using the value of the `ComboBox`. However, we explicitly set the culture by using a line like the following:

```
CurrentThread.CurrentCulture = new CultureInfo("de-DE")
```

However, this will very rarely be needed in a production application, since the system will set the current culture properties automatically at runtime based on OS settings. We can change many culture-related options in Windows by looking at Regional Options in the Control Panel.

One method used in the sample application that deserves another look is the `GetCultures(CultureTypes)` method. This method returns an array of `CultureInfo` objects filtered by the specified `CultureTypes`. In the case of our example application, we filtered by `SpecificCultures`. The possible values for `CultureTypes` are listed below:

- `AllCultures`: All cultures supported by the .NET Framework.
- `InstalledWin32Cultures`: All cultures that are installed on the system.
- `NeutralCultures`: All cultures that do not specify a country/region code.
- `SpecificCultures`: All cultures that contain both a language code and a country/region code.

It's important to note that globalization is based on the value of `CurrentCulture`, and requires a specific culture value. Localization, which we will discuss in the second half of this chapter, is based on the value of `CurrentUICulture` and can use either a specific or neutral culture value.

Culture-Sensitive Data

We will now take a look at each type of data that will be affected by globalization, when used in our application.

Calendars

The `System.Globalization` namespace contains a class to represent each calendar supported by the framework. We will not go into the details of each calendar implementation provided by the framework, but a list is provided below:

- Gregorian Calendar
- Hebrew Calendar
- Hijri Calendar

- Japanese Calendar
- Julian Calendar
- Korean Calendar
- Taiwan Calendar
- Thai Buddhist Calendar

Each of these calendar implementations derives from `System.Globalization.Calendar`. We can obtain a reference to the calendar object used by a specific culture by accessing the `Calendar` property of a `CultureInfo` object.

To demonstrate directly accessing a calendar object, the following line of code will return a Boolean value that indicates whether the year 2001 is a leap year for the current culture's calendar:

```
CurrentThread.CurrentCulture.Calendar.IsLeapYear(2001)
```

Currency

One area of globalization that requires some special attention is currency. As mentioned in our example application, the system will automatically apply the appropriate formatting for a currency value and use the culture-specific currency symbol.

The properties of the `NumberFormatInfo` class associated with culture-specific formatting of a currency value are as follows:

- `CurrencyNegativePattern`: How negative values are displayed. There are 16 possible values for this attribute and most just effect where the minus symbol, currency symbol, and value appear in relation to each other.
- `CurrencyPositivePattern`: How positive values are displayed. The possible values of this property just determine whether the currency symbol comes before or after the value.
- `CurrencySymbol`: The string to use as the currency symbol.
- `CurrencyGroupSizes`: The number of digits in each group to the left of the decimal separator.
- `CurrencyGroupSeparator`: The string used to separate groups of digits to the left of the decimal separator.
- `CurrencyDecimalDigits`: The number of decimal places to display for a currency value.
- `CurrencyDecimalSeparator`: The string used as the decimal separator.

None of these present a problem when the user provides all of the currency values. However, we could imagine a Windows Forms-based client application that connects to an auction application over the Internet. This auction site might provide all of its pricing in US dollars, while the user's current culture is Japanese-Japan. Without any intervention on the part of the developer, the price of that shiny red $50,000 Porsche will appear to the user as ¥50,000. This would be a very good deal at today's exchange rate (approximately $400). We can avoid this problem by explicitly setting the currency symbol. We will now look at how to do this.

The way in which numbers are displayed for a given culture can be overridden through the use of the `NumberFormatInfo` class. In the example outlined above, we can ensure that all amounts will be displayed as US dollars, but still allow all of the other culture-specific formatting by using the `CurrencySymbol` property as shown below:

```
NumberFormatInfo.CurrentInfo.CurrencySymbol = "$"
```

It doesn't matter where we set this property, as long as it is used before our application displays any currency data that will be affected.

Numeric Data

The culture-specific formatting done on our behalf by the .NET Framework for numeric data is straightforward, and rarely needs to be altered. However, as with currency, the attributes used for formatting numeric data can be accessed through the `NumberFormatInfo` class.

The relevant properties for displaying numeric data are listed below:

- `NumberNegativePattern`: This specifies how negative numbers are displayed. Options include displaying the minus sign before or after the value, or using parentheses to indicate a negative value.
- `NumberGroupSizes`: This specifies how many numbers constitute a group on the left side of the decimal separator. For example, a number displayed as 1,000.00 uses the value 3.
- `NumberGroupSeparator`: This specifies what character is used to separate groups on the left side of the decimal separator. For example, a number displayed as 1,000.00 uses the comma.
- `NumberDecimalDigits`: This specifies how many numbers are displayed to the right of the decimal separator. For example, a number displayed as 1,000.00 uses the value 2.
- `NumberDecimalSeparator`: This specifies what character to use as the decimal separator. For example, a number displayed as 1,000.00 uses the period.

These properties can be accessed in a manner similar to how we overrode the currency symbol in the previous section. For example, currency in the Japanese-Japan culture does not display any decimal digits. We could retrieve this type of information for the current culture by using the following:

```
Dim x As Integer
x = NumberFormatInfo.CurrentInfo.NumberDecimalDigits
```

String Sorting

The last culture-sensitive feature we will cover in this chapter is that of string sorting. The method `String.Compare` uses the `CompareInfo` property of the current culture to determine how to sort strings in a culture-specific manner. Once again, this is an area where we can let the system do all the dirty work on our behalf. Most of the options available cover things like whether sorts are case-sensitive, whether to ignore certain types of characters, and how to deal with specific things like the handling of certain Japanese characters.

Localization

This is where the real fun with internationalization begins. Instead of the system just formatting a piece of data based on cultural settings, localization requires us to build and deploy different copies of a resource for each culture we plan to support in our application. This allows the system to choose the appropriate resource to display based on the current culture. In this section, we will be looking at the following topics:

- Creating and using custom resources in our applications
- Building multiple versions of a form for different languages
- Using the WinRes tool to support translation of a UI without Visual Studio

All of the resource related tasks we will look at in this section use classes contained within the `System.Resources` namespace.

Even though the process of using resources is being presented here as a part of localization, building our application's UI using resource files can have many benefits that don't necessarily relate to internationalization. The biggest benefits revolve around the ability to separate resources from the application logic itself. This can provide the ability to change resources contained in satellite assemblies without having to recompile the application, and can also allow for easy localization of an application at a later time.

Creating and Using Resources

In general, a resource is any non-executable data that is logically deployed with an application. Resources can contain a variety of different data, including strings, images, and persisted objects. This allows us to build localized (translated) versions of these resources and have the application load the appropriate version at runtime, based on the value of the `CultureInfo.CurrentUICulture` property. Another advantage of using resources in our application is that it gives us the ability to change the resource data without having to recompile the application.

In this section, we will examine ways to manually create custom resource files and access them from code. However, in the last section of this chapter, we will build a multi-lingual application entirely with the visual tools supplied with Visual Studio and the SDK. This will include a demonstration on how to use WinRes thereby allowing a team of translators to translate different versions of a form for our application without having to (or being allowed to) see any of the source code and without needing to have Visual Studio on their machine.

Creating a Resource File

We will now focus on the most common ways of creating a resource file in a Windows Forms application using Visual Studio. Before we start looking at how to create our own resource file, we should take a look at how the Visual Studio Form Designer is already using resources in our applications behind the scenes.

Create a new VB.NET Windows Application and select the Show All Files option in the Solution Explorer. Then click to expand what now appears under the form in the Solution Explorer. There should be an additional file with the same name as the form but with a `.resx` extension as shown below:

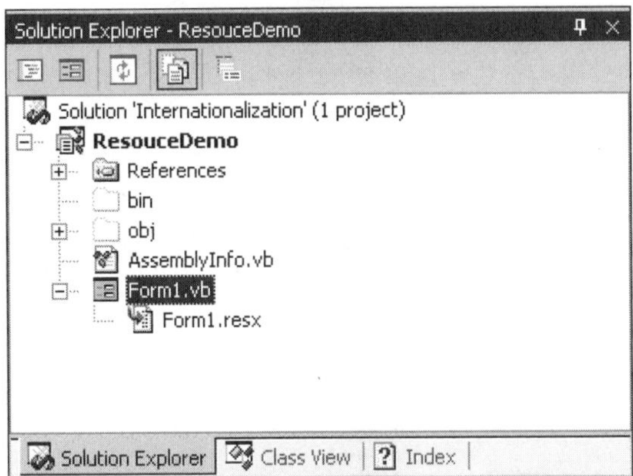

This file is created for us automatically by the Form Designer, and is really just an XML-based representation of what's on our form. This is in contrast to the text-base representation used by VB 6. We can look at the raw contents of this file by right-clicking the file and choosing to open it with the text editor. The extension `.resx` is used to represent the human readable source for a resource file. This file is then compiled into binary file with a `.resources` extension, and it is this file that is used by the application at runtime. However, we will not see this file when we build our application because the file is compiled into the application's `.exe` file. When we add additional resource files for localized versions of our form, we can deploy these in satellite assemblies to avoid having to recompile our application when adding or changing resources.

Fortunately, we don't need to try and understand everything needed to create a `.resx` file by hand because Microsoft has provided several different tools we can use when creating our own resource files. We will look at each of these tools in the following sections.

A String-Only Resource File

Often, there are certain strings that are potentially used in many different places in our application. In these cases, it's convenient to have a resource file that can be accessed by code on different forms in order to retrieve the appropriate string. The process of creating such a resource file has been made very easy in .NET.

Right-click on our project in Solution Explorer and choose to add a new item. Then, select Assembly Resource File from the dialog, as shown below:

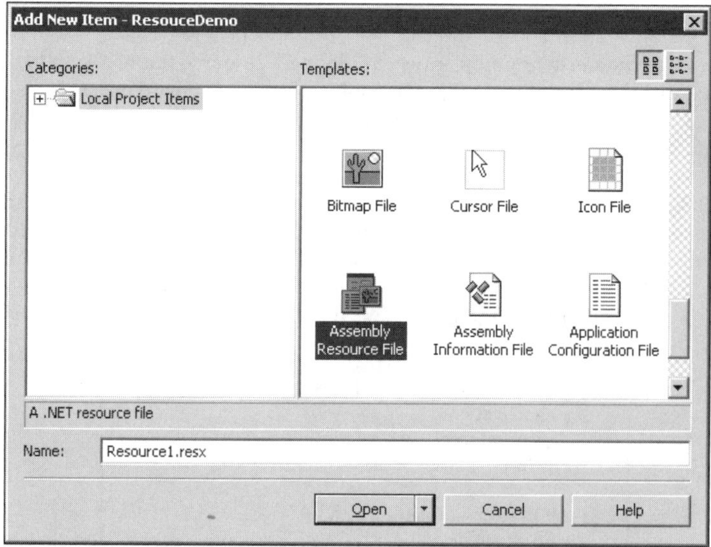

Once we click Open, the new resource file will be added to our project and the file will be opened in the Visual Studio resource file editor as shown below:

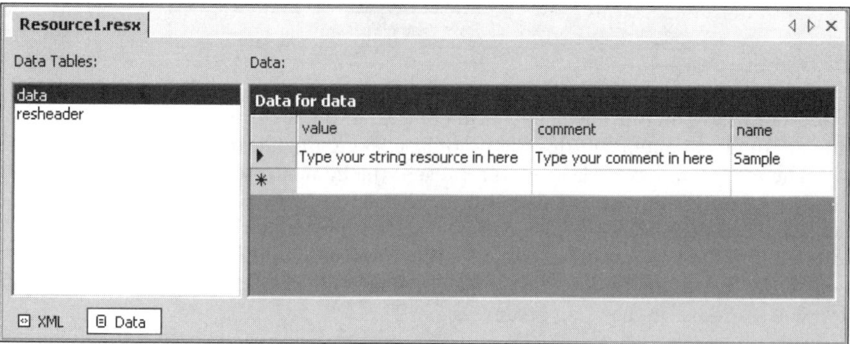

This editor allows us to add new string resources, and even edit the raw XML of the `.resx` file if we choose. We will look at how to retrieve these resources in code later, but right now let's look at another tool that provides much more flexibility.

International Characters

One question that many developers have when exploring the ability to make their application global-ready is simply, how to type foreign characters when using a US-English version of Windows. One utility that is useful in this regard is the Character Map utility, which is included with all versions of Windows, and is usually accessible from Start-Accessories. This utility allows you to see all of the characters that are available, and copy one or more to the clipboard. It also shows a keyboard shortcut that can be used to generate the selected character. This utility is shown below:

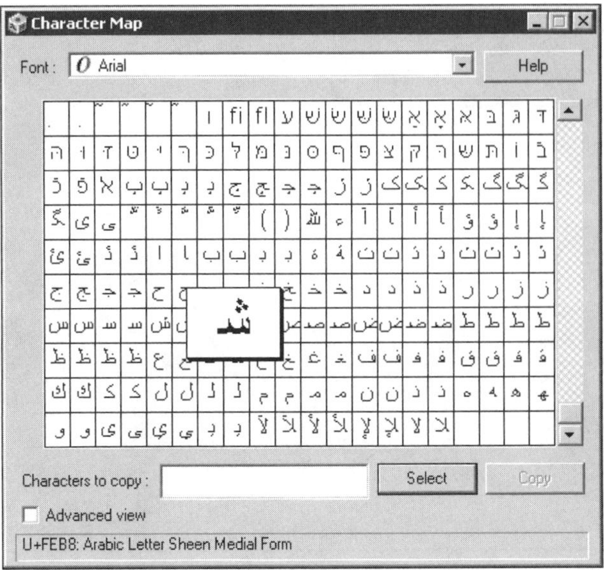

Once a character is selected it can be added to the text box by clicking Select. Clicking Copy will copy the characters to the clipboard. You can see in the example above that the key combination U+FEB8 will also generate the character.

> **There is one important note regarding the use of international charters and symbols. Not all of these characters and symbols are installed on all versions of Windows. For example, if you are working with a version of a form that has been translated into Korean, and you do not have the Korean language installed on your system, the text may not display correctly. However, this is usually not too big a problem for deployment, since an international version of Windows using Korean as the current culture will most likely have the characters and symbols available.**

Using ResGen to Create a Resource File

The most basic way to create a resource file is by using the command-line tool, `resgen.exe`. This tool is provided with the .NET SDK and can use a plain text or XML file to generate a `.resources` file. However, there are many visual tools provided with both the SDK and VS.NET that make this less necessary. Refer to the SDK for more information on the use of ResGen.

Using ResEditor to Create a Resource File

There is a really great tool for creating resource files which contain both text and image data. This tool is `ResEditor.exe` and although it's not integrated with Visual Studio, it is included as part of the .NET SDK. It may help to add this program as an 'External Tool' in the Visual Studio IDE by using the External Tools dialog under the Tools menu and adding a new entry that points to the `.exe` file. The tool is located in the `Framework.SDK\Samples\tutorials\resourcesandlocalization\reseditor` folder of the `Microsoft.NET` directory, but we will first need to build the application using the `.bat` file provided. The screenshot below shows what this tool looks like after adding a bitmap file:

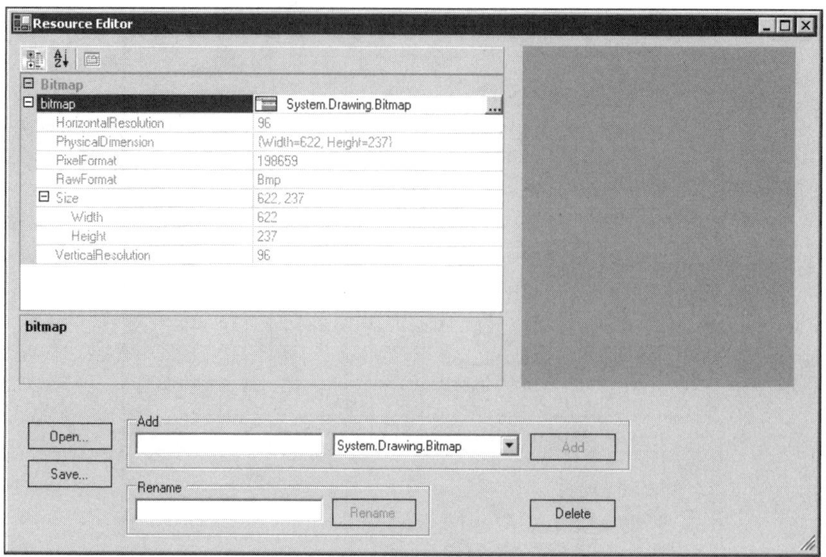

`ResEditor.exe` allows us to create and edit a resource file by using the familiar property grid. This tool also allows us to open and save both `.resx` files and compiled `.resources` files.

> **We can also create resource files programmatically by using an instance of the ResourceWriter class in the System.Resources namespace. However, this is rarely needed unless building a tool similar to ResEditor. Refer to the SDK documentation for more details on using a ResourceWriter.**

Retrieving Resources at Runtime

In this section, we will examine how to use code to access our resource file and retrieve both text and image data. The central class for working with resources at runtime is the `ResourceManager` class. A `ResourceManager` manages multiple resources from a common source that has a particular root name. The `ResourceManager` class has multiple constructors to support the retrieval of resources from assemblies and `.resources` files. The class also contains a static method that can be used to retrieve resources from stand-alone files such as images. Additionally, the `ResourceManager` class supports **fallback** resource lookup. This means that it uses region-independent and neutral cultures when resources matching the application's current specific culture are not provided.

As we saw from the previous sections on creating resource files, every resource is stored with a name. We will now use an instance of a `ResourceManager` and the name of the resource to retrieve it. The code below shows how to create a new `ResourceManager` object, based on the location of a `.resources` file:

```
Dim rm As ResourceManager = ResourceManager. _
CreateFileBasedResourceManager ("sample", ".", Nothing)
```

The method CreateFileBasedResourceManager takes three arguments. These arguments are the file, the location, and whether a non-default ResourceSet is to be used. The file is specified as the filename without the .resources extension. The location argument is relative to the application's base directory. So, in this case, we are creating a reference to the sample.resources file (first parameter) in the current directory (second parameter). The third parameter allows us to specify a custom ResourceSet, instead of the default runtime ResourceSet. Refer to the SDK for more details on the use of a custom ResourceSet.

To then retrieve a text resource, we simply use the GetString method of the ResourceManager and pass in the name of the desired resource, as shown below:

```
Dim myString As String = rm.GetString("textResourceName")
```

To retrieve an image resource we still need the name of the resource, but now we use the GetObject method of the ResourceManager object:

```
pictureBox1.Image = CType (rm.GetObject("imageResourceName", _
System.Drawing.Image))
```

We are doing a cast here using the CType method because the GetObject returns exactly that – a CObject type. We require an Image type so we can assign it to our PictureBox control.

Building Localizable Forms

Fortunately, Microsoft has provided exceptional support in Visual Studio for the most common task involved with building an application whose UI supports multiple languages. The support is built right into the Form Designer, and that is what we will look at in the example that follows. This is not to say that the material we covered in the previous sections on creating and retrieving resources can now be forgotten. Those techniques can still be very valuable in many circumstances.

We will begin by using the sample application we developed at the beginning of the chapter as the starting point for this example. This is necessary so that we have the ability to change the application's current culture at runtime.

The first addition to our original application will be a new form. We will build this new form to display a different version of itself, depending on the current culture. Add a new form to the project and drop a single Label control onto it. Then, change the text of the Label as shown below:

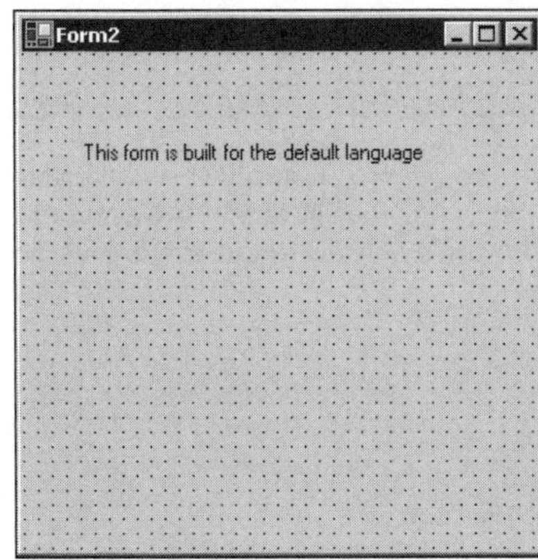

Now is when the magic happens. Go to the form's property window and change the `Localizable` property to `True`. Nothing much has happened yet. Now, change the `Language` property to `German`.

What has actually happened is that Visual Studio has automatically created an additional resource file for this form. We can see the evidence of this by selecting the Show All Files option in the Solution Explorer and examining what appears under `Form2.vb`. There are now two `.resx` files. One is named `Form2.resx` and the other is named `Form2.de.resx`. This is shown below:

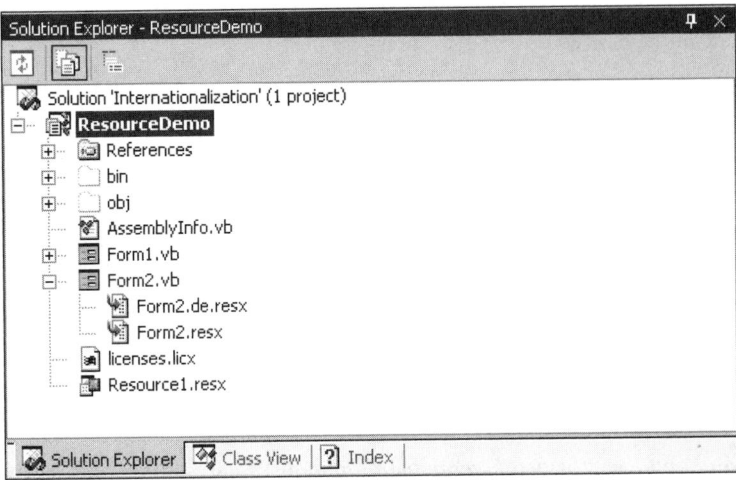

The tricky thing here is that even though there is still only one source code file, there are actually two separate visual copies of this form that can be edited. To illustrate this, with `German` still selected as the form's language, change the text of the `Label` control and resize the form to resemble something like the form shown below.

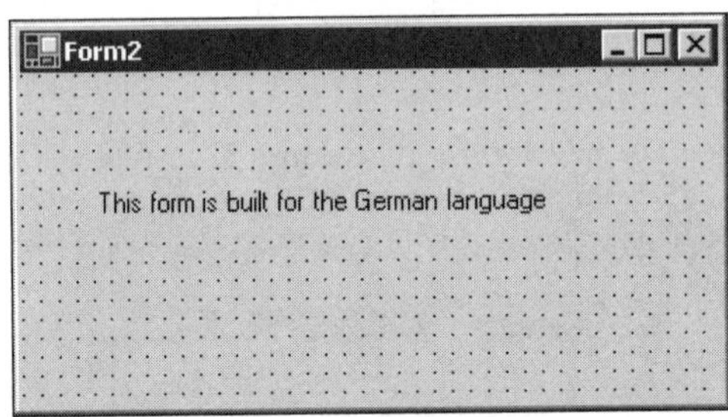

Now we just need to add two more things to our application before we can give it a trial run. Go back to `Form1` and add a command button below the set of labels we added at the beginning of the chapter. We don't need to change any of the button's properties but we do need to add the following lines of code to the button's `click` event:

```
Dim newForm As New Form2()
newForm.Show()
```

Secondly, add an additional line to the `SelectedIndexChanged` event of the `ComboBox`. The new line will change the `CurrentUICulture` and should appear right after where we change the `CurrentCulture`:

```
Thread.CurrentThread.CurrentCulture = ComboCulture.SelectedItem
Thread.CurrentThread.CurrentUICulture = ComboCulture.SelectedItem
```

As we said earlier in the chapter, while changing `CurrentCulture` will affect our `Label` controls, we must change the `CurrentUICulture` to have an effect on resource selection. Now we can go ahead and run the application:

When running the application, start off by clicking the button. We should see `Form2`, but with the label that says it's built for the default language.

Now close `Form2` and change the culture to any of the cultures that start with de. If we now click the button, we should see `Form2` pop-up again. However, this time it is much smaller and has the label that says it was built for the German language.

For one last experiment, close `Form2` again and change the culture to something other than en or de. We should see that the default version of `Form2` is displayed. This is another instance of the fallback behavior we discussed earlier. The system cannot find a matching specific culture, so it tries to find a matching neutral culture. Still no luck, so the default version is displayed.

In the next section, we will look at when this localization architecture really shines – when we want to have a non-programmer or third party actually translate the different versions of our forms into the appropriate languages.

Using WinRes to Support Localization

We saw in the previous section how to create multiple different visual representations of a form, each targeted for a specific language. Once this has been done, the next task is one of actually translating the UI for each of these versions into the appropriate language. What can make this task difficult is that the individuals who do the language translation are most often not the programmers. Sometimes these can be non-technical personnel in the same organization, but many times it can also involve a third party, such as a specialist technical translator.

Ideally, it would be great if the people doing the language translation could do so directly in the Form Designer. This would keep additional work required by the development team to a minimum and would also give the translators the ability to adjust the UI. For example, resizing a button that is too small to hold the Spanish translation of the button's text. There are however, many problems with this approach and some of these are listed below:

- Every person who has to translate the UI of a form would require a copy of Visual Studio on his or her machine.
- The source code of the application would be visible and, even worse, modifiable by the person doing the language translation. This is of course especially undesirable when using a third party for language support.
- Even when using a product like Visual Source Safe, it's not a very pleasant prospect to have several non-programmers opening the project and checking out files just to do language translation.

Fortunately, Microsoft has provided a tool to support localization that eliminates all of these issues. The tool is called the 'Windows Resource Localization Editor' or WinRes. WinRes is a Windows-based editor that allows the user to edit a form's `.resx` file with the same look and feel as Visual Studio, but without Visual Studio installed, or any source code from the application. WinRes is included as part of the SDK as `winres.exe`.

Using WinRes to open the `.resx` file for the default version of `Form2` in the previous example results in something like the following:

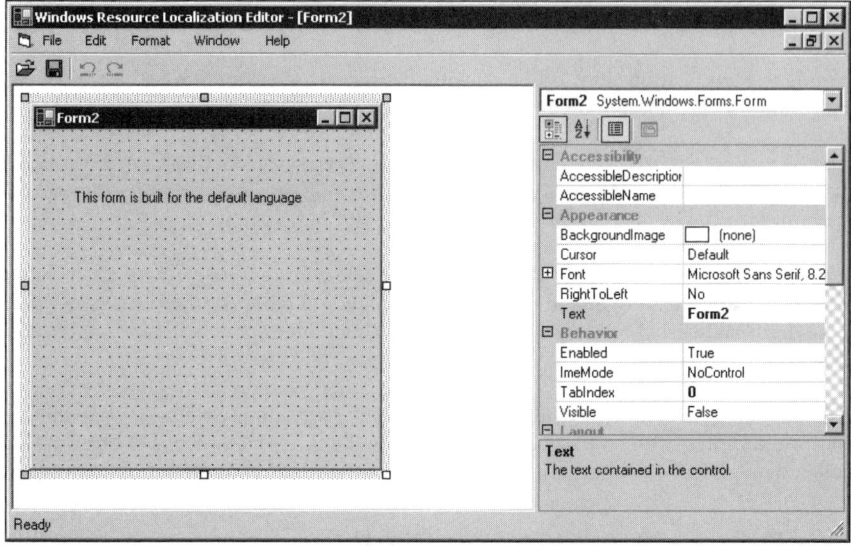

Using WinRes, we could choose each language we want to support using the form's property sheet in Visual Studio. This would automatically generate all the necessary `.resx` files. Then we could send these individual files out to one or several different third parties for language translation services. These other organizations could use WinRes to translate the forms or slightly modify the design if necessary and return them. All that would be necessary then would be to drop the `.resx` files back in to the project and compile.

Summary

As we can see, building a truly international-ready Windows application with .NET is a relatively painless process. Even if we never plan on translating any of our applications into other languages, we should at least be aware of what happens when one of our applications is run on a machine with different culture settings than our own. Hopefully, this chapter has also shown that using resources to make our core application as culture-neutral as possible can provide significant benefits. Most notably, it should be pointed out that having to retro-fit an existing US-only application to support other cultures could be a very tedious and expensive process.

Legend
- Concrete Class
- Abstract class

System.Windows.Forms

- System.Object
  - System.MarshalRefObject
    - System.ComponentMode.Component
      - CommonDialog
        - ColorDialog
        - FileDialog
        - FontDialog
        - PageSetupDialog
        - PrintDialog
      - ErrorProvider
      - HelpProvider
      - ImageList
      - Menu
        - ContextMenu
        - MainMenu
        - MenuItem
      - NotifyIcon
      - StatusBarPanel
      - Timer
      - ToolBarButton
      - ToolTip
      - Control
        - ButtonBase
          - Button
          - CheckBox
          - RadioButton
        - DataGrid
        - DateTimePicker
        - GroupBox
        - Label
          - LinkLabel
        - ListControl
          - ComboBox
          - ListBox
            - CheckedListBox
        - ListView
        - MonthCalendar
        - PictureBox
        - PrintReviewControl
        - ProgressBar
        - ScrollableControl
          - ContainerControl
            - Form
              - PrintPreviewDialog
              - ThreadExceptionDialog
            - PropertyGrid
            - UpDownBase
              - DomainUpDown
              - NumericUpDown
            - UserControl
          - Panel
            - TabPage
        - ScrollBar
          - HScrollBar
          - VScrollBar
        - Splitter
        - StatusBar
        - TabControl
        - TextBoxBase
          - RichTextBox
          - Textbox
        - ToolBar
        - TrackBar
        - TreeView
  - ListViewItem
  - TreeNode

14

Debugging and Optimization

For as long as programmers have been writing code, one common problem keeps replaying over and over – The Bugs! These can range from simple spelling errors in the code to more complex business logic errors that can be extremely difficult to find.

Debugging involves the use of tools and techniques that help developers remove bugs from applications before they are shipped out. We could create the world's best application and beta test it until it shines, but an end user can break it in the first five minutes.

Visual Studio.NET includes a lot of new features in the debugger, with a twist toward the new common language features built into .NET. In this chapter we will cover the following topics:

- Debugging features in VS.NET as they relate to Windows Forms.
- Optimization and Run-Time profiling techniques that can help us squeeze a little more performance from our applications.

What's New in Debugging in .NET

One of the best new features of Visual Studio.NET, is that we use the same IDE to create applications in VB, C#, or in VC++. In keeping with this, the same debugger also works across all the languages.

Because the debugger is integrated with all of the languages and the IDE, we can debug an application written in more than one language. This is especially important in .NET because we can create applications that use all three languages combined, and which call functions in the other languages. Without a common debugger, we would have to separately debug each and every function or piece of our application separately, in the language it was created in. The common debugger allows us to debug errors in the entire application, all at once.

We can debug code written in any of the languages under the CLR, including:

- Visual Basic.NET
- Visual C#.NET
- Visual C++.NET
- Managed Extensions for C++
- Script such ss VBScript or JScript
- SQL stored procedures

The debugger also allows the following debugging features:

- Debugging of Win32 applications written using COM.
- The ability to attach to a running application for debugging, even if that application is located on a remote computer, which is great for multi-tier applications that use a Windows Forms based user interface.
- The ability to debug multiple programs running in the IDE or as attached programs.
- Capability to perform Buffer Security checks.

Debugging of Native WIN32 Applications

The debugger in VS.NET is capable of debugging applications that have been written as native Win32 applications using Visual C++ 6.0. This allows us to use the same .NET debugger for our earlier applications, which prevents the need to have both IDEs installed on the computer.

Attach to Running Programs

This capability of the debugger allows us to perform actions such as debugging programs that were not created in Visual Studio.NET, (see the section above), debugging multiple applications simultaneously whether they are running in the IDE or not, debugging programs running on remote computers, debugging DLLs that are running in separate processes, and even allows the debugger to start automatically if an application crashes. We will show to attach to running code later in this chapter in the section entitled 'Attach the Debugger to a Running Process'.

The information presented in the debugger may be limited, as it depends on whether or not the application was compiled with debug information or not.

Buffer Security Checks

As most developers are probably aware, buffer overruns are becoming a popular means of getting around the security aspects of applications running on the Internet. By causing buffer overruns, computer crackers are able to exploit a security weakness in the application. This can, if the application has sufficient privileges, allow the cracker to gain access to the systems on which the software is running, and thereby gain administrative access to that system. Buffer overruns occur when return memory addresses are overwritten, effectively destroying data in adjoining memory locations.

By using the /GS option, we can inform the debugger to check for buffer overruns. It does so by inserting security checks into the source code for compilation.

Debugger Settings

In order to effectively use the debugger, we need to properly set it up for the debugging tasks that we're performing. This section will look at some of the settings available in the debugger and how to configure them. When working in the debugger, we can obtain help on the various windows and dialog boxes, by pressing the *F1* key.

Switching Between Debug and Release Configurations

Visual Studio.NET allows us to compile our application for two possible scenarios, namely Debug and Release. When first developing an application, it is best to use the Debug configuration, to ensure that debug symbols are placed within the code. This allows for easier and better debugging of the application, and is the default setting of the IDE when we create a new project.

> **Keep in mind that applications will run a little slower in Debug configuration, as there are no optimizations applied to the code, and the debug symbols will also make the code larger and slower.**

The Release configuration is the option to choose when we have finished debugging our application and are positive that it is ready to be sent to the end user. The code is fully optimized and all symbolic debug information is removed. This option gives us the fastest code possible. We can still include debug symbols outside of the code by creating PDB files. These files will be discussed later in the chapter.

As mentioned earlier, the Debug configuration is the default option that's selected by the IDE when we create a new application using the wizards. To change the option, all we have to do is select the appropriate option from the standard toolbar as shown in the following screenshot. For the purpose of testing the techniques described in this chapter, open the `WroxEdit application` which was created in Chapters 4 and 5.

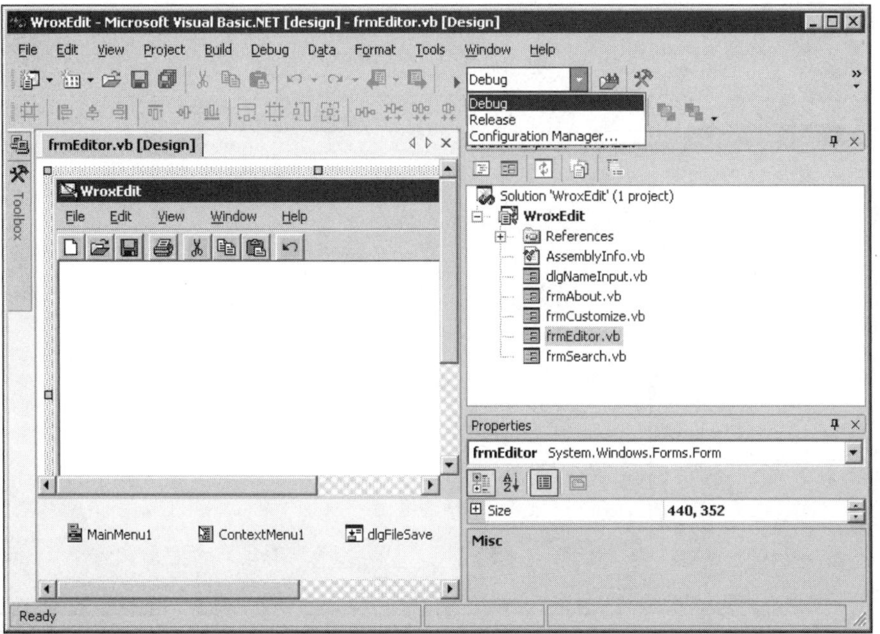

As we can see, the drop down shows the Debug and Release options, but also includes a Configuration Manager option. The Configuration Manager is used to configure the options for the build we have chosen. Choosing this option will display the Configuration Manager window as shown here:

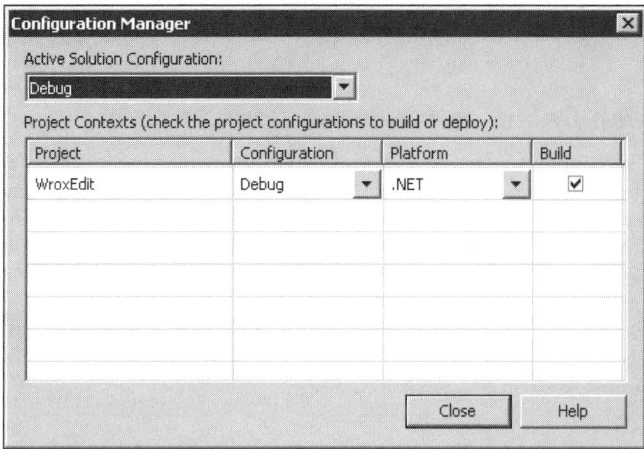

This allows us to choose the build configuration, such as Debug or Release, as well as indicating the platform that we want to compile for. At this time, the .NET platform is the only one available. The Build option becomes more useful when we have multiple projects open, and displayed in the Configuration Manager. It allows us to specify which projects to build using the current configuration.

We can also specify the build options, by selecting the project in the Project Explorer and then pressing *Shift+F4*, or by selecting the Property Pages option from the View menu. This will display the project's property pages as shown below:

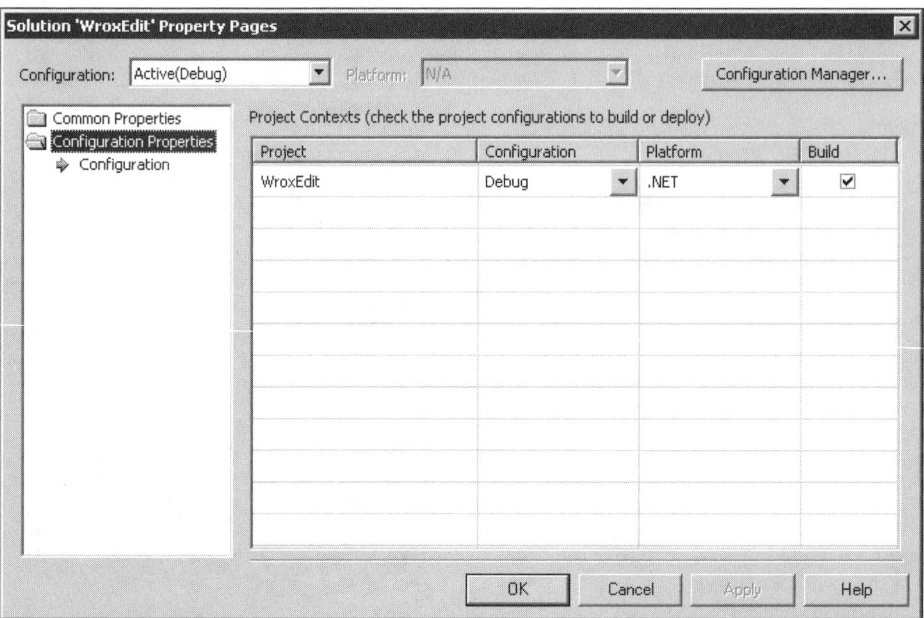

Select the Configuration Properties folder to display the setting shown here. As we can see, they are identical to the options available from the Configuration Manager used above.

Project Settings for Debugging

To set the properties of the project, open the Property Pages as discussed above. For our example, we only have one project in the IDE so we will work with that one application. Under the Common Properties folder, the first selection is the Startup Project. Ensure that the `WroxEdit` application is specified in the Single Startup Project drop down, and that the Single Startup Project radio button is checked off.

We should see that there is a grid in the lower portion of the property pages window. The first and only entry is the `WroxEdit` application. The second column is used to specify a startup option. Clicking the dropdown arrow allows us to check one of the following three options.

- None: Tells the IDE not to start this project when we run the debugger.
- Start: Will start the application specified when we start the debugger.
- Start Without Debugging: Causes the application to start but does not use debugging.

The next option available in Common Properties is the Project Dependencies option. There may be instances where we have projects that need to be built first because they contain code that this particular project relies on. One such instance might be if our Windows Forms code depends on a Windows Class Library project (DLL).

In order to debug the application we need to have the debug version of the DLL compiled and running. This option will allow us to specify which projects we want to build first, in order to properly debug this project. In order for this feature to work, we must have the additional project loaded in the IDE for them to appear in the Depends On list. Once we have the necessary projects loaded into the IDE, we must ensure that we have the main project selected. Open the Properties Pages and select the Project Dependencies option. We should now see the other projects displayed in the listbox. Place a check mark next to the projects that need to be built before this project, as shown here:

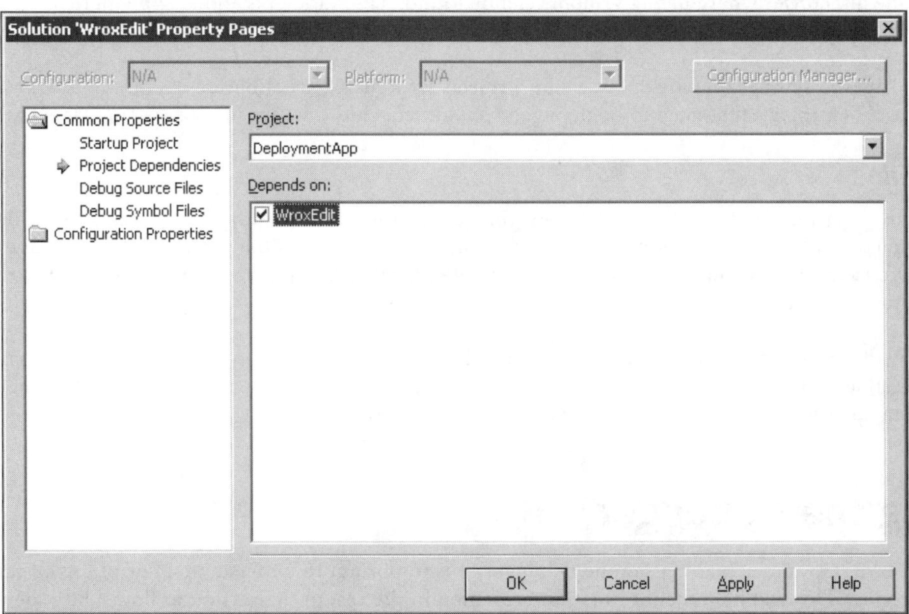

This will inform the IDE that it needs to build the checked applications first, before it builds and runs the current project in the debugger. This allows us to test the full functionality of the application, even though it relies on other projects.

The next option, Debug Source Files, allows us to specify additional locations for source files needed during the debugging process. In the first listbox, titled Search these paths for source files, we can include paths to search through for required source files. If there are source files that we wish to exclude, we can place those in the lower listbox, entitled Do not look for these source files.

The buttons on this page have the following functionality

Use this button to check the entries and verify them.

This button is used to create or insert a new line.

This button is used to remove a line or entry from the list box.

This button will move the selected entry down in the list.

This button will move the selected entry up in the list.

Placing the entries in a different order within the listboxes will cause the debugger to search the entries from top to bottom. If we have source files in one location that we use most often, place that location at the top of the list to speed up the searches.

The last option, Debug Symbol Files, is similar to the source files option. It allows us to specify and exclude directories where debug symbols can be found. The same operations apply here as with the Source Files option.

These are the settings that are available for projects written in Visual Basic.NET. Developers who have C# or C++ projects that need to be debugged should check the settings for those languages in MSDN.

PDB Files

A PDB (program database) file holds debugging information for the project in question. The file will hold incremental linking information for the debug configuration of the project. We don't have to worry about creating this file manually, as it will be created for us when we compile a debug configuration of the project in VB or C#.

The PDB file is named after the project, followed by the `.pdb` extension. For example, our `WroxEdit` application will have a PDB file named `WroxEdit2.pdb`. The PDB file must have the same name and timestamp as the binary executable being debugged or it will not load.

Using the Debugger

Before we step into actually using the debugger, it is important to understand a few of the basics of debugging. This will help the information presented in the rest of the section to flow a little better.

As we write our applications, we will inadvertently introduce errors into our code. The types of errors encountered will vary. Below we will look at some of the more common errors that occur in applications.

Syntax Errors

One of the first types of errors that we are likely to encounter is the **syntax error**, which is caused by the use of an improper syntax in our code. The compiler normally picks them up while we are writing our code, or when we try to build the project.

When we write our code and move to the next line, we should pay attention to any wavy lines that underline the code (In VB the wavy line is blue, and in C# it is red). If we see one of these lines, it is an indication that the line or portion of code underlined contains a syntax error. The error can be determined in one of two possible ways. Place the cursor over the section that contains the blue line and a tool tip will pop up indicating the source of the error. This is shown in the following screenshot:

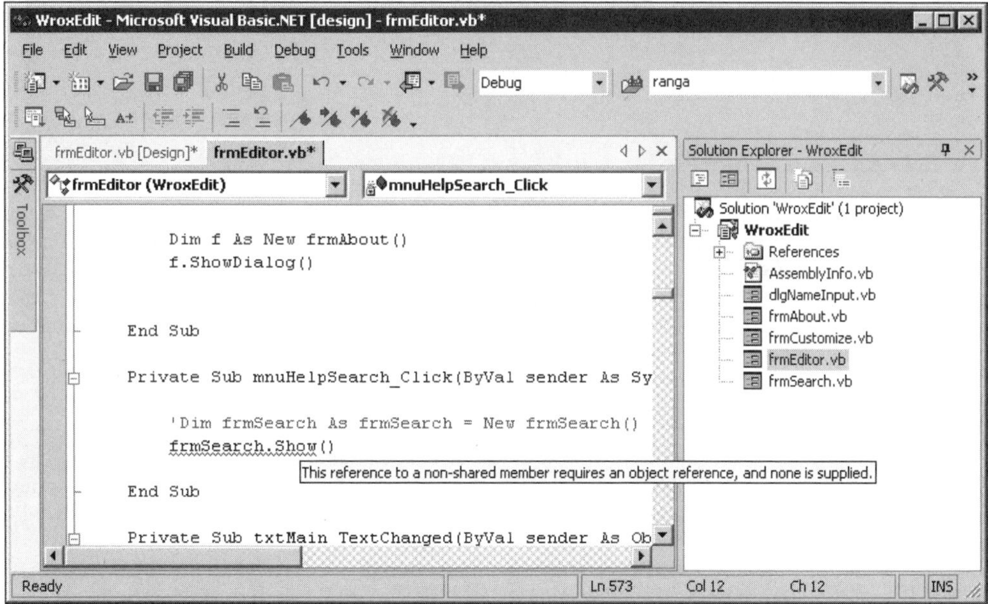

As we can see here, the tool tip offers some advice as to the error that is indicated by the blue wave line. In this instance, the declaration for the `frmSearch` form has been commented out, which causes the compiler to think that the object doesn't have a reference.

The other way that the compiler indicates an error of this type is to display it in the task list window at the bottom of the code window. This is shown below. If the error is not visible in the code window, double-clicking on the entry for the error in the task list will take us directly to the error in the code listing.

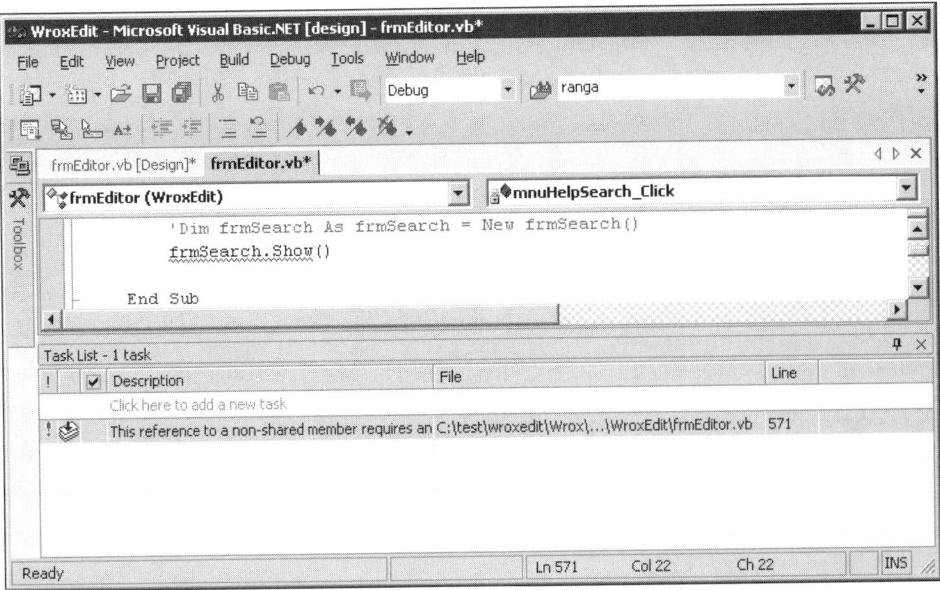

As we can see, the same error message that was displayed in the tool tip is shown here in the task list. The task list is not always visible, but can be displayed in one of two ways. We can either select View menu | Other Windows | Task List, or just build the project, and if any errors are present, the task list is displayed automatically by the IDE. Double-click each error to find it in the code window. We can also insert our own tasks in the task window. Search for the 'Task List' keyword to get more information on how to add tasks to the task list.

Semantic Errors

The second type of error is called a **semantic error**, which is a fancier term for a logic error. These types of errors are harder to find because they don't manifest themselves as errors that the compiler can catch. Instead, the program runs along just fine, but the end results aren't what they are supposed to be.

An example of this might be if we had created an application that worked with numbers, and we declared variables to hold the values of calculations as we worked through the program. However, at some point in time in the program, we were passing the values back and forth from a double to a single variable. We will lose precision, and the dollar values will not be displayed or entered correctly. Another example would be when a variable that is used to calculate the denominator of a fraction turns out to be zero at some point and crashes the program.

This is the type of error that will not be displayed or caught by the compiler. However it still creates a problem because our application will not perform as it is supposed to. For this type of error, we must use the other features of the debugger in the IDE to help us step through our code, and determine where the errors are occurring. Let's take a look...

Controlled Execution

When we talk about controlled execution, we refer to the commands that are available in the debugger that we use when debugging our code. The various ways to control the execution of the program with the debugger are explained in this section.

Start Command

In order to start debugging our application, we have to first start the debugger. We can do this by pressing *F5*.

Our program will continue executing until it either reaches a breakpoint or an exception occurs (or the program ends normally). Exceptions are the new term for errors in VB code, and they are now used across the more popular development languages, such as VB.NET, C# and Java.

If we have multiple projects, we can specify which project to start first for debugging by right-clicking the project in the project explorer, and choosing Set as Startup Project.

Stop Command

Within the IDE, we can stop the application from running in the debugger by choosing the Stop option from the Debug menu or by pressing the stop button on the toolbar:

Break Command

We can also cause the program execution to break, or pause, by choosing the Break All option from the Debug menu, pressing *CTRL+ALT+BREAK*, or pressing the Break button on the toolbar (adjacent and left of the stop option in the previous screenshot). This will cause the program to pause at the point when we chose the Break command. We can now view the variables in our code or inspect some of the other windows that were discussed earlier.

Click the Continue button (far left) to have the application continue execution.

Stepping through Code

Stepping through code is perhaps one of the most common tasks we will perform in the debugger when we have our application in a paused state. Stepping allows us to execute the code one line at a time, or one procedure or partial procedure at a time.

Within the debugger, we have three possible stepping options available to us. These are Step Into, Step Over and Step Out. We will take a look at each of these next.

Step Into

Using this command allows us to step through code, one line at a time. As an example of how this command works, open the `WroxEdit` application, and find a procedure that has multiple lines of code, such as the `mnuEditPreferences_Click` procedure. Place a breakpoint at the beginning of the procedure. In order to place a breakpoint, select a line of code and click in the gray bar to the left of that line of code. A red dot will appear, as shown below.

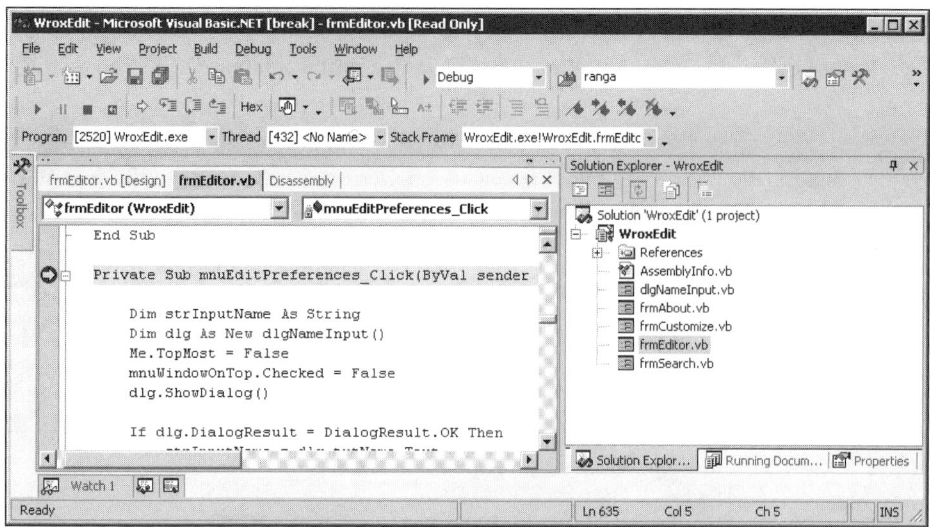

This will cause the application to pause at this location when we click this menu choice in WroxEdit. Run the application and select the menu as indicated to cause the application to pause. Once it is in break mode, we will see that the debug toolbar is displayed with the following buttons displayed on it:

Step Into is the highlighted button in this image. To its right is Step Over, followed by the Step Out button. With the program still in break mode, click the Step Into button once to see how the code is executed one line at a time, each time we click the button.

One thing we will notice is that if a procedure is called on a line of code, the execution switches immediately to that function call. Continuing to click the Step Into button will cause the code in the functions to also step one line at a time.

Step Out

We can use the Step Out command to step out of a function or procedure after stepping in a few lines. The code within the function or procedure is executed but we will not have to step into the function or procedure anymore. As an example, run the `WroxEdit` application again, and select its Edit | Preferences menu. This time, when we step through the code and execution switches to the `Public Sub New` procedure, select the Step Out command and watch how the execution steps out of the procedure and continues after the line of code that called the procedure. The code in the procedure still executes, but we don't have to keep using the Step Into command.

Step Over

The Step Over command is the last of the three commands available for stepping through code. This command is used to step over a function, causing the entire function to execute, and have the program break at the next line of code after the function call.

Each of these available commands allows us to have fine control over debugging our applications, one line or one function at a time.

The 'Stop' Keyword

We have already seen that we can halt our code at specific locations by placing breakpoints. So far we have done this by clicking at the desired location in the gray breakpoint bar in the left column of the code window.

Another option is to place the keyword `Stop` before the line of code we want to break at. As an example, place the `Stop` keyword at the same place we used for the breakpoint earlier and remove the breakpoint. Run the application and select the menu choice again. The program's execution will halt at the `Stop` statement just as it did for the breakpoint.

Setting an Execution Point

The debugger in Visual Studio.NET allows us to set the execution point to a different location in the program. A couple of reasons that we may want to perform this action is to either bypass a section of code that we know does not contain any bugs, similar to step out or step over, or to bypass a section that does contain a known bug, just to test the remaining portion of the function or code.

In order to change the execution point, our program must be in a Break state. We can use the same `Stop` statement that we placed in our code earlier to stop the execution.

When the program has halted, take a look in the gray margin and locate the yellow arrow. This is the indicator for where code execution currently is. To change the execution point, drag the yellow arrow to a new location in the code listing. As an example, drag the arrow to the line of code that is indicated here:

```
rk = Registry.LocalMachine.OpenSubKey("Software\WroxEdit", True)
```

Once the execution point has been placed at this line of code, click the Continue button on the debug toolbar to continue execution of the code. We should receive an error in the application.

The reason that this error is displayed is because we stepped over some code that was necessary. This is used to demonstrate a point about changing the location of execution in this manner. When we do so, we effectively skip all of the code that comes before. Unlike the step functions, the code that we bypass will not execute at all. Keep this in mind when choosing to use this functionality as we may skip over initialization or declaration code that is necessary.

Debugging Managed Code

In this section, we will look at debugging techniques for managed code in Visual Basic.NET. Managed code is code written to target the .NET framework, and the debugging techniques are a little different than the ones used outside the .NET framework. This section will look at the changes in debugging techniques for Visual Basic.NET, as well as some of the techniques used with managed code. We will also see that some of the debug windows that we can use as we debug our code also help us to decipher what is taking place.

The section will end with a look at assertions, a little more information on `Stop` statements, expressions, and a discussion on how to attach the debugger to a running process.

The Debug and Trace Classes

There are some changes in the methods and techniques used for debugging, and while some are not huge changes, they still require us to rethink, and apply different techniques for our debugging tasks.

One of the minor changes that have been made is in the `Debug` object that VB programmers are familiar with. When we wanted to display a variable's data value, or other information about some portion of the program as it was running, we would use the `Debug.Print` statement in the code of our application to print the information to the Immediate Window for inspection. In VB.NET the `Print` method is no longer a part of the `Debug` class. Instead, the `Debug` class, which belongs to the `System.Diagnostics` namespace, has four new methods namely `Debug.Write`, `Debug.WriteIf`, `Debug.WriteLine` and `Debug.WriteLineIf`. We will look at the two most commonly used methods here.

'Debug.Write'

This method will write information to what is known as the Listeners collection. Listeners are responsible for formatting the output of debug processes for display. If we use the `Debug.Write` method in our code, the information will be displayed in the Output window. As an example, enter the following line of code in the Edit | Preferences code in WroxEdit:

```
If dlg.DialogResult = DialogResult.OK Then
    strInputName = dlg.txtName.Text
    Debug.Write (strInputName)
    Dim rk As RegistryKey = _
    Registry.LocalMachine.OpenSubKey("Software", True)
```

This will cause the value that is entered in the Input box to be displayed in the Output window at the bottom of the IDE. If the output window is not displayed, select it from the View | Other Windows menu.

'Debug.WriteIf'

This function will perform the same task as the `Write` method, with one exception – it will only output the information if the condition is `True`. This is analogous to the `Watch` expression in VB6 that equates to breaking when the value is `True`. In this case however, the program execution will not break, but will instead output the value.

As an example of this, change the code in the `txtMain_TextChanged` event as seen here and then run the application again.

```
Private Sub txtMain_TextChanged(ByVal sender As Object, _
ByVal e As System.EventArgs) Handles txtMain.TextChanged
    blnIsDirty = True
    Debug.WriteIf(True, blnIsDirty)
End Sub
```

If we run the application and type a character in the text box we will see the value `True` printed in the Output window. We should be careful not to call any function within the `WriteIf` statement that may change the value of other variables.

Trace Class

Once our application is compiled with Release configuration, the methods from the `Debug` class are no longer available. They do not get compiled into the executable. We can use the `Trace` class, also in the `System.Diagnostics` namespace, to debug or monitor our application when it is compiled in a Release version. The methods in the `Trace` class allow us to place switches in our code that will write information to a log file, to a command prompt window or to some other available output medium. Use of these methods is a valuable resource in monitoring our applications in a production environment.

For now, we will move onto a discussion of the techniques used for debugging which will offer some information on how we can use some of the new features in debugging our applications.

Assertion

One of the techniques available to us in debugging is the **assertion**, which tests a condition in our code. If the assertion returns `True`, execution continues. However, if the assertion returns `False`, the application will enter Break mode. `Assert` is available in both the `Debug` and `Trace` classes. The `Assert` method can take up to three arguments, the first of which is mandatory, and is used as the condition to check. If the assertion fails, the optional second and third arguments will be used. These are string values that will be sent to the specified output device.

If we want to include this assertion into the compiled application, we will need to replace the `Debug.Assert` statement with a `Trace.Assert` statement. Be aware that there will be overhead in the application when we place the `Trace.Assert` statements in the code.

If we want `Trace` to work in our application, we can check the TRACE constant option in project properties as shown below:

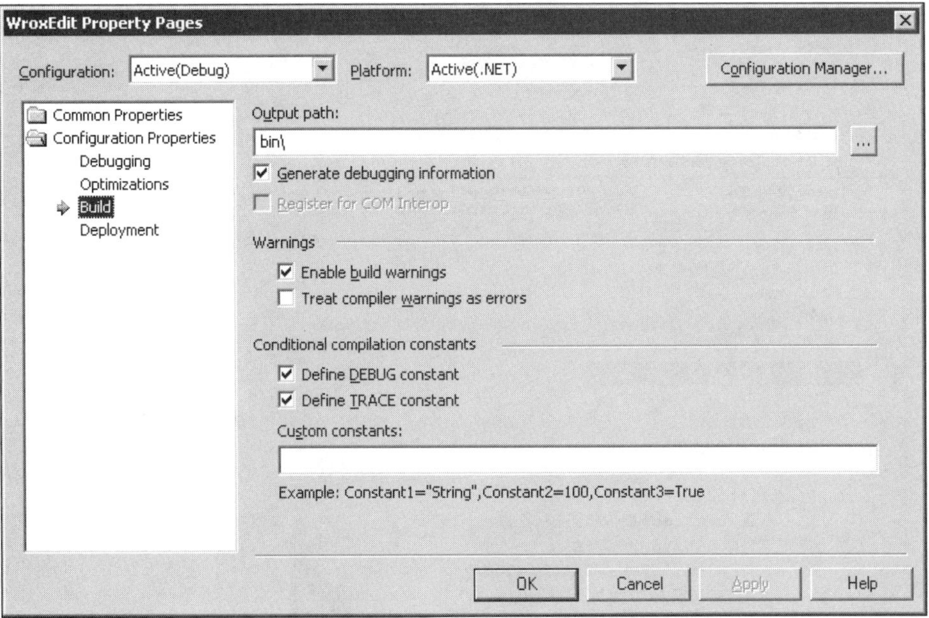

If we create assertions in our code using the Debug class, we must ensure that these assertions do not affect the outcome of any portion of our code. Remember, all Debug statements are removed from our code when we compile the application for release.

Using Diagnostic Messages in the Output Window

We have already seen an example of using the Debug.Write and Debug.WriteIf methods to display messages in the Output window for debugging purposes. Using the Debug or Trace class will produce the same effect when debugging our application in the IDE.

The Output window is only available while our application is running in the context of Visual Studio. The various methods will not display the output to that window in a compiled application. Also, remember that all Debug statements are removed from our code during compilation.

Debug Windows

As we work with the debugger we will use many different windows that help us debug our applications. We will take a brief look at each in this section.

Disassembly Window

This window is so named because it displays the disassembled code in Assembler format. Assembler is the closest thing to actual machine language and is rather cryptic to read, although some developers feel that it is easier to learn than any other language because there are fewer keywords.

To display the Disassembly window, our project must be in break mode, so we need to place a breakpoint in the code window as shown here:

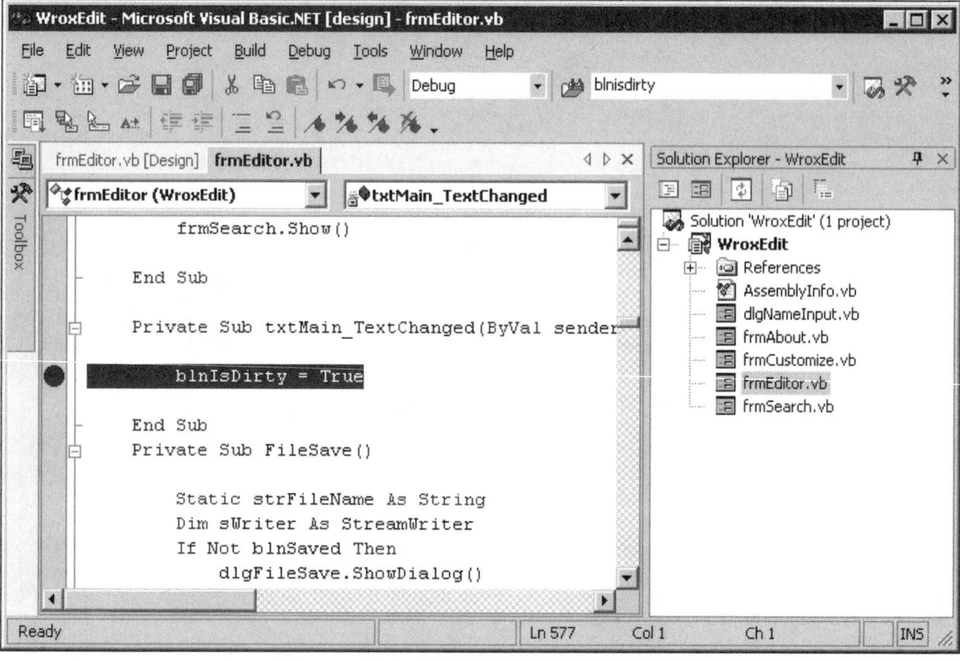

The breakpoint has been placed in the `TextChanged` event for the text box, so that it will be easy to cause the application to pause, simply by typing something into the text box. Run the application and type some text into the text box. Once we type, the application is placed in Break mode. We can now display the Disassembly window.

Select the Disassembly window from the Windows menu option of the Debug menu or press *CTRL+ALT+D*. We will see the window displayed as shown below:

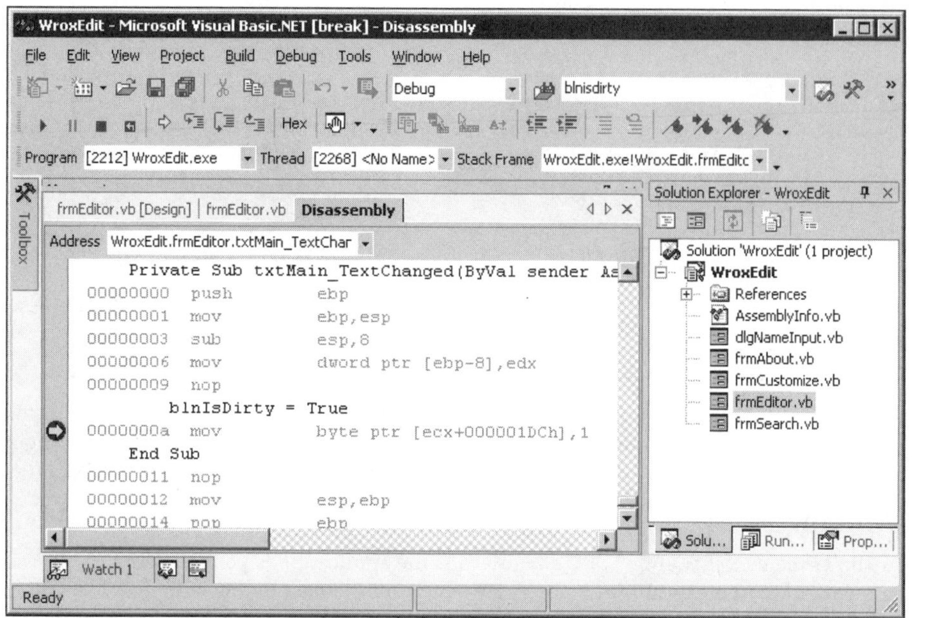

We can now see the assembly code that represents the actions our program is taking within the CPU and its registers.

Memory Window

An option that we would rarely use, but which can be useful, is the Memory window. We can use it to view the contents of memory that our application is using, and see what resides in those locations. This window is useful if we want to find out where .NET is storing our variables, or to find out some detail about pointers if we are using them in our code. An example of a Memory window is shown in the following screenshot:

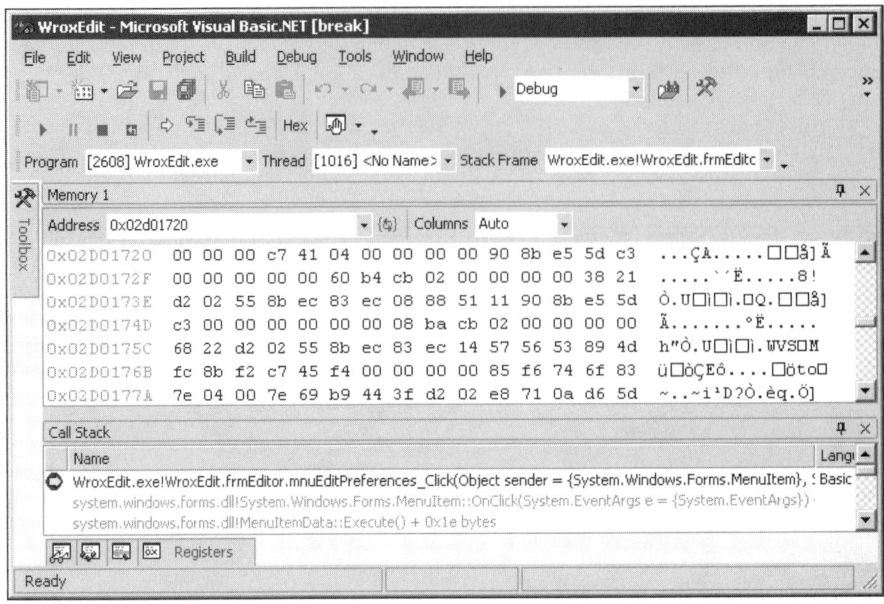

We can see that the memory address is indicated in the left column, the contents in hexadecimal format are displayed in the center column, and the equivalent ASCII representations are shown in the right column. For many VB programmers, this is a new feature that was not available before VB.NET.

Registers Window

This window shows the contents of the CPU's registers as the application is paused. The CPU uses these registers as a means of temporary storage while it is working on the data in the variables. The CPU copies the data from RAM into the registers and performs the necessary computation or comparison on them. The Registers window is displayed below:

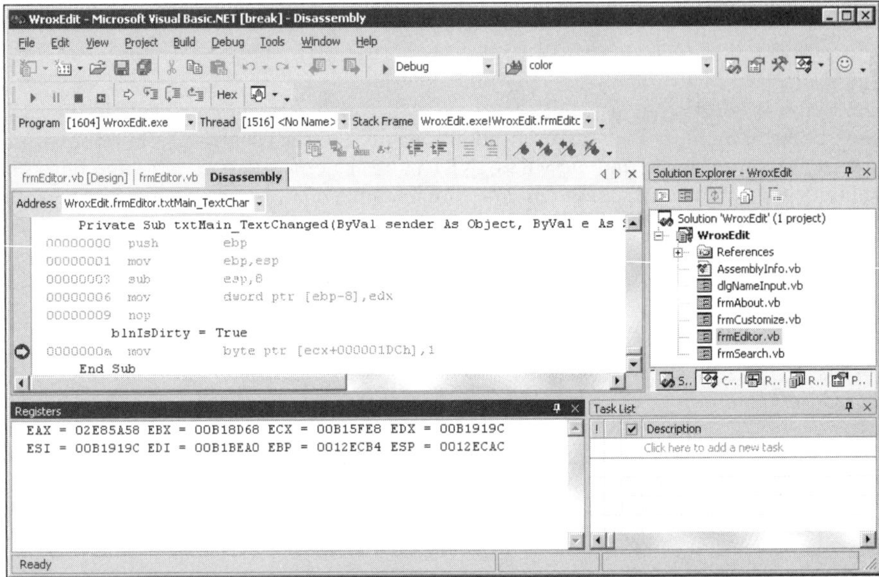

Breakpoints Window

The Breakpoints window shows us all the breakpoints that we have set in our code, and allows us to double-click one and go to that breakpoint in the code window. We can also clear a breakpoint from here by clearing the check mark from the box. It is also possible to specify conditions that should be met in order to break. We can also set the breakpoint to activate only if it is hit a certain number of times by specifying a hit count. A screenshot of the locals and breakpoints windows is shown below:

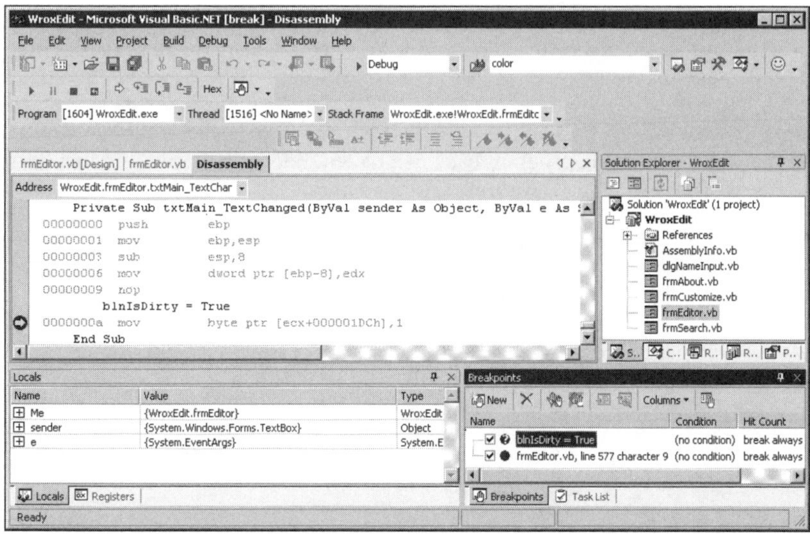

Autos Window

This window allows us to view variables from our application as they pertain to the current statement of execution and the previous statement. To display the Autos window, our application must be in Break mode. Once the program is in Break mode, select the Autos window from the Debug Windows menu to display the Autos window in the lower section of the IDE, as shown below:

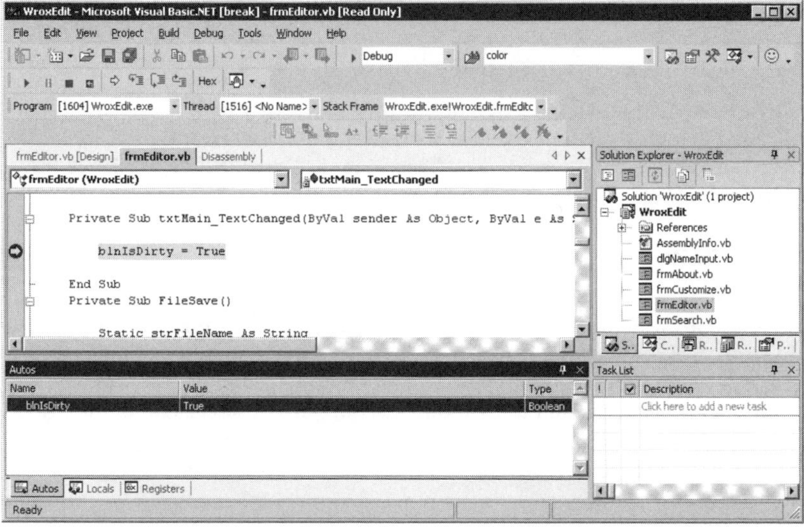

As we can see, the `blnIsDirty` variable is highlighted in the code window as the current statement, and is also displayed in the Autos window. The value is indicated as `False` because this statement has not been executed yet. We can also change the value of the variable in the Autos window by double-clicking in the Value column and changing it directly. We can also right-click in the Autos window to change the display to Hexadecimal to affect the display of the variables.

Locals Window

This window also requires the application to be in Break mode and is displayed using the same procedure as that for the Autos window. This window, however, displays all variables that are local to the context of the code that was executing as the program went to Break mode.

As an example, place a breakpoint back into the Preferences menu's click event, to stop the program execution in that event. Once the program has been halted, select the Locals window from the Debug | Windows menu to display the Locals window as shown here:

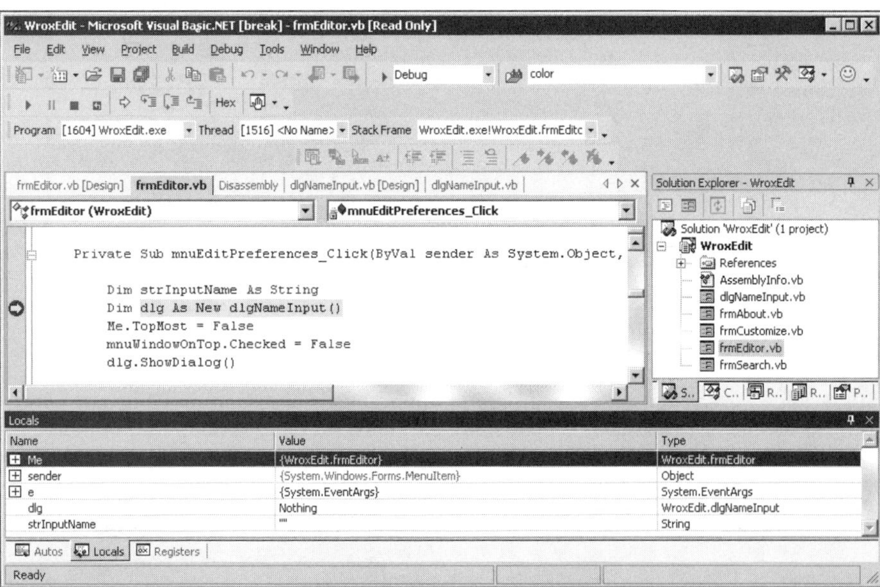

Note that all variables that are in the scope of this procedure are listed. Some have a plus (+) sign next to them indicating that they can be expanded to display additional information contained in variables such as objects, structures, enumerations, etc. This window also allows us to change the value of the variables in the same way as in the Autos window.

Me or This Window

This window is known as Me in Visual Basic or This in C++ and C#. We can display this window from the Debug Menu. This window displays the data types and variables that are a part of the current object that is in the context of the code being executed. In our earlier example, Me refers to the current form and all variables that are in that scope. These will all be displayed in the Me window, which allows us to change variables in the same fashion as that indicated already. A screenshot of the Me window with several controls is shown opposite:

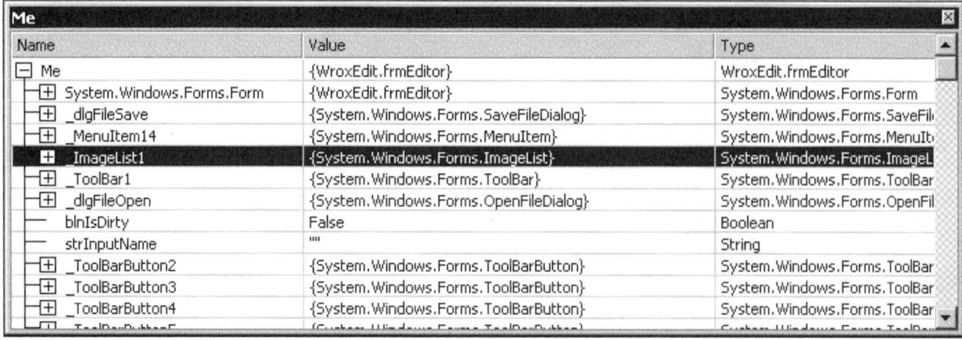

QuickWatch

We can watch the value of a variable or an expression by using the QuickWatch, or Watch window.

We can choose the QuickWatch option from the Debug menu. We can then type in a variable or expression name directly in the dialog box as shown here:

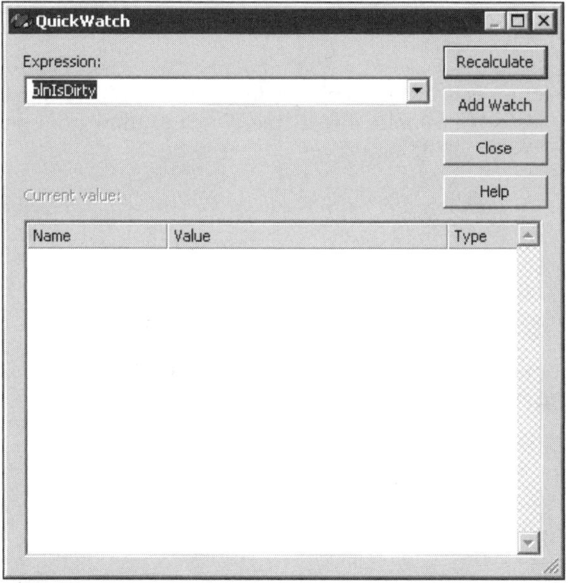

When we click Add Watch, the Watch window will be displayed in the lower portion of the IDE, with the expression or variable that we entered here.

Another way to display and add a quick watch is to right-click an expression in the code window and choose QuickWatch. If we right-click the `dlg` expression in the code window located directly underneath the breakpoint, and choose QuickWatch, the QuickWatch dialog is displayed with the object added as indicated here:

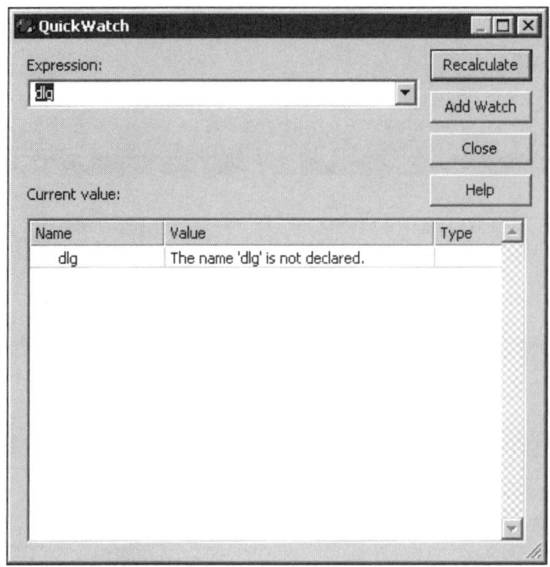

Watch Window

As we have already noted, we can add a Watch window to the IDE by using the Add Watch button from the QuickWatch dialog. We can also display the Watch window from the Debug menu. Visual Studio allows up to four Watch windows.

With this window open, we can view any expressions or variables that have been added, by right-clicking the variable or expression in the code window and choosing Add Watch from the pop up menu. We can use this window to monitor and/or change the values of the expressions and variables in our code. We can also view values in Hex format with this window, by choosing Hexadecimal display from the pop up menu for the window.

For more information on how the Registers window displays the information and allows us to change the data, review the MSDN documentation.

Call Stack Window

The Call Stack window gives information about which procedures have been called, and where execution is in the application at that moment. An example of this window is shown here:

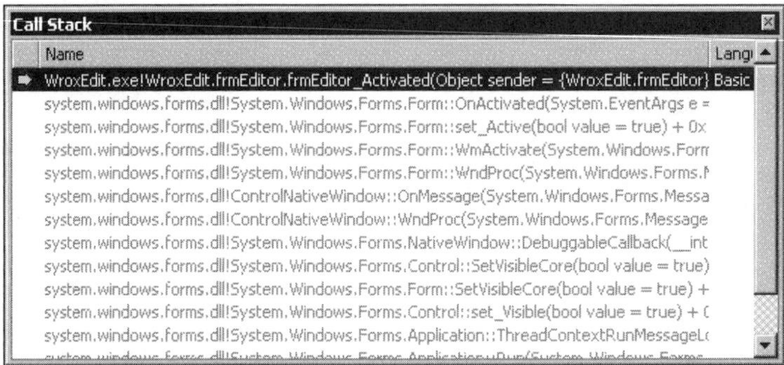

We can see that the stack pointer is located at the procedure that is currently executing. Note that the order of this window is from bottom to top. That is, the first procedure called is on the bottom of the list and the latest procedure called is on the top of the list.

Threads Window

If an application has more then one thread of execution, we can display those threads and switch to them using this window. The Threads window is shown in the screenshot below:

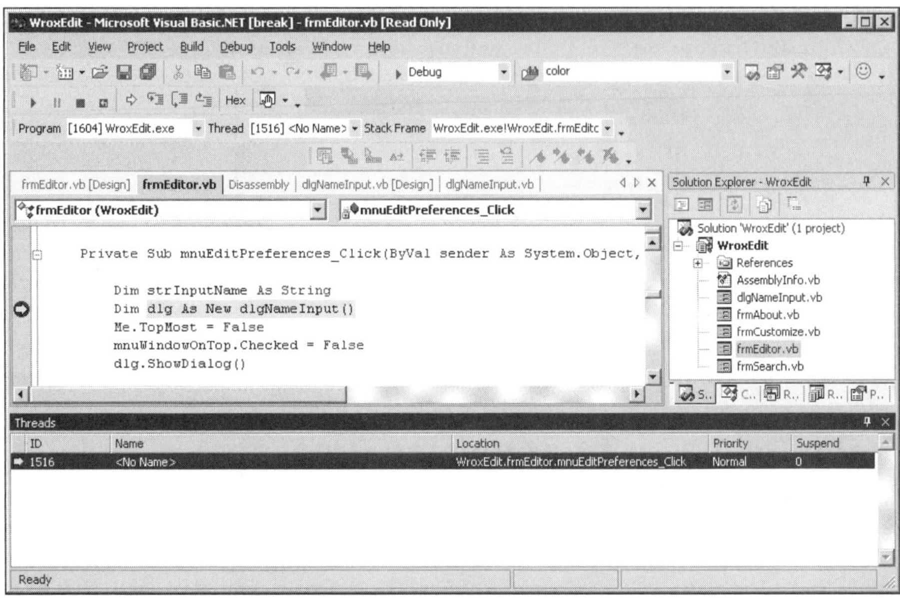

This window only shows one thread of execution, as that is all that we have in the `WroxEdit` application. If there were multiple threads running, they would all be displayed here and then we could right-click a thread in this window and choose Switch to Thread, to make that thread the active one in execution for testing purposes.

Modules Window

This window is used to display all modules used by our application. This includes Exe and Dll modules, including the runtime modules. The Modules window is shown here:

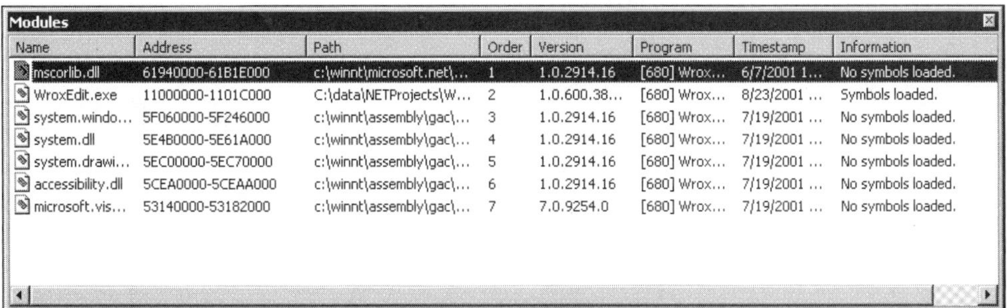

Note that the columns display the name of the module, the memory address where the module is loaded, and the full path to the Exe or Dll file. The modules are displayed in the order in which they were loaded by default. We can change the sort order by clicking on a column heading. The order will be sorted in ascending order with the first click, and then descending with the second click.

Immediate Window

The Immediate window can be used to interact with the program and find more information about the values of the variables and contents of the objects. We can type in commands and get results directly. A screenshot of an Immediate window is shown below. As you can see, the `Me` object's properties, such as its name, width, and text are queried and the output is received immediately in the window.

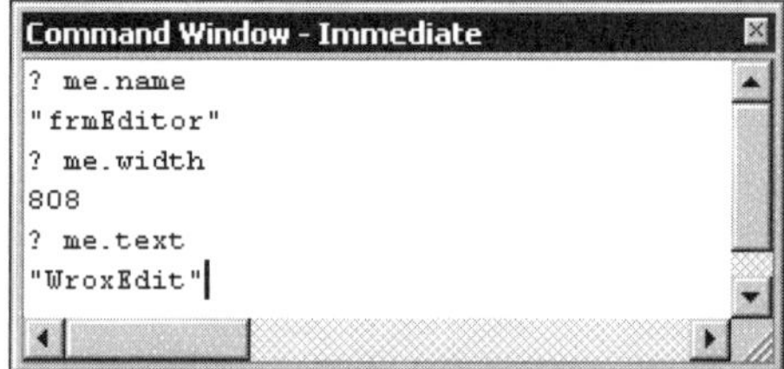

Now that we have an idea of all the different information available to us while debugging our application, we will move on to see how to attach our Windows Forms application to a running process.

Attach the Debugger to a Running Process

As we mentioned in the 'What's New' section of this chapter, we can attach to a running application, which is running outside of the Visual Studio.NET IDE by attaching to its process. This allows us to debug an application, that wasn't created in VS.NET, while it is executing. We can debug multiple applications that are running, debug applications running on remote computers, debug DLL files, and have the debugger start when an application crashes outside of the IDE.

To attach to a running program, we must follow these steps:

- With the IDE open, select the Processes option from the Debug menu. It should look something like the screenshot to the right:

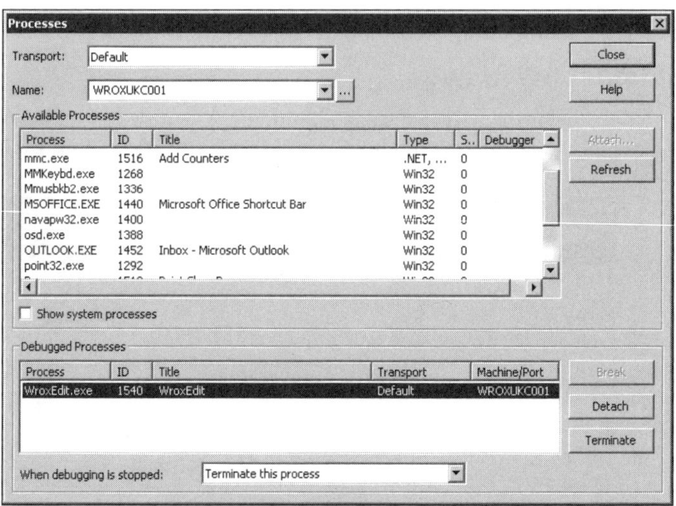

- Find the program we want to attach to, and select it.
- Click the Attach button.
- In the Attach to Process dialog that is displayed, select the process that you want to attach to and click the OK button. The process can be an application created by non-VS.NET languages. We should now see the process added to the Debugged Processes list at the bottom of the Processes window.
- Note the drop-down box at the very bottom of the Processes window. We can choose one of two possible actions to take when the debugger is stopped. We can either terminate the process, or detach our application from the process and leave the process running.

Handling Exceptions

Exceptions are errors that occur when the application is executing. As an example of an exception, comment out the line in our `WroxEdit` application in the Edit | Preferences menu that assigns the value returned from the input dialog to the `strInputName` variable as shown here.

```
If dlg.DialogResult = DialogResult.OK Then
' strInputName = dlg.txtName.Text
Dim rk As RegistryKey = _
Registry.LocalMachine.OpenSubKey("Software", True)
```

Run the application and try to set the user name. When we close the dialog by clicking OK, we will receive an exception error and a message box will appear informing us of this, as shown below:

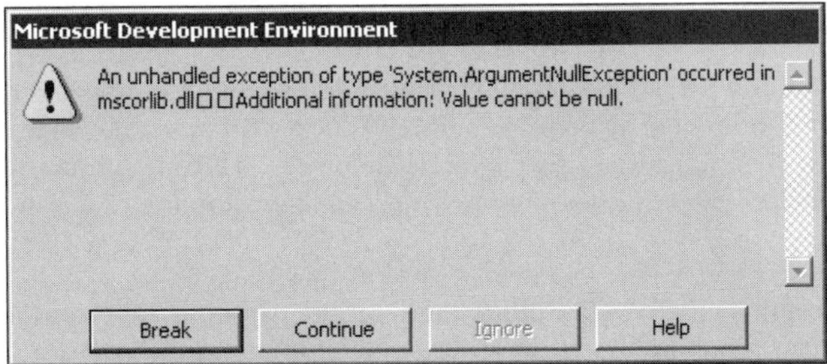

We are given two options on this message box. We can Break or Continue. Clicking Break will place the application in Break mode allowing us to research the error and check the state of variables. We cannot make any changes to code in this state. We must stop the debugger before doing so.

We can set the default behavior when an exception occurs in our application during debugging by choosing the Exceptions menu option from the Debug menu. This will present the following dialog box as shown overleaf:

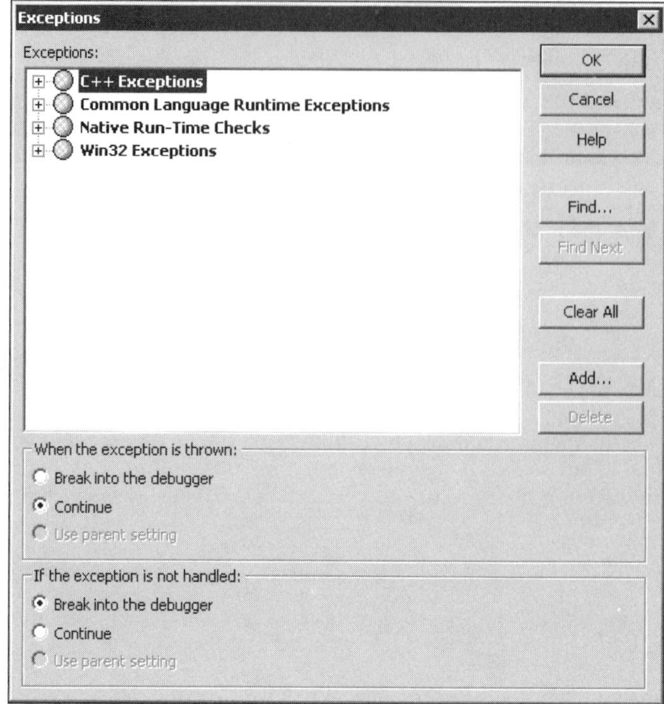

From here we can make choices based on the type of exceptions, but what we are really interested in is the default behavior located in the lower two sections of this dialog.

We can make choices for when an exception is thrown and when an unhandled exception is thrown. An unhandled exception is one that has no error handling code written to take appropriate action. We can either choose to have the application break into the debugger, which is similar to pressing the Break button on the error message box, or we can have the debugger stop the application by choosing the Continue option.

We can also add exceptions that are not present and set the default actions for those exceptions. As an example, let's take the exception that we have just created in our application, `System.ArgumentNullException`. This is not a part of the exception list, so we want to add it. Follow these steps to add the exception:

- Open the Exceptions dialog.
- Highlight the Common Language Runtime Exceptions category.
- Click the Add button and add `System.ArgumentNullException` in the textbox.
- Click the OK button.
- Expand the Common Language Runtime Exceptions category. We will also have to expand the System sub category.
- Highlight the newly added entry and change the two options for handling the exception to Continue.
- Click OK to close the dialog.

Run the application again and cause the same exception to be thrown. This time, the program automatically enters Continue mode.

To delete any exceptions that we have added, open the Exceptions dialog and select the added exception. Click the Delete button to remove the exception from the list. Choose the Clear All button to remove all user-added exceptions.

While the above method is useful, the standard way to handle exceptions is using the structured Try-Catch-Finally method of error handling.

Optimization and Run-Time Profiling

Optimizing is the process that programmers follow to ensure that they have the fastest and smallest possible assembly (Exe or Dll). This is achieved by following best coding practices as well as with the help of the VS.NET compiler itself.

The VS.NET compiler optimizes code as necessary. We can set the optimization request to the compiler in the properties window of the project as shown below:

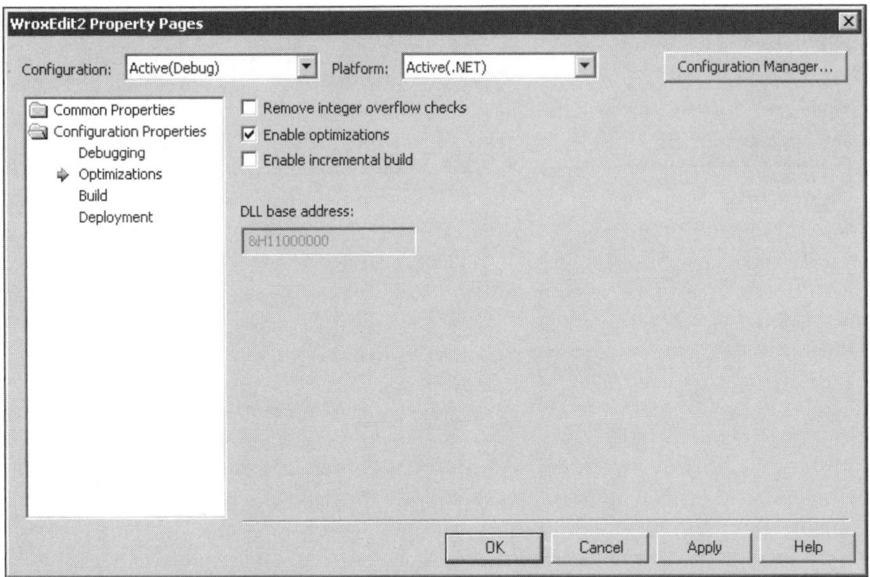

An important fact to remember when using optimization is that the debugging techniques may no longer work as we originally intended. The reason for this is that, during optimization, portions of code may be altered or removed altogether. We must test optimizations thoroughly if we have included trace-debugging options in our application.

Some developers prefer to optimize their code as they write it by following good coding practices. This involves steps such as ensuring that all variables are declared using the proper data types, using local variables and avoiding global variables whenever possible, using object variables with known class types, and using the data gathered about the application's performance from the performance counters.

Good coding practice and forethought given to optimization will produce the fastest code with the smallest memory footprint. In the following sections, we will see how to profile our Windows Forms application and gather statistics about the performance of the application.

Runtime Profiling

This concept deals with the monitoring of how our application performs as it is running in a production environment. There are a couple of tools available for us to use when profiling our application. These include the system monitor utility included in Windows NT/2000, known as `perfmon.exe` and the .NET performance counters API and the TaskManager.

`perfmon` is a system monitoring tool that can be invoked from the ControlPanel | Administrative Tools section in Windows 2000. This tool is helpful in determining the performance of applications. PerfMon can be started by typing:

```
C:\test> perfmon
```

at the command prompt, or at the Run option on the Start menu. The Performance monitoring utility is shown below:

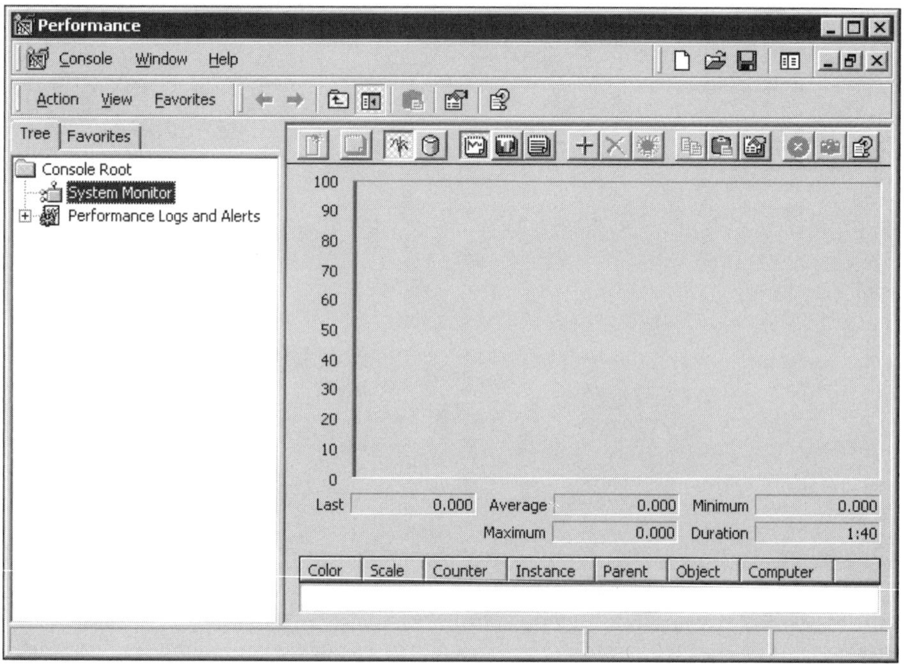

Notice that this utility offers us the choice of watching the performance from a graph, or from log files. We will concentrate on the graph portion for this explanation. To monitor the performance of our application, we need to add performance counters to the graph. Follow this procedure to add counters. The available counters will be discussed in the following sections.

- Open the `perfmon` utility if it is not already running.

- In the button bar above the graph window, select the Add button (addition symbol). The Add Counters dialog is displayed as shown here:

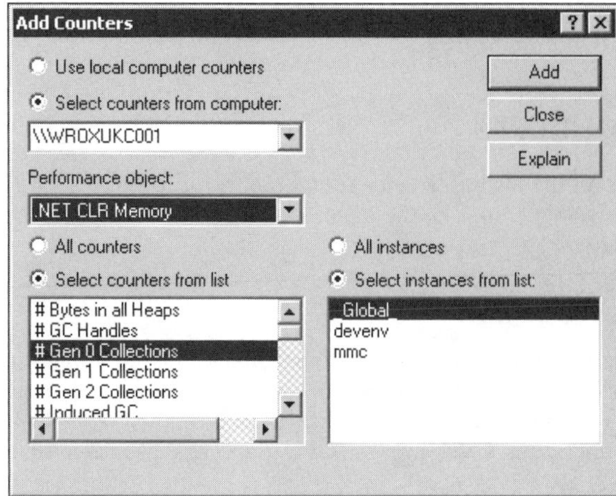

The meanings of the some of the counters will be discussed later in the chapter. We can also see an explanation of any counter by clicking on the Explain button and then selecting a counter.

Choose a counter, along with an instance, if any, and click Add. This will add the counter to the graph and we can view how that counter reacts as our application is running.

There are counters specifically for .NET within the list as well as the normal counters for CPU and memory resources. We can use a combination of these counters to monitor various aspects of our application. We don't necessarily have to choose all .NET counters either – the generic counters will provide performance information as well.

We have also looked at a Windows Forms component that can be used to monitor performance in Chapter 11 on components.

Monitoring Performance

As we have seen in the preceding section on Runtime Profiling, we can make use of the `perfmon` utility to monitor our application's performance. In this section we will take a look at some of the concepts involved in monitoring, such as the performance thresholds and counters. We will discuss what some of the counters are, and how we can manage them.

Performance Thresholds

When it comes to working with applications in the Windows environment, there is considerably more overhead than used to exist in the world of the DOS environment. This is mostly due to the requirements for the graphical aspects of applications in Windows. The handling of the graphical information for the purposes of painting the windows, 3D effects such as button clicks, and other aspects of the Windows GUI cause a considerable amount of data traffic within the computer in terms of messages. Windows uses messages to communicate with the program, RAM, and CPU within the computer to determine the state of windows and objects within those windows.

Performance is an issue for any program and after we have developed ours, we can begin to monitor its effects on the Windows environment, by monitoring performance counters as our application is running. We do this through the use of the performance counters and the `perfmon` utility. The next section will look at some available counters that we can add to the graph in `perfmon`, to watch how system resources react to our application.

Performance Counters

We can't possibly cover all the available counters that exist for use in the `perfmon` utility in one chapter, but we will mention a couple of the most important ones that we can use as we monitor our application's performance.

Processor, % Processor Time

This counter can be used to determine how much of the CPU's time our application takes as it executes and as we perform various tasks associated with the application. Add this counter to the graph and then start the `WroxEdit` application. Take a look at where the CPU usage is on the graph. Type in some characters in the textbox, or set the preferences, and watch how the CPU graph changes based on our actions.

Memory, Available MB

We can use the memory counters to see what effect our application has on available memory in the computer. We can add the counter and monitor the available memory before starting our application, and then see how it changes as we start and use the application. This can give us an idea of the memory footprint for the application.

These are two of the more popular counters that we can use, although there are numerous counters for each category. There are also some .NET counters available that allow us to monitor certain aspects in the .NET category.

The first category in the list is the .NET Exceptions. This category includes counters for exceptions thrown, exceptions thrown per second, filters per second, etc. For an explanation of each counter, highlight it and choose the Explain button.

The next category is the .NET CLR Interop category. This category includes counters for dealing with wrappers in COM objects, marshaling of arguments and return values, as well as type library imports and exports.

We can also add counters from the JIT category, which deals with operations specific to the Just In Time Compiler. The CLR Loading category deals with counters pertaining to the loading of our application and its behavior during loading.

We can also include counters for multi-threaded applications as well as counters specific to .NET memory allocation. The final two categories deal with counters relating to security and remote applications. We can use counters to help us to determine where we might apply some manual optimizations or change code to create faster execution.We can also use the tried and tested TaskManager. It gives good information about the processes that are running in the sytem and also gives information about memory and CPU consumption. Using the data gathered from these tools, we can optimize our application and produce the smallest and fastest code.

Summary

We started out by learning the debugging features in VS.NET and the different debug windows that are available to us while we program for the .NET program. We also saw how to profile our application and how to turn on the optimization feature in the compiler. The amount of debugging features available could actually warrant a book of its own, but hopefully the information presented will help in understanding the various features available while debugging and optimizing our code.

Legend: Concrete Class / Abstract class

System.Windows.Forms

- System.Object
  - System.MarshalRefObject
    - System.ComponentMode.Component
      - CommonDialog
        - ColorDialog
        - FileDialog
        - FontDialog
        - PageSetupDialog
        - PrintDialog
      - ErrorProvider
      - HelpProvider
      - ImageList
      - Menu
        - ContextMenu
        - MainMenu
        - MenuItem
      - NotifyIcon
      - StatusBarPanel
      - Timer
      - ToolBarButton
      - ToolTip
      - Control
        - ButtonBase
          - Button
          - CheckBox
          - RadioButton
        - DataGrid
        - DateTimePicker
        - GroupBox
        - Label
          - LinkLabel
        - ListControl
          - ComboBox
          - ListBox
            - CheckedListBox
        - ListView
        - MonthCalendar
        - PictureBox
        - PrintReviewControl
        - ProgressBar
        - ScrollableControl
          - ContainerControl
            - Form
              - PrintPreviewDialog
              - ThreadExceptionDialog
            - PropertyGrid
            - UpDownBase
              - DomainUpDown
              - NumericUpDown
            - UserControl
          - Panel
            - TabPage
        - ScrollBar
          - HScrollBar
          - VScrollBar
        - Splitter
        - StatusBar
        - TabControl
        - TextBoxBase
          - RichTextBox
          - Textbox
        - ToolBar
        - TrackBar
        - TreeView
  - ListViewItem
  - TreeNode

15

Packaging and Deployment

So far, we have seen how to create a Windows Forms application, compile, debug, and execute it. Now, it is time to package and deploy it in the target machines. In this chapter, we will cover the following topics:

- A brief overview of Windows Installer Technology and MSI (Microsoft Installer) package file
- How to use VS.NET to package and deploy a Windows Forms application

The Packaging and Deployment Process

We would typically develop a Windows Forms application in our development machine, which normally would be running Windows NT, Windows 2000 Professional, or Windows XP Professional. After testing the application on our development machine, we will need to package it and then deploy it. Since Windows Forms is a presentation layer tool, we will most probably deploy it in the user's machine, which can be running any of the Windows Operating System Versions (95/98/Me/NT/2000/XP etc.). If our Windows Forms application is used to configure a server application, then we will probably be deploying it on an NT/2000 Server.

The packaging and deployment process can be conceptually described using the following process:

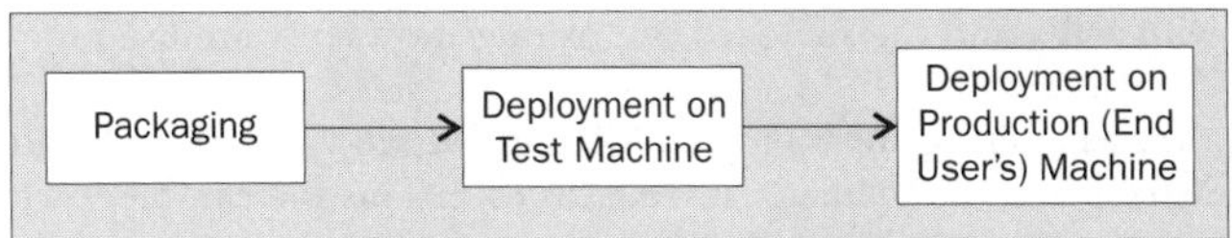

Packaging and deployment can be a complex subject, depending upon the number and types of components that are being deployed. Since this book specifically focuses on Windows Forms applications, this chapter will also focus on packaging and deployment from a Windows Forms application point of view.

Packaging

We can package a Windows Forms application in several ways, the most common being:

- Microsoft installer files (`.msi` files)
- Cab files for internet download (`.cab` files)
- Self extracting executable file (`.exe` files)

Tools available for packaging are:

- VS.NET, which uses the Windows Installer technology to create Microsoft Installer files
- Third party tools such as Installshield

It should be noted that, while Windows Installer technology is the preferred method of packaging.NET code, it is still possible to use the pre .NET methods of packaging, using non-Windows Installer technology.

Deployment

Deployment means installing all the components of an application from the package to the appropriate locations in the target machines. When deployment of a package is complete, its component files will have been copied to the application directory, shortcuts created on the desktop, program groups created in the start/programs menu, entries added to the registry if necessary, and so on.

A Windows Forms application can be deployed in several ways:

- Running the setup program, which will deploy the packaged components in the target machine
- Using the Internet to download and deploy the cab package
- Copying the files to the intended destination folders using `XCOPY`
- Using System Management Server to deploy the application to several target machines

Before looking at the specific features that Visual Studio .NET provides for this purpose, let's discuss some general issues regarding package and deployment.

Windows Installer

Windows Installer technology was introduced with Windows 2000 Server and, for the foreseeable future, all Microsoft software will be packaged using this installation technology. This installation technology is different from previous installation technologies such as the package and deployment wizard that comes with VB6, and the standard setups that most software used for deployment.

Windows Installer runs as a service in Windows NT and Windows 2000. In Windows 95 and 98 we can install it using a redistributable file named `instmsia.exe`. This file can be downloaded from MSDN, through http://msdn.microsoft.com/downloads/.

Once this file is installed in Win 95 and 98 machines, they will be ready to accept Windows Installer setup files, which have the `.msi` file extension.

The screenshot below shows the context menu that would appear if we right-click on an `msi` file:

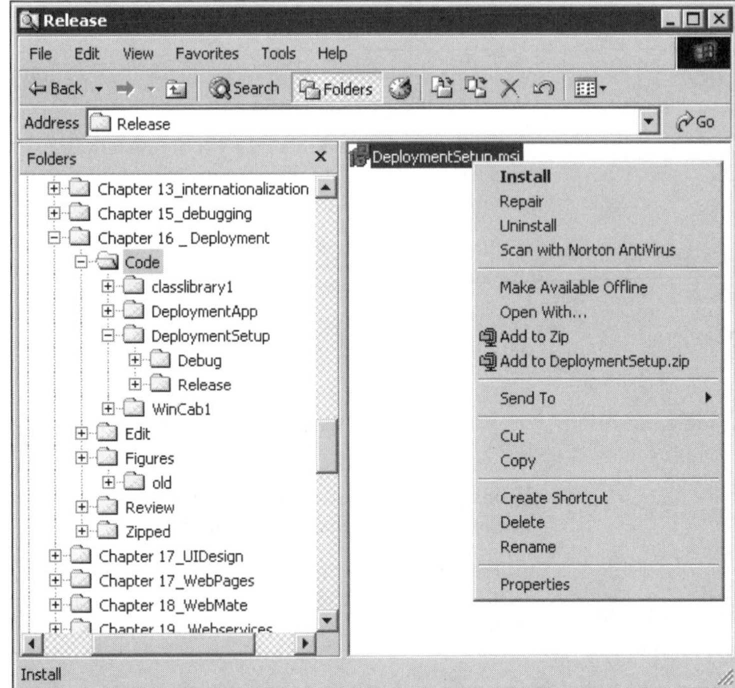

Windows Installer manages the installation and removal of applications by applying a set of centrally defined setup rules during the installation process. These setup rules control the installation and configuration of a new application. This service is used to modify, repair, or remove an existing application. The Windows Installer technology consists of the Windows Installer service for the Windows operating systems, and the package file format used to hold information regarding the application setup and installations. The `msi` file itself can be thought of as a database which keeps track of all the components, the rules that describe how and when they should be installed, and so on.

Installation Package File '.msi'

The `msi` package file is a relational database that stores all the instructions and data required to install (and uninstall) the program for several installation scenarios. For example, a package file could contain instructions for installing an application when a prior version of the application is already installed on the target machine. The package file could also contain instructions for installing the software on a computer where a previous version of that application has not been installed before. The package file may contain instructions for installing software for typical, standard, and custom installations.

Because the database is relational and installation events are stored in the `msi` database itself, changes made to one table are cascaded automatically throughout the database. This is a very efficient process for introducing consistent changes into the installation process and it simplifies customizing a large application or group of applications.

The following table describes the groups of related tables inside the `msi` package file:

Group	Description
Core table	Contains the features and components of the application and installer package.
File table	Contains the files associated with the installation package. Application files, resource files, and dependency files are all stored here.
Registry table	Contains the registry entries that need to be installed in the target.
System table	Tracks the tables and columns of the installation database.
Locator table	Used to search the registry, installer configuration data, directory tree, or `.ini` files for the unique signature of a file.
Program installation	Holds properties, bitmaps, shortcuts, and other elements needed for the application installation.
Installation procedure	Stores the information needed to manage the tasks performed during the installation by standard actions and custom actions.

Windows Installer is capable of performing a wide variety of tasks to handle various packaging and deployment scenarios. The following are some of the salient features of windows installer:

- **Restore to Original State**: Windows Installer keeps track of all changes made to the system during the application installation process. If the installation fails, Windows Installer can restore, or **roll back**, the system to its initial state. Since the `msi` package file itself is based on a relational database, the commit and rollback feature of database transactions is being applied to installation and removal of components. This is a very powerful feature that will enable us to keep the user's machine in a clean and consistent state. We will notice that when installation fails, the installation progress bar will move in the opposite direction.
- **Prevent Application Conflicts**: Windows Installer enforces installation rules that help to prevent conflicts with shared resources between existing applications. Such conflicts can be caused when an install operation makes updates to a dynamic link library (`.dll`) shared by an existing application, or when an operation deletes a dynamic link library shared by another application. We can check if a certain file exists, and then based on the result install or uninstall specific components.
- **UnInstall programs**: Windows Installer can reliably uninstall any program it previously installed. It removes all the associated registry entries and application files, except for those shared by other installed software. We can uninstall an application at any time after a successful installation.
- **Repair corrupted applications**: If any corruption in files is detected, Windows Installer repairs the application by recopying only those files found to be missing or corrupted.

- **Advertising (On Demand Installation)**: Windows Installer can be programmed to initially install a subset of an application. Later, additional components can be automatically installed when a user accesses features that require those components for the first time. This is known as advertising (also known as install on first use, or install on demand). For example, Windows Installer could install Microsoft Excel with a minimal set of features. The first time the user tries to use statistical analysis functions, Windows Installer would automatically install the statistical analysis component. Similarly, Windows Installer can also purge components that go unused in an application. For example, Windows Installer could be configured to remove the mail merge component if it goes unused for 90 days.
- **Unattended Installation**: Installation packages can be configured to require no installation process interaction from the user. Or it can be configured to display a dialog showing that the installation has completed. We can completely control the level of user interaction that we need with the installation process.

Windows Installer can be invoked from the command prompt using the `msiexec` command and supplying parameters to it. For example, to install a program called `MyProgramSetup.msi`, just type:

```
C:\> msiexec /i MyProgramSetup.msi
```

To uninstall it, use:

```
C:\> msiexec /x MyProgramSetup.msi
```

Complete details on all the switches available for `msiexec` can be found in the Windows 2000 help file under the Windows Installer/command-line switches subtopic.

The above overview of Windows Installer technology was intended to highlight the salient features. Investing time to understand the technology and figure out how to use it in a minimal scenario, as well as in the most complex scenario, is highly recommended in order to avoid installation problems. This is a complex technology by itself and you should refer to the Windows Installer SDK for more detailed information on the internals of the technology.

Typically, third party tools provide a more robust, feature rich installation software tool that will hide the complex internals of the Windows Installer. They also expose features of Windows Installer that are typically not exposed by VS.NET. Third party tools create a `setup.exe` program that will use the `msi` package file, whereas VS.NET does not create the `setup.exe` file. Windows Installer technology will greatly help Desktop Administrators using System Management Server to install, repair, modify and uninstall applications in a controlled manner.

Package and Deployment Using VS.NET

Having covered the Windows Installer briefly, let us now look at how VS.NET handles packaging and deployment. So far in this chapter, packaging and deployment were separately discussed to highlight the differences between the two. In practice though, they are regarded as one integrated process. Once we package an application, it is ready to be installed. Once a package is installed, it is considered deployed.

VS.NET uses the Windows Installer technology to package .NET code and create `msi` files. VS.NET comes with several template projects to create a setup project. It also comes with a Setup wizard to get us started. The screenshot below shows the options available:

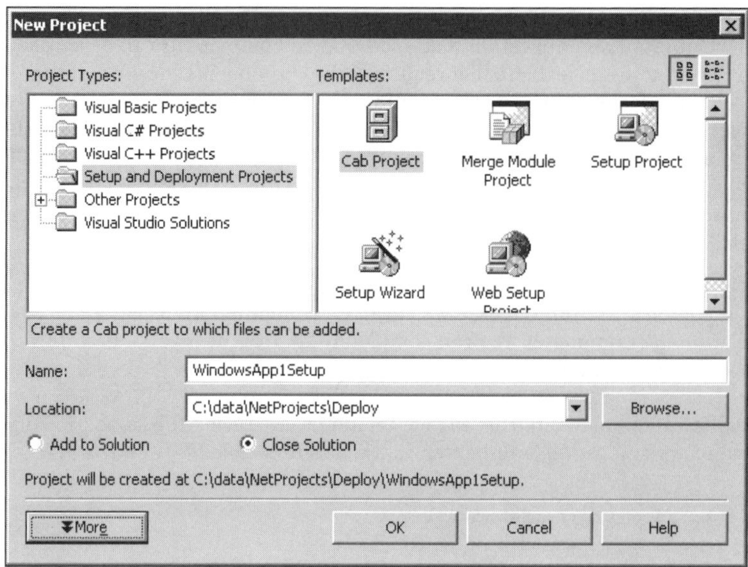

The following table is a brief description of the templates that are useful for a Windows Forms application:

Project Type	Purpose
Setup Project	Use this to create a setup program for our Windows Forms application.
Cab Project	Creates a cabinet file for downloading to a Web browser.
Setup Wizard	Will guide us in setting up a setup project quickly. We can customize it to add more files or exercise more control over our installation
Merge Module Project	Packages components that might be shared by multiple applications. For example, if our application consists of five utility files, then we can package those in a merge module project and incorporate them into any of our application installs.

Now let us consider packaging and deployment from a Windows Forms perspective only.

Packaging a Windows Forms Application

Most Windows Forms applications produce `exe` assemblies only. It is sufficient to deploy only the `exe` file, but they will also normally reference one or more custom class libraries. In this case the deployed application will not work without the class library. So, we need to package the `exe` and any referenced class library files, and then deploy the application. In .NET, unlike COM, class libraries are not registered in the registry so there is no need to run `regsvr32` on the class library. If we run the `regsvr32` on a .NET class library, we will not be able to register it and will get a "dll entry point not found" error message.

Remember that a project can have several configurations; the typical ones being Debug and Release. So, we can have a debug build and a release build of our Windows Forms application. Debug builds have extra debugging information in them and are not optimized for execution speed. Release builds are optimized for speed and don't have debugging information in them.

When the time comes to deploy, we may need to create a setup program for the release build to give to our testers. We may also want to have another setup program of our release build to give to select customers, but only show very limited features. Visual Studio will let us create two setup projects – one for the testers and one for the customers. Both these projects can reside alongside the Windows Forms project and all these projects can belong to one solution. This is a very useful way of organizing not only our projects, but also all the different setup and deployment scenarios associated with the Windows Forms project.

Let's run through a simple Windows Forms application, which makes calls to a managed dll, in order to demonstrate how to use the package and deployment projects that come with VS.NET.

- Open a new blank solution and name it `Deploy`.
- Under Project Types, select Visual Studio Solutions and click on Blank Solution.
- In the Name textbox, type 'Deploy' and choose the Location in which your `Deploy` folder will be created, as shown below. The Deploy folder will automatically contain the `Deploy.sln` solution file.

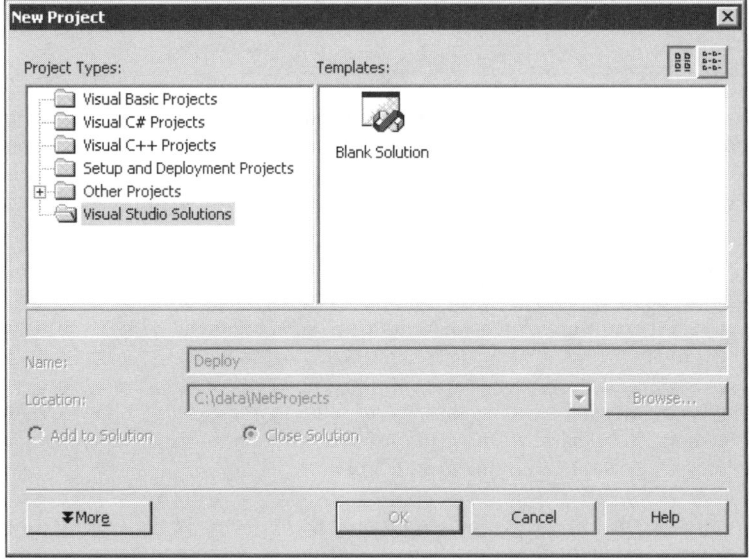

- Now add a `Class Library` solution by right-clicking on the solution and selecting Add Existing Project and selecting the `ClassLibrary1` project available from the Wrox site.
- Add the `DeploymentApp` VB.NET Windows Application project to this solution too.

At this point we should build the solution in order to make sure that both projects get built successfully. The following screenshot shows the output from the build. Note that the last line of the output window says "2 succeeded", and that the Debug configuration of the `DeploymentApp` and `ClassLibrary1` projects was built.

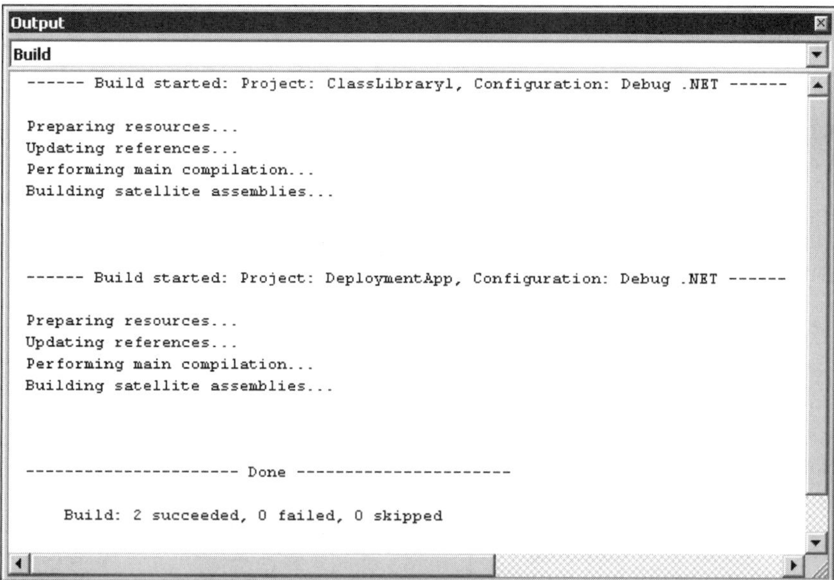
Output
Build
------ Build started: Project: ClassLibrary1, Configuration: Debug .NET ------
Preparing resources...
Updating references...
Performing main compilation...
Building satellite assemblies...
------ Build started: Project: DeploymentApp, Configuration: Debug .NET ------
Preparing resources...
Updating references...
Performing main compilation...
Building satellite assemblies...
---------------------- Done ----------------------
Build: 2 succeeded, 0 failed, 0 skipped

Now let's create a setup project. The setup project will package both the `DeploymentApp.exe` application and the `ClassLibrary1.dll` file and will create a setup program for installation on the user's machine.

- Add a new `Setup and Deployment` Project to our solution and select Setup Wizard.
- Name it '`DeploymentSetup`'. Note that this setup project will be created in ...`\Deploy\DeploymentSetup` folder.

A setup project wizard opens up, giving some basic information about what it will do. Click `Next` and move on to step 2 of 5.

In this step, the wizard asks us to choose the type of setup that we want. Choose 'Create a setup for a Windows application'. Note that this step also provides other options such as creating a CAB file for Internet download. Click Next and move to step 3 of 5.

In this step, we specify what files we want to package into our setup program. Since the setup project that we are creating is inside the `Deploy` solution, and since the solution has a `DeploymentApp` project and a `ClassLibrary1` project already in it, the wizard makes use of this information and provides a list of file groups that we will most likely need. In this case, the wizard lists the primary output from `DeploymentApp` project (which is `DeploymentApp.exe`), the primary output from `ClassLibrary1` (which is `ClassLibrary1.dll`), and other options such as source files and local resources. Select Primary output from DeploymentApp and Primary output from ClassLibrary1 as shown below:

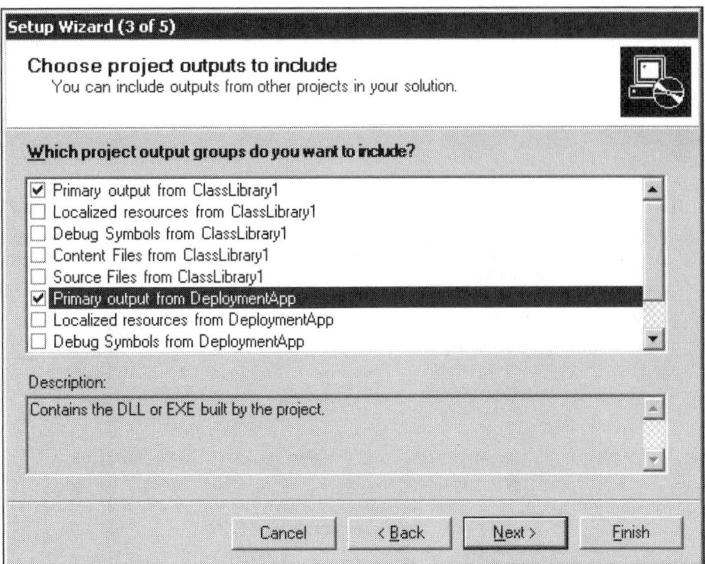

After clicking Next, the wizard gives us a chance to add additional files. We can include `Readme` files, a Frequently Asked Questions file, or any other file needed for our application here. Click Next and continue to the last step.

In step five (shown below), the wizard summarizes the options that we have chosen so far. Note carefully that the project groups chosen are listed and the name of the setup project and its location are also listed. Setup and deployment projects have a `.vdproj` (visual deployment project) file extension. Click Finish to let the wizard create the setup project.

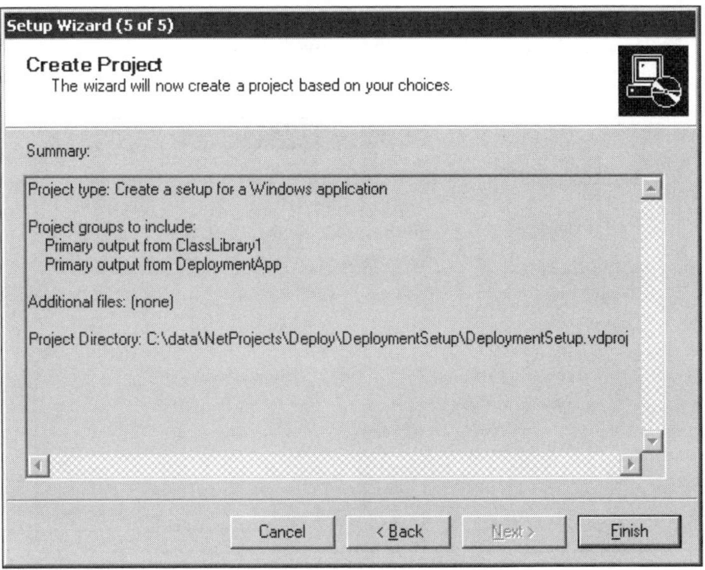

Now, as shown in the following screenshot, the `DeploymentSetup` project has been created inside the '`Deploy`' solution. The solution now has three projects, the `DeploymentApp` and `Classlibrary1` projects, and the `DeploymentSetup` project. Notice that the `DeploymentSetup` project also contains the primary output from `DeploymentApp` and `Classlibrary1`, which were the file groups that we supplied to the wizard.

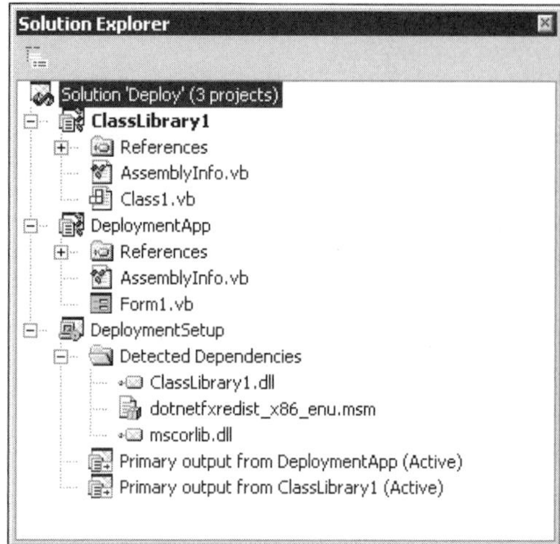

Remember that the wizard has only created the setup project till now, but has not built the project and created the setup installation file itself. Every project can have several configurations – the common ones being Debug and Release. Apart from each project having several configurations, the solution itself can have several configurations.

Set the active solution configuration to Release. To do this, go to the Build Menu and then Configuration Manager. In the configuration manager, select Release from the Active Solution Configuration dropdown and then make sure the individual project configurations are marked as release, as shown below:

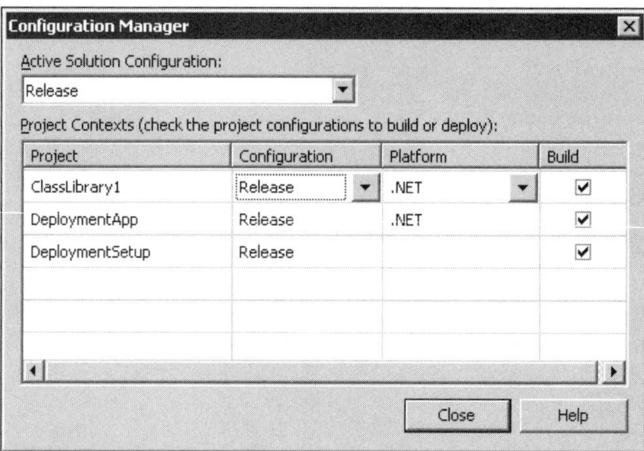

Build the setup project by right-clicking on the `DeploymentSetup` project node and choosing **Build**. We can choose **Rebuild** to incorporate the latest changes to our setup program. We don't have to build from scratch every time during the development stage, but it is a safe practice to build from scratch before final release. Note that building the setup project builds the Windows Forms and class library project as well as the setup project itself. This is because the `DeploymentSetup` project references the outputs of the Windows Forms and the class library projects. After the build is completed go to `...\Deploy\DeploymentSetup\Release` and we will find the `DeploymentSetup.msi` file. This is the package file that we will install in the target machine.

Deploying the 'DeploymentSetup' Setup

Now, let's deploy the package file to a target computer. For test purposes, we can deploy it to the same machine where we developed the `DeployApp` application.

Locate the `DeploymentSetup.msi` file in the `...\Deploy\DeploymentSetup\Release` folder, right-click on it and choose **Install** (or simply double-click on the `msi` file) – this will call up the Welcome screen shown here:

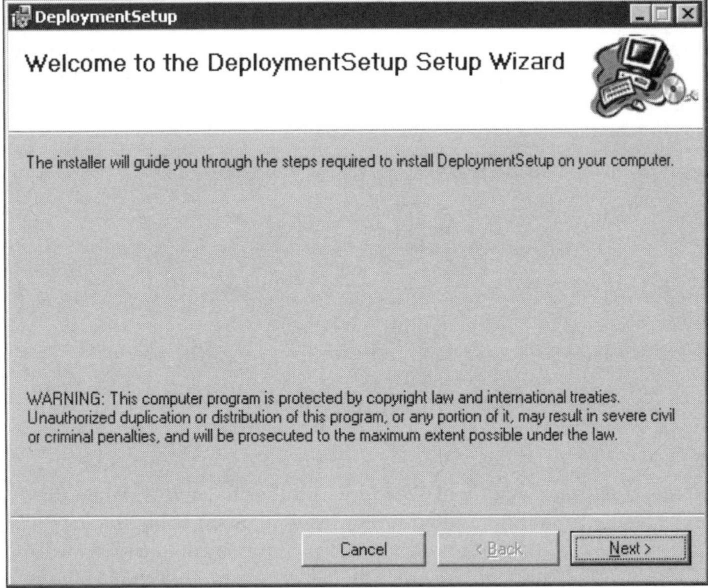

Click **Next**, and then provide the installation folder in which to install the application. After this, confirm the installation, and on the final screen we have the option to begin the installation process. After the installation is complete, we can go to the installation folder and view the `exe` and `dll` files. The screenshot overleaf shows the installed files:

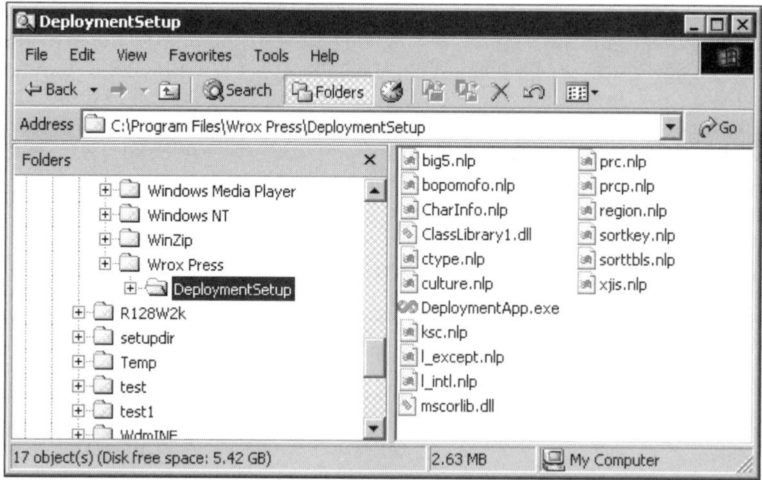

Remember, the deployment is successful only if the installed components run as intended and don't produce any runtime errors that are attributed to faulty installs. Run the program by double-clicking on the `DeploymentApp.exe` file and click on the buttons and verify it works – if it does we get presented with the following form:

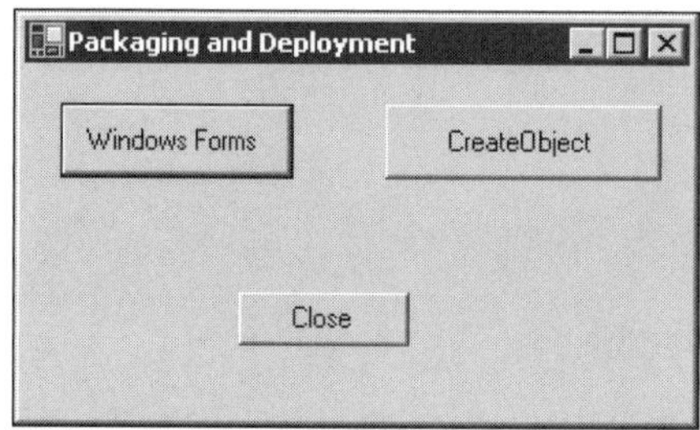

Repair

Now let's see the repairing functionality of Windows installer in action. Delete the `ClassLibrary1.dll` file from the installed folder (we will assume that the user has accidentally deleted the file). If we run the `DeploymentApp.exe` program again, an error will be generated when we click on the 'CreateObject' button. Now that the user has reported the problem to us, we don't have to run the installation again and install all the files again. We can just right-click on the `...\Deploy\DeploymentSetup\Release\DeploymentSetup.msi` file and choose Repair. After a few seconds, the missing file `Classlibrary1.dll` will be copied back to the correct folder.

In a corporate setting, the setup `msi` file may be in a CD-ROM or in a shared folder in the network. We can install it for the first time on the target machine by right-clicking on the setup `msi` file and choosing install or by double-clicking the `msi` file. We could also use System Management Server (SMS Server) to push the file to the user's desktop and install it for them remotely. After the install, the user's Add/Remove programs list in the control panel will have the entry for the application. Later when we want to uninstall or repair the application on a specific user's machine, we can locate the entry in the Control Panel | Add/Remove Programs list, choose the application and select Change, then Repair or Remove it.

Customizing the Installation

So far, we have seen how the setup wizard helps us to create a setup project quickly by asking us a few questions. There are, however, several other features in the setup project that the wizard does not expose to us. For example, adding a shortcut to the user's desktop, adding registry entries in the users machine, and others. After using the setup wizard and creating a `Setup` project, we can go back and customize it. By right-clicking on the `DeploymentSetup` project in the solution explorer and selecting the View menu, we can see several menu items for customizing the installation:

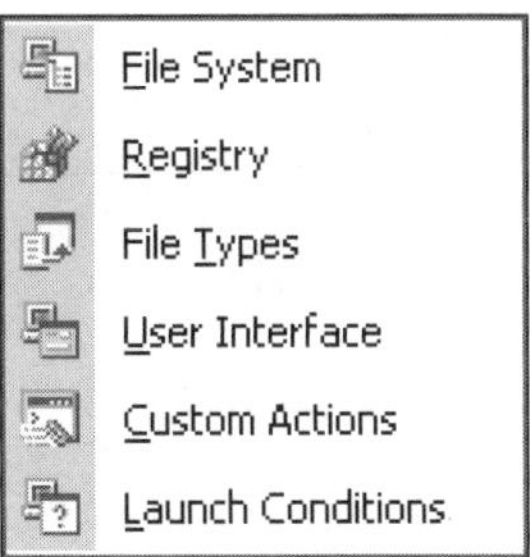

Each menu item will present us with an editor where we can customize the way the setup file will be packaged and deployed. For example, we can place shortcuts on the user's desktop using the File System editor, test whether a file already exists on a user's machine before beginning installation using the Launch Condition Editor, and so on. We will discuss some of the editors briefly and try out a few customizations to our `DeploymentSetup` project. We can also access these editors using View | Editor from the main menu on the top of the VS IDE.

File System Editor

The File System editor shows a snapshot of the file system on the target machine, as shown below:'

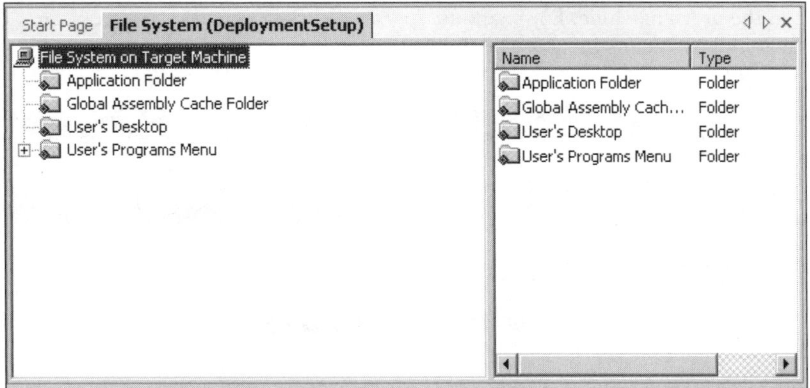

Let's customize our installation so that a shortcut to `DeploymentApp` is placed on the desktop, and also create a `DeploymentApp Program` group that contains the `DeploymentApp.exe` executable.

Right-click on the 'Primary output from DeploymentApp' list item on the right and select 'Create shortcut to primary output from DeploymentApp'. A shortcut will be created and will be listed in the Application Folder, which we can then rename to DeploymentApp.

Now let's create a program group in the user's start/programs menu. In the File System editor, select User's Programs Menu and select Add and then Folder. Rename the folder as `DeploymentApp` before going to the Application Folder. Then, copy the `DeploymentApp` shortcut to the `DeploymentApp` folder. Now create an additional shortcut for the output of `DeploymentApp` in the Applications folder.

After doing the above, we can build the setup project. Uninstall the previous version and then install the latest `DeploymentApp.msi` file. We can drag and drop the shortcut that is now present in the `DeploymetSetup` folder onto the desktop, and check to see that there is a `DeploymentApp` folder in the Start/Programs menu that also contains a shortcut to the `DeploymentApp` output.

Registry Editor

Right-click on the `DeploymentSetup` project and select View and then Registry. We will then be presented with several HKEY entries to which we can add entries. When we build the `Setup` project and run the installer, the registry entries will be added to the target machine. The screenshot below shows the registry editor:

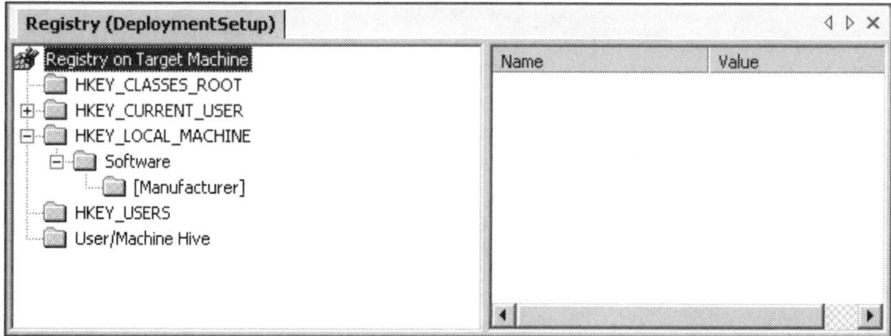

File Types Editor

If our application creates documents of a custom type, then we can associate that file type with our application in the user's machine. For example, we can associate `xyz` with `DeploymentApp` so that whenever files with extension `.xyz` are opened, an instance of `DeploymentApp` will be started and initialized with the `.xyz` file.

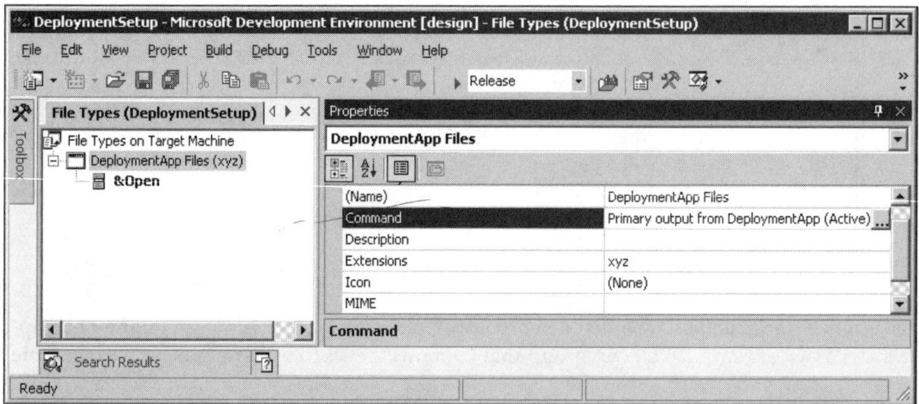

The above screenshot shows a file type `xyz` being associated with the primary output of `DeploymentApp`:

User Interface Editor

The User Interface Editor is used to customize the dialog boxes that are presented during the installation. It contains two sections: **Install** and **Administrative Install**. The Install section contains dialog boxes that will be displayed when the user runs the installer, and the Administrative section contains dialog boxes that will be displayed when a system administrator runs the installer.

By default a set of predefined dialog boxes are displayed in the editor. We can change the order in which the dialog boxes are shown, or even delete any or all of the dialog boxes. The types of dialog boxes that appear in a `Setup` project, by default, vary according to the project type. A Windows Forms application will have a different set of dialog boxes from a web application.

Predefined dialog boxes can be categorized as follows:

- Start dialog boxes are displayed before the installation begins. These dialog boxes are used to gather customer information or to allow the user to change the installation directory.
- A progress dialog box is displayed to provide feedback on the progress of an installation. It is during this stage that the files are copied to the target machine.
- End dialog boxes are displayed once the installation has finished successfully. Common uses are to notify the user that the installation is complete or to allow the user to launch the application.

Dialog boxes can be moved between category nodes via drag-and-drop or via the cut and paste commands on the Edit menu. We can also create our own custom dialog boxes and import them into the user interface editor. These custom dialog boxes must be created according to windows installer dialog specifications – and have the `.wid` file extension. Custom dialog boxes cannot be created using VS.NET. We need to use the Windows Installer SDK or third party tools to create them.

Adding Dialog Boxes

In the Start section of the Install tree, right-click and add the License Agreement dialog box. Move it up so that it appears after the Welcome dialog box. In the End section, add the Readme dialog and Register User dialog (screenshot below). Now build the `DeploymentSetup` project and run the `Setup` file.

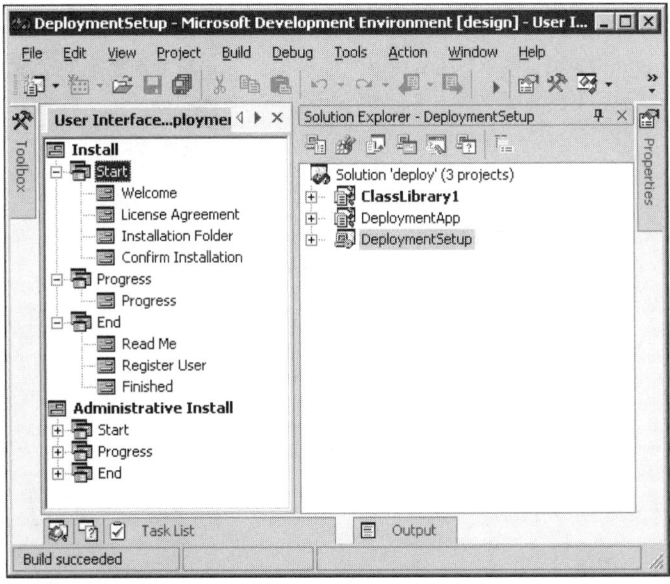

We will see the license dialog at the start of the installation, and the Readme file and Register User dialog box after the installation is complete. The installation itself happens during the progress section. Try experimenting with the various dialog boxes that come with VS.NET. Build and run the installation and notice the appearance of the License, Readme, and Register dialogs.

Launch Conditions

The Launch Conditions Editor allows us to specify conditions that must be met in order to successfully run an installation. For example, we might want to check for a specific version of an operating system – if a user attempts to install on a system that doesn't meet the condition, the installation will not occur.

Searches can be performed on a target computer to determine if a particular file, registry key, or Microsoft Windows Installer component exists. We can add a condition to check if the target operation system is Windows 95 or not and then proceed or stop the installation. Searches and conditional evaluations are performed at the beginning of an installation and are performed in the order that they are shown in the Launch Conditions Editor.

In the Launch Condition editor, under the Launch Conditions folder, add a new condition and name it `CheckNT`. The condition 'VersionNT >=500' will return `False` on a non-windows 2000 computer. In the property of `CheckNT`, select Condition and type 'VersionNT>=500' and in Message property type 'DeploymentApp is supported on Windows 2000 and later versions only'.

Now, if the project is run on a non-Windows 2000 computer. We will see a dialog box containing our error message, and the installation will abort.

There are several other launch predefined launch conditions in Windows Installer apart from VersionNT, such as Computer Name, Logon User, etc. Refer to the VS.NET documentation for more information on these and other launch conditions.

Packaging and Deploying Using CAB Files

In the beginning of this chapter, CAB files were listed as one of the options for packaging a Windows Forms application. We can package our files as CAB files and deploy them using Internet Explorer. Let's package the `DeploymentApp.exe` and `ClassLibrary1.dll` file in a CAB file.

In the `Deploy` Solution, add a new Setup and Deployment CAB Project, and specify the CAB project name as `DeploymentCab`.

In the solution explorer, right-click on the `DeploymentCAB` project node and select Add | Project Output. We will be presented with a window similar to the one shown below. From the Project combo box, select `DeploymentApp` project and then select Primary Output:

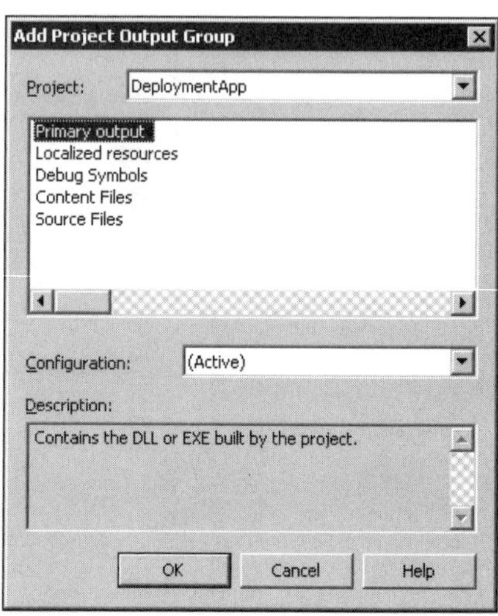

Repeat this step again, this time selecting the `ClassLibrary1` project and its primary output. Our solution explorer should look like the one shown in the following screenshot:

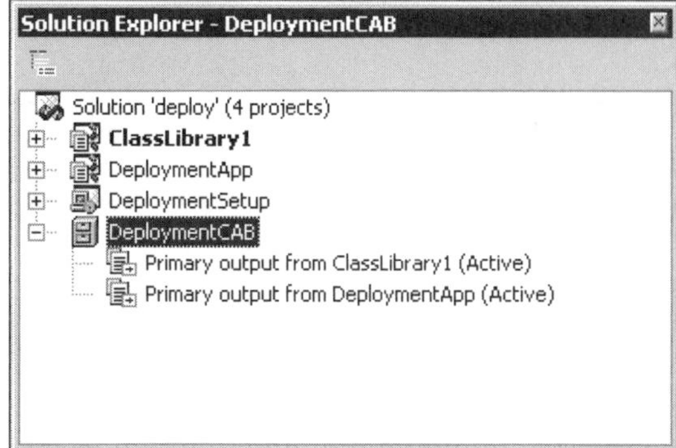

Now build the `DeploymentCAB` project and go to …\Deploy\DeploymentCAB and we should see the `DeploymentCAB.CAB` file. We can view the contents of the cab file using the `Expand` command with the `-d` parameter from the command prompt. The following screenshot shows the contents of the `DeploymentCAB` cab file using the `Expand` command:

This cab file can be downloaded to a client machine using a browser by referencing it in a web page.

Packaging and Deploying using Self Extracting Executable Files

VS.NET does not provide a feature by which we could wrap all the files that we need into a self-extracting file. Self-extracting files are used only on rare occasions for convenience. For example, the Windows Installer runtime files for Windows 95/98 are redistributed in a self-extracting file. Third party tools provide support for creating self-extracting files. While they are convenient to distribute patches, they don't afford control over the installation itself.

Deploying Using 'XCOPY'

XCOPY is a DOS command, and is an extended version of the COPY command. It can copy folders and create subfolders if they do not exist already in the target drive or machine.

Windows Forms applications and VS.NET applications can be deployed using XCOPY for quick installation to satisfy informal installation scenarios. This is a very important improvement over the registry dependent deployment of COM components. VS.NET code, whether Windows Forms or Library Class code, does not register itself in the system registry. Versioning information is stored in the assemblies themselves.

For example:

```
C:\> XCOPY A:\ C:\DeploymentApp
```

will copy all the files in the root directory of the A drive to the DeploymentApp directory of the C drive. If the DeploymentApp directory does not exist, XCOPY will prompt us to see if we want to create it. It won't, however, copy any subdirectories of A:\.

If we want XCOPY to create subfolders for us, then we can say:

```
C:\> XCOPY A:\ C:\DeploymentApp /s /e
```

This will copy all the files from A:\ to C:\DeploymentApp. It will also copy all the subfolders and the files in A:\ to the C drive, as a result of the /s (subfolder) switch. Any empty folders under A:\ are also copied to the C drive because of the /e switch. If we do not want the empty folder to be copied, remove the /e switch. Typing:

```
C:\> help XCOPY
```

will give us more information on XCOPY switches.

Uninstalling Windows Forms Applications

Windows Forms applications can be uninstalled in several ways:

- Simply delete the application files and the application folder and we are done. Since Windows Forms applications (and .NET applications in general) do not depend on the registry, just deleting the files is itself a clean way of uninstalling an application. Of course, if the application has desktop shortcuts or registry entries, we need to manually find and delete those too.
- We can right-click on the msi file, and choose UnInstall. This will delete the files and remove the desktop shortcuts and any registry entries.
- Use the windows Add/Remove Programs.

Deploying Using the Command Line

We can use the devenv command line program to deploy a project. For example, the following command will deploy the DeploymentSetup project in the Deploy solution:

```
C:\> devenv "c:\data\NETProjects\Deploy\Deploy.sln" /deploy /project
DeploymentAppSetup
```

More detailed information on the devenv command line program can be found in the MSDN library.

Summary

We began with an overview of the packaging and deployment process. Then we reviewed the important features of Windows Installer technology. A setup project and a CAB project were created and built. We verified the setup programs by installing them. We also customized the installation by adding shortcuts to the desktop and programs menu, by adding more dialogs and establishing a launch condition. The XCOPY method of deployment was highlighted as a quick and informal method of installing programs.

Legend
- Concrete Class
- Abstract class

System.Windows.Forms

- System.Object
  - System.MarshalRefObject
    - System.ComponentMode.Component
      - CommonDialog
        - ColorDialog
        - FileDialog
        - FontDialog
        - PageSetupDialog
        - PrintDialog
      - ErrorProvider
      - HelpProvider
      - ImageList
      - Menu
        - ContextMenu
        - MainMenu
        - MenuItem
      - NotifyIcon
      - StatusBarPanel
      - Timer
      - ToolBarButton
      - ToolTip
      - Control
        - ButtonBase
          - Button
          - CheckBox
          - RadioButton
        - DataGrid
        - DateTimePicker
        - GroupBox
        - Label
          - LinkLabel
        - ListControl
          - ComboBox
          - ListBox
            - CheckedListBox
        - ListView
        - MonthCalendar
        - PictureBox
        - PrintReviewControl
        - ProgressBar
        - ScrollableControl
          - ContainerControl
            - Form
              - PrintPreviewDialog
              - ThreadExceptionDialog
            - PropertyGrid
            - UpDownBase
              - DomainUpDown
              - NumericUpDown
            - UserControl
          - Panel
            - TabPage
        - ScrollBar
          - HScrollBar
          - VScrollBar
        - Splitter
        - StatusBar
        - TabControl
        - TextBoxBase
          - RichTextBox
          - Textbox
        - ToolBar
        - TrackBar
        - TreeView
    - ListViewItem
    - TreeNode

16

Web Services and Windows Forms (with the SDK)

Microsoft has worked very hard to make Visual Studio a wonderful tool for working in the .NET framework. However, many of the developers migrating to .NET are from backgrounds that encourage coding skills that do not specifically depend on having such a wonderful IDE to make the job of development easier.

The first .NET Framework beta was released well in advance of the Visual Studio.NET tool set and gave early adopters a real jump-start in getting skilled up in the .NET tools of their choice. In addition to this, the plethora of ASP and Java coders who spend many an hour code crunching in Notepad felt this was an environment that they could work well in. While Visual Basic developers anxiously awaited the release of the new version of VB, and C++ developers deliberated over whether managed or unmanaged C++ code was the option they wanted, the early adopters plugged away trying to find the treasures that existed in the Framework SDK. It quickly became apparent that some of the new tools in the Microsoft.NET framework were very appealing indeed, regardless of whether we were going to use Visual Studio or not.

This chapter will concentrate on getting access to Web Services inside a Windows Form without using the Visual Studio environment. We will only be using the Microsoft.NET Framework SDK, so a copy of the Microsoft.NET SDK will be needed to test any code examples. Don't forget to install the documentation, as it is invaluable. The SDK download ZIP can be found at http://msdn.microsoft.com/downloads.

Over the course of this chapter, we'll cover:

- What a Web Service is
- The Microsoft.NET Compilers

- How to hand code a Web Service that can be consumed by multiple clients
- Testing the Web Service
- Consuming a Web Service within a hand coded ASP.NET based application
- Consuming a Web Service within a hand coded Windows Forms based application
- Consuming a Web Service with the new HTTP classes – a variation on the Windows Form example

Before we begin with coding our example, we need to know something about what a Web Service actually is in the .NET framework. Let's have a quick overview.

What is a Web Service?

As we saw in Chapter 1, on top of the .NET services framework sit two application models: the Windows application model (Windows Forms) and the Web application model (Web Forms). Web Services sit alongside these application models in the ASP.NET application layer, but are independent of them. Most people (with good reason) think of Web Services as a purely web-based application tool set to be utilized by ASP.NET applications. This is the obvious place for them to fit, and they do fit there very well. Within the framework, however, Web Services are such a core element of the .NET Framework that they can also be used to enhance Windows Forms applications. Both can make use of remote functionality to complement their own application models.

Web Services offer a direct means for applications to interact with other web-based applications, because they are part of the ASP.NET application layer. We often hear them referred to as XML Web Services because they are usually based on XML. This was a conscious design decision by Microsoft because XML is text, and text can easily be passed through firewalls. This makes XML useful for working with data on the web. A Web Service is like a remote method (or set of methods) that can be accessed by any type of client that can handle the required inputs and return types. It can be thought of as somewhat similar to a DLL of methods that can be accessed remotely, a lot like DCOM (Distributed COM), or Java RMI (Remote Method Invocation). At a conceptual level, developers still integrate this business logic into applications by calling APIs. The difference is that these calls can be routed across the Internet to a service residing on a remote system, or routed locally around a network allowing grids of interconnected services to exist.

Developers can create a Web Service with ASP.NET by creating a file and saving it with an `.asmx` file extension. It can then simply be deployed as part of a web application, and is available as a Web Service.

Ordinary class methods are exposed as Web Service methods by marking them with the `[WebMethod]` attribute as shown below, and declaring them as public:

```
<%@ WebService Language="C#" Class="CheckService" %>

using System;
using System.Web.Services;
using System.Web.Util;

public class CheckService : WebService {
  [WebMethod] public String IntToWords(int inValue){
    return inValue.ToString();
  }
}
```

These specially marked methods can be invoked remotely by sending HTTP GET, HTTP POST or SOAP (Simple Object Access Protocol) requests to the URL of the .asmx file. Those interested in a comprehensive overview of SOAP can visit http://msdn.microsoft.com/msdnmag/issues/0800/webservice/webservice.asp.

The ASP.NET Web Services model by default assumes what is called a **stateless architecture**, and that is how we should view the results returned when invoking the methods of a Web Service. Web Services do not work like traditional executable programs do. They should be looked at as distinctly separate remote modules of business logic. We should not expect to make a call to a database via a Web Service and have the values returned from the database persisted between calls. We should instead pass the Web Service all of the information it requires to perform the task it has been designated to do, gathering the information required in our application, before invoking the Web Service.

Developers should design with this in mind, as stateless architectures are usually more scalable than stateful architectures. This is because the overhead of maintaining state on the server is avoided and there is less contention for limited resources. With Web Services, a new webmethod object is created each time a service request is received, the request is converted into a method call, and the object is destroyed once the method call returns. This maintains maximum efficiency on the Web Services Web Server. If a developer must add state to a Web Service, then he or she can use the ASP.NET State Management services to maintain state across requests. It is suggested that the reader refer to the documentation for information about this.

Web Services based on ASP.NET run in the Web application model, and as a result of this they obtain all of the security, deployment, and other benefits of that model. Applications that we develop will come to rely on the Web Services that we provide, and the more we integrate our services with the underlying model, the more complex our Web Services will become. It is critical that these services are completely dependable and always available. They should not (as far as is humanly possible) make mistakes, lose requests or corrupt data. Therefore testing by the developer should be carried out with vigor.

As this chapter will demonstrate, Windows Forms, Web Forms, and Web Services can be developed without the need for Visual Studio by using tools as simple as Notepad. We will, however, need to use one of the .NET compilers to compile our Windows Forms and to also compile a **proxy file**, which we'll discuss in detail later. We normally need to create a proxy file to access a Web Service (although we'll demonstrate a method of accessing Web Services without one later). With this in mind, it is important to spend a little time gaining a better understanding of the options available to the compiler. Refer to Chapter 2 for a list of the options.

While everything in this chapter will be developed locally, the principle for using remote and local Web Services is the same. Before we go ahead and use a Web Service though, we need to learn how to create one.

Creating a Web Service

In this section, we will create a Web Service with a real life objective. While it will not be fully functional, it will be capable of demonstrating how both Windows Forms and Web Forms clients can utilize a single Web Service without requiring any additional work to cater for both client types.

Creating a Web Service is no different from writing any other .NET class file with the exception of two things. Firstly, we must add a Web Service page directive to the top of the ASMX file, identifying the class name and the page language as follows:

```
<%@ WebService Language="C#" Class="CheckService" %>
```

> **Web Services are similar to `.aspx` pages but they have the extension `.asmx`. Like `.aspx` pages, they are automatically compiled when they are requested.**

Secondly, we must remember to define the methods that are available to be called as public Web Methods with the `WebMethod` attribute as follows:

```
[WebMethod] public String IntToWords(String inValue){
```

In this instance, we have added the `WebMethod` attribute to the method `IntToWords`.

Before that however, we will need to add a web application to our web server for the services application. It helps if you are familiar with the Internet Service Manager for your Windows version at this stage. For the purposes of this chapter, we have used Windows 2000 Advanced Server so the screenshots may not suit your particular version. If that is the case please refer to your web server documentation.

Start by creating a directory called `services` under the `inetpub\wwwroot` directory, and then open the Internet Service Manager. Navigate down the default tree to the directory called `services`, select action/properties, and then click create. Finally, name the application `services`. The Internet Services Manager should now look similar to that shown below. If your defaults don't match the screenshot you should change them to fit. Simply click OK and your web application should be created.

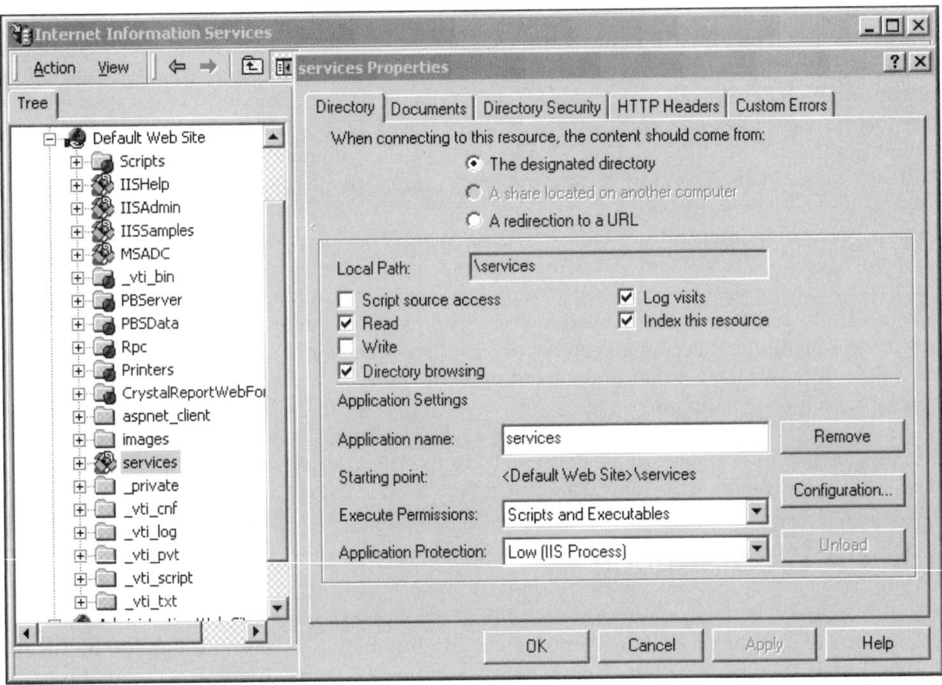

Now that we have a web application, we are going to create a credit card payment service that will be used by two fictitious companies to clear their credit card payments via a single banking service available from Wrox Bank. The Bank has two customers who have signed up to their new service:

- Craddocks Cosmetics: A trendy cosmetic and make up shop.
- Timney Trousers: A popular high street tailor with a comprehensive online shop.

Both have new computerized facilities based on .NET that allow the Wrox Bank to accept Credit Card payments on their behalf and manage their accounts for them. They have moved on from processing their own payments, and now rely on the new Wrox Bank payment service to manage their Credit Card transactions for them. With this approach, they have reduced their operational costs by outsourcing this expensive service to the Bank. Of course, this is a fictional scenario but it should allow us to see how flexible Web Services could be when used in a real business scenario.

The Web Service

The Web Service contains a single remote `WebMethod` interface called `clearCard`. It also contains a number of methods that have not been converted to `WebMethods`.

In the code example below, take notice of the following line:

```
[WebService(Namespace="clearingService")]
```

It is used to uniquely identify our Web Service. While it is not required for development and testing, it is a good idea to get into the habit of providing the Web Service with a unique name, perhaps even using full http addresses to the service, which is becoming the standard convention. The .asmx file consists of the following code which you should save in your services directory:

'ClearingService'

```
<%@ WebService Language="C#" Class="ClearingService" %>

using System;
using System.Web.Services;
using System.Web.Util;

[WebService(Namespace="clearingService")]

public class ClearingService {
  [WebMethod] public String clearCard(int CompanyID, string CardName,
              string CardNum, int ValidFromMonth,  int ValidFromYear,
              int ExpireOnMonth, int ExpireOnYear,  int TransactionValue){
    if(CompanyID == 1000 | CompanyID == 2000) {
      return "The Credit Card with name " + PCase(CardName)
              + "and Card Number " + CardNum + ", valid from "
              + ValidFromMonth.ToString("00", null) + "/"
              + ValidFromYear.ToString("00", null) + " until "
              + ExpireOnMonth.ToString("00", null)
              + "/" + ExpireOnYear.ToString("00", null)
              + " has been debited " + convert(TransactionValue)
              + " American Dollars to Company Account "
              + getCompanyName(CompanyID).ToString();
    } else {
      return "Invalid ID";
    }
  }
  string getCompanyName(int CompanyID) {
```

```
    string retVal = "";
    switch(CompanyID) {
      case 1000:
        retVal = " Craddocks Cosmetics ";
        break;
      case 2000:
        retVal = " Timneys Trousers ";
        break;
    }
    return retVal;
  }
  string[] wordArray = {" zero ", " one ", " two ", " three ",
           " four ", " five ", " six ", " seven ", " eight ",
           " nine ", " ten "," eleven "," twelve "," thirteen ",
           " fourteen "," fifteen "," sixteen "," seventeen ",
           " eighteen "," nineteen ", " twenty ", " thirty ",
           " forty "," fifty "," sixty "," seventy "," eighty ",
           " ninety ", "hundred and ", " thousand, ", " million, "};
  string getString(int inVal){
    string retVal = "";
    int tempVar;
    if (inVal > 999){
      return "Error 100";
    }
    if (inVal > 99) {
      tempVar = inVal / 100;
      inVal = inVal - (tempVar * 100);
      retVal = wordArray[tempVar] + " " + wordArray[28];
    }
    if (inVal > 20) {
      tempVar = inVal / 10;
      inVal = inVal - (tempVar * 10);
      retVal += wordArray[tempVar + 18].ToString().Trim()  + " ";
    }
    if (inVal > 0) {
      retVal += wordArray[inVal].ToString().Trim()  + " ";
    }
    return retVal.ToString().Trim();
  }
  string convert(int inVal) {
    int tempVar;
    string retVal = "";
    if (inVal > 999999999) {
      return "Number too large";
    }
    if (inVal > 999999) {
      tempVar = inVal / 1000000;
      inVal  = inVal - (tempVar * 1000000);
      retVal = getString(tempVar) + wordArray[30].ToString() + " ";
    }
    if (inVal > 999) {
      tempVar = inVal / 1000;
      retVal += getString(tempVar) + wordArray[29].ToString();
      inVal = inVal - (tempVar * 1000);
    }
```

```
    if (inVal > 0) {
      retVal += getString(inVal).ToString();
    }
    return retVal.Trim().ToString().Trim();
  }
  string PCase(string inVal) {
    string retVal = "";
    string s = inVal.ToLower().Trim();
    char[] separators = new char[] {' '};
    foreach (string sub in s.Split(separators)) {
      char[] subCharArray;
      subCharArray = sub.ToCharArray();
      string currentWord = subCharArray[0].ToString().ToUpper();
      for (int i = 1;i < subCharArray.Length; i++) {
        currentWord+= subCharArray[i].ToString();
      }
      retVal += currentWord + " " ;
    }
    return retVal;
  }
}
```

The bank has been quite good in setting up their service. They accept certain inputs and pass back a formatted confirmation message to the remote client, informing them that the card transaction has cleared. The example only simulates a database lookup to identify the company name using a simple `switch` method, and of course it does not carry out an actual card transaction or validation, but at least it validates the `CompanyID` field. We could enhance the service tremendously, even by only adding error trapping or actually linking it to a database. We could also make both the `PCase` method and the `convert` method used by the service internally into publicly available `WebMethods`. Simply add `[WebMethod] public` to each method to experiment.

If we save the code in our web application and call it via the web browser, we can see the web methods and the inputs required. For the purposes of this chapter, the `.asmx` file (`clearingService.asmx`) is saved in the following web application:

http://localhost/services/clearingService.asmx

Calling the `.asmx` file from the URL produces results similar to the following:

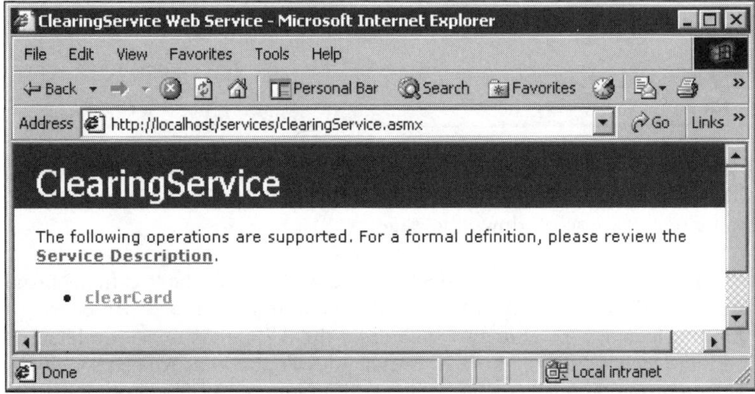

This is the Web Service runtime exposing the information that is publicly available about the Web Service to a remote client (often called a consumer). Of course, the only method it shows is the `clearCard` method. This is the only method we created as a `WebMethod`, so it is the only public method. The other thing it displays is the link to what is known as the service description often referred to as the WDSL file. We will come to that soon, but for now let's concentrate on the `clearCard` method.

Clicking on the `clearCard` method provides a Web Service interface for testing purposes, and to enable the remote consumer to manually identify how many fields are required and what type of fields need to be passed to the `WebMethod`:

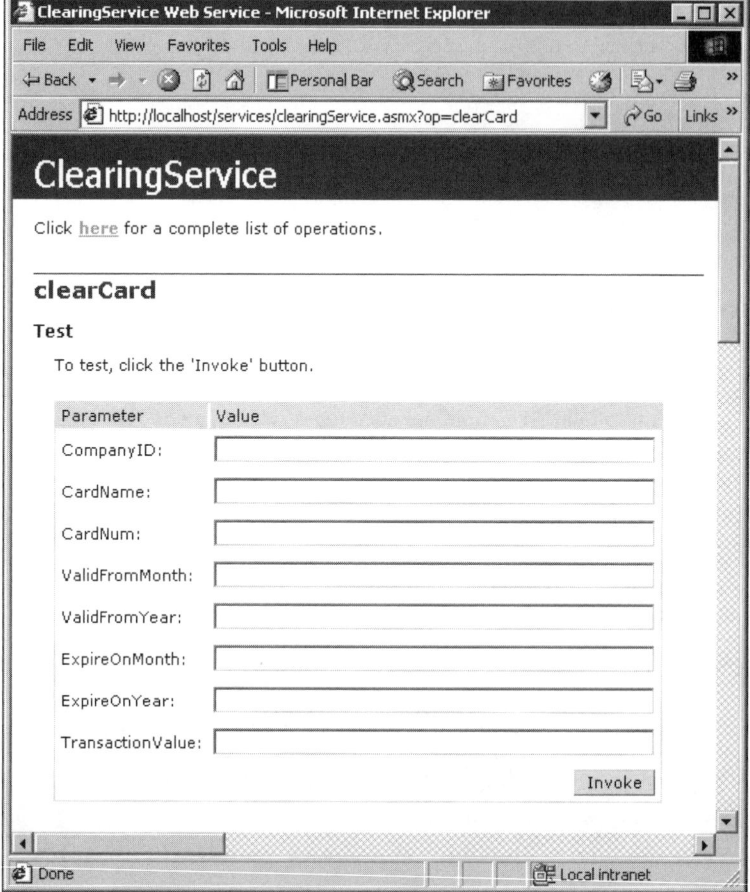

Below what is shown here are instructions on the type of parameters that need to be passed to consume the `WebMethod` via the three available protocols, HTTP GET, HTTP POST and SOAP. These instructions can be seen if we scroll down the page.

We can manually interact with the `clearCard` method by filling in the text fields provided (shown in the following screenshot) as we would with any ordinary web form. It is worth bearing in mind that we did not code this interface, it is provided by default by the ASP.NET object model at request time. This really is a useful interface for testing our Web Service development as we can see the methods directly, and see the results returned as XML strings. The result of any `WebMethod` call is a set of XML data.

If we fill in the details with data appropriate for this type of transaction we can test the output using values such as those shown in the following screenshot:

We get the results returned as a stream of XML data. This provides a common format of data to be disseminated by the various consumers of the Web Service. Pressing Invoke on the `WebForm` produces a new browser instance with results similar to that shown below:

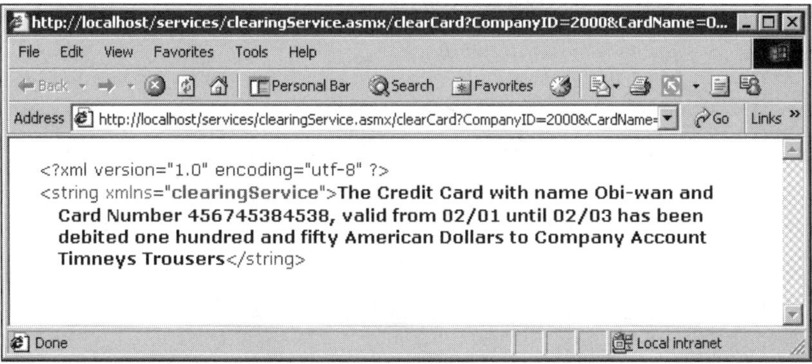

In this instance the parameters are passed as part of a GET request, which is the default for the test interface. So now that we have our functional Web Service, we need to create the clients that will consume the service.

Consuming a Web Service

There is a simple step-by-step approach to consuming Web Services from .NET clients. We use the `Wsdl.exe` (Web Service Description Language) application that is included with the SDK to create a proxy class that looks similar to the class `WebMethods` defined in the `.asmx` file. A proxy class is a representation of the methods available remotely without the functionality being held locally, but accessible locally. We then compile this and can use it just like any other DLL that we would use, without worrying about the underlying protocols required to access the Web Service `Web Methods`.

A WSDL file is an XML based file that describes the service in detail, outlining inputs, outputs and method names. It is provided for us by the Web Service and is normally referred to as a **service description**. We get the Service Description by calling the Web Service with the `?WSDL` switch appended to the end of the Web Service `.asmx` URL. This tells the Web Service runtime to provide the WSDL data we have requested. In the browser, type in the following URL:

```
http://localhost/services/clearingservice.asmx?WSDL
```

The result should be something similar to that shown below with XML continuing to the bottom of the browser:

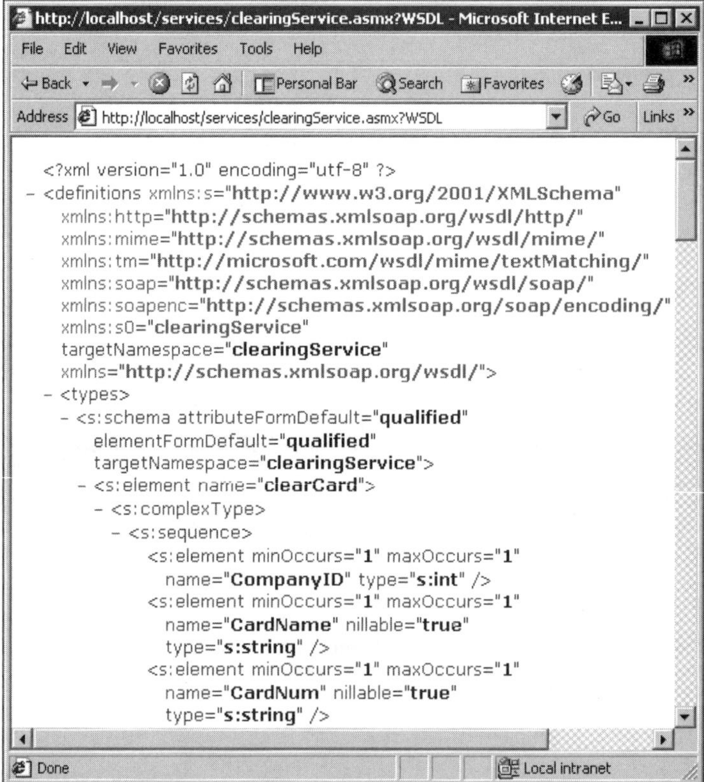

Save the WSDL file as `clearingservice.wsdl` in the same directory as our Web Service. Note that the browser may save this file with a `.XML` extension. If that occurs, simply rename the file.

Now we need to create a proxy file that we will compile into a DLL. It's a representation of the methods (without the method content) that our consuming client file can use. We can do this all manually, but by far the easiest approach is to create a simple batch file to execute the command line.

To do this, we create a batch file called `Build.bat` (saved in the same directory as the other files) as follows:

```
wsdl.exe /l:CSharp /n:ClearingServiceSpace /o:ClearingService.cs
         clearingservice.wsdl
csc /t:library /r:system.web.services.dll /r:system.xml.dll
    ClearingService.cs
```

Notice the switches we use here:

- `l`: Language, in this case C#
- `n`: The unique namespace which we will set as `ClearingServiceSpace`
- `o`: Signifies what our output file will be called
- `clearingservice.wsdl`: The name of the WSDL file we created earlier

There are many other switches for `WSDL.exe`, and we can have a look at them by simply typing:

```
C:\> WSDL
```

at the command prompt.

Notice that there are two lines in our batch file. The first line in the batch file creates the C# code required for the proxy stub, and automatically generates a `.cs` file. The second line of the batch file takes the automatically produced C# proxy stub code and compiles it to a DLL with the correct references required to compile the proxy source code into a DLL.

We should now have a C# DLL that is a local representation of our remote Web Service. Before we consume the Web Service, we will need to move the DLL to the `Bin` directory of our web application to enable `.aspx` pages to access it. Now is the time to create a `Bin` directory if one is not already present. If our web application root is `\services`, `Bin` will reside in `\services\Bin`.

We now have all of the files that we require to enable consumption of our custom Wrox Bank Web Service. Now all we need are the clients. To demonstrate multiple client types consuming the same Web Service we will create two clients. One will be for Timney Trousers who have invested heavily in browser based thin clients throughout their company, based on ASP.NET. The second is for Craddocks Cosmetics who favor more flexible and graphically intensive client side applications based on Windows Forms. We will begin with the ASP.NET application.

Consuming the Web Service via ASP.NET

ASP.NET Web Forms are used to create functionally 'thin' applications in which the primary user interface is a text-based browser. This could include HTML, WML, XML and whatever else we can serve over the web, such as e-commerce applications. They are typically thin client applications whose only dependency is that an appropriate browser exists on the client, be it a PC, WAP phone or a PDA.

Web Forms applications can take advantage of features built into the most recent browsers such as DHTML, and HTML 4.0, to enhance the user experience. The new .NET Web Forms components can automatically detect browser levels and render pages according to the technical level of the browser the client is using.

ASP.NET is very, very powerful as a web application development tool, and an excellent part of the whole .NET framework. The features added to supersede traditional ASP are rich and extensible. They are, however, beyond the scope of this chapter other than as a client to our Web Service. With that in mind we will assume that readers have enough ASPX or VB knowledge to understand the code example without requiring too much explanation. For a concise explanation of ASP.NET, try *Beginning ASP.NET, ISBN 1861005040*, published by Wrox Press.

So far in the chapter we have concentrated on C#. For the ASPX example we are going to utilize VB.NET to demonstrate that it is just as easy to use a Web Service in VB.NET as it is in C#.

To begin, we first need to create an `.aspx` file to call the Web Service. Take note of the `Import` statement on the first line: it is referencing back to the namespace we asked for when we compiled our proxy DLL in the `Build.bat` file earlier.

Open any text editor and create the following `clearingservice.aspx` page in the services directory:

```
<%@ Import Namespace="ClearingServiceSpace" %>
<%@ Page Language="VB" %>
<html>

   <script language="VB" runat="server" debug="true">

   ' declare our local variables

   Dim Op1 As Integer = 0
   Dim CompanyID As Integer = 0
   Dim CardName As String = ""
   Dim CardNum As String = ""
   Dim validFromMonth As Integer = 0
   Dim validFromYear As Integer = 0
   Dim ExpireOnMonth As Integer = 0
   Dim ExpireOnYear As Integer = 0
   Dim TransactionValue As Integer = 0
   Sub Submit_Click(Sender As Object, E As EventArgs)

      ' check integer inputs and assign submitted web form values
      ' to local variables for processing

      CompanyID = Int32.Parse(Operand1.Text)
      CardName = (Operand2.Text)
      CardNum  = (Operand3.Text)
      validFromMonth = Int32.Parse(Operand4.Text)
      validFromYear = Int32.Parse(Operand5.Text)
      ExpireOnMonth = Int32.Parse(Operand6.Text)
      ExpireOnYear = Int32.Parse(Operand7.Text)
      TransactionValue = Int32.Parse(Operand8.Text)
```

The next line shows the instantiation of the `ClearingService` proxy. We have a proxy to the remote Web Service, so we do not really need to know anything about the actual Web Service, only a simple method call in a DLL. We can easily use it in VB.NET because it's a DLL, even though it is also a C# proxy and a C# Web Service. The .NET interoperability capabilities handle this for us:

```
    Dim Service As ClearingService = New ClearingService()

    ' notice we have dim'd an instance of the ClearingService Class as
    ' Service

    Select (CType(sender,Control).ID)
       Case "GO" :
```

Next, we call the `clearCard` method (it's case-insensitive in VB.NET):

```
          Result.Text = "<b>" & Service.ClearCard(CompanyID, CardName,
          CardNum, ValidFromMonth, ValidFromYear, ExpireOnMonth,
          ExpireOnYear, TransactionValue ) & "</b>"
      End Select
  End Sub
  </script>
```

This next part of the script is the layout for the web interface. In this, we position the boxes and their labels, and use ASP code to assign references to the textboxes:

```
  <body style="font: 10pt verdana">
  <h4>Timneys Trousers Credit Card <br />Clearance Service</h4>

  <div style="padding:15,15,15,15; background-color:beige; width:300;
      border-color:black; border-width:1; border-style:solid">
     <asp:Label id="Result" runat="server"/>
  </div>

  <form runat="server">
  <div style="padding:15,15,15,15; background-color:beige; width:300;
   border-color:black; border-width:1; border-style:solid">

      Company ID: <br><asp:TextBox id="Operand1" Text="2000"
      runat="server"/><br>
      Card Name: <br><asp:TextBox id="Operand2" Text=""
                     runat="server"/><br>
      Card Number: <br><asp:TextBox id="Operand3" Text=""
      runat="server"/><br>

      Valid From: <br><asp:TextBox id="Operand4" Text="" runat="server"/>
      Month) <br><asp:TextBox id="Operand5" Text="" runat="server"/>
                  (Year)<br>

      Expires On: <br><asp:TextBox id="Operand6" Text="" runat="server"/>
      Month) <br><asp:TextBox id="Operand7" runat="server"/>
      (Year)<br>

      Transaction Value: <br><asp:TextBox id="Operand8" Text="0"
      runat="server"/><br>

  <input type="submit" id="GO" value="Process Transaction"
  OnServerClick="Submit_Click" runat="server">
  </div>
  </form>
</body>
</html>
```

Saving the `.aspx` code in our services web application as `clearingService.aspx` and calling it from a browser produces results similar to that shown below from the URL http://localhost/services/clearingservice.aspx:

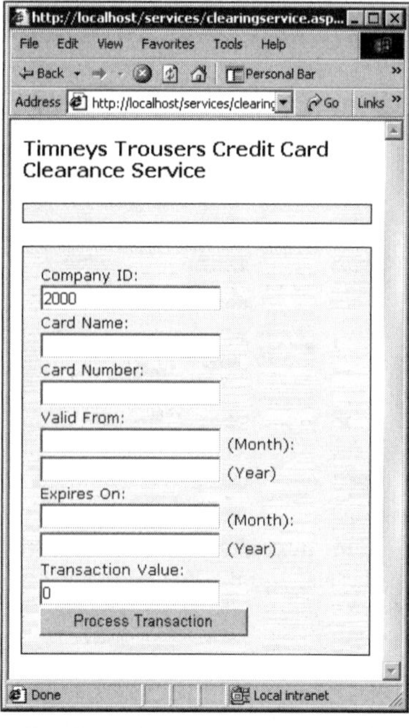

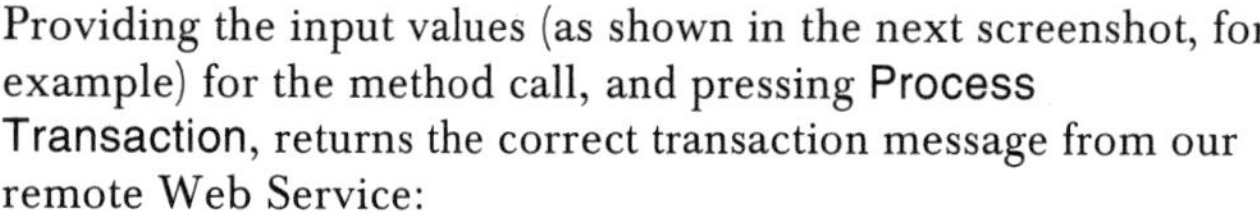

Providing the input values (as shown in the next screenshot, for example) for the method call, and pressing Process Transaction, returns the correct transaction message from our remote Web Service:

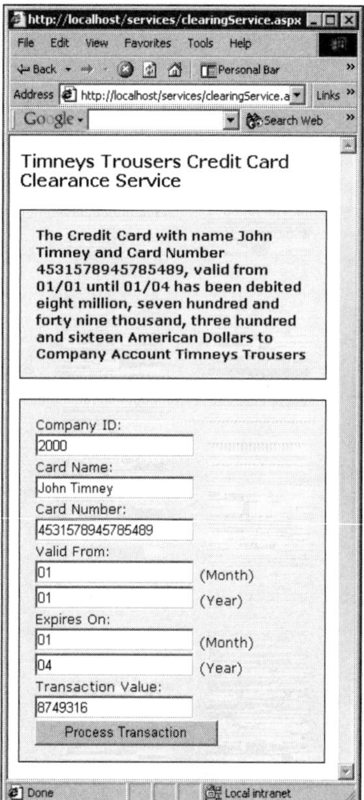

Consuming the Web Service via a Windows Form

As we have already seen in this book, Windows Forms are used to develop functionally 'rich' applications where the client computer is typically expected to handle the processing in an application. In the historical Microsoft model, this indicates that large chunks of code are typically coded into the application, and DLLs are created that ship with the application. In truth, this has not changed much – even with .NET – although deployment is significantly easier. Many Windows Forms applications would still probably expect to be entirely self-contained and perform all application processing on the user's computer, as rather 'fat' applications.

A Windows-based application that uses Windows Forms is built around a Microsoft Windows based framework, so it has access to system resources on the client computer. This includes local files, the Windows Registry, the printer, and so on. However, the framework is flexible enough to be implemented on any platform should someone take the time to do that. Windows Forms applications are our executable applications that are replacing legacy applications written using tools such as Visual Basic 6.

Now we will look at how to make a Windows Form from scratch with the SDK so that we are ready for deploying on any platform. The Windows Form will use our Web Service, thus allowing us to remove some of the processing burden out of the Windows Form and into a shared remote server, making the application somewhat thinner.

Developers might be pleasantly surprised to see that it is as easy to consume a Web Service from a Windows Form as it is from a Web Form. It is however slightly more difficult to create a Windows Form manually than to create a Web Form. To demonstrate this, we will create a very simple Windows Forms interface for Craddocks Cosmetics, to handle the credit card transactions from a client application, as opposed to a browser-based application. One thing to bear in mind when looking through this code is that the only critical part in utilizing the Web Service is the instantiation of the proxy DLL.

We will create a new C# Windows Form with eight inputs and a button for processing the transaction as shown below:

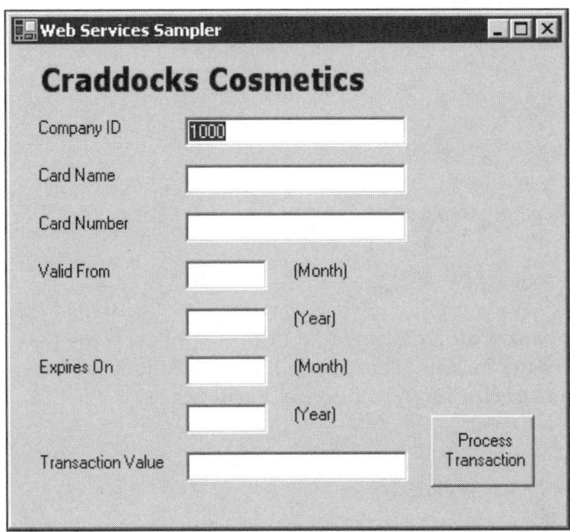

The code can look a little daunting at first, but it's really quite straightforward. Let's take a look.

Windows Form Service

We begin by giving our form a namespace to reside in. We will use `SimpleWebService` for ours, although if one is not specified it will take the default namespace. You can save these files in your `\Bin` directory for convenience, but they can be anywhere as long as the proxy DLL can be found:

```
namespace SimpleWebService {
```

Next, we declare the default system libraries we will use for form creation:

```
    using System;
    using System.ComponentModel;
    using System.Drawing;
    using System.Windows.Forms;
```

We now need to declare our class, which inherits from `System.Windows.Forms.Form`:

```
    public class webservices : System.Windows.Forms.Form {
```

Next, we declare the textboxes that we will use (for brevity's sake, we aren't going to include declarations two to seven since they are all the same):

```
        private System.ComponentModel.Container components;
        private System.Windows.Forms.TextBox textBox1;

        ...

        private System.Windows.Forms.TextBox textBox8;
```

Now, we will declare the labels:

```
        private System.Windows.Forms.Label label1;

        ...

        private System.Windows.Forms.Label label11;
```

We also require a button to process our transaction:

```
        private System.Windows.Forms.Button button1;
```

Additionally, we need a means of initializing and disposing of our Web Services Windows Form. We will add two methods to cater for this. These are common methods that could be added to any Windows Form. Notice that the constructor for Web Services carries the `InitializeComponent` method:

```
        public webservices() {
            InitializeComponent();
        }
        public override void Dispose() {
            base.Dispose();
            components.Dispose();
        }
```

Let's add the `InitializeComponent` method to the code. This contains the bulk of the code that is required for screen layout at initialization time. It tells the runtime what to put on the form container, and where:

```
    private void InitializeComponent() {
        this.components = new System.ComponentModel.Container();
```

Next, we instantiate the textboxes:

```
        this.textBox1 = new System.Windows.Forms.TextBox();

      ...

        this.textBox8 = new System.Windows.Forms.TextBox();
```

and then the labels:

```
        this.label1 = new System.Windows.Forms.Label();

      ...

        this.label11 = new System.Windows.Forms.Label();
```

Let's not forget the button:

```
        this.button1 = new System.Windows.Forms.Button();
```

Now we can set our basic screen layout size for when the Windows Form is first displayed:

```
        this.AutoScaleBaseSize = new System.Drawing.Size(5, 13);
        this.Text = "Web Services Sampler";
        this.ClientSize = new System.Drawing.Size(400, 500);
```

We have declared and instantiated elements of our Windows Form, but we have not actually told the runtime where to add these items to the form. We will do this now. Here, we add the textboxes we have instantiated, setting any default values or any absolute positioning:

```
        textBox1.Location = new System.Drawing.Point(120, 128);
        textBox1.Text = "2000";
        textBox1.TabIndex = 1;
        textBox1.Size = new System.Drawing.Size(152, 20);
        textBox2.Location = new System.Drawing.Point(120, 160);
        textBox2.TabIndex = 4;
        textBox2.Size = new System.Drawing.Size(152, 20);
        textBox3.Location = new System.Drawing.Point(120, 192);
        textBox3.TabIndex = 6;
        textBox3.Size = new System.Drawing.Size(152, 20);
        textBox4.Location = new System.Drawing.Point(120, 224);
        textBox4.TabIndex = 8;
        textBox4.Size = new System.Drawing.Size(56, 20);
        textBox5.Location = new System.Drawing.Point(120, 256);
        textBox5.TabIndex = 10;
        textBox5.Size = new System.Drawing.Size(56, 20);
        textBox6.Location = new System.Drawing.Point(120, 288);
        textBox6.TabIndex = 13;
        textBox6.Size = new System.Drawing.Size(56, 20);
```

```
        textBox7.Location = new System.Drawing.Point(120, 320);
        textBox7.TabIndex = 16;
        textBox7.Size = new System.Drawing.Size(56, 20);
        textBox8.Location = new System.Drawing.Point(120, 272);
        textBox8.TabIndex = 17;
        textBox8.Size = new System.Drawing.Size(152, 20);
```

Now we'll add the `Labels` we have instantiated, setting any default values or any absolute positioning:

```
        Label1.Location = new System.Drawing.Point(16, 128);
        Label1.Text = "Company ID";
        Label1.Size = new System.Drawing.Size(80, 16);
        Label1.TabIndex = 2;

        Label2.Location = new System.Drawing.Point(16, 160);
        Label2.Text = "Card Name";
        label2.Size = new System.Drawing.Size(64, 24);
        label2.TabIndex = 3;

        label3.Location = new System.Drawing.Point(16, 192);
        label3.Text = "Card Number";
        label3.Size = new System.Drawing.Size(80, 24);
        label3.TabIndex = 5;

        label4.Location = new System.Drawing.Point(16, 224);
        label4.Text = "Valid From";
        label4.Size = new System.Drawing.Size(64, 16);
        label4.TabIndex = 7;

        label5.Location = new System.Drawing.Point(192, 224);
        label5.Text = "(Month)";
        label5.Size = new System.Drawing.Size(64, 24);
        label5.TabIndex = 9;

        label6.Location = new System.Drawing.Point(192, 256);
        label6.Text = "(Year)";
        label6.Size = new System.Drawing.Size(48, 16);
        label6.TabIndex = 11;

        label7.Location = new System.Drawing.Point(16, 288);
        label7.Text = "Expires On";
        label7.Size = new System.Drawing.Size(72, 16);
        label7.TabIndex = 12;

        label8.Location = new System.Drawing.Point(192, 320);
        label8.Text = "(Year)";
        label8.Size = new System.Drawing.Size(48, 16);
        label8.TabIndex = 14;

        label9.Location = new System.Drawing.Point(192, 288);
        label9.Text = "(Month)";
        label9.Size = new System.Drawing.Size(64, 16);
        label9.TabIndex = 15;

        label10.Location = new System.Drawing.Point(16, 352);
        label10.Text = "Transaction Value";
        label10.Size = new System.Drawing.Size(96, 16);
        label10.TabIndex = 18;

        label11.Location = new System.Drawing.Point(16, 16);
        label11.Text = "Craddocks Cosmetics";
```

```
        label11.Size = new System.Drawing.Size(264, 88);
        label11.Font = new System.Drawing.Font("Tahoma", 16f,
            System.Drawing.FontStyle.Bold);
```

Here, we'll add the `Button` that we have instantiated, setting its default values or any absolute positioning. Also notice the addition of the `button1.click` event. We add the event at actual instantiation time, and the method called by the event later:

```
        button1.Location = new System.Drawing.Point(288, 328);
        button1.Size = new System.Drawing.Size(72, 48);
        button1.TabIndex = 19;
        button1.Text = "Process Transaction";
        button1.Click += new System.EventHandler(button1_Click);
```

We have declared and instantiated all of our controls for the window. However, the form is an aggregate of all of its contained controls, and our form does not yet 'know' of the existence of the controls. The following code creates the internal wiring between the form and its contained controls (once again we will only show the first and last declaration of each series):

```
        // actually add the controls to the form

        this.Controls.Add(textBox1);

        ...

        this.Controls.Add(textBox8);

        this.Controls.Add(label1);

        ...

        this.Controls.Add(label11);
        this.Controls.Add(button1);
    }
```

It looks like a lot, but it isn't really. The actual code is only a couple of hundred lines in total with everything added. So far all we have done is followed a step-by-step approach to laying out the screen. We have declared, initialized and added our components. This is a useful approach to manually building Windows Forms.

Before we compile it, though, let's add the button click method. We will enhance this in a short while to call our remote Web Service method `clearCard`. For now, an empty click event will do. This must be added now because in the initialization event we declared a `button1.click` event for the button we added, and the compiler will expect to find the method for the button click:

```
    private void button1_Click(object sender, System.EventArgs e) {}
```

Finally we need the `Main` method that is required to invoke the class when the `exe` is clicked, as well as the end brackets for the namespace and class file:

```
    public static void Main(string[] args) {
        Application.Run(new webservices());
    }
  }
}
```

We now have a GUI application (although it still needs compiling). Admittedly it's mostly non-functional, with the exceptions being that the fields can gather data and the button will accept key press events. Our Windows Form will also close gracefully because we added the correct dispose code. Save this as `WindowsFormService.cs`.

The next step is to add the code required to access our Web Service. We need to enhance the libraries we are using to include the proxy DLL we created earlier and a reference to the `System.Web.Services` namespace. Add the following to the code where we declared the default system libraries for form creation:

```
using clearingServiceSpace;
using System.Web.Services;
```

This gives us access to the library containing our Web Service proxy details. Now we can add the code to instantiate the DLL, and activate the `WebMethod` call. Add this code to the `button1.click` event. Notice how we convert the input values from text into whatever the appropriate individual `WebMethod` parameter value is:

```
    clearingService Service;
    Service = new clearingService();
    MessageBox.Show(Service.clearCard(Convert.ToInt32(textBox1.Text),
        textBox2.Text, textBox3.Text, Convert.ToInt32(textBox4.Text),
        Convert.ToInt32(textBox5.Text), Convert.ToInt32(textBox6.Text),
        Convert.ToInt32(textBox7.Text), Convert.ToInt32(textBox8.Text)));
```

Now we need to compile our application. The command is straightforward, but we need to make sure we add a reference to the `clearingService.DLL` file:

```
C:\inetpub\wwwroot\services\bin> csc /target:winexe /out:webservice.exe
/r:System.dll /r:System.Windows.Forms.dll /r:System.Drawing.dll
/r:clearingService.DLL /r:System.Web.Services.dll WindowsFormservice.cs
```

It's all on one line, which means a lot of typing, so you might like to put this into a batch file instead to save typing it all over again.

Running the executable is as easy as clicking on the resultant `webservice.exe` file. The results of completing the required fields and clicking Process Transaction are shown below:

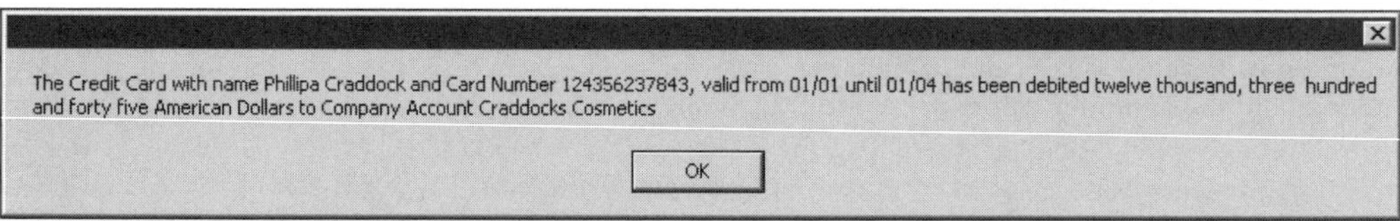

The Credit Card with name Phillipa Craddock and Card Number 124356237843, valid from 01/01 until 01/04 has been debited twelve thousand, three hundred and forty five American Dollars to Company Account Craddocks Cosmetics
OK

As we can see, the Windows Form has taken the input values and passed them to the Web Service `clearCard` remote method via the proxy DLL that we created earlier. It has taken the input values, which were only text, and converted them to the correct input values for the Web Service. It has called the remote method, and then returned a nicely formatted message to the user.

Consuming Web Services from Windows Forms without Using Proxy DLLs

The more familiar we become with Web Services, the more we will find that Microsoft is not the only company pushing the Web Services approach as an important model in their frameworks. The implication of this is that we may find, over time, that the approach shown so far in consuming Web Services from within Windows Forms might work with a Web Service produced in Java and hosted on a remote Apache server, for example. To get an appreciation of what is happening in the world of Web Services let's look at what some of the 'non-Microsoft' people are up to:

- IBM already provides the WSTK (Web Services Tool Kit) to help in converting existing Java classes and Enterprise JavaBeans into Web Services
- CapeConnect Two from Cape Clear Software goes a step further by providing a whole Web Services platform
- Application Server vendors such as BEA have announced support in their web servers to support Web Services

At the time of writing there is even a Java Specification request, JSR-109 (Implementing Enterprise Web Services) intended to define a programming model and architecture for implementing Web Services in Java.

The Linux community has also announced plans to 'embrace and extend' Microsoft's .NET initiative so that it works with the Linux Operating System. Microsoft has stated that it would help a certain vendor port major pieces of the .NET technology to FreeBSD, an open-source Linux competitor. .NET will become available to a far wider range of systems because of these developments.

It might be that standardizing outside of the Microsoft model might be a little less than straightforward in the next year or so, and it may be that some Web Services simply cannot be consumed using the Microsoft approach that developers will come to appreciate. Well, there is still some hope for .NET developers, because Microsoft saw fit to add in some excellent support for traditional HTTP that can be utilized from within our Windows Forms applications.

Extracting Results from a Remote Web Page

We will demonstrate how to extract the results from a remote web page using functionality provided in the `System.Net` and the `System.Web` classes. To demonstrate how to do this we will modify the Craddocks Cosmetics Windows Forms application to satisfy the Web Service inputs, using a traditional HTTP GET, without using the Web Service proxy DLL we created earlier. Instead, we will code directly to the remote page in a much more bespoke (some would say brute force) fashion.

Let's take a look at the code modification we need to make to the Windows Forms application. Copy the `WindowsFormService.cs` file we created earlier and open it with any editor.

We begin by altering the namespace – we will use `SimpleWebGet`. Remember, we must provide a namespace for our Windows Forms applications, so let's use one that at least refers to the purpose of the application:

```
namespace SimpleWebGet {

    using System;
    using System.ComponentModel;
    using System.Drawing;
    using System.Windows.Forms;
```

We need to add some additional references to make use of methods available in classes we have not yet come across. Notice that we have also removed some from the earlier code listing:

```
using System.Net;
using System.Text;
using System.IO;
using System.Web;
```

We must declare our class and instantiate the elements required to make the display. While the layout code remains the same, notice the removal of any reference to the Clearing Service Proxy DLL we created.

The real changes begin to occur in the `button1_Click` event. Modify (or remove and re-add) the `button1_Click` event to contain the following code:

```
private void button1_Click(object sender, System.EventArgs e) {
    String webServiceURL =
    "http://localhost/services/clearingservice.asmx/clearCard?" +
    "CompanyID=" + Convert.ToInt32(textBox1.Text) +
    "&CardName=" + HttpUtility.UrlEncode(textBox2.Text) +
    "&CardNum=" + HttpUtility.UrlEncode(textBox3.Text) +
    "&ValidFromMonth=" + Convert.ToInt32(textBox4.Text) +
    "&ValidFromYear=" + Convert.ToInt32(textBox5.Text) +
    "&ExpireOnMonth=" + Convert.ToInt32(textBox6.Text) +
    "&ExpireOnYear=" + Convert.ToInt32(textBox7.Text) +
    "&TransactionValue=" + Convert.ToInt32(textBox8.Text);
```

We have added a string to hold our URL. Developers familiar with URLs will recall seeing things like John%20Timney in the parameters. Take note of the %20. This is because web servers expect the data for request in a specific format. We won't explain too much about that, other than to say we need to convert the input field values from the Windows Forms application into valid URL Encoded values where needed. Typically, that means anything that is not a numeric. We will be issuing a GET request, therefore we must chain the input values on the URL line as Encoded values. The `HttpUtility` class provides methods for URL encoding and decoding when processing Web requests, which is why we added the class reference earlier.

What we will actually pass to the Web Service will eventually look similar to what we would see on the URL line of a web browser:

http://localhost/services/clearingservice.asmx/clearCard?CompanyID=1000&CardName=john&CardNum=1234&ValidFromMonth=01&ValidFromYear=01&ExpireOnMonth=01&ExpireOnYear=02&TransactionValue=123

Remember also that the Web Service passes back a string of data. This is an example of the string we get back:

```
<?xml version="1.0" encoding="utf-8" ?><string xmlns="clearingService">The
Credit Card with name John Timney and Card Number 1234, valid from 01/01 until
01/02 has been debited one hundred and twenty three American Dollars to
Company Account Craddocks Cosmetics</string>
```

As we always get back the same wrapper tags (`<string xmlns="clearingService">`, for example) it's quite easy to parse the string values out that we require. Of course, this is quite a simple example to parse and for more complex examples, it is suggested that readers take a look at the regular expression classes, or work out how to strip the XML values apart. Microsoft.NET has strong support for both regular expressions and XML. For this example a simple Substring approach will suffice.

Add the following code to the button click event to decompose the returned string accordingly:

```
        String htmlString = getWebService(webServiceURL);
        String startString = "ClearingService";
        String endString = "</string>";
        int StrStart = htmlString.ToLower().IndexOf(startString.ToLower()) +
        startString.Length + 2;
        int StrEnd = htmlString.IndexOf(endString);
        int StrLen = StrEnd - StrStart;
        MessageBox.Show(htmlString.Substring(StrStart, StrLen));
    }
```

Now add a method containing the code to actually perform the GET request, passing in the encoded URL *string* of data and receiving back a byte *stream* of data that we encode using the encoding format of choice and return as a `string`:

```
        private String getWebService(String URLString) {
            WebRequest req = WebRequest.Create(URLString);
            string htmlString = "";
            try {
                WebResponse result = req.GetResponse();
                Stream ReceiveStream = result.GetResponseStream();
                Byte[] read = new Byte[512];

                //read in chunks of 512 bytes

                int bytes = ReceiveStream.Read(read, 0, 512);
            while (bytes > 0) {
                Encoding encode = System.Text.Encoding.GetEncoding("utf-8");
                htmlString = htmlString + encode.GetString(read, 0, bytes);
                bytes = ReceiveStream.Read(read, 0, 512);
            }
        } catch(Exception) {
            htmlString = "Error retrieving page";
        }
            return htmlString;
        }
    }
}
```

Save it as `WindowsFormWeb.cs`, and compile it with the following:

```
C:\inetpub\wwwroot\services\bin> csc /target:winexe /out:webget.exe
/r:System.DLL /r:System.Windows.Forms.DLL
/r:System.Drawing.DLL /r:System.Web.DLL WindowsFormWeb.cs
```

Running the example again gives almost identical results, even though the technology used to consume the Web Service is very different, and actually quite simple to implement:

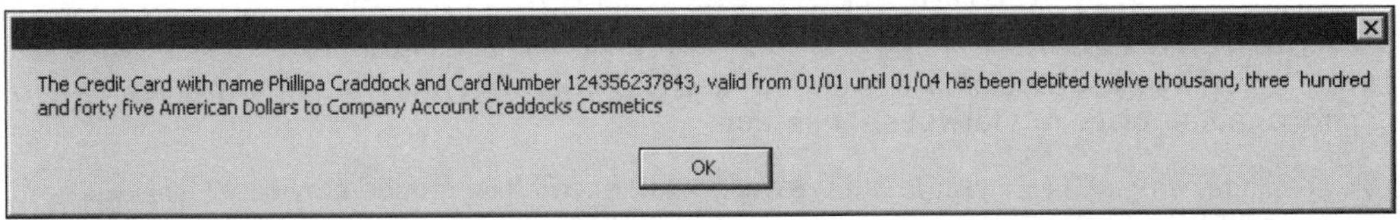
The Credit Card with name Phillipa Craddock and Card Number 124356237843, valid from 01/01 until 01/04 has been debited twelve thousand, three hundred and forty five American Dollars to Company Account Craddocks Cosmetics
OK

The example serves two purposes:

- It demonstrates how to access a Web Service without using the proxy DLL and WDSL approach, although it is strongly recommend that we use this whenever possible. This shows that whatever may happen in other technologies, there is likely to be an approach that will enable us to consume Web Service in our Windows Forms from within .NET.
- It also shows that it is possible using .NET to extract remote web pages without the need for third party components, or the thread safe XML HTTP objects favored by ASP and VB developers, which were usually required before .NET came along. Additionally, the code will also work quite happily in ASP.NET.

It is possible to further expand our example scenario used throughout this chapter. Dealing with a supplier who is not yet .NET enabled and does not serve information via Web Services, instead only having legacy Web Form interfaces (perhaps based on traditional ASP) would be one such example of this. The approach we have just demonstrated, however, would allow us to query those pages and still get the results in our Windows Forms, showing that we have the best of both worlds with the mixed and flexible approach that can be gained from using .NET.

Summary

It's very easy to use Web Services from any type of client once we have a basic grasp of the underlying technologies. This chapter has demonstrated a number of key things that help us make use of Web Services in our applications, and we have looked at the distinctions between Windows Forms, Web Forms, and Web Services.

We covered `Wsdl.exe` and saw a simple explanation of how to create a proxy DLL manually from a WSDL file for use by different consuming clients. Subsequently, we actually created the clients, an ASP.NET forms-based application written in VB.NET, and a Windows Form written in C#. We also saw how to build a Windows Forms application from top to bottom.

We then covered consuming Web Services when the Web Service vendor may not perhaps be adhering to the standards that we are looking to support in our applications, instead resorting to more traditional 'brute force' HTTP extraction approaches.

Quite a lot of information has been presented in this chapter, but it does not end there. What we have covered here is very focused, and targeted on how to consume a Web Service that we are already very familiar with, having created the service ourselves. To move forward there is one key area to look into, and that is the subject of Discovery.

Web Service Discovery is the process of locating and interrogating service descriptions defined in WSDL (Web Services Description Language). Through Web Service discovery, Web Service clients can learn that a Web Service exists, what its capabilities are, and how to properly interact with it. Using the .NET Framework SDK, we can use the Web Services Discovery Tool (`Disco.exe`) to enact the discovery process on a given URL. There is a very useful URL to help find out some more information about Web Service discovery, which at the time of writing can be found at http://msdn.microsoft.com/library/default.asp?url=/library/en-us/cpguidnf/html/cpconenablingdiscoveryforwebservice.asp

To conclude, why not pay a visit to http://www.gotdotnet.com/playground/services/? This site contains some useful Web Services that can be consumed from Windows Forms clients to help developers improve their skills even further.

Legend

- Concrete Class
- Abstract class

System.Windows.Forms

- System.Object
  - System.MarshalRefObject
    - System.ComponentMode.Component
      - CommonDialog
        - ColorDialog
        - FileDialog
        - FontDialog
        - PageSetupDialog
        - PrintDialog
      - ErrorProvider
      - HelpProvider
      - ImageList
      - Menu
        - ContextMenu
        - MainMenu
        - MenuItem
      - NotifyIcon
      - StatusBarPanel
      - Timer
      - ToolBarButton
      - ToolTip
      - Control
        - ButtonBase
          - Button
          - CheckBox
          - RadioButton
        - DataGrid
        - DateTimePicker
        - GroupBox
        - Label
          - LinkLabel
        - ListControl
          - ComboBox
          - ListBox
            - CheckedListBox
        - ListView
        - MonthCalendar
        - PictureBox
        - PrintReviewControl
        - ProgressBar
        - ScrollableControl
          - ContainerControl
            - Form
              - PrintPreviewDialog
              - ThreadExceptionDialog
            - PropertyGrid
            - UpDownBase
              - DomainUpDown
              - NumericUpDown
            - UserControl
          - Panel
            - TabPage
        - ScrollBar
          - HScrollBar
          - VScrollBar
        - Splitter
        - StatusBar
        - TabControl
        - TextBoxBase
          - RichTextBox
          - Textbox
        - ToolBar
        - TrackBar
        - TreeView
    - ListViewItem
    - TreeNode

17

Windows Forms in Web Pages

One nice feature of Windows Forms, working in conjunction with Internet Explorer version 6 upwards, is that Internet Explorer supports the downloading and displaying of controls within a web page using the HTML `<object>` tag. This is similar to the previous ability of Internet Explorer to display COM ActiveX controls, and of several web browsers to display Java applets. However, with Windows Forms this means that we can take advantage of all the other benefits offered by Windows Forms and the .NET environment, including the more sophisticated object model and the support in .NET for evidence-based security.

> *Note that this technology is not related to ASP.NET. ASP.NET allows compiled code and web controls to be run on the server in response to a web page request. Here we will be showing how to run Windows Forms controls on the client.*

In this chapter we will:

- Present an overview of mobile code technology.
- Discuss the implementation details, including how to build the assembly, where to place the files, the syntax in the HTML file, and how to run the application.
- Run through several examples.
- Demonstrate the security mechanisms in action.

This chapter requires that we set up and configure Microsoft's Web Server IIS (Internet Information Server). We will provide enough information so that you will be able to run the examples, but we will not attempt to cover it in detail.

Improvements and Constraints

The .NET platform delivers the capability of Windows Forms within web pages in a manner similar to Java applets. There are, however, benefits and constraints that we should be aware of.

The main benefits include:

- Improved performance over Java applets
- The ability to bring the richness of a Windows application to the web environment
- Automatic caching of JIT (Just In Time) compiled code on the client – the client only downloads the application when it changes

The constraints are:

- On the client side, only Microsoft operating systems are currently supported. However, when the .NET runtime becomes available for other platforms this restriction will be removed.
- Only IE (Internet Explorer) 6.0, the latest version at the time of writing, is supported.
- The .NET runtime must be installed on the client, which entails a hefty download, or a CD distribution. However, this restriction will become less of a problem in future since .NET will eventually be incorporated into the Windows operating system.
- On the server side, only Windows 2000 and above, and Microsoft IIS (Internet Information Server) 5.0 or later is supported.

This capability would typically be used on an Intranet or Extranet where we need to deploy an enterprise wide application that has the rich look and feel of a fat client application, but has the deployment and maintainability characteristics of a thin client, n-tier application. At this time, because of the constraints, it doesn't seem that this technology will be extensively used by web sites accessible by the public at large. If the efforts to move .NET to non-Microsoft environments are successful, and as Windows XP and IE 6.0 become much more common, this technique certainly will be a more viable one for public web sites.

There are few limits on the richness of the user interface that we can build using this system. All the capabilities of the Windows Forms class hierarchy are available to us when building our application. Using this technique, combined with the technique of consuming web services (see Chapter 16 on Web Services and Windows Forms), gives us a very powerful infrastructure for building state-of-the-art applications. To date, no other framework matches the distributed computing capabilities of .NET.

As an example, consider the case of a Customer Relationship Management system that we want to deploy for a worldwide sales and service force. We want a user interface that is richer than a typical browser interface. We want a drill-down approach into the data with a high degree of responsiveness for the user. They should be able to look at a customer, drill down to the products that the customer owns, drill down to the users of the products, and then see all customer contacts and user issues for each user. The user should be able to look at their data in a spreadsheet form, adjusting column widths, moving columns around, and saving their preferred configuration.

When entering records into the database, we have a requirement that we do extensive data validation before the record is added, and we should do the validation as the user moves from field to field. We may have a situation where the user may or may not be connected to the network at the time that they wish to add data. We need this application to be secure – only authenticated users should be able to access it.

Finally, we may have some interactive graphing requirements, where we need to put up a graph, and then allow the user to manipulate some of the parameters on which the graph is based, and get instantaneous feedback. Since we can specify the hardware and software configuration for all the users of this system, this would be an ideal system for implementation using this technique.

The advantage of using Windows Forms on the client for this sort of application – as compared with using, for example, ASP.NET pages – is that the responsiveness of the application is considerably increased since fewer round trips to the server need to be performed. In addition, since more processing is done on the client machines, the load on the server is reduced. On the other hand, ASP.NET pages would be more suitable if, for example, frequent accesses to a backend database on the server need to be made. Of course, there's nothing to stop us from writing an application that uses both technologies simultaneously, using ASP.NET to perform whatever processing is best suited to being done on the server, while displaying Windows Forms through the client web browser to provide the user with a rich client-side user interface and client-side processing.

Application Service Providers may also be very interested in this technology. They can develop a 'killer application' for their vertical market, and if the application is compelling enough, their users will be willing to install the appropriate browser and the .NET software. The service provider can quite easily implement a 'pay-per-use' model, or a model where the user pays for the data that they access, or even more sophisticated payment systems.

Overview of Mobile Code

Sometimes the technique of remote execution is referred to as **mobile code**, which Microsoft defines as software that is transmitted across a network from a remote server to a local computer, and then is executed locally. This is a form of distributed computing. The main difference between mobile code and traditional code is that mobile code does not need to be installed and executed by the user explicitly. Other examples of mobile code are ActiveX controls, Java applets, and script languages (JavaScript and VBScript) run by the browser.

As we saw in Chapter 1, Microsoft Intermediate Language (MSIL) is a CPU-independent instruction set that can be converted very efficiently to native code. When programmer-readable source code is compiled, it is placed in an assembly. Often code is compiled to a Portable Executable (PE) file and the assembly can be run as though it were an actual executable. When implementing mobile code however, we will compile it to an assembly that we will put into a DLL file. Then, using the HTML `<object>` tag in our web page, we will reference this assembly on the server. The browser (which at the time of writing must be IE 6.0), will automatically download the MSIL, cache it, compile it, and run it within the managed environment.

Mobile code under .NET treads lightly on the client machine. It doesn't need to modify the registry, and it can be removed easily. Limits can be placed so that only a given amount of cached mobile code can reside on the client machine at any given time. When the limit is reached, the .NET framework automatically removes the assemblies that were least recently used. Code that is removed does not leave any residue behind. Java applets certainly also tread lightly on the client machine, but they must usually be downloaded each time they are run, which is not an acceptable deployment method for large enterprise applications.

Mobile code under .NET supports an incremental download model. We don't need to download the entire application to start running it, and if some portion of the application is never run, we can configure our application so that it is never downloaded. We must make explicit design decisions to implement this by segmenting our application into appropriate assemblies based on the projected usage patterns of the application. So for example, we might put the core code that will be executed every time (or almost every time) a browser requests the control in one assembly, and then place code that will only be executed rarely, or if the end user selects certain options, in other assemblies.

In this chapter, we are going to implement mobile code only in the browser of a personal computer running a Microsoft operating system. However, it is worth pointing out that MSIL is targeted towards other devices, such as PDAs, mobile phones, and Internet appliances, which will therefore eventually also be able to download and run mobile code using similar principles, although that will not necessarily be in the context of a web browser.

Security

The managed environment is very important – it provides the security services that make it safe to run this code, since .NET is able to determine whether the code can be executed based not only on what the code attempts to do and what permissions the client user has on the local machine, but also based on how well trusted the server from which the code was downloaded is. It therefore protects against malicious code in a variety of ways, and if we have a server that is authenticated as a secure source for code, the managed environment can give more privileges to the mobile code.

An enterprise application with appropriate security may have a requirement of caching data locally so that the application can continue to run when the user is no longer connected. By explicitly giving permission to the server (an action that must be taken on each client), we can give the server permission to do such things as creating data files.

There are a variety of security schemes, from simple schemes that are good enough for situations with low security requirements, to the more sophisticated schemes, such as Kerberos Authentication Protocol. With appropriate application design and appropriate setup of the web server, we can deploy highly sensitive applications and data with a great degree of assurance of the integrity and confidentiality of our system.

Sometimes this security scheme is called 'evidence-based' security, which allows the user to execute mobile code safely from sources that have not been given a greater degree of permission. We can configure the client machine so that, based on both the identification and location of the publisher, additional permissions are given to the mobile code. Code that is not so identified can still be run safely, because the managed environment does not allow it to access files on the client (known as **sandboxing**), nor to adversely modify the client.

The security system also protects against 'spoofing', where malicious mobile code could put up dialog boxes in attempts to extract confidential information from the user. If the mobile code does not come from a trusted source, it will be distinctly visually marked as being mobile code – we'll see this later in the chapter. It can't put up a window that looks just like the login dialog box, tricking the user to enter user IDs and passwords that can then be transmitted to the outside world. We'll also see what this looks like.

Implementation Overview

Before we start building examples, we'll take a broad overview of the process of implementing mobile code.

The first step is to write a custom control class (usually in either C# or VB.NET, though of course you can alternatively write the class in managed C++ or in any other language that targets the .NET platform). Most commonly the class will be a user control, and so derive from `System.Windows.Forms.UserControl`. Depending on what we want our control to do on the web page, we can implement several types of functionality in our control:

- We can draw graphics by writing a `Paint` event handler.
- We can add child controls that will be contained in our control.
- We can write methods in our custom control that we can call from whatever client-side scripting language (either JavaScript or VBScript) we are using on our web page.
- We can put up Windows Forms message boxes, dialog boxes, and windows from our custom control. These dialog boxes and windows are instantiated on top of the browser, as separate windows.

We need to set the compilation options for our custom control to ensure that we generate a DLL assembly. It is convenient to modify the project properties so that the assembly is automatically placed in the same directory as our HTML file. The HTML and DLL file must be put into the same directory, and this directory needs to be mapped to a virtual directory within the home directory of IIS. We'll go through the process of creating the virtual directory and setting its execute permissions.

It is important that we carefully name our custom control and its namespace – we will need to refer to the control name and its namespace in our web page.

Then we need to create the HTML file. In this file we use the `<object>` tag to specify a reference to our assembly and its contained control. We can then use JavaScript to manipulate our custom control. As mentioned earlier, we can also use the `<object>` tag in an ASPX file but for simplicity in this chapter we'll stick to plain HTML files.

Before we can run our custom control, we need to install and configure IIS. We'll see a quick checklist on what must be done to configure IIS a little later on.

Note that for the controls to work properly, the web pages that contain mobile code **must** be hosted by IIS, and you must request them from the browser using the http protocol. Pages that contain plain HTML and do not contain components can be brought up in the browser just by entering their path on the hard disk into the address bar of the browser, but this is not possible with this type of page. This is because entering the path of the hard disk means that the file, rather than the http protocol, will be used to retrieve the page, which means that IIS will not be involved in retrieving and processing the page. That's fine for plain HTML pages in most cases, but where .NET components are concerned, IIS plays an important role in determining if the assembly needs to be downloaded to the client, and if it does, sending the assembly to the client.

Finally, we need to start our browser, and point it to our web page.

That was a broad overview of the process of writing and executing mobile code. Now, let's get down to looking at the examples.

Our Examples

The examples we will build over the course of this chapter are:

- **HelloWorldMobileCode:** The simplest example possible – HelloWorld Mobile Code. This example also shows calling a method in our custom control from JavaScript.
- **DialogBoxesExample:** This puts up a Windows Form that we will design with Visual Studio.
- **EmbedControlsExample:** We add Windows Forms control to our custom control, so that they have the appearance of being siblings to the other HTML controls on the page.
- **WriteFileExample:** We'll see what happens when we use a control that tries to do more than it has permission to do.

Before we start on these, however, we'll need to set up IIS.

Installation and Configuration of IIS

Bear in mind that the procedures presented here may change slightly based on the exact version of .NET and the operating system that you are running.

Installing IIS

If you are running Windows 2000 Server (or Advanced), IIS was installed by default. If you are using Windows 2000 Professional, you will need to install IIS if you have not done so already. To install IIS:

- Click Add/Remove Programs in the Control Panel.
- Click the Add/Remove Windows Component button. This brings up the first dialog box of the Windows Component wizard:

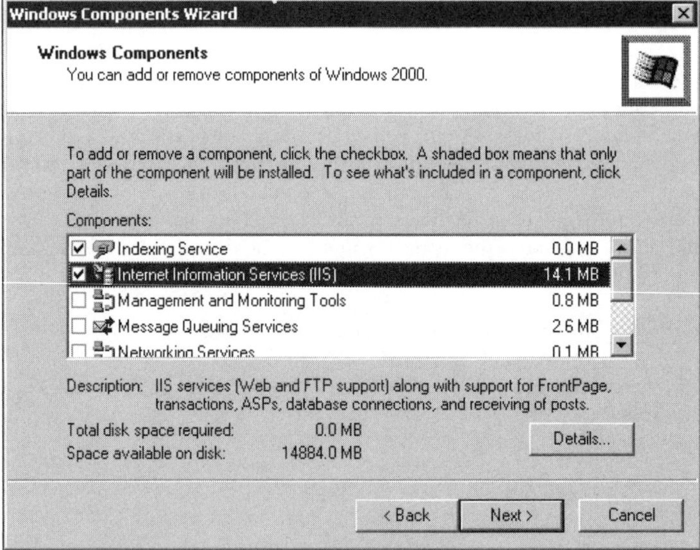

- Make sure that the check box in the list for Internet Information Services is checked.
- Click Next and follow the instructions.

Accessing IIS Documentation

If you have not yet read the IIS documentation, it is worthwhile to do so. To bring up IIS documentation, after installing IIS, you'll need to do this:

- From the Control Panel, click Administrative Tools.
- Click Internet Services Manager.
- Press F1 to bring up help.
- The right panel contains a link to the product documentation for IIS. Click on the link.

Alternatively, since you now have IIS running, we can go directly to the documentation by entering http://machine_name/iisHelp in the address bar of Internet Explorer, and in this URI, machine_name is the name of the server on which you have installed IIS (or just the string localhost if that is the same machine as the one you are currently logged in on).

Running the Permissions Wizard for IIS

After installing IIS, we may need to run the Permissions wizard:

- From the Control Panel, click Administrative Tools.
- Click Internet Services Manager.
- Expand the machine name, so that we can see entries on the hierarchical tool for Default FTP Site, Default Web Site, and Default SMTP Virtual Server.
- Right-click on Default Web Site, then select All Tasks / Permissions Wizard from the popup menu.
- Click Next.
- Click Inherit all security settings, and click Next.
- Click Replace all directory and file permissions (recommended), and click Next.
- Click Next.
- Click Finish.

Creating a Virtual Directory in IIS

We will put all of our examples into this directory.

- Create a directory named `C:\WindowsForms`. You can put this directory in another location if you choose, but you will need to refer to your new location as appropriate in these and other procedures.
- From the Control Panel, click Administrative Tools.
- Click Internet Services. This brings up the Internet Services Manager, an MMC snap-in used to administer IIS. Alternatively you can bring up the Internet Services Manager by running MMC from the command line, clicking on the Console | Add/Remove Snap-In menu item, and following the dialogs to add the Internet Information Services Snap-In.

- In the Internet Services Manager, right-click on the Default Web Site, and select New then Virtual Directory from the context menu, as shown in the following screenshot:

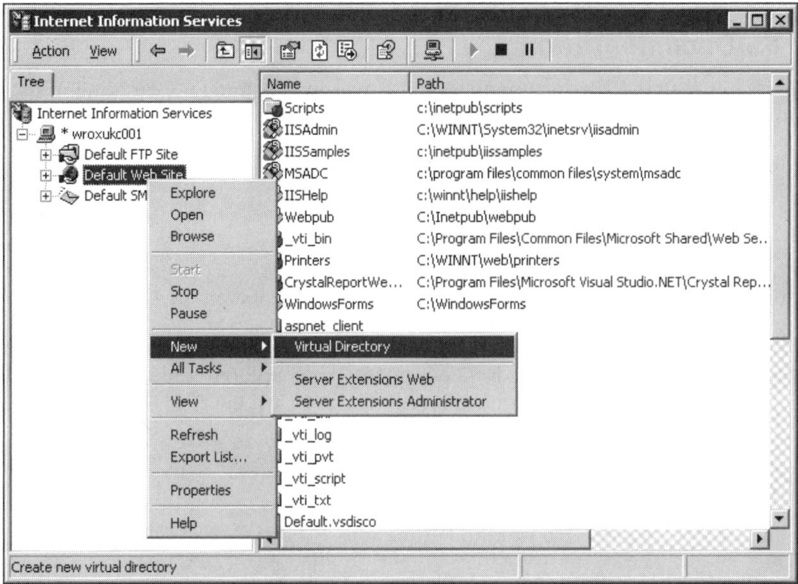

- Follow the instructions in the dialog boxes. The alias is the name by which the directory will be identified in HTTP requests. In this case we specify WindowsForms as the alias, and C:\WindowsForms as the path. This means that when an HTTP request comes in with the URI http://<ServerName>/WindowsForms/<FileName>, where <ServerName> is the name of the machine on which IIS is running, IIS will respond to the request by looking for the file C:\WindowsForms\<FileName>.

  Access permissions should be set to give at least Read access to clients for this virtual directory. For security reasons, you probably don't want to give any other permissions, though depending on the other files you wish to make available you may want to give script execution permission too. These are the default values anyway.

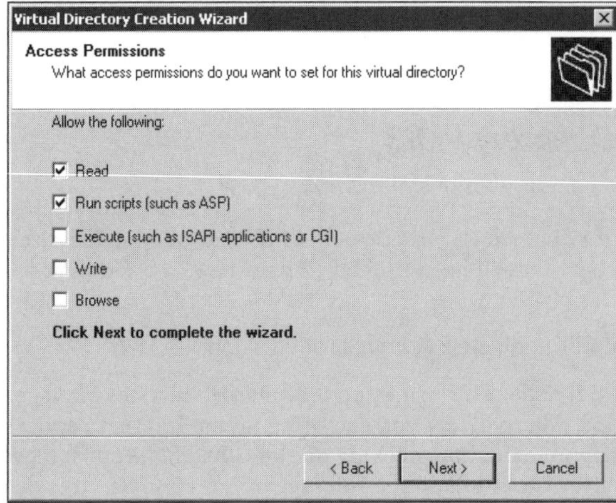

- Click OK, and close the Personal Web Manager.

As with any operating system, and any web server, there are many opportunities to create security holes. As an example, in the last procedure, if we had set Access Permissions to Write, and had set Application Permissions to Execute (including Scripts), we would have just granted anybody out on the web the ability to upload any program that they care to, and then execute that program on our web server. This program could do anything that it wanted to, including format our hard disk or get confidential files on our server and expose them to the world. Web security is a big subject, and can't be covered in this chapter, but be careful, and do enough research so that you are reasonably confident that you have created a secure system before going live with a web server.

Hello World Mobile Code

Our example is simple. We are going to use the tried and testing 'Hello World' example, but with a twist: this time, we'll be accessing it from a web page. In other words, we will write a short HTML page that displays the string, Hello World. But instead of displaying it using plain HTML, it will download a Windows Forms control from the web server that handles displaying of the text. We'll go through creation of the project here, but as usual the full code for the completed application can be downloaded from the Wrox Press web site.

To start off with, we will need to write the Windows Forms control that will be downloaded. To do this, we will write a user control that paints itself as the text, Hello World, on a yellow background.

Start Visual Studio, and create a new C# Windows Control Library project. Name the project HelloWorldMobileCode. This new project will be created with a user control named `UserControl1`. By default, the namespace for this user control is the name of our project, `HelloWorldMobileCode`.

We next add a `Paint` event to our user control. If necessary, review Chapter 6 on events for details on creating new events. In short, the procedure is:

- In the Design view, click on the user control to select it.
- Press F4 to bring up the properties window.
- Click the Events button on the tool bar (the yellow lightning bolt).
- Double-click on the `Paint` event. This will bring up the code editor window, with a newly created event handler for the `Paint` event. The insertion point will be placed in the newly created event handler.

Modify the event handler so that it contains the following code:

```
private void UserControl1_Paint(object sender,
        System.Windows.Forms.PaintEventArgs e)
{
    e.Graphics.FillRectangle(Brushes.Yellow, ClientRectangle);
    e.Graphics.DrawString("Hello World", Font, Brushes.Black, 10, 10);
}
```

We are going to add one more method, which displays Hello World in a message box, as opposed to painting it in the control's window directly, as the Paint event handler does), and which we will call from JavaScript in our web page. Add the following code to our custom control:

```
public void MyFunction()
{
    MessageBox.Show("Hello World!");
}
```

Next, we'll change the output path for our project so that after compilation it places the assembly in our new directory, C:\WindowsForms. Right-click on the project in the Solution Explorer and select Properties on the popup menu. In the left pane of the project properties window, click Configuration Properties. The default selection under Configuration Properties is Build, so we don't need to click it. Change Output Path in the right pane to C:\WindowsForms.

Save and build. Verify that `HelloWorldMobileCode.dll` has been placed in `C:\WindowsForms`.

Now, using any text editor, create a file with the following contents (we'll explain in it in a moment), name it `HelloWorldMobileCode.html`, and place this file in the directory C:\WindowsForms:

```
<html>
    <script language="JScript">
        function ExecuteMyFunction() {
            HelloWorldMobileCodeObjectID.MyFunction();
        }
    </script>
    <body>
        <p>Following is a user control that was written using the Windows
           Forms class library:
        <p>
    <object id = "HelloWorldMobileCodeObjectID"
        classid =
        "http:HelloWorldMobileCode.dll#HelloWorldMobileCode.UserControl1"
        height = "200"
        width = "200">
    </object>
    <p>
    <input type="button" value="Execute MyFunction"
        onclick="ExecuteMyFunction()">
    </body>
</html>
```

Now, start Internet Explorer 6.0. Enter the following address in the address bar: //localhost/WindowsForms/HelloWorldMobileCode.html.

If all went well, you will see the following web page:

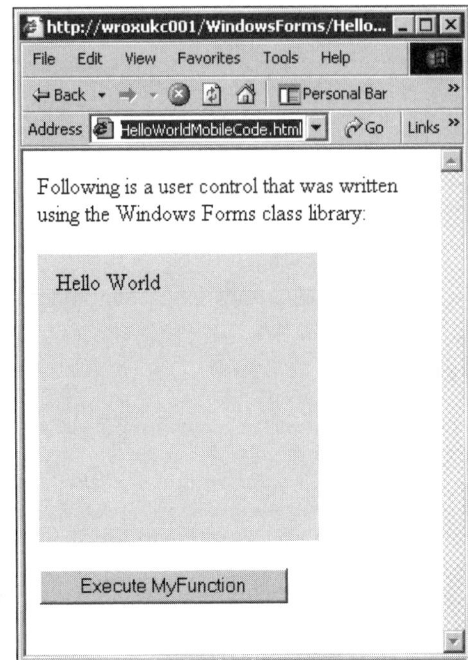

Clicking on the Execute MyFunction button will cause the control's `MyFunction` method to be called, displaying the Hello World dialog box.

The C# code is straightforward. It is identical to creating a small windows application, except that we compile it into a DLL instead of a Portable Executable file. We have seen similar code in many other places in this book.

If we are running IE on the local machine, and we attempt to modify our custom control and recompile it without closing Internet Explorer, we will get an error from Visual Studio telling us that it got an unexpected error creating the debug information. We must close Internet Explorer before we modify our custom control and recompile it. The reason for this is that as long as Internet Explorer is running on the local machine, the file is in use and so locked for writing operations. Hence Visual Studio.NET is unable to overwrite it with the newly compiled file.

The most interesting part of the HTML file is the `<object>` tag:

```
<object id="HelloWorldMobileCodeObjectID"
   classid="http:HelloWorldMobileCode.dll#HelloWorldMobileCode.UserControl1"
   height="200"
   width="200">
</object>
```

The `classid` needs to be formatted very carefully. We must specify the name of the DLL file, followed by the # symbol, followed by the namespace of our custom control, followed by a period (.), and finally, the name of the custom control.

The id attribute in the <object> tag above is the name by which this custom control will be known to scripting languages within this page. Notice that the scripting code refers to HelloWorldMobileCodeObjectID. Notice also, the JavaScript code that calls the method in our custom control:

```
<script language="JScript">
    function ExecuteMyFunction()
    {
        HelloWorldMobileCodeObjectID.MyFunction();
    }
</script>
```

This part of the HTML page demonstrates client-side interaction with the control.

Custom Dialog Boxes

In this example, we will demonstrate displaying of actual forms from a web page. We will design a couple of custom dialog boxes and compile them with our custom control into an assembly. We'll put these dialog boxes up when methods in our custom control are called by the client-side scripting language. We'll call these functions when buttons on our web page are pressed. This technique shows how we can have any number of forms that we can put up from a single web page, as well as showing client side interaction with the control.

Start Visual Studio, and create a new C# Windows Control Library project. Name the project DialogBoxesExample. This new project will be created with a user control named UserControl1. By default, the namespace for this user control is the name of our project, DialogBoxesExample.

Now, we'll build our first custom form. Select Project | Add Windows Form from the menu. Press OK to accept the default name of Form1. Drag two TextBox controls and a Button onto the form. Place them wherever you like. It should end up looking something like this:

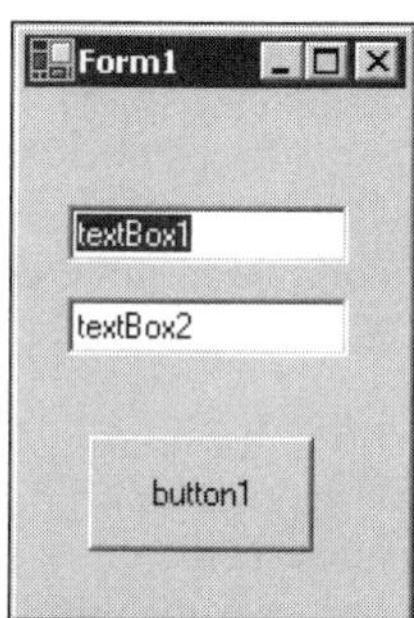

Now let's build our second form, make it so that it appears like this:

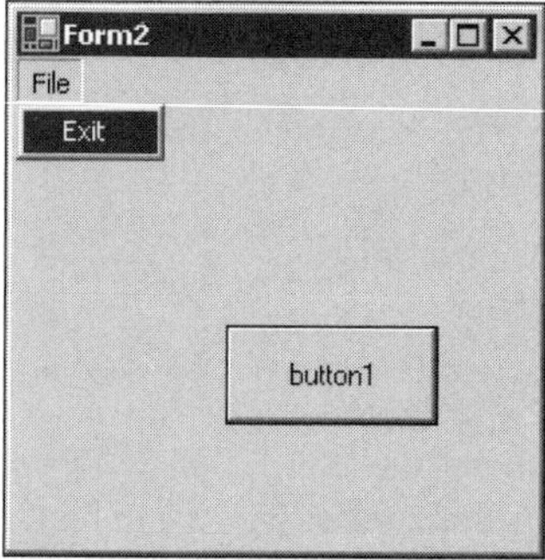

Double-click on the Exit menu item, and add the following code to the menu item event handler:

```
private void menuItem2_Click(object sender, System.EventArgs e)
{
    this.Close();
}
```

Add the following methods to the UserControl1 class in UserControl1.cs:

```
public void PutUpForm1()
{
    Form1 f = new Form1();
    f.Show();
}
public void PutUpForm2()
{
    Form2 f = new Form2();
    f.Show();
}
```

In the Properties window for the project, set the output directory to C:\WindowsForms and build the example.

Now create a file with the following contents, name it DialogBoxesExample.html, and place this file in the directory C:\WindowsForms:

```
<html>

<script language="JScript">

function PutUpForm1()
{
    DialogBoxesExampleObjectID.PutUpForm1();
}
function PutUpForm2()
{
    DialogBoxesExampleObjectID.PutUpForm2();
}

</script>
<body>
    <p>Press the buttons to put up examples of forms built using the
       Windows Forms class library:
    <p>
<input type="button" value="Put Up Form1" onclick="PutUpForm1()">
<input type="button" value="Put Up Form2" onclick="PutUpForm2()">
<object id="DialogBoxesExampleObjectID"
   classid="http:DialogBoxesExample.dll#DialogBoxesExample.UserControl1"
   height="0"
   width="0">
</object>
</body>
</html>
```

Now, start Internet Explorer 6.0. Enter the following address in the address bar: //localhost/WindowsForms/DialogBoxesExample.html (or, as usual, you can try running Internet Explorer on a different machine, in which case you should replace localhost in this URI with the name of the server, on which the web page and control have been installed).

The browser with the dialog boxes, after being run and after both buttons have been clicked, looks like this:

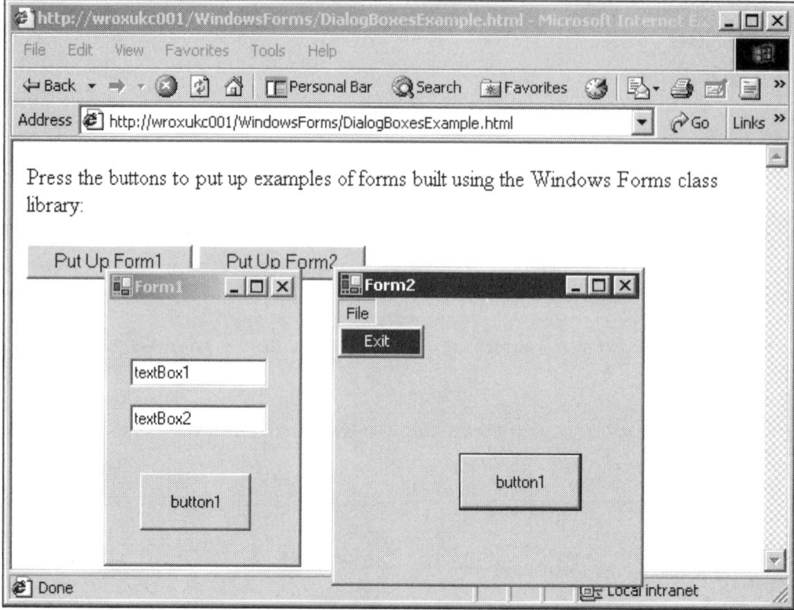

This example also shows the use of an invisible control. When we specify a height and width of the object as zero, it creates an invisible control:

```
<object id="DialogBoxesExampleObjectID"
    classid="http:DialogBoxesExample.dll#DialogBoxesExample.UserControl1"
    height="0"
    width="0">
</object>
```

This allows us to create a custom control that has functions that we can call from the scripting language, but which is itself invisible. This is potentially a powerful technique as it means that we can use the services of a .NET control that is intended to provide some other services to the web client (such as data access or validation), without actually being displayed as a control.

A Form within a Web Page

In this example, we will add some child controls to our custom control. This technique lets us put Windows Forms controls onto a web page in such a way that they look like siblings to traditional HTML controls. The result will be a web page that displays a form requesting some user input as shown:

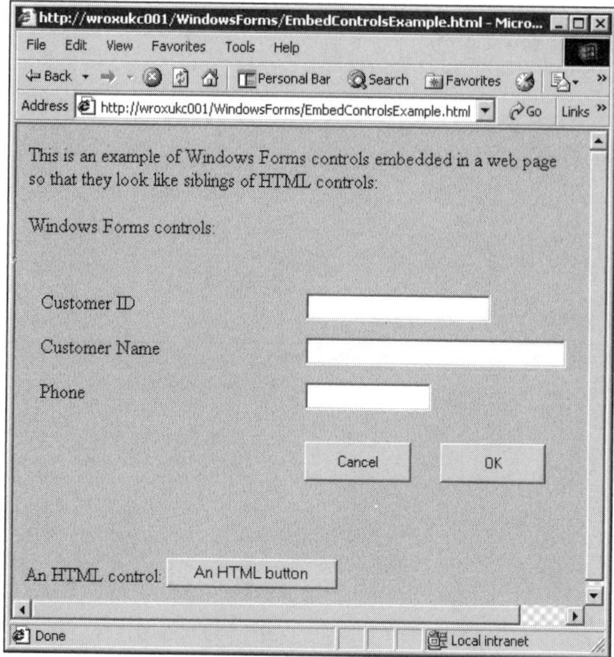

A similar effect could alternatively be achieved using Web Forms and ASP.NET pages, but our approach here, as remarked earlier, potentially allows a richer client-side user interface with fewer server round trips.

To write our control, we start Visual Studio and create a new C# Windows Control Library project. Name the project EmbedControlsExample. This new project will be created with a user control named `UserControl1`. By default, the namespace for this user control is the name of our project, EmbedControlsExample.

Resize the custom control and make it somewhat bigger. Add the TextBox controls, Label controls, and Button controls to our custom control. Set the FlatStyle property of the buttons to the value of System. Set the Font property on all of the TextBox controls to Arial 10 point. Clear the Text property of the TextBox controls. When you have finished, the design window will look something like this:

In the property window for the project, set the output directory to C:\WindowsForms and build the example.

Now create a file with the following contents, name it `EmbedControlsExample.html`, and place this file in the directory C:\WindowsForms:

```
<html>

<body bgcolor=silver>

<p>
This is an example of Windows Forms controls embedded in a web
page so that they look like siblings of HTML controls:
<p>
Windows Forms controls:
<p>
<object id="EmbedControlsExampleObjectID"
   classid="http:EmbedControlsExample.dll#EmbedControlsExample.UserControl1"
   height="220"
   width="500">
</object>
<p>
An HTML control:
<input type="button" value="An HTML button">

</body>

</html>
```

When IE and .NET render the custom control, they make the background color of the custom control the same color as the background of the web page, and they also make some adjustments to the colors of the child controls in our custom control. This behavior is implemented only if the background color of the custom control is not already the same color as the background of the web page. If the background color of the web page is white, the manipulations that IE does to the child control colors in our custom control do not look very nice, so the HTML for our page specifies a background color, as follows:

```
<body bgcolor=silver>
```

Note that the color called silver actually gets displayed as something that looks light gray.

This color is then the same color as the background color of our custom control, and thereby fixes the problem.

Writing to a File

The next example will attempt to write a file to the local file system, and shows security features of managed code.

Start Visual Studio, and create a new C# Windows Control Library project. Name the project `WriteFileExample`.

So that we can access the `StreamWriter` class, which is used to write to text files, without fully qualifying its name, add a `using` statement at the top of the file, as follows:

```
using System.IO;
```

Edit the code for `UserControl1.cs`, and add the following method to the class:

```
public void WriteToFile()
{
    StreamWriter strm = new
            StreamWriter("\\WindowsForms\\NewTextFile.txt", false);
    strm.WriteLine("This is some text");
    strm.Close();
}
```

As usual, in the property window for the project, set the output directory to C:\WindowsForms and build the example.

Now create a file with the following contents, name it `WriteFileExample.html`, and place this file in the directory C:\WindowsForms:

```
<html>

<script language="JScript">

function WriteToFile()
{
    WriteFileExampleObjectID.WriteToFile();
}

</script>

<body>

<p>Press the button to attempt to write to the local file system:
<p>
<input type="button" value="Write To File" onclick="WriteToFile()">

<object id="WriteFileExampleObjectID"
    classid="http:WriteFileExample.dll#WriteFileExample.UserControl1"
    height="0"
    width="0">
</object>

</body>

</html>
```

Assuming the browser is being run on a machine which has not been configured specifically to trust the server to write to files, when we put up the web page and click on the button, we get the following error:

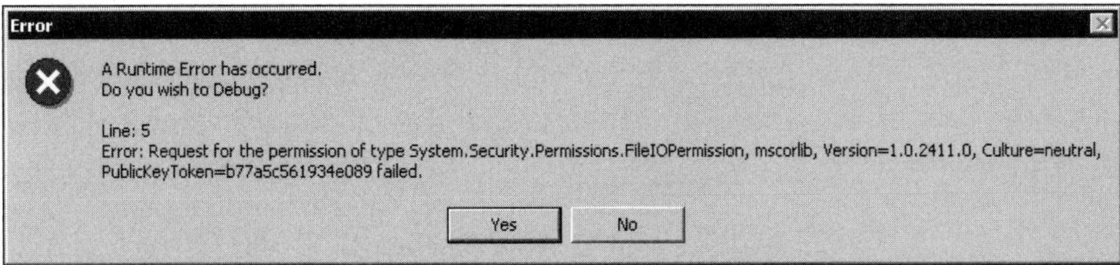

This error is fine – it's what we want here since the point of this example is to show that .NET security will step in and protect your client machine from potentially malicious actions by servers. Obviously if you do know what the control is doing and are happy to trust it, then you can configure the client machine to trust controls served up by that particular server to write to files – but doing so is beyond the scope of this chapter.

Preventing Spoof Controls

There is the potential that when a mobile code technology has the ability to create sophisticated user interfaces, malicious individuals or organizations in charge of web servers could write spoof controls that, for example, put up dialog boxes that trick the user on the client machine into divulging confidential information. To protect against this, when mobile code is run from an untrusted source, Internet Explorer puts up a note over the top of the dialog box explicitly informing the user that the application is not a trusted application. The user must click on the note before they can operate the dialog box. The note looks like this:

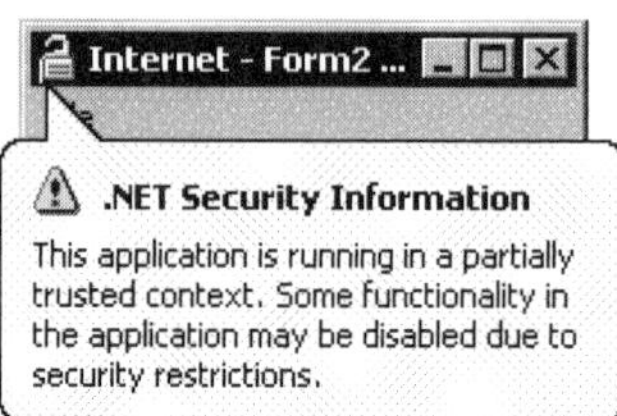

Summary

In this chapter, we saw how we can apply all that we have learned about building Windows Forms applications to building n-tier, thin client, zero-cost deployment applications. We can build Internet applications that have the look and feel of fat client Windows applications, but that have the maintainability characteristics and ease of deployment of a pure browser application.

We have seen a few of the capabilities of applications that are built using this fashion. We have gone through the exercise of writing the C# code to put up forms using this technique, and seen how to code HTML files that contain the custom controls.

We have understood some of the security considerations, and seen how users are protected from malicious code.

System.Object
System.MarshalRefObject
System.ComponentMode.Component
CommonDialog
ColorDialog
FileDialog
FontDialog
PageSetupDialog
PrintDialog
ErrorProvider
HelpProvider
ImageList
Menu
ContextMenu
MainMenu
MenuItem
NotifyIcon
StatusBarPanel
Timer
ToolBarButton
ToolTip
ListViewItem
TreeNode
Legend
Concrete Class
Abstract class
System.Windows.Forms
Control
ButtonBase
Button
CheckBox
RadioButton
DataGrid
DateTimePicker
GroupBox
Label
LinkLabel
ListControl
ComboBox
ListBox
CheckedListBox
ListView
MonthCalendar
PictureBox
PrintReviewControl
ProgressBar
ScrollableControl
ContainerControl
Form
PrintPreviewDialog
ThreadExceptionDialog
PropertyGrid
UpDownBase
DomainUpDown
NumericUpDown
UserControl
Panel
TabPage
ScrollBar
HScrollBar
VScrollBar
Splitter
StatusBar
TabControl
TextBoxBase
RichTextBox
Textbox
ToolBar
TrackBar
TreeView

18

Case Study: WebMate Web Site Development Environment

In this chapter we're going to examine WebMate – a real-life example of an application that's been written using Windows forms. Roughly speaking, WebMate can be thought of as a development environment aimed at assisting with the generation and maintenance of web pages for a web site. It is not purely a sample for this book; it's an application that has been used by the author for some time for web site maintenance purposes. When we say it is a developer environment – we really mean it! WebMate provides a user interface that has a lot of similarities with the Visual Studio .NET user interface, as can be seen from this screenshot of WebMate in action:

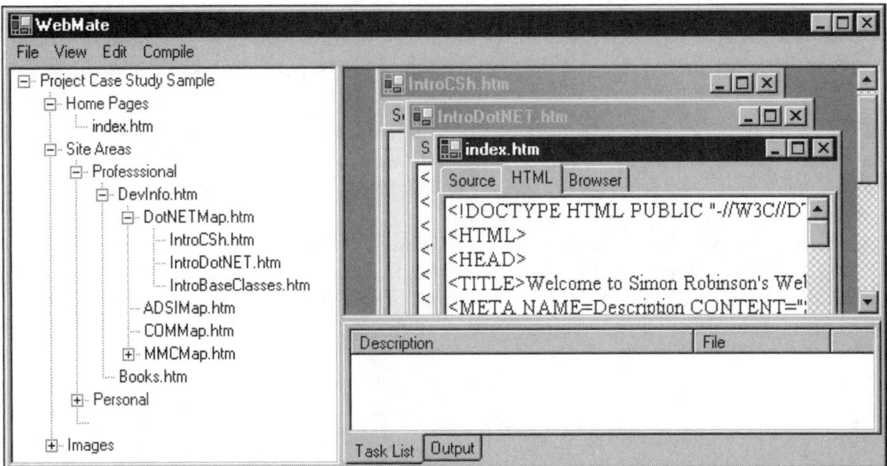

What we see here is an MDI application, which also features a couple of docked controls. These are a `TreeView` on the left, which displays the structure of the web site that is being written, and a tabbed control at the bottom, which displays data relating to the processing of the web site. The main area of the application contains a number of child windows. Each child window is devoted to the editing of one of the pages on the web site. Also notice that each child window contains a number of tabs that allow different views of that page.

Any developers who have ever looked at Visual Studio.NET (or at any of its predecessors, the VB, C++, and J++ developer environments for Visual Studio 6), and wondered how to write something with a similar user interface will find many of the answers here. Having said that, we should point out that there is no way we can develop something as sophisticated as Visual Studio.NET in one case study chapter! WebMate is much more restricted, and does not contain any windows other than ones displayed in the above screenshot. Also, unlike the docking controls in Visual Studio.NET, which can be freely moved around by the user, the controls in the WebMate remained firmly docked in the positions shown above (although they can still be resized). Despite that, it is quite a sophisticated Windows forms user interface we are going to develop. It has also been written with a strongly object-oriented methodology, making full use, for example, of implementation inheritance.

In summary, the main points about WebForms applications that this case study will illustrate are:

- Writing an object-oriented application that derives from the Microsoft standard Windows Forms controls where appropriate, in order to implement new functionality.
- Adding a sophisticated MDI user interface, in which various controls, notably a `TreeView`, interact with MDI child forms.
- Writing an application with developer environment-type features.
- Implementing intuitive and correct behavior for opening, saving, and creating new documents – in other words, making sure documents are saved correctly and no data is unintentionally lost (including coping with a situation where the user attempts to close an application when there are unsaved documents present).

We should point out, that since there is a limit to the size of application that we can cover in one chapter, the apparent sophistication of WebMate does come at a cost in terms of robustness, and in terms of fully implementing all the requirements for Windows GUI applications. In general, in a well-designed application (such as the WroxEdit application we saw earlier in the book), users should be able, for example, to access any of the features of the application through the mouse or keyboard. There ought to be appropriate main menu, toolbar, and context menu paths to access the main features.

> *Fully checking and supporting all possible inputs for WebMate would take a lot of work. So we have opted to present a more sophisticated though less robust user interface. In other words, a user probably won't have to try too hard to break the application by, for example, typing in silly input.*

We are going to start by having a look at precisely what WebMate is designed to do, and why it was written in the first place. Then we'll look at the application in action, going over how to use it. Finally, we'll look at the code and architecture behind WebMate. We'll focus in particular on the architectural principles and class hierarchy of the code.

Introducing WebMate

WebMate was written originally in order to assist the author in maintaining his web site, http://www.SimonRobinson.com. We can see why it is needed, by having a look at a typical page

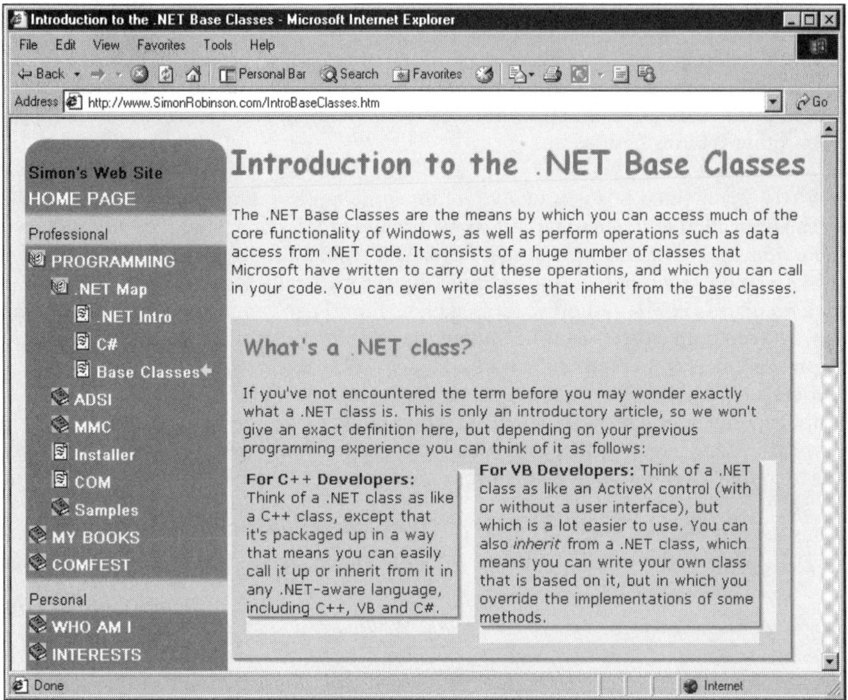

The page shown here contains an introduction to the .NET base-classes.

Note that, although we will be using this site to illustrate WebMate, and indeed the files that make up some of this site are included with the WebMate sample download, you shouldn't necessarily expect to find the site itself in the same state if you visit it. Also, be aware that, although you may run and test the sample code, and you may, if you wish, adapt it for the development of other web sites, the sample site itself (a subset of the author's own site) is copyright and may not be copied to other sites without explicit permission.

The site itself has quite a distinctive style, including the following features:

- Certain fonts and colors used (this is a black and white book, but if you look at the page, either on the web site or one of the sample downloads from Wrox, you'll find the color scheme is based on subtle shades of blue and purple!).
- There is a table of contents on the left. The table of contents shows that the site is arranged in a hierarchical, tree-like structure, so that by navigating the tree, we can get to any page on the site. It is also customized to each page, to show the location of that page in the site hierarchy. The table of contents also shows that the site is logically divided into a number of areas. The Home Page appears at the top of the table of contents, then areas such as Professional and Personal appear, each one highlighted in the table of contents. The actual site pages (other than the home page) are arranged in hierarchies within each of these site areas.

- Some highlighted areas within the body of each page are displayed with boxes that use a shading effect to make it appear that the area stands out from the page.

These features are not confined to this one page – every page on the site is designed to look similar. Many aspects of the site can easily be written by hand in HTML. The fonts and colors, for example, are defined in a style sheet. However, things like the table of contents are more problematic. The full site currently contains 60 pages, and adding a new page to the site means, in theory, that the table of contents might need to be changed in any or all of the other pages. Clearly, if this had to be done manually, it would be virtually impossible to make any substantial updates to the site! This alone would be sufficient to justify some sort of application that generated parts of the pages automatically. There are, however, other reasons besides this.

For example, the highlighted boxes actually require some quite complex HTML to make them display correctly. An application that generated the appropriate HTML code would greatly reduce the time involved in writing pages that contained these boxes. It would also be nice if coding up tags such as `<IMG>` and `<A>` could be simplified (for example, by automatically generating the alternative text for each image). Standard HTML authoring tools such as FrontPage cannot perform such specialized tasks, and this is why WebMate exists. WebMate allows us to write a site by simply creating a number of text files and typing in the text that forms the body of each web page. There is no need to manually type in HTML headers, etc. WebMate will process the pages to add the HTML headers, and will also automatically generate and insert all the HTML code required for the table of contents. This means that if we want to add a new page, we just write the body text for that page and insert it into the project, and WebMate will automatically update all the other pages on the site with the new table of contents.

The Web site consists entirely of HTML pages – it is not an ASP.NET application. WebMate exists to generate HTML pages and it should be noted is totally unconnected with Web Forms or ASP.NET.

> *You might be wondering why we don't simply use ASP.NET pages instead of HTML pages to allow the above tasks to be accomplished by ASP.NET controls when each page is requested. The answer is that the web site has been around since long before ASP.NET existed. At some point, the site will probably be upgraded to ASP.NET pages, but there would still be a need for some application like WebMate to maintain automatic records of the arrangement of pages in the resultant ASP.NET project.*

A Very Brief History of WebMate

WebMate was not originally a Windows Forms application. It was originally written in late 1999 as a VB6 application, and at the time, it did not have any GUI user interface. The web page files were simply edited in Notepad, or some other text editor. A layout file (which also had to be written by hand) defined the hierarchical structure of the site. WebMate was simply used to convert the text files into HTML files using the site layout file. This system was crude, but it provided sufficient automation to allow the site to be regularly updated.

When .NET appeared, offering the ease of VB-style UI coding, with the ability to easily write large object-oriented apps, I was curious to see how easy it would be to use Windows Forms to rewrite WebMate into a Windows application. An application that had a user interface that is sophisticated enough to allow most work involved in writing the site to be carried out from within the environment. The result is the C# program that is presented in this chapter.

> *WebMate does not deal with the uploading of files to the site – it is purely a local utility for generating the site on the local machine. There are plenty of ftp utilities around that make it easy to upload files, so there is little point duplicating this feature in the application.*

Using WebMate

When we first start-up WebMate, the individual controls (the `TreeView`, etc.) in the application are empty. As usual for an application that processes documents, we can either open a new document (a new **WebMate project** – each WebMate project represents a web site), or we can create a new document (project). Click File then New Project to create a new empty project, although as mentioned earlier, if you download WebMate from the Wrox web site, there is a sample project supplied with the code that you can open instead.

WebMate presents us with a dialog box asking for the name of the project. It will create a folder with this same name, so you shouldn't choose a name with any special characters in it:

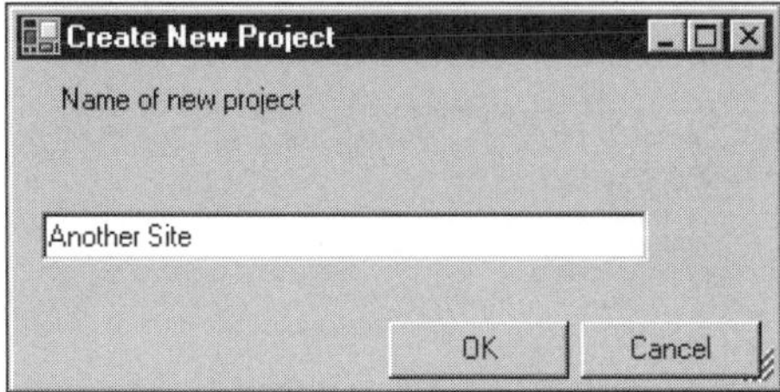

We don't get a choice of where the project goes. In order to keep things simple it is placed in a hard coded location: `C:\WebMate Projects\<Your chosen project name>`. (However, if we open an existing project, we do get the standard Open File dialog, which allows us to select location, so there's no problem if we want to move a project once we've created it.) After creating a new project, the tree view will look like this:

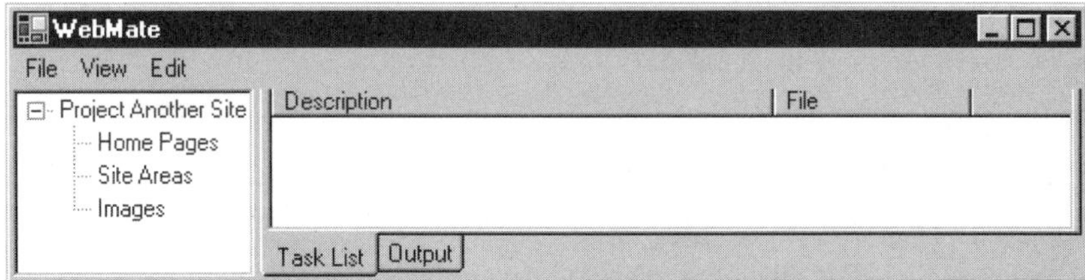

The tree view in WebMate is known as the **SiteExplorer**, since it allows us to navigate around the site, and serves an analogous purpose to the Solution Explorer of Visual Studio.NET. We don't yet have any files in the site but the outline structure is there. The nodes in the `TreeView` serve the following purposes:

Node	**Contains**
Home Pages	WebMate allows us to have more than one 'home page' (we might want to do this if we wish to offer alternative language versions, or a text-only version). On most Web sites, the home page is usually accessed without typing in any file name (for example, http://MyWeb site.com). However, since WebMate is not concerned with uploading the files to the server, as far as WebMate is concerned the only significance of a home page is that it appears highlighted in the table of contents. This means there's no problem with having more than one.

Table continued on following page

Node	Contains
Site Areas	The areas into which the site is divided (for example, Professional, Personal etc.). These are the areas marked in the table of contents for the site.
Images	Any image files that might be referenced from pages in the site.

We can also use Windows Explorer to examine the folder structure that WebMate has created:

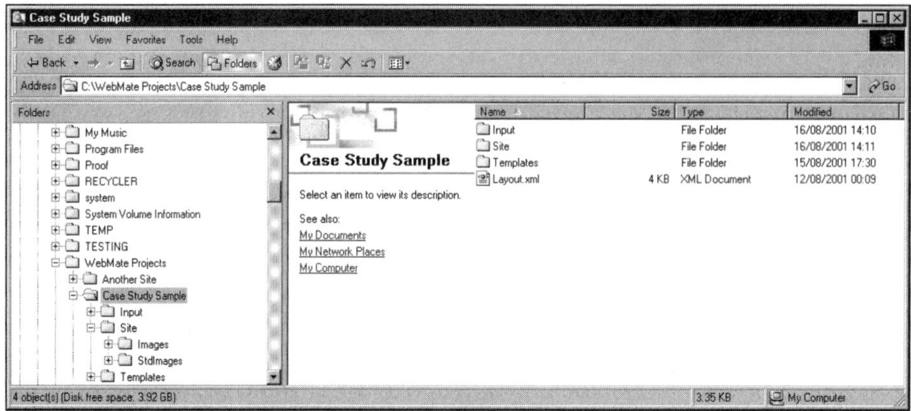

From this we can see that WebMate has created a folder for the project as a whole. It does this as soon as the new project is created. In that folder is a file called `layout.xml`. This file contains all the information about the site structure that WebMate needs. The file is in XML format, in keeping with the principle of .NET that we try to keep everything based on open standards if possible. There are also a number of folders in the project. These are:

Folder	Purpose
Input	Contains the text files that will be converted into pages on the site.
Site	Contains the site itself, as generated by WebMate.
Site/Images	Contains any image files used in the site. Note that, for simplicity, WebMate does not support any directory structure within the site, other than the folders that it itself has placed there.
Site/Std Images	This is similar to Site/Images, but it contains image files which WebMate itself inserts automatically, rather than ones that we have added to the site. Std Images includes the gif files for the rounded corners, and the various icons inside the table of contents. These files are not user-editable and do not appear in the SiteExplorer.
Templates	Container for any other files that WebMate might use in order to store information while we are working on the site.

Now that we have an empty site, we need to add some pages to it. There are two ways of doing this. The first way involves dragging and dropping files from Windows Explorer. We can do this if we already have files that we want to import into a WebMate project. The files should be plain text files (note: not HTML files – WebMate will ultimately convert the files to HTML format itself), and can be dropped into any part of the SiteExplorer that is able to act as a container for a web page. In practice, this means the Home Pages node, or any node that represents a file or site area already on the site. Dragging and dropping a file in this way means that WebMate will copy the file across to the Input folder in the project. Alternatively, if we want to create a new file from scratch, then we can go to the New menu and select New Web Page (or for a new home page, New Homepage). This will result in WebMate creating an empty text file ready for you to edit.

There is no menu option to import an existing file as a web page. As we mentioned earlier, the emphasis in the WebMate sample is on showing advanced sophisticated controls, rather than on sticking to standard Windows user guidelines. So, we will tend to find in WebMate, that there's only one way of accomplishing many tasks.

However, before we add any new files, we should add a couple of site areas (the Site Areas node can only contain site areas – it can't contain web pages directly. Recall that a site area is a set of pages that is listed together in the table of contents on the left of each web page). We do this from the New menu, selecting New Site Area. WebMate will look at the `SiteExplorer` in order to determine where to place the new site area, (or whatever new item we are trying to add). If a suitable item in the `SiteExplorer` is currently selected, WebMate will place the new item after that item or as a child of the item. If that is not possible (for example because no item in the `SiteExplorer` is selected or the selected item is unsuitable) then WebMate will find the first available position in the `SiteExplorer` tree at which the item in question can be added.

Once we have added a web page, we can edit the corresponding text file from within WebMate. All we do is navigate to that file in the `SiteExplorer` and double-click it (or hit the RETURN key). WebMate will open up a child window (which is known in the WebMate source code as a **FileForm**) that contains several tabs allowing us to edit and view the file. It will also activate the first tab, the Source tab, which is the one in which you can actually edit the file. The next screenshot shows the situation in which we've added a couple of files and site areas to the project and we are now editing the page DOTNetMap.

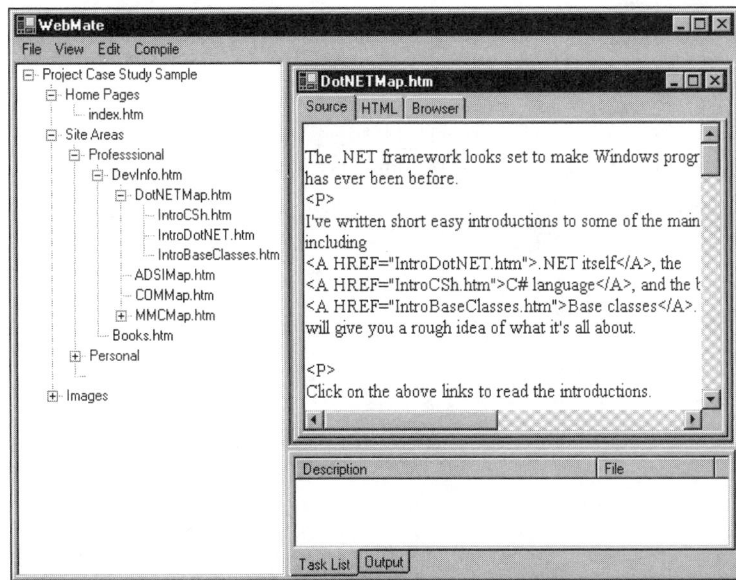

It can be seen from this screenshot that what we're typing isn't strictly HTML, although it appears to contain some HTML elements (it doesn't, for example, have an HTML header). This, apart from the ability to structure the site using the `SiteExplorer`, is the key to how WebMate simplifies the production of web pages.

The file being edited is a text file; it is stored with the extension `.txt`. The contents of this file are processed by WebMate to produce the corresponding HTML page. This means that the text we type into this file can contain HTML tags if we want – and these will be left unchanged by WebMate. However, WebMate will add all the required HTML headers at the start of the file, as well as the table of contents, and required trailing `</BODY></HTML>`, etc. tags at the end of the file. All we need to type in is the text for the main body of the page. After processing, this text will appear inside an HTML table cell in the final HTML document. However, WebMate is more powerful than that. It also recognizes a number of (what we will refer to as) **preprocessor directives**. These are commands that will be converted into HTML. As an example, the preprocessor directive, `*STARTPANELTABLE`, creates a raised table with the shading effect that we saw in the earlier screenshot of the `IntroBaseClasses.htm` page, while `*ENDPANELTABLE` marks the end of such a table. We will have a look at the full list of directives in the WebMate Preprocessor Directives section, later. If WebMate encounters a directive it does not understand, it will place an appropriate error message in the compiled HTML document.

Note that, as far as WebMate is concerned, we refer to the process of converting the directives to HTML as preprocessing, as this is done first. Next, the preprocessed HTML text is converted to a proper HTML page, by adding headers, and the table of contents, etc. We refer to this latter process as compiling.

The second tab in the child window, the HTML tab, simply shows the resultant HTML after WebMate has processed our source text. Compilation of the text file into an HTML page takes place automatically in the background, as soon as we select either the HTML or Browser tab, and is effectively instantaneous, so we never notice it happening. Alternatively, the Compile menu item under the File menu will cause all pages on the site to be compiled.

The textbox in this tab is disabled so its contents are not editable directly by the user:

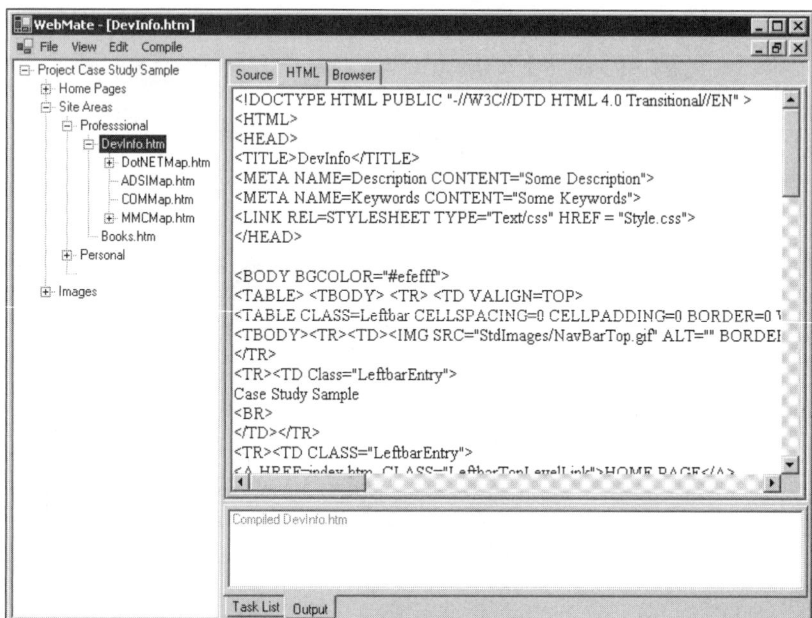

In this screenshot we notice that the Output tab of the lower tab control informs us that this text file was successfully converted to HTML. If there were any errors, these would be listed in the Task List tab.

The final tab (Browser) shows what the page will actually look like in Internet Explorer:

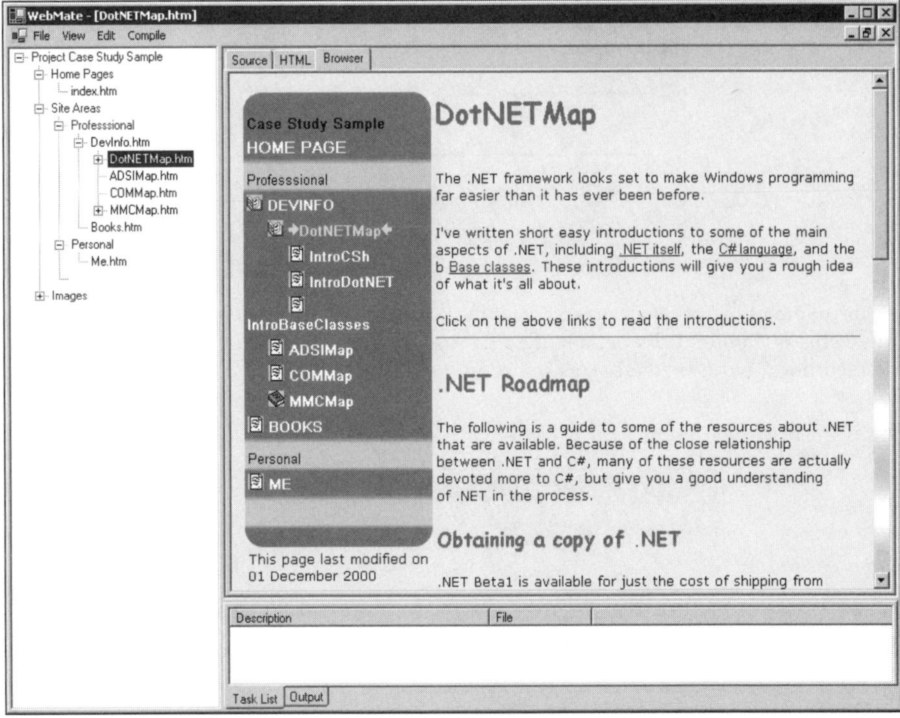

For this last screenshot, we've also maximized the child window, just to make the point that it is a real MDI child, with all the features we would expect from an MDI child window, including maximizing, minimizing, and resizing within the main window.

Finally, note that WebMate follows all the normal Windows user interface rules for keeping track of which files have been changed and ensuring we don't lose any data. So for example, if having just edited but not saved a page, we attempt to exit WebMate, we will be presented with something like this dialog:

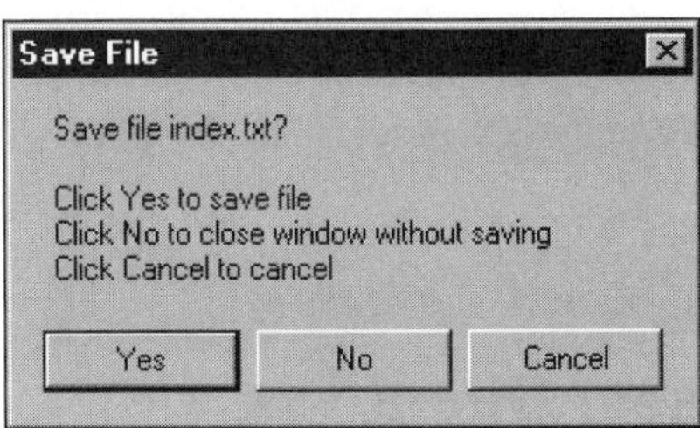

This might not look to significant, as we are all used to the fact that any well-written application that allows editing of documents will behave in this way. Nevertheless, it's significant here because we have to make sure we code up WebMate so that it does this! We'll see how this is done later in the chapter.

Project and Page Properties

WebMate also recognizes a number of properties, of both the project as a whole, and of each web page. These properties may be set, by selecting the item in question and clicking the Edit | Properties menu. If the node that represents the project is selected, this dialog is displayed:

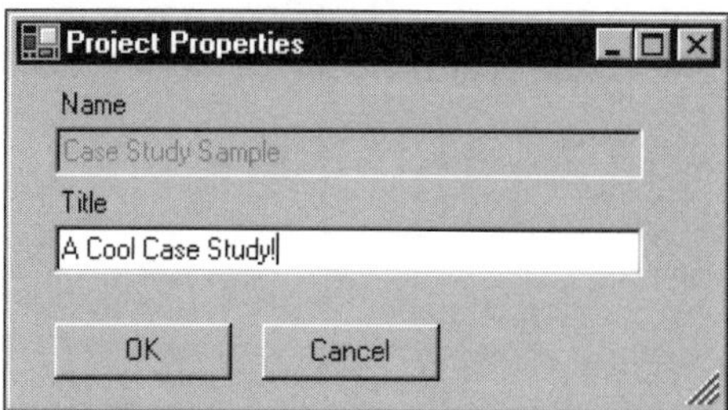

Name is the name of the project as recognized by WebMate, while Title is the text that appears at the top of the Table of Contents. By default, the title is set to the same text as the name (as happened in the earlier screenshots), but it is editable, as shown in the above dialog.

Individual web pages have rather more properties:

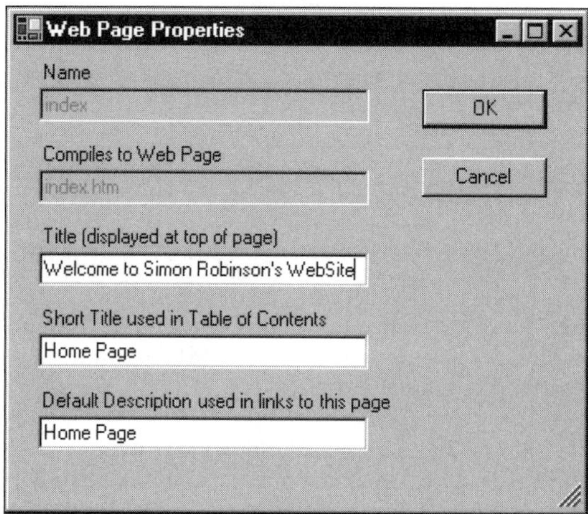

Again, Name is the generic name known to WebMate. The Web Page is the file name of the web page as it should be known on the compiled web site. The title is displayed at the top of the web page. The Short Title is the text describing that page as it appears in the table of contents, while the Default Description is what will be placed in a `*HLINK` preprocessor directive (covered in the next section) as the description of the target of a link to that page. The properties are all initialized to values based on Name when the page is first created, but most of them are editable via this dialog.

WebMate Preprocessor Directives

In this section, we will have a look at the directives that WebMate recognizes in text files. The directives are all indicated by an initial `*`. If a directive takes parameters, then these should follow in round brackets: `*HLINK(IntroCSharp)`. Several of the directives take optional parameters.

WebMate recognizes the following preprocessor directives:

Directive	Meaning
`*HLINK`	Creates an anchor `HLINK` reference, picking up the text that describes the reference from the name of the corresponding item in the project. For example, if the project contains a page known as IntroCSharp, which is compiled into the file `IntroCSharp.htm`, then the directive `*HLINK(IntroCSharp)` will be expanded into: `<A HREF="IntroCSharp.htm">Introduction to C#</A>.`
`*IMG`	Creates a link to an image. For example, if the project contains an image named Computer, which is stored in the file `Computer.jpg` and has the description, "Image of some computer", then the directive `*IMG(Computer)` will be expanded into: `<IMG SRC="Images/Computer.jpg" ALT="Image of some computer">.` `*IMG` can also optionally take extra parameters that represent the width and height of the image, if we wish to specify these.
`*STARTPANELTABLE`	Starts a raised table with a shadow. The color of the table can be optionally specified. We won't explain the HTML needed to do this here, since this is a Windows Forms book and not an HTML book, but it can be found in the source code for WebMate.
`*ENDPANELTABLE`	Ends the raised table. (If the corresponding *STARTPANELTABLE tag is missing this will lead to some strange HTML. A more sophisticated version of WebMate would raise such conditions as a compile error.)
`*REM`	The rest of the line is interpreted as a comment and is not passed through to the HTML file.
`*STAR`	Is converted to the `*` character. This is needed if the HTML file is to contain a `*` followed immediately by a letter (a-z, A-Z) since WebMate would interpret such a sequence in the source file as the start of a preprocessor directive.

Note that WebMate treats the preprocessor directives as case-insensitive.

One incredibly useful feature, which saves typing, is that WebMate will convert multiple new lines in the source text (that is, multiple carriage return-linefeed combinations) into HTML `<BR>` and `<P>` tags. A single new line will be ignored by WebMate. Two successive new lines will be converted into a `<BR>` tag. Three successive new lines will be converted to a `<P>` tag, while each subsequent successive new line will cause an extra `<BR>` tag to be added to the `<P>`.

Clearly, these preprocessor directives are quite restrictive. On their own, they are certainly not going to replace many of the HTML tags – hence the need to also place HTML tags in the source file. The importance of the preprocessor directives is that they save typing in certain key HTML constructs that occur repeatedly throughout the site. They also provide for some automation in the maintenance of the site. For example, if an image file is renamed, then there's no need to manually modify any HTML code if `*IMG` is used in place of the `<IMG>` element. This is because WebMate will automatically substitute the new file name wherever that image is referred to, when it recompiles the site.

Another benefit of WebMate that is slightly less obvious comes when we consider when a page was last updated. It is quite useful when browsing any site to know how out-of-date the information in a page is. WebMate automatically writes this information to each page compiled – but uses the last time that we edited the source text file. This means that the date placed in the page really will reflect the last time we changed the information in the body of the page, rather than, for example, minor changes to the table of contents caused by the addition of other pages to the site.

Although we have explained the preprocessor directives here so that you can use the WebMate sample, the code for the WebMate preprocessor / compiler won't be presented in this chapter since it is not relevant to Windows Forms. If you do want to examine this code you'll find it in the `Preprocessor.cs` and `Compiler.cs` files in the actual WebMate project. We will mention, though, that part of the code relies heavily on using regular expression technology from the .NET base-classes in the `System.Text.RegularExpressions` namespace to perform textual substitutions.

The Source Code

Now that we know how to use WebMate, let's have a look at the WebMate program itself. We will begin by looking at the object oriented architecture, and then look at the WebMate class hierarchy. Following that, we will look at various other topics including how to open and save projects, and how to edit Web pages.

Object-Oriented Architecture

As we would expect from a program written in an object-oriented language, WebMate contains a rich class hierarchy. In addition to this, since it is a Windows Forms application, many of the classes are derived from .NET base-classes in the `System.Windows.Forms` namespace.

In fact, object-oriented principles lie at the heart of the design of WebMate. Besides the fact that this means there is a rich class hierarchy based on implementation inheritance of classes, it also means that the different features of the program can be implemented locally within the most appropriate class.

To see what we mean by that statement, consider how we would have approached the program if we'd been coding in VB6. The heart of the program in VB6 would almost certainly have been the main `Form` object, representing the MDI form. There may have been additional dialog boxes, and we may have written some additional ActiveX controls.

Writing our own ActiveX controls can give some degree of object orientation, but in many VB programs, most code tends to be in the main `Form` object. This object takes all the event handlers for things such as mouse clicks, as well as selection of menu items and many of the other functions in the program, and usually grows 'spaghetti-like', to contain a huge range of functions and subs covering every aspect of the application.

By contrast, in WebMate, the class that represents the main window is a class called `WebMateForm`. This class is derived from `System.Windows.Forms.Form`, as we'd expect for Windows Forms application. However, in WebMate the `WebMateForm` class actually has very few responsibilities at all. Beyond instantiating the SiteExplorer and output controls, practically the only thing that `WebMateForm` does, is act as a container for those controls that are located in the MDI form, and supply the main menu, along with the event handlers for when the user selects menu items. Most of these handlers simply call methods in whatever other class is more suited to handle the particular event. In WebMate, just about everything is delegated to other classes on the basis that each class handles the work that is naturally its responsibility.

In a typical VB6 application, the SiteExplorer may well have been a `TreeView` control. However, in WebMate the SiteExplorer is an instance of a class called `SiteExplorer`, which is derived from `System.Windows.Forms.TreeView`. This means that it implements all the features of a standard `TreeView` control. The `SiteExplorer` class also knows how to handle, for example, drag-and-drop events that occur when the user drags a file into the SiteExplorer. Without implementation inheritance, these events would probably have been handled by the main form class – as would normally happen in VB6. In an object-oriented context, it makes more sense for the SiteExplorer itself to handle these, because these events only actually affect the SiteExplorer. Hence having the SiteExplorer handle drag-and-drop events makes for a cleaner separation of the different tasks in the program, with the result that the program is simpler to write and more maintainable.

This idea of objects taking responsibility for everything that is naturally their concern goes well beyond that. For example, consider the Project node inside the SiteExplorer. In WebMate, this node is not merely a simple tree node. A tree node, that is an instance of the .NET base-class, `System.Windows.Forms.TreeNode`, doesn't know how to do anything, except manage a node in a tree control. It can add children, and return some properties such as the text color and the background color, etc.

In WebMate, this node is an instance of a class called `ProjectNode`. `ProjectNode` is derived indirectly from `TreeNode`. In addition to the standard `TreeNode` methods and properties, `ProjectNode` is able to read the XML layout file that defines the project and so can set up the tree hierarchy below itself. Similarly, it can examine this TreeView hierarchy and use this to write out a new XML layout file. It can even tell when the tree structure has been modified and hence when the layout file needs to be saved before exiting the program. In other words, the `ProjectNode` isn't just a `TreeNode`: It manages the `TreeNode` and also manages the underlying object represented by the `TreeNode`. Since the two responsibilities are closely linked, it makes more sense for the `ProjectNode` to do this than for example the main form to handle the underlying project file represented by this `TreeNode`.

The list of specialized SiteExplorer nodes could go on. Nodes in the SiteExplorer that represents web pages are instances of the class `WebPageNode`. This class is also derived indirectly from `System.Windows.Forms.TreeNode`. In addition to basic `TreeNode` functionality, this class implements various properties of web pages that are recognized by WebMate (date last modified, title to be used in links to the Page, etc.), as well as maintaining a reference to the FileForm window that's used to edit that page, if one is open. The `Name` and `Title` properties, which are common to web pages and to the project as a whole, are maintained by a class, `UserNode`, which is a common base of `WebMateNode` and `ProjectNode`, lying between these classes and `TreeNode` in the inheritance hierarchy.

This object-oriented aspect of WebMate is something we should emphasize, as it provides huge benefits in maintainability that come from architecting any large project in this way. It is something that it would be well worth paying attention to when examining the source code for the project, especially for those who come from a Visual Basic background, and are therefore not used to programming in that style.

Of course, the above discussion shouldn't be taken to imply objects and inheritance did not exist at all in the pre-VB.NET days. VB6 does support interface inheritance, allowing objects to be encapsulated in each other and to expose interfaces, and a skilled VB developer will take advantage of this as far as possible. However, interface inheritance is geared more towards exposing contractual, fixed, interfaces to external applications (something not as relevant in the context of a single, self-contained application such as WebMate) and does not allow the direct specialization of objects in quite the way that implementation inheritance does.

Ex-C++ and Java developers will of course need no introduction to the kind of use of implementation inheritance discussed here. However, in the case of C++, before the days of .NET and Windows Forms, it was difficult to use implementation inheritance in the context of GUI classes in the way that we are doing here.

Coding the Project

As in any large project, there was inevitably some evolution (no matter how well planned the project appears to be at the start), with new classes appearing and existing classes taking on slightly different roles than those planned. Even so, writing of the code was kept relatively simple by having a good idea of the structure of the project before starting coding – in informal terms, a preliminary design was done. As we will see when we present the code, careful attention was also paid to using coding techniques that picked out potential bugs very early on.

The project itself is built as a single executable assembly.

We should mention that there is one disadvantage of using the implementation inheritance for Windows forms projects written using Visual Studio.NET. Namely, the design view in Visual Studio.NET, which we introduced in Chapter 2, doesn't really support this kind of inheritance. In other words, the design view expects us to place controls from the .NET base-classes onto forms using the toolbox. Although it is possible to customize the toolbox by adding our own controls, for example the WebMate `SiteExplorer` class, in practice the design view doesn't cope very well with this for the particular situation where our own controls are directly inherited from Windows Forms controls. As a result, the controls in WebMate were, in some cases, written by hand, rather than by dragging and dropping controls from the toolbox. In the code that we present in this chapter, we won't be particularly focusing on the code that instantiates the various controls, since that is all fairly routine Windows Forms code, and we have already encountered numerous examples of instantiating and displaying controls in previous chapters.

The following table will give you some idea of the procedures used for each of the controls and forms in WebMate.

Control	Procedure used to write code
`Main MDI Form`	Created as a new C# Windows Application project.
`All menus`	Created from Toolbox/Properties Window.
`SiteExplorer`	Class derived from `TreeView` – the code was written by hand. The `SiteExplorer` was added using the toolbox as a `TreeView` control, along with the corresponding splitter bar, then the VS.NET-generated code was modified by hand to change the `TreeView` instance to a `SiteExplorer` class instance.
`Output and TaskList Views`	The `TabControl` (a `System.Windows.Forms.TabControl` instance) containing these controls was added using the design view, along with the corresponding splitter bar. The output and task list views themselves are classes derived from `TabPage`, and the code to instantiate them as pages of the `TabControl` was added by hand.
`Child Form used to edit a web page`	Created as a new Form in the project.

Control	Procedure used to write code
View tabs in child form	The TabControl was added using the toolbox. The individual tabs within the TabControl are instances of classes specific to WebMate and derived from TabPage, and the code to instantiate these was added by hand. (Except that the browser control itself is a legacy ActiveX control added by the toolbox to a user control contained within the derived class.)

As noted in the above table, the controls used in WebMate include one legacy COM ActiveX control, the web browser used to display the Internet Explorer view of a web page. This is because at the time of writing there is no Windows Forms control available to perform that task. We examine the code used to add this control later in the chapter.

From this list we can see that where standard Windows Forms controls were used (as in the TabControls), these controls were typically added to the containing form using the toolbox and the Visual Studio.NET design view. For such controls this is usually the easiest way to get the code written. However, where controls were specialized to WebMate by deriving our own classes from the nearest corresponding Windows Forms control, we tended to simply add the code to instantiate the control manually. The main exception to this was the SiteExplorer, which was added as a TreeView control using the toolbox, and the code then customized by hand. The reason for this was so that a splitter control, in order to allow the SiteExplorer to be resized by the user, could also be added using the toolbox.

The main problem that prevented us from using the toolbox to add derived class instances was that our derived classes often contained setup code in the class constructor. If the class was added using the toolbox, Visual Studio.NET, in its attempt to be helpful, would actually read this code and duplicate it in the containing form's InitializeComponent method.

Unfortunately this meant that code would get executed twice when WebMate was run, resulting in runtime bugs. The design view, while useful for standard Windows Forms classes, isn't really intended to be used for derived classes in this way. Indeed, in order to prevent Visual Studio.NET from making unwanted changes to the instantiation of the SiteExplorer control, we eventually resorted to copying and pasting the main MDI form's InitializeComponent method to a new method, NoDesignInitializeComponent so that VS.NET couldn't fiddle with it!

```
#region Copied from Designer generated code so designer can't fiddle with it
/// <summary>
/// Required method for Designer support - do not modify
/// the contents of this method with the code editor.
/// </summary>
private void NoDesignInitializeComponent()
{
   this.splitter2 = new System.Windows.Forms.Splitter();
   this.splitter1 = new System.Windows.Forms.Splitter();
   // etc.
```

The old InitializeComponent method was retained, but the code to call it from the constructor commented out. In this way it could still be used to examine the menu items with the design view, but the code in it wouldn't get actually executed when WebMate was run.

```
public WebMateForm()
{
// removed because VS.NET keeps writing bugs into InitializeComponent()
//          InitializeComponent();
   NoDesignInitializeComponent();
   WebMateNode.InitializeNodes(siteExplorer, this);
   this.outputTabSet.TabPages.Add(taskList);
   this.outputTabSet.TabPages.Add(output);
}
```

These changes to the main MDI Form, WebMateForm, are unconventional, but at least it allowed us to get some use out of the design view, while still using our own specialized derived classes.

The disadvantage of not being able to fully use the VS.NET design view and, to some extent having to add our own workaround, was considered insignificant next to the huge maintainability benefits of using object-oriented principles in the code. The benefits of having Visual Studio write code automatically for us using the design view tends to remain constant, irrespective of the size of the project, whereas the benefits of using inheritance appropriately, and of using sound object-oriented principles are proportionately, far greater for large projects such as WebMate.

We're not going to attempt to present any of the standard code in WebMate that places controls on forms, etc. The rest of the book has adequately covered that kind of code. Instead, we'll focus on the implementation of more advanced features, such as the support for dragging and dropping files into the SiteExplorer. We will also examine how the object-oriented architecture works in practice.

Since WebMate is too large a project to realistically present more than a small proportion of its code in this chapter, we will take a task-oriented viewpoint. We will take a couple of the tasks that the user might perform while running WebMate, and work through the sequence of code that gets executed for each of these tasks. This means that we will see, in a natural way, how the flow of execution jumps between the various classes that make up the project. The tasks we will cover include opening a project (including saving any previous projects), and dragging and dropping files.

Before we do that, however, we will briefly review the WebMate class hierarchies.

WebMate Class Hierarchy

The classes that make up WebMate are as follows. (Note that all classes are in the namespace `Wrox.ProfessionalWindowsForms.WebMate`.)

Forms

All these classes are derived from `System.Windows.Forms.Form`.

Class	Purpose
`FileForm`	The child MDI form that allows editing of a file.
`InputDialog`	Utility class that represents a dialog box, which requests the user to input one string into a dialog box, and returns the result.
`ProjectPropertiesDialog`	The dialog (illustrated earlier) that allows the user to edit properties of a project.

Class	Purpose
WebMateForm	The parent MDI form for the application.
WebPagePropertiesDialog	The dialog (also illustrated earlier) that allows the user to edit properties of a web page within the project.

Controls

These controls are all derived from a .NET base-class in the `System.Windows.Forms` namespace:

Class	Derived From	Purpose
BrowserControl	UserControl	Container for the ActiveX web browser control that displays web pages.
BrowserView	TabPage	Displays compiled web pages visually (contains a `BrowserControl`).
HTMLView	TabPage	Displays compiled web pages in plain text (contains a `RichTextBox`).
OutputTabSet	TabControl	The tab control containing the task list and output views (contains `OutputView` and `TaskListView`).
OutputView	TabPage	Displays output from compilation process (contains a `TextBox`).
SiteExplorer	TreeView	The WebMate `SiteExplorer` window.
SourceView	TabPage	Tab that allows user to edit text files that will be compiled to web pages (contains a `RichTextBox`).
TaskListView	TabPage	Displays compilation errors (contains a `ListView`).

'TreeNode' Classes

These classes represent the various nodes in the SiteExplorer `TreeView`. They are derived either from `System.Windows.Forms.TreeNode` or from other WebMate `TreeNode`-derived classes:

Class	Derived From	Purpose
HomePagesNode	WebMateNode	Implements the `SiteExplorer` node that contains all home pages.
ImageNode	UserNode	Implements a `SiteExplorer` node that represents an image.
ImagesNode	WebMateNode	Implements the `SiteExplorer` node that contains all images.
ProjectNode	UserNode	Implements the `SiteExplorer` node that represents a complete project.

Table continued on following page

Class	Derived From	Purpose
`SiteAreaNode`	`UserNode`	Implements a `SiteExplorer` node that represents a site area.
`SiteAreasNode`	`WebMateNode`	Implements the `SiteExplorer` node that contains all site areas.
`UserNode`	`WebMateNode`	Abstract base-class that implements features of those `SiteExplorer` nodes that can be dynamically added to the project by the user.
`WebMateNode`	`TreeNode`	Abstract base-class that implements features common to all the nodes in the `SiteExplorer`.
`WebPageNode`	`UserNode`	Implements a `SiteExplorer` node that represents a web page.

Since the `TreeNode` classes form an integrated hierarchy, we will show a diagram of the hierarchy for just these classes:

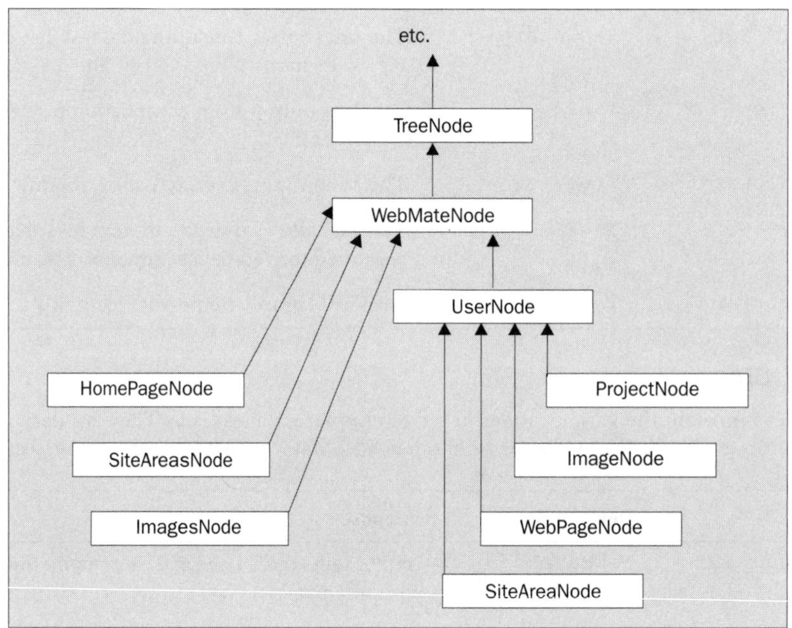

Other classes

These classes are all derived from classes in the `System` namespace:

Class	Derived From	Purpose
`Compiler`	`Object`	Compiles a web page.
`FilePaths`	`Object`	Contains strings that indicate various file and folder names used in WebMate. Never instantiated – all members are static.
`InsertLocation`	`ValueType`	Helper struct that indicates where a new item is to be added to the `SiteExplorer` tree. (NB. This is a struct, not a class.)
`MainProgram`	`Object`	Contains the static `Main` method that forms the entry point to WebMate.
`Preprocessor`	`Object`	Preprocesses a web page.

Saving a Project

Saving is a very important feature of any application that invites the user to edit any kind of document. There are several situations in which an application might be called upon to save a project – these include the user explicitly asking the application to do so, often by clicking on the appropriate menu option, or if the application is closed or a new project opened. We'll start off here by looking at what happens when the user clicks on the Save Site menu option in WebMate, though we will see later how other actions can feed into the same process of saving the project. Examining the process of saving a project will very clearly demonstrate how inheritance is used in combination with careful selection of which class is responsible for each action is used in the WebMate architecture.

As mentioned earlier, the main MDI menu options in WebMate tend to be handled by methods in the `WebMateForm` class, which represents the main MDI form. However, the handler for `SaveSite` does no more than delegate the task to the `SiteExplorer` object:

```
public class WebMateForm : System.Windows.Forms.Form
{
    private void OnFileSaveSite(object sender, System.EventArgs e)
    {
        SiteExplorer.Project.SaveRecursive();
    }
```

The above code snippet illustrates the way that we are going to present the code in this chapter: Rather than simply presenting the full definitions of each class we will simply work through the code that is actually executed in order to perform the task in question. The full class definitions are of course readily available with the source files for WebMate.

For the rest of this chapter we will be showing a large number of member functions and fields in a number of different classes. To make the code samples clearer we will normally prefix each piece of code with the declaration of the appropriate class as above, ignoring the fact that, in the actual code for WebMate, there will usually be a number of other functions and field declarations between the class declaration and the code we are examining.

We note in this code that SiteExplorer is a field in the WebMateForm class of type SiteExplorer and which is initialized to refer to the SiteExplorer control (which we recall is derived from TreeView).

```
public class WebMateForm : System.Windows.Forms.Form
{
    private Wrox.ProfessionalWindowsForms.WebMate.SiteExplorer siteExplorer;
```

In general though, we won't necessarily explicitly show the code for definitions of member fields where the meaning of those fields is obvious.

SiteExplorer.Project is a property in the SiteExplorer class of type ProjectNode, which is always initialized to refer to the TreeNode that represents the project as a whole. Since this node represents the project, it is considered the responsibility of this node to deal with loading and saving projects. Saving the project is done through its SaveRecursive method. The name SaveRecursive should give us some clue that this method is implemented to recursively run through the tree, saving any required file corresponding to each node.

In fact, SaveRecursive is not defined in ProjectNode at all – it's defined in the base-class, WebMateNode, since it's a method that needs to be implemented by all nodes, irrespective of their type. It looks like this:

```
    class WebMateNode : TreeNode
    {
        public virtual void SaveRecursive()
        {
            foreach (TreeNode node in this.Nodes)
            {
                WebMateNode child = node as WebMateNode;
                Debug.Assert(child != null);
                child.SaveRecursive();
            }
        }
...
```

This method simply runs through the children of a given tree node, calling itself against each of them. In order to do this it needs to cast each child to a WebMate node. Notice that we have used the Assert method of the System.Diagnostics.Debug class to verify that the result of the cast is not null. This method is used in debug builds to verify that the Boolean expression it has been passed evaluates to true, and it is extremely good practice to use it liberally throughout code since it ensures very early detection of a number of bugs.

Basically, whenever we see a point in the program at which some condition ought always to hold, then you can make sure this is the case by using Debug.Assert. The beauty of this method is that it is completely ignored by the compiler in release builds, and so will not impact either the program size or the performance when it ships the software. In this particular case, the Assert should never fail because in WebMate there should never be any tree nodes instantiated that are not actually instances of classes derived from WebMateNode.

You might, incidentally, wonder why we didn't simply write:

```
WebMateNode child = (WebMateNode)node;
```

In place of the lines:

```
WebMateNode child = node as WebMateNode;
Debug.Assert(child != null);
```

Both forms of code should have a similar effect. The reason for preferring the second form is that it will immediately break into the debugger, whereas the first will merely throw an `InvalidCastException`. Since we know that this should *never* happen if WebMate has been debugged correctly, exceptions are not really appropriate here. They are more appropriate for situations that happen rarely, but which are theoretically possible.

You also might wonder about the fact that our `SaveRecursive` method doesn't actually seem to do anything apart from run through all the nodes in the tree. When it reaches a node that has no children, the method will simply return immediately. However the key here is that we have defined `SaveRecursive` as a virtual method, which means it can be overridden. When we save the files, there are some types of node that don't have to do anything. The `ProjectNode` saves the XML layout file that defines the project. Each web page node is responsible for saving its corresponding text file and HTML file. However, some WebMate nodes do not represent objects that can or should be saved. Nodes such as the `ImagesNode`, the `SiteAreasNode`, and the `HomePagesNode` are simply containers for other nodes that are defined within the WebMate application. When we are saving the project, we simply require these nodes to pass the save operation on to their children, which is what the `SaveRecursive` method above does.

Referring back to the class hierarchy for WebMate nodes, we see that we have placed another abstract class (`UserNode`) to represent all nodes which are defined by the user, and which therefore might represent savable resources. `UserNode` supplies an override to `SaveRecursive`, which looks like this:

```
public abstract class UserNode : WebMateNode
{
    public override void SaveRecursive()
    {
        base.SaveRecursive();
        this.Save();
    }
```

This override still passes the `Save` method to all the children of this node, but also calls a method that saves this node, which is defined in `UserNode` as an abstract method.

```
public abstract class UserNode : WebMateNode
{
    public abstract void Save();
```

Since this method is abstract, it must be overridden by every class that derives from `UserNode`. There are several such classes, so we're not going to go over the details of the `Save` method for each one. For the case of `ProjectNode` class, `Save` uses a similar recursion technique to the one we have just seen to iterate through all the nodes, converting each node to an XML element, which is added to an XML document and saved as the `layout.xml` file. `ImageNode.Save` does nothing, since WebMate doesn't include the ability to edit images. (Even though this means we have to define a do-nothing override to `Save` in `ImageNode`, it was felt it was still better programming practice in this case to define `UserNode.Save` as abstract, thus ensuring that the compiler forces us to make a positive decision of how to implement `Save` for any `UserNode`-derived classes.)

Here we will only show the implementation of `Save` for `WebPageNode`. The implementation is actually quite simple, since the `WebPageNode` object itself doesn't have access to the text that needs to be saved. Knowledge of that text is in the `RichTextBox` inside the **Source** tab in the `FileForm` window associated with that file, assuming that one is open. If no such window is open then the user cannot have edited the file. The field `WebPageNode.editingForm` contains a reference to the `FileForm`. With that knowledge, you should be able to follow what this code does:

```
public class WebPageNode : UserNode
{
    public override void Save()
    {
        if (isDirty == false)
            return;
        Debug.Assert(this.editingForm != null);
        this.editingForm.SourceTab.SaveFile();
        IsDirty = false;
    }
```

The `SaveFile` method in the `SourceView` class that is called to actually save the data, uses the `RichTextBox.SaveFile` method, which is defined in the `RichTextBox` .NET base-class supplied by Microsoft.

```
public class SourceView
{
    public void SaveFile()
    {
        string fullPath = node.FullInputFilePath;
        textBox.SaveFile(fullPath, RichTextBoxStreamType.PlainText);
        FileInfo file = new FileInfo(fullPath);
        file.LastWriteTime = node.LastModifiedDate;
    }
```

This method actually calls back into the `WebPageNode` (represented by the node field) at a couple of points – in order to retrieve the full pathname of the text file (`node.FullInputFilePath`) and the date we wish to use as the last modified date (`WebPageNode.LastModifiedDate` property). `FileInfo`, incidentally, is a .NET base-class supplied by Microsoft which is defined in the `System.IO` namespace and which represents a file in a file system.

If your pre-.NET background is C++, you will probably have found it easy enough to follow the logic of what we've been doing so far, since the programming methodology we've been using is much the same as the approach you would normally use. If you have come from a VB background and are not used to classic implementation-inheritance-based object-oriented programming, then you might be thinking that the code presented above seems confusing, because of the way that we keep swapping from one class to another. The most obvious example of this being the way that the `WebPageNode.Save` method called up `SourceView.SaveFile` to save the file, but then this latter method promptly called back into the same `WebPageNode` object in order to find out where the file should be stored and what its last modified date should be!

Although this architecture looks strange at first sight, it really does make large projects easier to maintain. The overriding principle behind it is that – as mentioned earlier – each object has a certain area of responsibility, and each task that needs to be done is delegated to the appropriate object. In a non-object-oriented approach, we might have had the `WebMateForm` handle saving everything. This would save us from having to keep swapping between objects, but it would also mean that the class representing the main form would contain a huge and very hard-to-maintain mass of code.

The object-oriented approach, on the other hand, says that each object within the hierarchy of the project – in other words each node in the SiteExplorer – should know how to save itself. The ProjectNode knows how to save project layout files, while the WebPageNode knows how to save itself as an individual text file. In the case of WebPageNode, there is a further separation of responsibility, in that the WebPageNode knows where the text file it represents is and what its properties are and whether it needs to be saved, but it does not know what the contents of the file should be. That information is stored in the RichTextBox into which the user has been making their modifications to the file. This RichTextBox is managed by the **Source** tab in the file window, represented by our SourceView class.

Opening a Project

Opening an existing project is likely to be one of the first things you do when you run WebMate. A project is opened when the user clicks the **File | Open** menu. So the first thing that is executed is the handler for this menu item, which is a member method of the WebMateForm class, OnFileOpen:

```
public class WebMateForm : System.Windows.Forms.Form
{
private void OnFileOpen(object sender, System.EventArgs e)
    {
    // ask the user to save any existing project
    // Abandon open if the user cancels

        bool okToContinue = siteExplorer.SaveAndCloseProject();
            if (!okToContinue)
            return;

        dlgOpenProject = new OpenFileDialog();
        dlgOpenProject.Title = "Open Web site";
        dlgOpenProject.Filter = "WebMate Project Files (*.xml)|*.xml";
        dlgOpenProject.FileOk += new CancelEventHandler(this.OnOKOpenProject);
        dlgOpenProject.ShowDialog();
    }
...
```

The bulk of this method is given over to instantiating a standard Windows Forms OpenFileDialog. However, before this is done, a member method of the SiteExplorer object is called, SiteExplorer.SaveAndCloseProject. Recall that the WebMateForm.siteExplorer field contains a reference to the application's SiteExplorer control.

The purpose of calling this method is to make sure that we don't lose any data. WebMateForm.OnFileOpen has no way of knowing that we have only just started WebMate. For all it knows, we might have been editing another project, which we haven't yet saved. Therefore, WebMate, being a well-behaved application, needs to check whether this is the case, and if so it displays a suitable dialog box, asking the user what they want to do:

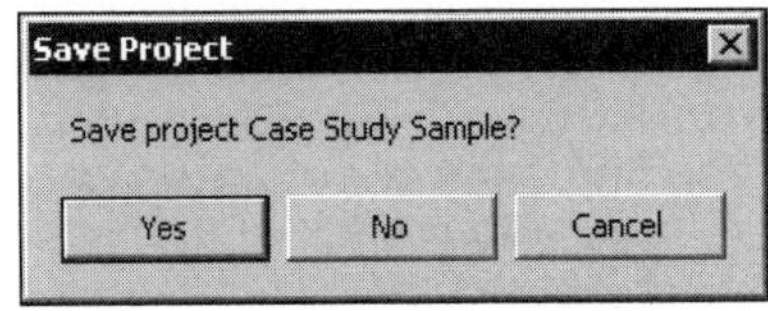

The code that handles this process is this:

```
public class SiteExplorer : System.Windows.Forms.TreeView
{
    public bool SaveAndCloseProject()
    {
        if (Project != null && Project.DirtyNodes > 0)
        {
            DialogResult result = MessageBox.Show("Save project " + Project.Name +
            "?", "Save Project", MessageBoxButtons.YesNoCancel);
            if (result == DialogResult.Cancel)
                return false;
            if (result == DialogResult.No)
                return true;
            Project.SaveRecursive();
        }
        return true;
    }
```

In order to understand this code we need to know that the `SiteExplorer.Project` property returns a reference to the node in the SiteExplorer that represents the project. This property is therefore of type `ProjectNode`. We will encounter this property frequently, since most of the other classes in the application frequently use this reference in order to access the project.

In the above code, we first check that the `Project` is not `null` (`null` meaning that no project has yet been loaded), and whether any files of the project are dirty (in other words, require saving; the `ProjectNode.DirtyNodes` property maintains a count of how many files are dirty).

There is nothing to do unless both of these conditions are true. (Notice how in the test, we make use of the fact that, in C#, conditional expressions are evaluated from left to right until a definite answer is obtained. Hence in the statement:

```
if (Project != null && Project.DirtyNodes > 0)
```

The computer will only examine the `Project.DirtyNodes` property if it has already determined that `Project` is not null – so there's no danger of a `null` reference exception being raised. This would not necessarily be the case in VB.NET.

If we discover that there are saved files in a current project, then we display the `MessageBox` shown in the previous screenshot, and take the appropriate action. If the user does request to save the project, then we do so by calling the `ProjectNode` class's `SaveRecursive` method which we have already examined, and which simply 'recurses' down through the tree, saving any node that requires saving.

Opening a New Project

Recall that we identified the project to be opened by asking the user to select it from a standard `OpenFileDialog`:

```
//in WebMateForm.OnFileOpen()
    dlgOpenProject = new OpenFileDialog();
    dlgOpenProject.Title = "Open Web site";
```

```
    dlgOpenProject.Filter = "WebMate Project Files (*.xml)|*.xml";
    dlgOpenProject.FileOk += new CancelEventHandler(this.OnOKOpenProject);
    dlgOpenProject.ShowDialog();
```

The highlighted line in this code tells us that we need to look in a method called `OnOKOpenProject` to see what happens when the user OKs the `OpenFileDialog`.

```
public class WebMateForm : System.Windows.Forms.Form
{
    private void OnOKOpenProject(object sender, CancelEventArgs e)
    {
        try
        {
            Debug.Assert(siteExplorer.Project == null ||
            !(siteExplorer.Project.IsDirty));
            ProjectNode newProject = new ProjectNode(dlgOpenProject.FileName);
            siteExplorer.ReplaceProject(newProject);
        }
        catch (Exception ex)
        {
             MessageBox.Show("Unable to complete operation: The following error
             occurred:\n\n" + ex.Message);
        }
    }
```

This method starts with a quick debugging check, to make sure that there really is no outstanding project to save. Then we simply instantiate a new `ProjectNode` object, passing it the full path name of the project layout file to be read in (note that `OpenFileDialog.FileName` returns the full path to the selected file). Then we call a method to replace the current `ProjectNode` in the `SiteExplorer` (if there is one), with the new one. So, our next step is to examine the constructor for `ProjectNode`:

```
public class ProjectNode : UserNode
{
    public ProjectNode(string path) : base("")
    {
        base.Text = "Project";
        this.LoadFromFile(path);
        this.ForeColor = Color.Blue;
    }
```

This constructor passes an empty string to the base `UserNode` constructor, which has been defined to require one parameter. Recall that in C#, as in VB.NET, constructors of all base-classes in a hierarchy always get executed when constructing a derived class instance. The string will actually be passed down on to the `WebMateNode` constructor, where it will be used to supply the name of the new node.

```
public abstract class UserNode : WebMateNode
{
public UserNode(string name) : base(name)
   {}
```

```
public abstract class WebMateNode : TreeNode
{
```

```
    public WebMateNode(string name)
    {
        this.name = name;
    }
```

The reason that the name of the node is passed down to the WebMateNode base-class is that all nodes have a name, and hence this field is considered the responsibility of the generic base-class. The reason that our ProjectNode constructor passes an empty string for this name is that we don't actually know what the name is going to be, until we have opened and read the file that describes the project. Hence, for the moment, we just pass an empty string, and we will change this field to the correct name as soon as we have read in the file. We have to pass in something because the only constructor available for UserNode and WebMateNode requires it.

The real work of setting up the new project node is done in the ProjectNode.LoadFromFile method. This method actually does a lot of work:

```
class ProjectNode : UserNode
{
    public void LoadFromFile(string solutionFile)
    {
        XmlElement xmlProject;

        XmlDocument xmlDoc = new XmlDocument();
        Stream strm = File.Open(solutionFile, FileMode.Open);
        xmlDoc.Load(strm);
        strm.Close();
        xmlProject = xmlDoc["Project"];
        CopyXmlChildrenToTree(xmlProject, this);

        base.Rename(xmlProject.Attributes["Name"].Value);
        this.Text = "Project " + base.Name;
        this.path = Path.GetDirectoryName(solutionFile);
        this.homePages = (HomePagesNode)this.Nodes[0];
        this.siteAreas = (SiteAreasNode)this.Nodes[1];
        this.images = (ImagesNode)this.Nodes[2];
    }
```

Although we have pointed out that the project layout file is an XML file, this is the first time that we've seen any code that actually manipulates this file. Naturally for an XML file, we will be using classes in the System.XML namespace. In general, LoadFromFile has to read in the XML file, examine the structure of the XML document, and set up the corresponding hierarchy of objects derived from WebMateNode. The first half of this method is devoted to that task.

The second half of LoadFromFile contains statements that initialize various fields of the ProjectNode class, based on the information contained in the file which is read in. Notice a call to base.Rename, which sets up the real name of the project. Rename is a virtual method defined in UserNode, which deals with the process of renaming an item. The base implementation simply changes the name field. However, the method is virtual, so it can be overridden by any classes that need to do other work in order to rename the underlying object. For example, WebPageNode overrides Rename to actually rename the text file that the node represents on the file system.

Other properties that are initialized in the `LoadFromFile` include `Text`, which is the property implemented in `TreeNode` which indicates the text to be displayed by the node in the containing tree control. `Path` will contain the full path name to the folder that contains this project on the file system, while `Homepages`, `SiteAreas` and `Images` are references to particular child nodes in this project that frequently need to be accessed by other parts of the application.

Now we'll have a closer look at the process of reading in the XML file. Reading in the file simply involves instantiating a new `System.Xml.XmlDocument` object and using its `Load` method to read the layout file into the document. The process of converting this XML document into a tree structure is done using the method `ProjectNode.CopyXmlChildrenToTree`. This method takes two parameters, which are references to the XML project to be converted and to the root of the tree. Since the root of the tree is just this project node, we pass in this reference as the second parameter.

In order to make this process of converting an XML file to a tree view structure easy, the XML files contain an XML document that has exactly the same structure as the node hierarchy in the `SiteExplorer`. In other words, where the top-level node in the `SiteExplorer` is the `ProjectNode`, the top-level element in the XML document is an element of type `Project`. Where the children of project in the tree `SiteExplorer` are the `HomePages` node, `SiteAreas` node, etc., the children of the project element in the XML document are nodes of type `HomePages`, `SiteAreas`, etc. We could go on, but you probably get the idea. As an example of a typical `layout.xml` file for a small project, the one for the project used in the earlier WebMate screenshots looks like this:

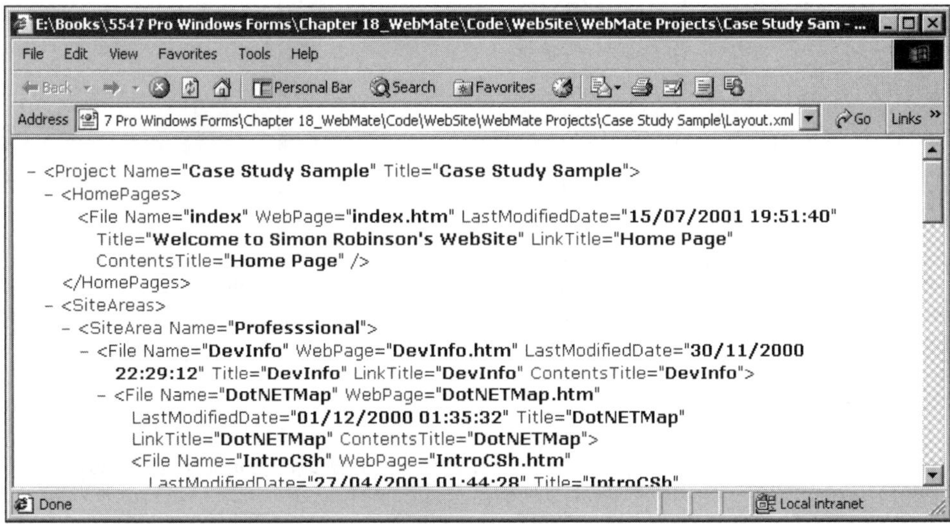

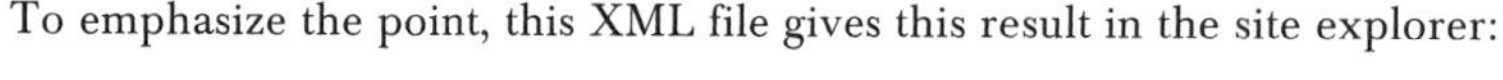

To emphasize the point, this XML file gives this result in the site explorer:

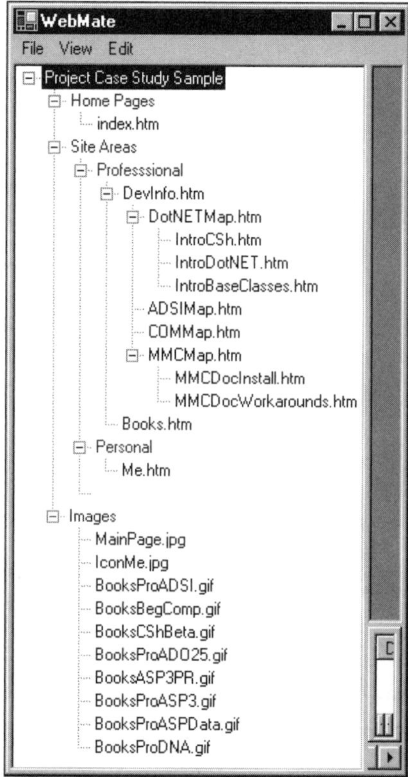

Comparing the screenshot and the XML file, we see that in the XML format, the name of the element indicates the type of node that it represents, while any attributes indicate the corresponding properties of the `WebMateNode` object in the `SiteExplorer`. None of the elements in the XML document has any values – the information is contained entirely in their names, their attributes, and in the arrangement of elements in the hierarchy.

> *If WebMate had been a larger commercial application then we would probably have wanted to supply an XML schema describing the structure of the document. However, for the intended use of WebMate I didn't consider it worthwhile spending the effort doing that. I think I can trust myself not to manually fiddle with the XML file and mess up its format!*

The exact correspondence between the hierarchy of the XML document and the hierarchy of the `SiteExplorer` makes for a very simple algorithm to convert the XML document to a `TreeNode` hierarchy: All we need to do is recursively work down through the XML document hierarchy, converting each element we find to the corresponding class of `TreeNode`, using the same technique that we saw used earlier for saving projects in `WebMateNode.SaveRecursive`. Here's what `CopyXmlChildrenToTree` looks like:

```
class ProjectNode : UserNode
{
    private void CopyXmlChildrenToTree(XmlNode xmlParent, TreeNode treeParent)
```

```
    {
        Debug.Assert(xmlParent is XmlElement);
        foreach (XmlNode xmlChild in xmlParent.ChildNodes)
        {
            Debug.Assert(xmlChild is XmlElement);
            TreeNode treeChild = WebMateNode.CreateTreeNode(xmlChild);
            treeParent.Nodes.Add(treeChild);
            CopyXmlChildrenToTree(xmlChild, treeChild);
        }
    }
```

`CopyXmlChildrenToTree` deals with navigating recursively down the XML document hierarchy. For each node found, it delegates responsibility for creating an appropriate `TreeNode` object to a method, `WebMateNode.CreateTreeNode`. This latter method takes an `XmlElement` as a parameter. It implements what is known as a **factory technique** (or **factory pattern**) for creating objects. Roughly speaking, the factory technique is where one object or class (often a base-class of the object to be instantiated) takes responsibility for instantiating another object, typically using a `switch` or other conditional statement, in order to determine the class of object to be instantiated. The implementation in this case is as follows:

```
public abstract class WebMateNode : TreeNode
{
    public static TreeNode CreateTreeNode (XmlNode node)
    {
        switch (node.Name)
        {
            case "HomePages":
                return new HomePagesNode();
            case "File":
                string name = node.Attributes["Name"].Value;
                string webPage = node.Attributes["WebPage"].Value;
                DateTime lastModifiedDate =
                DateTime.Parse(node.Attributes["LastModifiedDate"].Value);
                string title = node.Attributes["Title"].Value;
                string linkTitle = node.Attributes["LinkTitle"].Value;
                string contentsTitle = node.Attributes["ContentsTitle"].Value;
                return new WebPageNode(name, webPage, lastModifiedDate, title,
                linkTitle, contentsTitle);
            case "SiteArea":
                return new SiteAreaNode(node.Attributes["Name"].Value);
            case "SiteAreas":
                return new SiteAreasNode();
            case "Images":
                return new ImagesNode();
            case "Image":
                string imageName = node.Attributes["Name"].Value;
                string imageFile = node.Attributes["ImageFile"].Value;
                string altText = node.Attributes["AltText"].Value;
                return new ImageNode(imageName, imageFile, altText);

            default:
                throw new ControlFileException("Unknown Xml node: " +
                node.Name);
        }
    }
```

To some extent, factory creation methods depart from object-oriented principles, since it often means that, as in this case, a base-class needs to have knowledge of its derived classes hard coded into it. Usually, the idea of OOP is that derived classes know about the base-class, but base-classes have no knowledge of what classes may have been derived from them. This gives developers the freedom to derive other classes from a base-class in the future.

However, there are some situations, such as the situation here, where we need to instantiate an object that could be of any of a number of different classes, for which the factory technique is the most sensible option available. It is used in a few of the .NET base-classes, notably `System.Net.WebRequest`, and in the days of COM, a factory technique using a factory object known as the **class object** was employed for the creation of most COM objects. In our particular case, we could, as an alternative, avoid the factory pattern by having each container node create the nodes of the appropriate type. However, this has the disadvantage that we'd need to hard code the schema of the XML layout file into the code – and that hard-coded knowledge would be scattered across a large number of classes.

Using the factory pattern means we lose a certain amount of OOP methodology but don't need to hard-code the structure of the document into the program. As with any large project, there are normally a number of alternative ways to code up a solution, each with some benefits and disadvantages.

There is little point in looking at all the various constructors for the different types of node that can be called up by `WebMateNode.CreateTreeNode`. The constructors invoked by this method simply use their parameters to initialize member fields. The most complicated example is below:

```
public class WebPageNode : UserNode
{
    public WebPageNode(string inputFile, string webFile, DateTime
    lastModifiedDate, string title, string linkTitle, string contentsTitle)
     : base(inputFile)
    {
        this.inputFile = inputFile;
        this.webFile = webFile;
        base.Text = this.WebFile;
        this.lastModifiedDate = lastModifiedDate;
        this.title = title;
        this.linkTitle = linkTitle;
        this.contentsTitle = contentsTitle;
    }
...
```

We have already examined the one-parameter base `UserNode` constructor that is called by this `WebPageNode` constructor.

Up to this point, we have reviewed the entire process of instantiating a `ProjectNode` object. This contains all the information about the particular WebMate project, in the tree hierarchy below it. To complete the process of opening a new project, this `ProjectNode` needs to be added as a child to the `SiteExplorer` tree view, replacing any previous project. Recall from the `WebMateForm.OnOKOpenProject` method, which is the event handler called when the user clicks the OK button in the `OpenFile` dialog, that this is the last stage in opening the project:

```
// in WebMateNode.OnOKOpenProject
    Debugging.AssertFalse(siteExplorer.Project != null &&
    siteExplorer.Project.IsDirty);
    ProjectNode newProject = new ProjectNode(dlgOpenProject.FileName);
    siteExplorer.ReplaceProject(newProject);
```

This is the code for SiteExplorer.ReplaceProject:

```
class SiteExplorer : TreeView
{
    public void ReplaceProject(ProjectNode newProject)
    {
        Debug.Assert(project == null || !(project.IsDirty));
        project = newProject;
        this.Nodes.Clear();
        this.Nodes.Add(newProject);
        newProject.Expand();
    }
...
```

This method simply wraps up a debugging check on the status of any previous project along with a couple of calls to TreeView methods, to remove any previous nodes in the SiteExplorer and add the new one. We also called TreeView.Expand in order to make sure the project appears expanded initially. This is a little more friendly to the user, since if we don't do this automatically, clicking on the ProjectNode to expand it will almost certainly be the first thing the user does anyway.

We have now finished looking at the code that is executed when the user opts to open a project. Working through this code has given us a chance to see how .NET and Windows Forms allows us to use implementation-inheritance-based object-oriented programming in a reasonably sized GUI project. This OOP programming methodology was previously available to C++ developers before the days of .NET, but C++ developers didn't have such easy access to the classes and controls that makes Windows Forms programming so quick.

On the other hand, VB6 offered all the benefits of quick programming in a Windows environment, but at a cost of not supporting real object-oriented programming. With Windows Forms we get both, irrespective of whether we write our code in C# or VB.NET. This is important to emphasize. Although WebMate is written entirely in C#, all of the code that we've seen could equally well have been written in VB.NET. If that had been the case each method we have presented would have had the same structure, and the only significant difference is that we would simply have replaced C# syntax with VB.NET syntax, in each of the statements in the source code.

Although the code we have seen so far has demonstrated the object-oriented architecture of WebMate, we haven't really seen much code that specifically manipulates Windows forms. So, we are going to look at what happens when the user tries to drag and drop a file or files onto an existing project, and the WebMate code for this relies more heavily on the features implemented by the System.Windows.Forms base-classes.

Dragging and Dropping Files

Let's remind ourselves of the sequence of events that occurs when a drag/drop operation happens. When the user performs a drag/drop operation, and moves the mouse into a window (a form or control) with the left button depressed, the DragEnter event for that window is raised. As the user moves the mouse across the window, Windows continually raises the DragOver event, passing in the new coordinates of the mouse. If the user releases the mouse button over the window, thus completing the drag/drop operation, then the DragDrop event is raised, again with the coordinates of the mouse being passed in to the event handler.

Of course, if the user moves the mouse out of the window, the window will no longer receive the drag/drop and the DragLeave event is raised. In order to correctly handle drag/drop events, the SiteExplorer class will need to implement handlers for all four of these events with the exception of DragLeave. The handlers that we implement are SiteExplorer.OnDragEnter, SiteExplorer.OnDragOver and SiteExplorer.OnDragDrop.

Of these, OnDragEnter is the simplest. It simply needs to decide whether this particular drag/drop operation should be allowed. Since we are only supporting dragging and dropping of files, the condition we wish to impose is that the operation should only be permitted if the data the user is dragging consists of files to be dropped – not if any other form of data (for example, a selection from a Word document) is being dragged.

```
public SiteExplorer : TreeView
{
    protected void OnDragEnter(object sender, DragEventArgs e)
    {
        if (e.Data.GetData(DataFormats.FileDrop) != null)
        {
            e.Effect = DragDropEffects.Copy;
        }
            else
            e.Effect = DragDropEffects.None;
    }
...
```

As this code shows, we find out whether the data being dragged is a file, by actually attempting to retrieve the drag/drop data, which is available as the Data property of the DragEventArgs reference that handler receives, and requesting that the data be retrieved in FileDrop format. If the result is null, then we know that there is no point in allowing the operation. We disallow it by setting the Effect property of the DragEventArgs to None – this causes the mouse pointer to change to the 'disallowed' icon (usually a circle with a slash through it). Otherwise, we set the effect to Copy, causing the mouse pointer to change to the drag/copy icon. We do this to inform the user that the files being dragged will ultimately be copied across to the project's folder if the drag operation is successfully completed.

When implementing this sort of feature in our applications, we might additionally test whether the CTRL key was pressed – and set e.Effect to DragDropEffects.Copy if it is, or DragDropEffects.Move if it isn't, thus mimicking the behavior of Windows Explorer. We have chosen not to arrange that WebMate always copies files, because in this context, it might potentially be confusing to the user if he or she tries to place files into a WebMate project, and then finds they've been moved from their original locations. The really important thing, however, is to ensure that the cursor we select, via the Effect property, accurately reflects what our application is coded up to do if the user completes the drag/drop operation.

Next, we need to handle the DragOver event. The reason for handling this event is much the same as the reason for handling DragEnter – to check whether a drop operation will be allowed at the location where the mouse has moved to, and set the mouse pointer accordingly. This is to reflect the fact that even file drops can only be permitted on certain types of node. Files can be dropped into the ImagesNode (in which case we assume the dropped file(s) are images), into the HomePagesNode, any SiteAreaNode, or other WebPageNode (assuming the dropped file(s) are text files). If the mouse enters any of these nodes, then we need to ensure that the drag/drop effect is set to Copy. If the mouse enters any other node, then we need to ensure the effect is set to None. Additionally, it will provide useful extra feedback to the user if the node in question is selected and displayed as such, to make sure they know which node the drop will effect.

Note that we allow the drag effect to remain at `Copy` when the mouse is not over any node – this is done to make sure the user understands that, in principle, when the mouse first enters the `SiteExplorer`, the drag/drop operation will be permitted somewhere in the window.

This is the `OnDragOver` event handler:

```
public SiteExplorer : TreeView
{
    private void OnDragOver(object sender, System.Windows.Forms.DragEventArgs e)
    {
        Point pt = this.PointToClient(new Point(e.X, e.Y));
        TreeNode node = this.GetNodeAt(pt);
        if (node == null)
        {
            e.Effect = DragDropEffects.Copy;
            return;
        }
        if (node is WebPageNode || node is SiteAreaNode || node is HomePagesNode
        || node is ImagesNode)
        {
            e.Effect = DragDropEffects.Copy;
            this.SelectSiteExplorerNode(node);
        }
        else
        {
            e.Effect = DragDropEffects.None;
            this.SelectSiteExplorerNode(null);
        }
    }
 ...
```

This is rather more complex than `OnDragEnter` because of the need to determine which `TreeNode` the mouse is over, and to ensure that the node is displayed as selected. We can find out which node is selected by using the `TreeView.GetNodeAt` method, which takes the coordinates of a point relative to the top left corner of the client area of the tree view, and returns the node that is being displayed at that point (or `null` if there is no node at that point).

However, the `DragEventArgs` object gives us the location of the mouse in desktop coordinates (coordinates relative to the top left corner of the screen), so we need to convert the coordinates to client coordinates first. This is done using the method `PointToClient`, which `SiteExplorer` has inherited not directly from `TreeView` but ultimately from `Control`, one of the base-classes in `TreeView's` inheritance hierarchy.

Once we have identified the node in question, we can easily work out how to set the drag effect. If the returned `TreeNode` reference is `null`, we set the drag effect to `Copy` and then return. Otherwise, we examine what type of node we have and set the drag effect accordingly. We can identify the type of object the reference refers to by using C#'s `is` operator. In this case, whatever the class of node we identify, we also need to make sure that node is displayed as selected. This is the purpose of the `SelectSiteExplorerNode` method that is called. `SelectSiteExplorerNode` looks like this:

```
public SiteExplorer : TreeView
{
    protected void SelectSiteExplorerNode(TreeNode node)
    {
```

```
        if (this.selectedNode != node)
        {
            this.SelectedNode = node;
            this.Refresh();
            if (node != null)
            {
                node.Expand();
            }
        }
    }
...
```

SelectSiteExplorerNode takes as a parameter a reference to the TreeNode that we need to have selected. The first thing we do is compare it with the node that is actually selected at the present time. If the two are the same node, then there's nothing to be done. If they are different nodes, then we select the new node using the TreeView.SelectedNode property. Setting this property will select the node as far as the TreeView is concerned, but it won't actually cause what's displayed on the screen to change. To do that we need to call TreeView.Refresh to get the SiteExplorer to redraw itself. Finally, we expand out the newly selected node – just to be nice and helpful to the user.

Finally, we need to examine the handler for when the drop happens. This is going to be a much more complex process – up until now we have done little more than check whether we will allow a drag-drop event and set the mouse pointer accordingly. However, when the drop occurs we are going to have to attempt to insert the files into the project:

```
public SiteExplorer : TreeView
{
    protected void OnDragDrop(object sender, DragEventArgs e)
    {
        Point pt = this.PointToClient(new Point(e.X, e.Y));
        TreeNode node = this.GetNodeAt(pt);
        this.SelectSiteExplorerNode(node);

        object o = e.Data.GetData(DataFormats.FileDrop);
        string [] files = (string[])o;
        AddFilesToNode(node, files);
    }
...
```

OnDragDrop itself simply makes sure that the node in which we are attempting the drop is selected, then it retrieves the drag/drop data. Requesting the drag/drop data in FileDrop format retrieves an object (the class of which is unspecified), which can be cast to an array of strings. Each string in the array will then give the full pathname of the file (or one of the files) that has been dragged. OnDragDrop passes this array to AddFilesToNode in order to get the files actually inserted into the project if possible. AddFilesToNode is a large method, and is where most of the work of adding the files actually gets done.

Adding files is also an operation that can easily go wrong if the wrong type of files are being dropped (for example, files that turn out not to be text files are dropped into a site area), so you'll notice AddFilesToNode does much of its processing in a try block, in order to catch any exceptions that get thrown:

```
public SiteExplorer : TreeView
{
    public void AddFilesToNode(TreeNode node, string [] filePaths)
    {
        StringCollection failures = new StringCollection();
        this.BeginUpdate();
        foreach (string file in filePaths)
        {
            try
            {
                string fileName = Path.GetFileName(file);
                string fileRawName = Path.GetFileNameWithoutExtension(file);
                UserNode newNode;
                if (node is ImagesNode)
                {

                // we must be dragging an image. We won't bother checking file
                // extension since it's not possible to give a comprehensive list
                // of valid image extensions
                    if (Path.GetDirectoryName(file) != Project.FullImagesPath)
                    {
                        File.Copy(file, Path.Combine(Project.FullImagesPath,
                        fileName), false);
                        newNode = new ImageNode(new FileInfo(file));
                    }
                    else
                    {
                        // must be a text file drop ( a more sophisticated app
                        // would remove this restriction)
                        if (Path.GetExtension(file).ToUpper() != ".TXT")
                            throw new WebMateFileFormatException ("Not a .txt
                            file: " + file);
                        if (Path.GetDirectoryName(file) != Project.FullInputPath)
                            File.Copy(file, Path.Combine(Project.FullInputPath,
                            fileName), false);
                            newNode = new WebPageNode(new FileInfo(file));
                     }
                     node.Nodes.Add(newNode);
                     Project.IsDirty = true;
                     Project.Save();
                }
                catch (Exception e)
                {
                     failures.Add(e.Message);
                }
            }
            this.EndUpdate();

            if (failures.Count > 0)
            {
                StringBuilder sb = new StringBuilder(500);
                sb.Append("\nFAILED TO ADD TO PROJECT: \n\n");
                foreach (string failure in failures)
                {
                    sb.Append(failure);
                    sb.Append("\n");
```

```
            }
            MessageBox.Show(this.mainForm, sb.ToString(), "Add files to
            project");

        }
    }
```

The first thing we do in this method is to define a StringCollection called failures. This collection will hold the names of any files for which the drag/drop operation fails – so that we can display an appropriate message box to the user. Then we call the SiteExplorer class's BeginUpdate method. This method is inherited from System.Windows.Forms.Control. It informs the control that a number of changes are about to be made to it. For performance reasons, there's no point in the control attempting to redraw itself until all the changes are completed, which will be when the EndUpdate method is called. We do this because, if we add 10 files, for example, in quick succession, we don't want the SiteExplorer to redraw itself after each addition. That would not only hurt performance but also probably cause the user to see an unpleasant flickering effect.

The bulk of the method is then given over to a foreach loop that iterates through the files in the file drop, attempting to add each one to the project. Notice that the try block and corresponding catch handler are inside this loop. This ensures that, if the file drop fails for any one file, we continue to try adding the other files in the file drop. Before we examine the contents of this foreach loop, we'll jump to the end of the method to see an if statement (which checks to see if any failures actually occurred). If any did then we display a message box informing the user of the fact. The string to go in the message box is constructed using a StringBuilder object from the System.Text namespace for performance reasons. If more than two or three modifications are likely to be made to the same string, then using a StringBuilder improves performance by saving on memory allocation and copying operations.

Now we'll examine what happens in the foreach loop when WebMate attempts to add a file to the project. First, we use a couple of static methods from System.IO.Path to retrieve different portions of the name of the file. Path.GetFileName retrieves the name of the file given the full path name. For example, supplied with C:\My Documents\index.txt, it will return index.txt. Path.GetFileNameWithoutExtension does the same thing, but knocks off the extension – so in this example it will return the string index:

```
string fileName = Path.GetFileName(file);
string fileRawName = Path.GetFileNameWithoutExtension(file);
```

Next, we use an if statement to check whether the node we are dragging the files into is the ImagesNode. If so, we are attempting to insert an image – otherwise the user must be attempting to insert a web page. If we are inserting an image, we copy the file across to the project's ImagesDirectory if it is not already there (we check this using the Path.GetDirectoryName static method, which returns the path of the directory containing a file – so, for our example it would return C:\MyDocuments). Note that no check is made to see if the file is of an appropriate file type here, though in a more sophisticated application some kind of check would be important.

Doing this kind of check is potentially problematic because of the large and growing number of different image formats. The FullImagesPath property of our ProjectNode class returns the folder in the project that holds the images – probably something like C:\WebMate Projects\Site\Images, and Path.Combine combines elements of a file path together. We then instantiate an ImageNode object that represents a node in the SiteExplorer, which corresponds to an image. The ImageNode constructor we use looks like this:

```
public class ImageNode : UserNode
{
    public ImageNode(FileInfo file)
     : base(Path.GetFileNameWithoutExtension(file.Name))
    {
        Debug.Assert(file.Exists);
        this.imageFile = file.Name;
        base.Text = this.imageFile;
        this.altText = "Picture of " +
        Path.GetFileNameWithoutExtension(file.Name);
    }
```

The `ImageNode.altText` field represents the text that `WebMateNode` will insert for the HTML ALT property of the `<IMG>` element if it encounters a `*IMG` directive in any page it is compiling. We set it to a default string here, but the user can change it later if they wish via the **Properties** dialog for that `ImagesNode`.

If the user is trying to drop a web page into the project, the procedure is basically the same, except that we additionally check whether the file concerned is a text file – by examining the file extension – and reject it if it isn't. In either case, we need to add the newly created node that represents the file, to the node to which it was dragged. Then we mark the project itself as modified, and immediately save it, ensuring that details of the new file are stored in the project's `layout.xml` file. We are not examining the `ProjectNode.Save` method in this chapter, but it is available with the download on the Wrox Press web site.

Editing a Web Page

We will now examine how WebMate allows the user to examine and modify individual web pages.

WebMate allows the user two possible ways of electing to edit a page. The user can either double-click on the page in the `SiteExplorer`, or, with the page already selected in `SiteExplorer`, hit the return key. This leads to two event handlers `OnDoubleClick` and `OnKeyPress`, both in the `SiteExplorer` class:

```
public class SiteExplorer : TreeView
{
    private void OnDoubleClick(object sender, System.EventArgs e)
    {
        EditNode();
    }

    protected override void OnKeyPress(System.Windows.Forms.KeyPressEventArgs e)
    {
        if (e.KeyChar == 13)
        {
            OnEditNode();
            e.Handled = true;
        }
    base.OnKeyPress(e);
    }
...
```

From this code, we gather that SiteExplorer.EditNode is the method that really handles this process, and the two event handlers shown here simply ensure that EditNode can be called either through the mouse, or by the keyboard. We also note that, just for a change, we've handled the KeyPress event by overriding the one-parameter Control.OnKeyPress method instead of adding our own separate event handler. Note also that in our override of OnKeyPress, we specifically set the Handled property of the EventArgs parameter to True to indicate the event has been handled if the user hits RETURN and we display the corresponding child form. This prevents the computer from bleeping when RETURN is pressed.

Now we'll examine EditNode:

```
public class SiteExplorer : TreeView
{
    private void EditNode()
    {
        TreeNode selectedNode = this.SelectedNode;
        WebPageNode selectedFileNode = selectedNode as WebPageNode;
        if (selectedFileNode != null)
        {
            selectedFileNode.CreateForm();
        }
    }
...
```

So EditNode simply checks whether the double-click or return has happened with an editable WebPageNode selected, and if so calls another method, WebPageNode.CreateForm. CreateForm does the work of instantiating a child window, in which to edit the web page.

```
public class WebPageNode : TreeView
{
    public override void CreateForm()
    {
        if (editingForm == null)
        {
            FileForm newForm = new FileForm(mainForm, TheSiteExplorer, this);
            editingForm = newForm;
            newForm.Show();
        }
        else
        {
            editingForm.Activate();
            if (editingForm.WindowState == FormWindowState.Minimized)
            editingForm.WindowState = FormWindowState.Normal;
        }
    }
...
```

Note that CreateForm is declared as override. It is actually declared as a do-nothing virtual method in the base-class WebMateNode. The reason it is declared in that manner, is in case in future we decide to add implementations of it to other types of node (for example to edit images).

CreateForm first checks to see if an appropriate child window (represented by a FileForm object) is already open. Clearly if one has already been created, we need to activate the existing one rather than create a new one. If such a form exists, the WebPageNode.editingForm field of the relevant WebPageNode object in the tree view will indicate this. If this property is not null, then we simply activate the form referred to so that it receives the focus. We also ensure that the form is not minimized by restoring it, if need be. A slightly more sophisticated application would probably check the state of other child windows to determine whether to restore or to maximize the form.

If editingForm is null then we know that no child form that allows editing of this page currently exists, so we create a new one, and call its Show method to make it visible. Creating a new child window involves nothing more than calling the FileForm constructor, since all the work involved in setting up the form is handled by this constructor. In this code, we've also indicated the declarations of several of the fields in FileForm:

```
public class FileForm : Form
{
    private System.Windows.Forms.TabControl viewTabs;

    private SiteExplorer siteExplorer;
    private WebPageNode fileNode;
    private SourceView sourceTab;
    private HtmlView htmlTab;
    private BrowserView webTab;
    private ProjectNode project;

    public FileForm(Form parent, SiteExplorer siteExplorer, WebPageNode fileNode)
    {

        // Required for Windows Form Designer support

        InitializeComponent();
        this.MdiParent = parent;
        this.siteExplorer = siteExplorer;
        this.project = siteExplorer.Project;
        this.fileNode = fileNode;
        this.Text = fileNode.WebFile;

        sourceTab = new SourceView(fileNode);
        sourceTab.Text = "Source";
        viewTabs.TabPages.Add(sourceTab);

        htmlTab = new HtmlView(fileNode);
        htmlTab.Text = "HTML";
        viewTabs.TabPages.Add(htmlTab);

        webTab = new WebPageView(this);
        webTab.Text = "Browser";
        viewTabs.TabPages.Add(webTab);

        viewTabs.SelectedIndexChanged += new EventHandler(OnChangeTab);

    }
...
```

The InitializeComponent method called from this constructor is the Visual Studio.NET-supplied method, which contains code to set up the main menu for this child form, and to place the TabControl viewTabs in the window. We have not inherited any new class from System.Windows.Forms.TabControl, but used this class directly, since we don't need the tab control to implement any new behavior. The WebMate-specific code comes in the individual tab pages, the **Source**, **HTML**, and **Browser** tabs, which are therefore implemented as our own derived classes (all derived from TabControl): SourceView, HTMLView and BrowserView.

Since InitializeComponent contains only standard Visual Studio.NET-generated code, we won't show that method here. We will note, however, that the Dock property of viewTabs is set to DockStyle.Fill.

The remainder of the FileForm constructor consists of field initializations, as well as one manually added event handler, and should be self-explanatory. The event handler, OnChangeTab, deals with the situation when the user changes between tabs, and we will examine it in the *Viewing the Results ofEditing a Web Page* section, below.

In order to complete looking at what happens when the FileForm object is created, we need to examine the constructors for the three tab views. The first, SourceView, looks as follows. Notice in the code, that the tab contains a RichTextBox, the code for which was added by hand rather than using the Visual Studio.NET design view:

```
public class SourceView : System.Windows.Forms.TabPage
{
    private RichTextBox textBox;
    private WebPageNode node;

    public SourceView(WebPageNode node)
    {
        this.node = node;
        textBox = new RichTextBox();
        textBox.Parent = this;
        textBox.DetectUrls = false;
        textBox.Dock = DockStyle.Fill;
        textBox.Show();
        textBox.Font = new Font("Times New Roman", 11);
        textBox.WordWrap = false;
        textBox.LoadFile(node.FullInputFilePath,
            RichTextBoxStreamType.PlainText);
        textBox.TextChanged += new EventHandler(OnTextChanged);
    }
...
```

The above code should be self-explanatory. It sets up the behavior of the RichTextBox, reads the file containing the source text, and loads the contents of this file into the RichTextBox. Although not strictly part of the process of setting up the child form, we will briefly note the implementation of the OnTextChanged event handler. In general, System.Windows.Forms.RichTextBox is able to carry out all the processing required when the user modifies the text in the textbox. The one extra thing we need to add is to ensure the corresponding WebPageNode in the SiteExplorer knows that the text has changed, which means that the page will need to be saved (as well as recompiled to the actual HTML page):

```
public class SourceView : System.Windows.Forms.TabPage
{
    protected void OnTextChanged(object sender, EventArgs e)
    {
        node.IsDirty = true;
        node.NeedsCompiling = true;
    }
```

The constructor for the `HTMLView` class is very similar. Note that in this case, however, the contained `RichTextBox` is read only. Also, there is no need to actually load any text into this textbox at construction time, since the active, visible tab is always set to be the source tab initially. Text is added to this `RichTextBox` if the user actually selects to view this tab, and is dealt with in the `FileForm.OnChangeTab` event handler, which we will examine soon.

```
public class HtmlView : System.Windows.Forms.TabPage
{
    private RichTextBox textBox;
    private WebPageNode node;

    public HtmlView(WebPageNode node)
    {
        this.node = node;
        textBox = new RichTextBox();
        textBox.Parent = this;
        textBox.DetectUrls = false;
        textBox.ReadOnly = true;
        textBox.Dock = DockStyle.Fill;
        textBox.Font = new Font("Times New Roman", 11);
        textBox.WordWrap = false;
        textBox.Show();
    }
...
```

The `BrowserView` constructor is similar, but in this case we instantiate a contained user control, `BrowserControl`, which is a class that we have derived from `UserControl`:

```
public class BrowserView : System.Windows.Forms.TabPage
{
    private FileForm fileForm;
    private BrowserControl browserControl = new BrowserControl();

    public BrowserView(FileForm fileForm)
    {
        this.InitializeComponent();
        this.fileForm = fileForm;
        browserControl.Parent = this;
        browserControl.Show();
    }
...
```

The reason for the existence of `BrowserControl` is to contain the actual web browser control. The reason that we haven't simply placed a web browser control directly in the `BrowserView` control, is that this does not appear to be possible using the Visual Studio code generation wizards. At the time of writing, there is no .NET control available that will perform the functionality of Internet Explorer in displaying web pages. In order to achieve this task, we need to resort to a legacy ActiveX control – the web browser stored in the Dll, `shdocvw.dll`.

Now, despite the earlier comments regarding the relative advantages of object-oriented programming versus automatic code generation, incorporating an ActiveX control can require some fiddly code, which it is preferable to have Visual Studio.NET write automatically for us. We simply use the Customize Toolbox dialog (which is brought up by right-clicking over the toolbox) to add the Microsoft Web Browser control to the toolbox. For a more detailed look at adding and using ActiveX controls, see Chapter 9 on Menus, Toolbars, and Other Controls.

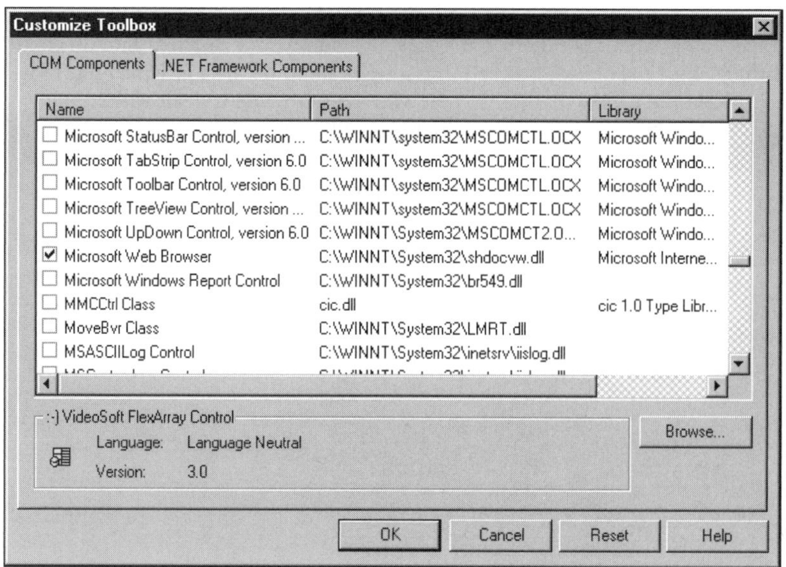

Then we can simply drag and drop the web browser control onto a form or control in the design view, just as we would for any .NET base-class control. However, at the time of writing, this is only possible if the control on which we are placing the legacy COM control is either a form (derived from `System.Windows.Forms.Form`), or a user control (derived from `System.Windows.Forms.UserControl`). Since a control derived from `UserControl` cannot also be derived from `System.Windows.Forms.TabPage`, and cannot therefore be a tab page, we need an intermediate `BrowserControl` object between the `BrowserView` and the actual web browser.

The constructor for the `BrowserControl` class is entirely Visual Studio.NET-generated:

```
public class BrowserControl : System.Windows.Forms.UserControl
{
    private AxSHDocVw.AxWebBrowser axWebBrowser1;
    /// <summary>
    /// Required designer variable.
    /// </summary>
    private System.ComponentModel.Container components = null;

    public BrowserControl()
    {
        // This call is required by the Windows.Forms Form Designer.
        InitializeComponent();
    }
...
```

This completes the code that is executed in order to set up a child window when the user double-clicks (or hits *Return*) on a `SiteExplorer` node, in order to indicate that they want to edit a web page.

Viewing the Results of Editing a Web Page

We have already covered the editing process itself – this is handled mostly by the RichTextBox control in the SourceView object using code in the Windows Forms base-classes, with little need for additional support from WebMate code. The same really applies to saving files – we saw the bulk of the code required to save edited files when we examined the process of opening a project. In this section, we need examine only the additional code required to enable the user to view the results of their editing, in the HTML and View tabs.

Since the FileForm form is always initially displayed with the Source tab activated, the user can only view the other tabs by changing tabs. This means that we can execute the code needed to correctly display the other tabs from within the FileForm class's OnChangeTab event handler. The handler itself is, basically, no more than a switch statement:

```
public class FileForm : Form
{
    void OnChangeTab(object sender, EventArgs e)
    {
        switch (viewTabs.SelectedIndex)
        {
            case 0:
                break;
            case 1:
                OnSelectHtmlTab();
                break;
            case 2:
                OnSelectWebTab();
                break;
            default:
                Debug.Assert (false);
                break;
        }
    }
...
```

If the user selects the first (Source) tab then there is no action to be taken, since this tab contains only user-editable text. Let's see what happens when the HTML tab is selected by looking at the OnSelectHtmlTab method.

```
public class FileForm : Form
{
protected void OnSelectHtmlTab()
    {
        CompileIfNeeded();
        string outputFilePath = Path.Combine(project.FullSitePath,
        fileNode.WebFile);
        htmlTab.Navigate(outputFilePath);
    }
...
```

We will not examine the CompileIfNeeded method, since we're regarding the compilation process itself as beyond the scope of this chapter. Briefly, it checks the WebPageNode to see whether any changes to any files since the last compile, indicate the need for a recompile of the page, and then calls up the compiler and preprocessor if a compilation is required. We then work out the path at which the compiled (or perhaps newly compiled) HTML file can be found, and pass this path to the HtmlView.Navigate method, which displays the contents of this file (as plain text, not as a web page, in the RichTextBox):

```
public class HtmlView : System.Windows.Forms.TabPage
{
public void Navigate(string htmlFile)
    {
        textBox.LoadFile(htmlFile, RichTextBoxStreamType.PlainText);
    }
...
```

You may wonder what the point of the additional method call is, just for the sake of a single statement, but again it assists encapsulation and object-oriented programming. It is the responsibility of the child FileForm to detect that a different tab has been selected, and the responsibility of the newly selected tab to load any data it needs in order to display itself correctly. Encapsulating the statement in this way will make it easier, if in future we need to change the implementation of the task of reading a file.

This code is all we need in order to display the HTML view is in the FileForm class's OnSelectWebTab method. Displaying the **Browser** view is however a little more complex. This is what happens:

```
public class FileForm : Form
{
    protected void OnSelectWebTab()
    {
        CompileIfNeeded();
        string outputFilePath = Path.Combine(project.FullSitePath,
        fileNode.WebFile);
        webTab.Navigate(outputFilePath);
    }
...
```

So far, this looks like the same sequence for when the **HTML** Tab is selected, but the BrowserView.Navigate method opens up rather more code. First, the request is passed through to the contained BrowserControl object:

```
public class BrowserView : System.Windows.Forms.TabPage
{
    public void Navigate(string url)
    {
        browserControl.Navigate(url);
    }
...
```

The Navigate method of the BrowserControl class in turn passes this request on to the web browser itself, but only after checking its own size on the screen:

```
public class BrowserControl : System.Windows.Forms.UserControl
{
public void Navigate(string url)
    {
        ResizeBrowser();
        object flags = (object)0;
        object refObj = new object();
        this.axWebBrowser1.Navigate(url, ref flags, ref refObj, ref refObj,
        ref refObj);
    }
...
```

The call to `ResizeBrowser` ensures that the web browser control is the correct size to completely fill the `BrowserControl` control (and hence to fill the **Browser** view tab). It looks like this:

```
public class BrowserControl : System.Windows.Forms.UserControl
{
    public void ResizeBrowser()
    {
        axWebBrowser1.Left = 0;
        axWebBrowser1.Top = 0;
        axWebBrowser1.Width = this.ClientRectangle.Right;
        axWebBrowser1.Height = this.ClientRectangle.Bottom;
    }
```

The reason for this method is that, unlike the new .NET controls, the legacy ActiveX browser control does not have a `Dock` property that can be set to ensure the control completely fills its container. Hence, we have to achieve the same effect manually, by making sure it has the correct size and location every time it is displayed. We also need to do this if the **Browser** view tab is ever resized (this can happen if the user resizes, restores or maximizes the containing `FileForm` form). Hence, the `BrowserView` class needs to implement the additional `OnResize` event handler:

```
public class BrowserView : System.Windows.Forms.TabPage
{
    public void OnResize(object sender, System.EventArgs e)
    {
        browserControl.ResizeBrowser();
    }
...
```

This completes the code required to display the different views of the compiled web page. However, in order for the code to run correctly while debugging (though not after shipping), we need to modify the Visual Studio.NET's settings for exceptions.

> *We need to explicitly set Visual Studio.NET to continue whenever any exception in the namespace* `System.Runtime.InterOpServices` *is thrown.*

The reason for this is that the .NET COM `interop` classes that have been written in order to interface with legacy ActiveX controls appear to work by sometimes internally and harmlessly throwing and handling their own exceptions – this certainly happens when the web browser control is displayed using the current build of .NET. We certainly don't want to break into the debugger when any of these exceptions are thrown.

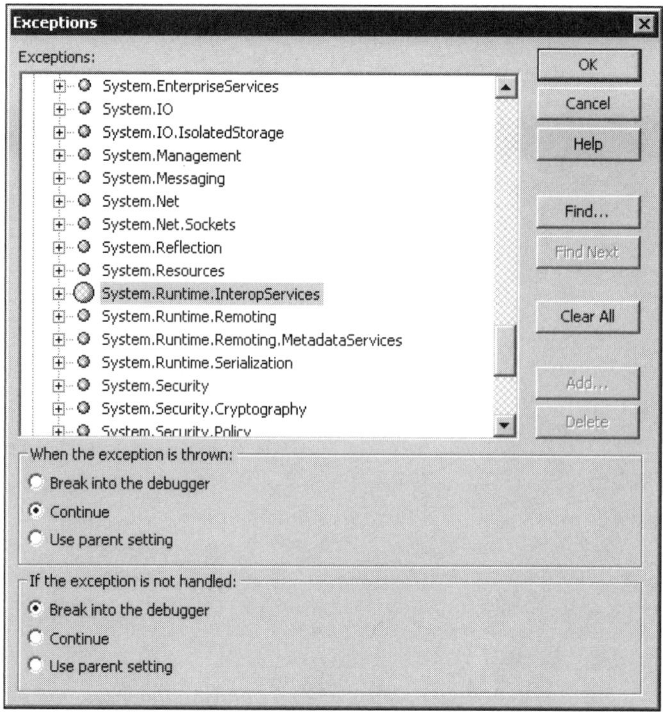

Making this change ensures that, even if while debugging we choose to set up Visual Studio.NET to break into the debugger for other exceptions, the web browser control will still be displayed correctly.

Closing WebMate

The final areas of code we will examine are those methods that are invoked when the user closes WebMate. This is not a process that can be left entirely to the Windows Forms base-classes, because of the risk that there might be unsaved files in the project the user has been editing. If this is the case, then we need to ask the user what to do – whether the files should be saved or not.

We need to cover two separate situations. The first is when the user closes a child `FileForm` window, and the second is when the user closes WebMate itself. Both situations are dealt with by providing handlers for the `Closing` event of the relevant form.

Closing the Child Form

The `OnClosing` event handler for this situation looks like this:

```
public class FileForm : Form
{
    protected override void OnClosing(CancelEventArgs e)
    {
        if (fileNode.IsDirty)
        {
            string message = "Save file " + fileNode.InputFile + ".txt?\n\nClick
            Yes to save file\nClick No to close window without saving\nClick
```

```
            Cancel to cancel";
            DialogResult result = MessageBox.Show(message, "Save File",
            MessageBoxButtons.YesNoCancel);
            switch (result)
            {
                case DialogResult.Yes:
                    this.fileNode.Save();
                    break;
                case DialogResult.No:
                    break;
                case DialogResult.Cancel:
                    e.Cancel = true;
                    break;
            }
            }
            if (e.Cancel == false)
            {
                fileNode.IsDirty = false;
                fileNode.EditingForm = null;
            }
            base.OnClosing(e);
        }
...
```

In this case, we've chosen to implement the handler by overriding the base-class handler rather than by adding our own. This has the advantage here of ensuring that we can explicitly see that our handler code is executed first – which may be important if our code detects that the close operation should be cancelled.

This code should be largely self-explanatory. We first check whether the file this form represents has been modified since last saving. If `WebMateNode.IsDirty` returns `False` then there's no problem and we can go ahead with closing the form. Otherwise, we display a message box asking the user what to do, and take the appropriate action. In either event we set the `IsDirty` and `EditingForm` properties of the `WebMateNode` object that represents this form, so that this object knows that there is no longer a child window representing this object and that this web page no longer needs saving.

Closing WebMate

The handler that's invoked if we try to close the entire WebMate application looks a bit simpler. This is because the code used to check if anything needs saving in the entire project, to display the appropriate message box, and take the appropriate action, has already been written. We saw it earlier in the `SiteExplorer.SaveAndCloseProject` method, which we examined as the first stage in the process of opening a project. Recall that this method returns `True` if the operation to close the current project can continue. Armed with this information, we can understand how `WebMateForm.OnClosing` works:

```
public class WebMateForm : System.Windows.Forms.Form
{
    private void OnClosing(object sender, System.ComponentModel.CancelEventArgs e)
    {
        bool okToContinue = siteExplorer.SaveAndCloseProject();
        if (!okToContinue)
        {
            e.Cancel = true;
            return;
        }
    }
...
```

This is as far as we are going to go in examining the source code for WebMate. A number of aspects of the code were not covered here, including creating a new project, setting and examining the properties of items, and deleting items. However, the tasks that we have examined should be sufficient to give an idea of how to write a sophisticated Windows Forms application.

Summary

In this case study chapter, we have seen an example of Windows Forms in action in a real-life project that had a sophisticated user interface. We examined the code that gets executed when a number of different tasks are performed by the project, including:

- Opening a project
- Saving a project
- Dragging and dropping files
- Editing a page
- Closing WebMate

In particular, we paid attention to the way that Windows Forms allows an object-oriented architecture to be used with GUI controls.

Of course, there's no reason not to build on WebMate, or any of the other examples we saw in this book. At any rate, we are now ready to create our own professional Windows Forms applications. Good Luck!

- System.Object
  - System.MarshalRefObject
    - System.ComponentMode.Component
      - CommonDialog
        - ColorDialog
        - FileDialog
        - FontDialog
        - PageSetupDialog
        - PrintDialog
      - ErrorProvider
      - HelpProvider
      - ImageList
      - Menu
        - ContextMenu
        - MainMenu
        - MenuItem
      - NotifyIcon
      - StatusBarPanel
      - Timer
      - ToolBarButton
      - ToolTip
      - Control
        - ButtonBase
          - Button
          - CheckBox
          - RadioButton
        - DataGrid
        - DateTimePicker
        - GroupBox
        - Label
          - LinkLabel
        - ListControl
          - ComboBox
          - ListBox
            - CheckedListBox
        - ListView
        - MonthCalendar
        - PictureBox
        - PrintReviewControl
        - ProgressBar
        - ScrollableControl
          - ContainerControl
            - Form
              - PrintPreviewDialog
              - ThreadExceptionDialog
            - PropertyGrid
            - UpDownBase
              - DomainUpDown
              - NumericUpDown
            - UserControl
          - Panel
            - TabPage
        - ScrollBar
          - HScrollBar
          - VScrollBar
        - Splitter
        - StatusBar
        - TabControl
        - TextBoxBase
          - RichTextBox
          - Textbox
        - ToolBar
        - TrackBar
        - TreeView
  - ListViewItem
  - TreeNode

System.Windows.Forms

Legend: Concrete Class; Abstract class

Index

Symbols

A

B

C

D

E

F

G

H

I

J

K

L

M

N

O

P

Q

R

S

U

V

X

Z

Wrox writes books for you. Any suggestions, or ideas about how you want information given in your ideal book will be studied by our team. Your comments are always valued at Wrox.

Free phone in USA 800-USE-WROX
Fax (312) 893 8001

UK Tel.: (0121) 687 4100 Fax: (0121) 687 4101

Professional Windows Forms – Registration Card

Name ____________________

Address ____________________

____

____

____

City __________ State/Region __________

Country __________ Postcode/Zip __________

E-Mail ____________________

Occupation ____________________

How did you hear about this book?

- ❒ Book review (name) ____________
- ❒ Advertisement (name) ____________
- ❒ Recommendation ____________
- ❒ Catalog ____________
- ❒ Other ____________

Where did you buy this book?

- ❒ Bookstore (name) __________ City __________
- ❒ Computer store (name) ____________
- ❒ Mail order ____________
- ❒ Other ____________

What influenced you in the purchase of this book?

❒ Cover Design ❒ Contents ❒ Other (please specify):

____

How did you rate the overall content of this book?

❒ Excellent ❒ Good ❒ Average ❒ Poor

What did you find most useful about this book? ____________

____

____

What did you find least useful about this book? ____________

____

____

Please add any additional comments. ____________

____

____

What other subjects will you buy a computer book on soon?

____

What is the best computer book you have used this year?

Note: This information will only be used to keep you updated about new Wrox Press titles and will not be used for any other purpose or passed to any other third party.

Note: If you post the bounce back card below in the UK, please send it to:

Wrox Press Limited, Arden House, 1102 Warwick Road,
Acocks Green, Birmingham B27 6HB. UK.

Computer Book Publishers

NO POSTAGE
NECESSARY
IF MAILED
IN THE
UNITED STATES

BUSINESS REPLY MAIL

FIRST CLASS MAIL PERMIT#64 CHICAGO, IL

POSTAGE WILL BE PAID BY ADDRESSEE

WROX PRESS INC.,
29 S. LA SALLE ST.,
SUITE 520
CHICAGO IL 60603-USA